THE
ECUMENICAL ADVANCE

A HISTORY OF
THE ECUMENICAL MOVEMENT
VOLUME 2
1948–1968

D1596674

THE
ECUMENICAL ADVANCE

A HISTORY OF
THE ECUMENICAL MOVEMENT
VOLUME 2
1948–1968

EDITED BY

HAROLD E. FEY

Second edition
with updated bibliography

—

WORLD COUNCIL OF CHURCHES
GENEVA

First published in 1970 by SPCK, London,
and The Westminster Press, Philadelphia
Second edition, 1986

ISBN 2-8254-0872-7

© 1970 World Council of Churches, Geneva, Switzerland

Cover design: Rob Lucas

CONTENTS

74339

ABBREVIATIONS

AAS	*Acta Apostolicae Sedis*
A.A C.C.	All Africa Conference of Churches
A.C.T.S.	Advisory Committee for Technical Services
A.F.P.R.O.	Action for Food Production
Amsterdam	*The First Assembly of the World Council of Churches*, ed. W. A. Visser 't Hooft. London, S.C.M. Press, 1949
A.P.I.D.E.P.	Association Protestante Internationale des Prêts (International Protestant Loan Association)
B.B.C.	British Broadcasting Corporation
B.W.A.	Baptist World Alliance
C.A.S.A.	Christian Agency for Social Action (National Christian Council of India)
C.B.M.S.	Conference of British Missionary Societies
C.C.I.A.	The Commission of the Churches on International Affairs
C.C.L.A.	Committee on Co-operation in Latin America
C.C.S.A.	Christian Committee for Service in Algeria
C.E.C.	Conference of European Churches
C.E.L.A.M.	The Latin American Episcopal Council (Roman Catholic)
C.E.L.A.D.E.C.	The Latin American Commission on Christian Education (Protestant)
C.I.M.A.D.E.	Comité Inter-mouvements auprès des Evacués
C.J.D.P.	The Commission on a Just and Durable Peace
C.O.R.A.G.S.	Committee on Relief and Gift Supplies (National Christian Council of India)
C.U.P.S.A.	Casa Unida de Publicaciones, S.A. (Mexico D.F.)
C.R.O.P.	Christian Rural Organization Programme
C.W.M.E.	Council on World Missions and Evangelism
C.W.S.	Church World Service
D.F.M.	Division of Foreign Missions
D.I.C.A.R.W.S.	Division of Inter-Church Aid, Refugee, and World Service

D.I.C.A.S.R.	Department of Inter-Church Aid and Service to Refugees
D.W.M.E.	Division of World Mission and Evangelism
E.A.C.C.	East Asia Christian Conference
E.C.L.O.F.	The Ecumenical Church Loan Fund
ECOSOC	Economic and Social Council of the U.N.
Edinburgh	*The Second World Conference on Faith and Order*, ed. Leonard Hodgson. New York, The Macmillan Company, 1938
E.P.E.A.A.	Ecumenical Programme for Emergency Action in Africa
Evanston	*The Evanston Report: The Second Assembly of the World Council of Churches, 1954*, ed. W. A. Visser 't Hooft. New York, Harper and Brothers Publishers, 1955
Faith and Order	Commission on Faith and Order of the World Council of Churches
F.A.O.	Food and Agriculture Organization of the United Nations, Rome
FO No.	Refers to Faith and Order Numbered Paper, New Series
F.W.C.C.	Society of Friends World Committee for Consultation
H.E.K.D.	Hilfswerk der Evangelischen Kirchen in Deutschland (Relief Work of the Protestant Churches in Germany)
H.E.K.S.	Hilfswerk der Evangelischen Kirchen der Schweiz (The Swiss Protestant Churches Relief Agency)
I.C.C.	International Congregational Council
I.C.C.C.	International Council of Christian Churches
I.C.E.M.	Intergovernmental Committee for European Migration
I.L.O.	International Labour Organization, Geneva
I.M.C.	International Missionary Council
IRM	*International Review of Missions*
I.R.O.	International Refugee Organization
I.S.A.L.	Iglesia y Sociedad en America Latina (Church and Society in Latin America)
Lausanne	*Faith and Order: Proceedings of the World Conference, Lausanne, 3–21 August 1927*, ed. H. N. Bate. London, S.C.M. Press, 1927
Life and Work	The Universal Christian Council on Life and Work; first meeting, Stockholm 1925
Lund	*The Third World Conference on Faith and Order*, ed. Oliver S. Tomkins. London, S.C.M. Press, 1953
L.W.F.	Lutheran World Federation, Geneva

Montreal	*The Fourth World Conference on Faith and Order*, ed. P. C. Rodger and Lukas Vischer. London, S.C.M. Press, 1964
MRCC	Refers to the Minutes and Reports of the Central Committee of the year in question
M.R.I.	Mutual Responsibility and Interdependence in the Body of Christ
N.C.C.C.U.S.A.	National Council of Churches of Christ of the United States of America
N.E.C.C.	Near East Christian Council
New Delhi	*The New Delhi Report: The Third Assembly of the World Council of Churches, 1961*, ed. W. A. Visser 't Hooft. New York, Association Press, 1962
N.S.C.F.	National Student Christian Federation
Oxford	Conference on Church, Community, and State, Oxford, England, 1937
P.C.C.	Pacific Conference of Churches
R.A.V.E.M.C.O.	Radio, Visual Education, and Mass Communication of the Division of Foreign Missions of N.C.C.C.U.S.A.
S.C.M.	Student Christian Movement
S.A.S.P.	Committee on Specialized Assistance to Social Projects
S.P.C.K.	Society for Promoting Christian Knowledge
S.V.M.	Student Volunteer Movement
U.L.A.J.E.	Union of Latin American Evangelical Youth
U.C.M.	University Christian Movement
U.N.	United Nations Organization
U.N.E.L.A.M.	The Provisional Committee on Christian Unity in Latin America
U.N.E.S.C.O.	United Nations Educational, Scientific, and Cultural Organization
U.N.C.T.A.D.	United Nations Conference on Trade and Development
U.N.H.C.R.	United Nations High Commission for Refugees
U.N.I.C.E.F.	United Nations Children's Fund
U.N.R.R.A.	United Nations Relief and Rehabilitation Agency
U.N.R.W.A.	United Nations Relief and Works Agency
Uppsala	*The Uppsala Report 1968: Official Report of the Fourth Assembly of the World Council of Churches, Uppsala 4–20 July 1968*
U.S.C.L.	United Society for Christian Literature
U.S.E.P.	United States Escapee Programme

W.A.R.C.	World Alliance of Reformed Churches
W.C.C.	World Council of Churches
W.C.C.E.	World Council of Christian Education
W.M.C.	World Methodist Council
World Alliance	World Alliance of Reformed Churches
W.S.C.F.	World Student Christian Federation
Y.M.C.A.	Young Men's Christian Association
Y.W.C.A.	Young Women's Christian Association

CONTRIBUTORS TO THIS VOLUME

PAUL R. ABRECHT is Executive Secretary of the Department on Church and Society of the World Council of Churches. A Baptist minister, he is an honours graduate in economics of the University of California and holds a divinity degree from Union Theological Seminary, New York. He is the author of *The Churches and Rapid Social Change* (1961) and other studies. He was also editor of the important series of four books which were published in 1966 in connection with the world conference on "Christians in the Technical and Social Revolutions of Our Time", of which conference he was the secretary responsible for organization.

EUGENE CARSON BLAKE became the second General Secretary of the World Council of Churches in 1966. For the previous fifteen years he was Stated Clerk of the United Presbyterian Church in the U.S.A. Under his leadership the United Presbyterian Church became active in the civil rights movement. He was active in the preparation of the first new American Presbyterian confession of faith since 1648 and initiated the Consultation on Church Union, in which nine denominations are now seeking to form a Church "truly catholic, truly evangelical, and truly reformed". Dr Blake has long been actively engaged in the ecumenical movement. He was President of the National Council of Churches in the U.S.A. and continued on its General Board until he went to Geneva. In the W.C.C. he was a member of the policy-making Central Committee and of its Executive Committee, was Chairman of the Division of Inter-Church Aid and Chairman of the Finance Committee. He studied at Princeton and Edinburgh and once taught at Forman Christian College, Lahore, India. He served pastorates in New York and California, has received honorary degrees from eighteen colleges and universities, and is the author of four books.

DAVID LAWRENCE EDWARDS, a priest of the Church of England, has been Dean of King's College, Cambridge, since 1966. Born in 1929, he was formerly a Fellow of All Souls College, Oxford, and Editor of the Student Christian Movement Press, London. He lectures in modern church history in Cambridge University and is the author of eight books.

HAROLD E. FEY was Editor of the *Christian Century*, Chicago, from 1956 until he retired in 1964. Later he served for four years as Visiting Professor of Christian Social Ethics in Christian Theological Seminary, Indianapolis. He received his theological degree from Yale Divinity School, served as pastor of congregations of the Christian Church, Disciples of Christ, taught as a missionary in Union Theological Seminary, Manila, Philippine Islands, was Editor of *World Call*, a Christian Church monthly magazine, and was U.S. Secretary for the Fellowship of Reconciliation. He is a member of the Executive Committee of the Council on Christian Unity of the Christian Church, Disciples of Christ and represents his Church on some committees of the National Council of Churches. He joined the editorial staff of the *Christian Century* in 1940 and is the author of several books. His home is in Indianapolis.

MEREDITH B. HANDSPICKER is a native of Malden, Massachusetts and a professor in Andover-Newton Theological Seminary near Boston. He graduated from Bates College, Maine, *summa cum laude* in Philosophy. He received the B.D. degree from Yale Divinity School *magna cum laude* and later received the M.A. and the Ph.D. at Yale. He was Secretary of the Faith and Order Department of the W.C.C. from 1963 to 1967. He is a minister of the United Church of Christ.

VASIL T. ISTAVRIDIS is a lay theologian of the Greek Orthodox Church. He graduated from the Theological School of Halki, Istanbul, where he is teaching modern church history, including the history of the ecumenical movement. He also studied at Andover-Newton Theological Seminary and at Boston University, receiving the Th.D. degree from the latter institution. He is the author of pamphlets and books on inter-Church relations, including the theological dialogue between Orthodox and Anglicans, on the history of the ecumenical movement, and on great ecumenists. He is a member of the World Council Central Committee. He has participated in many ecumenical gatherings.

HANFRIED KRÜGER first studied law, then turned to theology and comparative religion, receiving his Ph.D. in 1937. His thesis which he wrote under Professor Friedrich Heiler in Marburg, was on "Verständnis und Wertung der Mystik im neueren Protestantismus". He served as an assistant minister from 1938 to 1940 in Hannover and Loccum in the Evangelical Church of Hannover and from 1941 to 1943 in Hannover and from 1943 to 1951 in Lauenstein, Hannover. From 1951 to 1953 he worked in church administration in Hannover. In 1953 he became Secretary for Ecumenical Affairs in the Foreign Relations Office of the E.K.D. in Frankfurt/Main. As head of the Ökumenische Centrale and chief editor of the quarterly journal *Ökumenische Rundschau* since 1956, he was appointed Secretary of the Deutscher Ökumenischer Studienausschuss from 1956 to 1967 and also Secretary of the Arbeitsgemeinschaft Christlicher Kirchen in Deutschland since 1963.

HANS JOCHEN MARGULL has since 1967 been Professor of Missions at the University of Hamburg, Germany, from which university he received the Th.D. degree in 1958. He was a missionary of the United Presbyterian Church (U.S.A.) to the United Church in Japan from 1965 to 1967. Earlier he headed the Department on Studies in Evangelism of the World Council of Churches and earlier still was a student minister in Germany. A Lutheran, he studied at Griefswald Halle, Mainz, and New York Theological Seminary. He is the author of three books, one of which was published in Japanese.

GEOFFREY MURRAY is information officer of the Division of Inter-Church Aid, Refugee, and World Service of the World Council of Churches. Before joining the staff of the W.C.C. early in 1961 he spent thirty-two years as a newspaper reporter on the *Daily Express, Daily Mirror, Daily Dispatch,* and *News Chronicle* of London, broken only by four years' service with the Royal Air Force during the Second World War. He is now Geneva correspondent of the *Christian Century.* He is the author of six books and has attended and reported many ecumenical meetings.

J. E. LESSLIE NEWBIGIN is Bishop of the diocese of Madura and Ramnad of the Church of South India. He was and continues to be an ordained minister of the Church of Scotland. He was present at the founding of the World Council of Churches in 1948 and served as Chairman of the commission which wrote the statement on the theme of the Second W.C.C. Assembly in 1954. He was Secretary of the International Missionary Council from 1959 to 1961 and Director of the W.C.C. Division of World Mission and Evangelism from 1961 to 1965, when he was elected bishop. He was a Secretary of the Student Christian Movement for two years after he received the M.A. degree from Cambridge University. He is the author of nine published books.

O. FREDERICK NOLDE of New York City was Director of the World Council of Churches Commission of the Churches on International Affairs from 1946 to 1968 and since 1948 an Associate General Secretary of the World Council. He is unofficially recognized to be the chief architect of the article on freedom of thought, conscience, and religion in the Universal Declaration of Human Rights, proclaimed by the United Nations in 1948. For more than two decades he has been a spokesman for the W.C.C. and the C.C.I.A. before the United Nations and intergovernmental conferences in New York, Geneva, Paris, Berlin, Seoul, and elsewhere. His representations have sought, among other objectives, the cessation of nuclear weapons testing, disarmament, and the peaceful settlement of international disputes. Dr Nolde holds degrees from Muhlenberg College, the Lutheran Theological Seminary at Philadelphia, and the University of Pennsylvania. He served as pastor, as professor, and later as dean of the graduate school at Lutheran Theological Seminary. He has several honorary degrees.

FRANK SHORT, now minister of the Sherborne Congregational Church in England, was from 1953 to 1965 Asia Secretary and General Secretary of the Conference of Missionary Societies in Great Britain and Ireland. From 1926 to 1953 he was a missionary in China of the London Missionary Society, serving in the last four years of that period as Secretary of the China Council of the L.M.S. and as representative of the L.M.S. in South Asia. From 1961 to 1965 he was a member of the Committee on National Council of Churches relationships of the Division of World Mission and Evangelism of the World Council of Churches.

LUKAS VISCHER, an ordained minister of the Swiss Reformed Church, is the Director of the Secretariat on Faith and Order of the World Council of Churches. He has been associated with the W.C.C. since 1961. He served as one of the World Council's observers at all four sessions of the Second Vatican Council. A native of Basle, he studied at the Universities of Basle, Strasbourg, Göttingen, and Oxford. His Th.D. degree in early church history came from the University of Basle. Before joining the World Council staff, he was for eight years pastor in Herblingen, Switzerland. He has written several books and articles dealing with the ecumenical movement.

W. A. VISSER 'T HOOFT was General Secretary of the World Council of Churches from 1948 to 1966 and was made Honorary President in 1968 by the Fourth Assembly of the W.C.C. He is an ordained minister of the Netherlands Reformed Church and of the Protestant Church of Geneva. His doctoral thesis at the University of Leyden on "The Background of the Social Gospel in America" became the first of the dozen books he wrote. Beginning with the Stockholm Conference on Life and Work in 1925 and work with the International Y.M.C.A. and the World's Student Christian Federation, his ecumenical interest and service has been lifelong. In 1938 he became General Secretary of the Provisional Committee of the World Council of Churches and ten years later General Secretary of the World Council of Churches. He received honorary degrees from many of the world's leading universities, was honoured by the Ecumenical Patriarch of Constantinople and the Orthodox Church of Russia, and received high honours from the governments of The Netherlands, France, and Germany. During his administration the World Council of Churches moved from tentative and provisional beginnings to becoming the acknowledged chief instrument and channel of the ecumenical movement.

HANS-RUEDI WEBER is Associate Director of the Ecumenical Institute of the World Council of Churches at Chateau de Bossey near Geneva. He was appointed to this post in 1961. A Swiss Reformed pastor, he was Executive Secretary of the World Council's Department of the Laity from 1955 to 1961. Earlier he was a missionary to Central Celebes and Java in Indonesia and Secretary of the Student Christian Movement in Switzerland. Dr Weber received the Bachelor of Theology degree from the University of Berne, a diploma from the W.C.C.'s Graduate School, and a doctorate in Theology from the University of Geneva. Dr Weber is the author of books published in English, French, and German.

INTRODUCTION

The present volume is a sequel to *A History of the Ecumenical Movement 1517–1948*, edited by Ruth Rouse and Stephen C. Neill, which was published in 1954. It differs from that volume in that this book covers only the twenty-year period from 1948 to 1968, whereas the former volume covered more than four centuries (1517–1948). This book is smaller in size and is intended to be of interest to the much wider public which is now following the development of the ecumenical movement.

It may be thought that, if history is written so close to the event, the authors will have difficulty in seeing actions in their proper perspective. Each of the distinguished authors who have contributed to the present volume is aware of this difficulty and is prepared to leave historians who write in the future to place events in a different light from that in which they now appear. But we believe that our contributors are rendering a service of genuine importance in running the risks involved in evaluating developments so close to their happening. The last two decades have been rich in important events and, as this record shows, full of promise for the decade which we are now entering. This is sufficient justification for what is here attempted.

Here it should be emphasized that the ecumenical movement must not be regarded as identical with the World Council of Churches, nor has the latter ever claimed to be its only expression. Nevertheless, it is universally recognized that the World Council occupies in it a place of special responsibility, being at present the most strongly organized inter-Church body for promoting the aims of the movement. This explains why so many of the following pages are devoted to the developments of the World Council and to what it has been able to accomplish in promoting the cause of ecumenism during the first years of its existence.

The development of the World Council during the last twenty years has had three main aspects. In the first place, its membership has greatly increased. The Churches whose delegates met at Amsterdam in 1948 and on 23 August sealed this pact of fraternity, were 147 in number, Protestant, Anglican, Orthodox, and Old Catholic. Today the member Churches are 235. The increase is mainly due to the fact that several of the great Orthodox Churches entered into membership in 1961, and equally a large number of young Churches in Asia, Africa, Latin America, and Oceania, which had recently become independent. Orthodoxy, which for too long had been a minority in the ecumenical movement, has thus been able to exercise increasing influence and to make its full contribution. On the other hand, the increased number of Churches from the Third World has given the World Council a more universal character. Thus the centre of gravity has shifted considerably in two ways: confessionally the Reformation Churches are less prominent, regionally the Western Churches are less dominant.

Secondly, ecumenism is interpreted today in a wider sense than it was in 1948. It has been increasingly realized that unity is not an end in itself and should not be sought for its own sake but rather to accomplish more effectively God's purpose for all mankind. In 1951 the Central Committee proclaimed that unity and mission are inseparable realities. The vital link between them was forged in 1961 when the International Missionary Council was integrated into the World Council of Churches. Mission is no longer regarded as a form of "one way traffic" from "Christian" Europe and America to the "pagan" continents, but the task of the whole Church in the world as a whole. Moreover, this concept was broadened at the Fourth Assembly of the W.C.C. at Uppsala in its discussion of catholicity to say that the mission is to the whole person in the whole society, with all its principalities and powers, in every country.

This leads to the third aspect of development which is visible not only within the World Council but within the entire ecumenical movement: the increasing concern for the world and its problems. The World Council has constantly reminded its members that the Church does not live for itself and that its vocation is to serve mankind. For that reason it has drawn them into more and more extensive programmes of inter-Church aid and relief, service to refugees, and help in regions of rapid social change. Simultaneously the World Council organized regular studies of all kinds on social and international problems to inspire and guide the Churches' action. So doing it has been faithful to the heritage of the "Life and Work Movement" founded in 1925 at the Stockholm Conference. Finally, the World Conference on "Church and Society" held in Geneva in 1966 and the Uppsala Assembly have, as will be seen in these pages, plunged the Churches into the heart of the human crisis.

All these developments are direct continuations of ecumenical efforts of the past whose vitality is expressed in the deepening and expanding process described here. But near the end of the period reviewed in this volume an event of great significance occurred which marks a turning-point in the history of the ecumenical movement, namely the Second Vatican Council (1962–5). While the Roman Catholic Church had previously maintained an attitude of extreme reserve with regard to the ecumenical movement, it now decided to associate itself with it and to participate actively in the dialogue which the World Council has encouraged for many years. A significant change has taken place in the atmosphere of the relations between the Roman Catholic Church and non-Roman Christendom, and this has opened the way to an era of trust and co-operation in many fields.

The above comments suffice to show that "movement" is the right word to associate with ecumenical. This movement is assuming new forms to meet new conditions. It is impossible to foresee what shapes will emerge in the future, since the world and the Churches are passing through a deep crisis. The younger generation is judging all existing institutions. The World Council of Churches is not exempt from their scrutiny. Within the Church, young Christians do not conceal the fact that their conception of Christian unity and action differs from that of the older generation. But the ecumenical movement has clearly been guided by God in the past, and this is sufficient guarantee for its future.

The committee which assumes responsibility for the publication of this volume on the History of the Ecumenical Movement 1948–68 has been fortunate to secure as editor Dr Harold E. Fey, whose great experience in such matters particularly qualifies him for this delicate task. We wish to express our gratitude for the distinguished manner in which he has accomplished this task.

In closing, the Committee wishes to express its deep appreciation to the Christian Church, Disciples of Christ, to its Council on Christian Unity and to its "Week of Compassion" for generously providing funds which made possible the writing, editing, and publication of this continuation of the History of the Ecumenical Movement, as they did for the previous volume, *A History of the Ecumenical Movement 1517–1948.*

HENRI D'ESPINE
Chairman of the Committee
on Ecumenical History.

PREFACE TO THE SECOND EDITION

Although there are other histories of the ecumenical movement, these two volumes — *A History of the Ecumenical Movement 1517-1948* and *The Ecumenical Advance 1948-1968* — originally published jointly by SPCK and the Westminster Press, still represent the only "official" literature on the subject. The World Council of Churches itself was involved in the choice of writers and editors and in the final production of the volumes. The aim was to present a detailed and impartial account of the many ecumenical impulses, initiatives and activities during these centuries, and to make a systematic survey of the ecumenical history of the churches.

Taking the Reformation as its starting point, the first volume covers four centuries of varied endeavours towards church unity in Europe and North America. In particular it deals with the Faith and Order, World Mission and Evangelism and Life and Work movements in the twentieth century, which led to the formation of the World Council of Churches.

The second volume is mainly concerned with developments within the World Council, its programmes and activities, from 1948 through the Fourth Assembly at Uppsala in 1968. It also includes chapters on the Orthodox and Roman Catholic involvement in the ecumenical movement, on the origin and growth of national and regional councils of churches, and on the part played by confessional families in the ecumenical movement from 1948 onwards.

It has often been pointed out that as the ecumenical pioneers of the twentieth century pass from the scene, we suffer from a loss of "ecumenical memory". Even those committed to the ecumenical cause often work with only limited knowledge of past ecumenical efforts and of the continuity in the programmes, concerns and activities of the World Council of Churches and other ecumenical bodies since 1948. These volumes continue to refresh our memory and can broaden our perspective. For, when the past is forgotten, the present loses perspective and the future lacks direction. More recent trends and developments, which have become increasingly complex and controversial, can be recorded and evaluated only if the challenge, the vision and the enthusiasm of earlier decades are newly experienced.

These two volumes have been out of print for some years. It is our hope that their republication now, with a new bibliography included in the second volume, will be of help to both individuals and institutions.

Emilio Castro
Geneva, August 1986

1

The General
Ecumenical Development
since 1948

W. A. VISSER 'T HOOFT

The Third Generation

By 1948 the ecumenical movement could look back on two important periods of its life.

The first had been the period of the pioneers. A small group of men had begun to plant the ecumenical idea in the minds of church leaders. The initiatives they took were due to their own conviction and imagination rather than to any widespread movement in the Churches. So they met with a good deal of resistance and scepticism. But they had that patient tenacity which comes from devotion to a great spiritual cause. Two laymen, John R. Mott and J. H. Oldham, succeeded in 1910 in bringing the missionary forces together. A missionary bishop and a lawyer, Charles Brent and Robert Gardiner, created "Faith and Order" and prepared the Lausanne Conference of 1927. An archbishop, Nathan Söderblom, was able to organize almost singlehandedly the first conference on "Life and Work" in Stockholm in 1925. Another layman, Sir Willoughby Dickinson, with the support of a German professor, Friedrich Siegmund-Schultze, built the World Alliance for Friendship through the Churches. In the meantime another spontaneous initiative had been taken in Constantinople by Archbishop Germanos, who was also largely responsible for bringing the Greek Orthodox Churches into the ecumenical bodies.

This period is therefore characterized by numerous energetic initiatives which led to the formation of a variety of ecumenical bodies, each of which had its loyal adherents in the Churches, but none of which was considered by the Churches as their own instrument for ecumenical action.

The second period was that of the architects who sought to give a more clearly defined shape to the ecumenical movement. The outstanding names are William Temple, J. H. Oldham, William Adams Brown, Archbishop Germanos (Thyateira), George Bell (Chichester), Marc Boegner, Alphons Koechlin, William Paton. Theirs was a threefold task: to arrive at an integration of the ecumenical bodies, to relate these bodies more directly to the Churches, and to work out a specific programme of common action. By 1937, at the time of the Oxford and Edinburgh conferences, a specific plan could be submitted. It was proposed to bring Faith and Order and Life and Work together in a single organization. Close relationship would be established between the new body and the International Missionary Council. A year later in Utrecht a representative conference of the Churches elaborated the Constitution of the World Council of Churches. But this second period had to last longer than was expected. The Second World War came and the first Assembly which was to have been held in 1941 could not meet until 1948. This proved to be to the advantage of the movement, for in the war years the ecumenical convictions were tested and deepened.

The year 1948 marked the beginning of the third period. A new generation took over. We can call it the generation of the builders. Among the leaders in this new period there were only a few who had known the period of the pioneers—George Bell (died 1958), Alphons Koechlin (died 1965), Yngve Brilioth (died 1959), Otto Dibelius (died 1967), Hamilcar Alivisatos. The task was now to ensure that the ecumenical movement should really become ecumenical, that it should become the ecumenical movement of the Churches, and that it should develop adequate structures.

At the time of the first Assembly in 1948, the World Council was still far from representing all of Christendom. It is true that through the International Missionary Council, through confessional alliances, through the Y.M.C.A., Y.W.C.A., and the World Student Christian Federation, Christian leaders in Asia, Africa, and Latin America were in contact with Christians in other countries. But the Churches of these continents were not yet in regular communication with the Churches in other parts of the world and had no independent centres of initiative. At the Amsterdam Assembly of 1948 the number of representatives of the younger Churches was so limited that they "were swamped in a sea of delegates from older churches" and that "their opinion on many issues was not clearly heard".[1]

At the same time Eastern Orthodoxy was in those days only represented by the Greek-speaking Orthodox Churches. The other Orthodox Churches which had taken part in the Moscow Church Conference of 1948 had decided against participation in the World Council of Churches.

In the Roman Catholic Church a small group of theologians had begun to show their deep interest in ecumenism, but the Church as such stood aloof and did not give permission to such Roman Catholic observers as had been invited to attend the Amsterdam Assembly.

Thus the ecumenical movement of 1948 had its geographical and confessional limitations. The story of the years since 1948 is essentially the story of the process through which the ecumenical movement became universalized. It is a story of ecumenical mobilization of practically all Christian Churches.

The Historical Context of the Ecumenical Mobilization

The fast development of the ecumenical movement from a relatively esoteric concern of individual Christians with a great vision in some of the Churches to a widespread movement of thought and life affecting all the Churches in one way or another obliges us to inquire why this new factor in church history appeared at this particular time. What was the historical context in which this rediscovery of the universal dimension of the Christian faith took place?

We can only note the most essential features of the changed situation of the Church. These can be summarized as follows:

Precisely at the time when the world is being unified and a world civilization begins to take shape, the world position of Christianity is undermined and the process of estrangement between Church and world becomes increasingly acute and manifest.

These three related developments are so well known that they need little comment. Powerful forces make the many separate worlds of yesterday into one world. The unity of mankind is no longer a pious dream; it becomes a practical necessity as the interdependence of the nations grows and all are confronted with the same opportunities and the same dangers. A world

[1] Chandran Devanesan in *Ecumenical Review*, vol. i (January 1949), p. 143.

civilization comes into being, but it takes the form of a Great Society based on the dynamic forces of technology and economic development in which Christian values play a minor role. At the same time the world position of Christianity, which had been a position of privilege in the period when governments of traditionally Christian countries were in direct or indirect control of most of the world, is severely shaken when in many of the newly independent nations the national revival leads also to a resurgence of the indigenous religions. And a very large part of the world, including Russia with its ancient Christian tradition and China, a country which had often been considered one of the most promising mission fields, came under the domination of an ideology which sought to replace Christianity.

The third development is the most complex. The estrangement between the Church and the world has in it an element of emancipation, of a natural affirmation of the autonomy of culture over against a Church which had too often sought to keep the world under its tutelage. On the other hand, secularism can take an aggressively anti-Christian form and develop ideologies which become practically pseudo-religions. But there is another element in the estrangement between Church and world. It is the new sense of the integrity of the Church and the refusal on the part of Christians to accept a coexistence with the world in which Christianity loses its identity. The estrangement is not only due to Karl Marx or to Auguste Comte and Friedrich Nietzsche. It is also due to Kierkegaard, Karl Barth, Nicolai Berdyaev, and the men of the confessing Church in Germany and other countries. There had to be a 'No' to a wrong relation between Church and world before there could again be a 'Yes' and a new turning to the world on the basis of a clearer conception of Church and world.

Does this context then explain the emergence of the ecumenical movement? Sociologists will be inclined to answer this question affirmatively and to interpret the ecumenical movement as the response of the Churches to external challenges, threats, and pressures. Theologians will be inclined to deny such sociological conditioning and point out that the movement is fundamentally a rediscovery and reaffirmation of a dimension of truth which is inherent in the very nature of the Church from the beginning. It would seem that there is more truth in the sociological interpretation than most theologians are willing to admit and more truth in the theological understanding than the sociologists accept.

That the theologians have a strong point can be shown by the fact that the ecumenical movement has not followed what may be called the line of least cultural resistance. If the movement had been essentially a response to an external threat, it would surely have organized itself as a movement to defend traditional Western civilization against its enemies inside and outside the camp. But this has not happened. On the contrary the ecumenical movement has been a critical element in Western culture and sought to find new answers to the problems of relations between the ideological West and the ideological East, or between the traditionally Christian countries and those dominated by other religions, answers which grew out of Christian convictions rather than out of traditional cultural attitudes. It must also be remembered that the ecumenical movement has shown that it is not dependent upon the ups and downs of internationalism and that during the Second World War and again during the post-war tensions it has shown that it can transcend the socio-political forces which drive men apart.

On the other hand, the sociologists are surely right if they maintain that the development of the ecumenical movement has been helped and intensified by the historical situation in which the Churches find themselves in this period of their history. The recall to the universal dimension of the faith has found a wider echo in our time because the Church cannot perform its calling in the "one world" if it remains divided and provincial in its outlook. Roger Mehl puts the matter clearly: "To say that the ecumenical movement was born in a given sociological context, to say that its birth and its development have been favoured, influenced and orientated by a certain number of sociological facts, does not mean at all to pronounce a judgment on the significance of the movement."[1] For that significance lies ultimately on the common recapturing of the simple biblical truth that the Church as the people of God and the body of Christ must exemplify in this world how God gathers men together from the ends of the earth in order to live as a new humanity.

Return to the Source

Already during the 1930s and 1940s the *Biblical Renewal*[2] had been a powerful factor in bringing Christians of different traditions together. This had been shown in the life of the Christian youth movements and particularly at the World Conference of Christian Youth in Amsterdam, 1939. In the post-war years it was increasingly realized that the Word of God was "the true bond of ecumenical unity". At a World Council meeting in Oxford 1949, biblical scholars from many confessions issued a statement concerning "guiding principles for the interpretation of the Bible" and said: "We have found a measure of agreement that surprised us all . . . . It is an actual experience within the ecumenical movement that, when we meet together, with pre-suppositions of which we may be largely unconscious, and bring these suppositions to the judgement of Scripture, some of the very difficulties are removed which prevent the Gospel from being heard."[3]

This insight that the Bible provided the true meeting ground led to increased emphasis on Bible study in ecumenical meetings, including the W.C.C. Assemblies. It led also to the insertion in the basis of the W.C.C. of the words "according to the Scriptures". The addition of these words was a recognition of the place which the Bible had in fact occupied in the development of the ecumenical movement. Without the common biblical theology the ecumenical movement would have had no backbone. The deepest motive for the seeking of unity was the biblical conception of the gathering into one of the people of God by the Lord Jesus Christ.

[1] *Traité de Sociologie du Protestantisme*, pp. 185–6.
[2] Title of a book by Suzanne de Diétrich (1945) in the Series "Ecclesia Militans" under the auspices of the W.C.C.
[3] *Biblical Authority for Today*. London 1951.

But the return to the source did not only affect the member Churches of the World Council. In the Roman Catholic Church there had been a most remarkable revival of Bible study and of concern for the use of the Bible by the faithful. Thus, as Cardinal Bea has said, the desire to go back to the pure sources of our faith is today a common characteristic of all of Christendom.[1] For the first time Bible translations were being prepared by scholars of all confessions together. And the first results of this common translation work show a surprising consensus, not only concerning the best rendering of the original into modern languages, but also concerning the meaning of the text.

This common return to the source could not fail to have a decisive influence on the ecumenical dialogue. This became visible in the formulations concerning the relation between Scripture and tradition which have been given on the one hand by the Montreal Conference on Faith and Order and on the other hand by the Second Vatican Council. For these formulations show that in this crucial matter the various confessional positions are not as far apart as earlier generations have thought. There are still real divergences to be overcome; but it is already the case that in biblical research and biblical theology all the Churches have now the opportunity and the duty to learn from each other and to enrich each other. This is a great promise for the healthy development of the ecumenical movement.

The Churches Accept Responsibility

In the period before the creation of the World Council of Churches the relationship of the Churches to the ecumenical bodies remained undefined. The Churches were asked to send delegates to world conferences, but these world conferences set up their own continuation committees which were responsible for ongoing work. When the plan to form the World Council was launched, all Churches had to consider whether they would accept responsibility for, and a commitment to, an ongoing organization which would be the expression of their will "to stay together" and which would be controlled by them. Thus from 1948 onwards a new ecumenical situation was created. Ecumenism had no longer that informal character which it had had so far. The largest, most conspicuous, and comprehensive part of the ecumenical movement had become an instrument of the Churches.

There were those who were unhappy about this development. They feared that the movement would lose its spontaneous character and that the voice of the prophets would no longer be heard. On the other hand, most of the men who had played such a large role in the creation of the early ecumenical movement were convinced that the time had come to give the movement firm rootage in the life of the Churches. It was not that suddenly the movement was captured by church administrators. It was rather that laymen such as Oldham and Mott and church leaders who were of a prophetic rather than of a bureaucratic type such as William Temple, George Bell, and William Adams Brown saw clearly that in order to make the ecumenical movement

[1] *Gedanken zum Theologischen Wörterbuch zum Neuen Testament.* Juli 1964.

relevant to the actual life of the Churches the Churches should be asked to accept a specific responsibility for its life. It was not intended that the World Council would in any way seek to have a monopoly or a hegemony. It was realized that the independent movements which had paved the way would continue to make their own specific contribution to the ecumenical cause.

During the following years the advantages of the new situation became clear. For in this way ecumenism penetrated far more deeply into the life of the Churches than it could have done if the Council had not been a Council of Churches. And it can be said that most member Churches have at least shown in the financial assistance given to the W.C.C., in sending their delegates to meetings, and in many other ways that they took their membership seriously. It is true that there was another side to the picture. Far too often W.C.C. initiatives did not meet with any considerable response in the member Churches. Too few of the Churches had set up an adequate structure to deal with ecumenical matters. Too many letters remained unanswered. Too few of the decisions of Assemblies or Central Committee have been seriously considered and ratified by member Churches. But this was not so much due to any unwillingness of the Churches to play their part as to the fact that they were unprepared for quick and sometimes stormy ecumenical developments.

The men who had worked out the W.C.C. plan, and very especially Dr J. H. Oldham, had had in mind that the W.C.C. would use for its work not only the service of the official church leaders, but also "lay people holding posts of responsibility and influence in the secular world", for such men would be needed if the Church would give a relevant witness in the modern world.[1] This principle has been observed in many aspects of the work of the World Council, more especially in its work on social and international problems. Many laymen, who do not regard themselves as official representatives of their Churches, have played a very considerable part in the conferences and in the study and work of the World Council. This is illustrated by the fact that the important World Conference on Church and Society in 1966 was largely composed of such laymen, whose names had been approved by the Churches concerned. It was therefore considered to be a conference speaking to the Churches and the World Council rather than speaking on behalf of the Churches and the World Council. In this and other ways laymen, and also theologians invited as experts rather than as official church leaders, have made a very great contribution to the ecumenical movement. But this is not an adequate solution of the problem of the place of laymen in the responsible leadership of the World Council.

It is true that a number of laymen have served on the official organs of the W.C.C. But the original intention that they should have a very considerable voice in the leadership has not been fulfilled. The Constitution of the W.C.C. as adopted at Utrecht and Amsterdam instructed the Central Committee to urge the Churches to ensure that approximately one third of the Assembly should consist of lay persons, men and women. But this goal has not been attained. Too few Churches are willing to carry out in practice what the whole

[1] Report of the "Committee of Thirty-Five" to the Oxford and Edinburgh Conferences in 1937.

ecumenical family has so often said about the place of the laity, both men and women, in the life of the Church.

The Search for Renewal

The call to the Churches concerning the first Assembly of the World Council of Churches had said: "Our first and deepest need is not new organization, but the renewal, or rather the rebirth, of the actual churches." And both in the preparatory volumes for the Assembly and at the Assembly itself there had been strong emphasis on the relation between unity and renewal. "We pray for the churches' renewal as we pray for their unity. As Christ purifies us by His Spirit we shall find that we are drawn together and that there is no gain in unity unless it is unity in truth and holiness."[1]

Thus from the outset the World Council realized that unity could come only through shared renewal. During the war years and those immediately following, many movements of renewal had sprung up in the Churches and the World Council sought to make whatever inspiration and new ideas were found in each place available for the whole fellowship. The Ecumenical Institute which began to operate in 1947 and the first director of which was a prophet of church renewal (Dr Hendrik Kraemer) stood for "the reawakening of the Church through the spiritual mobilization of the laity". Before long a secretariat and later a department for the laity were organized with the same purpose. And in many other aspects of the Council's life the theme of church renewal became a dominating theme.

These first years after the Assembly were years of great hopes concerning the renewal of the Churches. Many Churches had found new life as they had been confronted with modern forms of paganism and had begun to transform their obsolete institutional structures. There was a new realization that not only in the so-called mission field but in all parts of the world the Churches were called to a comprehensive evangelistic and missionary approach. New forms of the Christian ministry were being worked out. And even more important, it was widely understood that, as the Evanston Assembly put it, "An immense opportunity is open to the churches in the world through their laity not to be seized for ecclesiastical domination, but for Christian witness."

It cannot be denied that the movement for church renewal has produced results and that these results are to a considerable extent due to the mutual stimulation and inspiration which could take place only because there was an ecumenical movement. Many Churches have a new conception of their mission in and to the world and created new structures to fulfil that mission. Evangelical academies and similar institutions in many countries have been "energizing centres". The "Kirchentag", of which Dr Reinhold von Thadden was the pioneer, has not only in Germany but also in other places injected fertile ideas into the life of the Churches. The youth movements, both those under church auspices and those which have an independent existence, notably the World's Student Christian Federation with its studies and conferences on "The Life and Mission of the Church", have made their contribu-

[1] Report of the first section of the Amsterdam Assembly.

tion through sharp, but also constructive, criticism of the ecclesiastical established order. But it is also true that the renewal of the life in the Churches has not been as deep and as widespread as had been hoped in the early years of the Council's life. Many, especially among the younger generation, felt a sense of deep disappointment. Why had the renewal movement not transformed church life more thoroughly? Was it due to a lack of spiritual depth and dynamic or to the institutional immobilism of the ecclesiastical structure or to both? The ecumenical movement itself made the issue of institutionalism a main subject of study.[1] But it cannot be said that adequate answers have been given to the basic issue.

As the Second Vatican Council became a council of *aggiornamento* and in Roman Catholic theology the theme of "reform—an essential element in the Church" (as Cardinal Döpfner formulated it) came to the fore, all open-minded Christians became confronted in a new way with the great theme of renewal. Once again the struggle for renewal in one Church stimulated and challenged the other Churches. In this field especially there is every reason to apply the principle dear to the ecumenical pioneer, Abbé Couturier, that the true ecumenical way is the way of "spiritual emulation". The greatest contribution to unity will be made by the Church which is most ready to let itself be thoroughly renewed by the Holy Spirit.

The Common Calling to Mission

The first effective initiatives leading to ecumenical co-operation had been taken by the missionary movement and had inspired the pioneers of co-operation between the Churches. But the missionary movement had created its own strong organization under the dynamic leadership of such men as John R. Mott, J. H. Oldham, William Paton. This International Missionary Council, based on the national councils and missionary councils, was in the 1920s and 1930s much ahead of all other ecumenical bodies in clarity of purpose and efficacy. On the other hand, the men of the I.M.C. became increasingly involved in the other ecumenical movements. By the time of the Madras Conference of 1938 it was clear that some link would have to be established between the I.M.C. and the World Council of Churches. It was therefore decided at the first Assembly of the W.C.C. in Amsterdam that the two bodies should be known as being "in association with" each other.

This arrangement proved to be useful, but, as co-operation became more intensive, the question as to the maintaining of two separate organizations became increasingly insistent. The strongest demand for full integration came from the Churches in Asia and Africa. They desired to be in full partnership with the Churches in Europe and America and to participate in the ecumenical movement of the Churches, and they found it difficult to have to deal with two different world organizations. In the countries of the older Churches the problem was, however, that the responsibility for missions was often in the hands of missionary societies which had grown up because the Churches had

[1] *Institutionalism and Church Unity* (a study prepared under the auspices of Faith and Order). New York 1963.

not waked up to their missionary calling. Would an integration of I.M.C. and W.C.C. not lead to a weakening rather than to a deepening of concern for the evangelization of the world? Were the Churches ready to accept their responsibility for the world-wide apostolate?

In the ten years between 1948 and 1958 these questions were discussed with great intensity. It was found that owing to the new realization of the position of the Church in a "non-Christian world" and owing to the rediscovery of the missionary nature of the Church itself many Churches were now eager to take their full share in the common missionary task. Thus by 1958 it was possible for both I.M.C. and W.C.C. to decide that they would work towards a full integration of the two bodies. The integration took place at the New Delhi Assembly in 1961.

Fears which had been expressed in some quarters that a considerable part of the constituency of the International Missionary Council would not desire to co-operate with the integrated council, did not materialize, for only very few members of the I.M.C. remained outside the new Division of World Mission and Evangelism. Even a short time after the date of integration it was truthfully said that it seemed that the two bodies had been together for many years.

Although Churches and missionary bodies in each country remained free to follow or not to follow the international pattern, the integration of I.M.C. and W.C.C. led to similar action in a good many national situations. Thus the Churches have accepted more direct and definite responsibility for missionary activity and the missionary societies have related themselves more closely to the Churches. This was all the more necessary since not only outside, but also within the Churches, radical questions were raised with regard to missions. These had not only to do with missionary policies, but with the very *raison d'être* of missions. The modern mood of relativism and of syncretism made its influence felt. The true *raison d'être* of missions as a constraint put on the Church by its Lord, which had nothing to do with cultural imperialism, needed to be clarified by the whole ecumenical fellowship. And it had to be shown that there was no difference in principle between the evangelistic task in continents of Christian tradition and that in continents where other religions dominated. In all six continents the Church was called to mission. This was the theme worked out in the World Council Assemblies and in the Mexico meeting of the Commission of World Mission and Evangelism. At the same time the Evangelism Department of the W.C.C. concentrated on the study of "the missionary structure of the congregation". This study met with stronger response than any other study undertaken by the W.C.C. in recent years.

Coming to grips with the World

The Oxford Conference on Life and Work in 1937 had helped many Churches to realize that the Church had a prophetic mission towards society. And the experience of the war years made it very clear that one of the principal tasks of the Church was to perform the "office of the watchman". Thus many Churches which had taken for granted that the civilization in which they lived was and would remain a Christianized civilization realized suddenly that the very foundations of their society were shaking and began to rediscover the social dimension of their calling. Churches which had been silent about the great human issues of our time and had lived a self-centred existence began to speak out. They found that, while their voice was no longer a dominant voice, they could nevertheless help their members to steer a Christian course in their daily life and exert a not inconsiderable amount of influence on public opinion.

But they found at the same time that with regard to the basic issues of our time their witness would have to be a common witness. In this respect especially the statement of the Stockholm Conference was applicable: "The world is too strong for a divided Church." Thus the task to formulate common Christian convictions concerning those social and international problems which were of world-wide dimensions was to a large extent entrusted to the organs of the ecumenical movement.

A passage from the consultation on the future of the Commission of the Churches on International Affairs (C.C.I.A.), held in 1967 in Scheveningen, shows clearly that this concern belongs to the nature of the ecumenical movement. It said:

> We draw attention to the providential reality ... that precisely at the time when the unity of mankind is becoming an inescapable fact, the privilege of ecumenical fellowship is being progressively realized by the churches. The discovery of their unity, transcending without destroying the ecclesiastical traditions and national loyalties of Christians throughout the world, gives churches a new perspective from which they may come to more objective judgment of the conflicts of our time.[1]

It was also increasingly understood that neither the world nor the church membership would listen to a mere repetition of statements concerning general Christian principles. On the other hand, the Churches had no right to express a conviction about specific world problems unless they could do so on the basis of a thorough study of the issues undertaken by men whose competence would be respected. That is why the Commission of the Churches on International Affairs was formed as a body of church people who had experience in the field of international affairs and who were served by a permanent staff of men in daily contact with international developments. That is why in the realm of Church and Society very concrete studies were undertaken on the implications of "rapid social change" for the Churches in many parts of the world. And that is why the World Conference on Church and Society in 1966 concentrated on such concrete human issues as the problems of development and the relations between the affluent nations and the nations engaged in a desperate struggle against poverty.

It is a remarkable fact that in spite of the extreme variety of national, political, and theological background it has so often been possible to arrive at a common mind about difficult and controversial problems. There were, of course, also a number of questions, some of them crucial, on which no such *communis opinio* was reached and it became clear that the ecumenical

---

[1] *Ecumenical Review*, vol. xix (July 1967), p. 317.

movement can never "rest on its laurels" and that every new generation has to go through its own struggle to find a common basis for witness and action. Towards the end of our period new possibilities of consultation and co-operation in the field of social and international issues between the W.C.C. and the Roman Catholic Church began to materialize. When one compares what the World Conference on Church and Society said about the issues of world economic justice and development with the recommendations made in the papal encyclical *Populorum progressio* one finds that a substantial consensus in this crucial subject is developing.

The Impact of Asia, Africa, and Latin America

At the beginning of our 1958–68 period, the status of the younger Churches in the ecumenical movement was still ambiguous and uncertain. Only twenty-four of these Churches had joined the World Council. So they represented a small minority. And within their different regions they had little contact with each other. Most younger Churches knew a great deal more about the Churches in the country from which their missionaries had come than about the Churches in their own part of the world. But in the years since 1948 very many younger Churches became members of the Council. This meant that "they were recognized as equals of the older churches" and "this enabled them to gain a new sense of their own destiny in the economy of God in the world".[1] But they would not be able to fulfil their ecumenical calling unless they could come together on a regional or continental level in order to learn from each other, to undertake common tasks, and to bring their specific contribution to the whole movement.

The Asians led the way. In a series of meetings from 1949 onwards, plans were defined and the East Asia Christian Conference came into being. Africa, ·Latin America, and the Pacific Islands followed a few years later.

This development of a regional ecumenism was in no way a withdrawal from the world-wide movement. On the contrary. It was an effort to formulate more clearly what were the specific concerns of each region and what contribution it could make to the whole. At the same time it was realized that the great question how to bring the Christian message to the peoples of Asia or Africa in a manner truly comprehensible in the indigenous cultural situations, but with full loyalty to the essential content of the gospel, was a question which could best be answered by the Churches together, continent by continent.

Thus a whole new dimension was added to the ecumenical movement. This became increasingly clear at the meetings of the Central Committee and of the Assemblies of the World Council. The issues being discussed were no longer only those which were of greater concern to Europe and North America. The Central Committee meetings in Lucknow 1952 and Enugu 1965 and the Assembly at New Delhi were opportunities for confrontation with the realities of the Asian and African situation. And the World Conference on Church and Society in Geneva 1966 was in fact a dialogue between the

[1] V. E. Devadutt in *Lessons for Tomorrow's Mission* (W.S.C.F. 1960), p. 213.

"North" and the "South" in which the voices of Asians, Africans, and Latin Americans were heard as never before in the ecumenical movement.

The impact of the Churches of these continents on the ecumenical movement can be summarized in the following points:

1. They have helped the other Churches to realize that the position of Christianity in the world is that of a minority the future of which depends on its missionary energy.

2. They contribute to the creation of a different sense of proportion in doctrinal and theological matters. For the issues which are crucial for them are not the traditional interconfessional issues, but rather the issues of a right interpretation of basic Christian truth in terms of cultures dominated by other religions.

3. They help the other Churches to face the problem of world poverty hunger, and underdevelopment as the number one problem for humanity and as an inescapable challenge to all Christians.

The ecumenical movement is still not fully ecumenical in so far as in its concerns, in its leadership, in the composition of many of its meetings, older Churches hold a dominating position. But progress in the direction of a truly effective participation of the total Christian family has been made.

The Impact of Eastern Orthodoxy

One of the earliest initiatives to arrive at the creation of a fellowship of Churches had been taken in 1920 by the Ecumenical Patriarchate of Constantinople, and a number of Orthodox Churches had taken part in the ecumenical meetings of the 1920s and 1930s. But by the time of the Amsterdam Assembly of 1948 only a few had accepted membership in the W.C.C. and only two (the Ecumenical Patriarchate and the Church of Greece) had been able to send delegations to Amsterdam. Attempts made to arrive at a fraternal discussion with the Moscow Patriarchate had failed. The situation was similar in other ecumenical organizations. That large part of Eastern Orthodoxy which lived in the countries under a communist regime was for the time being unable to maintain contacts with other Churches. It is true that Orthodox leaders in Western Europe and the U.S.A. continued to make a valuable contribution, but the general situation remained, nevertheless, that during a considerable period the Orthodox Churches were not present on the ecumenical scene in such numbers and with such weight that they could make their voice sufficiently heard.

The situation began to change after the Evanston Assembly of 1954. After a period of correspondence delegations of the Orthodox Church of Russia and of the W.C.C. met in Utrecht 1958 and found a basis for closer relations. Visits of W.C.C. leaders and staff-members to Russia and of Russian Church leaders to Geneva were arranged. Many questions were clarified.

In 1961 the Orthodox Churches of Russia, Rumania, Bulgaria, and Poland became members of the W.C.C. They were followed by other Orthodox

Churches and also by other Eastern Churches, notably the Armenian Church, so that by 1964 practically all large Churches of Eastern tradition were actively participating in the movement. The persistent policy of co-operation with, and support of, the W.C.C. maintained by Patriarch Athenagoras of Constantinople was an important element in this development.

In the meantime the Orthodox Churches had also to consider what should be their attitude to the Second Vatican Council to which they were asked to send observers. This led to a series of meetings of Orthodox Church leaders at which decisions were taken concerning the policy of the Orthodox Churches in the new ecumenical situation. Unprecedented personal contacts were established when Pope Paul VI and Patriarch Athenagoras of Constantinople met in Jerusalem, later in Constantinople and in Rome, and when dignitaries of several Orthodox Churches visited Rome.

This was therefore the period in which Eastern Christianity began to make its impact felt in the ecumenical movement. The Montreal Faith and Order Report 1963 said: "For the first time in the Faith and Order dialogue, the Eastern Orthodox and other Eastern Churches have been strongly represented in our meetings. A new dimension of Faith and Order has opened up and we can only begin to see its future possibilities."[1] These last words deserve emphasis. The active participation of the Eastern Churches, not only in Faith and Order meetings, but in the conferences on Church and Society, on international affairs and many others has made a real difference to the ecumenical movement. They have raised questions about the place of worship among the concerns of the ecumenical movement. They have added new dimensions to the discussion on ecclesiology by maintaining at the same time a high doctrine of the Church and a strong emphasis on the autonomy of each national Church. On the other hand, the ecumenical movement has made it necessary for them to face anew the issue of the Church's responsibility in the field of social ethics. But it must also be said that after so many centuries of separation between East and West and at a time when many of the Orthodox Churches are living under great external pressures, it is still exceedingly difficult to arrive at a full sharing between the Christian East and the Christian West. Neither in the West nor in the East has enough been done to find and prepare men for the task of ecumenical interpretation and cross-fertilization between two main parts of Christendom which have been separated for ten centuries.

The Roman Catholic Church
Enters upon the Ecumenical Scene

Individual Roman Catholics had shown deep interest in the ecumenical movement since its beginning and in the 1930s small groups of Roman Catholics, Protestants, and Orthodox had come together quietly to explore the possibilities of a dialogue. The World's Student Christian Federation was a pioneer in this field. The attendance was largely from some of the countries of western Europe. During the Second World War many new contacts were established.

[1] Montreal, p. 56.

B

Not only in the countries where Roman Catholics and Protestants were both in conflict with national socialism, but also in Great Britain, there were conversations at the level of the hierarchy, and in some cases common declarations were issued. It was therefore hoped that a number of individually invited Roman Catholic observers would be allowed to attend the first World Council Assembly, but this hope was not fulfilled. In 1949 the Vatican defined its attitude to the ecumenical movement (*De motione ecumenica*) and recognized the significance of the ecumenical movement. It was also stated that no Roman Catholics should attend international ecumenical meetings unless they had permission to do so from the Vatican. When the Second Assembly took place in 1954, the Roman Catholic Archbishop of Chicago forbade any Roman Catholics to attend the meeting in Evanston, a suburb of Chicago.

In the meantime the informal theological contacts had been intensified. Roman Catholic ecumenists made increasingly helpful contributions to the ecumenical discussion. The questions they raised about the nature and policies of the World Council stimulated the Council to clarify its position. Thus the important Toronto declaration of 1950 on "The Church, the Churches and the World Council of Churches" was at least in part an answer to questions which Roman Catholic theologians had raised.

A new situation was created in 1960 when Pope John XXIII created the Secretariat for the Promotion of Unity among Christians. Up to that moment the W.C.C. or other ecumenical organizations had no "address" in the Roman Catholic Church to which they could turn to discuss specific problems of relationships or of common concern. From that moment onwards there was regular consultation. Cardinal Bea, who headed the new secretariat, went out of his way to facilitate personal contacts with leaders of the W.C.C. and of the different Churches. Thus it became possible to have at the Third Assembly a group of Roman Catholic observers designated by the Roman Catholic Church, and thus it came about that observers from many confessional bodies, from the W.C.C. and from some Churches, attended the Second Vatican Council. Their role at the Council went far beyond observing and really led to a real dialogue about the great themes on the agenda of the Council. The Decree on Ecumenism which the Council adopted opened new doors for ecumenical contacts. Its definition of ecumenism had a good deal in common with that underlying the life of the W.C.C.; but the difference between the two conceptions was that the Vatican Council thinks in terms of a bringing of the other Churches to a renewed and more truly catholic Roman Catholic Church, whereas the ecumenism of the W.C.C. considers the question of the ultimate form of unity as an open question the answer to which will have to be found during the common ecumenical pilgrimage.

An important result of the new situation was the creation of a Joint Working Group between the Roman Catholic Church and the W.C.C. During the short time of its existence this group has already shown its usefulness as a platform for the discussion of common concerns. Its reports have been well received by the Central Committee of the W.C.C. and by the Vatican authorities.

The ecumenical mobilization of the Roman Catholics has modified the ecumenical situation very profoundly. Both at the international and at the national level there has been a tremendous increase in opportunities for contact, for serious conversation, and for practical co-operation. It was inevitable that these new and unexpected possibilities came to occupy the centre of the ecumenical stage. It seemed for a time as if the one and only important ecumenical problem was that of the relations between the Roman Catholic Church and other Churches. And there was a good deal of naive optimism about the removal of age-old divisions in the very near future. Some people declared that the centre of the ecumenical movement had shifted and that the ecumenical initiative had passed to the Roman Catholic Church. But they forget that ecumenism is not a game of football. There is no place in the ecumenical movement for a form of competition which seeks to eliminate other participants. For that would be to deny the very principle of gathering and the creation of true fellowship.

There is a place in the ecumenical movement for what the Abbé Couturier called "spiritual emulation", that is, for mutual stimulation to deeper and better Christian obedience and discipleship. Now the ecumenical movement as it had taken shape in the W.C.C. had been a stimulus for the Roman Catholic Church. Similarly, the entrance of the Roman Catholic Church upon the ecumenical scene has stimulated and will continue to stimulate the W.C.C. and its member Churches. It has not only led many Churches to rethink their attitude to the Roman Catholic Church, but it has led them to ask again whether they themselves were sufficiently active in the cause of church unity. Thus it is shown again that the cause of ecumenism is indivisible, that, as the Decree on Ecumenism of the Second Vatican Council said, there is one ecumenical movement, and that the spiritual gift of the active desire for unity, as all spiritual gifts, is given for the common good of the whole People of God.

Confessional Consciousness

Most confessions or denominations had developed their own federations, alliances, or organs of consultation before the ecumenical movement took shape. But in the period after the Second World War most of them re-organized themselves and became more active than they had been before, and some developed a strong secretariat and undertook a wide variety of tasks.

This development was partly due to the specific needs of their member Churches, but it was also due to the emergence of the ecumenical movement. The new unprecedented ecumenical situation obliged each confession to consider anew what position it should take with regard to the issues of church unity, and this led naturally to a new reflection on the significance of the common confessional heritage. All has to ask: What can our confessional family contribute to the wider ecumenical family? What is the basic truth for which it must stand at all cost?

It was equally inevitable that the growth of the confessional bodies would create problems of relationship between these bodies and the W.C.C. There were the practical problems such as the demands in time, in energy, in finance which the W.C.C. and the confessional bodies were making on the same Churches. There was the fundamental issue of the relative claims of confessional unity and of unity on the national scale. Fortunately most of these bodies were willing and eager to co-operate with the World Council and the World Council itself understood that the support of these bodies was essential for its own development. Thus regular means of consultation were developed and it proved possible to remove a number of misunderstandings.

In recent years several of the confessional families have found a very important role in paving the way for church unity by entering in dialogue with other confessions. In this respect the invitation issued by the Roman Catholic Church to all confessional bodies to send observers to the Second Vatican Council has had important consequences. As the confessional families reflected on their attitude to the Roman Catholic Church and in many cases agreed to enter into conversation with the Roman Catholic Church, they realized that more could and should be done on a world level about conversations with the other confessions. The more specific discussions on reunion will have to a very large extent to take place on a national level, but discussions on the world level can prepare the way. Thus we find in recent years that a whole network of interconfessional dialogue is developing.

Evangelical Critique of Ecumenism

During the period concerned the growing influence of the ecumenical movement also led to growing criticism on the part of Christians who mistrusted the basic motives of the movement. The wilder form of opposition, expressing itself in accusations that the movement was infiltrated by communists or that it was scheming to gather all the Churches under the authority of the Pope, created a certain amount of confusion among ignorant people, but never had enough backing of responsible churchmen to become a real problem. But the criticism that came from responsible conservative Evangelical circles had to do with real issues which had to be faced. For these issues were important in themselves, and failure to answer them could lead to increasing estrangement between the ecumenism of the W.C.C. and the ecumenism of evangelical bodies, some of which had a considerable following in member Churches of the W.C.C.

The main issue was ecclesiological in character. Is the unity of which the New Testament speaks to be conceived exclusively as a "spiritual" and "invisible" unity or as a unity which must also find concrete structural expression in the life of the Church? The W.C.C. made it clear, very particularly in its New Delhi statement on unity, that, while it could not choose for any particular form of unity, it stood for unity which would express itself in tangible form. This stand was not taken because of a desire for the concentration of ecclesiastical power, or in order to increase the influence of the Church in the world, but rather because, according to the Scriptures, it is an essential part of the calling and witness of the Church to manifest the oneness of the people of God.

It was stressed again and again that the W.C.C. Churches did not conceive such concrete unity as the centralized unity of a super-Church, that real unity did not mean uniformity, and that it was out of the question that any of these Churches would give up the spiritual independence which they cherished so greatly. The suspicion that there was an ecumenical conspiracy to create a vast and powerful ecclesiastical machinery of world-wide dimensions has not yet been removed. But, as the Central Committee of the W.C.C. noted in 1966, "In those Evangelical circles where ecumenism has been suspect hitherto, there are now increasing signs of concern about Christian unity."[1] There were other points of criticism. Many Evangelicals feared that the ecumenical movement would lead to theological relativism or even syncretism. This fear is not wholly unfounded since there are a certain number of people in several of the member Churches of the W.C.C. whose "ecumenism" takes the form of a theological indifferentism or of a general embracing of all religions. The W.C.C. has, however, been able to answer that the main thrust of its theological studies and pronouncements has been clearly biblical and christocentric and that the basic principle of its ecumenism has always been that unity at the expense of truth is not unity at all.

Perhaps the most relevant question raised by the conservative Evangelicals has been whether the ecumenical movement has concentrated its energies too much on social and international problems and neglected the primary task of mission and evangelism. The question is all the more relevant since a comparison between the W.C.C. Churches and the evangelical bodies shows that the latter are spending a much greater proportion of their resources of men and money on evangelism and foreign missions. But the great question arises: What is evangelism? Is the Church evangelistic only if it preaches the gospel to individuals? Or is it also evangelistic if it throws the light of the gospel on the great human problems of our time? The debate continues and both partners in the conversation have to learn from each other. For, as the Central Committee of the W.C.C. said in 1965: "The member churches of the World Council, which have already experienced something of the mutual correction and edification which is made possible by our common membership in the Council, need also the contribution of these evangelical churches...."

Churchly Ecumenism Challenged

We have noted that during the 1930s and 1940s there had been a "rediscovery of the Church".[2] This had been partly due to the convergent development in biblical theology, so that it was possible to speak of a "new consensus" of scholars from differing confessions concerning the decisive place of the Church in the New Testament. But it was also the consequence drawn from the church conflicts first in Germany, then in the occupied countries, in which it had been shown that the Christian cause could be defended only by confessing Churches deeply conscious of their God-given mission. Moreover, the witness which had to be given to society, national or international, at a time

---

[1] MRCC (Geneva 1966), p. 72.
[2] See *A History of the Ecumenical Movement 1517–1948*, ed. Rouse and Neill, pp. 574 and 700.

of the shaking of the foundations could be effective only if it was given by Churches who could speak on behalf of a coherent community of the faithful. The fact that with the creation of the World Council of Churches the ecumenical movement became more definitely "churchly" in character was therefore widely accepted as a necessary development.

But not many years later the question was raised whether this emphasis on the Church was really justified. Had the movement not lost some of its spontaneity and of its revolutionary character by linking itself so closely to the Churches? Was there not a danger that the World Council, which had begun its life with a very small staff working in a chalet and in wooden barracks and which within twenty years had become a considerable organization housed in impressive buildings, was itself becoming the victim of the iron law of institutional development? Some began to use the word "ecumenical bureaucracy".

And there was an even deeper issue. Was it right to be so strongly concerned about the formation of an *oikoumene* of the Churches? Should not the original meaning of *oikoumene*, namely "the whole inhabited world", become the true focus of the movement, so that it should be really concerned with the world rather than with the Church?

These ideas met with considerable response among young people who were deeply disappointed by the lack of effective renewal in the Churches and by the slowness of advance toward church unity. They received further encouragement from the more general anti-institutional wave which became a characteristic of the life of the younger generation in the 1960s. The result has been the growth of various forms of spontaneous ecumenism, outside or in very undefined relation with the ecumenical movement of the Churches. In so far as these forms of ecumenism are completely unrelated to the life of the Churches and combat not only institutionalism but also the very existence of institutions, they are not likely to have a lasting effect. For no spiritual movement can make any real impression on the course of church history or world history unless it becomes incarnate in some tangible (and that means some institutional) form. It was precisely the concern for relevance to the new world situation which led the men of 1937 to the conclusion that the ecumenical movement should have a more definite shape. But in so far as these new movements seek to act as pioneers for the Churches, to challenge bureaucratic and immobile structures, and to make imaginative experiments, they may render a service similar to that which was rendered by the Christian youth movements in the early days of the ecumenical movement.

The fact that the ecumenical movement has continued to grow is not in itself a cause for alarm, but for gratitude. For that growth has been a response to a great need in the life of the Church. And the churchly *oikoumene* can only serve the world *oikoumene* if it develops adequate instruments for the fulfilment of its task. Moreover, whether a movement becomes institutionalist and bureaucratic is far more a problem of quality than of quantity. The best answer to institutionalism is therefore to ensure that within the given institutions it is the calling rather than the organization, the goal rather than the means, which dominate.

Theological Tensions

The 1930s and 1940s were a period of remarkable convergence in theological thought. The ecumenical movement had helped to overcome divisions and was in turn greatly strengthened by the common turning to a biblical theology with strong emphasis on the calling of the Church in the world. By the time of the Oxford Conference 1937, the tension between the "activist" and the "otherworldly" theologies had lost a good deal of its sharpness because the world situation had forced the "activists" to revise their optimistic view of history and had forced the "otherworldly" to take the task of the Church in society more seriously. There remained enough important theological problems, such as those between the "Catholic" and the "Protestant" conceptions of the Church, but in 1941 a Dominican, Father F. M. Braun, could write that "a new consensus"[1] was emerging in this respect. And the Amsterdam Assembly 1948, while stressing the very real difference between the "Catholic" and "Protestant" conceptions, found a substantial consensus on "the Universal Church in God's design". It said: "Beneath these disagreements we find an agreement in a unity which drew us together and will not let us go."[2]

During the years of preparation for the Second Assembly with its main theme "Christ the Hope of the World", there was again a lively discussion concerning the meaning and relevance of eschatology. The Advisory Committee on the main theme, composed of Christian thinkers of extremely varied background, had a hard time arriving at a common document and the Assembly did not accept it as its own word. But the Assembly admitted that the report "exhibits a substantial ecumenical consensus" and that "it indicates the direction in which we must all move".[3] And there can be no doubt that the report exerted a wide influence in the following years. The revision of the Basis of the W.C.C. 1961, so that it included a definite reference to the authority of the holy Scriptures and an explicit statement concerning the Trinity was also a sign of growing consensus. And the most impressive aspect of the theological development was that Roman Catholic, Orthodox, and Protestant were not only learning from each other, but that they discovered large areas of agreement about theological issues which had kept them apart for many centuries.

But the story of theology, as the story of human thought generally, is a story of ever new beginnings. And so during the period many of the results of the theological work of earlier generations were again called in question. There is practically no Church which escapes this theological shaking of the foundations. The Roman Catholic theologian Karl Rahner speaks of a sense of "historical dizziness". Now it is inevitable that in a time of intensive inter-Church contacts, new movements of thought cross the frontiers of the confessions. And so the new divergence of convictions concerning demythologization and *Heilsgeschichte*, concerning the "end of religion" and the meaning of secularism, concerning existentialism and the "death of God", is

[1] F. M. Braun. *Aspects nouveaux du problème de l'Église* (Fribourg 1941), chapter 3.
[2] Amsterdam, p. 55.   [3] Evanston, p. 70.

not one between the different confessions, but a subject of debate within each confession and within the ecumenical movement as a whole.

This "transconfessional" character of the great theological debates of recent years is bound to have considerable effect on the relations between the Churches. Already the representatives of the new theological currents in the different Churches have a stronger bond among themselves across confessional frontiers than they have with many of their fellow-churchmen who do not accept the new ideas. This brings an element of confusion into the inter-Church situation, but it may also help to show that many of the old lines of division and demarcation are no longer the truly important ones. The Commission on Faith and Order is deeply aware of this new situation and has therefore decided that it must not only be concerned with the "controversies which have their origin in the past", but also with the "new threats to unity" and that in its future work priority should be given to the great controversies of today.

For the ecumenical movement as a whole the question arises whether out of the present theological tensions a new consensus will emerge which can serve as a foundation for the common witness and the common task. There is no reason to deplore the fact that new situations require the reformulation of the truth, but there is every reason to be watchful that the basic insights which have created the ecumenical movement and kept it alive will not be lost in the process of rethinking.

Non-Theological Tensions

The hope which many had expressed that after the Second World War the ecumenical ship could sail on less troubled waters was not fulfilled. The postwar period became a period of acute political tensions and conflicts and these had considerable repercussions on inter-Church relations. The ecumenical movement could have taken one of two lines of least resistance. It could have identified itself uncritically with one particular power-constellation or one ideology. The temptation to do this was all the greater, since in the first years after the Amsterdam Assembly only very few Churches in communist countries could participate in the life of the movement. Voices were not wanting which urged the World Council to enter into alliance with the Western powers and to defend their policies without reserve. But the ecumenical movement had learned the important lesson that its strength could consist only in its integrity and independence as a movement exclusively motivated by Christian convictions and constantly concerned about the maintenance of fellowship between Christians in all parts of the world and living under the most diverse political regimes.

The other line of least resistance would have been to decide that, in view of the repercussions which statements on controversial issues might have for the cohesion of the movement, the World Council should remain silent concerning such issues. Many times the W.C.C. has been warned that if it continued to speak out on the burning issues of international relations it would surely endanger its own life. But the ecumenical movement had precisely become relevant when it had become a fellowship of common convictions and for common witness and sought to throw the light of the gospel upon the grave issues facing mankind. An ecumenical movement which would proclaim only vague generalities could hardly expect to be taken seriously by the Churches and by the world.

The dilemma created by the duty to witness to justice and peace and the duty to maintain fellowship led to a number of greater and smaller crises. At the time of the war in Korea, during the Hungarian crisis and the Suez War, at the moment of the Cuba conflict, and on a number of other occasions the responsible committees of the Council or its officers made specific declarations. In doing so they sought to take their stand on principles which had been adopted by the Assemblies. More frequently the officers of the Commission of the Churches on International Affairs expressed their mind concerning possible solutions of international problems. In many cases these statements were well received. In some cases they led to a good deal of controversy within the movement. It is, however, remarkable that in no case did they lead to a real break in the ecumenical fellowship. The decision of three Dutch Reformed Churches in South Africa to leave the Council is no exception, since their decision was mainly based on the rejection of the report of the Cottesloe Conference[1] which had been approved overwhelmingly by their own chosen delegates.

When, by the time of the Third Assembly in New Delhi 1961, the Churches of Russia, Rumania, Bulgaria as well as a large number of Churches from Asia and Africa had joined, the W.C.C. became a body in which nearly all the international tensions of our time were at least potentially reflected. And at each meeting of the Central or Executive Committees or of the C.C.I.A. some of these tensions had to be dealt with and if possible overcome. It cannot be said that the attempt was always successful. But it can be said that on the whole the struggle to arrive at a common mind has often strengthened rather than weakened the sense of common sharing in a fellowship which transcends all political divisions. Thus at the World Conference on Church and Society hard words were said by the representatives of the poorer nations to those of the rich nations and vice versa, but it was precisely on the basis of this frankness that it became possible to reach a common mind on many important problems.

The experience of these years shows how difficult it is for all Churches to rise above the necessarily limited viewpoint of their national and social environment, but it has also shown that it is precisely through the ecumenical encounter that the necessary mutual correction can take place so that the Churches can arrive at a more objective judgement concerning the road to true peace and real justice.

The W.C.C. was, however, by no means the only Christian body to deal with international problems and non-theological tensions between Christians. During the period under discussion there was a considerable improvement

---

[1] The Cottesloe Conference was a meeting of delegates of the W.C.C. member Churches in South Africa together with a small delegation of the W.C.C. It dealt with the Christian attitude to race relations in South Africa.

in the relations between the Roman Catholic Church and the Churches in communist countries and even an improvement in its relations with some of the governments of these countries. The great exception remained China. Contacts with Christians in China became fewer and fewer in spite of all attempts to restore fellowship. This was even true in the case of the Prague Peace Conference which in the beginning had had participants from the Chinese Churches. That Peace Conference played an important role in bringing Christian leaders from eastern Europe together and in promoting a dialogue between them and Christians from countries in the West, in Asia, Africa, and Latin America. It is not organized as a body representing all the Churches in an official way and considers its task as complementary to the work of the W.C.C. From time to time discussions have taken place between the W.C.C. and the Prague Peace Conference in order to clarify the position of each body in relation to the other.

The Growing Ecumenical Network

International ecumenism had received much of its original inspiration from national bodies, very especially from the Federal Council of Churches in the U.S.A. But the emergence of the ecumenical movement on the world level led to the formation of national councils in many countries in which such councils did not yet exist. Where these councils were well organized and co-operated with the World Council, or where they were member councils of the International Missionary Council and became members of the new Division of Missions and Evangelism of the W.C.C., they helped greatly in relating the programme of the world bodies to the Churches. It was in the realm of inter-Church aid, relief work, and service to refugees that the most effective system of continuous co-operation was elaborated. For the first time in church history the Churches possessed an instrument of service through which they could act speedily and efficiently whenever a great human need had to be met in any part of the world.

It must be added that in many places there has been a considerable development of ecumenical activity on the local level. There are still cities and villages where local congregations belonging to church bodies which are active in the ecumenical movement have little contact with each other. But the number of local councils which understand that ecumenism begins at home is growing, and it is increasingly understood that local councils should not only be concerned with common practical problems, but also with a real spiritual sharing between the Churches.

The regional (continental) councils have been created in the period since the Amsterdam Assembly. They are of varying strength, but several of them have already become indispensable instruments for ecumenical action and it is largely due to their work that each continent can now make its voice heard in the world-wide dialogue.

With regard to ecumenical education there was also considerable progress. Ecumenism became under a variety of names a recognized subject of study in many theological faculties and colleges. Ecumenical Institutes were formed in many places. It can be said that the number of people who give full time to the service of the ecumenical cause on the international, national, and local level has increased beyond anything which the most optimistic supporters of the ecumenical movement had conceived possible in 1948.

The more specialized movements, which are organizationally independent, but collaborate in many ways with the W.C.C. and with the Churches, remained as indispensable for the ecumenical movement as a whole as they had been before the formation of the World Council of Churches, for they performed tasks which could not, at least not in the same way, be performed by the Churches or the W.C.C. All of them had to face new problems and discovered new opportunities as the ecumenical movement advanced. Thus the United Bible Societies entered in consultation with the authorities of the Roman Catholic Church about common translations of the Scriptures. And the Y.M.C.A., Y.W.C.A., and the W.S.C.F. also developed their relations with Roman Catholic youth organizations.

What was Achieved and What was Not Achieved?

The strength and weakness of the ecumenical movement as it developed during the last twenty years can be summarized in the following seven points— five of them dealing with points of strength and two of them dealing with points of weakness.

The points of strength would seem to be the following:

1. All Churches have been obliged to respond to the fundamental question which the ecumenical movement puts before them, the question of their relation to other Churches, the question of their obedience to the original mandate to gather with the Lord of the Church the dispersed children of God into one. Every Church must make up its mind about this new fact in the history of the Church, that the Churches after centuries in isolation and self-centredness are again turning towards each other and seeking to manifest that the bond of common faith in Jesus Christ must lead to a common life and a common witness.

2. The Churches live again as members of a family, a family in which there is still a great deal of friction and misunderstanding, but a family which cannot fail to realize that it has a common history and a common destiny, that it has its own identity and its own ethos and that its members need to support each other and to share their spiritual and material gifts. The times when Churches could live as self-contained entities is irrevocably gone. Theology can no longer be carried on in the form of confessional monologue.

3. The existence of the ecumenical movement has given encouragement to Churches which are under the pressure of a hostile environment or live a very isolated existence. For them the sense of belonging to a world-wide fellowship has an existential significance which it can hardly have in the same way in Churches living in more favourable external conditions.

4. The ecumenical movement has enabled the Churches to render a common

witness at the world level. In a time in which the grave human issues are issues of global dimensions the Churches can hardly make their voice heard if they do not speak together and if they do not speak in terms of the total world situation. The ecumenical movement has shown that their common faith enables the Churches to arrive at common convictions concerning the tensions and conflicts of our time and so to help in breaking through the deadlock situations which are characteristic of international life in our time.

5. The ecumenical movement has enabled the Churches to practise solidarity in their relations with each other and to become an effective instrument for the meeting of human need in all parts of the world.

The points of weakness would seem to be the following:

1. The ecumenical movement cannot yet claim that very significant results have been reached with regard to church unity. The word "unity" is here taken in the wider sense, for the ecumenical movement must not be judged exclusively by the number of organizational unions, but also by the other ways in which growing fellowship expresses itself, such as intercommunion. With regard to actual unions it can be said that a considerable number of Churches have become united with each other. While in most cases these Churches belonged to the same or closely related confessional families, the trend toward interconfessional unions is increasing. It is also true that a very large number of Churches are at present in negotiation with each other about unity. But few of these schemes are as yet approaching the moment of completion and realization.

With regard to full intercommunion there has been some progress. But in many circles, notably among the young, there is a sense of disappointment that after several decades of living together the Churches have not solved this distressing problem.

Thus the ecumenical movement has now reached a critical stage. Will it be content with that by no means inconsiderable, but nevertheless very incomplete, form of unity which it has already achieved? Or will it press on to that full unity which alone is worthy of the Church of Christ and which is the deepest *raison d'être* of the movement itself.

2. The ecumenical movement is not sufficiently rooted in the life of the local congregations. In spite of all attempts made to educate church members for participation in the ecumenical enterprise the movement is still too much an army with many generals and officers, but with too few soldiers. It would seem that not enough has been done to show that the ecumenical concern is not to be conceived as one of the many concerns in which a local congregation may take interest, but as a concern which arises out of the very nature of the Church. It is clear that real advance towards full unity will be made only if in the coming years local congregations and their members discover that to follow Christ means to follow him in his work of the building on the one Body, his Body.

2

The Life and Activities
of the World Council of Churches

H. KRÜGER

Defining the Nature and Function
of the World Council of Churches,
from the Toronto Statement (*1950*)
to the Ecumenical Way (*1966*)

It is a noteworthy fact that the World Council "in process of formation" had to solve extremely far-reaching and important problems during the formative years between 1938 and 1948, before it had been officially constituted. It is also noteworthy that it existed for several years before it rendered an account of its own nature. At Amsterdam the Assembly adopted a statement from the Provisional Committee on the "Nature of the Council".[1] It is quite natural that in those first years many misunderstandings arose, especially from the Orthodox side, about the nature and purpose of the W.C.C. because a body of this kind had never existed before. Until then ecumenical relationships had been comparatively loose and non-committal. Through the formation of the W.C.C. they were now raised to an official level, and the member Churches were compelled to understand clearly their own status in this new fellowship. The comments and reflections were summed up in a draft entitled "The Ecclesiological Significance of the World Council of Churches" which was submitted to the Central Committee at Toronto in 1950. This formed the basis for the famous "Toronto statement" which clearly defined the relation of the member Churches to one another.[2]

The Toronto statement declares: "The World Council of Churches is not and must never become a Super-Church" (III. 1). Its competence does not even cover union negotiations; its purpose is "to bring the churches into living contact with each other" (III. 2). The W.C.C. has no ecclesiology of its own (III. 3), therefore no Church is obliged to change its own ecclesiology (III. 4) nor to accept "a specific doctrine concerning the nature of Church unity" (III. 5). The basis for fellowship in the W.C.C. is merely "the common recognition that Christ is the Divine Head of the body" (IV. 1). Admittedly the Churches belonging to the W.C.C. recognize "that the membership of the Church of Christ is more inclusive than the membership of their own Church body" (IV. 3); but this does imply "that each Church must regard the other member churches as churches in the true and full sense of the word". But "they recognize one another as serving the One Lord" (IV. 4) and "recognize in other churches elements of the true Church" (IV. 5). It is on this basis that they seek "a common witness before the world" (IV. 6), "render assistance to each other in case of need, and refrain from such actions as are incompatible with brotherly relationships" (IV. 7). "The member churches enter into spiritual relationships through which they seek to learn from each other and to give help to each other in order that the body of Christ may be built up and that the life of the churches may be renewed" (IV. 8).

All this sounds very cautious and reserved. Clearly it was intended more to describe the existing situation than to point towards a future goal, in order that all the member Churches might participate and co-operate. (This

[1] Amsterdam, pp. 127–8.   [2] *The First Six Years, 1948–1954*, pp. 113–19.

reticence applied not only to the Orthodox Churches but also to many Reformation Churches.) It is only with extreme caution that reference is made in the last paragraph to "a very real unity" which has repeatedly "been discovered in ecumenical meetings". "It exists and we receive it again and again as an unmerited gift from the Lord. We praise God for this foretaste of the unity of His People and continue hopefully with the work to which He has called us together. For the Council exists to serve the churches as they prepare to meet their Lord Who knows only *one* flock."

At the Third Assembly of the W.C.C. at New Delhi (1961) the Toronto statement was confirmed (see report of the section on "Unity", paras. 4, 49, and 50), because it "still best expresses our understanding of the Council's nature" (para. 48). However, the developments of the last ten years force us "to seek further clarification". "Mere insistence upon deeper study will not guarantee fresh insight. We are learning what the Council is by *living* together within it." "Nevertheless, the need for careful reflection on the theological meaning of our new life in the Council continues to be unfulfilled" (para. 48). "At least we are able to say that the World Council is not something wholly other than the member churches. It is the churches in continuing council" (para. 49).

Following the reconsideration in New Delhi, the question was taken up again at the Fourth World Conference on Faith and Order held at Montreal (1963), at which the theme "The Church and the World Council of Churches" was one of the questions dealt with by a subcommittee of the Section on "The Church in the Purpose of God" (para. 48). Certain tendencies to concede that the World Council of Churches bears certain marks which are marks of the Church of Christ were energetically opposed, especially by the Orthodox, because this would change the nature and basic assumptions of the W.C.C. The crucial sentence in the final report is the following: "The Council is not the Church; it is not seeking to be a Church or *the* Church", but it "offers itself as a servant of the churches and of the Church".[1] On the other hand, this statement was also made:

> The Council gratefully acknowledges that in sustained fellowship it has received something new, an enrichment of our Christian existence and a new vision of our Christian task in the world . . . . We do not concur in the precise definition of this experience, but we are agreed that it is a new dimension in the Council. We therefore express the ardent wish that this new experience should grow and increase steadily through God's help and guidance, leading us to final unity.

At Montreal the hope had been expressed that the Central Committee would devote further attention to this matter. At the Central Committee held at Rochester, U.S.A., in the same year the General Secretary, Dr Visser 't Hooft, therefore spoke on the subject "What can we say together about the meaning of membership in the World Council of Churches?"[2] While conceding that the Toronto statement had "rendered very good service", Dr Visser 't Hooft said:

[1] Montreal, pp. 48–9.   [2] MRCC (Rochester, U.S.A. 1963), pp. 134–8.

[It had been] criticized because its concept of the World Council of Churches was static rather than dynamic. . . . The Toronto statement and other documents of the council had not ascribed ecclesiological quality (in the strict sense of the word) to the W.C.C. But had the churches in the Council not learned something as they had lived together? Was there a growth in fellowship which should express itself in a deeper and richer self-understanding of the Council and did that experience not force us to admit that the nature of the Council should be described in ecclesiological categories? Several theologians have answered this question in the affirmative and speak of the W.C.C. as *une réalité ecclésiale*.

Dr Visser 't Hooft then drew attention to three issues important for future discussion of the meaning of membership in the W.C.C.

1. The Churches had not yet developed the categories of thought which can adequately describe the "ecumenical experience", which is a completely new experience in church history. Remarkably enough, the various confessional world bodies had also left the problem of their own ecclesiological character largely unsolved. "We try to define ecumenical realities in the thought-forms of a pre-ecumenical age." An additional difficulty is that Churches employ different terminologies in approaching the questions.

2. Another question that must be raised was whether the ecumenical experience can be described in terms "which are wholly or partly institutional".

3. The W.C.C. did not want to become a "Super-Church", and must not do so; but could one describe it in ecclesiological terms "without erroneously implying that the World Council is after all in some sense the Church and that membership in it adds something to the ecclesiological reality of its member churches"?

What were the implications of the above questions? (said Dr Visser 't Hooft):

> We should find a way to express what God has given to the churches in and through their fellowship in the Council, but we must ensure that we express it in such a way that the very provisional nature of the Council is clearly understood and that there cannot arise any confusion between that provisional unity and the unity which belongs to the Church Universal. Also: As churches live, speak, act together *a new reality* begins to emerge. . . . We cannot possibly call it the *Una Sancta*. . . . What we can say is that we receive together spiritual gifts which are signs of that oneness which was at the beginning when "the company of those who believed were of one heart and soul" (Acts 4. 32) and a first fruit of that oneness which will come into existence when all who bear the name of Christ will have been fully gathered together by the Lord of the Church.

Dr Visser 't Hooft insisted that "we must carefully distinguish between the World Council of Churches and this new ecumenical reality", because the ecumenical movement was wider than the World Council of Churches, and if the description of the emerging ecumenical reality were transferred to the World Council this would be "to confuse the instrument with the product". In conclusion Dr Visser 't Hooft proposed that the member Churches be requested to give further attention to this question. But he wisely added, "It is better to live with a reality which transcends definition than to live with a definition which claims more substance than exists in reality."

The anticipated critical response came in the ensuing discussion. The fact was stressed again from the Orthodox side that "the Orthodox Church could never regard the World Council as a Church". But also with respect to the conservative Evangelicals Dr Hendrikus Berkhof, among others, pointed out: "We can live beyond Toronto, but we cannot formulate beyond Toronto."[1]

Similar reserve was shown by the member Churches to whom the document was sent, in the name of the Central Committee, for study and comment. It was evident that the overwhelming majority of the member Churches had not reached the point in their own thinking which would enable them to formulate in precise terms their understanding and the nature of their membership in the World Council. In some cases, however, this reserve may have been motivated by the fear that they would have to draw practical conclusions from recognizing the theological significance of the W.C.C., that is, to concede to it greater power and authority.

This experience paved the way for another document entitled *The Ecumenical Way* which was discussed by the Central Committee in Geneva in 1966.[2] This document was not concerned with describing the nature of the W.C.C. or its self-understanding; it was rather an attempt to take stock of the situation and to agree upon the policy of the World Council. The document was also sent to the national and regional Christian Councils and to the confessional organizations. It was also intended as a basis for discussion in local congregations and at inter-Church conferences; it stressed the work done by the W.C.C., on which emphasis had already been laid at New Delhi ("All in each place") and at Montreal. This document also says something about the W.C.C. (IV. paras. 12 and 13); it stresses the need for flexibility in the institutions of the W.C.C., for spiritual inspiration and renewal, and its responsibility for the world.

The response to this document was astonishingly meagre. On the one hand, the lack of balance in its thinking and formulation was more strongly criticized than usual. On the other hand (as Lukas Vischer stated in 1967 to the Central Committee at Heraklion), some of the comments made one feel "something of a hope and an expectation that the World Council will give pastoral help to the churches, and especially to the local churches".[3] Vischer comes to the sober conclusion:

> Both the document itself and especially the answers show that the discussion on the meaning of the World Council has come to a dead end. No helpful suggestions have been made from any quarter. The discussion is confined to agreement, or more often disagreement, with the Toronto statement of 1950, and when one has finished reading the replies one has the feeling that one has been turning round in circles to no purpose. When a discussion comes to a dead

[1] MRCC (Rochester, U.S.A. 1963), pp. 17–21.
[2] MRCC (Geneva 1966), pp. 89–92 (original form) and pp. 70–5 (final form).
[3] MRCC (Heraklion 1967), pp. 130–1.

end, the wisest thing is to leave it alone for a time. The great questions raised by the present situation cannot be directly included in a discussion on the nature of the World Council.

However, the document has helped to strengthen the forward movement. The views expressed require courageous action on the part of the W.C.C., and this is perhaps the most promising aspect of the whole question.

This confirms the statement made by Dr Visser 't Hooft that the self-understanding of the World Council of Churches, and the importance which its member Churches attach to their membership in it, must be built up step by step through living and working together, before they can be defined in words. Surely it should be emphasized that two decades is much too short a time for there to be any consensus among the member Churches on the ecclesiological significance of the W.C.C. However, despite all the sober conclusions, one should not disregard the dynamism which is at work within the growing fellowship of Churches, which was described by Edmund Schlink in his address at the Lund Conference in the following manner:

> Let us therefore hurry forward on this way and not stand still. Let us look forward. Let not our eyes be held to the present, but let us tear our eyes away from the visible divisions which we have not yet overcome, and let us look firmly to the One Lord towards whom we are moving. In the view ahead, in the expectation of the Coming Judge of the World and the Redeemer, we shall recognize the temporary character and the lack of finality of many things which divide us now.[1]

The Basis of the W.C.C. Clarified[2]

In Article I of its Constitution the World Council defined its "Basis" as follows: "The World Council of Churches is a fellowship of churches which accept our Lord Jesus Christ as God and Saviour."[3] Already at Amsterdam, however, the desire was expressed "for clarification or amplification of the affirmation of the Christian faith set forth in the Basis of the Council". Although the Assembly held the view "that the Basis set forth in the Constitution is adequate for the present purposes of the World Council of Churches", those Churches which desired the Basis to be changed were requested to present their desires in writing to the Central Committee for study, and the Central Committee was instructed to keep its study of possible changes within the christological principle set forth in the present Basis.[4]

At the meeting of the Central Committee in Toronto (1950) Dr Visser 't Hooft reported for the first time that one member Church had proposed an amendment (Remonstrant Church of Holland), but action on the request was postponed until the next meeting of the Central Committee.[5] Later on the Society of Friends of Philadelphia and Vicinity, and then the Presbyterian Church of Australia, sent in proposals for amending the Basis. At Rolle in 1951 a subcommittee was appointed (consisting of Douglas Horton, Georges

---

[1] *Ecumenical Review*, vol. v (October 1952), p. 36.
[2] See Wolfdieter Theurer, *Die trinitarische Basis des ORK*. Frankfurt-am-Main 1967.
[3] Amsterdam, p. 197.   [4] Ibid., pp. 115 ff.   [5] MRCC (Toronto 1950), p. 53.

Florovsky, and Anders Nygren) to which Dr Visser 't Hooft presented a memorandum dated 1 October 1951.[1] At the next meeting of the Central Committee in Lucknow the subcommittee reported that it had received a great deal of material to work on.[2] It was not considered necessary to change the Basis, but the Assembly should explain that the incarnation and the Trinity were implicit in the Amsterdam Basis. The Assembly should also define the meaning of the Basis, and for this the subcommittee presented a draft.

Shortly before the Second Assembly of the W.C.C. at Evanston (1954) the Church of Norway came forward with the suggestion that the words "in accordance with Holy Scripture" be added to the Basis,[3] but the proposal was received too late to be considered by the Second Assembly. At Evanston a "Statement on the purpose and function of the Basis" was accepted,[4] saying that the Basis performs three functions: it indicates the nature of the ecumenical fellowship, provides the orientation point for the work which the World Council undertakes, and indicates the range of the fellowship which the member Churches seek to establish. It stated that "while the Basis is less than a confession, it is much more than a mere formula or agreement".

At Evanston the new Central Committee appointed a new subcomittee, under the chairmanship of Dr E. A. Payne, to examine the Norwegian proposal and other requests for amendments relating to the Trinity.[5] In the negotiations which followed the desire soon became apparent for the Basis to be extended on biblical and trinitarian lines. In October 1956 Dr Payne and Dr Visser 't Hooft sent a memorandum to a number of theologians and church leaders asking for their personal comments; these would be submitted to the subcommittee at its meeting before the Central Committee in New Haven in 1957. The answers received showed that a change in the formulation of the Basis was considered inadvisable at that time, although the arguments in favour of doing so were in many cases admitted. At New Haven the subcommittee then submitted a full report to the Central Committee; this contained not only the changes proposed by Churches and individuals, but also the draft of a new formulation.[6]

> The World Council of Churches is a fellowship of Churches which, in accordance with Holy Scripture, confess our Lord Jesus Christ as the Son of God who was made man for our salvation, in whom the Father was revealed, and to whom the Holy Spirit bears witness guiding us into all the truth.

After a long discussion[7] it was decided to defer decision until 1958, and in the meantime to ask the members of the Central Committee to reflect on the matter and to consult with members of their Churches. At the Central Committee held in 1958 at Nyborg there was no time to examine this question, so that it had to be deferred until the following year. Dr Payne also

---

[1] MRCC (Rolle 1951), pp. 20ff.
[2] MRCC (Lucknow 1952–3), pp. 35f and Appendix VIII, pp. 95f.
[3] Evanston, p. 215.   [4] Ibid., pp. 306f.   [5] MRCC (Evanston 1954), p. 13.
[6] MRCC (New Haven 1957), Appendix XXII, pp. 132–5.
[7] MRCC (New Haven 1957), pp. 67–9.

stated that the number of comments received had been disappointingly small.[1]

For the Central Committee in Rhodes in 1959 the subcommittee submitted an expansion of the existing Basis[2], which was adopted by the Central Committee. The Faith and Order Commission was requested to make a study of the declaration suggested at New Haven and also the real nature and function of the Basis of the W.C.C. If the Faith and Order Commission undertook this task, the fact would be reported by the Central Committee to the member Churches and to the Third Assembly, together with an account of the study and discussion of the matter since the Evanston Assembly in 1954. At the same time it would be made clear that the Central Committee was in no way opposed to the suggested additional affirmations, believing them to be in accord with the beliefs of the member Churches.

Things then developed so rapidly, to a large extent owing to the stimulus of Dr Visser 't Hooft, that the Faith and Order Commission did not need to undertake this task. Prompted by Orthodox recommendations, in January 1960 Dr Visser 't Hooft proposed the following formulation:

> The World Council of Churches is a fellowship of churches which believe in Jesus Christ and which under the guidance of the Holy Spirit seek to fulfil together their common calling to manifest their unity as children of one heavenly Father.[3]

The following month the Executive Committee, meeting in Buenos Aires, agreed to another proposal, which read as follows:

> The World Council of Churches is a fellowship of churches which, under the guidance of the Holy Spirit and according to the Scriptures, confess the Lord Jesus Christ as God and Saviour and therefore seek to fulfil together their common calling to the glory of God the Father.[4]

The Executive Committee decided to pass on this proposal to the subcommittee on the Basis and, if it agreed, to take all the steps required to prepare for the acceptance of this new formulation of the Basis at the Third Assembly. Dr Payne reported to the Central Committee, which met at St Andrews in August 1960, about the latest developments. At the suggestion of Policy Reference Committee III, the Central Committee then decided on the existing form of the Basis to be submitted to the Third Assembly:

> The World Council of Churches is a fellowship of churches which confess the Lord Jesus Christ as God the Saviour according to the Scriptures and therefore seek to fulfil together their common calling to the glory of the one God, Father, Son and Holy Spirit.

In this connection the Central Committee again stressed the fact that the Basis had never been intended to be a creed nor as a full statement of the Christian faith, but merely "to say what holds us together in the World

---

[1] MRCC (Nyborg 1958), p. 66.   [2] MRCC (Rhodes 1959), pp. 201f.

[3] Letter from Visser 't Hooft dated 4 January 1960 to Fry, Payne, Bridston. Copy in W.C.C. archive "The Basis After Evanston".

[4] See minutes of meeting of Executive Committee, 8–12 February 1960, W.C.C. archive "The Basis after Evanston".

Council, what is the starting-point of our conversation and the foundation of our collaboration". The proposed new formulation was merely an expansion of what was already contained in the existing Basis. It was important to mention this, in order to avoid misunderstandings, and to fulfil widespread wishes. Four specific changes had been requested:

    (i) the substitution of the word "confess" for "accept";

    (ii) the use of "the" instead of "our" before "Lord Jesus Christ";

    (iii) the addition of the phrase "according to the Scriptures"; this goes back to the earliest Christian confessions of faith and stresses the authority of Scripture for all Christians;

    (iv) the trinitarian character of the Basis is in line with the statement adopted at Evanston. The end and object of our fellowship together is acknowledged by adding the phrase "and therefore seek to fulfil together their common calling to the Glory of God".[1]

The concluding sentence brings out the missionary element which became a strong influence on the ecumenical fellowship through the integration with the International Missionary Council at New Delhi.

Admittedly the discussions at New Delhi did not run as smoothly as those at St Andrews. Objections were raised by some Baptists, Mennonites, Remonstrants, and Quakers mainly to the words "God and Saviour", which existed already in the old version of the Basis. However, the result of the ballot showed a majority of far more than the two-thirds required: 383 in favour, thirty-six against, and seven abstentions.[2] After years of discussion, the acceptance of the new Basis sharpened the self-understanding of the W.C.C. and served to strengthen its inner coherence.

The Significance of the Three Assemblies

In order to evaluate rightly the importance of the Assemblies, it is essential to take as the norm the constitutional functions and powers of the W.C.C., of which the Assembly is "the principal authority" (Constitution, V. (i)). Paragraph III of the Constitution lists the functions of the W.C.C. as defined at New Delhi, including its missionary task and its relations with national and regional Christian Councils:

    (i) To carry on the work of the world movements for Faith and Order and Life and Work and of the International Missionary Council.

    (ii) To facilitate common action by the churches.

    (iii) To promote co-operation in study.

    (iv) To promote the growth of ecumenical and missionary consciousness in the members of all churches.

    (v) To support the churches in their world-wide missionary and evangelistic task.

    (vi) To establish and maintain relations with national and regional councils, world confessional bodies, and other ecumenical organizations.

    (vii) To call world conferences on specific subjects as occasion may require, such conferences being empowered to publish their own findings.[3]

[1] MRCC (St Andrews 1960), pp. 211f.   [2] New Delhi, pp. 152–9.
[3] Ibid., pp. 426–7.

In paragraph IV of the Constitution the Authority, which provides a framework for the above functions, is defined:

> The World Council shall offer counsel and provide opportunity of united action in matters of common interest.

> It may take action on behalf of constituent churches in such matters as one or more of them may commit to it.

> It shall have authority to call regional and world conferences on specific subjects as occasion may require.

> The World Council shall not legislate for the churches; nor shall it act for them in any manner except as indicated above or as may hereafter be specified by the constituent churches.

From these aspects and in accordance with these norms, how are the first three Assemblies to be evaluated? How did they fulfil their mandate and what were their particular characteristics?

Amsterdam

The first Assembly held at Amsterdam, 22 August–4 September 1948, and attended by 351 delegates representing 145 Churches from forty-four countries, can be regarded as the point at which the nascent W.C.C. gathered the ecumenical community to take stock of the Churches' position, and tried to point out the responsibility of world Christendom in face of the upheavals caused by the Second World War. Here on 23 August the World Council was unanimously declared to be constituted, at a plenary session chaired by the Archbishop of Canterbury, Dr Geoffrey Fisher. The resolution was submitted by Pastor Marc Boegner in the name of the Committee of Fourteen and the Provisional Committee. The great moment had come when "the churches themselves assumed responsibility for the ecumenical movement and conversely the ecumenical movement won a secure foundation in the life of the churches".[1] The Message of the Assembly expressed this fact as follows:

> Christ has made us His own, and He is not divided. In seeking Him we can find one another. Here at Amsterdam we have committed ourselves afresh to Him, and have covenanted with one another in constituting this World Council of Churches. We intend to stay together.

The "nature of the Council" was more closely defined in a separate statement.[2] It was clearly stated that the churches had decided to make common cause in accordance with the will of the Lord of the Church. Where this common way would lead them was unforeseeable. But, to quote the Report of Section I, "We acknowledge that He is powerfully at work amongst us to lead us further to goals which we but dimly discern."[3]

To what extent did the First Assembly take account of these aims and follow them up? This question cannot be answered by generalizations or by impressions based on feelings; it can only be answered by listening intently

---

[1] Visser 't Hooft. See *A History of the Ecumenical Movement, 1517–1948*, p. 720.
[2] Amsterdam, pp. 9 and 127f.   [3] Ibid., p. 56.

to the trends and the achievements of the separate Sections and Commissions. The general theme of the Assembly was "Man's Disorder and God's Design".

The themes of the four Sections were derived from it:

1. The Universal Church in God's Design.
2. The Church's Witness to God's Design.
3. The Church and the Disorder of Society.
4. The Church and the International Disorder.

Against the background of the widely differing political situations and church traditions it was, of course, impossible to expect the Sections to come to homogeneous findings. However, they manifested their common readiness and their conviction that they should bear witness of God's design as a factor bringing order into a disordered and disrupted world.

The theological groundwork (Section I), in which Karl Barth and Michael Ramsey participated, expressed the indissoluble connection between unity and inner renewal: "We pray for the churches' renewal as we pray for their unity. As Christ purifies us by His Spirit we shall find that we are drawn together and that there is no gain in unity unless it is unity in truth and holiness."[1] At the same time the Report of Section I speaks of the basis of the fellowship within the W.C.C.: "The World Council of Churches has come into existence because we have already recognized a responsibility to one another's churches in our Lord Jesus Christ."[2] This basic undertone continues as a strong influence right up to the document on Proselytism in 1960. The simplified distinction drawn in this Section between a "Protestant" and a "Catholic" type of Church, as being the deepest of all our differences, later seemed to be inadequate.

In Section II it was strongly realized for the first time that evangelism is the common task of all the Churches, and that "the present day is the beginning of a new epoch of missionary enterprise".[3] No distinction is drawn any longer between mission and evangelism, because it must be recognized that the traditional distinction between the "Christian" and "non-Christian" countries no longer exists.[4] Above all, however, a strong appeal was addressed to "the laity": "This is the day of opportunity for the lay membership of the Church."[5] The question of the training of the laity was examined by a special committee, which took as its starting-point the experience of the Ecumenical Institute at Bossey.[6] The report of the committee on "The Life and Work of Women in the Church" was on the same lines.[7] Recognition of the importance of the laity in the Church was one of the outstanding features of the Amsterdam Assembly. It found strong expression also in the reports of Sections III and IV in which the lay delegates to the Assembly played a decisive role.

It is to Section III that the ecumenical discussion during the years that followed owes the concept of "the responsible society" as an alternative to capitalism on the one hand and communism on the other. In order "to prevent an undue centralization of power in modern technically organized

---

[1] Amsterdam, p. 56. [2] Ibid., p. 57. [3] Ibid., p. 66. [4] Ibid., p. 66.
[5] Ibid., p. 68. [6] Ibid., pp. 153–6. [7] Ibid., pp. 146–8.

communities" it was suggested that society should have "a rich variety of smaller forms of community",[1] which would ensure scope for personal responsibility.

The fact that Section IV included such divergent attitudes as those of Professor J. Hromadka and John Foster Dulles and was able to support them shows the strength of a fellowship like that of the newly formed W.C.C., and put it to the test for the first time. Two points which arose in Section IV deserve special mention owing to their significance for the Assembly as a whole and for the future of the W.C.C.: (a) the rejection of war in principle ("war is contrary to the will of God") but also the inability to accept this attitude unanimously as Christians;[2] (b) the clear political statement that "Christianity cannot be equated with any" political system.[3] Every kind of tyranny and imperialism was a call for struggle, and for efforts to secure human rights and basic liberties, especially religious liberty.

If one tries to evaluate the Amsterdam Assembly as a whole one can say that it was no longer marked by the enthusiasm and optimism which had dominated some earlier conferences. It was too close to the Second World War for that. On the other hand, the First Assembly gave evidence of the Churches' sense of common responsibility in service to the world, as required by "God's design" in Christ. It was taken far more seriously than during the first decade of the ecumenical movement. Joint action by the Churches of this kind could spring only from their unity in Christ, which was maintained in inner renewal and in responsibility for one another.

Evanston

The work of Amsterdam was continued by the Second Assembly of the W.C.C. held at Evanston, U.S.A., 15–31 August 1954 and attended by 502 delegates from 161 member Churches. Especially important was the fact that the Second Assembly was held in the U.S.A. and gave the strongest member Churches an opportunity to acquaint themselves directly and immediately with the W.C.C.

At Amsterdam the Churches had announced their intention "to stay together". At Evanston they expressed their desire "to grow together" with certain reservations: "We dedicate ourselves to God anew, that He may enable us to grow together."[4] It was this deep sense of belonging together and of the responsibility which it implied that enabled the Assembly to tackle the main theme "Christ—the Hope of the World", theologically an extremely difficult one. Compared with Amsterdam this theme clearly represented a turning towards the centre which linked together all the Churches belonging to the World Council. However, this theme now gave rise to differing opinions. The concept of the Christian hope held by the European Churches tended to be eschatological, whereas the concept of the American Churches was more optimistic and more concerned with the Christian's hope in this world here and now. The statement on the report of the Advisory Commission on the Main Theme, in which body eminent theologians had co-

---

[1] Amsterdam, p. 77.   [2] Ibid., p. 89.   [3] Ibid., p. 91.   [4] Evanston, p. 91.

operated for years, said that "sharp differences in theological viewpoint were expressed" in the discussion. "The note of joyous affirmation and radiant expectancy which should mark a statement of the Christian hope does not sufficiently illuminate the report." The statement draws attention to certain important omissions: "The present work of the Holy Spirit in the Church and the world; specific reference to 'signs of hope'; adequate treatment of the theme of creation and cosmic redemption."

"We are not agreed on the relationship between the Christian's hope here and now, and his ultimate hope", said the Second Assembly. However, the report was submitted to the Churches with the desire "that all who read it will be moved to give utterance to the Christian hope in their own words and with the additions which their thought and prayer discover".[1] A discordant note was introduced by the reference to the hope of Israel (Rom. 9—11) which was finally omitted after a heated debate. However, repercussions of the debate were felt for a long time, and the disagreement of the outvoted minority had to be recorded at the plenary session. The vote showed first that many did not recognize that the Jewish people occupy a special place in the history of salvation, and second that some delegates were motivated by political considerations.

The connection between the Sections and the Main Theme was a very loose one, if it existed at all (to quote Walter Freytag). The Sections continued the trends stressed at Amsterdam (and Section I also continued the work of the Third Conference of Faith and Order held at Lund in 1952). This time there were six Sections:

1. Our Oneness in Christ and our Disunity as Churches.
2. The Mission of the Church to those outside her Life.
3. The Responsible Society in a World Perspective.
4. Christians in the Struggle for World Community.
5. The Churches amid Racial and Ethnic Tensions.
6. The Laity: the Christian in his Vocation.

The so-called "Younger Churches", except those in China, were much more strongly represented than at Amsterdam, and their presence was felt in many ways (especially when discussing the unity of the Church) in the form of an impatient urge for concrete action. Moreover, the missionary dimension, which had been so characteristic of Amsterdam, was missing at Evanston, for instance in the Report of Section I. However, to quote Walter Freytag again: "Yet it must be stated that the report on Evanston offers the most biblical testimony yet given by any ecumenical world gathering."[2] It showed that the W.C.C. was penetrating more deeply into holy Scripture, which was helping it to become clearer theologically in every sphere, and helping the Churches to discover their common convictions.

In continuation of the ideas worked out at Amsterdam, the missionary task of the laity was also strongly stressed (Section II). Section VI combined it with important considerations about "the Christian concept of work" in order to "bridge the gulf between the Church and the world".

[1] Evanston, pp. 70f.   [2] *Ecumenical Review*, vol. vii (*October 1954*), p. 12.

The Amsterdam phrase "the responsible society" was more clearly defined at Evanston; it was made clear that it did not indicate "an alternative social or political system" but "a criterion by which we judge all existing social orders and at the same time a standard to guide us in the specific choices we have to make" (Section III. I.7). The simplified distinction between two opposing economic systems which dominated the discussions at Amsterdam was superseded at Evanston by more careful differentiations. Priority was given especially to the social and economic "problems in the economically underdeveloped regions" (Section III), a question to which the W.C.C. paid increasing attention. In Sections IV and V the Second Assembly again affirmed its responsibility for international peace and justice and issued an appeal to governments urging the prohibition of all weapons of mass destruction, and abstention from aggression. The Assembly also issued statements on religious liberty and on "inter-group relations" (insisting on racial equality). Both themes had been introduced at Amsterdam (see Amsterdam Report, Section VI). As a result of the Assembly's report on "The Churches amid Racial and Ethnic Tensions" a department for racial and ethnic relations was set up within the W.C.C. This was followed in 1958 by the setting up of a secretariat on questions concerning religious liberty.

New Delhi

The years between the Assembly at Evanston and that at New Delhi (1954–61) were crucial for the development of the W.C.C. both internally and externally. The Third Assembly was held at New Delhi, 19 November–5 December 1961. It was attended by 577 delegates from just under 200 member Churches, as well as by a large number of advisers, youth delegates, fraternal delegates, observers, and visitors. The main theme "Jesus Christ—the Light of the World" continued the Christocentric line of the W.C.C., extending it now into the sphere of the non-Christian religions. It was liable to misinterpretation in view of the fact that light is one of the symbols that appear in the Asian religions. In order to avoid being misunderstood as syncretism, the theme therefore had to be worked out with great care on its biblical basis. This time the main theme was not given great precedence, as had been the case at Evanston; it was merely regarded as a guiding principle. The deliberations were to spring from the ongoing work of the W.C.C., and not be forced into the formula of a dominating main theme. On the other hand, an effort was made to ensure that the main theme permeated the sections and influenced them more than it had done at Evanston.

The Third Assembly may be summed up from two aspects: its external extension and its internal strengthening.

1. At New Delhi twenty-three more Churches were admitted to membership of the W.C.C., bringing the number of member Churches up to 198. The new member Churches included three groups:

(*a*) The Orthodox Churches of eastern Europe, whose adhesion was rightly regarded as extremely important by the General Secretary. Dr Visser 't Hooft said: "In this way a tremendous opportunity is offered to us, the opportunity to ensure that a real spiritual dialogue shall take place between the Eastern Churches and the churches which have their origin in the West. If we accept this opportunity our ecumenical task will not become easier, but we shall surely be greatly enriched."[1]

(*b*) Younger Churches joined in sufficient strength to make their influence felt. Of the twenty-three new member Churches, eleven were in Africa, five in Asia, and two in South America. Only five were from Europe or North America. Altogether eighteen of the twenty-three new member Churches belonged to the "Third World".

(*c*) The two Pentecostal Churches from Chile formed a bridge to the Evangelical Churches, most of which dissociated themselves from the W.C.C. and still do so. The application of these Churches for membership was equally important theologically, because it brought out the pneumatological aspect of the theological discussion in the ecumenical movement.

The World Council was also very considerably extended externally through its integration with the International Missionary Council at the Third Assembly.

2. The tremendous variety of ecumenical work was summed up at New Delhi under three points, so as to concentrate the discussion and in order to relate the three aspects to one another. They were: Witness, Service, and Unity. The internal norm for this was the new Basis, the external point of reference was "the local Church" which (to quote Dr Visser 't Hooft in his report) must be made "ready for unity" in accordance with the statement "All in each place". As compared with the assemblies at Amsterdam and Evanston, therefore, the emphasis had clearly shifted from the individual to the local congregation.

The main theme "Jesus Christ—the Light of the World" had testified to the uniqueness of Christ. On the other hand, in the section on "Witness" a theological problem arose which has continued to preoccupy the W.C.C. ever since: the influence of Christ in other religions, i.e. to what extent God's action in the non-Christian religions is in accordance with the Christian faith, and what possibilities might arise from it, for instance in connection with the Asian form of Christianity. This logical conclusion from the universal implications of the Lordship of God and of the salvation of Christ as well as consideration of the changes in the other religions led the section on "Witness" to make pronouncements like the following:

> The Church is sent, knowing that God has not left himself without witness even among men who do not yet know Christ, and knowing also that the reconciliation wrought through Christ embraces all creation and the whole of mankind. . . . In the churches, we have but little understanding of the wisdom, love and power which God has given to men of other faiths and of no faith, or of the changes wrought in other faiths by their long encounter with Christianity. We must take up the conversations about Christ with them,

[1] *Ecumenical Review*, vol. xiv (January 1962), p. 222.

knowing that Christ addresses them through us and us through them" (Report of Section on "Witness", III. 7).[1]

"In solidarity with all men" new structures and new forms of witness were sought, in which the "laity" must occupy a definite status. (This met with some objections, not only from the Orthodox, because it seemed to devalue the status of the traditional ministry. This difference is constantly coming up in many spheres of the ecumenical conversation.)

The same concept of "solidarity" was also taken up by the Section on "Service" as a link with the call "to participate in service in all these areas of the contemporary world" (para. 4).[2] But by relating it clearly to God's love for men, a distinction was drawn between Christian service and mere philanthrophy (para. 1). The Section on "Service" already revealed a characteristic which became even more apparent at the World Conference on Church and Society in Geneva in 1966: it lacked a substantial, valid theological foundation, and among so many different kinds of Churches it was almost impossible to achieve one. The primary aim of the section was to face the problems of political, economic, and social change, and thus to help the "younger Churches" in their situation. Christians were therefore warned against all forms of conformity with past or present social systems. As at Amsterdam, the section refused to identify itself with any economic, social, or political system, and stressed the importance of human dignity. The absolute Lordship of Jesus Christ over history is the main concept running through the whole report, for he makes it "possible for a Christian to live (or die) with integrity under any political system; it is possible for the Church to obey its Lord in all kinds of external circumstances" (Report of Section on Service, para. 34).[3]

The Section on "Unity" centred around the so-called "unity formula of New Delhi", which had been worked out at the meeting of the Faith and Order Commission at St Andrews in 1960. Here at the highest level of the Assembly the section endeavoured to define the aim of unity which had given rise to the W.C.C. and which inspired it:

> We believe that the unity which is both God's will and his gift to his Church is being made visible as all in each place who are baptized into Jesus Christ and confess him as Lord and Saviour are brought by the Holy Spirit into one fully committed fellowship, holding the one apostolic faith, preaching the one Gospel, breaking the one bread, joining in common prayer, and having a corporate life reaching out in witness and service to all and who at the same time are united with the whole Christian fellowship in all places and all ages in such wise that ministry and members are accepted by all, and that all can act and speak together as occasion requires for the tasks to which God calls his people. It is for such unity that we believe we must pray and work (Report of Section on Unity, para. 2).[4]

Realizing the inadequacy of what had previously been said, the above was an attempt to describe the common task without giving a "definition of

[1] New Delhi, pp. 81–2.   [2] Ibid., p. 94.   [3] Ibid., p. 100.   [4] Ibid., p. 116.

the Church", so as to emerge at last from an "ecclesiological docetism" (Edmund Schlink). Admittedly the separate formulas and concepts needed to be implemented, and this urgent task was not tackled seriously enough by the member Churches during the years that followed. But at New Delhi the aim was to arrive at concrete conclusions, as is shown by the "implications" which the section tried to draw for the life of the local Churches, the confessions, and the ecumenical movement. It even recommended taking "responsible risk" (para. 30). The W.C.C. was urged to extend its "educative function" (para. 42d) and to play a more active part in negotiations for union (para. 45g).[1]

Altogether the tendency at New Delhi was to strengthen the position of the W.C.C. Thus the Policy Reference Committee recommended "that the Council should give its member churches spiritual and practical guidance in a Christian approach to the actual questions and problems of our day, such as materialism, secularism, peace and war, and social justice. The W.C.C. should certainly not wait to be pushed into critical situations, but should always take the lead and initiative in asking. What is the command of our Lord in the present time? At the same time, the churches themselves should be encouraged to bring their requests in this regard before the W.C.C."[2]

Thus between the First and Third Assemblies, the World Council, as "the ecumenical conscience of the churches", became more and more the mouthpiece of the member Churches. This was shown at New Delhi in a renewed stand on religious liberty, a resolution on anti-semitism, a stand on international crises, a message to the Christians in South Africa, and an "Appeal to all Governments and Peoples".[3] At the same time the W.C.C. assumed increasing responsibility for relief to people in distress, refugees and victims of natural catastrophes all over the world. After three assemblies the ecumenical fellowship had stood the test. The Churches' desire to stay together (Amsterdam) and to grow together (Evanston) had developed into joint progress in assuming new tasks (New Delhi). This tremendous task of ecumenical unity, renewal, and co-operation was re-examined at Uppsala in 1968 in the light of the promise of the Lord when he shall return, "Behold I make all things new!"

The Work of the Central Committee and the Executive Committee

The Constitution of the W.C.C. (para. V (ii)) defined the powers of the Central Committee. The Central Committee originally consisted of ninety members; at New Delhi the number was raised to 100, at Uppsala to 120. The definition follows: "It shall, between meetings of the Assembly, carry out the Assembly's instructions and exercise its functions, except that of amending the Constitution, or modifying the allocation of its own members."[4] The Central Committee shall meet normally once every calendar year, and shall have power to appoint its own executive committee. The Executive Committee (originally consisting of twelve members, since New Delhi fourteen

[1] New Delhi, p. 130.   [2] Ibid., p. 145   [3] Ibid., p. 280.   [4] Ibid., p. 428.

members, and since Uppsala sixteen members) shall meet twice a year. It shall carry out the decisions of the Central Committee, just as the latter carries out the decisions of the Assembly (Rules of the W.C.C., VI (2)).[1]

It is a noteworthy fact that during the course of time the importance of the Executive Committee has increased, and it has become more independent of the Central Committee, so that it often gave the impression of controlling the Central Committee instead of carrying out the latter's instructions. To a considerable extent this is due to the fact that during the time between the assemblies the membership of the Executive Committee has remained almost unchanged, in spite of re-elections every year; this has given it a great deal of stability. This trend has also been encouraged by the two chairmen of the Central Committee (or/and Executive Committee): the Bishop of Chichester, Dr Bell (1948–54) whose cordial, friendly character did so much to establish friendly contacts between others, and Dr Franklin Clark Fry of the Lutheran Church of America (1954–68) whose gift of leadership was respected by all, and who carried out his duties as chairman combining authority with humour. He was ably assisted by Dr Ernest Payne and, after 1966, by Dr Russell Chandran.

Both the Central Committee and the Executive Committee have met in different places nearly every time, so as to get to know all the member Churches and to strengthen their sense of solidarity with the World Council. During the years between the Amsterdam and Evanston Assemblies the Central Committee met in Holland, England, Canada, Switzerland, and India. During the time between the Evanston and New Delhi Assemblies it met in Switzerland, Hungary, the U.S.A., Denmark, Greece, and Scotland. During the years between the New Delhi and Uppsala Assemblies it met in France, the U.S.A., Nigeria, Switzerland, and Greece. In addition, both the Central and Executive Committees held meeting in connection with each of the assemblies. As well as meeting at the same time as the Central Committee, the Executive Committee also held separate meetings, for instance in Germany (1954), Australia (1956), Latin America (1960), and the U.S.S.R. (1964).

The Central Committee and also the Executive Committee might easily have confined themselves exclusively to the organizational tasks entrusted to them by the Assembly, or which arose in course of time. The danger that they would do this was increased owing to the shortness of their meetings. However, both the Central and Executive Committees resisted these temptations and kept their attention fixed on the basic themes which needed consideration both for the development of the ecumenical fellowship within the World Council and for the fulfilment of its responsibilities outside. In addition to the Toronto statement (already mentioned) *The Church, the Churches, and the World Council of Churches* (1950) and the statement entitled *The Ecumenical Way* (1966), these included the statement of the Central Committee at Rolle (1951) "The Calling of the Church to Mission and to Unity",[2] and the report on "Christian Witness, Proselytism and Religious Liberty in the setting of the World Council of Churches", drawn up by a committee under the chairmanship of Bishop Angus Dun and approved first at the

[1] New Delhi, p. 435.   [2] *The First Six Years*, p. 124.

Central Committee in Galyatetö in 1956, and then in its final form at St Andrews in 1960, which defined the relation of the member Churches to each other;[1] it was accepted by the Assembly at New Delhi and commended to the Churches.

In relation to the secular sphere a number of statements were made (mainly drafted by the Commission of the Churches on International Affairs) on Religious Liberty and Freedom of Conscience, on the menace of nuclear warfare, on the problems of disarmament, and on special political danger spots such as Korea (1950). (The resolution on Korea aroused considerable tensions and differences within the W.C.C., which led to the resignation of one of its Presidents, Dr T. C. Chao of China.) Statements were also made on the war in Vietnam and on the conflict between Israel and Egypt. The question may be asked: What purposes are served by making all these statements concerning events in the world? The booklet *New Delhi to Uppsala* draws attention to their threefold purpose: "First, to serve as a crystalization point for world Christian opinion; second, to help the member churches in deciding what stand they should take; third, to give World Council spokesmen, particularly the Commission of the Churches on International Affairs, a firm foundation for the approaches which they make to international governmental bodies and individual governments" (English edn, p. 10).

There is therefore no question of making normative statements which would be binding upon the member Churches, or which would oblige them to take certain steps. None of the resolutions passed by the World Council of Churches does so. They become binding only if they are accepted by the member Churches. The W.C.C. wants only to be the "instrument" of the Churches; it offers itself as a help in guiding them in their further reflections and practical conclusions. It cannot and must not depart from this principle if it is to remain meaningful as the point of intersection and the co-ordinating centre of all the Christian traditions and systems of thought.

But even when the deliberations did not result in any special pronouncements, recommendations, or resolutions, the Central Committee has always been ready to learn about current problems which concern the whole ecumenical movement, and has discussed them, so as not to become drowned under the weight of routine business, but to remain constantly on the alert and ready to assume responsibility for its task. The socio-ethical issues ranged from "responsible parenthood and the problem of population" to the fundamental questions of Christian unity, evangelism, and joint responsibility for inter-Church aid and relief projects. In addition the Central Committee is responsible for a third category of spiritual leadership and guidance: the tremendous number of study projects started by the Central Committee either on its own account or through the competent divisions and departments.

Among these studies mention should be made of the following: "The Lordship of Christ over the World and the Church" (1955-9),[2] "Christians and the Prevention of War in an Atomic Age—a theological discussion" (also started in 1955), the extensive studies on "Rapid Social Change"

[1] *Evanston to New Delhi*, Appendix VIII, paras. 239-45.
[2] Ibid., paras. 34, 35.

(1955–60), and the study projects decided upon at New Delhi: "The Finality of Christ in the Age of Universal History"[1] and "The Missionary Structure of the Congregation".[2]

All this demands a great deal of time and energy from the members of the Central Committee and Executive Committee, for in addition to the actual meetings nearly all the members are engaged in work in committees and study groups whose purpose is to promote the development of the whole work of the W.C.C. In his report of the Assembly at New Delhi, Dr Fry said: "Practically nothing occurs in the Council's life between Assemblies that lies outside the portfolio of the Central Committee."[3] The Central Committee has therefore become the real power-field and radiation-centre of the W.C.C., not only in regard to the organization for which it is responsible, but also in its influence upon the Churches, many of which do not yet possess the necessary channels to carry out what has already been approved at the highest level.

Structure, Staff, and Headquarters

1. *Structure* The structures assumed by an organization are not to be regarded as unimportant. Its effectiveness will always depend on whether it finds suitable forms for its work. In this respect the W.C.C. has always shown flexibility, but without falling into arbitrary experimentation or improvization. *Life and Work* and *Faith and Order* already had decades of organizational experience behind them, which they contributed to the World Council. The rapid growth in the membership of the W.C.C. and the increased demands made upon it caused the Central Committee three years after Amsterdam to set up a "Committee on Structure and Functioning" to examine the organization and working of the W.C.C.; this committee presented a long report to the Central Committee at Lucknow in 1953,[4] which was followed by an equally long debate. The proposals were re-examined and thoroughly discussed at the Evanston Assembly.[5] The sub-division into divisions and departments formed the structural basis for the years that followed and "has given much greater coherence to the work of the Council".[6] There were to be three main divisions concerned with Studies, Inter-Church Aid, and Ecumenical Action. The heads of these three divisions are at the same time Associate General Secretaries. Discussion continued, however, about this pattern of organization and whether it was permanently suited to the work of the Council or should be changed.

One important change made at Evanston was the decision that the Presidents could no longer be re-elected. This caused some misgivings, because the Anglicans (for instance) were anxious that the Archbishop of Canterbury should always be one of the Presidents of the W.C.C. It was felt, however, that by electing new presidents at each Assembly more Churches and countries could be involved in the work of the Council.

---

[1] New Delhi, p. 165.   [2] Ibid., p. 195.   [3] Ibid., p. 338.
[4] MRCC (Lucknow 1953).   [5] Evanston, pp. 174–214.
[6] *Evanston to New Delhi*, para. 26.

After Evanston the plans for the integration of the International Missionary Council with the World Council of Churches (see Section 6 below) made it necessary to consider further changes of structure. These were studied by the Committee on Programme and Finance, of which the Chairman was Dr Eugene Carson Blake. The findings of this committee concerning the organization of the W.C.C. are contained in its report to the Assembly at New Delhi.[1] In the view of the committee, it was too soon to make basic changes. However, attention may be drawn to some points in the report because they reflect certain tendencies. For instance, it was proposed to appoint a "Committee on National Council Relationships" to give "continuous attention to the development of relationships of mutual helpfulness between the W.C.C. and national and regional councils of churches and Christian councils". The position of Faith and Order was also strengthened; it was not promoted to the status of a division, but it was given scope to have more influence on the ecumenical work as a whole and its staff was increased. The staff of the General Secretariat was also increased. Lastly, it was proposed that there be a "Staff Co-ordinating and Advisory Committee on Studies" to co-ordinate the study work of the different divisions; this was made urgently necessary by the organizational extension of the W.C.C. The Assembly passed the report, instructing the Central Committee to take the necessary steps to examine the organizational structure within two years.[2]

In accordance with the instructions of the New Delhi Assembly, the Central Committee at Rochester (1963) appointed a committee to examine the structure of the W.C.C. with Norman Goodall as chairman. This committee was to study and consider how the separate aspects of the work of the W.C.C. could best be co-ordinated, in the light of the suggestions already made. This committee presented its first report at Enugu.[3] Among other things, Faith and Order was given the status of an autonomous secretariat of the Faith and Order Commission. lodged within the Division of Studies and having representation in the Staff Executive Group; but the nomination of Assistant General Secretaries was still postponed.

The committee presented another report in 1967 at the meeting of the Central Committee in Crete.[4] The Central Committee approved the committee's view that no change should be made yet in the structure of the divisions. It was decided to reconstitute the committee with Bishop James K. Matthews as chairman and to ask it to present a report to the Central Committee immediately before Uppsala. The Assembly at Uppsala appointed a new committee on structure, which undertook to examine the existing structures within three years, taking due account of new factors such as regional developments, relations to non-member Churches, and to the Roman Catholic Church. This presents a broad field to the W.C.C. in which it will need greater dynamism through more intensive concentration and more rational application of its strength.

2. *Staff* However, what use would the most perfect structures be without

[1] New Delhi, pp. 351–7.   [2] Ibid., pp. 351–7.   [3] MRCC (Enugu 1965), pp. 102–16.
[4] MRCC (Heraklion 1967), pp. 122–6.

the men and women who fill them with life and spirit? During the twenty years since it was formed the W.C.C. has been blessed with persons who devoted their whole energies to the W.C.C. The problem of suitable staff is particularly difficult in the W.C.C. because account has to be taken not only of personal abilities but also of the person's confessional and geographical background. The Geneva staff must reflect the membership of the Churches which belong to it.

Continuity was maintained with the earlier stages of the ecumenical movement thanks to the outstanding personality of Dr Visser 't Hooft, who was General Secretary for eighteen years (1948–66). In him great theological, linguistic, and spiritual gifts were combined with a capacity for organization and leadership which made him the real inspiration and architect of the W.C.C. When Dr Visser 't Hooft made it known at the age of sixty-five (in 1965) that he wished to retire in order to devote himself to writing and other scholarly work, the Central Committee was confronted by an extremely important task—that of choosing a new General Secretary. At Rochester in 1963 the Executive Committee (through the Central Committee) proposed the appointment of a nominations committee. However, the Central Committee took up a suggestion, made by the Bishop of Winchester, that the Executive Committee should act as a nominations committee. At Tutzing (1964) the Executive Committee decided to propose to the Central Committee the Reverend Patrick C. Rodger (from the Episcopal Church of Scotland), Executive Secretary of the Department of Faith and Order, as Dr Visser 't Hooft's successor. At the same time Dr Visser 't Hooft was asked to continue in his position until 1966. Before this nomination was presented to the Central Committee, the news was given to the press by the Executive Committee and some of the member Churches expressed negative reactions, not against the person nominated, but against the procedure whereby the Central Committee found itself confronted with a *fait accompli*.

At the meeting of the Central Committee at Enugu (1965) the Executive Committee still maintained its nomination of the Reverend Patrick C. Rodger, but the Central Committee could not agree about the nomination. It wanted to have more scope for choice between several candidates, especially in view of the different concepts held about the office of General Secretary. Owing to the personality of Dr Visser 't Hooft this position had never been defined; he had been General Secretary for nearly two decades and had carried out his functions in a way that no one else could hope to emulate. At the Central Committee meeting in Geneva (1966) the only name presented for consideration by the new nominations committee (appointed at Enugu) was that of Dr Eugene Carson Blake, who since 1951 had been Stated Clerk of the United Presbyterian Church in the U.S.A. He was elected almost unanimously. Dr Visser 't Hooft still remained available in an advisory capacity.

If one were to mention other members of the Geneva staff, this would imply that others who were not mentioned were less important. However, a few names must be noted among those who helped to build up the W.C.C. both organizationally and inwardly. During the first years of the W.C.C.'s existence Oliver S. Tomkins and Stephen Neill were working in the General

Secretariat. The ever-growing tasks of the Division of Inter-Church Aid, Refugee and World Service were directed first by Dr Robert Mackie, then by Dr Leslie Cooke. The work of the Commission of the Churches for International Affairs is indissolubly bound up with the names of Sir Kenneth Grubb and Dr O. Frederick Nolde, who showed themselves prudent advisers in difficult situations for the W.C.C. and its member Churches, and who also acted as the mouthpiece of the W.C.C. in relations with governments and international organizations.

Madeleine Barot of France untiringly reminded the W.C.C. of the concerns of women in the Churches. The Division of Studies was first under the direction of Nils Ehrenström (1948–54) and then of Robert Bilheimer (1954–63). A large number of study projects were undertaken. Father Paul Verghese contributed immensely to the Division of Ecumenical Action as its Director from 1962–7. The work of the Ecumenical Institute at Bossey, set going by Hendrik Kraemer in co-operation with Suzanne de Diétrich, continued from 1955–66 under Professor H. H. Wolf and since then under Professor N. A. Nissiotis. The burden of responsibility for financial affairs was borne by Frank Northam. The Information Department was first under John Garrett, then under Philippe Maury until his death in 1967. The question of religious liberty benefited greatly from the expert knowledge of Dr Carillo de Albornoz. The W.C.C. office in New York was run for many years by H. S. Leiper, S. McCrea Cavert, and Roswell P. Barnes; now Dr Eugene Smith succeeds them. The late Z. K. Matthews served as the first Area Secretary for Africa within D.I.C.A.R.W.S. Many many more names could be mentioned.

Nor should the many secretaries and staff members be forgotten who carried out different functions at the W.C.C. for longer or shorter periods. Without their help and knowledge the W.C.C. could never have carried out its world-wide tasks.

The Assembly at Amsterdam had given its approval to a staff of thirty-six executive secretaries. However, owing to the initial difficulties (for instance the Information Department had not yet been set up) this number was not reached. In 1968 the staff is made up as follows: executive, ninety-seven; administrative, secretarial, and clerical staff, 130; mail, telephone, cyclostyle, and other ancillary services, twenty-four; total 251. People outside are often astonished that the W.C.C. is able to cope with such tremendous tasks with such a comparatively small staff.

3. *Headquarters* As the staff increased, the premises at No. 17 route de Malagnou, Geneva, became more and more inadequate. Already soon after the Evanston Assembly the Executive Committee had appointed a "Headquarters Committee" to examine the question of office accommodation. At the Central Committee at Davos in 1955 permission was given to work out plans to build on the same site, but owing to lack of space the plan had to be abandoned. After long negotiations with the authorities of the City and Canton of Geneva, the W.C.C. exchanged the site in the route de Malagnou for a site four times the size in Grand-Saconnex, an area of Geneva devoted

to international organizations. The new address is 150 Route de Ferney, 1211 Geneva 20.

In order to cover the cost of building, the Central Committee appointed a committee whose chairman was Bishop Henry Knox Sherrill, one of the Presidents of the W.C.C. at that time. Thanks to generous financial aid from many of the member Churches, from individuals, and from foundations the new building was erected and was occupied in April 1964. It was officially consecrated in July 1965 on the occasion of the meeting of the Executive Committee. It contains an adequate number of offices, which were extended in 1968 by adding two more floors to one of the wings, so that it can now accommodate ten world confessional bodies and ecumenical organizations. It also has several spacious meeting-rooms, which enabled the Central Committee to be held there in 1966, and also the World Conference on Church and Society in the same year. The chapel is open to all the member Churches for worship, and is used by the staff for services and intercession. The library and archives have been greatly extended and occupy a separate building, so that the new headquarters is becoming an "ecumenical centre" to which people come to work and to visit from all over the world.[1]

Integration of the I.M.C. and the W.C.C.[2]

One of the most decisive events in the life of the W.C.C. was the integration of the International Missionary Council with the World Council of Churches. It was the outcome of an inner necessity based on the basic ecumenical approach that unity and mission are both essential aspects of the Churches; that it is the Church's mission which has revealed the necessity of its unity, and that mission has been one of the main roots of the ecumenical movement. This conviction carried even more weight than organizational considerations and practical demands. At Amsterdam John A. Mackay had said: "The Ecumenical Church is a child of the missionary movement" for "the Christian Church, to be truly the Church, must be a missionary as well as a worshipping Church".[3]

The relations between the I.M.C. and the W.C.C. had grown constantly closer since 1938.[4] The Joint Committee set up in 1939 became the basis for joint projects such as the Commission of the Churches for International Affairs founded in 1946, the East Asia Secretariat (1949) which was developed in 1957 into the East Asian Christian Conference, the Ecumenical Press Service (started in 1948), and (in accordance with a decision by the Evanston Assembly in 1954) the Study Division of the W.C.C. In addition the two organizations co-operated closely in inter-Church aid projects. After the Amsterdam Assembly both organizations officially added the words "in association with" the other one to their own title.

Dr Mackay presented a report to the Central Committee at Lucknow in

---

[1] Cf. *Evanston to New Delhi*, pp. 21f; New Delhi, p. 75; *New Delhi to Uppsala*, p. 17.
[2] Cf. *Why Integration?* by Ernest A. Payne and David G. Moses. London 1957.
[3] Amsterdam, p. 26.
[4] *A History of the Ecumenical Movement, 1517–1948*, pp. 398–400, 414–16.

1953 in which he said that the Joint Committee of the I.M.C. and the W.C.C. (at its meeting in London in 1952) had come to the conclusion: "It is clear that we are approaching the time when we must look to some corporate form of the two organizations."[1] However, in the report made by the Joint Committee at Evanston the question of full integration was still left open.[2]

At the meeting of the Central Committee at Davos the following year, the Joint Committee (which had Henry P. Van Dusen as its chairman and Norman Goodall as its secretary) stated that more than half the work of the W.C.C. was already being done jointly with the I.M.C.: "There was general agreement that the committee should not immediately concentrate on the question of the possible integration of the W.C.C. and the I.M.C. While the consideration of this issue is the direct responsibility of the committee, its solution is likely to be reached more effectively if time is taken to develop co-operation further."[3]

In its report to the Central Committee at Galyatetö in 1956 the Joint Committee affirmed its conviction that the time had come "when the W.C.C. and I.M.C. should consider afresh the possibility of an integration of the two councils. The committee regards it as imperative that any such integration should be in a form which ensures that missions belong to the heart of the ecumenical movement." Three reasons were given for the new development: the deepening missionary consciousness of the Churches, the ever closer working relationships necessitating processes which go beyond "association", and the increasing overlap in membership. The Central Committee instructed the Joint Committee "to undertake the formulation—in the fullest possible consultation with all concerned—of a draft Plan of Integration for presentation to the W.C.C. Central Committee in 1957 and to the I.M.C. Assembly at the Gold Coast in December–January 1957-8".[4]

The membership of the Joint Committee was increased from twelve to twenty, and it then presented its report to the Central Committee at New Haven in 1957. It made provision for the creation of a Commission on World Mission and Evangelism (similar to the Commission on Faith and Order) which would carry out its work through a "Division on World Mission and Evangelism" (an additional division of the W.C.C.). Care must also be taken to ensure that missionary concerns were adequately represented on the Executive and Central Committees and in the other divisions of the W.C.C.[5]

Although the draft had been kept very flexible and allowed scope for modifications, the tremendous difficulties presented by integration had to be faced. In the first place, the W.C.C. was composed of Churches, whereas the I.M.C. members were national and regional Christian Councils which often included in their membership missionary organizations or Church-bodies which did not want to be associated with the W.C.C., for example, certain fundamentalist groups. Should the I.M.C. break off its connection with these groups for the sake of integration with the W.C.C.? Misgivings on this score

---

[1] MRCC (Lucknow 1953), p. 46.   [2] Evanston, p. 322.
[3] MRCC (Davos 1955), p. 121.   [4] MRCC (Galyatetö 1956), pp 110f.
[5] MRCC (New Haven 1957), pp. 44f, 116–22.

were expressed at the meetings of the Central Committee at New Haven and the following year at Nyborg by representatives of Norway and France.

Furthermore, anxiety was felt that the I.M.C. (if it became a commission within the W.C.C.) might become neutralized and restricted in its action in the same way as the Faith and Order movement seemed to some people to have been. Similar views were expressed at the World Mission Conference in Ghana (28 December 1957–8 January 1958). At that conference the proposed integration was approved by fifty-eight votes to seven; at the same time strong sympathy was expressed for the misgivings of some missionary councils (especially in Africa, Latin America, and Scandinavia) and assurance was given that the plan for integration would be re-examined accordingly. A request was made at Ghana that the next Assembly of the W.C.C. be postponed from 1960 to 1961, so as to enable all the questions raised to be clarified; this proposal was also approved by the Central Committee of the W.C.C. in 1958.

However, some of the member Churches of the W.C.C. expressed strong reserve toward the proposed integration. In this case it was the Orthodox who were afraid that the character of the W.C.C. as a Council of Churches would be menaced by the merger with the I.M.C. They also feared that a "mammoth organization" would be produced, which would present dangers, and that the project was not yet ripe because the nature and tasks of the W.C.C. had not yet found sufficient understanding in the local Churches. Moreover, as most of the mission work was run by Protestant missions, the W.C.C. would (they maintained) become more and more "pan-Protestant" in its policy. Criticisms of this kind were voiced at the Central Committees at New Haven, Nyborg, and Rhodes.

Under such circumstances the idea of integration was slow in gaining ground on both sides. Until the Central Committee met at Rhodes in 1959 only forty-six of the 171 member Churches had expressed their opinion about integration with the I.M.C.; of these, forty-four were in agreement. By the same date twenty-two of the thirty-eight councils belonging to the I.M.C. had expressed themselves in favour of the merger, and three had declared themselves opposed (Norway, Belgium, and Brazil). One council had left the I.M.C. (the Belgian Congo). The tensions did not by any means die down at the Central Committee meeting at St Andrews in 1960. There was still a real fear that the question of integration might create a breach within the W.C.C. and within the I.M.C., because of the disagreement of the Orthodox and fundamentalist Churches.

But by the time of the meeting at St Andrews the difference with the Orthodox Churches had largely been resolved. The Orthodox Churches had avoided adopting any official attitude towards integration, and some of the Orthodox members of the Central Committee exercised "fraternal abstention" when the final vote was taken, while others (including the delegates from the Church of Greece) actually voted in favour. This may have been partly due to the plan to modify the Basis and to draw up the document concerning Proselytism. Many Orthodox may have been influenced by the fact that through integrating the W.C.C. and I.M.C. it would be easier to keep control over tendencies to proselytize. At the final vote there was an overwhelming majority in favour of integration. There was only one vote against it (by the Old Catholic representative) and three abstentions (including the Church of Norway, where the situation is particularly complicated).

Thus it was assured beforehand that integration would be accepted at New Delhi. At the last meeting of the I.M.C. immediately before the Assembly it gave its official approval to integration, and the plan was then accepted as it stood by the Assembly with all the changes which it involved in the constitution and the rules of the W.C.C. without a single dissenting vote. The chairman at that meeting, Archbishop Iakovos, then solemnly declared that "these two Councils are now united in one body with the name of the World Council of Churches".[1]

At the opening session of the Assembly, Bishop Lesslie Newbigin, then General Secretary of the I.M.C., had spoken on the theme "The Missionary Dimension of the Ecumenical Movement". He strongly advocated integration. He stressed the fact that no movement has the right to call itself ecumenical unless it does its utmost to bring the gospel to the whole world. "For the churches which constitute the World Council this means the acknowledgement that the missionary task is no less central to the life of the Church than the pursuit of renewal and unity."[2]

It was the positive conclusion of decades of development; but at the same time the Churches belonging to the World Council had confirmed their responsibility for their united mission to the world.

Growth of W.C.C. Membership[3]

In the rules of the W.C.C., the following criteria for membership are laid down, in addition to the primary requirement of the constitution that Churches eligible for consideration for membership shall be those "which express their agreement with the Basis" (Rules of the W.C.C., I. (3)):

(a) *Autonomy* An autonomous Church is one which, while recognizing the essential interdependence of the churches, particularly those of the same confession, is responsible to no other Church for the conduct of its own life.

(b) *Stability* A Church should not be admitted unless it has given sufficient evidence of stability in life and organization to become recognized as a Church by its sister churches.

(c) *Size*

(d) *Relationship with other Churches*

(The last two criteria are not defined in the Rules.)

Furthermore, "Before churches which are recognized as full members of one of the confessional or denominational world alliances with which the Council co-operates are admitted, the advice of these world alliances shall be sought" (I(4)). The same applies to Churches which belong to a Council

[1] New Delhi, p. 60.   [2] Ibid., p. 4.   [3] Ibid., p. 430.

associated with the W.C.C. or affiliated to the Commission on World Mission and Evangelism (I (5)). The application for membership must be approved by a majority of two-thirds at the Assembly or between assemblies in the Central Committee. The Central Committee shall then inform all the member Churches, "and unless objection is received from more than one-third of the member churches within six months the applicants shall be declared elected" (Constitution, II).[1]

The report entitled *The First Six Years, 1948–1954* (p. 9) states that "all churches which by the time of the Amsterdam Assembly had taken official action to join the World Council have remained members." The only withdrawal was the Baptist Union of Wales and Monmouthshire which did so "in view of the fact that many of its local churches had also membership in the Baptist Union of Great Britain and Ireland". Since 1948 nine Churches had been admitted into membership, bringing the total membership (immediately before the Evanston Assembly) to 161 Churches. The report said that the membership was still weak in Africa and Latin America. In Africa "the situation is slowly improving as mission churches become autonomous churches and apply for membership. In Latin America special efforts will have to be made to interpret the true character of the World Council." The hesitant attitude of the Orthodox Churches was not mentioned. At Amsterdam the only Orthodox Churches represented were the Church of Greece, the Ecumenical Patriarchate of Constantinople, the small national Eastern Orthodox Churches, the Russian Orthodox Church in Exile, and the Rumanian Orthodox Episcopate in America. However, the old Patriarchates of Alexandria, Antioch, and Jerusalem soon associated themselves.

The report *Evanston to New Delhi, 1954–1961* stated that during those seven years nineteen more churches had joined, including eight from Africa and five from Asia. Geographically the smallest number of member Churches was in Latin America. No reference was made either to the fact that no other Orthodox Churches had applied for membership. However, after 1957 negotiations opened with the Russian Orthodox Church, which were soon to alter the situation.

The largest expansion in membership took place at New Delhi when twenty-three new Churches joined the W.C.C. (see New Delhi, p. 9). This brought the number of member Churches up to 198. Although the Protestant Churches of Czechoslovakia, Hungary, and Poland had been represented in the W.C.C. from the beginning, relations with eastern Europe were greatly strengthened by the accession of the Orthodox Churches of Russia, Bulgaria, Rumania, and Poland. During the years which followed other Churches from eastern Europe (both Orthodox and non-Orthodox) also joined the W.C.C., so that it could now claim to be a fairly complete representation of non-Roman Catholic Christendom. The number of member Churches in Asia and especially in Africa also increased. The report *From New Delhi to Uppsala, 1961–1968* (p. 10) stated that if the Churches which joined at the New Delhi Assembly are added to those which joined since that date, twenty-one African Churches and seven Churches of the Eastern Orthodox

[1] New Delhi, p. 426.

tradition had been added to the membership up to 1966. The report also stated that two Pentecostalist Churches from Chile were accepted into membership, thus forming the first bridge to church bodies of a specially Evangelical character. However, the attitude of these groups to the W.C.C. is still marked by reservations, for different reasons. In order to enable smaller Churches with fewer than 10,000 members to co-operate in the W.C.C. (this being the minimum number fixed for membership of the W.C.C.) the New Delhi Assembly created the category of "associated Churches". This was in recognition of the fact that, if a large number of very small Churches became actual members, it would be almost impossible to allocate places at the Assembly. On the other hand, the W.C.C. wanted to strengthen the fellow-ship between itself and these small Churches, which were often living in a non-Christian environment, if they fulfilled all the other conditions for membership. Since New Delhi twelve Churches became "associated" with the W.C.C. They can send observers to the Assembly.

Before Uppsala the total number of member Churches was 232. Attention must, however, be drawn to the fact that the actual figures do not always reflect the size of the W.C.C. membership. For instance, some Churches which have merged in a union count in future only as one single Church, and do not need to apply for membership again.

The rapid growth of the W.C.C. has admittedly been offset by some painful setbacks. Because of the Korean crisis in 1951 the four member Churches in China withdrew from co-operation in the W.C.C., although they did not formally cancel their membership. Nevertheless, Bishop K. H. Ting of China attended the Central Committee meeting of Galyatetö in 1956. In 1955 the Baptist Union of Scotland withdrew from the W.C.C. In 1961 the three Dutch Reformed Churches in South Africa (the two Synods of the Transvaal and the Cape of the main Dutch Reformed Church, and the small Dutch Reformed Church of Africa) left the W.C.C. owing to basic differences of opinion on the policy of apartheid (which the W.C.C. had tried in vain to overcome). In 1963 the Union of Baptist Churches in the Netherlands decided to cancel their membership in the W.C.C. and in future merely to send observers to its conferences, because the W.C.C. (they alleged) was marked by "the imperialism of the national churches, *rapprochement* with the Catholic Church, the danger of Marxist infiltration, ecumenical impatience and a theology of relativism". In the latter case some misunderstandings may have crept in.

Relations with Regional Bodies

From the very outset the W.C.C. has fostered relations with National Councils of Churches and National Christian Councils, and later with regional organizations, and sought their co-operation in solving ecumenical tasks on the regional level. These efforts are described in Chapters 3 and 4 of this volume, and so will not be discussed here.

Relations with Confessional Bodies

The relations between the W.C.C. and the confessional and denominational bodies promoting ecumenism on the regional level presented comparatively few problems. The difficulties were far greater in the relations between the W.C.C. and the confessional world organizations, which vary widely in character and structure. Here it had to deal with definitely confessional bodies on a world level—confessional bodies which felt obliged to foster their own particular church tradition or confessional consciousness, and to make it clear. From the outset the W.C.C. has endeavoured to transform the differences into creative tensions. Of course, a basic attitude which is definitely confessional is always in danger of leading to isolation from other confessions and to theological rigidity (or even theological self-righteousness). The leaders of the W.C.C. have therefore never been afraid to point out the dangers of such trends. On the other hand, they have constantly stressed the fact that clear knowledge of one's own theological standpoint and of one's own church tradition are indispensable for a fruitful ecumenical conversation. For this reason, from the very outset the W.C.C. has sought contact with the confessional world bodies and other ecumenical organizations. This is laid down in the Constitution of the W.C.C., in Articles III and VII, where it is stated that "such world confessional associations and such ecumenical organizations as may be designated by the Central Committee may be invited to send representatives to the sessions of the Assembly and of the Central Committee in a consultative capacity".

It is noteworthy that simultaneously with the extension and strengthening of the W.C.C., the confessional world bodies were also growing larger and stronger. The Report *The First Six Years, 1948–1954* says: "It would seem that this development is due partly to the increased sense of solidarity and the desire to help churches which belong to the same confessional family, and partly to the desire to clarify the specific position of a particular confession in the wider ecumenical conversation" (p. 16). The problems which arise are evident: overlapping in the practical work, divided loyalties, and the anxious question "how the growth of a strong confessional consciousness will affect the ecumenical situation".[1] In its reports the W.C.C. was able to state again and again that the co-operation with the world confessional bodies (especially in the field of Inter-Church Aid) was making good progress, and that many of these world confessional bodies had clearly expressed their desire "to take their part in the ecumenical movement and to support the World Council of Churches".[2]

(The relation between confessional families and the ecumenical movement is discussed at greater length in Chapter 5 of this volume.)

Criticisms, Misunderstandings, and Opposition

It is absolutely inevitable that a phenomenon as significant as the World Council of Churches in its impact on church history and world history should

[1] *The First Six Years, 1948–1954*, p. 16. [2] *Evanston to New Delhi, 1954–1961*, para. 16.

encounter criticism from outside. Criticism acts as a healthy corrective. In addition the Council must constantly re-examine its own form and its own action. The W.C.C. has from the outset always tried to exercise self-criticism of this kind. It is not necessary to repeat here what Dr Visser 't Hooft has stated in the first chapter of this book. I will merely complement and underline certain points. The W.C.C. has always been prepared to remember that primarily it is not an organization but a movement, and that it must remain so. Some of the pioneers of the 1920s and 1930s were filled with misgivings when the dynamic ecumenical movement (marked by the personalities of great leaders) developed in 1948 into "a fellowship of Churches". They were afraid that the *élan* of the first decades might become smothered by a fixed form of organization. It was not primarily the younger generation which protested against the institutionalization and bureaucratization of the ecumenical movement. Among the middle generation and the older generation also there have always been men who realized the gulf between "movement" and "institution". In this connection mention should be made of the book *Unity in Mid-Career*, edited by Keith R. Bridston and Walter D. Wagoner (New York 1963).

When the question arose of building a new headquarters for the W.C.C. in Geneva, *The British Weekly* brought out an anxious article entitled "Movement or Monument?" Similar examples could be quoted indefinitely. Every movement (whether secular or church) sooner or later reaches the critical phase between the uncontrolled dynamic of its birth and the time when it has to become institutionalized and to have fixed working forms. It must be admitted, however, that the W.C.C. has always remained aware of this tension. It has never claimed that the whole ecumenical movement is contained within its own divisions, committees, and conferences, nor has the W.C.C. any desire to channel the ecumenical movement in this way. Again and again it has been affirmed that the ecumenical movement is something far more extensive than the World Council. Again and again the World Council has accepted suggestions from ecumenical groups and associations outside its own organization, and has tried to establish contacts with them.

It is not surprising that a fellowship as heterogeneous as the W.C.C. has difficulty in arriving at joint statements on theology, or even on political and social questions. Western and Eastern traditions, loyalty to Scripture alone and loyalty to tradition, free parish structure and sacramental liturgical structures, loyalty to the confessional tradition and strong insistence on unity, widely differing political views (from east and west and from the Third World)—all these coexist within the W.C.C. and rub along together day in day out. But they do so on their common Basis in which they "confess the Lord Jesus Christ as God and Saviour according to the Scriptures and therefore seek to fulfil together their common calling to the glory of the one God, Father, Son, and Holy Spirit".

The divergences which arise, therefore, are not "criticisms"; they are inherent in the nature of the ecumenical fellowship and of the ecumenical dialogue. The contribution which the Roman Catholic Church has to make in its dialogue with the W.C.C. also belongs to a different category.

On the other hand, the W.C.C. does receive criticism from many Evangelical groups as represented, for example, in the World Evangelical Fellowship, which even misunderstand and misinterpret it. These criticisms range from theological questions to political suspicions. Again and again the W.C.C. is attacked because it tolerates within its own fellowship Churches which embrace in their membership both active, committed Christians and Christians whose relation to the Church is more nominal than real. The critics overlook the fact that the fellowship of Churches belonging to the W.C.C. have made it their aim to help one another (through the power of the gospel) to undertake inner renewal and to educate their members to become real, conscious Christians. Instead of holding aloof, those Christian groups whose first concern is the genuine conversion of their own members to Christ would fulfil their particular task far better if they tried to express their concept of what it means to be a Christian within the framework of the other Churches.

The same applies to the criticism (often made by the Evangelical groups) that the W.C.C.'s contacts with the Orthodox Churches and with the Roman Catholic Church during the last few years have assumed undue importance. As a result of several Orthodox Churches having joined the W.C.C. in the early 1960s, and of the Second Vatican Council, certain tendencies towards "over-compensation" can be discerned in the work of the W.C.C., some of which may be described as "the need to make up for lost time"—because intensive official conversations with the above-mentioned Churches had been difficult or impossible for several decades. Now they are open.

However, the W.C.C. has always made it absolutely clear that the dialogue with the Roman Catholic Church must be carried on within the framework of the whole concept of ecumenism, in such a way that it promotes the formation and extension of relations to other Churches: "It is important to ensure that new relationships are developed in such a way that existing relationships are deepened and strengthened, and that freedom is retained for the fuller development of fellowship among all Christians."[1] In the same connection stress was laid on the fact that the contribution of the so-called "Evangelical Churches" is indispensable for the W.C.C., and the importance of seizing opportunities for mutual discussion and co-operation with them. Those member Churches which had "Evangelical" trends and groups within their own congregations were requested to "seek ways by which this witness may be more adequately represented in the life of the World Council" in view of the fact that their "theological convictions, spiritual experience, and missionary zeal might well find more vital expression in the life of the Council".[2] The W.C.C. has repeatedly made similar statements urging the Churches not only to listen to the criticisms and warnings of the conservative Evangelicals, but also to learn something from the Christian life that they practise and from their exemplary efforts for mission and evangelism. Since no official connection could be established with the conservative Evangelicals, the W.C.C. has tried to make contacts with them unofficially through

[1] MRCC (Enugu 1965), p. 38.   [2] MRCC (Enugu 1965), p. 40.

consultations. In many cases this has helped to clear up misunderstandings and has furthered mutual understanding.

During the last few years the appearance of so-called "modern theology" has aroused considerable misgivings among conservative Evangelicals. They have criticized the W.C.C. for allowing exponents of this "modern theology" to speak at ecumenical conferences and to contribute to ecumenical statements, thus endangering the unchangeable bases of the biblical message. However, through authorized spokesmen, the W.C.C. has more than once unmistakably made it clear that it takes its stand on the whole biblical message of salvation centred in Christ in its trinitarian interpretation.[1] On the other hand, the W.C.C. cannot and must not close its eyes to the new trends in theology nor to their disturbing effect on its own member Churches.

The W.C.C. certainly does not support these extremist trends which have strayed away from the centre of the Christian faith, and this is what the conservative Evangelicals fail to understand. But the W.C.C. cannot shirk facing the challenge of the modern theology, which has caused a great deal of confusion within its member Churches. Just because of its responsibility for those Churches, the W.C.C. must try to clarify these modern trends. In doing so the W.C.C. must carefully avoid giving the impression of being a doctrinal authority of any kind. That would help to justify the criticism that it wants to set itself up as a super-Church.[2]

In the cases described above there may be some ground for criticism or for misunderstanding. But the "International Council of Christian Churches" is an entirely different matter. This is a definite countermovement to the W.C.C. led by Dr Carl McIntire; the fundamentalist groups belonging to it are small, but extremely active.

This association, which was founded in 1948 parallel with the Amsterdam Assembly, accuses the W.C.C. of modernism and relativism in relation to the basic truths of the Bible, of fraternizing with the Roman Catholic Church, of compromising with communism, and of promoting pacifism. It is not an over-simplification to say that the I.C.C.C. is an isolated group and that its assertions are absurd. Misconceptions and suspicions of the same kind extend deep down into the member Churches belonging to the W.C.C., and the latter will have to strive continually to convince the Churches, and secular public opinion also, by clarity in its attitude and precision in its statements concerning its policy and its aims.

Where the W.C.C. has Succeeded and Where it has Failed

In this swiftly moving age the tendency is rather to register failures or inadequacies than to recognize progress and success resulting from the efforts of many generations. This applies also to the ecumenical movement. It is only the oldest people living today who can remember the complete lack of connection which formerly existed between the Churches, the divisions

---

[1] MRCC (Heraklion 1967), pp. 100–4 (Report of the General Secretary, Dr Blake).

[2] See W. A. Visser 't Hooft, "The Super Church and the Ecumenical Movement", in *Ecumenical Review* vol. x (July 1958), pp. 365–85.

and conflicts which had continued for centuries and were taken for granted and passed on, and the consequent prejudice against other Churches or religious groups and condemnation of them. The far-reaching changes in the relations between the Churches, thanks to the ecumenical movement, are simply taken for granted today. Many people fail to realize how much work and effort had to be made for decades by men and women in all Churches before the present state of ecumenical fellowship was attained. In all its statements the W.C.C. has constantly made it clear that this fellowship cannot be understood in the sense of an easy-going ignoring of existing differences.

The sole aim of the W.C.C. was to bring the Churches out of their isolation and to draw them into consultation with one another; in this the W.C.C. merely wanted to be an instrument and to provide a basis. After twenty years' experience the W.C.C. has definitely shown that it has achieved this aim in all essentials. In the W.C.C. and through it the Churches have not only learned to know and understand each other better; they have also realized afresh their responsibility for each other and for service to the world. Smaller Churches, or Churches which were persecuted and which were obliged to live in isolation, have experienced the strengthening fellowship of world Christendom through their membership of the W.C.C. Their mutual support in emergencies through world-wide relief projects has created a sense of belonging to one single family, which is felt even in the local congregations. Most important of all, the Churches which belong to the W.C.C. are compelled all the time to examine themselves and to strive for renewal, by listening together to the Word of God and by learning from one another.

Against this background of achievement certain weaknesses do admittedly still exist, and also certain dangers of wrong development. Have the member Churches fully recognized all the obligations which spring from their membership in the World Council? When the World Council sends out questionnaires or asks the Churches to pronounce their opinion, it finds again and again that the response from the member Churches is extremely small. In some cases this may be due to the lack, in some Churches, of organs to deal with such tasks. On the other hand, the W.C.C. cannot fulfil its many different tasks unless its thought and action is adequately supported by its member Churches. Otherwise the balance would shift from the life of the member Churches to the Geneva headquarters, which would conjure up the spectre of "secretariocracy".

Is it not possible that this lack of response is due to the fact that the delegates who attend the assemblies and who sit on the executive committees of the W.C.C. have too little contact with their own Churches, and that they do too little to relate their work in the W.C.C. to the life of their home-Churches and carry it out there? It is an old complaint that is constantly heard in the local congregations that the W.C.C. is an affair for theologians and church leaders; and hitherto the W.C.C. has not succeeded in proving this criticism groundless.

This brings us to the most painful gap in the whole network of ecumenical work: the fact that it is inadequately rooted in the local Churches. It would be over-simple to generalize about this. The reasons for it differ widely. They range from lack of attention to the ecumenical movement during the theological training to the indifferent introversion of the local Churches. Admittedly, during the past decades a great improvement has taken place in this respect and grass-roots co-operation between congregations is growing, even when their Churches or denominations remain apart. But ultimately the future of the ecumenical movement will depend on whether it succeeds in uniting "all in each place" in joint witness and service. The separation and the opposition between the Christian Churches on the local level was the starting-point of the ecumenical movement; it is therefore only on the local level that it can come to fulfilment.

This certainly does not mean that (as many people fear) the question of truth should be regarded as relative, and that priority should be given to a pragmatic solution for unity on the local level. But the W.C.C. and its member Churches must constantly face the question how the ecumenical agreements and resolutions are being carried out in practice. Eminent theologians such as Professor Edmund Schlink have often remarked resignedly that in W.C.C. commissions agreements about important theological questions have been reached without the member Churches afterwards hearing anything about them, not to mention doing anything to put the agreements into practice. Furthermore, in the 1950s Professor Walter Freytag once expressed his concern about the fact that even within ecumenical commissions the members themselves often did not remember, and consequently did not apply, what had been said and done on the same question years before, or even decades before. This also involves a structural problem at ecumenical conferences. Up to the present the W.C.C. has not succeeded in developing conference-procedure which will ensure that the participants are not overwhelmed with material, and which will also ensure that adequate time is available for examining and dealing with questions. It is evident that the W.C.C. might lag fatally behind the Roman Catholic Church's precise doctrinal statements because its own statements are not sufficiently mature or not adequately formulated. Only by concentration of emphasis, continuity and tenacious dynamism can the fellowship of Churches belonging to the W.C.C. be obedient to the call which has gathered them together under their one Lord and has placed them on the path of discipleship.

3

Out of
All Continents and Nations

A REVIEW OF REGIONAL DEVELOPMENTS
IN THE ECUMENICAL MOVEMENT

HANS-RUEDI WEBER

When on 23 August 1948 the World Council of Churches was solemnly inaugurated, the non-Western delegates had mixed feelings. On the one hand, they rejoiced in the fact that now as younger Churches they could meet with the older Churches on an equal level, as sisters rather than as daughters. On the other hand, however, they had serious apprehensions.

Beyond Western Parochialism

The major apprehension concerned the question whether the newly created body would not have a one-sided Western character. The two movements which merged—"Life and Work" and "Faith and Order"—had in their history shown little awareness of the pioneering ecumenical work being done outside eastern and western Europe and North America. "Faith and Order" conferences had several times been shocked out of their Western parochialism by people such as Bishop Azariah from South India; but these incidents had little consequence. For "Faith and Order" the "East" remained the Orthodox Churches, and only at Lund in 1952 did this movement begin to grow aware of the challenging significance of the existence of younger Churches in the non-Western world. No wonder that the Amsterdam statements about unity disappointed in particular the Indians, who less than eleven months earlier had seen the inauguration of the Church of South India. D. T. Niles expressed their feelings in a telling image: "The older churches were discussing the reasons and circumstances which had led to their earlier divorce: the younger churches were only just getting married and did not wish to be asked their opinion on the subjects which had led to the quarrels between the older churches."[1]

In the "Life and Work" movement Western parochialism reigned no less. Indeed, it was not until the W.C.C. study on "Our common Christian responsibility towards areas of rapid social change" (1955–61) that the "Life and Work" stream of the ecumenical movement became aware of the challenges of revolutionary Asia, Africa, and Latin America for Christian social thinking and action. At the first W.C.C. assembly, however, the treatment of the East–West conflict still gave the impression that the East ended with the Bosporus, as C. Devanesen observed.[2]

Such Western parochialism had been gradually overcome in the ecumenical youth movements and—with a delay of about one generation—in the International Missionary Council. They were not among the founding organizations of the W.C.C., but in all continents they had formed many of the actual and potential W.C.C. leaders, who immediately struggled for breaking through the traditional Western parochialism and worked hard for the manifestation of true universality. In 1947 W. A. Visser 't Hooft said in his report to the Provisional Committee of the W.C.C.: "It is . . . important that the younger churches should participate very fully in the setting up of the Council in order that they may make their full contribution to it and consider it from the start

[1] Amsterdam Series, 1948, vol. v, p. 62.
[2] "Post Amsterdam Thought from a Younger Churchman", in the *Ecumenical Review*, vol. i (January 1949), p. 143.

as their own instrument of ecumenical fellowship and action."[1] In the same year Stephen C. Neill was sent as an ecumenical ambassador to Asia and early in 1948 a special Far Eastern Commission was set up in Manila. Moreover, since its first meeting in 1946 the Joint Committee of the I.M.C. and the W.C.C. played an important role in letting the voice of the younger Churches be heard. As a result of all these initiatives, among the 351 official delegates at the Amsterdam Assembly there sat twenty-six nationals from Asia, six nationals from Africa, three Latin Americans, one from the Near East, but none yet from the Pacific.

Despite these efforts to make the W.C.C. an instrument of and for the Churches in all continents, P. D. Devanandan later confessed:

> Some of us from the so-called younger churches left Amsterdam with a heavy heart, because we could not help feeling that somehow we did not belong. The entire trend of discussion veered round problems of life and thought which primarily concerned the older churches. Moreover, we gained the impression, rightly or wrongly, that we were being made to think and act in accordance with the ideas, doctrinal and political, which are current in the older churches.[2]

This *malaise* came partly from a strong emphasis on the confessional loyalty in the early W.C.C., revealed by a significant change in the rules about the principles of representation. In the earliest draft of the W.C.C. constitution (1938) the membership in the Assembly and Central Committee was to be chosen according to a regional principle.[3] At Amsterdam this rule was changed and the accepted constitution says that seats must be allocated "due regard being given to such factors as numerical size, adequate confessional representation and adequate geographic distribution".[4] The confessional and the proportionate numerical representation were therefore set beside or even before the regional representation. Many delegates from the younger Churches who were involved in union negotiations had hoped that the W.C.C. would give a clear priority to the regional over the confessional loyalty. This did not happen and younger churchmen ever since have raised the question whether the W.C.C. does not foster an inter-confessional ecumenism at the expense of the equally important, perhaps even more important, inter-regional aspect of the ecumenical movement. "To us of the younger churches it is the international nature of our faith that strikes the imagination; . . . to us it is vital that ecumenical Christianity be both international and missionary."[5]

The insistence on the region does not therefore spring from an isolationist

---

[1] W.C.C. Buck Hill Falls Meeting, 1947, MRCC, p. 54. He did not tire of insisting on this point; cf. his reports to the W.C.C. Central Committee in Amsterdam 1948, MRCC, p. 30; in Chichester 1949, MRCC, pp. 65ff.

[2] *Ecumenical Review* vol. iv (January 1952), p. 163.

[3] G. K. A. Bell, ed., *Documents on Christian Unity* (Third Series, London 1948), pp. 294ff. This was in accordance with the proposal of the Committee of Thirty-Five in 1937; cf. *Oxford Series* (1937), vol. viii, p. 280.

[4] Amsterdam Series 1948, vol. v, p. 199. Cf. also the article by O. S. Tomkins on "Regional and confessional loyalties in the Universal Church", in Amsterdam Series 1948, vol. i, pp. 135–46.

[5] P. D. Devanandan, "The ecumenical movement and the younger churches", Amsterdam Series 1948, vol. i, pp. 152ff.

regionalism with the aim to counterbalance the factual Western parochialism of most ecumenical organizations by creating an Asian, African, or Latin American parochialism. The deepest motive is the concern that the Church become truly catholic (out of all the nations of the earth) and truly missionary (sent to all the nations of the earth). Ecumenical regionalism is an act of obedience. This was clearly expressed in the solemn declaration which inaugurated in 1959 the first regional ecumenical body: "Believing that the purpose of God for the churches in East Asia is life together in a common obedience to Him for the doing of His will in the world, the East Asia Christian Conference is hereby constituted."[1]

It is interesting to note that a similar movement from one-sided Western and inter-confessional ecumenism to regional developments and an emphasis on inter-continental ecumenism is present within the Roman Catholic Church. The Second Vatican Council defined the ecumenical movement as "those activities and enterprises which, according to various needs of the Church and opportune occasions, are started and organized for the fostering of unity among Christians".[2] Unity is seen here exclusively as unity with "the separated brethren", with the Churches and ecclesial communions separated from the Roman Apostolic See. Only the interconfessional aspect of the ecumenical movement is emphasized which reflects the concern of the Western Roman Catholic ecumenists. The Second Vatican Council, however, has also brought to the fore the intercontinental aspect of the ecumenical movement, although this happened not so much through the influence of the ecumenists and under the subject of ecumenism, but through the influence of the bishops from Africa, Asia, and Latin America and under the subjects of catholicity and mission. The Church is seen as the sacrament of the salvation of the world and of the unity of mankind. In this connection the necessary regional development is strongly emphasized. In order that the Church become truly catholic, particular Churches in the different regions and nations must retain their own traditions and thus contribute through their special gifts to the good of the other parts and of the whole of the Church.[3] This catholic nature of the Church makes her missionary and leads to the establishment of particular Churches in the different regions of the world.[4] It is a pity that in the documents of Vatican II this necessity of regional developments within the Church in order that she may be truly catholic and missionary has not been recognized as a primary *ecumenical* concern.

The Asian Region

When in 1921 the Far Eastern Olympic Games were held in Shanghai, the Chinese Y.M.C.A. took the initiative of organizing what was probably the first Asian Christian meeting. Asian Christians had, of course, met earlier at

[1] E.A.C.C. Inaugural Assembly at Kuala Lumpur, 1959, *Report*, p. 10.
[2] *Decree on Ecumenism*, no. 4.
[3] *Dogmatic Constitution on the Church*, no. 13.
[4] *Decree on the Missionary Activity of the Church*, nos. 1, 19–22.

world meetings. The world conference of the World's Student Christian Federation in Tokyo in 1907 was an especially important step in this Asian Christian self-discovery. Yet until 1921 no special initiative was taken to gather Asian Christians together. The experiment must have been convincing because only one year later, in 1922, at the World Student Christian Federation (W.S.C.F.) world conference in Peking, it was recommended "that an international conference in the Far East be continued regularly as a means to promote co-operation between the Eastern Movements and to make them know and understand one another better".[1] However, the birth pangs of the Asian revolution prevented early fulfilment of such plans for regular co-operation.

The uniting force still came from outside Asia, especially in the dynamic person of John R. Mott. His travels through Asia—first in 1895-7, then in 1907, in 1912-13, and many times later—set the ecumenical movement in motion in that continent. Many of its leaders were discovered and given confidence and training by him. He organized the visiting of Asian Christians among themselves, for instance the important visit of T. Z. Koo from China to the students in India in 1922. Most Asian National Christian Councils are the fruit of J. R. Mott's initiative. It was therefore a proper expression of gratitude when one of the first actions taken by the E.A.C.C. at its inaugural assembly was the inauguration of the "John R. Mott Lectures".

The above-mentioned Peking resolution was first implemented at Tjiteureup on Java in September 1933. The young Student Christian Movement of Java had invited its sister student movements from Asia and Australasia for a meeting which in a remarkable way foreshadowed the discussions of the I.M.C. assembly in Tambaram, India in December 1938 and of the later E.A.C.C. meetings. Because the living Christ, his uniqueness and finality, was put in the centre of the common study, it became possible to discuss in a very frank way such delicate subjects as colonialism and nationalism, the relationship between the Asian Church and Western missionary societies, the attitude of Christian faith to the syncretism and the religions of Asia.

These were subjects taken up five years later at Tambaram. There for the first time nationals of the lands of younger Churches formed a small majority of official delegates in a Christian world assembly, and among them were almost all the future leaders of the E.A.C.C. A deep solidarity in faith between Asian Christians had become a reality. This was forcefully demonstrated by the fellowship between the Chinese and Japanese delegations, even though their countries were at war with one another. "Wherever we looked we saw Chinese and Japanese together", wrote an African delegate.[2] This already existing fellowship in Christ had now also to receive a visible, organizational expression.

Communications from the Chinese and Japanese National Christian Councils about the desirability of a far eastern office of the I.M.C. were considered at Tambaram, and one year later A. L. Warnshuis was appointed

---

[1] W.S.C.F. General Committee (Peking 1922), *Minutes*, p. 27. Cf. also H.-R. Weber, *Asia and the Ecumenical Movement 1895–1961* (London 1966), pp. 277–92.

[2] M. T. Soga, quoted in R. I. Seabury, *Daughter of Africa* (Boston 1945), p. 75.

secretary of this office. But war intervened. The Geneva meeting of the I.M.C. committee in 1945 had again to decide on this matter, this time on the basis of a proposal sent by the Chinese and the Indian National Councils of Churches. This proposal set out the following long-term objectives for the planned East Asia Regional Committee:

(i) To promote and give expression to the spirit of Christian unity among the churches of East Asia. (ii) To promote fellowship and mutual helpfulness among Christians in East Asia through conference, exchange of delegations and such other measures as may be agreed upon. (iii) To promote a sense of the responsibility of the churches in East Asia for the Christian witness and for the building up of the churches in this area. (iv) To deepen the unity of the churches in East Asia with the world Church. (v) To bring to the life of the world Church the distinctive contribution of the churches in East Asia.[1]

The memorandum states clearly the purpose of an Asian regional body within and for the ecumenical movement. It was interesting, however, how differently this aim was interpreted in action by the existing Western ecumenical organizations and by the Asian Christians. The Joint Committee of the I.M.C. and W.C.C. thought in terms of an *office* and in 1947 approved such an ecumenical organizational structure. Yet in a special consultative session held in July 1947 during the I.M.C. meeting in Whitby, Asians showed little enthusiasm for such an office. What they wanted was an opportunity for consulting together, as R. D. Manikam reported in their name:

Prior to the establishment of an East Asia office . . . preliminary steps should be taken immediately to plan for an East Asia conference, whereby representatives of the churches can share their experience and concern, join in meditation and prayer and make common plans for participating more fully in the life of the ecumenical Church.[2]

The first East Asian Christian Conference met at Bangkok in December 1949. Although organized by a Chinese (S. C. Leung), China was absent for the first time. Having surveyed the contemporary situation in the Asian Churches and discussed their common task, the conference decided to appoint an Asian as their "ambassadorial representative". One year later R. B. Manikam from India began to fulfil this function. Especially in the years 1952-3 Asia became the scene of perhaps too many ecumenical gatherings organized by the W.C.C. and other agencies. Probably the most important was the study conference for East Asia at Lucknow, India, where Asian Christians prepared their contribution to the W.C.C. assembly in Evanston.

In July 1955 the Asia Council on Ecumenical Mission held its first meeting in Hong Kong. This organization was created mainly by Presbyterian and United Church mission boards and their daughter Churches in East Asia in order to stimulate inter-Church aid and exchange of personnel. The creation of this body accelerated the plans for establishing a more representative regional church conference. When in March 1957 the Second East Asian Christian Conference met therefore in the thoroughly Asian atmosphere of

[1] I.M.C. Committee (Geneva 1946), *Minutes*, p. 46.
[2] I.M.C. Committee (Whitby 1947), *Minutes*, p. 32.

the small fishing village, Prapat, in revolutionary Indonesia, firm proposals were drawn up for creating the E.A.C.C. The core of the mobile E.A.C.C. staff team began to work, each secretary based in his home country and working from there: D. T. Niles from Ceylon, U Kyaw Than from Burma, and Alan Brash from New Zealand.

This last name indicates an important development. Many had feared that the meeting in Prapat might become a mere ecclesiastical replica of the Asian–African Bandung conference in 1955, where a political power bloc formed itself over against the western nations. But true ecumenical regionalism has nothing to do with the forming of continental or racial power blocs. One of the first acts of the chairman at Prapat was therefore to move the delegates from Australia and New Zealand from the observers section into the full membership section. Ever since the Churches in Australia and New Zealand have played an important role in the E.A.C.C.

The E.A.C.C. assembly has so far met three times: for its inaugural assembly in Kuala Lumpur, Malaya in May 1959, and twice in Bangkok, Thailand, in February–March 1964 and January–February 1968. Typical, especially for the first of these, were the outstanding contributions which Asian laymen made to its deliberations. The assemblies have authorized a series of important consultations. In India, Japan, the Philippines, Korea, and Indonesia the consultations on "New Patterns of Christian Service" (1960–2) showed the present Asian Christian thinking about the relationship between social service and social action as well as the trend from separate Christian service institutions to the involvement of Christians in state and secular service programmes. The "situation conferences" in India, Japan, and Singapore tried to discern what joint action for mission means today in the three major areas of East Asia. A meeting in Hong Kong in 1966 and one in Seoul in 1967 summed up present Asian thinking and convictions about Faith and Order and Church and Society matters respectively. This is only a very selective list of meetings, by-passing many consultations organized by E.A.C.C. committees and excluding those organized by the various Asian study centres and by the W.C.C.; and not least the third assembly of the W.C.C. at New Delhi in 1961.

The E.A.C.C. assemblies also authorized and surveyed a growing number of inter-Church aid and missionary projects. Deeply involved with the questions of the home and family life, the E.A.C.C. has stimulated much concern in the Asian Churches about planned parenthood. The exchange of fraternal workers within Asia and the sending of Asian missionaries—over two hundred are now listed—were fostered. Asian churches remain thus no longer merely receiving Churches. This is also true financially. Between fifteen and twenty thousand U.S. dollars a year are given by Asian Christians in response to W.C.C. emergency appeals for aid somewhere in the world. Especially significant was the establishment of the Asian Christian Service in Vietnam where through the costly service of the E.A.C.C. area personnel Asian Churches fulfil together their ministry of reconciliation. This short and incomplete list shows that the E.A.C.C. is not only a ferment of ideas—although this aspect of regional developments is emphasized in the description of this chapter—but also a programme of common witness and service.

What is the purpose of all these projects and meetings? D. T. Niles, the retiring E.A.C.C. general secretary, said in his ten-years report: "The complex of ideas and principles within which our churches in East Asia usually functioned was within the context of world denominations and confessions. The E.A.C.C. helped to provide the other eye with which the churches could look at their work and witness." Thus it helped to build up "within the life of each church and country a group of men and women, both older and younger, who are willing to probe the frontiers of the Christian enterprise" and "to give to these frontiersmen a sense of solidarity, encouragement and sharpened insight". "All we have sought to do is to inject into situations ideas which we felt were right at this time, to get key individuals in every country committed to these ideas, and then to put pressure behind these ideas so as to make costly any attempt to disregard them."[1] If this is a fair description of the E.A.C.C.'s work, then it is essential to examine which ideas were studied in order to understand the main thrust of the Asian regional body. The earlier mentioned John R. Mott Lectures are a helpful guide for such an examination.

The first John R. Mott lecture series (1959) stood under the theme, "A decisive hour for the Christian mission".[2] First, some Western friends were asked to situate the Asian churches within the ecumenical movement. This led up to the much noted lecture by D. T. Niles on "A Church and Its 'Selfhood' " which became a programme because it expressed in a prophetic way what had to be said at that time and place. Just as a child suddenly says "I" and his self thus ceases to be a mere object, so Asian Churches have become conscious of their self-hood. This happened in their worship, in their mission to a given place and in their secular engagement, i.e. Christian involvement in the political, economic, and social affairs. However, this self-hood can grow only in relationship with other "selves". For a long time relationships have existed between Churches and their missionary agencies in the West with the Churches in Asia, but the relationships do not yet sufficiently take account of the newly acquired selfhood of Asian Churches. D. T. Niles therefore spelled out what changes are overdue in these missionary relationships. There are also growing relationships of conversation, belonging, and oneness among the Asian Churches themselves. Now "the E.A.C.C. is one more expression of this growth of the churches in Asia into selfhood. It is the instrument of our resolve to be churches together here in Asia. It is to be the means by which we enter into a meaningful participation in the missionary task of the Church."

The second John R. Mott lecture series (1961) dealt with the subject "Christ's Ministry and Ours",[3] emphasizing the ministry of the laity. The main speaker, Masao Takenaka from Japan, pointed especially to the New Testament image of the Church as the community of the first fruits of the new humanity.

> It somehow transcends the notion of a majority or minority situation. It gives a real qualitative representation rather than one determined by quantitative

[1] D. T. Niles, "Ideas and Services", unpublished manuscript.
[2] *A Decisive Hour for the Christian Mission* (London 1960), p. 96.
[3] Published in *The South East Asia Journal of Theology*, III. 3 (January 1962), p. 18.

number. A Christian layman in industrial society, no matter how insignificant he appears to be, is a first fruit in that particular and concrete place. He is a pledge of the Holy Spirit that the great harvest is to come. I believe this concept of the first fruits gives real strength and support to Christian presence and involvement in a concrete place of work and living in our Asian setting.

Takenaka and the other lecturers then spelled out what such a qualitative representation means for the everyday life of ordinary Christians and for the ministries and structures of Asian church life.

Under the title "Grace and Apostleship"[1] the third series of the John R. Mott lectures (1964) continued the reflection on the themes of the first two series, but the main accent lay now on the understanding of the tides of history. M. M. Thomas showed that ever since the Bangkok meeting in 1949 the E.A.C.C. has overcome the traditional pietistic indifference to the tides of history. At the inaugural assembly at Kuala Lumpur in 1959 it was even stated that "the Church must endeavour to discern how Christ is at work in the revolutions of contemporary Asia; releasing new creative forces, judging idolatry and false gods, leading people to a decision for or against him and gathering to himself those who respond in faith to him, in order to send them back into the world to be witnesses to his Kingship".

It was a sign of healthy realism that in his 1964 lecture M. M. Thomas concentrated on the forces which tend to betray the promises of God in the revolutionary tides of Asia. He thus showed how the tide of nationalism brings for Asia the danger to pass from the traditional conformist collectivism to the modern technical mass society without having discovered the human person and the personal community. Similarly the true humanity which Christ reveals can be endangered by the negative aspects of the tides of growing group consciousness, or by the tide of growing economic tension between the rich nations of the North and the poor nations of the South.

Having reflected on the necessary selfhood which the Asian Churches need for fulfilling their task in new Asia, having rediscovered the ministry of the laity, their vocation to be the first fruits of the new humanity, and having now also made a realistic appraisal of the Asian scene, the time was ripe to think about the theme "Confessing the Faith in Asia Today".[2] This was the subject of the fourth series of the John R. Mott lectures (1966). The fact that among the seven lecturers only two were Asian nationals shows the awareness of the E.A.C.C. that while Christ has to be confessed in the concrete region of Asia today, this confession must happen in full communion with the Church universal. This, however, does not mean that the Churches in Asia can simply take over the confessions of the Western Churches. C. H. Hwang said:

> The sad thing is that, before becoming first a confessing Church in the missionary situation, the younger churches were prematurely projected into a "confessional" situation which was not their own, that is, before they knew and became a Community of Christ they were told to become a Presbyterian, Lutheran,

---

[1] Published in *The South East Asia Journal of Theology*, v. 4 (April 1964).

[2] *The South East Asia Journal of Theology*, viii. 3 (January 1967). C. H. Hwang's lecture in the same journal, viii. 1–2, pp. 77f.

Methodist or Anglican Church. They were divided without even being able to know why. I believe that the way to recover the unity of the Church on the road is to return to the confessing church first, and only secondly to become a confessional church, and hold steadfastly the second within the context of the first. Finally, I believe that God has once again put not only the younger churches but also the older churches and the ancient churches in a new missionary situation—not only in Asia today but also in the world today—so that we may learn our way back to the unity of the *confessio viatorum*.

Such a *confessio viatorum* is not in the first place the affair of theologians but of the pilgrim people. It was therefore right and according to the best tradition of the E.A.C.C. that also an Asian layman, T. B. Simatupang, was asked to speak on this theme.

The African Region

Within the cataclysms of modern African history the Church can survive only if it struggles with the following tasks: Will it be able to build up a Christian family life for Africa without becoming legalistic and disregarding the African social heritage? Will Christians overcome the fear of sorcery and witchcraft which survives even among many sophisticated African believers and nevertheless have a sympathetic approach to the old African world view? Will the Church be able to stem the growing proliferation of separatist sects without losing the positive search for community and indigenization which finds expression in these movements? To this list of C. P. Groves, the foremost historian of the Church in Africa,[1] new challenges must be added today: What is the role of the Church in the midst of the clash of cultures? What contribution can Christians make for abolishing the economic exploitation of the African peoples and for nation-building?

In the predominantly autobiographical novels of contemporary African writers such questions appear again and again. How do Christians in Africa answer these challenges? What insights have they gained to contribute to the Church universal? An important beginning of the answer to these questions is the way in which African Christians and Churches increasingly learn to face the above-mentioned challenges together, to consult with one another and support one another in their discipleship.

Unfortunately, William Carey's "pleasing dream" of 1806—to hold from 1810 onwards decennial world missionary conferences at the Cape of Good Hope—was never realized, otherwise Africa's ecumenical history might have begun already at the beginning of the nineteenth century. In actual fact the earliest interdenominational missionary conference met only in 1904 in Johannesburg. At that time South Africa was already active in the World Student Christian Federation, because only one year after the foundation of the Federation at Vadstena in 1895 one of its founder members, Luther Wishard, had helped to establish the mostly Dutch South African Student Christian Association. In 1906 John R. Mott visited South Africa for the first

[1] C. P. Groves, *The Planting of Christianity in Africa*, vol. iv (London 1958), pp. 315–56.

time. It was not until the 1920s, however, that Africa was discovered in ecumenical history.

This discovery happened in Asia. At the World Student Christian Federation meeting at Peking in 1922, for the first time a son of Africa was asked to speak at a world conference—the American Negro Willis King, who was later the Methodist bishop in Liberia. He made a deep impression, and the important policy decisions made in Peking concerning race relations and the building up of ecumenical student work in Africa was to a great extent due to him. One and a half decades later it was again in Asia, at the I.M.C. assembly in Tambaram, that for the first time Africa was well represented in a world gathering and experienced the dynamic of the ecumenical movement. "My journey out of Africa turned me from a South African into an African. Madras made me a world Christian", wrote Mina T. Soga.[1] The First Asio-African Conference in Bandung, Indonesia in 1955, strengthened the African political leaders in their quest for a free Africa, and this movement in turn influenced the African Churches' quest for selfhood.

Meanwhile James E. K. Aggrey from the Gold Coast had been fighting relentlessly for understanding and sympathy for Africa and its people among the Christians in North America and Great Britain. In 1921 he attended the first meeting of the I.M.C. at Lake Mohonk, New York and was appointed a member of the Council. One year later he appealed to the Foreign Missions Conference of North America:

> Give us a full-rounded chance. The sea of difference between you and us should be no more. The sea of our failure to bring any contribution to the Kingdom of God shall be no more. You white folks may bring your gold, your great banks and your big buildings, your sanitation and other marvellous achievements to the manger, but that will not be enough. Let the Chinese and the Japanese and the Indians bring their frankincense of ceremony, but that will not be enough. We black people must step in with our myrrh of child-like faith. . . . If you take our child-likeness, our love for God, our belief in humanity, our belief in God, and our love for you, whether you hate us or not, then the gifts will be complete. . . . God grant that you who have heard . . . this plea from Africa will trust us, will come and educate us, and will give us a chance to make that contribution to the world which is in the design of God.[2]

"Come and educate us!" This call was heard by Europe and North America. During the next decades the Christian commitment for education in Africa became a first attempt to see Africa as a whole. In 1920–1 an educational survey commission was sent by the U.S.A. Foreign Missions Conference and the Phelps-Stokes Fund to Central, West, and South Africa, and in 1923–4 a second commission, mainly British, surveyed East Africa. Both were led by Jesse Jones and in both Aggrey collaborated. Meanwhile, one of the greatest ecumenical pioneers, the I.M.C. secretary J. H. Oldham, became almost totally absorbed in African affairs. He was the prime mover for the first international conference on the Christian Mission in Africa.

[1] R. I. Seabury, op.cit., p. 77.

[2] Edwin W. Smith, *Aggrey in Africa* (London 1929), pp. 188f.

It met in September 1926, not in Africa but in Le Zoute, Belgium.[1] In the same year the Institute of African Languages and Culture was launched in London, and in 1929 the I.M.C. created its International Committee on Christian Literature for Africa. Five years later John R. Mott became instrumental in getting Christian Councils started in Southern and Central Africa.

After the inquiries made in the 1920s in the field of general and religious education, the Tambaram assembly of the I.M.C. decided in 1938 that a comprehensive inquiry be made concerning the present condition of theological education. Especially in Africa the great lack of adequately trained ministers had become a major obstacle to the growth of the Church. "It is impossible to exaggerate the importance of the work of those who teach theology and train ministers of the African Churches." This first conclusion of the inquiry led immediately to the second one, namely the obligation for co-operation in theological training.

> The judgement of the succeeding generation may well be that the fateful issue of our own time for the advance or the decline of Protestant Christianity in Africa was the achievement or refusal of Christian co-operation; and that the issue was basically determined in the type, spirit, and quality of the schools for pastors.[2]

In the post-war years some experiments in joint theological training appeared (Limuru in Kenya, Trinity College in Kumasi, the Yaounde theological faculty, etc.). A meeting of representatives of Protestant missions and Churches was held at Leopoldville, and by 1955 there were Christian Councils in fourteen African territories, although only three of these—Belgian Congo, Sierra Leone, and South Africa—were affiliated to the I.M.C.

In the new Africa where in the period between 1958 and 1961 eighteen nations reached independence, intercontinental co-operation was indeed needed. But were the Western missionary organizations and the African Churches ready for it? "The tendency was unmistakably for the extension of confessional organizations rather than for the fostering of inter-confessional unions."[3] The clearest sign of this trend is the fact that the first (Church or secular) All Africa Conference which met in Africa itself was organized by the Lutheran World Federation. In 1955 it called together the memorable All AfricaLutheran Conference on the slopes of Mount Kilimanjaro at Marangu, Tanganyika. The stated purpose of that meeting was to bring all the Lutheran Churches and mission fields in Africa out of isolation in order that they might begin to think as an African Lutheran Church and see the vision of the Christian Church throughout the whole continent of Africa.

The enthusiastic reports of delegates and visitors—out of a total of 168 participants 116 were Africans—show that this purpose was achieved despite the great difficulties of communication. Undoubtedly a real community has

---

[1] The special Africa issue of *IRM* (July 1926), with the preparatory papers for the Le Zoute Conference, gives an excellent survey of Africa in the 1920s and the task which the Church faced then in that continent.

[2] *Survey of the Training of the Ministry in Africa*, Part iii, p. 61 and Part ii, p. 95.

[3] C. P. Groves, op.cit., vol. iv (London 1958), p. 305; cf. pp. 304–7.

grown among Lutherans in Africa. Yet for the African delegates the discovery was not so much Lutheranism as the Church in Africa. This appeared especially in the discussions on faith and confession. The call for a *confessio Africana* was strong and the Marangu report recommends that "a comprehensive confessional statement—*confessio Africana*—may be worked out, not necessarily replacing the old confessions, but amplifying the Lutheran teaching in terms and in a language which will be understood by the modern African".[1]

Unfortunately, the two following All Africa Lutheran Conferences did not go very far in implementing this recommendation. At Antsirabé in 1960 the accent lay on "the faith of our fathers", and at Addis Ababa in 1965 only Josiah Kibira came back to the Marangu recommendation in his courageous keynote address where he said:

> Theologically, there is a lack of freedom of mind. With the exception of a few cases, we can hardly think independently. We depend mostly on advisers from Europe and America. Our theological boards are very inadequate as long as they reflect American, Swedish or German Lutheran theologies rather than African theologies. . . . And yet we must stress the universality of Christ's Church. We must guard ourselves against an African church and against what we mean by a *confessio Africana*. Yet the question is this: how long must we depend on the European churches to do our thinking in the very things we wish to do?[2]

Kibira struggled here with the basic issue of true regionalism in the ecumenical movement. Regionalism does not aim at a Church and confession which is more Asian or African than Christian. It wants to maintain the universality of Christ's Church. But, at the same time, it wants to counterbalance the existing strong European and American character of the present manifestation of Christ's Church. Churches and theologians of the West had taken Aggrey's words about the African child-like faith too literally. Dr Akanu (formerly Sir Francis) Ibiam once said that to many white missionaries "Africa must stay where she is—the baby of the world—not only in political affairs, or in economic matters, or sociologically, but even in church life and Christian emancipation".[3] In order to grow out of this tutelage ecumenical regionalism aims at creating structures in which there is freedom of mind for Christians in a given region to think, confess, and act according to God's will for this region. Kibira's problem was that a Lutheran or any other confessional all Africa conference is not the best possible structure for such a freedom of mind. Meanwhile, a better structure had been created, although it still has many growing-pains: the All Africa Conference of Churches (A.A.C.C.).

Over New Year 1957-8 an ecumenical body, the I.M.C., held for the first time a world assembly in Africa, at Accra in Ghana. This provided a good occasion for organizing the first representative All Africa Church Conference which met at Ibadan, Nigeria in January 1958. The conference was held under

[1] Marangu Report (Geneva 1956), p. 48.
[2] Addis Ababa Report (Geneva 1966), p. 19.
[3] *Witnesses Together*, E.A.C.C. Kuala Lumpur Report, p. 146.

the auspices of the Christian Council of Nigeria although the initiative had mainly come from the I.M.C. A largely African committee had worked out the programme which under the general theme "The Church in Changing Africa" included lectures and discussion groups on (i) the Church, youth and the family, (ii) the Church and economic life, (iii) the Church and citizenship, (iv) the Church and culture, and (v) the growing Church. Among the 195 people who actually attended, ninety-six represented the Churches in twenty-five African countries and territories. An open and flexible programme, together with the corporate Bible studies, ensured that the purpose of the meeting was achieved: the African Christian self-discovery and a first grasp of the task ahead.

The discovery was sometimes painful, not only because there exists no *lingua franca* for Africa, but because Africa is culturally, racially, politically, and ecclesiastically such a diverse and torn-apart continent. Alan Paton from South Africa, for instance, introduced himself to the conference as "a native of Africa, though a white one as you can see". The delegates were impressed both by the planned church union in Nigeria and by the reports about the Prapat conference and its resolve to create the E.A.C.C. Despite all tensions and difficulties, they opted for a visible organizational expression of the unity which they had already found and whose strengthening they felt to be imperative. A provisional committee was named and Ibadan 1958 became for the A.A.C.C. what Bangkok 1955 and Prapat 1957 had been for the E.A.C.C.

Youth pressed forward. With the help of the ecumenical world youth organizations they expressed strongly their aspirations in the All Africa Christian Youth Assembly at Nairobi in December 1962. Meanwhile Donald M'Timkulu from South Africa had been appointed to organize the inaugural assembly of the A.A.C.C. It met at Kampala, Uganda in April 1963 bringing together representatives from some 100 Churches and forty-two countries in Africa. The presence of three official observers from the Roman Catholic Church was a sign of the changing climate. In Uganda Anglicans and Catholics fought and killed one another in 1892. Now, since January 1964, the two Churches are together in Uganda's Christian Council.

At the opening of the assembly the delegates voted unanimously for the establishment of the A.A.C.C., an act which after a solemn silence was loudly heralded by the beating of African drums. The constitution—with almost the same preamble as that of the E.A.C.C.—and the future work commissions of the A.A.C.C. were shaped and accepted. The commissions are: (i) the life of the Church, dealing with the forms of worship, evangelization, and the training of ministers and the laity; (ii) social, national, and international responsibility of the Church, including especially the search for a true Christian family life in Africa; (iii) youth, to continue the work begun at Nairobi; (iv) education, with the subdivisions of formal education and Christian education; (v) literature and mass communication. In the course of the next years an A.A.C.C. secretariat was built up, stationed first at the Mindolo Ecumenical Centre at Kitwe, Zambia and since 1965 in Nairobi. The growing A.A.C.C. staff now helps the A.A.C.C. commissions to fulfil their task. Only a few examples can be mentioned which show that African Christians begin to face the earlier-mentioned questions which are decisive for the Church's mission to modern Africa.

The emergency situations created by civil wars, race discrimination, refugees, and hunger, become a severe test for the community of Churches which develops in the A.A.C.C. A continent-wide survey of the needs in Africa was made for the W.C.C. by the late Z. K. Matthews and Sir Hugh Foot. An ecumenical emergency fund for Africa was created, which makes it possible to operate service and training projects all over the continent.

True Christian family life and, related to it, the question of church discipline, remain burning issues. Ever since the first work group at the Ibadan conference discussed that subject, the A.A.C.C. and W.C.C. have jointly sponsored mobile teams and meetings for consulting and advising the African Churches in this field. Immediately before the Kampala Assembly, a two-month seminar on the Christian home and family life worked out recommendations on such controversial questions as bride price, polygamy, family planning, and prostitution. No less urgent remains the question of the Christian participation in nation-building and economic development. The results of the W.C.C. study on rapid social change in Africa were therefore summarized in a preparatory volume for the Kampala Assembly. In January 1965 a remarkable group of African laymen and church leaders met at Enugu, Nigeria for discerning "The Christian Response to the African Revolution". Having thus both in study and action been involved as Christians in the African revolution the Africans were well prepared for contributing to the World Conference on Church and Society at Geneva in 1966, and their interventions often astonished, irritated, and enlightened participants from the West.

The basic theological question which must be studied in the African context is the relationship between "Biblical Revelation and African Beliefs". This was the subject of the first consultation of African theologians which met in January 1966 at Ibadan. Unless this relationship is studied and the gospel preached in its context, fear of sorcery and witchcraft will remain smouldering under the surface of Christian belief. This study also emphasizes elements of the biblical message which have been neglected by Western Christians, for example, the importance of sacrifice and Christ's victory over the powers and principalities. Many other initiatives were taken by the A.A.C.C., usually in collaboration with ecumenical world organizations: the conference on Christian Education in a Changing Africa over New Year 1962–3 at Salisbury, work in the field of race relations, contact with African separatist movements, evangelism in urban Africa, the survey and consultation on the evangelization of West Africa, leadership training courses for the laity and ministers, seminars for African writers, artists, and specialists in mass media, work in collaboration with the World Council of Christian Education which held its fourth world institute at Nairobi in July 1967.

Africa is no longer "the baby of the world" but is coming of age. Helped by the A.A.C.C., the Churches in Africa began to face together their costly vocation of which the inaugural assembly's message said:

Here in Kampala at the tombs of the first Baganda martyrs, we have been reminded of all the saints who died for His cause on this continent. We share the burden of all on this continent who suffer persecution, oppression and injustice in any form and from whomsoever. We have been made conscious that the faithful proclamation of Christ as the only Saviour of the world may, even in our day, have to be tried out by a Cross and martyrdom.[1]

Other Regional Developments

Space does not allow as extensive a description of the origin and development of other regional bodies as that which we have given to the Asian and African scene. In any case the E.A.C.C. and the A.A.C.C. have pioneered on this way of ecumenical regionalism and they have gone furthest so far. The reasons for establishing regional conferences or councils of Churches are essentially the same in all continents, although the special characteristics of the Churches and the society in each region mark both the specific form and tempo of each regional development.

Near East

In between Asia and Africa lies the geographically ill-defined region of the Near (or Middle) East. It is the cradle of Judaism, Christianity, and Islam. The characteristics of this immensely diverse region, from Morocco to Iran and from Turkey to central Sudan, are the dominance of Islam, the Arab–Israeli tension, political instability, oil, and poverty. Christians form a small minority, deeply divided among various ancient Eastern Churches, Roman Catholics, and numerous Protestant bodies. The wounds of the Crusades are still open. Proselytism by Protestants and Roman Catholics among the ancient Eastern Christians and, more recently, political divisions and the unresolved refugee problem have created an atmosphere of mistrust in which co-operation and common worship, study, and action are extremely difficult.

The first stimulus for a common Christian approach in this area came from an I.M.C. conference on missions to Moslems at Lucknow in 1911. Later, from February to April 1924, John R. Mott conducted a series of "Moslem conferences" in Algeria, Egypt, Lebanon, and Iraq, leading up to a general conference in Jerusalem in April 1924. In its findings the first proposal for an area council is made. Together with a Christian Literature Committee for Moslems—also an outcome of the Jerusalem conference—the planned area council was constituted in 1927 (since 1929 called the Near East Christian Council (N.E.C.C.). Unlike the E.A.C.C. and the A.A.C.C., it is not based on the prior foundation of National Christian Councils in the area, and stands thus half way between a national and a regional body. The work of the N.E.C.C. was from its beginning very much hampered by the fact that its leadership came mainly from foreign missionaries and that it remained almost exclusively Protestant in an area where the ancient Orthodox Churches form the majority.

[1] *Drumbeats from Kampala*, p. 16.

D

The Christian approach to Islam remains a major concern for the N.E.C.C. From 1957 to 1962, for instance, the exemplary study pamphlet series *Operation Reach* was published in order to prepare Christians in the Near East for their missionary encounter with Moslems. Each study contains the exposition of a salient theme in Islamics and a meditation on the truth of the gospel in an Islamic context. One of these meditations deals with an art which not only Christians in the Near East but in all continents must learn, namely "the art of being a minority".[1] Annual summer schools helping missionaries and church leaders to understand Moslems and to witness to Christ in a Moslem world are organized in Jerusalem and Isfahan.

Much of this work was focused in a study conference held in April 1959 at Asmara in Eritrea. The conference message expressed a distinctive new spirit in the Christian approach to Moslems:

> We have been conscious of the failure of the Church, both in the past and now, to live and act according to the measure . . . of God's seeking, suffering, re-deeming love, demonstrated in Christ and His Cross. With penitence and humility we confess our need for cleansing and a new spirit of respect and friendship for Moslems, through which the barriers of suspicion and fear will disappear. . . . We wish to relate the Christian message constructively to Islamic thought and experience and to enter as fully as we may into areas of mutural practical concern.[2]

The missionary aspect of the N.E.C.C. continues equally in its work of co-ordinating Christian literature. The Council sponsored in 1960 a three weeks Christian writers institute in Alexandria. In 1961 it reorganized and expanded its literature department. In the same year it also began its partner-ship with "The Radio Voice of the Gospel", the Lutheran radio station in Addis Ababa, Ethiopia.

One of the most important results of the Asmara Conference was the participation of delegates from the ancient Orthodox Churches. The Ethiopian Church delegation gradually progressed, for instance, from complaint about Protestant mission efforts proselytizing among Orthodox to an awakening interest in the task of the whole Church to bear witness to Christ among Moslems and people of other faiths. This beginning of an understanding between Protestant and Orthodox was partly a result of the growing Protest-ant–Orthodox community in the W.C.C. Moreover, vigorous Orthodox youth movements had sprung up in the Near East which were no longer content with the merely Protestant character of the N.E.C.C. In ecumenical work camps held in the Near East young Orthodox and Protestants had discovered one another. After Easter 1955 an ecumenical youth leaders con-sultation was held in Beirut. Jointly sponsored by the World Student Christian Federation and the W.C.C. youth department, Gabi Habib began work in the whole Near East region from 1964 onwards. In July 1964 a Middle East Youth and Student Assembly was held in Broumana, Lebanon.

[1] K. Cragg, "The Art of Being a Minority", in *Operation Reach* (Beirut March-April 1959), pp. 6–18.
[2] *The Christian Faith and the Contemporary Middle Eastern World: Report of the Asmara study conference*. New York 1959.

Another strong stimulus for making the N.E.C.C. confessionally more representative is mentioned by its long-time secretary, Harry Dorman:

> The plan of integration of the W.C.C. and the I.M.C. has accentuated the special problems and opportunities which confront the ecumenical movement in the Near East. . . . Here the great majority of Christians belong to the ancient eastern churches, many of which have been unsympathetic with the modern missionary movement from the West. . . . What does integration imply for this situation?[1]

The first implication had to be a change in the N.E.C.C. itself. In 1964 the N.E.C.C. changed its name to become "The Near East Council of Churches". The crucial paragraph of the revised N.E.C.C. constitution now reads:

> The aims of the N.E.C.C. are to aid the Church in the Near East in her proclamation to all men of the gospel of salvation through Jesus Christ; to give expression to the unity of churches in this task; and to relate the gospel to the many problems which confront men and nations in the Near East.

The first step in doing this is seen in the promotion of "fellowship among churches working in the area so that all may bring into the common treasury the riches of their own traditions and spiritual experience".[2] In 1964 still only one Orthodox Church, the Syrian Orthodox Patriarchate, sent delegates to the N.E.C.C. This situation has not changed substantially, although since 1965 for the first time a national, Albert Isteero from the Coptic Evangelical Church in Egypt, has been general secretary of the N.E.C.C.

The strongest impetus for a much greater fellowship among Christians in the Near East is undoubtedly the emergency situation created by the Arab–Israeli wars and the seemingly insoluble refugee problem. In the service to refugees, Orthodox, Protestant, and Roman Catholic Christians have met. Whether this service be done under the auspices of the N.E.C.C., the W.C.C., or any other religious or secular agency, here is a common task. In May 1951 the I.M.C. and W.C.C. held therefore a conference on refugees in Beirut, in order to begin to co-ordinate the work done by many Protestants and the N.E.C.C. Committee for Refugee Work with both state and intergovernmental agencies and the ancient Orthodox communities. A second conference was held at the same place and under the same auspices in May 1956. The full participation of several outstanding Orthodox leaders in this second Beirut conference helped much to foster a community of service among Protestants and Orthodox in the area.

Despite this beginning of co-operation, the time seems not yet ripe for Christians in the Near East to face their greatest theological issue, namely the dialogue between the sons of Abraham—Jews, Christians, and Moslems. "In a Near Eastern setting it is impossible today to deal with the problem posed by Romans 9—11 and with the related problem of the use of the Old Testament in Christian worship."[3] Yet exactly this encounter of Jewish, Christian, and

[1] Harry Dorman, "Churches and Missions in the Near East", in *IRM* (1962), p. 42.

[2] *The Constitutions of the Near East Council of Churches*, as revised at the Fourteenth Plenary Meeting of the Council at Cairo, 14–17 April 1964.

[3] Horace M. McMullen, "Spiritual aspects of the plight of Arab refugees: a report from the second Beirut Conference", in *IRM* (1957), p. 57.

Moslem faiths and what Christians can learn from it and contribute to it will be the major theological task of the N.E.C.C.

Europe and North America

The ecumenical history of Europe and North America and the general ecumenical history are so intimately intermingled that it is difficult to distinguish between the two. General ecumenical history has still a strongly Western character in its thought-forms and procedures, its committee membership and staff, its meeting-places and languages. The headquarters of almost all ecumenical organizations are now in Geneva and—last but not least—the Vatican is in Rome. The staff of all world organizations has therefore functioned for the ecumenical movement in the whole world but simultaneously and especially in Europe and North America.

North America remains the only continent which has no distinct regional body. This is mainly due to the fact that especially in the U.S.A. a strong National Council has been built up which, together with the Canadian Council of Churches, almost covers the whole continent.[1] Whenever necessary these two councils consult and collaborate together. The New York office of the W.C.C. links the U.S.A. member Churches with the Geneva headquarters, and it organizes yearly a conference of these member Churches which make up about thirty per cent of the W.C.C. constituency and upon whom the W.C.C. largely depends financially. The absence of a regional body has not excluded North American regional initiatives. The laymen's conference held at Buffalo in 1952 on "The Christian in his Daily Work", the North American Youth Assembly at Ann Arbor in 1961, and, more important still, the excellently prepared North American Faith and Order conference at Oberlin in 1957, show what can be done regionally even without an established regional organization.

In 1939 Europe once again became the battlefield of the world. Contrary to experience in the 1914–18 war, however, in the Second World War the fellowship of Christians never ceased, and the W.C.C. in process of formation played no small role in maintaining contacts. The story of the church struggles in Europe, of the various church renewal movements which sprang from it, and the remarkable story of inter-Church aid in post-war Europe belongs to the general ecumenical history. The largest operation of the W.C.C., the Division of Inter-Church Aid and Service to Refugees, worked almost exclusively for Europe until 1955, after which concrete plans were made to develop its work outside Europe. This giving and receiving of aid created a bond among European Churches which was not broken even when political divisions made contacts between eastern and western European countries difficult or impossible. The friendship which had grown in the courses of the Ecumenical Institute at Bossey near Geneva, in the European rest house "Casa Locarno" in southern Switzerland, in the German "Kirchentag", and in other meeting-places or movements, survived the years of separation

[1] Cf. *The History of the Ecumenical Movement, 1517–1948*, pp. 256–9, 518f, 621–4, the chapter on National Councils in this volume, and the definitive book by S. McCrea Cavert, *The American Churches in the Ecumenical Movement: 1900–1968* (New York 1968).

between the East and the West. Gradually this newly discovered solidarity of Christians in Europe had to find organizational expression.

In April 1947 the Ecumenical Institute called together the leaders of the lay training centres and vocational groups which sprang up simultaneously in many European countries just after the war. This group continued to meet and in 1957 it constituted itself as the Directors Association of Laymen's Colleges in Europe with annual meetings and a full-time secretariat. From 1947 onwards national church youth secretaries in Europe met annually to review and plan their work together. At the Amsterdam assembly of the W.C.C. the organization of regional laymen's conferences was proposed and the first of these met in July 1951 at Bad Boll in Germany. One of the leaders of this meeting wrote later:

> The conference in Bad Boll noted that anyone on the Continent desiring to say something of sound value concerning political, social or cultural problems needs to examine those problems in an overall European perspective, and thence to extend the lines of that perspective out into the world as a whole. Any attempt to renounce large-scale co-operation would be turning our backs on reality.[1]

A few months earlier the Europeans present at the W.C.C. Central Committee at Rolle began to discuss plans for a conference of Churches in Europe, and these discussions were continued in 1952 at the Faith and Order Conference at Lund. So the "Prapat" for Europe was planned.

At Brussels in 1955 a German and a Dutch church leader, Ernst Wilm and Egbert Emmen, were asked to investigate the possibility of calling an unofficial conference of European Churches. This conference met in May 1957 at Liselund in Denmark. Because the initiative came mainly from Reformed and United Churches, many large Lutheran Churches were cautious about committing themselves. Also the Anglican and the Orthodox were not yet represented except by a delegate of the ecumenical patriarchate. But delegates came from both the East and West of Europe. Especially for the participants of the small Protestant minority Churches in the U.S.S.R., Poland, Czechoslovakia, Hungary, Yugoslavia, and Greece as well as for those of the Latin countries of Europe, this meeting proved to be a great event.

Much work had still to be done in order to gather a more representative European conference. Nevertheless, this minor miracle happened in January 1959 at Nyborg in Denmark. This time a number of the larger Lutheran, Anglican, and Orthodox Churches were represented. Organizationally things remained open, but the "Conference of European Churches" (C.E.C.) had become a fact. The series of "Nyborgs" in the now famous hotel at Nyborgstrand in Denmark had begun. Nyborg II met in October 1960. Two years later Nyborg III decided to give C.E.C. a more definite structure. The inaugural C.E.C. assembly, Nyborg IV, revived the old Christian symbol of the Church as a ship, because it met in October 1964 on board M.S. "Bornholm". Participants from the German Democratic Republic had *visa* diffi-

---

[1] "The European Laymen's Conference", in *Laymen's Work* (Geneva), no. 2 (November 1951), p. 19.

culties. The organizers therefore decided to charter a Danish ship and to take the East German delegation on board at sea, on the international line between Denmark and Sweden, off Malmö.

This seafaring assembly adopted the constitution of the C.E.C., but did not yet give the European regional body adequate means for work. But three years later, at Nyborg V, meeting at Pörtschach in Austria, the budget of C.E.C. was increased fourfold. G. G. Williams from Wales was appointed as a full-time secretary and he took up office in 1968. Meanwhile the presidency of C.E.C. had also been enlarged in order to have an adequate representation of the Orthodox and the Anglican Churches at the highest level. This is the organizational history of C.E.C. What are its major concerns, visions, and worries?

The meetings of C.E.C. give European church leaders the opportunity to reflect together periodically about the Church's task in divided Europe and the changing world. The subjects which were presented in the Nyborg lectures, discussed in preparatory committees and in the conference study groups give, therefore, an interesting survey of what is "in the air" on the European continent. At Liselund (1957) the proclamation of the one gospel in a divided Europe and the responsibility for one another among the Churches in the East and the West were the themes considered. The phenomenon of secularization in the modern technical society, where the Constantinian era has come to its end, was at the centre of deliberations at Nyborg I (1959) which also asked whether indeed a common heritage and a common task exist for the Churches in Europe.

Nyborg II (1960) studied this common task: the service which the Churches render to one another and which they have to render to a European society which is dechristianized and threatened by war. This led Nyborg III (1962) to consider the Churches of Europe and the crisis of modern man. Under this general theme an evaluation of European humanism was made and man's encounter with Christ and the renewal of the Church for a new service were studied. Perhaps the two most urgent tasks in this new service were then discussed at Nyborg IV (1964): the living together of continents and thus the commitment of European Churches to other continents and the living together as generations in the present tension between the generations. Nyborg V (1967) finally looked at some special new emphases in the European Churches' task to serve and reconcile, for example, in the new situations created by specialization and man's isolation in society and by the increased leisure time.

Some of the most outstanding Protestant and Orthodox thinkers in East and West Europe were found to introduce these subjects. The Nyborg Reports, in which these lectures are printed, remain thus most valuable documents. Why is it then that C.E.C. still does not seem to have come into its own? Why this persistent feeling of crisis in the European regional body? At least three reasons can be given:

The C.E.C. participants lists reveal impressive European church representation. The Russian Orthodox Church, for instance, sent delegates to the Nyborg conferences before it became a member of the W.C.C. There are eighteen European Churches at present members of the C.E.C. which are not members of the W.C.C. Yet the same lists reveal that despite the increasing lay participation the C.E.C. is still basically an assembly of bishops, church presidents, and pastors. The first impetus for collaboration among Christians in Europe had come from the laity. Yet most of the vision and vigour of these European youth and lay movements seem to have gone into the life of the W.C.C. rather than of the C.E.C. An example is the first European ecumenical youth assembly which met in July 1960 at Lausanne. Little of its impatience, for instance with regard to intercommunion and the renewal of the local Church, seems to have spilled over into C.E.C.

There are too many other groups, events, and movements in European church life which go alongside the work of C.E.C. and partly overlap with it. These include the Conference of the Protestant Churches in Latin countries of Europe, the work done in Europe by confessional world bodies, the Committee on Christian Responsibility for European Co-operation, the ecumenical work done by the Taizé Community and other Christian organizations. Moreover, in the same period when the Nyborg conferences began, the Prague Peace Conference was convened. Although this is not a regional, but is intentionally at least a world organization, it gathers the same or a similar group of people and discusses similar subjects as C.E.C.

The greatest handicap for a European regional church body, however, is Europe itself, its division of languages, cultures, and political barriers. The fact that Nyborg IV had to meet on the high sea is but one illustration. German, French, Russian, and English are used as conference languages and nevertheless many delegates have to speak in a language other than their own. When the linguistic problem is solved, the deeper problems of understanding begin, those between Protestant and Orthodox, between church leaders from the East and from the West. Yet exactly this unsettled mosaic of Europe calls for the reconciling community of those who preach the *one* gospel in a divided continent.

Latin America[1]

The ecumenical pioneer in Latin America was the Committee on Co-operation in Latin America (C.C.L.A.), originating in North America. Its history goes back to a controversial decision of the world missionary conference at Edinburgh in 1910. The planning committee had decided in 1908 that only societies sending missionaries "among non-Christian peoples" would be eligible for membership in the conference. The interpretation of this clause aroused hot discussions in the further preparation and at the conference itself, creating for J. H. Oldham his "gravest issue" as the conference secretary. In particular the Europeans who disliked the work of American evangelists among Catholics in Latin countries of Europe kept strictly to the principle of the planning committee, excluding thus from consideration at Edinburgh also missions to Latin America, except those to the non-Christian Indians. Under the leadership of Robert E. Speer, many North Americans who had a better knowledge of the actual situation in Latin America pleaded for the inclusion

[1] Some of the following information has been provided by Louis Odell from Uruguay who kindly wrote a memorandum about regional developments in Latin America.

of missions in that continent. They lost their cause but organized at Edinburgh itself two informal meetings on Latin America.

The controversial exclusion of Latin America drew much attention to that continent. As an outcome of the discussions at Edinburgh, the U.S.A. Foreign Missions Conference appointed in March 1913 a tentative committee on co-operation in Latin America. Thus the hispanic and traditionally Roman Catholic continent of Latin America became increasingly a "mission-field" for Anglo-Saxon, North American missionary societies. Among these the conservative evangelical faith missions, which do not collaborate with ecumenical world bodies, and more recently the rapidly growing Pentecostal movements, form the large majority.

With John R. Mott as secretary of the above-mentioned committee, the first Congress on Christian Work in Latin America became a notable ecumenical event. It met in February 1916 at Panama. Its programme was a near replica of the Edinburgh conference, and with regard to participants it did even better: of the 230 official delegates twenty-one were Latin Americans. Roman Catholics had been invited but did not attend. The congress unanimously asked the organizing committee to be its continuing organization and the C.C.L.A. was thus constituted. In the following two months deputations of congress members visited Peru, Chile, Argentina, Brazil, Colombia, Cuba, and Puerto Rico and held follow-up conferences in these countries.

In April 1925 a second congress was held in Montevideo, Uruguay, this time not for the whole of Latin America, but for South America only. With Spanish as the congress language, Latin American Protestantism showed its vigour and leadership capacity. While at Panama effective evangelization had been stressed, the Montevideo congress emphasized also strongly the Churches' social responsibility. Organized and led completely by Spanish speaking Evangelicals, the Evangelical Congress for Mexico, Central America, and the Caribbean area at Havana in June 1929 had an even more clearly Latin American character. "Latinization" was the key word and W. R. Hogg writes that "probably never before in any 'missionary conference' had the missionary voice been so silent—that of the indigenous church so pronounced".[1] At this congress the establishment of a Latin American Evangelical Federation was recommended for the first time.

Almost twenty years after the Havana congress investigations were made whether the Caribbean area should not have its own regional ecumenical body. Staff visits were made, especially by the late E. J. Bingle,[2] and a consultation was held in May 1957 at San German, Puerto Rico. Regional work in the realms of Christian education and of Christian marriage and family life were initiated, but so far little progress was made in establishing a Caribbean conference of Churches.

The above-mentioned congresses and the continuing work of C.C.L.A. were instrumental in creating a series of National Christian Councils. That of Puerto Rico was founded as early as in 1905, followed by those of Mexico

[1] W. R. Hogg, *Ecumenical Foundations* (New York 1952), p. 268.

[2] Cf. E. J. Bingle, *Cuba to Surinam: Report of a Journey in the Caribbean* (I.M.C., London, 1954).

in 1928, Brazil in 1934, the River Plate (Argentina, Uruguay, and Paraguay) and Jamaica in 1939, Peru in 1940, Chile and Cuba in 1941. These councils worked in a fruitful way together with the C.C.L.A. It must not be over-looked, however, that the co-operative ventures raised more interest in the "historical" Churches. At the Montevideo meeting the new anti-ecumenical Christian Missionary Alliance and the Evangelical Union of South America participated. But this was not going to last. In the tremendous growth of Evangelicals in Latin America—from about 12,500 in 1900 to about 9,000,000 in 1961—the mostly anti-ecumenical faith missions and later the Pentecostal movement became much stronger than the "historical" Churches. This new situation and the growing Latin American consciousness called for a re-consideration of the co-ordinating structures, all the more so when after the war the C.C.L.A. became an area committee of the Division of Foreign Mission, in the National Council of Churches of the U.S.A.

Upon the initiative of the National Christian Councils in Mexico and the River Plate, Latin American leaders organized what they called the First Latin American Evangelical Conference. It met in July 1949 in Buenos Aires. This small study conference considered the background of Protestantism in Latin America, its message and the strategies and priorities of its mission. The report laid great emphasis on the study of the Bible so that every member can become an evangelist. "For the Evangelical Christian, evangelism is a matter of life or death. Every Evangelical Christian should be aflame for the redemption of his neighbours who do not know the depth of the grace of our Lord."[1]

Due to the lack of a continuation committee, almost twelve years passed before the Second Latin American Evangelical Conference met in July/August 1961, in Lima, Peru. The 220 delegates and visitors represented thirty-four denominations in all Latin American countries with the exception of Panama and Nicaragua. Reading the reports of Buenos Aires and Lima one is struck by the great difference of emphasis. In Lima all the speakers were Latin Americans and a new generation of leaders became vocal and set the pattern. This change of atmosphere is perhaps clearest in the different ways the two meetings spoke about the role of laymen. "In the first conference, we find the traditional emphasis on the work of laymen as helpers to pastors, as instru-ments for securing individual conversions and the growth of the congrega-tions. The means of evangelism are focused on the same purpose. The second conference took seriously the structures of society and the need to change these structures through the presence within them of the Christian laity."[2]

How did this change happen? Through the services of C.C.L.A. and several ecumenical world bodies such as the World Council of Christian Education and the ecumenical youth organizations an increasing number of young Latin American Evangelicals had come into contact with the ecumenical movement. Already in 1941 at a meeting in Lima the Union of Latin American

---

[1] B. Foster Stockwell, "Latin American Evangelical Conference", in *IRM* (1950), p. 80.
[2] A. E. Fernandez Arlt, "The Laity in the Latin American Evangelical Churches", in Stephen C. Neill and H. R. Weber, ed., *The Layman in Christian History* (London 1963), p. 372.

Evangelical Youth (U.L.A.J.E.) had been formed which held several continent-wide congresses and leadership training seminars. The 1956 congress in
Baranquilla, Columbia had, for instance, the following courageous and
confident theme for a revolutionary continent: "Religious liberty and social
justice: Good news to the poor. To the captives, liberty". From 1951 the
World Student Christian Federation had greatly intensified its work in Latin
America, and Valdo Galland was appointed as its travelling secretary for that
continent. From November 1956 to February 1957 an ecumenical youth
team extensively visited Latin America.

Even more important was the impact of the W.C.C.'s Church and Society
department's study on rapid social change. National consultations on the
Christian responsibility in society were held in Brazil (1955, 1957, 1960) and
in the River Plate area (1957, 1959). Other areas were visited by staff. In 1959
a bulletin on Church and Society was spontaneously started in Uruguay, as a
local initiative. This bulletin later became the magazine *Christianismo y
Sociedad*, the official organ of Iglesia y Sociedad en América Latina (I.S.A.L.).
The response that the rapid social change study had in Brazil and the River
Plate area led to the convocation prior to the Lima conference of the First
Latin American Consultation on Church and Society. It was held in Huam-
pani, near Lima, in July 1961. As a result of this consultation the Latin
American Commission on Church and Society (I.S.A.L.) was constituted in
February, 1962 and has been active ever since. Parallel to the Huampani
consultation another one was held to deal with problems of Christian educa-
tion which again in 1962 led to the formal constitution of the Latin American
Commission on Christian Education (C.E.L.A.D.E.C.). U.L.A.J.E. held
further congresses in 1961 and 1966. Through the work of the Theological
Education Fund the collaboration between theological colleges is growing.

All these developments call for a Latin American regional body. Yet the
Lima conference had established a continuation committee with only a
rotating secretaryship from one National Christian Council to the other. As
many expected, this did not work. A new step forward came when on the
occasion of the first I.S.A.L. consultation on Christian social action and
service the presidents of several National Christian Councils met and strongly
emphasized the need for a continental confederation of Evangelicals in the
"Declaration of Corcovado" (Brazil), in September 1963. One year later, in a
meeting at Montevideo, Uruguay, the formal decision was adopted to create
the long-expected regional body, the Provisional Committee on Christian
Unity in Latin America (U.N.E.L.A.M.) and Emilio Castro was appointed
its part-time secretary. This committee is now co-ordinating and fostering the
ecumenical forces in the midst of the very precarious ecumenical situation of
Latin America.

Nowhere else is there more mistrust of, and mal-information concerning,
the ecumenical movement than in Latin America. In particular those groups
in which the leadership is still in the hands of the conservative evangelical
missionaries are against a common worship, service, and witness. Nowhere
else does the present *aggiornamento* of the Roman Catholic Church affect
Evangelicals more than in Latin America. During these last years many young

Evangelicals have found much more understanding and support in their social and political commitment from progressive Roman Catholic priests and bishops than from their own church leaders. I.S.A.L. and other progressive evangelical groups work increasingly together with Roman Catholics and the already existing Roman Catholic regional body (C.E.L.A.M.—the Latin American Episcopal Council). An anti-Catholic evangelical regional body will therefore not find much enthusiasm among younger Latin American Evangelicals.

Added to mistrust from the faith missions and the changing relationships with the Roman Catholics is a great theological uncertainty among the ecumenically minded Evangelicals themselves.

> We are going to and fro between two heresies: the fundamentalistic, which tends to ignore the fact that Christ reconciled the world unto himself and the other that insinuates and forgets at the same time the call to faith, conversion, decision as well as to biblical eschatology; the former denies the fact that faith creates a necessary change, the latter speaks about identification and incarnation irresponsibly in an "impressionistic" manner, without seeking for the biblical affirmations.[1]

How is it possible to combine a strong concern for social action with the great heritage of Latin American evangelical commitment to evangelism? What is the specific task of Latin American Evangelicals in a continent where a strong minority of the leadership in the Roman Catholic Church is involved in a far-reaching *aggiornamento*? How to maintain and deepen the fellowship with conservative evangelical faith missions and the Pentecostal movement and at the same time grow in communion with the Catholic, Orthodox, and historic Protestant streams of Christianity? These are some of the questions with which Latin American Evangelicals must struggle and where they have to make their contribution to the ecumenical movement.

The Pacific

In no region of the world was a regional development pastorally more needed than in the Pacific. Although jet aeroplanes now criss-cross that immense area between the Americas and Asia, life behind the reefs of the Pacific islands still remains very isolated, self-sufficient, and, to the problem-ridden Western visitor, strangely harmonious. On some islands there exists an intact *corpus Christianum*, while in some mountain valleys of New Guinea the first contacts between the Church and only recently discovered tribes are just beginning. The consecutive invasions of soldiers during the war and of tourists after the war, the threat of atomic fall-out through the testing of bombs, the ferment of new ideas and expectations in the minds of young people who are no longer at ease in a patriarchal and static society and Church—all these factors of change have forced Christians in the Pacific to face their common plight and their common task.

In February 1959 a number of Churches and missions in the Pacific area asked the I.M.C. to organize a regional conference. A small advisory group

---

[1] *America Hoy—Iglesia y Sociedad en America Latina* (Montevideo 1966), p. 54.

met in Suva, Fiji in March 1960 and planned the conference and its preparatory work. Five topics were chosen to be considered in lectures and study
groups: (1) the ministry; (2) the unfinished evangelistic task; (3) the relevance
of the gospel to the changing conditions of life in the Pacific; (4) the place of
young people in the life of the Church; and (5) the Christian family. Behind
these topics, which could have been chosen in almost every region of the
world, lies a deeper one. It shows the great discernment of the advisory group
meeting at Suva that it so clearly recognized this fact and wrote to the
Churches:

> In the days before the coming of the Gospel, men's lives were ruled largely by
> fear. The coming of Christianity wrought a marvellous change in the life of
> our peoples. But we have to ask, "Did the coming of Christianity mean that
> fear was replaced by love, or did it mean that men transferred their fear to a
> new object and began to fear God with a pagan fear?" . . . Our churches often
> seem to be more governed by fear than by love, more concerned to enforce
> conformity to certain laws of behaviour than to show their love to God by
> loving and forgiving others. It sometimes seems that our churches are places
> where certain standards are demanded, rather than places where God gives
> sinners forgiveness and victory over sin.[1]

The deepest aim of this first conference of Churches and missions in the
Pacific was thus nothing less than a reformation. With a view to this the
Churches were asked to pray for the conference and to make a self-examination
concerning the themes proposed in the light of the message of Paul's letter to
the Galatians.

Probably no ecumenical event in the post-war ecumenical history has been
so fervently prepared in local groups of a whole region and has been carried
so intensely by the prayer of ordinary Christians as this first Pacific conference
which met at Malua on the island of Samoa in April–May 1961. It became
much more than a planning conference for establishing a new regional body
within the ecumenical movement, although it fulfilled this function according
to the now well-known pattern of appointing a continuation-committee,
authorizing the work of a regional secretary, and preparing the way for a later
inaugural assembly. This conference became in fact a reformation event, and
in the conference Bible studies Paul's letter to the Galatians spoke in a disturbing and renewing way to the basic topic which the advisory group had so
clearly outlined. The daily "news-sessions" also helped much to break the
isolation of life behind the reefs, so that the conference report was rightly
called "Beyond the Reef".

The continuation committee immediately began its work, planning the
continued study of the five conference subjects and appointing Vavae Toma
from Samoa as the regional secretary. He became a pastoral visitor to the
isolated Churches on the Pacific islands. Immediately after the Samoa Conference the Theological Education Fund convened a consultation at Suva in
Fiji and it was here that plans for a united Pacific theological college were
discussed. After difficult negotiations this college became a reality in April

---

[1] *Beyond the Reef: Records of the Conference of Churches and Missions in the Pacific*
(London 1961), pp. 7f.

1966, at Suva. It now plays an important role in helping the coming leadership of the Pacific Churches to discern together God's will for the Pacific region.

At the meeting of the continuation committee at Tonga in 1965 the plans were finalized for the inaugural assembly of the Pacific Conference of Churches (P.C.C.). It was held in May–June 1966 at Chapanehe on the island of Lifou in the Loyalty Islands. The topics chosen for discussion were education, marriage, custom, stewardship, and citizenship. Simultaneously with the P.C.C. a number of National Christian Councils came into being. Such councils were founded in the New Hebrides and Fiji Islands, then the Melanesian Council of Churches was formed, one of whose first tasks is to co-operate with the Roman Catholics in establishing a joint Christian centre at the University planned for Port Moresby. Other councils are now planned in the Solomon Islands and the Samoan group.

Due to the work of the continuation committee, its study commissions and the visits of Vavae Toma—since 1967 succeeded by Setareki Tuilovoni from Fiji—the Churches had come to know one another better. At the Lifou assembly the accent lay therefore no longer in the first place on the meeting and hearing from one another, but on the planning for doing things together. The Second Vatican Council begins to bear fruit and in Samoa and Tonga Protestants and Roman Catholics are now working together on a common vernacular version of the Bible. As in other areas, so also in the Pacific the regional body which was only just created is already too narrow for the widening scope of the ecumenical movement.

This quick journey through the *oikoumene* has shown that virtually in all continents regional ecumenical bodies now exist. This is a new fact in ecumenical history. It must be taken seriously by National Christian Councils and its member Churches. This new fact must also influence the central operations, emphases, and structures of the W.C.C. and other world ecumenical bodies. A beginning has been made for the executives of the various regional bodies to consult together (meetings in Geneva in 1965 and 1967), and the Uppsala Assembly of the W.C.C. has authorized the appointment of a new associate general secretary for relationships with national and regional councils.

Regional ecumenical bodies have their particular dangers.[1] They could easily become either continental ecclesiastical power blocs or mere administrative outposts of ecumenical world organizations. In both cases they would hinder rather than foster the full participation of local Churches in the ecumenical movement. The foregoing description of the beginning of these regional bodies shows, however, that such dangers are clearly faced. Regional

---

[1] For an analysis of the promises and dangers of regional ecumenical bodies see, for example, W. A. Visser 't Hooft, "Die Bedeutung der Regionalen Kirchlichen Zusammenarbeit für die Oekumeniche Bewegung", in *Die europäische Christenheit in der heutigen sakularisierten Welt* (Zurich 1960), pp. 118–23; U Kyaw Than, "East of New Delhi: Regionalism or Centralism?" in K. R. Bridston and W. D. Wagoner, ed., *Unity in Mid-Career* (New York 1963), pp. 57–67; Heinrich Meyer, "Regionalismus und Konfessionalismus", *Oekumenische Rundschau* (1961), pp. 197–208.

ecumenism must not be overstressed. In many central ecumenical issues the real divisions go now not only across confessional families but also right across continental boundaries. Nevertheless, the future may show that the intercontinental character of the ecumenical movement is equally, or perhaps even more, important than its interconfessional character. God's liberating Word is witnessed to all nations and continents. Out of all nations and continents the Church is called to be the first fruits of a new humanity.

4

National Councils of Churches

FRANK SHORT

INTRODUCTION

Dr J. H. Oldham, as far back as 1922, wrote of the proposed formation of National Christian Councils as "New Spiritual Adventures in the Mission Field".[1] They were to be the visible organs through which units and common purpose would find expression. Richey Hogg, in *Ecumenical Foundations*, refers to Dr Mott's judgement, "My first and my greatest contribution to the International Missionary Council was to bring about the formation of the National Christian Councils" (p. 156). Hogg also links the International Missionary Council, the National Christian Councils, and the younger Churches, in his statement, "For years no other body existed to knit the younger Churches, through the National Christian Councils, into the organized fabric of world Christianity" (p. 283).

K. S. Latourette, in the summary to his chapter on "Ecumenical Bearings of the Missionary Movement and the International Missionary Council" in *A History of the Ecumenical Movement 1517-1948* (pp. 401-2), notes that the younger Churches had a mounting share in the ecumenical movement and that their most numerous forms of ecumenical experiment were co-operative ventures undertaken by national and regional units, which had been drawn into a global structure through the International Missionary Council. These comments indicate the significance of Christian Councils for the ecumenical movement, and the importance of the contribution they were then making to its development. The question may well be asked if the National Christian Councils have fulfilled the expectation and promise of these earlier years.

The Growth of the National Christian Councils

In 1910 there were only two National Christian Councils through which limited co-operation was possible. By 1928, at the time of the Jerusalem Meeting of the International Missionary Council, there were twenty-three; by 1938, the year of the Madras Conference, there were twenty-six, and a decade later there were thirty.

It is instructive to look at the list of the thirty councils which were members of the International Missionary Council at the end of 1948. (The list appears at the end of the January 1949 issue of *International Review of Missions*.)

Australia   National Missionary Council of Australia.
Belgium   Conseil missionaire Protestant de Belgique.
Brazil   Confederacao Evangelica do Brasil.
Ceylon   National Christian Council.
China   National Christian Council.
Congo   Conseil Protestant du Congo.
Denmark   Dansk Missionsraad.
Finland   Suomen Lahetysneuvosto.
France   Société des Missions Évangéliques de Paris.
Germany   Deutscher Evangelischer Missionsrat.
Great Britain   Conference of Missionary Societies in Great Britain and Ireland.

[1] *International Review of Missions*, vol. ii, no. 44, pp. 526-50.

India and Pakistan   National Christian Council of India, Pakistan, and Burma.
Japan   National Christian Council.
Korea   National Christian Council.
Latin America   Committee on Co-operation.
Malaya   Christian Council.
Mexico   Concilio Nacional Evangelico de Mexico.
Near East   Near East Christian Council for Missionary Co-operation.
Netherlands   Nederlandsche Zendings-Raad.
Netherlands Indies   Zendings Consulaat.
New Zealand   National Missionary Council of New Zealand.
Norway   Norsk Misjonsrad.
Philippine Islands   Philippine Federation of Evangelical Churches.
Puerto Rico   Association of Evangelical Churches.
River Plate   Confederacion de Iglesias Evangelicas del Rico de la Plate (Argentina, Paraguay, Uruguay).
Siam   National Christian Council of Siam.
South Africa   Christian Council of South Africa.
Sweden   Svenska Missionsradet.
Switzerland   Schweizerischer Evangelischer Missionsrat. Conseil Suisse des Missions Evangeliques.
United States and Canada   Foreign Missions Conference of North America.

Richey Hogg had commented (p. 253) that in 1928 the National Christian Councils encircled the globe and could spread and implement the decisions of the Jerusalem Conference. The progressive growth in the number of such Councils incorporated still further areas of the world, and brought them increasingly within the area of impact of the subsequent gatherings of the International Missionary Council.

These Councils of Churches and missionary societies, and the national or regional missionary agencies, now existed in every continent. Those in the "sending" countries, lands of the missionary agencies, included two Councils or comparable bodies in Australia and New Zealand, ten in Europe, and one in North America. In the "receiving" countries, lands of the younger Churches, there were five in Latin America, nine in Asia, and three in Africa and the Near East.

Nor was that all. In addition to these member bodies of the International Missionary Council there were, in 1948, twenty-two other co-operative organizations, of one kind or another, in different parts of the world, with which the International Missionary Council was in touch. They are listed in the January 1949 issue of International Review of Missions. Thirteen of them were in African territories, one was in Asia, four were in the West Indies, and four were in Latin America. They varied from Evangelical Alliances, Social Welfare Councils, Councils of Churches, to Inter-Mission Councils or other forms of missionary co-operation. Ten of them subsequently became members of the International Missionary Council.

When it is remembered that the functions of the International Missionary Council had been defined, in part, in its Constitution as:

To stimulate thinking and investigation on questions related to the mission and expansion of Christianity in all the world. . . . To help to co-ordinate the activities of the national missionary organizations and Christian Councils of the different countries, and to bring about united action where necessary in missionary matters . . .

it is not difficult to see the measure of the possible contribution of this network of Christian councils to the furtherance of ecumenical idea and action in the field of mission. Moreover, a study of the reports of the meetings of the International Missionary Council at Jerusalem, Madras, Whitby, Willingen, and Ghana, reveals how wide were the interests and concerns in which the member councils were involved. There was not much that had its place in the growth of the Church, in its witness and its service, which was absent from international consideration, and from challenge to these national organs of co-operation.

CHANGE AND DEVELOPMENT
IN NATIONAL CHRISTIAN COUNCILS

1

A study of the 1948 membership of the International Missionary Council reveals already some of the changes and developments which would occur more frequently in the next two decades. The changes in the political structure of nations in Asia and Africa which would arise from the ending of the colonial era were already foreshadowed. The National Christian Council of India, Burma, and Ceylon had become the National Christian Council of India, Pakistan, and Burma. Ceylon had already become a separate member council. Within a few years Burma, Pakistan, and India would each have separate National Christian Councils. The Christian Council of Malaya became the Council of Churches in Malaysia and Singapore reflecting the separate independence of both Malaya and Singapore. The Zendings Consulaat of the Netherlands Indies would cease to be a member council, and in 1952 its place would be taken by the National Council of Churches in Indonesia.

Comparable changes were to take place, somewhat later, in Africa—though for the most part in councils which were not then members of the International Missionary Council. New nations were established, some with names which replaced those of earlier colonial days. Ghana (Gold Coast), Madagascar, Rhodesia, Sierra Leone, and Zambia (Northern Rhodesia) became member councils between the years 1954 and 1961. New names which occur in the 1968 list of non-member councils include Uganda, Burundi, Rwanda, Malawi (Nyasaland), Tanzania (Tanganyika). In a word, existing councils adjusted themselves to their changed political situation, and they together with newly formed councils sought to respond to the challenges of the new era.

Changes occurred also in Latin America. The Committee on Co-operation in Latin America withdrew from separate membership of the International Missionary Council on the ground that it was strictly a committee of the division of foreign missions of the National Council of Churches in the U.S.A. (N.C.C.C.U.S.A.). The River Plate Federation of Evangelical Churches withdrew in 1963, when Federations of Evangelical Churches in Argentina and Uruguay and the Evangelical Council of Chile became separate affiliated councils of the Commission on World Mission and Evangelism of the World Council of Churches. In 1952 the Cuban Council of Evangelical Churches became a member council of the International Missionary Council, as did the Jamaica Christian Council in 1954, and in 1967 the Christian Council of Trinidad and Tobago became an Affiliated Council of the Commission on World Mission and Evangelism.

2

The process by which missionary councils developed into Christian Councils, and then, even if not always in name, into Councils of Churches, was already far advanced by 1948. In the following period it was to be carried further, and that in a variety of ways.

(a) In Asia and in Africa it was realized increasingly that it was inappropriate, and that for many reasons, for missionary agencies as such to have membership in a National Christian Council. While their financial contribution was useful, and even necessary, their membership both obscured the nature of the council, and diminished its effective relationship to government and community. The National Christian Council of India is a typical example of this development. Under its constitution the Council was a Council of Churches and Missions. Between the years 1950 and 1956 there was considerable discussion on the desirability of the Council becoming a Council of Churches only.

The Asia Secretary of the Conference of British Missionary Societies visited India in the autumn of 1955, and conferred with the National Christian Council. He was made aware of the importance which was attached to the closest relationship of the Council with the Churches of India, and of the desire that the consequent amendment of the Constitution should not endanger the financial support given by the co-operating missionary agencies. The Conference accepted the recommendation which he made in his report

> That the National Christian Council of India be informed that British missionary societies represented in the Conference no longer desire direct representation on the Council, and that they suggest the constitution of the Council should be reviewed in the light of this action with a view to securing the maximum responsible relationship with the Churches of India.[1]

In the revised constitution of 1956 it was determined that "only organized Church bodies are entitled to direct representation in the Council". Missions still not integrated in a Church in India could become associate members. Missionaries might still serve on the Council as the elected representatives of the Church with which they were associated. Thereafter, and not only in India, the Christian Councils became increasingly Councils of Churches.

(b) There has been notable development in the Near East. In 1948 the Council was the Near East Christian Council for Missionary Co-operation. It later became the Near East Christian Council, and more recently still the Near East Council of Churches. Contemporary ecumenical developments, the

[1] C.B.M.S., A/5/56.

political struggles and tensions of the area, the vast and continuing problem of the Arab refugees, have combined to bring the Churches of the region into new and closer ecumenical relationship.

(c) Developments have also taken place in the missionary councils of the West. Member bodies of the International Missionary Council in 1948 included the National Missionary Councils of Australia and New Zealand, the Conference of Missionary Societies of Great Britain and Ireland, and the Foreign Missions Conference of North America (the U.S.A. and Canada). The first has now become the Division of Mission of the Australian Council of Churches. The second member body is now the National Council of Churches of New Zealand—which is of interest in that it has a "Commission on Overseas Mission and Inter-Church Aid" thus following the pattern set by the East Asia Christian Conference. The Conference of British Missionary Societies alone remains unchanged in its status of "In association with the British Council of Churches", though the pattern of future relationship has recently been under discussion.

Developments in North America have been far-reaching. The Foreign Missions Conference of North America, which had begun its notable history as far back as 1893, in 1950 became the Division of Foreign Missions of the National Council of the Churches of Christ in the United States of America. That organization, so well known by its initials N.C.C.C.U.S.A., was the long-considered development of the Federal Council of the Churches of Christ in America, which had been founded in 1908. Professor K. S. Latourette, in the Rouse–Neill volume (p. 374), gives a vivid description of "the ever widening scope of co-operation" in and through the Foreign Missions Conference which had been achieved by 1948. In a later chapter of the same book (pp. 623f) Miss Rouse records the birth of the National Council, and the "euthanasia" of the old Federal Council, involving the union, towards the end of 1950, of eight separate national councils, which included, in addition to the Federal Council and the Foreign Missions Conference, Councils for Home Missions, Religious Education, Higher Education, Missionary Education, Stewardship, and the Council of Church Women. Miss Rouse's last word on this transformed Council is that it "united practically all organized aspects of the Churches' common life in an ecclesiastically-constituted organ of common action. This is a long step towards a practically united Church in the United States. It is the longest step, short of organic union, as yet taken in any country towards union among the Churches" (p. 624).

The Council was still not satisfied with its structure, and discussion continued for some years on the future pattern of organization. The completion of the massive and impressive Inter-Church Center at 475 Riverside Drive, New York, and its official opening on 29 May 1960 brought many member units into the one building, and so facilitated closer relationship between the member Churches and also with the various organs of co-operative activity. In the later reorganization the Division of Foreign Missions became the Division of Overseas Ministries—in part a recognition of the ambiguity and misunderstanding generally associated with the words "foreign" and "missions".

A detailed account of the N.C.C.C.U.S.A. is included in a book by Dr Samuel McCrea Cavert on "American Churches in the Ecumenical Movement", published in 1968 by Association Press, New York.

The discussions which led to the formation of the N.C.C.C.U.S.A. were paralleled by discussions in Canada which in 1944 resulted in the formation of the Canadian Council of Churches. In 1946 a separate Canadian Overseas Mission Council came into being, which in 1952 became the Department of Overseas Missions of the Canadian Council of Churches. The Constitution of the Council of Churches provided for the maintenance of close relationship with, *inter alia*, the Council of the Churches in the U.S.A., and the Department of Overseas Mission entered into a new fraternal relationship with the Division of Foreign Missions of the N.C.C.C.U.S.A. While it is the N.C.C.C. U.S.A. which is now affiliated to the Commission on World Mission of the World Council of Churches, where Canada is concerned it is the Department of Overseas Missions which is so affiliated.

The Relation of the National Christian Councils to the Ecumenical Movement

Many National Christian Councils, particularly in the lands of the so-called younger Churches, owed their origin to the initiative of the International Missionary Council, and for much of the period up to 1948, through their membership in that Council, they were an important and integral part of the ecumenical movement.

But in the period covered by the present volume their place in, and their relationship to, the ecumenical movement has been subject to considerable development. The changes which took place in the years 1948–68 affected their relationship to the World Council of Churches, to the International Missionary Council, and to the regional ecumenical organizations which came into existence in the second half of the period.

The main story of these developments will be told in other chapters of this history, but no account of the National Christian Councils would be complete without reference to these far-reaching changes in their relationships and in their activities.

Relationship of National Christian Councils to the World Council of Churches

While it has been emphasized repeatedly that the World Council of Churches is essentially and necessarily a Council of Churches, and the International Missionary Council was basically and creatively a Council of Councils, the World Council of Churches from a very early date realized the potential importance of National Christian Councils for the furtherance of its own work and influence, and the International Missionary Council always needed close and intimate touch with the churches related to its member councils.

74339

It is, therefore, not surprising that as early as September 1948 the Central Committee of the World Council of Churches decided that some constituent councils of the International Missionary Council in "younger Church areas" should be invited to assist the World Council of Churches in the promotion of its activities. Such Councils would have an opportunity to send representatives to meetings of the Assembly and of the Central Committee. On the other hand, the World Council, in the promotion of its departmental activities, would work normally through the offices of the National Christian Councils with which it had this relationship. At the same time provision was made for working relationships with a number of "nation-wide councils" in lands of the "older Churches".

The Second W.C.C. Assembly at Evanston made provision for a more formal working relationship of National Christian Councils with the World Council by creating a category of "associated councils". By the time of the Third Assembly at New Delhi, eighteen councils had accepted the invitation to become thus associated. These included councils in Asia, Australasia, Europe, and North America.

The importance of this development for the understanding of the nature and significance of the contribution made by the National Christian Councils to the ecumenical movement is indicated by the extent to which these councils had become the normal channel for the interpretation, support, and implementation of World Council activities. The meetings of National Christian Councils provided opportunity for the discussion of World Council proposals in the context of local situations. Some councils reproduced in their own structures some parts of the departmental organization in the World Council of Churches. This development not only recognized the growing commitment of the National Christian Councils to the life and work of the ecumenical movement, but progressively increased their involvement in that movement, both in the work of the World Council of Churches itself, and in ecumenical activities in their several areas.

In September 1967 there were twenty-three of these Associated Councils of the World Council of Churches. Only two of them are in Africa (Rhodesia and South Africa), seven are in Asia (Burma, Ceylon, India, Indonesia, Japan, Malaysia, Philippines), two are in Australasia (Australia and New Zealand), ten are in Europe (Austria, Czechoslovakia, Denmark, Finland, Germany, Hungary, Netherlands, Poland, Sweden, and Great Britain), and two are in North America (Canada and the U.S.A.).

While there are gaps in the territories so represented, notably in Africa and in Latin America, it is obvious that the contribution which the twenty-three associated councils can make to the ecumenical movement is considerable, and indeed is necessary if the ecumenical is to become rooted in the local situation.

The Relationship of National Christian Councils to the International Missionary Council

The history of the relationship of National Christian Councils to the International Missionary Council has been spelled out in detail in the two volumes, *A History of the Ecumenical Movement* and *Ecumenical Foundations*. But the end of 1961 was to see the conclusion of the story of the International Missionary Council as such, and its integration in the World Council of Churches as its Division and Commission on World Mission and Evangelism. The member councils of the International Missionary Council became affiliated councils of the C.W.M.E., and so entered into a new and direct relationship with the World Council of Churches.

There was an inevitability about this development. As far back as 1946 the joint committee of the W.C.C. and the I.M.C. had called attention to the common origin and the common calling and purpose of the two bodies, and had seen the necessity of steps being taken which would "quicken the mission-consciousness of the churches and the Church-consciousness of missions". Something more than being "in association with each other" was necessary if the theological insights of the relation of Church and mission, and of mission and unity, were to govern the relationship of the W.C.C. and the I.M.C. within the ecumenical movement.

The member councils of the I.M.C. did not accept readily the proposals for the integration of the two bodies, and it speaks volumes for the patient wisdom of the joint committee and of its two parent bodies that the Third Assembly at New Delhi was able to carry through the impressive act of integration.

The mind of the member councils had been made plain at the Ghana Assembly of the International Missionary Council in December 1957–January 1958.[1] The debate revealed that, while there was strong support for integration from some councils, and a favourable attitude to it in others, serious reservations existed in parts of Latin America and Africa and by certain councils in northern Europe.

To some extent these reservations derived from misunderstanding concerning the World Council of Churches. Delegates could not be unaware of prevalent propaganda which charged the World Council with intent to become a "super-Church", with having an inadequate doctrinal basis, and with lacking real evangelistic concern.

To some extent these reservations derived from a fear that integration would result in the creation of a mammoth and bureaucratic organization in which missionary vision and thrust would be lost. To a much larger extent reservation and misgiving arose from the fear that integration would have a divisive effect within the constituent councils of the International Missionary Council, and would endanger the maintenance of existing co-operation between member bodies who were in sympathy with the ecumenical movement, and those who, for varying reasons, were not.

The long resolution which the Ghana Assembly passed accepted in principle the integration of the two bodies and adjudged the draft plan prepared by the joint committee of both organizations to be a "generally suitable instrument for integration". It recognized the sincere and deep concern of those who feared that integration might result in the relinquishment of the

[1] See *Report*, pp. 156–700.

purposes for which the International Missionary Council had been founded, and instructed its Secretariat to give special attention to ways in which misunderstanding of the World Council of Churches and ignorance about the existing relations between that body and the International Missionary Council could be removed.

The Assembly commended the draft plan to its member organizations for further study, but realized that it would be impossible for its consideration, and consequent action upon it, to be completed in time for the Assembly of the World Council of Churches which it was proposed to hold in 1960. The World Council was therefore invited to postpone its Assembly until 1961.

The additional year gave an opportunity for detailed study of the plan by member councils of the International Missionary Council, and for consultation with its secretaries. It was possible for many misgivings to be removed, and for some councils to make provision within their constitutions for the continued participation of member societies who were unable to give approval to the proposed integration with the World Council of Churches.

The draft plan had wisely provided that all constituent councils of the International Missionary Council at the time of integration would automatically become "affiliated" members of the Commission on World Mission and Evangelism of the World Council of Churches. When the final Assembly of the International Missionary Council was held in New Delhi in November 1961, it was able to confirm the approval given by its administrative committee to the plan for integration with the knowledge that only two member Councils had withdrawn from membership—the Congo Protestant Council and the Norway Missionary Council.

The action of the Congo Protestant Council had been taken at an early stage in the discussion on integration. It arose from a desire to maintain the unity of the council, when faced with pressure exerted by related missionary agencies with headquarters in the United States which strenuously opposed any association with the World Council of Churches. The action of the Norway Missionary Council sprang in part from the nature of its relationship with the Churches of Norway, in part from theological fears concerning the World Council itself, and in part from the fear that integration would result in a weakening of concern for the missionary task of the Church.

It is probably worth while to record that the membership of the Commission is comprised of eighty representatives of affiliated councils, and thirty-five who are nominated by the Central Committee of the World Council of Churches. This act in itself betokens the way in which the Churches and the missionary agencies, now integrated in the World Council of Churches, are both involved in the task of world missionary service and evangelism.

The Constitution of the World Council of Churches makes it clear that the old member councils of the International Missionary Council, now either "affiliated" to the Commission on World Mission, or "associated" with the World Council as a whole, or having both these relationships, can rightly feel that the mission-consciousness of the Churches and the church-consciousness of missions has been "quickened", and the purpose which had so long governed the I.M.C.: "To deepen the sense of missionary obligation in the churches throughout the world and to further the effective proclamation to all men of the Gospel of Jesus Christ, as Lord and Saviour" has been more than safeguarded.

For the functions of the World Council of Churches now include: "to promote the growth of ecumenical and missionary consciousness in the members of all churches; to support the Churches in their world-wide missionary and evangelistic task". And the aim of the Commission on World Missions and Evangelism is defined as: "to further the proclamation to the whole world of the Gospel of Jesus Christ, to the end that all men may believe in Him and be saved".

Moreover, it is of importance to the affiliated and associated councils that the missionary task of the Church now has relevance for each and all of the departments and divisions within the World Council structure. And it could be that the advantages of the location of the Commission and Division within the Ecumenical Centre in Geneva more than outweigh the disadvantages which some feared might arise from the concentration of the whole of the integrated structure in that city.

National Councils in association with the World Council of Churches

Australian Council of Churches
Ökumenischer Rat der Kirchen in Österreich
Burma Christian Council
Canadian Council of Churches
National Christian Council of Ceylon
Ecumenical Council of Churches in Czechoslovakia
Ecumenical Council in Denmark
Ecumenical Council of Finland
Arbeitsgeneinschaft Christlicher Kirchen in Deutschland
Ecumenical Council of Churches in Hungary
National Christian Council of India
Council of Churches in Indonesia
National Christian Council of Japan
Council of Churches in Malaysia and Singapore
Ecumenical Council of Churches in the Netherlands
National Council of Churches in New Zealand
National Council of Churches in the Philippines
Polish Ecumenical Council
The Christian Council of Rhodesia
South African Council of Churches
Swedish Ecumenical Council
The British Council of Churches
National Council of the Churches of Christ in the U.S.A.
Ecumenical Council of Churches in Yugoslavia

Regional Ecumenical Developments and National Christian Councils

This history and significance of the regional ecumenical developments which have taken place in the decades covered by this volume are dealt with in another chapter. It is necessary, however, to refer briefly in this chapter to the effect of this development on the life and work of National Christian Councils. The East Asia Christian Conference, which in many ways pioneered regional developments, illustrates what is probably common, in varying degree, to all such developments.

There was a concern for a regional area as such, and a recognition of common problems and tasks within that area, which it was felt should be shared by all Churches and councils within that area. Immediately a new relatedness was created within the region which brought councils and Churches into a fellowship of knowledge and service. In the case of East Asia it encompasses those Churches and councils in lands stretching from India and Pakistan to Japan, and down to Australia and New Zealand. And it has to be remembered that it brought together representative Christians who otherwise would never have met. And the same process of making the remote near has taken place in Africa with the organization of the All Africa Conference of Churches.

Secondly, in the same way as Latourette states that the "compelling motive" of the various forms of co-operation which he had been describing[1] was evangelism, so again the compelling motive behind the Asian regional development was a passion for mission. It had been evidenced by the earlier Asia Council on Ecumenical Mission. It was evidenced by the passionate words of Bishop Enrique Sobrepena of the Philippines at Prapat, when he spoke of the Asian Churches being "haunted by a sense of mission". It was evidenced by the themes of successive assemblies. At Prapat in 1957 it was "The Common Evangelistic Task". At Kuala Lumpur in 1959 it was "Witnesses Together". And at Kuala Lumpur there began a consciousness of the extent and significance of Asian participation in missionary service. Nor has evangelism been absent from the concerns of African regional development. It is impossible to overestimate the importance of this missionary emphasis for the work of the associated National Christian Councils and Churches. At a time when the missionary emphasis was diminishing in Christian Councils this concern for mission was both an inspiration and a challenge.

Thirdly, there has been manifested a concern for the political, economic, industrial, and social issues of the region, and for the relation of the Christian gospel to those issues. In illustration it is enough to recall that the theme arising from the Bangkok Assembly of the E.A.C.C. (1964) was "The Christian Community within the Human Community", and to point to the work of the Bangalore Christian Institute for the Study of Religion and Society, and its relationship to the National Christian Council of India. The activities of the All Africa Conference of Churches amply provide evidence of a like

[1] *A History of the Ecumenical Movement, 1517–1948*, p. 402.

development. Again, the agenda of Christian Councils has had to find place for this range of issues, as well as for the other concerns which arise from regional ecumenicity.

In brief, this regional development has added another dimension to the task of National Christian Councils. Over and above national responsibilities and world ecumenical commitment there is now the pressure of regional concerns and activities.

The continental area of Latin America, which lacks organized expression of regional development comparable to that in Asia, Africa, or the Pacific, has experienced similarly the pressure of this regional dimension through the involvement of National Christian Councils in co-operative activities on a continental basis. Latin American Evangelical Conferences have been held in Argentina in 1949, and in Peru in 1961. and a third conference is being planned to meet in Brazil in February 1969. This co-operative relationship has been expressed in other fields of common concern such as literature, youth work, education, audio-visual aids, and radio evangelism. Regional organization is following in the wake of these developments. In 1961 two Latin American Commissions were formed—one on Christian Education and the other on Church and Society. There have also been developments leading towards a permanent organization for Evangelical co-operation in Latin America. In this connection a "Provisional Committee for Evangelical Unity" was formed at a consultation held in Uruguay in December 1964.

The Committee on National Council Relationships

The draft plan for the integration of the World Council of Churches and the International Missionary Council asked the Central Committee of the World Council of Churches to consider the appointment of a Standing Committee on National Council Relationships so that continuous attention might be given to relationships of mutual helpfulness with all national and regional councils.

Enough has already been written in this chapter to indicate the complexity of national council relationships within the structure of the ecumenical movement. Affiliated councils share in the policy making of the Commission on World Mission, while associated councils, of which the affiliated council may be a part, may be invited to send representatives to meetings of the Central Committee, but without vote. Similarly the importance of these councils for the furtherance of the ecumenical movement and activity has been duly noted.

In 1961 the Third Assembly, meeting at New Delhi, the Assembly of integration, did appoint such a committee within the General Secretariat, and gave to it a mandate which included:

> The functions of the committee shall be:
> i to develop patterns of relationship and co-operation whereby the World Council of Churches and national councils of churches and other Christian councils can strengthen each other and best serve the needs of their constituencies;

ii to assist such councils in utilizing the resources of the World Council of Churches and to assist the divisions of the World Council to relate their programmes to the needs of such councils;

iii to keep before all the divisions and departments of the World Council and its member churches the significance of such councils in the fulfilment of the purposes of the ecumenical movement; and

iv to recommend to the Central Committee ways in which such councils can participate most effectively in the life of the World Council.

The committee had its first meeting in Paris in 1962. It met again in Rochester, New York, in 1963, and again in Enugu, Nigeria, in 1965.

From its inception the committee became aware of two difficulties. Meetings of the committee were necessarily held around the time of meetings of other World Council committees. Many of the members were also involved in some of these meetings, and so found it difficult to attend throughout the sessions of the Committee on National Council Relationships. Further, the committee quickly realized that its work would make greater demands on the time of its secretary than his total commitments would permit.

The Paris meeting was important because it both indicated the range of questions and issues which came properly within the terms of its mandate, and also outlined matters of major importance which would continue to engage the committee in its subsequent meetings. The committee was impressed with the number and range of contacts which were being maintained between Christian Councils and the World Council of Churches. It was said that the various divisions of the World Council were in regular co-operation with nearly thirty councils which were neither "associated" nor "affiliated". The committee was conscious also of the wide diversities between councils. They differed in basis of membership, aim, function, structure, and resources. It was thought that a thorough study needed to be made of the nature and scale of the services a council might properly undertake, of the financial support of councils, of the role of councils within the ecumenical movement, and of the constitutional position of councils in the World Council of Churches.

The committee found reason to emphasize the need for constant co-ordination between the divisions and departments of the World Council in their dealings with Christian Councils. It believed that, as the interdependence of the World Council and other Christian Councils grew, it would be important to keep under review the formal relationships between them.

The subject of the nature of Christian Councils in relation to their financial support was considered again at the Rochester meeting of the committee. The following statement was adopted:

A Christian Council is primarily a representative body for the churches within its own area. Its effective witness to the wider significance of the ecumenical movement depends on this basic requirement, and if this representative character is weak or ambiguous all its work suffers, no matter what resources it may have at its disposal from outside its area. In particular, a Christian council should be able to act in relation to the government of its country, and be recognized by the people, as the responsible voice of the churches in that country. Otherwise its integrity is challenged.

The meeting at Enugu carried the discussion on the financial support of Christian Councils still further, and decided to explore the possibility of establishing a mutual assistance fund for National Christian Councils which needed financial aid beyond the resources which they received from their member organizations.

This continuing discussion revealed the perplexities and complexities, which over several decades had troubled the International Missionary Council in its consideration of the support of Christian Councils in days of increasing national sensitivity. And it was still found impossible to assemble factual data about financial support being received susceptible of accurate analysis and interpretation.

The inherent difficulty of reaching conclusions on a problem which involved a wide diversity of circumstances and need, and which might hold promise of assisting Christian Councils in their growth and service within and beyond their own land, and that without endangering their self-hood and integrity, pointed inexorably to the need of an officer within the World Council structure who would be able to devote the whole of his time to the fulfilment of the mandate given to the Committee on National Council Relationships. Such an appointment was approved at the Fourth Assembly of the W.C.C., meeting at Uppsala, Sweden in 1968.

The Contribution of the Ecumenical Movement to National Christian Councils

National Christian Councils, in their varied manifestations, regional councils and conferences, and the integrated World Council of Churches itself, are all expressions of the ever-widening involvement of the "parts" of the Christian family with its "whole", and with the totality of the Christian task and witness inherent in the Lordship of Jesus Christ. Through it the individual Christian in his local congregation has his place and responsibility in the ecumenical movement.

It is not that all Churches and missionary agencies are equally committed everywhere to, or associated with, this inclusive ecumenical relationship. There are exceptions in every land. In some cases the reason rests in theological belief. In others, the desire of even a majority of members on a Christian Council to retain in its local fellowship a minority of members for whom an association with the World Council of Churches is not possible inhibits any formal relationship with the World Council or with its Commission on World Mission and Evangelism. In some cases, particularly in Latin America and parts of Africa, interest in the ecumenical movement is hindered and limited by the pressure of related missions whose headquarters are opposed to any association with the ecumenical structure, and to any involvement in ecumenical activity. In still other cases the political situation in a country may limit the free association of council and Church with the wider relationships of ecumenical organization and responsibility. Even so, it is frequently and increasingly true that there are avenues of communication and of service which are able to link the ecumenical movement with councils which, while seeking to further co-operation and unity in their own lands, are unable to be responsibly related to the ecumenical movement beyond their borders.

The provision in the constitution of the World Council of Churches for relationship with national and regional councils states that "the purpose of such working relationships shall be to help national councils in their work". It would be possible to write exhaustively of the actual help which is given by or through the World Council of Churches to national Christian Councils in almost every aspect of their work.

At a relatively low level, and even if it be true that almost insoluble problems have been involved, it remains a fact that the financial aid which has been given to councils, first through the International Missionary Council and its agencies, latterly through affiliated councils of the C.W.M.E., and increasingly through the Division of Inter-Church Aid, Refugee, and World Service, has not only over the years amounted to very considerable sums of money, but has enabled those councils to undertake a range of work and service on behalf of their member Churches and of the communities in which they are set which otherwise it would have been impossible to fulfil.

Further, in almost every one of the activities pursued by Christian Councils, there is within the World Council structure continuing creative thought and experiment and potential assistance which can be made available to the national councils for their challenge, inspiration, and help. Through the divisions of the World Council, such as World Mission and Evangelism, Studies, Ecumenical Action, and Inter-Church Aid, through the Commission of the Churches on International Affairs, and, above all, through the personal visitation by members of the World Council staff, the National Councils are encouraged and helped in the varied tasks they attempt to perform on behalf of their member bodies.

In a memorandum written by Mr Louis Odell on "The relationship of the National Christian Councils of Latin America to the Ecumenical Movement", acknowledgement is made of the important part played by the Division of Inter-Church Aid, Refugee, and World Service in creating a better climate of relationship between the National Christian Councils and the ecumenical movement. He says: "As a result of the creation of the Secretariat for Latin America within the Division of Inter-Church Aid, Refugee, and World Service, ecumenical relationships are improving, and are gaining noticeable importance. Regular visits to Latin America, the formulation of projects, the search for ecumenical support, the conduct of studies, and the exchange of information, have meant a more complete understanding of the nature of the World Council of Churches, and of its role vis-à-vis the Churches, the will of God, and Christian unity. As a result, a better and more creative association with the World Council of Churches has been established, and relationship has become possible with Churches and councils which were traditionally opposed to the ecumenical movement, and, consequently, fresh avenues of communication and mutual collaboration have been opened.

Of even greater importance and significance is the help derived by national councils from their involvement in the ecumenical movement. In it they not only have a vision of the "whole" in the realm of the life and witness of the Church, but through their relationship with it they are involved in participation in it, in both study and action, in fellowship with the representatives of other Christian councils, and to the enrichment of their service for the Kingdom of God in their own lands. To be engaged with Christians of other continents, from other confessions, and from differing background and circumstance, in the consideration of any of the varied ecumenical activities in which the World Council of Churches is engaged, is to be immeasurably enriched in the understanding of the world task of the Church, and uplifted by the consciousness of having some part in that task in the sometimes lonely and difficult situation in which Christian councils may at times be placed.

The Contribution of National Christian Councils to the Ecumenical Movement

The provision in the Constitution of the World Council of Churches for relationship with national councils also states that "the purpose of such working relationships shall be . . . to encourage them to help the World Council of Churches in the promotion of ecumenical activities in the area concerned . . .". There has been ample recognition that, in the same way as the International Missionary Council depended upon its member councils for the furtherance of its work and policies, so the World Council has needed the co-operation and participation of national and other councils.

Documents of the Joint Committee of the World Council of Churches and the International Missionary Council contain such statements as:

> In the day to day work of the W.C.C. there is a growing dependence on the service of national councils.[1]

> The W.C.C. has always recognized the vital role national and other Christian councils occupy in the ecumenical movement. The W.C.C. has also acknowledged its dependence on the co-operation of Christian councils in the furtherance of its own policy and programmes. While the primary point of reference from the W.C.C. is to its member churches, divisions and departments habitually correspond with Christian councils, engage their interest and activity in studies and projects, work through them to a growing extent, and often respond to initiatives taken by the councils.[2]

In a document on the "Relationship of the Division of Inter-Church Aid and Service to Refugees and National Councils of Churches and National Christian Councils" it is stated: "The programme of the Division is commended to the member churches mainly through departments of National Councils of Churches, and resources for the programme are collected mainly through the same channels."

The nature of the services rendered by Christian Councils to the ecumenical movement naturally will differ according to the variations in their own

[1] Joint Committee 10/8.   [2] Joint Committee, September 1961.

structure, resources, and function. Some have been able to assist considerably with service connected with arrangements for meetings of Assemblies and committees of the W.C.C., and in other ways are able to assist in the promotion and furtherance of its programmes and policies. Inevitably the requests made for assistance are greater in the case of some councils than others. But the Christian Council, whatever its structure and function, makes a contribution by its very existence. It is part of the structure of co-operation and unity which links Church with Church and other Christian agencies in the area, and therefore has a necessary place in the structures of co-operation which link the Churches of a given area with those of other lands and continents. It is part of a complete chain of co-operation and communication which stretches from the individual Christian to the W.C.C., and which reaches back from the W.C.C. to the local congregation and its individual members. As Dr Oldham argued in his article on "New Spiritual Adventures in the Mission Field", "If our unity is real, and we have a common purpose, these must express themselves through some visible organ."[1] And such organs of co-operation are necessary for the fulfilment of the tasks of the World Council of Churches, and of the ecumenical movement as a whole.

Probably the greatest contribution made by the National Christian Councils and regional organizations to the ecumenical movement has been in the outstanding leadership which has been made available for the service of that movement. It has come from every continent, and has continued from 1910 until the present day. It would be invidious, and maybe tedious, to begin to name them. But a study of reports of assemblies, commissions, and the like, over the years would provide frequent evidence of the contribution in vision and outlook of those who have had much of their training in and through their service to National Christian Councils. This contribution has involved equally valuable participation in the work of the committees of the various departments and activities of the World Council—representing a costly contribution by the national councils themselves in the time and service of their secretaries released for ecumenical service. Admittedly, in the process, the national councils have gained from the added experience of their officers which flowed back into the life and work of the councils to which they belonged.

Nor is it possible to measure the influence of Christian Councils, particularly in the lands of the younger Churches, in their insistence on facing the realities of the ecumenical challenge in the context of their own situation, in which traditional confessional pressures have sometimes become entrenched.

It is not without meaning and challenge for the ecumenical movement as a whole that the National Council of Churches in Indonesia, founded in 1950, defines its aims and functions as:

> Establish one Christian Church in Indonesia, promote and execute co-operation according to agreements among Churches: establish relations with mission and ecumenical bodies at home and abroad: seek to enlarge and deepen present ecumenical relations: represent Churches in dealing with government in matters of common interest.

[1] *IRM*, no. 44 (1922), p. 547.

E

The Ecclesiological Significance of Christian Councils

Towards the end of the period covered by this history there has been considerable interest concerning the ecclesiological significance of Christian Councils—the World Council of Churches itself as well as the National Christian Councils. A document produced by the joint committee of the World Council of Churches and the International Missionary Council in July 1960 raises the issue in this way:

> The increasing importance of national and regional councils, not only as useful adjuncts to the World Council of Churches and valuable aids to ecumenical experience, but as a fundamental part of the structure of the ecumenical movement gives importance to the insistent question—What is the ecclesiological significance of councils?

In reporting to the Central Committee, after its first meeting in Paris in August 1962, the Committee on National Council Relationships "noted with appreciation that in the forthcoming World Conference on Faith and Order provision is being made for consideration of what has been termed 'the ecclesiological significance of Christian Councils'."

The Fourth World Conference on Faith and Order (Montreal 1963) did give some consideration to the issue, and took note of the report of the National Council of Churches in the U.S.A. of "the Ecclesiological Significance of Councils of Churches", and an essay by the Reverend Kenneth Slack of the British Council of Churches. The section report on "The Church and the World Council of Churches", apart from commenting on the ambiguity involved in the English expression "councils of churches", is chiefly concerned with the World Council of Churches, and that without "presuming to give a definite answer".

An article by Dr Lukas Vischer entitled "Christian Councils—their Future as Instruments of the Ecumenical Movement"[1] does, however, attempt to deal precisely with the question: What is the ecclesiological significance of Christian Councils? It merits close study, and should occasion considerable debate. He is aware that the character, structure, and powers of Christian Councils vary so greatly that any ecclesiological formula is bound to be inadequate. But, he says,

> However great the difficulties may be, the question of the ecclesiological significance of Christian councils needs to be kept in view. The very inability to state what they ecclesiologically are shows at least one thing with unmistakable clarity; they are in fact an ecclesiological anomaly which ought not to continue indefinitely in its present form.

Dr Vischer's conclusion is that Christian Councils can fulfil their function only if they are understood as transitional institutions which overcome the ecclesiological anomaly of division, and make increasingly visible the unity which binds the Churches together. He shares the belief that a conciliar structure belongs to the very essence of the Church, and believes that in the

[1] *Study Encounter*, June 1968.

new period in the history of Christian Councils which is now beginning, the structure of Councils should be modified to meet the challenges represented by the increasing number of Churches seeking union with each other, and by the willingness of Roman Catholic local Churches, in some places, to join Christian Councils as full members.

The next volume of ecumenical history will reveal the extent to which National Christian Councils themselves have found the answers to questions as to their nature and ecclesiological significance, and the extent to which they have been led to modify their structures and functions.

5

Confessional Families
and the Ecumenical Movement

HAROLD E. FEY

During the two decades covered by this history, relations between confessional families and the ecumenical movement assumed new importance and complexity. Attempts to deal with these relations required sharper definitions. Definitions of confessionalism were not easy to make because no two denominational groupings found the same meaning in the word or in the reality it signified. So clarification efforts became adventures in self-examination. In 1967, after other names had been discarded as unsatisfactory, the secretaries of the world confessional groups adopted the term "world confessional families". They said the families consist of "the various Christian traditions taken as a whole. Each world confessional family consists of Churches belonging to the same tradition and held together by this common heritage; they are conscious of living in the same universal fellowship and give to this consciousness at least some structured visible expression."[1]

Beginnings of Confessional Organizations

The forms of these "structured visible expressions" vary greatly. One confessional family has a thousand employees and annual budgets in the millions. Several have small but highly competent staffs and moderate budgets. Others are served by part-time secretaries without assistance who earn their living at other tasks. Some had origins which preceded the modern ecumenical movement by many decades. Others were formed or assumed their present level of activities since the World Council of Churches was officially launched in 1948. Anglicans deny that theirs is a confessional grouping and they did not in fact develop a continuing organization until after 1958. But the first Lambeth Conference, which began the process of consultation, was held in 1867. The "Alliance of Reformed Churches Throughout the World holding the Presbyterian System" was the first formally organized confessional family. It was launched in 1875 and held its first meeting in 1877. The Methodists started holding "World Ecumenical Conferences" in 1881 but did not organize their World Methodist Council until 1951. The Lutherans did not begin the process of consultation until 1923, when the Lutheran World Conference began to meet, and did not launch the Lutheran World Federation until 1947. Today it is the largest of all.

Nevertheless, difficult as they are to define and varied as they are in their "structured visible expressions", the world confessional families are very much alive and must be taken into account in their relationship with the ecumenical movement. In their beginnings they were in fact the principal existing forms of the ecumenical movement, giving the members of their Churches a new consciousness of universality through the discovery of the world-wide dimensions of their own fellowships. Many of their leaders participated in the formation of the World Council of Churches and today have positions of leadership in it.

In the last two decades confessional groupings have increased in strength and in scope of work. At the same time their status has paradoxically been limited by the growth of the ecumenical movement. While today some church-

[1] Report of Secretaries of World Confessional Families. Geneva 1967.

men within these groupings and more outside of them consider that they have become a hindrance to the ecumenical movement, confessional organizations continue. Shorn of any claim to absolutism that may ever have been attributed to them, they seek and generally find constructive roles as they examine their reasons for separate existence and their unquestionably expanding and deepening relations with other confessional families.

While the World Council of Churches is not the ecumenical movement, its emergence and development has been and is a prominent factor in that movement. The issue of confessionalism has been a matter that has had to be considered since the earliest meetings for planning of the W.C.C. The first meeting for definitive projection of the W.C.C. was held in Utrecht, Holland in 1938. Here Lutherans argued that membership in the W.C.C. should consist of Churches and that seats in its Assembly and Central Committee should be allocated on a confessional basis. According to church historian Abdel Ross Wentz, the Lutheran representative said:

> It is our conviction that the World Council itself will move more quickly and more certainly towards a united testimony before the world if the churches themselves associated in confessional groups are permitted to speak frankly with one another in friendly comparison of views—far more quickly and certainly than if Christians speak with one another as national or geographical groups. The way to a united Christian testimony before the world of today would be rendered more difficult by sectionalism than by sectarianism.

His argument for membership by Churches prevailed; but the attempt to associate Churches in confessional blocs within the structure of the W.C.C. did not prevail.

After the Second World War, when the committee on arrangements for the Amsterdam Assembly met in England, the same argument was put forward. In reply the committee held that invitations had already been issued and that the basis of membership in the World Council would have to be settled when the First Assembly met. Following this meeting but before Amsterdam, Henry Pitney Van Dusen, President of Union Theological Seminary, New York, wrote that the confessional issue would be "much the most explosive issue and one which is most likely to erupt with some sharpness on the floor of the Assembly". He said that tension was between regionalism and nationalism on the one hand and denominationalism or confessionalism on the other. "The interests of confessionalism are being urged by some Orthodox and Anglican churchmen, by a few Reformed or Presbyterian leaders, but most convincedly and insistently by certain spokesmen for American Lutheranism."[1]

Confessionalism and the W.C.C.

When the Lutheran World Federation was formed in 1947 at Lund, Sweden, Bishop Anders Nygren and others continued to advocate a confessional basis for the W.C.C. The General Secretary of the W.C.C. provisional committee

[1] *Christianity and Crisis*, vol. viii, no. 7.

appeared before the Lund conference and appealed for support in the following carefully chosen words:

> The World Council is deeply aware of the fact that the ecumenical task can only be performed if the main confessional federations and alliances perform their task of bringing the churches of their confessional family together in close fellowship and so prepare the way for the even greater and more difficult task of establishing the wider ecumenical Christian brotherhood.

The breadth of vision which turned an either–or into a both–and approach finally won the day.

The issue was resolved when the Amsterdam Assembly adopted the formula proposed by the provisional committee: "Seats in the Assembly shall be allocated to the member churches by the Central Committee, due regard being given to such factors as numerical size, adequate confessional representation and adequate geographical distribution." This was a compromise. The formula recognized the existence of confessional groups; but the basis of membership was still Churches, not confessional groups.[1]

The Amsterdam Assembly also approved the following additional action:

> The Constitution of the Council authorizes the Council to establish consultative relationships with denominational federations to send representatives to the Assembly and the Central Committee in a consultative capacity. The provisional Committee recommends that these bodies should be especially consulted with regard to membership of Churches of their confession. In so far as they enter into the field of inter-church aid and reconstruction they should, furthermore, be invited to relate their activities as closely as possible to the Council's reconstruction department. It is inevitable that in their manifold approaches to the churches the activities of the Council and of the confessional federations overlap to some extent. It is therefore most desirable that regular contacts be maintained between the executive officers concerned. And the most appropriate solutions would be that as many of the federations as possible should follow the example of those which have set up offices in Geneva or sent special representatives to Geneva.

This compromise did not lay to rest all the concerns which were inherent in the situation, particularly as confessional groups developed a new vigour following the formation of the World Council of Churches. So Charles Ranson spoke for others as well as for himself when he addressed the board of directors of the London Missionary Society on 19 September 1951. He said:

> The growth of the World Council of Churches and the ecumenical idea has stimulated a revival of organized confessionalism. There are two aspects of this development. One is tremendously important and potentially creative. This is the concern which has quite properly developed within the churches that they shall understand deeply their own heritage and thus be able to talk with meaning and realism with other churches with whom they are in ecumenical conversation.

[1] See Abdel Ross Wentz, *The Lutheran Churches and the Ecumenical Movement* in *World Lutheranism Today: A Tribute to Anders Nygren* (Oxford: Rock Island, Illinois 1950).

The other aspect, which gives real cause for concern to those of us whose interest lies largely in the life of the younger churches, is the way this is expressing itself organizationally in world-wide confessional bodies. These tend to project themselves across the world and to fasten upon the younger churches those leading strings from which we have been trying to free them for many years. The real growing points of ecumenicity today are in the life of the younger churches. The real driving force in this organized confessionalism which is in danger of hardening into ecumenical sectarianism lies in the older Christendom, often among people who have no conception of the implications of what they are doing for the life of the younger churches.[1]

The emphasis in this statement was prophetic, for in the years since Dr Ranson spoke, the most searching questions concerning the effect of confessional activities have come from the East Asia Christian Council.

Co-operation in Compassion

In the first decade following the Second World War major ecumenical energies were absorbed by work to relieve suffering humanity and to repair war damage to church structures and relationships. Inter-Church aid and help for refugees, first within Europe and then in widening circles throughout the world, became a major preoccupation of confessional and ecumenical organizations alike. Many Churches co-ordinated their efforts under the World Council, whose substantial humanitarian efforts are described in Chapter 8 of this book. Others channeled some resources of man-power and materials through the W.C.C. and with them carried on denominational enterprises for their own most afflicted people.

Because vastly more Lutherans were uprooted and more Lutheran Churches were disrupted by reason of the struggle in Europe than were members or Churches of other Protestant groups, the Lutheran World Federation organized its own massive programme of assistance to refugees and aid to Churches. The achievements of the L.W.F. in relief, resettlement, and reconstruction constitute an heroic chapter in church history. Abroad, work that began during the war as service to "orphaned missions" expanded in various directions, one of which was resettlement of European and other refugees. It is important to recognize that while this work was done under the auspices of the L.W.F., a confessional organization, the L.W.F. also assisted the efforts of other ecumenical organizations and was assisted by them as resources permitted. While the L.W.F. still carries on a large programme, the trend is towards more co-operation rather than towards more competition.

By 1957 the immediate urgencies of the post-war crisis were tapering off and the Churches could once more turn to examining their relationships with one another. The Second World Assembly, held in 1954 at Evanston, Illinois, had invited observers from non-member Churches, but had not otherwise disturbed the balance of ecumenical/confessional relationships. Because confessional organizations were growing in strength, the impression spread that they might be heading towards a collision course with ecumenical institutions,

---

[1] Quoted by Michael Hollis in *Mission, Unity and Truth* (London 1967), p. 10.

which were also gaining acceptance. Even those who did not hold this view recognized that consultation was required to take into account changes in relationships and attitudes. The increase in the number of Churches which were uniting with other Churches or were engaged in negotiations looking toward union was also a factor. So the time was ripe for representatives of confessional organizations to meet to discuss their relationships with each other and with the W.C.C. This began in 1957.

Since 1957 the officers of fourteen world confessional families have met in Geneva, generally annually, for conversations among themselves and with members of the staff of the World Council of Churches. Not all are represented at every meeting. The families whose representatives have met are the Anglican Communion, the Baptist World Alliance, the Ecumenical Patriarchate (Constantinople), the Friends World Committee for Consultation, the International Congregational Council, the Lutheran World Federation, the Mennonite World Conference, the Old Catholic Church, the Pentecostal World Conference, the Patriarchate of Moscow, the Salvation Army, the World Convention of Churches of Christ, the Methodist World Council, and the World Alliance of Reformed Churches. The Standing Committee of Oriental Orthodox Churches joined the conversations in 1967.

Annual Meeting of Confessional Representatives

How did the meetings of confessional bodies begin? It is significant that the initiative was taken by one of them. At the 1956 meeting of the executive committee of the World Alliance of Reformed Churches in Prague, President John A. Mackay of the W.A.R.C. spoke of the rebirth of churchmanship and of the importance of the ecumenical movement. He then described "the resurgence of confessionalism" as a positive factor. The new confessionalism differed from the old, he said, in that there was now no disposition to "absolutize their several confessional structures or loyalties. No single confession believes that it represents the one and only Church of Christ, the Una Sancta." But each seeks to make its specific contribution to the "ecumenical treasure house of Christian faith and life".

Since confessional movements and the ecumenical movement are growing side by side, he said, they could either collide or co-operate. Dr Mackay thought that, if co-operation is to result, "the confessional movement must be taken seriously by the World Council of Churches". He therefore proposed that "confessional leaders come together for the exchange of information and the discussion of policies in an atmosphere of Christian confidence". He had talked with W.C.C. leaders and said they favoured confessional leaders conferring on an autonomous basis. Later that morning the executive committee of the W.A.R.C. voted to sponsor an invitation to confessional leaders to meet informally to explore prospects of co-operation.

The informal gathering was held at New Haven when the Central Committee of the W.C.C. met during the following summer, 1957. Leaders of seven confessional groups got together and approved the idea of a larger meeting of presidents and secretaries of confessional groups. This larger meeting was held at the W.C.C. in the autumn of the same year. The W.A.R.C. suggestions for the agenda were comprehensive. As they were stated by the W.A.R.C. executive group in 1957 they included:

> ... frank and friendly discussion of the place of confessionalism in the ecumenical movement; the contribution which a resurgent confessionalism can make to the enrichment of that movement; the points at which, if any, confessionalism becomes a threat to that growing oneness in Christ which ecumenical movement seeks; the ways in which the commitment of the churches to the ecumenical movement presupposes some restraint on the consciousness and practice of mission on the part of confessional groups with reference to each other.

In some sense these points have constituted the agenda of each meeting of confessional leaders since 1957.[1]

While the conferences have always been held under the auspices of the confessional groups themselves, meetings have been held at the World Council of Churches headquarters and staff members of that organization have been welcome contributors to the discussions. As a matter of fact, the initiation of this series of annual conferences of leaders of confessional organizations was most welcome to W.C.C. leaders. The issue of ecumenical/confessional relationships was recognized to require discussion. Here was a way that discussion could begin. The struggle of confessional groups to define their own character has been helped, even if it is not solved, by sharing with others having like problems. Relationships between confessional families and the ecumenical movement have benefited from open confrontation of issues. Again, issues have not been finally resolved, but they have been clarified and put on the way to resolution because, as Dr Mackay said, the tendency to absolutize confessional structures or loyalties is a thing of the past.

The point of view from which these conversations proceeded was that taken by Henry Carter, a British Methodist, who wrote:

> The ecumenical movement has taken two forms, inter- and intra-confessional, and Methodism as a world-wide confession is explicitly related to both. It might seem that a major and divisive issue confronts us here. To pursue the line of confessional activity with only intermittent regard for the call of the Universal Church would mean intensification of denominational feelings and policy, with heightening of barriers against unity. To respond to the Universal Church with scant concern for confessional loyalty and duty, as though the ecumenical movement could here and now dissolve that elemental bond, would scatter, not conserve, the spiritual treasure which the confession holds in trust. Yet the bare statement of the issue in this way points to the true line of action. The recognition that inter- and intra-confessional movements have progressed side by side and stage by stage points to an unfolding purpose, to which churches of many confessions and in all parts of the world have become sensitive and responsive. We can thankfully acknowledge the continuing guidance of Divine Spirit on the way that leads to the true unity and wholeness of Christ's Church, the Una Sancta.[2]

[1] From the minutes of the executive committee of the World Alliance of Reformed Churches, 1956, at Prague, and 1957, at Stoney Point, New York.

[2] *The Methodist Heritage* (London 1951), p. 218.

The early years of the conferences of representatives of confessional families were not notably productive. But the passage of time and the proddings of providence working through events finally combined to break down reticence and to open the minds of confessional leaders to one another. At first each was so preoccupied with the practicalities of confessional ministries that serious theological conversation was difficult. The result was that it was easier to make ecumenical affirmations than it was to study and work together. It was, after all, the Churches which commanded the major resources of men and money. These made it possible for church leaders to launch enterprises which they considered to be ecumenical in spirit yet which were confessional in personnel, orientation, and result. Lack of patience with theological discussion on the nature of the one Church under its one Lord encouraged unilateral action and short-circuited possible ecumenical achievements. This was not changed until voices began to be raised, especially by the youth of the Churches, which questioned the seriousness of ecumenical commitments which expressed themselves verbally in terms of identity with the ecumenical movement, but structurally, financially, and empirically in pre-ecumenical terms.

Ecumenical Evangelism

Another factor which was at work was what might be called ecumenical evangelism. It found expression at the crucial time when the ecumenical movement had to move past its initial stage or die in its infancy. One example of many that might be cited was heard at the service which was held in Oslo Cathedral during the 1961 meeting of the World Methodist Council: W. A. Visser 't Hooft preached from the text in Romans 15 which was adapted for his closing words. He declared that, while some people consider that the very existence of the denominations constitutes a difficulty for the ecumenical movement, there are many "extremely positive elements" in the denominational heritage. He hoped that the time would never come when Methodists would not express their gratitude for John Wesley. He urged them to share their spiritual heritage. But there is a denominationalism, he said, which expresses itself in "spiritual laziness, in withdrawing, in refusing to face the consequences of a real confrontation with other denominations" for fear of the sacrifices which might be demanded. This kind of denominationalism, he said, was bad. So also is the ecclesiastical power politics which uses confessional words and forms as levers to achieve its ends. Then he came to the point:

> But there is one more thing [said Dr Visser 't Hooft]. Do we always remember that denominations by their nature are provisional in character, or do we sometimes think and speak about them as if they were final embodiments of Christian truth? Now Martin Luther and John Calvin and John Wesley have all made it abundantly clear that they did not think of the church formation which they saw growing up in their lifetime as the last word. On the contrary, they all thought in terms of the Church Catholic and prayed for the restoration of the full catholicity and unity of the church. And should we be more

confessional than our confessional leaders? More confessional than Luther or Calvin, or more than Wesley? Surely not!... What we need most of all from you is precisely that desire which is also at the heart of Methodism, which was surely in the heart of John Wesley, that desire to render a more obedient, a more convincing witness than the world has seen for many centuries to the unity, to the universality of the people of God and the Body of Christ. May the God of steadfastness and encouragement grant you to live in such harmony with one another—yes, with one another as Methodists, but also with all who call upon the name of the Lord Jesus Christ, in accord with Jesus Christ, that together you may with one voice glorify the God and Father of our Lord Jesus Christ.[1]

A major factor in raising the confessional question in inescapable form was the action of a new regional ecumenical organization—the East Asia Christian Conference. Meeting at Bangalore, India in 1961, the E.A.C.C. declared that "the very vitality of these confessional loyalties often create serious obstacles in the life of the younger churches". This touched upon the sensitive issue which had set the ecumenical movement on its way at the world mission conference in Edinburgh in 1910, namely that of churchly divisions throwing a road block in the way of the world mission which had been entrusted to the Church by its Lord. The timing of the E.A.C.C. was perfect, since the Third Assembly of the World Council of Churches was about to be held in New Delhi. It could hardly afford to ignore the challenge.

The Asian Challenge to Confessionalism

New Delhi did not ignore the question, but also it did not face it squarely. In the report of the section on Church Unity, which made the famous "all in each place" statement, the Assembly noted that most of the confessional organizations existed many years before the founding of the World Council. This was an interesting but not a relevant point. It affirmed that "their purpose is not only to clarify and strengthen confessional understanding and loyalty but to serve responsibly in the wider ecumenical movement. But opinion is divided today over the effects of their existence and work upon the participation of their churches in the movement for unity and upon the course they ought to take in the future."

The New Delhi Assembly observed that some believe that a deeper understanding of the various confessions is necessary if the quest for unity in the truth is at length to be successful, and that it is the duty of the confessional organizations to advance that deeper understanding. On the other hand, the Churches have in their membership leaders who see world confessional bodies as a threat to wider unity, particularly in Asia and Africa. The New Delhi Assembly had already agreed to its famous statement concerning "the centrality of unity of all Christians *in each place* which must of course always seek to be a 'unity of the truth'". It therefore concluded that, if the leaders of confessional bodies believe this, "they will not consider the union of one of

---

[1] *Proceedings of the Tenth World Methodist Conference, Oslo, Norway, 1961* (London: Nashville 1961), p. 280.

their churches as a loss, but as a gain for the whole Church. And a service can be rendered to such churches if the confessional bodies assist them in the responsible study of all issues which are involved in the proposed union."

This observation represented a legitimate hope but it did not attempt to resolve the questions involved in the simultaneous rise of the ecumenical movement and increase in the strength of the confessional bodies. Some of these questions appeared in the *Ecumenical Review* for October 1964. They had been raised by the East Asia Christian Conference Assembly which met in Bangkok in February of that year. The E.A.C.C. Assembly recommended that the E.A.C.C. executive group bring together representatives of confessional bodies and of the younger Churches in a "major consultation". The question the Assembly raised for discussion suggests the nature of the continuing dialogue over confessionalism in so far as it concerns the mission of the Church.

Affirming their belief that "the Church is One Body, the Body of Christ", the Asian Churches pointed out that they are moving toward autonomy, not merely to achieve organizational independence, but also so that each Church will "find its own selfhood, being able under God to make its own response to its Lord in the specific situation it has been called to mission". Therefore, "on such a matter as church union, a church must make up its own mind and accept the consequences of its own obedience". Since the parent churches are involved, "they too must decide how best to help in the process of decision-making without violating their own integrity or that of the younger churches". The Bangkok Assembly called on confessional bodies to give help to Churches of the same family "within the framework of the total ecumenical operation". Moreover, the Assembly summoned confessional organizations to make plans which "strengthen and do not weaken the movements toward larger cooperation, closer co-ordination [and] joint action for mission and unity".

The East Asia churchmen asked confessional organizations to work within the ecumenical movement to help people within their respective families to understand how the Asian Churches see and are trying to interpret the Christian faith. An informational role which each confessional body should undertake ought also to be carried out concerning the experiences of Christians in other confessional families "so that they can take courage and pray intelligently for each other". Before these organizations carry out these essentially theological functions, their Asian colleagues asked them to face three hard questions:

1. Do the world confessional organizations rest on a theological principle or do they simply gather together Churches because of a common history and tradition?

2. Even where world confessional organizations are seeking to preserve for the universal Church some fundamental insight into an aspect of Christian truth, is this best done by an organization built around that truth?

3. Are the confessions and doctrines which are the historical basis of these world confessional organizations living realities among the people in these confessional families?

E.A.C.C. approach to "Big Three"

Finally, these Asian Churchmen ventured to doubt the relevance and use-fulness of world meetings which had been proposed by various confessional bodies. Instead, the E.A.C.C. churchmen asked them "to support the ecumenical programmes that are now developing for the handling of these issues". They then addressed directly the World Methodist Council, the Anglican Communion, and the Lutheran World Federation. To the Methodists, who were reported to be rethinking their organizational structure, Bangkok asked that the World Council of Churches and the regional conferences of Asia and Africa be consulted about plans. Asian churchmen also warned that, while Methodist Churches of the United States, Great Britain, and Europe face similar problems and so might profitably confer on them, they should not assume that this was true of the Churches of Asia. There, "the issues lie between the churches together and the world", they said.

Turning then to the Anglican Communion, the Bangkok Assembly noted that, since Anglican officers are being appointed to serve in regions of Asia, these officers and the metropolitans in the area should meet with the working committee of the East Asia Christian Conference to deal with problems of inter-Church aid, joint action for mission, and "the growing together of the churches in each local area". The E.A.C.C. also sought information on the sponsorship and powers of the Anglican regional officers, and asked that this new initiative should "not isolate the Anglican churches from other churches and from giving aid to and receiving from them".

The Bangkok Assembly finally appealed to the Lutheran World Federation "to make it entirely clear that Lutheran Churches in Asia, which are involved in discussion of proposals for church union, will have full encouragement and help from other Lutheran Churches in the world in seeking a basis of union which is in conformity with holy Scripture. Only so will it be clear that the Lutheran World Federation is not a step towards a World Lutheran Church." It also asked if the L.W.F. "could consider making its present inter-Church aid operation one more closely integrated with the work of" the division of Inter-Church Aid of the World Council of Churches and also with that of the E.A.C.C. Later the L.W.F. did vote to assure Lutheran Churches which might enter into unions that they would not suffer loss of funds or man-power by such action.

Bangkok appealed to all confessional organizations to recognize that, as the Churches of a region unite, it will be increasingly important that such regional ecumenical organizations be strengthened.

> There are always risks involved when the churches reflect a common ethnic origin or common nationality or a common economic status. These risks can be provided against only by strengthening conciliar structures that cross all national and ethnic dividing lines. The ultimate aim must be the restoration of the one Holy Church, to the end that the united church in any one area will have an organic place in the Church Universal.

Immediate results from these appeals were not expected and did not appear.

World conferences or conventions of world confessional bodies continued to meet. But in East Asia a series of "situation conferences" were held by the E.A.C.C. Out of these came a positive proposal for "Joint Action in Mission". The idea was that in the great areas of responsibility in which the missions held a common mandate united efforts could still go forward unhindered by confessional differences. The idea was excellent; performance on it was slow in starting. But the request of the E.A.C.C. for an enlarged meeting of the world confessional bodies was not forgotten, and soon plans for it entered the active stage.

Confessional Representatives' Response

The enlarged meeting was held in Geneva, on 12 and 13 October 1965. Thirty-three representatives of nine world confessional bodies gathered. With them were three staff members from the Lutheran World Federation, three from the World Presbyterian Alliance, and ten persons from the staff of the World Council of Churches. The representation was: Anglican four, Baptist World Alliance five, Friends World Committee for Consultation three, International Congregational Council two, Lutheran World Federation four, Salvation Army three, World Convention of Churches of Christ three, World Methodist Council six, and World Presbyterian Alliance three.

World confessional groups which did not send representatives to this meeting were the Old Catholic Church, the Mennonite World Conference, whose executive cannot remember receiving any correspondence about it, the Pentecostal World Conference, the Ecumenical Patriarchate (Istanbul), and the Patriarchate of Moscow. Notably missing from the conference also were representatives of the younger Churches of Asia, Africa, and Latin America. With the exception of one staff member of the World Council and one executive of a mission board, all of the participants were North Americans or Europeans.

The 1965 conference accepted without changes the working definitions of "confessional bodies" which had been adopted in 1962, although by this time questions were being raised concerning its adequacy. After two days of discussion the conference adopted a set of findings which represented its consensus. Originally they were largely the work of W. A. Visser 't Hooft, the general secretary of the World Council of Churches, but were accepted as a fair statement of the level of agreement which had been reached.

As published in the *Ecumenical Review* (vol. xviii, 1966, pp. 91ff) under the title "Statement of a Joint Consultation Concerning Confessional Movements and Mission and Unity", the statement said that during recent years officers of the world confessional bodies had been meeting regularly "for conversations among themselves about matters of common interest. Since 1962 much of the discussion has centred upon the role of the confessional bodies in the ecumenical movement." The statement then outlined the purpose of the present meeting between "representatives of the mission agencies of the churches to discuss the significance of the confessional movement for the task of the churches in mission and unity". It said that it was hoped that the consultation would result in a much wider discussion and continuing conversation. It repeated the 1962 definition of confessional bodies and then said:

> We believe that to think and act as if the historic confessional church families represent the only spiritual reality to be taken seriously is to live in the "pre-ecumenical" age. In that sense the statement of a Lutheran theologian that the confessional era is at an end is true. On the other hand, we believe that to think and act as if the fully ecumenical age had been reached, in which confessional disagreements have been overcome and in which it is possible to think only in terms of an integrated world-wide Christian community is premature and therefore also unrealistic. It is characteristic of the present period of church history that the Church lives "between the times" when the confessions remain the main expressions of its life but in which these confessions have all to answer the ecumenical questions: "What is the relevance of the faith that all the confessions hold in common for their relationships to each other and for the unity and mission of the Church of Christ today?" and "How can they express in common witness and new ecclesiastical structure" the unity in Christ which exists already and for which they are responsible to our Lord for the sake of the world?

The Geneva conference then posed a set of questions of principle and another set of questions of function which it had been led to confront and which it believed the Churches must face. The first question of principle was: "How does the Church confess Christ in a true and contemporary way both in its witness and its structure?" While historic confessions of the faith had arisen from an endeavour to state what it meant in specific situations to be faithful to the word of God, what should happen now that the situations have changed? So also with ecclesiastical structures; they had been formed to meet specific challenges, but now other challenges are raised.

> Within their four walls the separate churches tend to speak at times as though their specific confessional traditions were the only criteria of truth. Yet in the arena of ecumenical encounter and partnership in mission they find themselves compelled to think of their confessions and structures in a new perspective and therefore open to development and reconciliation.

So ecumenical experience leads to a new appraisal of traditions and structures. How then "define theologically the relationship between the One Faith in which all are baptized and the 'confessions' which certain churches or groups of churches feel called in obedience to the Gospel to make separately?"

What Answer to Youth?

The second question of principle asked how the Churches can deal with their young people who take seriously the "ecumenical imperatives"? Often the result is that young people revolt when church leaders proclaim their determination to work for renewal through unity and mission, yet cling tenaciously to the *status quo*. This intensifies the conflict between generations within the Church. The effects of this revolt on students who are subjected to confessionally oriented theological education is particularly serious for them and for the Church. The third question of principle arises within Churches whose confessional stand or form of ecclesiastical structure has become the subject of tension or division within the church body. While leaders give "the appearance of solidarity" on confessional or ecclesiastical matters, they and the world often know that the appearance does not always correspond with the reality. To a greater or lesser extent this is the case in every denomination. Obviously this is "a matter for the most serious consideration".

The question of function raised by the 1965 conference of confessional bodies dealt with such matters as what is or should be the relation of the confessional movements to the "conciliar ecumenical movement and the future of the total mission of the Church"? National Christian Councils provide forums for discussion of important issues and provide facilities for common action in missionary and evangelistic tasks of the Churches, such as "Joint Action for Mission". This is an important and urgent issue. Also the Churches must ask: "What relation has the confessional and ecumenical understanding of the Churches to their processes of decision-making in respect of their upbuilding of the Church and their mission to the world?" The answer involves pastoral care, education, church extension, and missionary activities which in turn affect the Churches' use of money and personnel.

A noticeable discrepancy between ecumenical affirmation in one direction and expenditure of money in other directions, said the conference, does the Church no good. So the Churches must ask themselves: "How can we establish the criteria of responsible partnership between the affluent and the needy on the one hand, and between confessional bodies and National Councils on the other?" This is also applied both to decision-making and to the allocation of funds. For example, what happens when a Church or church agency is asked to help other Churches "with which they are not in theological agreement or in full communion?" Some agreed criteria for responsible partnership are called for.

Finally the 1965 conference asked: What should be the relationship of the united Churches to the confessional bodies of which the uniting Churches were members? And what priority should be given to regional ecumenical organizations in the development by a Church of its missionary strategy? The statement ended with recognition that the answer to these questions would not easily be found, since the consequences of whatever decision is reached on them will be far-reaching. But "we have formulated these questions in the hope that God may be pleased to use the discussions which they will provoke to further his purpose of unity for his people".

So the questions which came into the open at Bangalore and had echoed through the discussions at New Delhi and in other conferences were further emphasized and deepened at Geneva. They were more readily asked than answered; but there was no doubt that they had deeply penetrated the consciousness of leaders of the confessional bodies. In respect of the original impetus for asking the questions, Geneva left something to be desired, for the younger Churches were not represented by their own people. But confessionalism had arisen in the West, and so it was necessary that it be considered by Western Christians. They may be sure that Christians in other parts of the world are not indifferent to it. Westerners were more intimately concerned with its origins and could conceivably do most to reconcile confessionalism and ecumenism. The discussion might have profited if the younger Churches had been represented; but they had raised the question in such a way that henceforth it could not be ignored, whether or not they were present.

Comment which followed the Geneva conference varied. One participant noted that "the spirit of caution" was pronounced. He cited as evidence the fact that a spokesman for the International Congregational Council had received no support when he proposed as a question to be included in the concluding statement of the meeting: "Under what circumstances can we feel that the confessional bodies have fulfilled their function and can disappear as such?" The I.C.C. representative received no encouragement and the question was not included. The conference had the opportunity to advance "Joint Action for Mission" which had been launched in the Situation Conference in Asia and had subsequently been endorsed by the W.C.C. Division of World Mission and Evangelism at its meeting in Mexico City. But the idea of Joint Action for Mission received inadequate attention at Geneva and was "only slowly, very slowly, being implemented" anywhere.

Another line of comment noted that the prevailing definition of "confessional bodies" was such that Orthodox, Anglican, and Roman Catholic Churches would have difficulty in recognizing themselves in it. Does the fellowship between confessional bodies consist solely in the fact that each has specific convictions of a doctrinal or ecclesiological character to support, as Lukas Vischer asked in an article written in August 1966? This is, as he noted, clearly a "pre-ecumenical" definition, an "ecumenical formalism which does not do justice to reality". The deeper question, which must be faced in an ecumenical context, arises between Churches, such as the Orthodox and the Roman Catholic on the one hand and the Western confessional bodies on the other, concerning whether church structures must be fashioned on the historical model of the first centuries or may follow synodical principles which evolved much later and influenced not only ecclesiastical but parliamentary institutions.

Merging of Confessional Organizations

Denominational forms of Christian association are provisional, argued W. A. Visser 't Hooft before the Methodists at Oslo. Now it begins to appear that organizations of confessional families, which have evolved in relatively recent times, may also be regarded as provisional. The World Alliance of Reformed Churches and the International Congregational Council have taken decisive steps towards merging in 1970. The merger of two confessional organizations is, so far as we are aware, without precedent in modern times. This one is therefore a matter of exceptional interest.

"Over ten years of prayerful and harmonious discussions between the International Congregational Council and the World Alliance of Reformed

Churches", wrote General Secretary Marcel Pradervand of the W.A.R.C., "have taken place on the questions of closer relations between the two world families of churches". Conversations were officially approved on both sides by repeated actions as the discussions moved forward step by step towards merger. Official visitors or fraternal delegates were present at meetings of both organizations since 1958. Staff and officers have also kept in regular contact. A joint committee was formed in 1964 to prepare and present principles and proposals concerning relations between the two bodies.

A factor which contributed substantially towards union between the World Alliance and the I.C.C. was the fact that four of the twenty-one members of the I.C.C. are also members of the W.A.R.C. These are the United Churches of Canada, Jamaica and Grand Cayman, the United States, and Zambia. The I.C.C. is also "in fellowship" with four other United Churches which are members of the alliance. They are the Church of Christ in China, the United Church of North India, the United Church in Japan, and the United Church of Christ in the Philippines. In addition, Congregational and Presbyterian Churches are looking forward to union between themselves in Australia, New Zealand, and Great Britain, Union negotiations have begun in South Africa, Scotland and the Netherlands. The I.C.C. has member Churches in Argentina, Brazil, Czechoslovakia, Finland, Guyana, Madagascar, Samoa, South Africa, and Sweden. In many of these places ties exist or are being created with one or another of the 101 member Churches of the Alliance, which has twenty-eight members in Africa, twenty in Asia, three in Australia, twenty-eight in Europe, twelve in Latin America, and ten in North America.

A statement of "Principles", from which the factual data above has been taken, was circulated among I.C.C. and W.A.R.C. members. It also says:

> Both organizations have consistently gone on record in recognition and support of United Churches. Nearly all of their members are presently engaged in some form of church union negotiation or exploration which are in position to do so, in many instances involving the relations with churches belonging to traditions not normally associated with the names Congregational, Presbyterian or Reformed. In each case the intention has been to enter into a fuller relation with other Christian brethren, within one church, Catholic and Reformed. Accordingly, in principle the name "Reformed" by which these churches express their desire to be "continually reformed according to the Word of God" is applicable to any church which holds that same desire. Likewise, the name "Catholic" they would also claim for themselves, as representing their acknowledgement of Christ's presence even among the diverse fragments of a divided church, their identification with all the struggles of the Church and with its whole sanctified life throughout human history, and their will to live under and to pray for that fullness of community which Christ alone can bring, by the Witness of the Gospel and the power of the Holy Spirit.

Another ground for union is found in the fact that sixty-one of the Alliance's 101 members and seventeen of the I.C.C.'s twenty-one members are members of the World Council of Churches. The Principles express the desire of both families of Churches "to do nothing separately which can be done in co-operation and to enter as fully as facilities allow into its (the W.C.C.'s) programme, especially in the area of studies. We do not wish to administer Inter-Church Aid or other similar funds, but prefer to support aid programmes of the World Council of Churches, providing special counsel on the situation of minority churches." The Principles and proposals for union were adopted by the executive committees of the two organizations in 1966.

The draft constitution which is proposed for adoption in 1970 states that "the Church is founded solely upon Jesus Christ as Lord and . . . is one Body in the communion of the Holy Spirit under the headship of the one Lord, Jesus Christ". After outlining the histories of the two organizations, the constitution declares that they are joined into one organization under the name "The World Alliance of Reformed Churches (Presbyterian and Congregational)" and in shorter form: "The World Alliance of Reformed Churches".

It is significant that the W.A.R.C./I.C.C. merger will be open-ended, assuming that the constitution is adopted as proposed. Article II on membership, says that

> Any church which accepts Jesus Christ as Lord and Saviour, which holds the Scriptures of the Old and New Testaments to be the supreme authority in matters of faith and life; acknowledges the need for the continuing reformation of the Church catholic; whose position in faith and evangelism is in general agreement with that of the historic Reformed confessions, recognizing that the Reformed tradition is a biblical, evangelical and doctrinal ethos, rather than a narrow and exclusive definition of faith and order, shall be eligible for admission to the Alliance.

Article II concludes:

> United Churches which share this understanding of the nature and calling of the Church shall be eligible for admission. Membership in the Alliance does not restrict the relationship of any Church with other Churches or with other inter-Church bodies.

The ecumenical purpose which is exemplified in the merger and is implicit in the histories of the merged confessional bodies will be continued under the new World Alliance of Reformed Churches. Article III, section 9 of the proposed constitution states that a purpose of the Alliance shall be

> to facilitate the contribution to the ecumenical movement of the experiences and insights which the churches within the Reformed family have been given in their history, and to share with churches of other traditions within that movement, and particularly in the World Council of Churches, in the discovery of forms of church life and practice which will enable the people of God more fully to understand and express together God's will for his people.

The Alliance is to meet in General Council ordinarily once in five years. In the interval an executive committee serves in its stead, having full powers to speak and act for the Alliance in conformity with its constitution.

Member bodies of the W.A.R.C. and I.C.C. were asked to report their actions, favourable or unfavourable, on the proposals for merger by 30 June 1968. Officials of both families of Churches met at Uppsala at the time of the

Fourth Assembly of the World Council of Churches to receive the actions of the Churches, to summarize them, and to announce the result. Since the result is favourable, the Twentieth General Council of the World Alliance of Reformed Churches will become the Uniting Council.

Self-Evaluation of Confessional Families

After ten years of annual meetings, the secretaries of world confessional families produced a document at their 1967 meeting which will probably stand for some time as a statement of "the Place of World Confessional Families in the Ecumenical Movement". We quoted their definition for the term at the beginning of this chapter. Their statement explained that members of some families have a strong consciousness of belonging together as a universal fellowship, but others are hardly aware of any such bond. Some made the visible structure of their universal fellowship a part of their ecclesiology, while others think of structure as a "mere organizational convenience". Differences are explained in part by historical origins, in part by teachings about the nature of the Church, in part by relations with other Churches. Even the term confessional is misleading, says the statement, for not all families are bound together mainly by their "confession of faith". Not all depend upon organization to furnish the bond between Churches. "World Communion" is acceptable to some "because it points to the Eucharist as a bond of unity and even families which have not yet realized full communion are earnestly seeking to establish it as soon as possible". So families, which maintain unity in spite of diversity, seems to be the best term.

The 1967 statement recognized that world families are an historical fact and are "at present a necessity". Each Church has to give some expression to its universal character; but on the world scale this still adds up to division. So there is a necessary connection between world families and the World Council of Churches. Both are elements in the ecumenical movement. The W.C.C. reminds the world families of their limits and roles in the ecumenical movement. It gives them a place "to meet and co-operate" and thus to realize a fuller universality than any single world family will ever be able to realize. The world families remind the W.C.C. "that there is a true universality only if it is rooted in truth". Hence the W.C.C. and the families are interdependent.

Recognition of this interdependence, says the 1967 statement, leads to four conclusions. One is the need for contacts between the W.C.C. and the families and between the families themselves; if the ecumenical movement is to be furthered, these contacts should be co-ordinated. Second, there is need for greater exchange of information and co-ordination of studies. W.C.C. studies are mainly directed towards furthering the ecumenical task; world family studies "aim at clarifying the contribution to the ecumenical movement of churches within one tradition". The two kinds of studies should be related, for both are concerned with the theological problem of the catholicity of the Church and its practical results. The world families therefore welcome the invitation of the Secretariat of Faith and Order to appoint liaison officers for this purpose.

Third, more use should be made of the possibilities for practical co-operation between world families. These include the field of inter-Church aid, where W.C.C./L.W.F. co-operation is already widespread, and joint consultation and action for mission. Also in the Church's witness in international affairs an extension of the co-operation which already exists would be practical and much more effective. The revised constitution of the C.C.I.A. makes this possible. Finally, the multiplying problems of religious liberty in many countries invite closer W.C.C./World Families co-operation and co-ordination.

The statement ended with a paragraph which shows as clearly as anything that has been said by an ecumenical body in the direction in which the Churches are being moved:

> The number of churches engaged in union negotiations is rising. World Families whose member churches are committed to union require further conversations about the problems arising from this commitment. Everything possible should be done by the Confessional Families together, and by the Confessional Families and the World Council of Churches to encourage the realization of further unity among the churches.

Confessional Family Organizations

Brief descriptions of eleven of the world confessional family organizations follow. Each of these is entitled to appoint advisers to the Central Committee and to the Assemblies of the World Council of Churches. Each is invited to send representatives of the annual meetings of World Confessional families at Geneva and usually does so. In addition, the Ecumenical Patriarchate of Constantinople, the Patriarchate of Moscow, the Standing Committee of the Oriental Orthodox Churches, and the Pentecostal World Conference are entitled to appoint W.C.C. advisers and to be represented at annual meetings of the Confessional families at Geneva. Descriptions of the Orthodox Churches appear in Chapter 11 of this book.

The Anglican Communion

The Anglican communion consists of nineteen independent, autonomous, national, and regional churches, having a total membership of forty million. (See World Christian Handbook.) Its central office in London, established as recently as 1963, is directed in 1968 by Bishop Ralph Stanley Dean, who is secretary of "the Advisory Council on Missionary Strategy". The name Anglican does not appear in the title, although Bishop Dean is in fact also executive officer of the Anglican Communion and secretary to the Lambeth Conference, which meets each decade. All but one of the nineteen Churches are members of the World Council of Churches. In pointing out that "the Anglican is not a confessional body in the ordinary sense of the term" and that Anglican Churches are independent and autonomous, Bishop Dean notes:

> They are bound together chiefly by the fact that each is in communion with the See of Canterbury and with each other. There is no specifically Anglican Confession of Faith; there is no central authoritative structure; there is no

longer even one book of Common Prayer, for at least eight different rites now obtain, though all partake of a common shape of the liturgy. The Anglican Communion holds to the Holy Scriptures, the Catholic creeds of the undivided church, the Dominical Sacraments and the threefold order of bishops, priests and deacons.

The Advisory Council on Missionary Strategy operates under the terms of a document called *Mutual Responsibility and Interdependence in the Body of Christ*. While it was criticized at first as a step toward pan-Anglicanism, criticisms have abated as it is seen to be a channel of communication within the Anglican Communion and with the Church of Christ as a whole. In the last twenty years, the five new indigenous national Churches which have emerged within the Anglican Communion have all become constituent members of the World Council of Churches. Since Anglican provinces and dioceses in many parts of the world are included in plans for united Churches in their area, the Advisory Council on Missionary Strategy recommends that where such a scheme for church unity is approved by the province concerned, "the contribution brought to it by Anglicans should be in every way as whole-hearted and complete as possible". The council says these contributions should include capital and development funds and that financial or personal support from outside the area "should not be lessened because of the partici-pation of the church in unity Schemes". Unity conversations and negotiations in various stages and in many countries now include the Consultation on Church Union in America, dialogues with Orthodox and Roman Catholics, official visits between the Archbishop of Canterbury and their highest officials, and in some cases official commissions for continuing study.

The Baptist World Alliance

The Baptist World Alliance is a voluntary association between Baptists in seventy-eight unions or conventions of Churches having a total membership in 1968 of 25,914,000. An additional three million Baptists belong to Churches which are not members of the Alliance. The Alliance has headquarters in London and in Washington. It holds congresses every five years and publishes a monthly journal, "The Baptist World". Dr Josef Nordenhaug, its executive secretary, lives in Washington. Eleven of the seventy-eight member denomina-tions are members of the World Council of Churches. The B.W.A. exists to increase fellowship and co-operation between Baptist Churches. It is specifi-cally enjoined against interfering with the independence of member Churches or the administrative functions of existing organizations.

A 144-person executive committee governs the B.W.A. between Congresses. Each member body elects at least one representative. About two-thirds of the budget of the Baptist World Alliance comes from the ten-million member Southern Baptist Convention (U.S.A.) whose only official ecumenical rela-tionship on a membership basis is with the B.W.A. The B.W.A. was not represented by observers at the Second Vatican Council, but did authorize its general secretary to send observers to the meeting in Rome on the Lay Apostolate in 1967. The B.W.A. has a relief department; but several of its member Churches contribute to human need through the Inter-Church Aid department of the W.C.C. and through Church World Service in the U.S.A. Regional sub-organizations of the B.W.A. exist in North America, where nine-tenths of all Baptists live, and in Europe. The B.W.A. has study commissions working on Baptist doctrine, mission and evangelism, religious liberty and human rights, Christian teaching and training, and co-operative Christianity. The last of these commissions was authorized in 1967.

Friends World Committee for Consultation

Forty-six "Yearly Meetings" of the Society of Friends form the Friends World Committee for Consultation, which has an office in Birmingham, England. It was created in 1937, at a world conference in the U.S.A. The first such world conference was held in London in 1920. A few Yearly Meetings are not represented in F.W.C.C., being mainly those in the Evangelical Friends Alliance. About 200,000 persons form the membership of the Society of Friends.

The F.W.C.C. is not in any sense a controlling body. It seeks to encourage consultation and help Friends understand the world-wide character of the Society, to strengthen the spiritual life within the Society, to keep under review the Quaker contribution in world affairs, and "to promote understanding between Friends of all countries and members of other branches of the Christian Church and with members of other religious faiths". The World Committee sent observers to the Second Vatican Council, to the Prague Christian Peace Conference, and it sends representatives to participate in the International Association for Liberal Christianity and Religious Freedom.

The Friends United Meeting and the Friends General Conference, both of the U.S.A., were among the 147 Churches which constituted the World Council of Churches in 1948. They include over half the total membership of the Society of Friends in the world. Yearly Meetings hold membership in the National Councils of Churches in the United States, Canada, the Netherlands, Ireland, Australia, New Zealand, Madagascar, Pemba, and Rhodesia. Mrs Blanche Shaffer is general secretary of the F.W.C.C.

The International Congregational Council

The International Congregational Council was founded in London in 1891 as an *ad hoc* gathering without permanent organization. It was reorganized in 1949 as a constitutional body with staff. It holds assemblies every four or five years. It does not regard itself as a confessional body and plans to merge with the World Alliance of Reformed Churches in 1970. Its head offices are in London. Dr Ralph R. G. Calder is its executive secretary.

In 1966, when it held its tenth assembly, representatives of seventeen constituent member Churches met at Swansea, United Kingdom. The largest Congregational Church, having about 1,250,000 members, entered the United Church of Christ, U.S.A. in 1957, but this did not invalidate its tie to the I.C.C., which has several United Churches in its membership. In fact, about seventy-five per cent of members of Churches in the I.C.C. belong to United Churches. Other Churches are considering mergers.

From its earliest meeting the I.C.C. had an ecumenical purpose, inviting discussion on Congregationalism's relationship with the "Church Catholic". The 1966 Assembly "agreed without dissent" to approve the proposed merger of the I.C.C. with the World Alliance of Reformed Churches. "At the same time", Dr Calder wrote, "there remains a strong conviction among many that certain Congregational (though not denominational) convictions as to the liberty of the Christian man, and as to the dangers of ecclesiastical uniformity and rigidity and particularly as to the essential wrongness of clericalism, call for some form of continued witness, whether it calls itself Congregational or not."

The Lutheran World Federation

The largest and one of the most distinctively "Confessional" bodies is the Lutheran World Federation, which has in its membership a large share of the 72,500,000 Lutherans in the world. It is about a year older than the World Council of Churches, with which it shares the Ecumenical Centre in Geneva. Its total number of employees is around 1,000. In Geneva it has a staff of over sixty persons, of whom twenty-one are executives. The L.W.F. general secretary is Mr Andre Appel. The Federation was constituted in 1947; it succeeded a more loosely knit consultative organization called the Lutheran World Convention, which held its first world meeting in 1923. The *Lutheran World*, which the L.W.F. publishes quarterly, has a circulation of 4,000. It takes a leading part in the discussion of relations between confessionalism and the ecumenical movement. Lutheran world assemblies are held at six-year intervals.

The Lutheran World Federation is a "free association of Lutheran churches". According to its constitution,

> It shall not exercise churchly functions on its own authority, nor shall it have power to legislate for the churches belonging to it or to limit the autonomy of any member church.

Its functions are:

> to further a united witness before the world to the gospel of Jesus Christ as the power of God for salvation; cultivate unity of faith and confession among the Lutheran Churches of the world; develop fellowship and co-operation in study among Lutherans; foster Lutheran interest in, concern for, and partici- pation in, ecumenical movements; support Lutheran Churches and groups as they endeavour to meet the spiritual needs of other Lutheran Churches and groups to help meet physical needs.

It can take action on behalf of one or more member Churches in such matters as they commit to it.

The L.W.F. service for refugees has since 1947 provided new homelands for over 100,000 refugees. The World Service division of L.W.F. handles relief commodities and assistance to the value of $10 million per year; its other budgets total around $3 million. In its earliest years most of its money came from the United States; now gifts from Germany and Sweden exceed those from the U.S.A. The L.W.F. owns and operates the Radio Voice of the Gospel, a powerful station costing $1.5 million located in Ethiopia, which makes half of its broadcast time available to Churches affiliated with the W.C.C. The L.W.F. also established the Lutheran Foundation for Inter-Confessional Research at Strasbourg, France, which carries on study in basic theological problems, currently those concerned with Roman Catholic/ Protestant questions.

Its world missions department grew out of the needs of "orphaned missions" during the Second World War and now serves Churches and missions in Asia and Africa. A final area of work is the L.W.F. Community Development Liaison and Validation service. It serves as a link between Lutheran Churches and operating projects of general welfare or economic development and fund-raising agencies with resources to put into such activities. Co-operation between the W.C.C. and the L.W.F. is continuous and many-sided. Carl H. Mau, Jr, associate general secretary of the L.W.F., says of the two organizations: "Their continued close coexistence to the present day has undoubtedly contributed greatly to the influence that each has had on the other and to the mutual understanding of their respective purposes that exists between them, particularly on the staff level."

The late Franklin Clark Fry, then President of the L.W.F., said at the opening of its Fourth Assembly:

> We in Helsinki are here consciously as a part of the Church of God. We make no pretence to be the whole of it. We would do violence both to our fathers and to ourselves, and of course also to the truth, if we were to do so, for our fathers designed the noble expositions of the Word of God to which we hold, not as partisan documents, but as ecumenical confessions. As their sons we are prepared in spirit to reach out to brethren everywhere in a search for the fuller oneness of all who call Christ Lord in the midst of a hostile world, on the basis of a common adherence to him who is and who teaches the truth.[1]

Old Catholic Churches

Old Catholic Churches of Austria, Germany, the Netherlands, Switzerland, the Polish-Catholic Church in Poland, and the Polish National Catholic Church in America are members of the World Council of Churches. The Old Catholic Churches in Czechoslovakia and Yugoslavia are not yet members. Old Catholic Churches are self-governing national Churches but one in the faith, deriving their origins from Latin Christendom. The International Conferences of the Old Catholic Bishops, founded in 1889 as the Union of Utrecht, expressed their unity. The first originated in Holland in 1723, when the Chapter of Utrecht maintained its ancient right to elect the Archbishop of Utrecht, against the opposition of Rome. The term "Old Catholic" was adopted to mean original Catholicism. The Old Catholic Churches of Germany, Switzerland, and Austria were formed in 1870 in consequence of their protest against the dogmas of the First Vatican Council concerning papal supremacy and papal infallibility. The Polish National Catholic Church in America was constituted between 1897 and 1907; the Churches in Czechoslovakia, Poland, and Yugoslavia after the First World War. Old

[1] *Proceedings of the Fourth Assembly of the Lutheran World Federation* (Helsinki, 30 July to 11 August 1963), p. 37. Published by the Lutheran World Federation, Geneva.

Catholic Churches are found in eight countries and have a total of around 500,000 members. They have missions in France and Italy.

On 7 November 1966 Cardinal Alfrink of the Roman Catholic Church, at a public ceremony in the Old Catholic cathedral in Utrecht, announced that the Roman Catholic Church renounced the requirement that the Old Catholic Church accept papal condemnations of the Old Catholic Church concerning Jansenism, especially the papal statements issued in 1665 and 1713. Since Cardinal Alfrink's pronouncement at Utrecht, official dialogues between the Old Catholic Churches and the Roman Catholic Church have begun in Holland, Germany, Austria, and Switzerland. Consistent with their inter-communion with the Anglican Communion, the Old Catholic Churches support an Anglican mission in South Africa. They are studying the union discussions between the Anglican and Methodist Churches. Also, the dialogue between Old Catholic and Orthodox Churches has taken on new vigour. In Switzerland they shared in the preparation of a document on mixed marriages, published by the Federation of Swiss Protestant Churches and the Roman Catholic Bishop's Conference. In 1965 the Old Catholic Churches extended their intercommunion with the Anglicans to the Episcopal Reformed Church of Spain, the Lusitanian Church (Portugal), and the Independent Church of the Philippines.

The Salvation Army

So far as the ecumenical movement is concerned, the Salvation Army is regarded as a Church, so it is represented in meetings of the World Confessional Bodies. It works in seventy countries and has 18,563 officers (or ministers) who preach the gospel in 146 languages through 16,190 preaching stations. It publishes 129 periodicals with a circulation of over two million. The Army conducts social service programmes through 2,000 social centres, sixty-nine hospitals, and over 800 day schools. Its primary aim is "to proclaim the Gospel of the Lord Jesus Christ to men, women and young people untouched or uninfluenced by the Gospel and to develop its membership into a fighting force of God".[1]

The headquarters of the Salvation Army is in London, where its work began in 1865. The General of the Army is elected by a high council consisting of Salvation Army leaders from all over the world. World leaders meet at agreed intervals to review work and to plan further advance. Relationships between the Army and the historic Churches are marked by free and friendly co-operation. It is a long-established rule with the Army not to proselytize and not to criticize the doctrine, worship, or organization of Churches. The Salvation Army is a full member of the World Council of Churches and has been since its beginning. Commissioner F. A. Evans says:

> There has been no change in the relationship of the Salvation Army with the W.C.C. during the last twenty years except a growing awareness of the usefulness of the W.C.C. and a greater desire to enter into fraternal relationship with all members.

[1] Figures from *The Salvation Army Year Book, 1967*. Published by Salvation Publishing and Supplies Ltd, London W.C.1.

Mennonite World Conference

Organized in 1925, the Mennonite World Conference is generally represented in the meeting of confessional organizations in Geneva. The Mennonites of the Netherlands are members of the World Council of Churches. Several North American Mennonite Conferences are members of the National Association of Evangelicals. The number of Mennonites in the world is estimated to be 400,000.

In the forty-two years between the first and the eighth world conferences, the Mennonites set up a General Council, which normally meets annually. Its executive secretary, Cornelius J. Dyck, is a full-time faculty member of the Mennonite Biblical Seminary. The office of the council is now located in Elkhart, Indiana, but is "passed around as the brotherhood sees fit". In addition, there is a Mennonite Central Committee, which was organized in 1920 as a relief and service agency. Its headquarters are in Akron, Ohio. It carries on humanitarian work in Vietnam, India, Africa, Latin America, and elsewhere. Co-operation in relief and humanitarian work has allayed Mennonite fear of "entangling alliances", so that Professor Dyck says:

> There seems to have emerged a new readiness on the part of Mennonites to dialogue with any and all who are willing and to leave the fruit of such encounter to future developments.

World Alliance of Reformed Churches

The oldest of the organized confessional families came into existence in 1875 as the "Alliance of Reformed Churches Throughout the World Holding the Presbyterian System". Its first assembly was held in Edinburgh in 1877. Present were delegates representing forty-one Churches in fourteen countries. Now the Alliance serves 109 churches of the Reformed Church Family in seventy countries, having a total membership of around 55 million. Renamed the World Alliance of Reformed Churches, its budget is less than $100,000. Its staff numbers seven. Its offices were moved from Edinburgh to Geneva in 1948 and are now in the Ecumenical Centre. Its general secretary is Marcel Pradervand.

The Alliance holds a world meeting every five or six years. An area council meets in Europe about as often; the North American area council meets annually. Fully ninety-five per cent of all Reformed and Presbyterian Churches hold membership in the Alliance, and sixty-two of the 109 member Churches of the W.A.R.C. are also members of the World Council of Churches. They have furnished a considerable share of the W.C.C. leadership. In 1951 the W.A.R.C. executive committee declared:

> The Reformed tradition in post-Reformation Christianity is thus by nature ecumenical, that is to say, it is committed to the pursuit of Christian unity upon the basis of loyal commitment to the essential verities in the Christian faith.

In its meeting held in 1949, the Executive Committee of the Alliance set forth its programme as (*a*) support for Inter-Church Aid as administered by the World Council of Churches, (*b*) development of contacts between

Churches and ecumenical organizations, and (c) engagement in common study. In 1954 the General Council of the Alliance reaffirmed the position previously taken concerning Inter-Church Aid, saying that the Alliance "is not organized for the administration of inter-church aid and does not propose so to organize because of the conviction of many of our churches that the giving and receiving of aid has implications beyond our Reformed family". It was through the initiative of the Alliance that representatives of confessional families first began to hold meetings in 1957. The Alliance persistently tries to act as an intermediary between the ecumenical movement and those Reformed Churches which remain outside it. The World Alliance and the International Congregational Council plan to merge in 1970.

World Convention of the Churches of Christ (Disciples)

The World Convention of the Churches of Christ (Disciples) was begun in 1930 in the United States, where about nine-tenths of the two million members of Churches belonging to the Convention live. Its office is in New York, although the denominational offices are in Indianapolis. The Reverend L. V. Kirkpatrick is its executive secretary. Its principal activity is to hold a world convention at five-year intervals. Each convention elects an executive committee to which the executive secretary is responsible. In the intervals between conventions work is carried on through four committees: study, finance, programme, and inter-faith relations.

The preamble to the constitution of the World Convention says: "The World Convention of Churches of Christ (Disciples) exists in order to show more fully the essential oneness of the churches in the Lord Jesus Christ". Other purposes named are to "impart inspiration", to "cultivate fellowship", and to "promote unity". The executive says that "the World Convention considers its ecumenical responsibilities include helping to maintain ecumenical dialogue within the world family of Churches of Christ and Disciples of Christ itself". This is not easy, as the following paragraph will suggest:

The Christian Church, Disciples of Christ, is by far the largest denomination of this "confessional family", assuming that this term applies. It is a member of the World and National Councils of Churches and of the Consultation on Church Union. Since 1961 conversations looking toward church union have been carried on under the auspices of the Consultation. Considerable progress has been made. So the preoccupations of "co-operative" Disciples with union and the confessional preoccupations of Churches which think ecumenically only in denominational terms tend to diverge. These divergencies widen as the movements for and against union grow. What will be the role of the World Convention in the event its largest constituent denomination enters into a United Church does not yet appear.

The World Methodist Council

Twenty Methodist denominations having Churches in eighty-six countries make up the association known as the World Methodist Council. It has offices in London and Lake Junaluska, North Carolina and has voted to set up an office in Geneva. The Handbook of Information of the World Methodist Council says that there are in the world 18,824,352 Methodists, of whom over 14 million are in North America.[1]

The World Methodist Council was formed in 1951. It succeeded a series of Methodist ecumenical conferences, held at intervals beginning in 1881. When the W.M.C. was formed, the launching conference adopted a message to the Methodists of the world which said, *inter alia*,

> We wish to affirm explicitly that, far from being in rivalry with the World Council of Churches, or wishing to isolate ourselves from the movement toward the reunion of the churches, our purpose in promoting the closer unity of Methodism is that this may make a stronger contribution to the larger unity of Christ's Church throughout the world.

The W.M.C. holds conferences at intervals of several years, the last being held in London in 1966. The 1961 revision of its constitution set as the first purpose "to deepen the fellowship of the Methodist people . . .". The second was "to foster Methodist participation in the ecumenical movement and to promote the unity of Methodist witness and service in that movement". The third was "to advance unity of theological and moral standards in the Methodist churches of the world". The principal activity under this head is the Oxford Theological Institute, held for ten days every two or three years, in which around 100 Methodists participate. The W.M.C. also has a committee which studies all union proposals which involve Methodists and offers advice when requested. The organization also arranges the exchange of preachers.

The Methodist Church in the United States (which became the United Methodist Church in 1968) has included in its organization congregations, conferences, and episcopal areas in many countries. The 1968 general conference, in which the Methodist and the Evangelical United Brethren Churches became the United Methodist Church, granted twenty-eight annual conferences in fourteen countries permission to become autonomous bodies or to merge with other Churches. Since the United Methodist Church itself is a member of the Consultation on Church Union in the U.S.A. and the Methodist Church in Great Britain is considering reunion with the Church of England, it is safe to predict that the World Methodist Structure Congress, which is to be held before or during 1972, will not suffer for lack of business to discuss. Where the World Methodist Council will emerge from this discussion it is impossible to predict.

Since many confessional families confront similar problems, it seems likely that discussions between world confessional families will sharply increase in vigour and relevance in the near future.

---

[1] *World Methodist Council Handbook of Information, 1966–1971.* Published by the secretariat, W.M.C., Lake Junaluska, N.C., U.S.A.).

6

Faith and Order 1948–1968

MEREDITH B. HANDSPICKER

F

Introduction

> St Paul strikes sectarianism of all ages between the eyes by calling divisions "carnal" ... Division in the eyes of this intense man is fatal to the life of the church.[1]

Bishop Charles Brent was also "an intense man". Deeply moved by the great World Missionary Conference in Edinburgh in 1910, he was instrumental in having his Church, the Protestant Episcopal Church in the U.S.A., issue a call later that year which invited "all Christian bodies throughout the world which accept our Lord Jesus Christ as God and Saviour" to send delegates to a world conference to discuss questions "pertaining to the Faith and Order of the Church of Christ".[2] Divisions and divisiveness mark the life of the Church of Christ. Such division mars the effectiveness of the Church, and strikes at the very nature of the Church, its unity. "God calls man to unity—his ideal. Man calls to God for unity—his need."[3] Divided, the Church gets in its own way.

"The Faith and Order movement at its best is solely concerned with the truth."[4] Tissington Tatlow closes his history of Faith and Order up to 1948 with these words. The unity which the movement seeks is not obtained through ecclesiastical joinery, nor by compromise in matters of faith. Woven together in the complex motivation which gives life to the movement are a number of convictions: first, that the Church is intended by its Lord to be one; second, that only a truly united Church can function effectively in fulfilling its mission; third, that only in a Church which is one can the fullness of Christian truth be discerned.

In Lausanne Bishop Brent took as his text John 17. 20–3: "That they may be one ... that the world may believe". This has been a favourite text in the ecumenical movement; but the conviction that unity is of the essence of the Church rests not on this one text, but on the whole tenor of the apostolic writings.

In the British Faith and Order Conference in 1964, the theme of the meeting was "One Church, Renewed for Mission". The then chairman of the Faith and Order Working Committee, Dr Oliver Tomkins, the Bishop of Bristol, presided. In his remarks to the conference Bishop Tomkins noted that the missionary orientation of Faith and Order sought to insure that in coming into union we do not merely continue to follow old patterns, but discern the shape of the Church God demands of us today.

The concern for truth is manifest in the commission given to negotiators in Australia from the Congregational, Methodist, and Presbyterian Churches: to discover not "how we can reduce the different traditions to a common

---

[1] Bishop Charles Brent, "The Call to Unity", Lausanne, p. 6.

[2] Ibid., p. vii. For the history of Faith and Order prior to 1948 the reader is referred to the proceedings of both the Lausanne Conference and the Edinburgh Conference, the numbered papers in the "Old Series", Rouse and Neill, *A History of the Ecumenical Movement*, pp. 405ff, and relevant sections of Vischer, *A Documentary History of the Faith and Order Movement*.

[3] Ibid., p. 7.   [4] Rouse and Neill, op. cit., p. 441.

factor", but rather to seek the fullness of "what we must confess together today as the Faith of the Church".[1]

How have these motivations led to action? In what ways has the Faith and Order movement sought to bring about the unity of the Church, its more effective missionary thrust, and its growth into the fullness of Christian truth? Its work has been guided by two principles, first articulated in the constitution accepted in 1948: to draw the Churches out of isolation into conference, and to leave to the Churches all initiatives towards reunion with one another.[2]

As a Commission of the World Council, Faith and Order has kept its traditional function of "calling the churches out of isolation into conference". Membership in the Commission is not tied to membership in the World Council, nor is invitation to World Conferences on Faith and Order. Thus at the theological heart of the Council is a Commission now having among its membership not only representatives of conservative Protestant Churches and Pentecostal groups who do not feel able to join the Council, but Roman Catholic representatives as well. This *can* insure that the Council does not itself develop a provincial outlook which becomes that of just one more ecclesiastical in-group. Later in this chapter we shall examine in detail the kinds of study and activities by which Faith and Order has sought to deepen understanding among the Churches and open up possibilities for greater unity.

But while Faith and Order exists to serve church unity, the second principle in its constitution states that only the Churches themselves are competent to initiate actual negotiations for unity. Such initiatives have been going on for a long while, and the results have been recorded in surveys of union negotiations.[3] While initiative continues to remain with the Churches, we shall see how Faith and Order has become more and more involved in the movement towards union.

One way to examine the growth of a movement would be to trace its development chronologically: What did it do from one important conference to another? Those who wish to trace the history of Faith and Order in this manner can be aided by the summary histories prepared for each Assembly of the World Council.[4] Such a study can well supplement the approach taken in this chapter, which will be to examine the various studies undertaken by the Faith and Order Commission in order to discover what development has occurred, and what consensus has been reached, in each area of concern. This will provide a record of how Faith and Order has sought to be true to its vocation to seek the truth.

But truth is never sought abstractly. The search is both pragmatic and

[1] *Ecumenical Review*, vol. xviii, (July 1966), p. 362.

[2] FO, no. 1, p. 68. Compare FO, no. 50, p. 169 for the current wording.

[3] The first such was published by H. Paul Dougless, *A Decade of Objective Progress in Church Unity: 1927–1936*. New York 1937. It was followed by a survey made by Stephen Neill, *Towards Church Union: 1937–1952*. London 1952. Since then biennial surveys have been prepared by the Faith and Order Secretariat and published in the *Ecumenical Review*, April 1954, October 1955, April 1957, January 1960, April 1962, July 1964, and July 1966.

[4] *The First Six Years: 1948–1954*. Geneva 1964. *Evanston to New Delhi: 1954–1961*. Geneva 1961. *New Delhi to Uppsala: 1961–1968*. Geneva 1968.

personal. In this case the search is for the sake of church unity; we shall therefore turn after a survey of the studies to an examination of Faith and Order in relation to the movement for church union. The search is carried out by persons; we shall in closing discuss the people of Faith and Order, those individuals and their organizational means of co-operation whereby the work of Faith and Order has been carried forward.

Faith and Order Studies

The Nature of Unity

Competing claims and counter-claims compound confusion. The missionary task of the Church and its claim to preach the truth are impeded by disunity and divisiveness. But in our search together for unity, what is the nature of the goal which we are seeking? At the beginning of Faith and Order work, there was but a listing of differing viewpoints concerning the nature of unity.[1] By 1937 the delegates to Edinburgh had a somewhat clearer vision of the goal, which is to "realize the idea of the Church as one living body, worshipping and serving God in Christ".[2] This would involve both an inner spiritual unity and that outward unity "which expresses itself in mutual recognition, co-operative action, and corporate or institutional unity".[3]

At Amsterdam the basis for the search for outward unity was articulated: "God has *given* to His people in Jesus Christ a unity which is His creation and not our achievement".[4] The authors of this statement, coming from the section on "The Universal Church in God's Design", included some of the outstanding theological figures of the day: Karl Barth, Edmund Schlink, K. E. Skydsgaard, George Florovsky, and Douglas Horton—the latter four all to be exceptionally active in subsequent Faith and Order work. They wrought well, for this notion of the givenness of our unity undergirded all subsequent Faith and Order discussion of the nature of the unity we seek. Broad lines were indicated concerning the latter by the Amsterdam section on "The Church's Witness to God's Design"; the Churches were called to "move forward, as God guides them, to further unity in faith, in fellowship, at the table of the Lord, and in united proclamation of the word of life".[5]

The theme of "outward" unity which was introduced at Edinburgh was further developed at the Third World Conference in Lund, 1952. "We are agreed that there are not two churches, one visible and the other invisible, but one Church which must find visible expression on earth."[6] While the delegates differed on whether certain doctrinal, sacramental, and ministerial forms are of the essence of the Church, they looked forward to a time when all Christians could have unrestricted communion in sacrament and fellowship with each other.

Insistence on the visibility of unity was at variance with another World Council document on "The Church, the Churches and the World Council of Churches", adopted by the Central Committee at Toronto in 1950. There it

---

[1] Lausanne, pp. 465ff.   [2] Edinburgh, p. 250.   [3] Ibid., p. 259.
[4] Amsterdam, p. 51 (italics inserted).   [5] Ibid., p. 69.   [6] Lund, p. 33.

was clearly stated that "membership in the World Council does not imply the acceptance of a specific doctrine concerning the nature of church unity".[1] Among the various options listed in the statement was one which "held that visible unity is inessential or even undesirable."[2] The main point of this earlier statement was the insistence that no doctrine concerning church unity was a prerequisite for membership in the Council. But to insist that for this reason no growth in consensus among the members could be achieved would be to cut at the very heart of the ecumenical movement and to rest satisfied with the *status quo*. Lund was one more step in moving away from the *status quo*. It indicated a growing agreement on the "notes of unity"—one of these was to be "visibility".

At the Evanston Assembly in 1954 the givenness of our unity was assumed, as was our task to manifest it "not for the sake of the Church as an historical society, but for the sake of the world". "The being and unity of the Church belong to Christ and therefore to His mission."[3] The Assembly also underscored the dynamic inherent in the ecumenical movement—its opposition to the *status quo*. Reaffirming the Amsterdam covenant to "stay together", the Assembly stated, "But beyond that, as the Holy Spirit may guide us, we intend to unite."[4] If this were to be the intention, a still clearer vision of the goal was necessary.

Such a situation challenged Faith and Order to rethink its own role in the ecumenical movement. In 1957 a committee, chaired by Dr Oliver Tomkins, was constituted to study "The Future of Faith and Order",[5] and it brought in its interim report the next year. While it agreed that no one definition of unity can be demanded as a condition of membership in the Council, it nevertheless underscored the task of Faith and Order "to stand for the unity of the Church as the will of God, and for a ceaseless effort to know what obedience to that will means concretely."[6] In that same year, 1958, Bishop Lesslie Newbigin, a member of the committee, published a book in which he developed his own vision of unity. In part he said,

> For myself I do not believe that we can be content with anything less than a form of unity which enables all who confess Christ as Lord to be recognizably one family in each place and all places, united in the visible bonds of word, sacrament, ministry and congregational fellowship, and in the invisible bond which the Spirit Himself creates through these means, one family offering to all men everywhere the secret of reconciliation with God the Father.[7]

In 1959 Bishop Newbigin presented the Working Committee with a paper detailing his views of the nature of "churchly unity".[8] After revision this was added to the beginning of the report on the Future of Faith and Order which was then submitted to the Central Committee of the World Council meeting in Rhodes that year, further revised by the Commission in 1960, and this introductory section sent on for consideration by the section on Unity at the

[1] Vischer, op. cit., p. 171.   [2] Loc. cit.   [3] Evanston, p. 85.
[4] Ibid., p. 90.   [5] FO, no. 25, p. 28.   [6] FO, no. 26, p. 47.
[7] Lesslie Newbigin, *One Body, One Gospel, One World* (London 1958), p. 56.
[8] FO, no. 27, p. 2.

Assembly in New Delhi, 1961.[1] This led to the now-famous New Delhi Statement on Unity, which the Assembly voted to approve and commend to the Churches "for study and appropriate action". The key paragraph, a sentence of Pauline complexity, indicates the growth in consensus on unity since Lausanne.

> We believe that the unity which is both God's will and his gift to his Church is being made visible as all in each place who are baptized into Jesus Christ and confess him as Lord and Saviour are brought by the Holy Spirit into one fully committed fellowship, holding the one apostolic faith, preaching the one Gospel, breaking the one bread, joining in common prayer, and having a corporate life reaching out in witness and service to all and who at the same time are united with the whole Christian fellowship in all places and all ages in such wise that ministry and members are accepted by all, and that all can act and speak together as occasion requires for the tasks to which God calls his people.
>
> It is for such unity that we believe we must pray and work.[2]

While there was a dearth of official church reaction, the phrase "all in each place" caught the imagination of churchmen all over the world. The power of the phrase is evident in the response it evoked from the British Faith and Order Conference in 1964. There the section on "All in Each Place" issued a call to the British Council of Churches to covenant to reach union by an agreed date, hopefully not later than 1980.[3] Perhaps one reason for the warm reception of the statement was its concreteness. Lund had agreed that the quest of the ecumenical movement is for visible unity; in the New Delhi Statement the marks of such unity were spelled out and the implications made clear for the Church "in each place". This brought abstract theorizing down to earth, and the implications of church union for the "grassroots" were specific. Faith and Order was at last beginning to fill in the picture of the kind of unity we are seeking together. Men and women could see what this would mean for them in the places where they lived out their lives.

Criticisms came in, however. While the goal was stated, the way to it was not. While the unity of all in each place was spelled out, the relationship of those in one "place" to those in other "places" was not. The catholicity of the Church was indicated ("united with the whole Christian fellowship in all places and all ages"), but its "marks" were not given.

Further impetus was given to consider catholicity by the calling of the Second Vatican Council in 1962. A number of Faith and Order Commission members were observers at the Council, and Professor K. E. Skydsgaard of Denmark and the then Research Secretary of the Commission, Dr Lukas Vischer, were at all its sessions. This increase in communication was furthered by the presence of Roman Catholic observers at the Fourth World Conference on Faith and Order in Montreal in 1963. There one evening session was devoted

---

[1] See MRCC (1959), pp. 175ff; FO, no. 31, pp. 113ff.
[2] New Delhi, p. 116. A collection of reactions to the statement compiled from press reports, articles, and official church actions, was prepared by Mr Mark Santer and is in the Faith and Order archives.
[3] *Unity Begins at Home* (London 1964), p. 77.

to a consideration of catholicity;[1] an address on "Protestant Catholicity" was delivered at an ecumenical rally during the conference; and the sections themselves grappled with the question.

Both Section I on "The Church in the Purpose of God" and V on "All in Each Place" discussed catholicity in terms of its "qualitative" character. It was discerned in terms of the participation of each Church or congregation in Christ, and therefore related to Churches of other times and places. The whole Catholic Church is present in every local congregation gathered for the hearing of the Word and the celebration of the Lord's Supper.[2] Granted that this is the heart of catholicity, what does it mean for the organized life of the Churches?

At its meeting in Aarhus in 1964 the Working Committee appointed some of its number, together with consultants, to pursue the study of unity. Their report was presented to the Commission in Bristol in 1967 and accepted as the basis for discussion in Section I of the Assembly in Uppsala in 1968.[3] Entitled "The Holy Spirit and the Catholicity of the Church", this document seeks to supplement the christological definition of catholicity adumbrated at Montreal, to root it clearly in the trinitarian faith, and to pursue further the meaning of the phrase in the New Delhi Statement: "are brought together by the Holy Spirit into one fully committed fellowship". The kernel of this document is found in two questions: "When will God's gift of unity in the Spirit lead us to a visible union of all Christians? How can we find one common life in which it is not necessary to press forms and ways into a single mould?"[4]

Unlike the New Delhi Statement, this latest attempt to articulate the nature of the unity we seek does not have one compendious paragraph summarizing its conclusions. It is perhaps too early for that. But it expresses a clear hope that the Churches of the world will be able to speak and act together, perhaps through a universal council "which will speak of the faith which all confess and the obedience to which all are called". In its[5] concluding sentence the commentary on the statement specifies the ultimate aim of the unity we seek, for it is more than just the unity of the Church. "Christians work in the certainty that the unity and destiny of the human race depends upon the faithfulness of God."[6]

One can discern clearly a growing consensus among the member Churches of the World Council since 1948. In Amsterdam they "intended to stay together"; at Lund unity was sought by focusing on the common centre, Christ; in New Delhi they affirmed the oneness of "all in each place"; at Montreal they sought for catholicity amongst the diversity of theologies; at Bristol they began to take steps to indicate what catholicity implies. The twenty years have been difficult ones. Often the goal has not seemed clear

---

[1] Addresses were given by Archpriest Vitaly Borovoy of the Russian Orthodox Church, and Professor Claude Welch of the Methodist Church, U.S.A. For the full texts see the *Ecumenical Review* (October 1963), pp. 26–42.

[2] See Montreal, pp. 45f (para. 24) and pp. 80ff.

[3] For the full text see *Drafts for Sections* (Geneva 1968), pp. 7–27.

[4] Ibid., p. 11.   [5] Ibid., p. 18.   [6] Ibid., p. 27.

when the exigencies of immediate problems clouded one's vision. Yet seen in short compass the progress towards clarifying the kind of unity sought by the ecumenical movement has been steady and cumulative. Only the future actions of Churches and Christians all over the globe will demonstrate what real authority this growth in consensus exercises. But this consensus concerning church unity is not without roots. It has been supported by a sub-structure of other Faith and Order studies.

Ecclesiology

We have so far examined one aspect of this topic, namely the nature of church unity. To deal in full with Faith and Order's work on the doctrine of the Church over the past twenty years would be impossible in the scope of this chapter. The reader is therefore referred to the documents cited in the course of this section; not only would a wealth of material have to be covered, scores of theologians and churchmen would have to be mentioned as well. What we shall be examining is the result of hundreds of man-hours, miles of travel, and scholarly dedication. This is true of all Faith and Order work, for at bottom it is a highly personal affair.

In order to grasp what has happened in the course of the last twenty years, we shall try to see whether any overall pattern has emerged. The best way to begin is to see the state of affairs shortly after 1948. The Edinburgh Conference had laid plans for international theological commissions. Between 1948 and the Lund Conference in 1952 these commissions were drawing the results of their work together. The preparatory volume for Lund entitled "The Nature of the Church" is an excellent indication of where Faith and Order had come in ecclesiology. It is, in effect, a monument to what has been termed "comparative ecclesiology". Its essays describe different Churches and communions in terms of their "distinctives". It is also the end of a road. In "A Word to the Churches" the Lund Conference reported:

> We have seen clearly that we can make no real advance towards unity if we only compare our several conceptions of the nature of the Church and the traditions in which they are embodied.[1]

To get beyond this impasse, the Conference recommended that in the future, Faith and Order treat the doctrine of the Church "in close relation both to the doctrine of Christ and to the doctrine of the Holy Spirit".[2] Rather than to compare positions, people from all Churches were asked to study together the relationship between God and his Church. The full trinitarian thrust was made clear in a recommendation from the next World Conference, held at Montreal in 1963. There the section on "The Church in the Purpose of God" requested further study of "the proper relation of creation and redemption".[3]

It would appear in retrospect that the study of the doctrine of the Church over the past twenty years has in fact been carried on at least implicitly with reference to a trinitarian understanding of God. This becomes clearer as we

---

[1] Lund, p. 15.   [2] Ibid., p. 22.   [3] Montreal, p. 43n.

look at the various studies and see from what perspective they view the Church.

A need was felt as far back as 1937 to study the Church as a part of the created order. An American group had been working on "the non-theological factors in the making and unmaking of church union". More accurately these factors can be termed those aspects of the Church which characterize it as an organization among other organizations. A letter by Professor C. H. Dodd, read at the Commission meeting in 1949, spoke of "unavowed motives in ecumenical discussions". These concerns were then discussed in more detail just prior to Lund at the Ecumenical Institute in Bossey. The group concluded: "Such factors have acquired enormous power over us. They are not incidental: they are compounded of the very stuff of earthly history and human sin."[1] As Dr Ernest Payne later observed, if a thorough study in the area of the so-called "non-theological "factors were pursued it would have finally to deal with the Christian doctrine of creation and history.[2]

Many factors could be studied. The Commission decided in 1955 to isolate "institutionalism" for examination and constituted a study commission for the purpose. In its interim report published in 1961 the study commission put the problem clearly:

> Granted that institutions are an integral aspect of the divine–human nature of the Church, the question inevitably arises: On what basis is it possible to distinguish between constitutive and permanent and, on the other hand, derivative and historically variable features?[3]

Sociological analysis and case studies were pursued to seek further clarification of the problem. The study brought to awareness the intransigent quality of "organizational inertia" whereby the Church, along with other institutions, has a built-in resistance to change.[4] In its pursuit of sociological analysis the study has enabled the theological questions to be posed more precisely and pointedly.

Further work along these lines was recommended by the Commission in Aarhus in 1964 when it initiated a study entitled "Spirit, Order and Organization". Careful empirical study was to be continued; but the aim would be to analyse the process of change, rather than the resistance to change, in the Church. In such a way it was hoped that the relationship between the Holy Spirit and the Church would be clarified. Yet here too the Church itself would be studied empirically, namely as a part of the created order.[5]

For the most part the study of institutionalism had proceeded only partially aware of its theological rootage. However, at Montreal the desire for an

---

[1] C. H. Dodd, G. R. Cragg, Jacques Ellul, *Social and Cultural Factors in Church Divisions*, FO, no. 10, p. 32.

[2] FO, no. 17, p. 37.

[3] *The Old and the New in the Church* (London 1961), FO, no. 34, p. 78.

[4] The final report of the Commission is published in *Faith and Order Findings*, ed. Paul S. Minear (London 1963). Numerous essays and case-studies written in the course of study can be found in *Institutionalism and Church Unity*, ed. Nils Ehrenstrom and Walter G. Muelder (New York 1963).

[5] See FO, no. 44, pp. 58ff.; FO, no. 50, p. 156.

explicit examination of the Church in relation to creation was forcefully made. Because of the recommendations from that conference the Commission instituted a study in 1964 entitled "Creation, New Creation and the Unity of the Church". This took Faith and Order into the realm of more general theological study. But this was necessary both because the Church is rooted in the world, and because of increasing controversy over the proper relationship between Church and world, redemption and creation.

The first stage in this study was completed with the presentation of the report "God in Nature and History" to the Commission meeting in Bristol in 1967. It was largely drafted by Professor Hendrikus Berkhof of the Netherlands, and many people had had a part in the work. Historians, natural scientists, and behavioural scientists, as well as theologians, had entered into the discussion. After examining the various ways in which one can speak of the relationship between God and the world, the document points to the ambiguities involved in judgements concerning this relationship, and draws some consequences for our understanding of the Church.

The Christian has to know for himself where he sees the forces of the Spirit at work, so that he can support them, and where he sees the forces of darkness at work, so that he can resist them. But while we need to interpret history, there is no clear authority. Our various interpretations call for "confirmation, amendment or rejection by the common body of Christ".[1] For this reason the widest possible participation is desired and the need for the ecumenical movement itself is emphasized. Not only individuals but Churches must "wrestle to find a common interpretation of the contemporary situation, as the basis for their common endeavour".[2]

After accepting the document on "God in Nature and History" as the first stage of this new work, the Commission authorized as a second stage a study of "Man in Nature and History". In part this study is seen as "preventive medicine"—attempting to avoid new and different schisms over theological differences. As Tissington Tatlow had observed in his history of Faith and Order, today on no major theological question "do the dividing lines exactly correspond with denominational allegiance". He noted that this fluidity might betoken "the dawn of a much wider unity or of a different pattern of schism".[3] After noting the difficulties of the "generation gap" in the ecumenical movement, and the desire especially of the younger generation for involvement "in the world", the Bishop of Bristol, Dr Oliver Tomkins, spoke in his closing remarks at the Commission meeting in 1967 of this "new dimension" in Faith and Order work. This new study on "Man in Nature and History" is important, for "it is the task of Faith and Order to discern the New Man in Christ: to discern what is the form of a true humanity. To see the answer to that question is to understand afresh the form of the Church. The New Man cannot be a schizophrenic. A divided Church obscures from humanity the form of its own destiny."[4]

[1] *New Directions in Faith and Order*, FO, no. 50, p. 30.
[2] Loc. cit.
[3] Rouse and Neill, op. cit., p. 441.
[4] FO, no. 50, p. 164.

The institutionalism study, and those which followed it, had studied the Church as a created organization, part and parcel of the area open to sociological inquiry. In these new studies, however, the focus was on the manner in which the Church could respond to the work of God in the created order. In both cases we discover more about the Church in its relation to creation.

Major ecclesiological study between Lund and Montreal was carried out by the Theological Commission on Christ and the Church. Its interim report "One Lord, One Baptism" had as its subtitle "The Divine Trinity and the Unity of the Church."[1] The task was considered to involve an acknowledgement of the unity which exists already among the Churches, a unity in Christ and in the Spirit, and a drawing of the consequences for the actual life of the Churches in their search for outward unity. Among the salient points of the report were its insistence upon the inextricable relation of the Church to creation; its integral relationship to the Israel of God called prior to Christ; the distinct life of the Church based on the life, death, and resurrection of Christ; and the basis of the Church's unity in the perfect unity of the triune God.[2]

The study was primarily preoccupied with the redemptive function of the Church. In the accompanying paper on baptism emphasis is placed on baptism based upon the "efficacy of Christ's saving act". Starting from this point we can think of all other rites of the Church "as dependent upon and in various ways renewing or more specifically expressing the fulness of baptism itself".[3]

"Christ and the Church", the final report of the theological commission, was received by Section I on "The Church in the Purpose of God" at Montreal. It was in two parts, one from a North American section and one from a European section.[4] While both worked along different lines, the stress, as is indicated by the title, was on "Christ and the Church". The Church was seen as "grounded in the eternal purpose of the Father to send his Son Jesus Christ into the world".[5] Yet neither document was truly accepted as a basis for work. The make-up of the section membership can help explain this. Prominent in the discussion were Professors Ernst Käsemann and Eduard Schweitzer; both brought the tools of post-Bultmannian scholarship to bear in criticism of the documents. But articulate Orthodox members resisted their emphasis on *theologia crucis* at the expense of *theologia gloriae*. Reformed and Lutheran members split over the question of the relationship of the Church to creation and redemption. Further creative complications arose from hearty participation in the discussion by observers from the Roman Catholic Church, the Lutheran Church–Missouri Synod, and the Southern Baptist Convention.

While the Lund method of focusing on the relation between God and the Church had been used in the preparation of the two documents, discussion in the section made it clear that "comparative ecclesiology" is still a necessary

[1] *One Lord, One Baptism* (London 1960), FO, no. 29.
[2] Ibid., pp. 13f.   [3] Ibid., p. 70.
[4] See *Faith and Order Findings*, ed. Paul S. Minear. London 1963.
[5] Ibid., p. 38 of FO, no. 38.

ecumenical tool. The report itself indicated this when it pointed to "elements of tension which we neither minimize nor disguise". It went on to indicate that these differences reflect the present ecumenical situation, and that "the growth of the World Council of Churches has enlarged the areas of possible disagreement".[1] At New Delhi in 1961 many Orthodox Churches had been admitted into membership in the Council, as well as two Pentecostal Churches. Added to this was increased Roman Catholic participation. This led Montreal to be described as a "promising chaos": a chaos, because the growth in membership meant that achieved consensus needed to be rethought and achieved again; promising, because of the much wider constituency which was now involved in ecumenical discussion.[2]

While the report of the Montreal section did not contain much that was an "advance" over previous work, it led, through the very disagreements which were revealed in the discussion, to new avenues of Faith and Order study. We have already mentioned the study on "Creation, New Creation and the Unity of the Church". But additional studies were also approved by the Commission in 1964. A study on "The Church and the Jewish People" was initiated, which helped the self-understanding of the Church through an examination of its relationship with biblical Israel, and tried to clarify Christian–Jewish relationships today.[3]

Other studies indicate the desire to examine more carefully the relationship between the Church and the Holy Spirit. We have seen above how this gave new direction to the study of the empirical nature of the Church with the study of "Spirit, Order and Organization". Further concentration on the work of the Holy Spirit was evoked by the Montreal section's insistence that the nature of conciliarity, both in ecclesiology proper and in evaluating the role of "councils of churches", needed thorough study.[4] In discussing "Christ, the Church and the Churches", the section placed great emphasis on the Church as "both present in, and one with, the local congregation gathered for the hearing of the Word and the celebration of the Lord's Supper".[5] This reinforced the work of Section IV on "Worship and the Oneness of Christ's Church" and led to the institution of a study on "The Eucharist: a Sacrament of Unity".[6] These latter two studies received impetus from other quarters as well. Their results will be reported below.

At Lund an era of study in comparative ecclesiology ended. A new method was begun with promise in the work of the theological commissions, especially that on "Church and the Church". But with the growth of the World Council, and wider participation even by non-member Churches in its deliberations, some retrenchment had to be made. Yet after the "promising chaos" of Montreal new studies were conceived, quickly initiated, and interim reports were ready in a scant three years. When one views the study programme from 1948 to 1968 one discovers that, viewed as a whole, discussion of ecclesiology in fact was carried on in a trinitarian context. In diverse ways the nature of the

---

[1] Montreal, p. 41 (paras. 8 and 9).
[2] Ibid., p. 7.
[3] See Montreal, p. 44, no. 1; FO, no. 44, p. 42; FO, no. 50, pp. 69–82.
[4] Montreal, pp. 48ff.   [5] Ibid., pp. 45f.   [6] FO, no. 44, p. 54.

Church was studied in relation to creation, redemption, and the ongoing life of the Church as the fellowship of the Holy Spirit.

Most important, in the process of study scholars and churchmen of the Roman Catholic and Protestant West and of the Orthodox East, from the developed countries of North America and Europe and the developing countries of Asia, Latin America, and Africa, have worked together. What remains, and it is a large task indeed, is to see the fruits of their common labour communicated to the vast memberships of their Churches across the globe.

Worship

Study of worship has had a continuing role in Faith and Order. As important, however, has been the corporate worship which always has characterized meetings of the Commission and World Conferences. Here direct knowledge of other traditions was possible, and this informed the study process.

In the early stages comparative studies played an important role. In preparation for the Lund Conference a volume entitled *Ways of Worship* was prepared to provide information on worship in the various traditions.[1] It was basically a comparative study. The subsequent work of the section on worship at Lund made clear that consensus in this area was still not possible. The "unsolved problems" listed were too many to recount. Differences existed between "low" and "high" Church; there was much disagreement in the discussion of the Eucharist and concerning the relation between Word and Sacrament. Clearly much work remained to be done.

Also under discussion at Lund was the preparatory volume on *Intercommunion*.[2] It contained both historical studies on the problem in different ages and a section on comparative attitudes and practices. In discussing the preparatory volume, the Conference noted that the urgent desire for fellowship in the Eucharist "is very widely felt in all parts of the world". But ultimately, it noted, the urgency "comes from our Lord's call to us".[3] While not making notable progress toward solving problems, the Conference did make recommendations concerning communion services at ecumenical gatherings.[4]

Subsequent to Lund study in worship was carried on by an international theological commission with three sections, each with a different mandate. One was based in East Asia, one in Europe, and one in North America.[5] Reports from each group were presented to the Montreal Conference in 1963.[6]

Whereas at Lund a good deal of consensus was reached concerning Christ and the Church, and at Montreal deeper disagreements were revealed, with

[1] *Ways of Worship*, edited by Pehr Edwall, Eric Hayman, and Wm. D. Maxwell London 1951.

[2] *Intercommunion*, ed. Donald Baillie and John Marsh. London 1952.

[3] Ibid., pp. 49f.

[4] Ibid., p. 58. Note the revisions in these recommendations made at the Montreal Conference in 1963: Montreal, pp. 79f.

[5] FO, no. 17, pp. 25ff.

[6] *Faith and Order Findings*, ed. Paul S. Minear. London 1936. FO, no. 39.

regard to worship the process was reversed. A large measure of agreement was in fact registered by the section on "Worship and the Oneness of Christ's Church" in 1963. For instance, the section could state that despite many disagreements regarding Holy Communion, they could agree that the Eucharist is "a sacrament of the presence of the crucified and glorified Christ until he come, and a means whereby the sacrifice of the cross, which we proclaim, is operative within the Church".[1] Growth together in the ecumenical movement had made all Churches more deeply committed to sacramental worship and liturgical renewal. Agreement on the "presence" of Christ in the Eucharist, and on its sacrificial character, were significant advances over the disagreements at Lund.

The consensus which was evident at Montreal was no abstract agreement among liturgiologists; it was a consensus deeply rooted in common commitment to the celebrative, educative, and missionary character of the worship of Christ's Church. The growing liturgical sensitivity was not an attempt to revive traditional forms, for when a man has a living faith in God he should be encouraged to express it "in spontaneous praise and thanksgiving".[2] A growing agreement on the sacramental character of the Church's worship was evident in the work of the section; but this agreement was focused on the contemporaneity of the traditional and the spontaneity of the orderly.

After Montreal the Commission decided to centre study on the Eucharist and authorized a study in 1964 entitled "The Eucharist: A Sacrament of Unity". To aid the study Professor J. J. von Allmen of Switzerland was commissioned to write an essay as an aid to discussion, and this was published in 1967 after it had been discussed and revised by an international theological commission.[3] This provided further basis for discussion by the theological commission, whose work was presented to the Commission at its meeting in Bristol in 1967.

In this report major emphasis was placed on an analysis of the Eucharist in terms of its "anamnetic and epikletic" character, namely in terms of the way it functions as representation and anticipation, and the way in which it necessarily includes the invocation of the Holy Spirit. Further, the report speaks of the catholic character of the Eucharist, and carries on the emphasis made in Montreal on the local eucharistic fellowship as having "the fulness of catholicity".[4] Therefore, lack of local unity is a challenge to "Christians in that place": "A mockery is made of the Eucharist when walls of separation destroyed by Christ on his cross are allowed to persist: those between races, nationalities, tongues, classes, congregations, confessions, etc."[5]

One can see even in this cursory review that the work of studies such as this one feeds into our general understanding of the nature of the Church. This emphasis on the "qualitative catholicity" of the local eucharistic fellowship helps one understand better the nature of the Church, the kind of unity sought "in each place", and the way in which Churches in one place are related to those in other places and times.

[1] Montreal, p. 93 (para. 117).   [2] Ibid., p. 76.
[3] J. J. von Allmen, *The Lord's Supper*. London 1969.
[4] FO, no. 50, pp. 61–3.   [5] Ibid., p. 63.

In plans for further study the Commission in 1967 picked up the other theme in the Montreal report on worship, and in the interim report on "Christ and the Church". It proposed that further study in worship might "find its focus in the relation of Baptism and the Eucharist".[1] This theme, plus further work on the knotty problem of intercommunion, continues the work of Faith and Order in the area of worship.

Ministry

Questions of "order" are among the thorniest which face Churches in union negotiations or discussions of full eucharistic fellowship. It is therefore surprising that in recent years study in this area has not evoked more interest from the Churches. It was not always so.

At Lausanne in 1927 delegates focused on what appeared to them to be three major forms of church order: episcopal, presbyteral, and congregational. In their report they maintained that "these several elements must all, under conditions which require further study, have an appropriate place in the order of life of a reunited Church".[2] In surveys of present plans of union one discovers that in most cases provision is made to weave these three elements together, a healthy legacy from the early days of Faith and Order. Edinburgh in 1937 continued study in this area under the title "Ministry and Sacraments". For the most part the section's report merely listed various positions.[3] Little progress was made at Lund. Discussion centred on what constitutes a "valid" ministry.[4]

Direct study of the ministry ceased, really, between Edinburgh in 1937 and Montreal in 1963, at the very time when church union negotiations were increasing. At Montreal, since no special material had been prepared, the section on "The Redemptive Work of Christ and the Ministry of His Church" used some material from the report on "Christ and the Church", a bulletin (no. 15) prepared by the Laity Department, and documents from the Division of World Mission and Evangelism.

At Montreal discussion centred not on types of order, nor on the "validity" of orders, but on the ordained ministry as such. Beginning with an affirmation of "the recovery of the biblical teaching about the royal priesthood of the whole people of God", the report then goes on rather wryly to acknowledge that the Church "has always had and (so far as we know) always must have what we may call a 'special ministry' ".[5] The emphasis is on the ministry of the whole body; the ordained ministry is seen as one among "the differing gifts bestowed by the Spirit".[6] All in the section agreed that orderly transmission of authority is normally "an essential part of the means by which the Church is kept from generation to generation in the apostolic faith". But then the traditional differences emerged, ranging from the Orthodox insistence upon "unbroken succession of episcopal ordination from the apostles" to Quaker insistence that there is not sufficient New Testament authority to warrant

---

[1] FO, no. 50, p. 156.   [2] Lausanne, p. 469.   [3] Edinburgh, pp. 245-9.
[4] Lund, pp. 255 and 266.   [5] Montreal, p. 62 (paras. 77 and 80).
[6] Ibid., p. 65 (para. 92).

ordination.[1] Increasing consensus on the theological bases of ministry has not yet led to greater agreement on matters of order.

After Montreal the Commission authorized, at its meeting in 1964, a study on "Christ, the Holy Spirit and the Ministry". Yet this study itself suffered from "a relative lack of support".[2] No findings were available to be presented to the Commission at its meeting in 1967. At that time, however, the decision was made to tackle the central problem head on. The study would focus on ordination. Use could be made of the not insignificant materials already collected; growing consensus in other areas of ecclesiology might provide new insights. Such a study, with the growth of union negotiations over the face of the earth, is both necessary and long overdue.

One can only speculate on the reasons why such a central question of church order has received such scant attention and evoked little support from churchmen. It is at least possible that part of the "hidden agenda" in discussions concerning order is the institutional identity of church bodies, and, for that matter, the self-identity of churchmen and ministers as well. The very fact that for many Churches order provides the main thread of continuity, at least in their own self-understanding, means that reaction to change in this order will be strong. "Organizational inertia" mounts to a well-nigh immovable force where organizational identity is in question. Continued probing of what had been termed "non-theological factors" may be necessary in conjunction with study of the specifically theological aspects of order.

Tradition and traditions

Early discussion in this area centred on "Scripture and tradition", the proper relation between the two, and the use of creeds.[3] It was mainly an intra-Western discussion between those of Catholic and Protestant persuasions. Orthodoxy's influence was felt more strongly at Edinburgh, and the definition of tradition offered by that conference in 1937, "the living stream of the Church's life", opened the vistas of discussion.[4] It prompted one Western Free-Church theologian to observe that theologians of Churches other than Orthodox need now "to look again at their own understanding of tradition".[5]

Lund did not deal specifically with this area of study; but concern with the question ran through many areas of its work. The very next year, in 1953, the Working Committee of the commission discussed the topic,[6] and in 1954 the Faith and Order Commission authorized a Theologian Commission on Tradition and Traditions.[7] Its two sections, European and North American, published interim reports in 1961.[8] They approached their task differently, the European group centring on the dogmatic issue of Scripture and tradition, while the North American group took a more historical perspective, attempting to discover whether "it is intelligible to speak of the identity and continuity of the Christian *reality* in historical terms".[9]

[1] Montreal, pp. 65f (para. 95).   [2] FO, no. 50, p. 144.   [3] Lausanne, pp. 466f.
[4] Edinburgh, p. 229.
[5] Daniel Jenkins, *Tradition, Freedom and the Spirit* (Philadelphia 1951), p. 16.
[6] FO, no. 17, pp. 33f.   [7] FO, no. 21, p. 28.
[8] *The Old and the New in the Church*. London 1961. FO, no. 34.   [9] Ibid., p. 14.

With diverse approaches, the final reports nevertheless showed a large measure of agreement, especially in the use of terms. Slight differences in usage were resolved in the final report of the Montreal Conference itself in 1963:

> By *the Tradition* is meant the Gospel itself, transmitted from generation to generation in and by the Church, Christ himself present in the life of the Church. By tradition is meant the traditionary process. The term *traditions* is used in two senses, to indicate both the diversity of forms of expression and also what we call confessional traditions, for instance the Lutheran tradition or the Reformed tradition.[1]

This is a working out of the implications of the Edinburgh definition of tradition as the "ongoing life of the Church". With such an understanding, what is transmitted in tradition is "the Christian faith, not only as a sum of tenets, but as a living reality transmitted through the operation of the Holy Spirit".[2]

A common awareness of *the Tradition,* and an affirmation that it is one indication of the unity which is given in Christ to the Church, led to questions about the ways in which "the traditionary process" operates in our Churches, especially in Christian education. The New Delhi Assembly had already asked the Youth Department to engage in a study of catechetical materials; the Montreal Conference recommended a similar course of action to the Faith and Order Secretariat.[3] Collaboration between these two departments and the World Council on Christian Education began soon afterwards and the Commission approved the study in 1964.[4] A consultation in 1965 produced an interim report[5] which was widely circulated for comment, and an international drafting committee prepared the final report which was approved by all three groups for publication in 1967.[6] Its recommendations include common preparation of educational materials and ecumenical Christian education in local centres. The purpose of the report was to indicate to our Churches how they can bring their educational programmes in line with the ecumenical commitments they have made, and to grow in both.

Highly technical scholarly work was necessary in the area of Tradition and traditions as well. The first study of this type was a patristics study group. It met in Paris in 1962 in response to the request made at New Delhi that the Commission "establish a programme of joint study of theological problems by Orthodox and non-Orthodox theologians".[7] The group examined St Basil's treatise on the Holy Spirit in order (1) to clarify the authority and significance of the Fathers of the early centuries, and (2) to establish some hermeneutical principles for work in patristics. Its conclusions were reported to the Commission meeting in 1967.[8]

---

[1] Montreal, p. 50 (para. 39).   [2] Ibid., p. 52 (para. 46).
[3] New Delhi, pp. 221f; Montreal, pp. 60f (paras. 74–6).
[4] FO, no. 44, pp. 36 and 42.   [5] *Risk.* January 1966.
[6] *World Christian Education.* January 1968. Reprints are available under the title *Ecumenical Commitment and Christian Education.* Geneva 1968.
[7] FO, no. 50, p. 120; FO, no. 48, p. 12.
[8] FO, no. 50, pp. 41–8.

Two other studies in this general area of Tradition and traditions were also requested at New Delhi: one on the function of Councils throughout the history of the Church, and the other on the problem of theological discourse, including the problem of hermeneutics.[1] The first of these, like the study of patristics, was made up of an equal number of Orthodox and non-Orthodox scholars. It studied the conciliar process in the ancient Church. Among its conclusions were the following: conciliarity belongs necessarily to the life of the Church; conciliar processes continue in the separated Churches. But because of separation we have not had a genuine ecumenical council since the early centuries. This is desirable still, and the ecumenical movement, and the World Council of Churches "can be seen as a tool for the preparation of a true Ecumenical Council".[2] The work of this group will be combined with that of the patristic study group and centre on the Council of Chalcedon and its reception by the Churches.[3]

An examination of "Biblical Hermeneutics and its Significance for the Ecumenical Movement" started in 1964, jointly sponsored by the Division of Studies. An interim report was presented to the Commission in 1964,[4] and five regional groups in Europe and North America were formed to carry the work further. The final report, prepared by an international consultation in 1967, indicated that a consensus was gained on the use of literary and historical methods and on the process of interpretation in general. In addition it made some observations about the present stage of ecumenical discussion on the Bible.[5] Its report was received by the Commission in 1967, and further study was authorized on the topic "The Authority of the Bible".[6]

Throughout these studies in Tradition and traditions, whether of Christian education or of patristics, run themes which are crucial for the everyday life of Christians and therefore for the unity of the Church. Basically one can say that they deal with authority for Christian living. They deal with the passing on of the gospel, and with its appropriation in understanding. All these studies indicate that it is only as the gospel itself is continually re-appropriated that it is effective in guiding the Church's worship, witness, and service in the world.

Summary

Of necessity this summary has been cursory, yet it is clear what a wide range of studies underlies Faith and Order's attempt to discern (1) the nature of the unity we seek, and (2) the path to take towards that goal. Clearly the beginning of the path lies in understanding one another. The task of "comparative ecclesiology" is a continuing one. But then comes the arduous task of attempting to discern the shape of a common life in the future for Churches which are now separated. Then comes the even more difficult task of creating that

---

[1] New Delhi, pp. 174 and 173.   [2] FO, no. 50, pp. 57f.   [3] Ibid., p. 58.
[4] FO, no. 44, pp. 61ff.   [5] FO, no. 50, pp. 32–41.
[6] FO, no. 50, p. 156. Compare the results of this study with those reached at an Ecumenical Study Conference sponsored by the Study Department on the World Council at Oxford in 1949. *Biblical Authority for Today*, ed. Alan Richardson and Wolfgang Schweitzer (Philadelphia 1951), pp. 270–6.

life together in united Churches. This is what the movement toward church union is all about, and to it we now turn.

Faith and Order and Church Union

Stephen Neill surveyed with remarkable completeness the development of "Plans of Union and Reunion: 1910-1948" in the previous volume of this series.[1] Since that time, as we have mentioned above, there have been regular surveys published, and for the reader wishing detailed analysis these are indispensable.[2] Within the confines of this chapter we can but examine the general relationship of Faith and Order to the movement towards church union.

The church union movement

Movement for the unification of Churches has been an aspect of the ecumenical movement which proceeded quite independently of its varied organizational forms. In brief, there can be little causal connection drawn, say, between Life and Work, Faith and Order, or the World Council on the one hand and the unions which have been achieved. There has been parallel growth and an increasing rate of growth.

Between 1925, the year of the first Conference on Life and Work, and 1948, the founding of the World Council, nineteen united Churches were formed, including fifty-seven Churches in fifteen countries. Between 1948 and 1966 (the last year for which figures are available as I write) twenty-three more united Churches were formed, including seventy-four more Churches. That this movement is world-wide is indicated by the fact that these unions took place on all six continents and included a total of twenty-one countries.[3]

The movement continues, for in 1966 there were 121 different Churches involved in forty-six negotiations, again on all six continents. More significantly, these new figures indicate an increase in negotiations which seek to transcend confessional or polity barriers. Of the unions since 1925, about one-third transcended such barriers, while of negotiations now under way two-thirds seek to overcome these significant differences.[4]

Issues in church union

Among most of the Churches which have already joined, or are about to join, doctrinal issues seem to be least important. The main exception to this is in highly confessional Churches such as the Lutheran Church of Australia or between such Churches as the Reformed Presbyterian Church and the Orthodox Presbyterian Church in the United States. This is not to say that doctrine is unimportant for these churches, but that it is not primarily a divisive issue. For example, the proposed uniting Church in Australia has as the first fruit of negotiations a forty-four page pamphlet on "The Faith of the Church".

[1] Rouse and Neill, op. cit., pp. 445-508.   [2] See above, p. 146, n. 3.
[3] M. B. Handspicker, "Church Union" in *World Christian Handbook* (1968), ed. H. Wakelin Coxill and Sir Kenneth Grubb. London 1968.
[4] Ibid.

Where doctrinal differences do exist among churchmen negotiating for union such differences do not follow denominational lines. They are differences which exist within all the Churches.

From the beginning the issue which was most difficult to overcome was church order or polity. Since 1925 only one negotiation, that which led to the Church of South India, has succeeded in uniting a Church with bishops in the apostolic succession with non-episcopally ordered Churches. Only a few negotiations succeeded across Congregational–Presbyterian polity lines before 1948, although now difficulties here have lessened—to the extent that the International Congregational Council and the World Alliance of Reformed Churches propose to merge in 1970. But in some unions of this type dissident groups have broken away from or refused to enter the united Church. This is most notable in the United Church of Canada, with the continuation of the Presbyterian Church, and in the United Church of Christ in the United States, with a continuing association of Congregational Churches.

The inclusion of the historic episcopate in the Chicago–Lambeth Quadrilateral of the Anglican Communion as a "non-negotiable" item has meant that episcopacy is an issue in any negotiation where Anglicans are involved.[1] At present they are working towards union in sixteen negotiations. In the course of time, however, consensus has been developing that the historic episcopate, usually in a modified form, is a desirable element in the ordering of church life.[2] Certainly the early agreement at Lausanne that both Congregational, Presbyterian, and Episcopal elements were desirable had some influence in developing this consensus. More recently the decision by the negotiating committee of the Presbyterian, Methodist, and Congregational Churches in Australia to have a church order with bishops in the historic episcopate has been evidence that choice of such an order is not merely an expedient to enable episcopal and non-episcopal Churches to unite, since none of these Churches is at present episcopally ordered.[3]

The major issue at present takes a twofold form: the unification of ministries and the order of the united Church. The first is seen in discussions such as those in Great Britain between Anglicans and Methodists where the proposed "Service of Reconciliation" between ministries and memberships has caused much discussion.[4] At the moment one live option seems to be that used in forming the Church of South India, where all ministers of the uniting Churches were accepted into the ministry of the united Church, with all subsequent ministers receiving episcopal ordination. The other was devised in the course of discussions in North India and Ceylon; here bishops of the united Church will receive into their jurisdiction ministers of the uniting Churches with the laying on of hands and prayer.[5] At issue in this latter is

---

[1] See Rouse and Neill, op. cit., pp. 264ff.   [2] See FO, no. 43, p. 4.

[3] See *The Church: Its Nature, Function and Ordering* (Melbourne 1963).

[4] *Conversations between the Church of England and the Methodist Church.* London 1963. *Relations between The Church of England and the Methodist Church.* London 1965. *Towards Reconciliation.* London 1967. *Anglican–Methodist Union in Wales.* Penarth 1965.

[5] See, for example *Scheme of Church Union in Ceylon.* Third rev. ed., 1955, as amended in 1963 (Colombo 1964, pp. 10–27). Other similar schemes, each with some differences, are found in the North India plan, and those for union in Ghana and Nigeria.

whether it truly recognizes the validity of all the ministries being united, a question also raised about Anglican–Methodist plans in Great Britain. In attempting to interpret the first plan for scrupulous Anglicans an increasing number of theologians are contending that acceptance by a bishop in the historic episcopate, and acceptance of that bishop's jurisdiction, constitutes a "valid" ministry.

Such discussion about the ministry of a united Church, and the uniting of ministries, led the Very Reverend Patrick C. Rodger, when he was a member of the Faith and Order Secretariat, to observe that in the eyes of many laymen "church union negotiations seem to be mainly ministers discussing the ministry". The fact that this does seem to be one of the major issues makes all the more regrettable the lack of attention paid to the ministry in Faith and Order studies of the past few decades. The problems in this area are both helped and hindered by an increasing focus on the ministry of the whole people of God— both in ecumenical discussion and in church union plans as well. All the more reason, therefore, for thorough and swift study by Faith and Order of the ministry of the Church and its ordering.

Another sub-issue in the discussion of ministry seems an impending obstacle to church union in some parts of the world. Negotiations in Asia, Australasia, the United Kingdom, and North America are under way between Churches which have ordained women presbyters and those who refuse ordination to women. While an increasing number of theologians, including Roman Catholics, see no theological issue here, the sociological and psychological issues are by no means insignificant. Faith and Order has begun work in this area, most recently with its publication of a study entitled *Concerning the Ordination of Women*,[1] More thorough work is still needed, especially since, while the practice of ordaining women differs between Churches, differing attitudes towards their ordination obtain within almost all Churches.

This discussion of issues has been limited to two areas: polity and ministry. This is not because these are the only issues in church union, but because they are the most widespread. Stephen Neill, in his earlier survey, noted that "only a full-scale survey could give an idea of the range of problems that have had to be faced, the variety and ingenuity of the solutions that have been tried".[2] These issues vary not only with the denominations involved, but according to the places and times negotiations are carried on. Issues which were once church-divisive, such as the relation between Scripture and tradition, sacramental theology, and even church discipline, are still divisive in some contexts. But increasingly these are becoming issues more of church unity than of church union. In other words, these are differences within the various Churches. Already we have mentioned the issue of the relationship between Church and world as having the incipient power of schism—across denominational and confessional lines. In these various areas the future function of Faith and Order may increasingly come to be prevention of schism or of "ecclesiastical drop-outs".

---

[1] Geneva 1965.   [2] Rouse and Neill, op, cit., p. 448.

Faith and Order in Church Union

While the role of Faith and Order with regard to particular initiatives for union is still strictly circumscribed, in recent years it has been able to participate with more direct effectiveness in furthering initiatives already taken. The surveys of negotiations help to provide a network of communications among the negotiating committees. The Secretariat has now been asked to use this network to channel information about successes in one area to others facing similar problems, and to communicate information about World Council studies which may aid negotiating committees.[1] This will help remedy the real deficiency to date in communicating the results of ecumenical study to the places where it can help to effect change.

Another area where Faith and Order could have been of help for a long time was that of providing consultants for negotiators. This would provide expertise garnered from other negotiations, or from study, for committees requesting it. As far back as 1955 the Working Committee suggested that church union committees, where possible, should invite the Faith and Order secretary to "sit with the negotiating committee as an observer or consultant".[2] Some felt that this was exceeding Faith and Order's mandate. Strenuous discussion occurred on the topic at the Central Committee meeting in 1959.[3] The first visit of Faith and Order consultants occurred that year, but since then these visits have not only increased in number, but are understood to be a regular part of the work of the Secretariat.

Finally, one can only say that while there may be little direct relationship between the work of Faith and Order and the movements toward unity, it is clear that its study and discussion have helped to create an ethos conducive to union. Further, many individuals intimately involved in negotiating are themselves in part formed by their work in Faith and Order. Informal and *ad hoc* though they may be, the links between Faith and Order and union negotiations are strong.

One way in which these have been strengthened is through consultation among negotiators from various parts of the world. At first only unofficial consultations were held at times when large numbers of people were gathered at an Assembly. Such were held after Lund, and the Evanston and New Delhi Assemblies.[4] In 1964 the Commission authorized the calling of a large consultation, and this was held at the Ecumenical Institute in Bossey, Switzerland in April 1967.[5] Recommendations were submitted by the consultation to the Faith and Order Commission, and among them was a request that the Secretariat continue to organize such meetings.[6] Representatives from union committees and united Churches had discovered that such direct consultation provided clarity of communication unavailable in any other way.

---

[1] FO, no. 50, p. 148.   [2] FO, no. 22, p. 17.
[3] MRCC (1959), pp. 33ff, 175ff.   [4] FO, no. 22, p. 17.
[5] FO, no. 44, p. 34. See *Midstream*, vol. vi, no. 3, for texts of the meeting.
[6] FO, no. 50, p. 149.

Summary

Faith and Order provides a favourable climate for union, and its studies undergird the movement so far as they are known and used. In addition, the work of the Secretariat serves to communicate information, and to bring knowledgeable people together. But at this point a suggestion may be made. It is time that a volume similar to those prepared by H. Paul Douglass and Stephen Neill was published. The biennial surveys keep those who are interested up to date. But periodic reviews and assessments of longer periods of time are a continuing need in this area.

The People and Organization of Faith and Order

People give Faith and Order its life and its style. The very beginnings are inconceivable without the fire of Bishop Charles Brent and the dogged devotion of Robert Gardiner. This has continued to be the case since its merger into the World Council of Churches in 1948. One important change took place at that time: Faith and Order was to have a full-time secretary in the person of the Reverend Oliver Tomkins, although he would have offices in both London and Geneva. Dr Leonard Hodgson would continue as theological secretary, and the indefatigable archivist of Faith and Order, Dr Floyd Tomkins held the title of associate secretary in America. These men, together with the Chairman of the Commission, Bishop Yngve Brilioth of Sweden and the Vice-Chairman, Principal R. Newton Flew, oversaw the work of the theological commissions as they prepared for the Lund Conference.

Yet the real work of Faith and Order is carried out by numberless persons whose names would take pages to list. Here we can but indicate officers and staff. But the international theological commissions of the earlier days of Faith and Order, and the numerous committees and study groups which have characterized its work since 1964, are the backbone of Faith and Order study. For the days between 1948 and 1963, the names of those to be mentioned are clear. The officers of the theological and study commissions are those who bore the brunt of preparation. Prior to Lund there were three such. For the Commission on the Church Dr R. Newton Flew was Chairman, Professor K. E. Skysgaard, Vice-Chairman, Dean C. T. Craig, Chairman of the American group, and the Reverend Kenneth Riches, Secretary. The group working on "Ways of Worship" was chaired by Professor G. van der Leeuw, with Dr H. Asmussen as Vice-Chairman, Professor W. J. Kooiman as Secretary and Mr W. Vos as Co-Secretary. That working on "Intercommunion" had as Chairman Professor Donald M. Baillie, with Professor H. S. Alivisatos as Vice-Chairman and Professor John Marsh as Secretary.

The list lengthens after Lund, when Faith and Order was preparing for Montreal in 1963. That stepchild of Faith and Order study, the Study Commission on Institutionalism, was chaired by Dean Walter Meulder and had as Secretary Professor Nils Ehrenstrom—probably the only commission officered completely by men from the same theological faculty. The North American section on Christ and the Church was chaired consecutively by Professors Robert Calhoun and W. Norman Pittenger, with Professors

G. R. Cragg and Claude Welch as Secretaries. In Europe this theological commission had as officers Bishop Anders Nygren and Professor G. W. H. Lampe.

A variety of style of work is indicated by the varied ways in which the sections of the Commission on Worship were organized. In North America Professor Joseph Sittler served as Chairman. In Europe the officers included Professor Regin Prenter as Chairman and Principal A. Raymond George as Secretary. But in Asia, where the distances to be travelled were considerable, officers multiplied: Principal J. Russel Chandran was Chairman, with Bishop Lakdasa de Mel and President C. Kishi as Vice-Chairmen and Dr J. R. Fleming as Secretary.

Finally, the Commission on Tradition and Traditions, composed of two sections, had as North American officers, Professor Albert C. Outler as Chairman, Father Georges Florovsky as Vice-Chairman, and Professor David Hay as Secretary. In Europe the section was chaired by Professor K. E. Skydsgaard with Professor S. L. Greenslade as Vice-Chairman.

This listing of names is only to indicate the spread of responsibility in any Faith and Order study. It is possible within a short compass to give names only for the work done prior to 1964. Since its meeting in Aarhus the Commission has adopted a varied method of study which involves many more *ad hoc* committees in addition to study commissions. An indication of what this means can be found in the list of participants in Faith and Order studies included in *New Directions in Faith and Order*.[1] In contrast to the three groups working prior to Lund, and the four prior to Montreal, the report lists eleven separate studies, two of them with five sub-groups each.

Recent proliferation of studies has been made possible because of changes in the organization of Faith and Order. This too can be traced through the succession of persons involved in the work of the Commission. After Lund 1952, Bishop Brilioth's work as Chairman was complemented by the work of Dr Oliver Tomkins as Chairman of the Working Committee—an organizational differentiation to enhance the work of Faith and Order. When Dr Tomkins left as Secretary he was replaced by Dr J. Robert Nelson, who continued through 1957. That year leadership changed in two ways, with Dr Keith Bridston coming to Faith and Order as Secretary, and Dean Douglas Horton replacing Bishop Brilioth as Chairman.

From 1957 onward "The Future of Faith and Order" was a continuing subject of discussion. Drafts of a report on the topic were submitted to the Central Committee in the years 1957, 1959, and 1960.[2] A number of important changes in Faith and Order's functioning were rendered possible through the action of the Central Committee of the World Council in 1960: (1) the secretariat would report to the Central Committee each year on issues in the realm of unity; (2) time at assemblies would continue to be allotted for discussion of unity; (3) provisions would be made from time to time for

[1] FO, no. 50, pp. 174–8.
[2] FO, no. 26, pp. 47ff; 27, pp. 23ff; 31, pp. 113ff. For one man's view of what was at stake, see Keith Bridston, "Domesticating the Revolution", *Unity in Mid-Career*, ed. Keith Bridston and Walter D. Wagoner (New York 1963), pp. 30–46.

World Conferences; (4) the staff of Faith and Order would be increased to three, and the director of the secretariat would be a member of the Staff Executive Group, the staff policy-making body in Geneva.

In 1961 the staff changed again, this time increasing in numbers. Professor Paul Minear became Director, the Reverend Patrick C. Rodger, Executive Secretary, and Dr Lukas Vischer, Research Secretary. This was the staff which took care of the final organization of the Montreal World Conference on Faith and Order in 1963. Since that time the secretariat has been maintained at full strength, with Dr M. B. Handspicker coming on the staff as Assistant Secretary in 1963 when Professor Minear returned to his teaching and became Chairman of the Commission, and Archpriest Vitaly Borovoy becoming Associate Director when, in 1966, Patrick Rodger left the staff and Dr Vischer became Director. The secretariat's work has also been augmented by assistant secretaries seconded from member Churches, the Reverend Reinhard Groscurth coming in 1966 and Dr John Zizioulas in 1968.

Faith and Order's future in 1967 was placed in the hands of new chairmen of both the Commission, Professor H. H. Harms, and the Working Committee, Professor J. Robert Nelson. The resignation of Dr Minear saw a former Director and Chairman of the Commission cease his official connection with the Commission. That of Dr Oliver Tomkins, the Bishop of Bristol, ended a relationship which had begun in 1948 with his election as Secretary, and which was continued from 1952 to 1968 by a sixteen-year tenure as Chairman of the Working Committee.

For a full history of the "people of Faith and Order", in distinction from this history of a commission, a department, and a secretariat, many more pages would be needed. Faith and Order work has, thankfully, spread wider and wider—both in terms of the people involved and the organizational means whereby they are involved. National Faith and Order conferences have been held in Australia and New Zealand, in North America, the British Isles, and East Asia. Regional conferences have taken place within numerous countries, including those in the British Isles, North America, India, and others. Lay groups have become involved, especially through the series of "Living Room Dialogues" in the United States, and study groups sponsored by the ecumenical secretariat of the Evangelical Church in Germany. Faith and Order secretaries, and even multiple-staffed secretariats, have been constituted by national and regional councils of Churches.

Here is where we see the continuing character of Faith and Order as a movement. In the World Council of Churches, Faith and Order has become a secretariat within an institution, a needed ecumenical institution. But this institutional position enables it to encourage and support further work outside its specific oversight. The spirit which encouraged and inflamed Bishop Brent still finds ways to continue, and the institutional and organizational forms, while continually having to be reviewed, can aid and abet this spirit.

Church union committees, theological commissions, *ad hoc* study groups, laymen talking in living rooms or academies, conferences at retreat centres or universities, working committees, the Commission, the Secretariat—each and every one of these groups is part of that movement which is seeking the union of Christ's Church according to his will, and in his own time.

Conclusion

In the early 1930s Abbé Paul Couturier of Lyons sought a formula of prayer in which all could unite to pray for the unity of the Church. He advocated that we pray that "our Lord would grant to His Church on earth that peace and unity which were in His mind and purpose, when, on the eve of His Passion, He prayed that all might be one".[1] In 1941, in large part as a result of this change in intention, Faith and Order changed its week of prayer (which had been started in 1920) to coincide with the Week of Prayer for Christian Unity, celebrated annually in most parts of the world from 18 to 25 January. This "spiritual ecumenism" has been important to the Faith and Order movement from the outset, and the now widespread observance of the Week testifies to a growing response on the part of all Christians to the appeal for their participation.

Prayer for unity is an act in which all Christians, from whatever station in life or part of the world, can participate. It can involve a change of heart and a new breadth of vision for those who engage in it. It is essential if the work of Faith and Order is to take root in the vast constituencies of our Churches.

Faith and Order began as a movement among people deeply interested in the unity of the Church for the sake of its mission. Through the years both the scope of its work and its organization and methods developed slowly but surely.

With the formation of the World Council in 1948 the ecumenical movement became increasingly institutionalized. This had to be the case if the movement was to effect change in the institutions we call Churches. During the life of the Council it is not surprising to find growing concern for the "future of Faith and Order". The movement, if it were to continue as a movement, had to have adequate organizational form, determined by its own missionary and theological dynamic.

As the future breaks before us, it is clear that further growth and change in the work of Faith and Order is mandatory. Broader participation by the membership of all of our Churches has to come if unity is to be achieved— or received. Prayer and study are ways in which many can become involved. The so-called "grassroots" are increasingly leaping over the boundaries set by church discipline. A growing "anonymous ecumenical movement" threatens subtle schism if organizational intertia continues to block movements toward union.

The goal of the movement is "One Church Renewed for Mission". Bishop Tomkins, when still Secretary of the Department, observed that the function of the ecumenical movement can best be understood by analogy to the work of the physician.

> As the physician pursues the treatment in his relentless mercy, the patient's early hopes of cure and sense of greater strength may well have to be followed

[1] Rouse and Neill, op. cit., p. 348.

by a phase in which knowledge of unsuspected depths in his disease, the discovery of vitiation in organs he thought were healthy, must be the prelude to more lasting cure. Today we dare not speak of the unity of the Church without also speaking of its *renewal*.[1]

This is eminently still the case; renewal is the necessary prelude to true unity. But in addition we must grapple with issues which, while they have not yet divided the Church, promise division, alienation, or growing apathy. Whether one speaks of the "anonymous ecumenical movement" or the "underground church", one points to a reality of increasing power. There is the threat of a "horizontal schism" threatening all our Churches. The reasons for this are many, but perhaps a key one is seen in differing attitudes towards the world. Many Christians are now discerning the activity of the Spirit in the emergence of free nations, in international groupings, and in projects where Christians and non-Christians seek together for peace and justice in the new social structures created by the technological revolution overtaking all societies.

Other Christians see the Church as the ark of salvation, as a means to escape from the ambiguities and negativities of the world in which they live. It is a means of disengagement rather than a source of power and inspiration for engagement. The former group often finds little to inspire them in the internal life of organized Churches, and disparages worship and organized communal life. The latter group sees engagement and action in the world as a threat to the *status quo*, including that of the Churches.

In the midst of this increasing polarization, the work of Faith and Order is pastoral as well as theological. It needs to seek the roots of reconciliation between these two poles, and there are the resources within the Churches to accomplish this. Many of our churchmen, clergy as well as laymen, unite within themselves a deep spiritual life with a lively engagement with the problems of the contemporary world. The tragedy is that many of these folk, including large numbers of our younger churchmen, find neither spiritual resources nor the mutual support of a loving community within the organized life of our Churches.

The Bishop of Bristol's remarks are still germane. Renewal is the prerequisite of unity if we are not to unite organizations and programmes which are engaged in doing what need not be done, or even what ought not to be done. In its recent forays into more general theological issues, such as "God in Nature and History" and "Man in Nature and History", Faith and Order promises to regain its function as the theological *avant garde* of the ecumenical movement. Continuing, persistent, and courageous effort is necessary if Faith and Order is to fulfil its contemporary function of preserving unity, as well as its historical function of furthering reunion.

[1] FO, no. 2, p. 16.

7
Mission to Six Continents

LESSLIE NEWBIGIN

The Context

The two decades with which this history deals were a period in which the foreign missionary movement of the non-Roman Catholic Churches faced the most profound crisis of its history. Six factors combined to create this crisis of missions.

1. The Dismantling of the Colonial Empires

The opinion that missions were simply the spiritual and cultural aspect of western colonialism has been so often expressed as to risk being accepted as part of the unexamined mythology of our time. Careful historical study (for example in *Colonialism and Christian Missions*, by S. C. Neill) shows that the facts are far more complex than this simple statement allows. Nevertheless, it is a fact that the colonial systems of the western powers provided for the most part the political and cultural framework within which missions operated in most parts of what is now called the "third world" during the century and a half prior to 1947. That year, in which the Indian sub-continent became independent of British rule, may be taken as the starting-point of the process of decolonization which has been almost completed within less than twenty years. A change so profound and so rapid, which removed within a few years the framework within which missions had been operating for two centuries, could not fail to shake profoundly the whole missionary movement, even though the discerning missionary leaders had been for many years advocating and preparing for the liberation of the dependent peoples, and even though the work of missions was itself one of the most powerful forces preparing for that liberation.

2. The End of Missions in China

The most massive effort of Protestant missions during the century preceding the period of this survey had been directed to China. At the World Missionary Conference at Tambaram in 1938, the Chinese delegation had been outstanding in quality. The Chinese Church, though small, seemed full of immense promise. Yet, within a few years of the establishment of communist rule in China, missions had been completely eliminated from the country and much of the fruit of their century of work had apparently been destroyed. This shattering event led to much searching of heart among those responsible for leadership in the foreign missionary movement. It helped to produce a sense of crisis, though it is to be doubted whether the rethinking was sufficiently profound. Perhaps the most searching questions arise from the fact—generally accepted—that the communist government in China has been able to accomplish many of the reforms for which missions were the early advocates but which they were not strong enough to complete. The end of missions in China has therefore raised very profound questions regarding the relation of the Christian world mission to the whole world-wide process of secularization, and to the exercise of political power.

173

3. The Growth of a Sense of Global Human Interdependence

One of the most important spiritual facts of this twenty-year period is the growth, among ordinary men and women in all continents, of the feeling that the human race is a single entity bound together for better for worse, facing common problems, threatened by common dangers, and seeking common goals. It is true that the colossal exception to this was China; indeed one can say that the Chinese people, constituting one quarter of the human race, were completely absent from the developing ecumenical story which this chapter records. Moreover, towards the end of the twenty-year period there were many evidences that a movement of separatism, leading to the break-up of nations or to acute conflicts within them, was gathering force. Nevertheless, it remains true that, during the period of our survey, and for the people involved in the story, the growth of a sense of global interdependence was one of the most important elements in the spiritual climate.

Much of the power of missions had come from their appeal to the sense of what is beyond the frontiers of normal experience. The appeal to go "to the ends of the earth", evoked not only echoes of the "Great Commission", but also led to a deep response from that in every man which wants to press beyond the known to the unknown. Livingstone's vision of "the smoke of a thousand villages which have never yet heard the Gospel" spoke not only to the believer in every Christian, but also to the explorer in every man. In the decades under review, missions have had to come to terms with the fact that the "frontier" in that sense no longer exists. The world has become one parish, in a sense different from that which was in John Wesley's mind. Everything is part of one world. The question arises whether "foreign missions", as distinct from the general duty of witness which rests upon every Christian everywhere, have any distinctive *raison d'être*.

4. The Growth of the Concept of "Development"

A few years before the period under review began, the British Parliament had voted a small sum for "development" in the colonies. In the course of the subsequent years the conviction that it was the duty of the "developed" nations to aid the others towards a higher standard of life became one of the dominating ideas of international life. This was partly rooted in the expansion of the idea of the welfare state, partly no doubt in the sense of moral obligation towards peoples who had formerly been in subjection to the great powers, partly in economic self-interest, and partly in the growing conviction that mankind has the technical resources to banish poverty and create decent living conditions for all. As the sense of a single global community grew stronger, so also did the sense that an obligation rested upon the wealthy nations to help the poorer to raise their standards of living. This conviction found expression in many ways—from voluntary movements among students to "miss a meal" in order to help some development scheme in India, to massive programmes under the U.N. "Development Decade". On the other hand, this movement had an interesting effect upon the relations between missions and governments: as the governments of the western powers began to interest themselves in development they discovered that missions sent from their own countries had been engaged in development (though innocent of the word) for many decades, and found it convenient to use the help of missions for their programmes. On the other hand, many former supporters of missions began to feel that "development aid" was the modern equivalent for the missionary activities of the past. The acceptable ideal was no longer the man who went across the frontier to unknown lands to preach the gospel; it was rather the man who went as a teacher, a technician, a health worker, to help needy brethren in the one human family. The great programmes of Inter-Church Aid seemed to some to offer a more acceptable way of helping one's neighbour than the kind of missionary work which was felt to carry too much of the old arrogance of the colonial era. Even Christian congregations would offer resources for work abroad on the condition that they should not be used for anything connected with missions.

5. The Crisis of Faith in the West

This is something which it is difficult to describe, because both writer and readers are in the midst of it. Nevertheless, it must be referred to as one of the potent factors shaping missionary thinking and action during the period of our study. There is, firstly, the long-term questioning of the very foundations of faith which may be said to have been an essential element of Protestantism ever since the eighteenth century and which from time to time produces a spiritual situation out of which foreign missions simply cannot come. Secondly, and more exactly to our present point, there is the dissolution of the "Christendom" situation in the western world, which results in an increasingly sharp separation between missions on the one hand and the general cultural and political influence of the western nations on the other. And finally, there is the very marked change in the years following 1947 which may be characterized in two ways. On the one hand, a chronic bad conscience has seized the western white man in his relations with the rest of the world so that he fears above everything else the charge of arrogance. On the other hand, a profound crisis of faith within the Western Churches has led to a loss of conviction that there is anything in the Christian faith which is so vital that without it men will perish.

In so far as the overwhelming preponderance of missionary activity in the past two centuries has been from the Western Churches, this crisis of faith, allied to the wider factors to which reference has been made, has created a situation for missions which shakes them to their foundations. Perhaps the impact of this crisis upon the work of foreign missions was delayed by the fact that those concerned were thinking more about the meeting of the gospel with the traditional non-Christian religions than about the meeting of the gospel with the anti-traditional secularized societies of the West. As the movement towards a "six-continent approach" developed, it became clear that there was a gulf between the language used in discussions of "the theology of missions" and the language which the normal western Christian used about his own belief. By the end of the period under survey the gulf had become apparent, and the resultant spiritual problem had become inescapable.

G

6. The Growth of the Ecumenical Movement

The fruit of the work of missions has been the creation of a world-wide family of Churches. But the very existence of these Churches calls for a profound re-examination of the nature of the missionary movement itself. Is the work of missions done when the Church has been planted in every nation? Does the task not now rest upon the Church in each nation, rather than upon the foreign missionary? What, then, is the further need for the mission? These questions were present in missionary discussions long before the period we are now reviewing, but they could not be pressed with their full force while the "younger Churches" were isolated from one another and dependent for contact with the rest of the Christian world solely upon their parent missions. The development of the International Missionary Council brought able representatives of the younger Churches together periodically on a world level, and helped to bring pressure on missions to face this question. But it was when the World Council of Churches became fully organized, and brought together as equal members the young Churches of Asia, Africa, and Latin America and the older Churches from which the missions had been sent, that this question became inescapable.

Within the growing fellowship of the World Council an increasingly rich exchange of thought, experience, personnel, and resources began to develop. The younger Churches found themselves related to, and stimulated by, the other Churches in all kinds of new ways. In the growing programmes of inter-Church aid they found themselves sharing in help from older Churches quite outside the old missionary channels. To an increasing number of people it seemed that this pattern of interdependence within one world-wide Church represented the true pattern for the future, and that the type of organization developed by foreign missions should be completely discarded. The intimate association, leading in 1961 to complete integration, between the International Missionary Council and the World Council of Churches, ensured that the debate was conducted within one fellowship. Nevertheless, the questions put. from the side of the World Council of Churches, and the issues raised by the W.C.C.'s programme of inter-Church aid, were among the factors which compelled a radical rethinking of the nature of the missionary task in an era of global interdependence.

Whitby to Amsterdam

The World Missionary Conference which met at Tambaram, India in 1938 dramatized for a very great number of people the fact that the Christian Church had become a truly world-wide company. The place of meeting had been shifted from China because of the outbreak of war there. The shadow of a demonic totalitarianism lay over the world. Tambaram, with the excellent work done in making it widely known, shone as a beacon of hope to Christians in many lands. The darkness of the world made its light shine brighter. The famous words spoken by William Temple at his enthronement as Archbishop of Canterbury during the darkest days of the war had as their background the vivid realization which Tambaram had given of the existence of a world-wide Christian family as the "great new fact of our time".

As soon as possible after the war, the International Missionary Council convened a world consultation at Whitby, Ontario. The title of the volume which embodies the record of this meeting—"Renewal and Advance"—well indicates its dominant mood. Even during the terrible period of war, the International Missionary Council had been able to maintain to a remarkable degree the fabric of co-operation, especially through the vast programme of support for "orphaned missions". Now in 1947 the world-wide family which had met at Tambaram could meet again. There was joy and confidence in planning for the future. It had not yet become clear how drastic were the changes which the world had undergone as the result of the convulsions of the war years. The complete extinction of the colonial pattern, most dramatically in China, but also throughout the rest of Asia and Africa, was still in the future. The extent of the spiritual damage which the old Christendom had suffered could not yet be assessed. The call was to go forward with renewed courage, and in the confidence that the world was eager to hear the gospel. "Expectant Evangelism" was one of the two distinctive slogans of the meeting. The other was "Partnership in Obedience", and to this phrase we have to give some attention.

The problem of the relation between missionary bodies in the West and the "younger Churches" which were the fruit of their labour in the East and South, had been already for several decades the dominating problem for missions. In the prevailing atmosphere of the colonial era it was not easy for missions to develop a satisfactory relation with the Churches which they still regarded as their children. The various programmes for devolution of responsibility from mission to Church did not have smooth sailing. At the Whitby meeting, the representatives of the older and younger Churches met separately to discuss this matter. The findings of the two groups showed such a remarkable measure of agreement that the conference was able to come with great unanimity to a common statement. The key phrase was "partnership in obedience". Older and younger Churches were equally called to accept the responsibility of mission, and they were to work in an equal partnership, each contributing the gifts that God had given.

The context of this partnership was still the missionary task in the "non-Christian world". Attention was focused, as was natural in a gathering sponsored by the International Missionary Council, upon the task in the traditional "mission lands". The fact that the "younger Churches" are also partners with the older in the evangelization of Europe and North America had not yet become clear.

In the following year (1948) the World Council of Churches was constituted at the Amsterdam Assembly. The International Missionary Council was to be in a relation of "association" with the new body, and very many of those who had been leaders at the Whitby meeting were prominent in the discussions at Amsterdam. One of the four sections into which the Assembly divided was concerned with the missionary and evangelistic task of the Church. Nevertheless, there were very marked differences between the Amsterdam discussions and those of Whitby. At Amsterdam those who were involved in what were traditionally called "foreign missions", whether as missionaries or as "younger churchmen", were a minority. The context was certainly fully ecumenical. It was concerned with all the six continents. But the point of view was that of the Christian dealing with his non-Christian neighbour. The particular problems which haunt every discussion held under the rubric "to the ends of the earth" were absent. The discussion reflected the growing uncertainty within Christendom about the whole matter of evangelism. Significantly the closing chapter of the volume dealing with this section is headed: "Is there a problem of evangelism?" One could say that this discussion was about evangelism in six continents, rather than about mission to six continents. The question had not yet been raised which would dominate the discussion ten years later: "Is there a specifically missionary task which is, on the one hand, more than the evangelism of one's neighbours, and is, on the other, valid even when the geographical division of the world into "Christian" and "Mission" lands is no longer valid?"

Willingen

Five years after Whitby, in 1952, the International Missionary Council convened a major meeting at Willingen in Germany. This meeting was widely thought at the time to have failed in its major task. But subsequent history has shown that it was in fact one of the most significant in the series of world missionary conferences.

The primary purpose for which the meeting was called was a profound rethinking of the nature of the missionary obligation of the Church. In a phrase which was frequently used in the course of the preparatory work, there was felt to be urgent need for a "theology of missions". The very foundations of the whole missionary movement were in need of re-examination; and the changes in the world were so revolutionary as to raise the question whether missions in the traditional sense were not already a thing of the past. When Canon Max Warren told the conference: "We have to be ready to see the day of missions, as we have known them, as having already come to an end", he was expressing the central questioning which had led to the calling of the conference. When the conference documents were assembled in one volume, they were given the title: "Mission under the Cross", for, in the words of Dr Norman Goodall, the editor: "The moments at which the whole gathering felt itself most surely under the leading of God . . . were those in which the Cross and its 'hiddenness' were the focus of worship and the theme of exposition."

Two issues dominated the discussions of the section which was charged with the preparation of a statement on the missionary obligation of the Church. On the one hand, a sharp attack was launched, primarily by J. C. Hoekendijk of the Netherlands, against the Church-centric view of missions which was implied by the title of the study, and which had been dominant in the thinking of the I.M.C. since the Tambaram conference. On the other hand, and closely related to the first, there was a strong effort made, especially by the North American study group which had prepared for the conference, to relate the missionary task to the signs of Christ's present sovereignty in the secular world. In the time available at the conference the group could not produce a statement which commanded the assent of the whole gathering. A substitute document was prepared which, without really coming to grips with these two issues, nevertheless gave a clear affirmation of the basis of the missionary calling of the Church in the being of the Triune God himself.

While the Willingen meeting could not reach an acceptable reconciliation of these theological tensions, its work has proved fruitful in the subsequent years. The affirmation that the mission is the *Missio Dei*, and that mission belongs to the very being of the Church itself, has been determinative of much later thinking. The statement of Willingen that "there is no participation in Christ without participation in His mission to the world" has reverberated down the subsequent years. At the same time those who struggled unsuccessfully at Willingen to develop a doctrine of mission which takes more account of what God is doing in the world outside the Church have been justified by subsequent developments in thought. It has become plain that a completely "Churchcentric" theology of mission is inadequate. The mission of God is more than Church extension. The question of the relation of Church to mission is a matter of continuing debate, but there is no doubt that Willingen gave the debate much of its direction and its power.

Beside the theological question which was the main reason for meeting, Willingen was the starting-point of a number of lines of thought and experiment which have been important in subsequent ecumenical history.

New forms of ministry

Tambaram had given much attention to the need for a more adequately trained professional ministry. Willingen asked whether a full-time paid ministry is "fundamental to the nature of the Christian ministry, or is it an uncritical transplantation to another soil of what was appropriate to a different environment?" The call to examine this question was repeated at the Ghana Assembly of the I.M.C. in 1957 and has led to the widespread ecumenical study of forms of the ministry which is still going on.

The role of the layman abroad in the mission of the Church

One of the most important words spoken at the Willingen Assembly was the call of Canon Max Warren for "an entirely new type of missionary activity to be developed alongside the traditional modes".

> We need [he said] to envisage men and women of scientific training who will be ready to give their service in development schemes, going to their work as ordinary salaried officials and bringing their expert knowledge to bear on some local situation. But they will go, not merely as those whose Christian convictions are marginal to their work . . . Rather they will go with a vocation consciously and deliberately to seek to work out a distinctive and purified technology in the light of Christian insights.

The Assembly drew attention to the fact that while there were 300 Swiss missionaries serving abroad, there were 65,000 Swiss serving abroad in secular occupations, and to the plans developed by the Swiss Missions Council for the training of Christians going abroad in such service. The birth of the movement of "development" which was to become so prominent in the 1960s, constituted a challenge to the Churches to a new kind of missionary action. Though Willingen called for action to follow up the call of Canon Warren, it must be admitted that the response came only slowly. It was not until 1960 that the I.M.C. appointed a Secretary (Dr Paul Löffler) for this specific purpose.

The Creation of Regional Study Centres

During a visit to India prior to the Willingen meeting, H. Kraemer had expressed the opinion that the Church there lacked the means of coming into direct contact at a deep level with the thought of the country. There was need for the creation of some sort of centre at which men with adequate specialist training could devote time to study, research, and promotion of dialogue with representatives of living movements of thought outside the Church. This conviction was shared with others, at an informal meeting at Willingen convened by Glora M. Wysner, and a recommendation was made to the I.M.C. favouring "the establishment of regional centres for study and research on questions related to the work of the Christian mission and the growth of the Church, affording opportunity to individuals and groups for study, writing, training and conference, and also undertaking the publication of relevant studies and research". This recommendation was taken up vigorously by the I.M.C. Dr Wysner undertook a journey in the Near East and Asia as the result of which plans were developed for study centres in Jerusalem and Bangalore and other places. With steady encouragement this programme has developed greatly during the subsequent years, and the chain of study centres in Asia, Africa, and Latin America is now playing an important role in the mission of the Church.

Missionary Mobility

During the debates at Willingen there was a sharp attack upon the immobility of missions. "It was roundly declared that the greater part of the contribution of the Western Churches towards the world mission of the Church, in service and money, was no longer employed on the frontier between Church and the world; it was absorbed in the support of a relatively static, long-established Christian enterprise."[1] In response to this challenge separate sessions of the delegates of younger and older Churches were held at which the question was asked: How can the Church recover its missionary initiative and achieve greater mobility? No very clear directives emerged from these discussions; but the conviction was registered that new patterns of partnership were needed if mobility was to be recovered. This conviction was to bear fruit later in the concept of "Joint Action for Mission". At the same time the Assembly

[1] N. Goodall, ed., *Missions under the Cross* (London 1953), pp. 18–19.

devoted a considerable amount of time to the place of institutions in the mission of the Church, and drew up a series of criteria which were to be widely influential during the subsequent decade.

Mission and Unity

The Assembly also adopted a statement on "The Calling of the Church to Mission and Unity", which echoed much of what had been said in the preceding year in a document prepared by the Central Committee of the World Council of Churches at Rolle, Switzerland. The statement urged member councils to seek fresh ways of relating themselves to the work of the Commission on Faith and Order of the W.C.C. At the same time the Administrative Committee of the I.M.C. had before it a formal letter from the Joint Committee of the I.M.C./W.C.C. which asked it to consider seriously the implications for practical life of the statement made at Rolle:

> It is clear in the New Testament that the Church is called at the same time to proclaim the Gospel to the whole world and to manifest in and to that world the fellowship and unity which is in Christ. These two aspects of the calling of the Church are interdependent . . . Can we articulate clearly how these two are related to each other; and can we express in the life of our congregations, our churches and our ecumenical movements this fundamental unity?[1]

In response to this call, the I.M.C. made a series of practical recommendations for further co-operation, especially in the fields of Faith and Order and Inter-Church Aid. This latter area of co-operation was soon to dominate the further discussion of relationships between the two world bodies.

Towards Integration from Evanston

The next major world gathering was the Second Assembly of the World Council of Churches at Evanston in 1954. The attention which was directed to Christian eschatology, especially in the preparatory studies on the main theme, powerfully influenced the thinking of the Churches about their missionary task—for a true theology of missions must be intimately related to eschatology. The Assembly did not, however, produce any explicit new thinking on missionary questions. The section on evangelism did not feel itself called to discuss the specific problems which arise for foreign missions from the fact that their "home base" has become world-wide. The Assembly did, however, take important practical steps leading further towards the integration of the I.M.C. and the World Council. It had before it both the Rolle statement and the correspondence arising therefrom, and also the report of the East Asian Study Consultation at Lucknow (December 1952) which had called for more serious consideration of the relation between the two world bodies. The Assembly decided to reconstitute the Joint Committee with a full-time secretariat, and also to constitute a joint Division of Studies to serve both Councils. It also took note of the experience gained through the appointment of R. B. Manikam as joint Secretary for the two bodies in East Asia, and recommended that the I.M.C., on behalf of both bodies, should

[1] MRCC (Willingen 1952), pp. 34–5.

take the initiative in exploring the possibility of further co-operative action in Africa. The Joint Committee, with Norman Goodall as its full-time Secretary and Henry P. Van Dusen as its Chairman, began a vigorous new phase of its existence.

Its first meeting following Evanston took place in July 1955. It had before it the findings of the recent meeting organized by the Division of Inter-Church Aid at Les Rasses, Switzerland on world needs and strategy. The pressure of human needs and the growing obligation of "development" were compelling Christians to think in much more far-reaching terms about the world and about the service of the Churches. The joint committee noted that in responding to the call to a wider, more far-reaching, and more positive service by all the Churches to one another, and by all the Churches together to human needs throughout the world, further questions are bound to arise calling for joint consideration by W.C.C. and I.M.C. The Division of Inter-Church Aid now felt itself called to enter with massive programmes of aid into the areas in which the missionary societies had long been at work. These societies had been for many decades seeking to lead the Churches to financial self-support and had therefore been reducing the level of aid for on-going work. There was anxiety lest the coming in of large new resources from organizations which were interested in service rather than in mission might both hinder the development of self-support and also deflect the younger Churches from their missionary task. Many years were to be spent in seeking to define the relations between inter-Church aid and mission in such a way as to do justice to both. In the meantime, however, the joint committee recorded its opinion that it "should not immediately concentrate on the question of the possible 'integration' of the World Council of Churches and of the International Missionary Council. While the consideration of this issue is the direct responsibility of the committee, its solution is likely to be reached more effectively if time is taken to develop co-operation together."

A year later, the perspective had changed. The joint committee in 1956 found itself compelled "to recommend to the parent bodies that in the opinion of the joint committee the time has come when consideration should be given to the possibility of full integration between the World Council of Churches and the International Missionary Council, subject to an adequate safeguarding in any plan of integration of the distinctive expression of the mission of the Church as this has been embodied in the International Missionary Council".

The last phrase in this minute voices the anxiety expressed by some missionary leaders that the integration of the two bodies might lead to the pushing of missionary concern to the periphery. Much of the missionary thrust of the preceding century had come from bodies organized independently of the great Churches, and often against their opposition. Was it possible now to trust the Churches with the responsibility for world mission? In answer to this it was pointed out that the strong theological movements of the time were rediscovering, from one angle or another, the missionary nature of the Church. From the point of view of the W.C.C. it was a matter of its spiritual health whether it could go on saying that mission belongs to the very nature of the Church without becoming involved in the life of missions. The question, to quote Dr Visser 't Hooft at the 1956 meeting, was not one of "churchifying mission but of mobilizing the Church for its mission".

At the same meeting (Herrenalb 1956) the joint committee approved of a "list of categories of need for which Inter-Church Aid might seek the support of the churches" for aid to Churches in Asia, Africa, and Latin America. These included, in addition to emergency needs, projects designed to strengthen the Churches' witness or service which went beyond their existing resources. The way was thus opened up for a massive contribution from wealthier Churches through channels other than the traditional missionary channels.

As the result of the 1956 decision on integration, a meeting was held at Lambeth Palace in April 1957, which drafted a plan of integration between the two world bodies for submission to the joint committee. This plan came before the joint committee in July of the same year and after very full discussions an amendment was adopted for presentation to the two bodies. The discussion clearly revealed both the reasons which led many in both councils to seek integration and also the strength of the resistance which could be expected from both sides. On the one hand, the World Council had in its membership Orthodox Churches whose direct experience of Protestant missions had been gained through the work of bodies which had built up Churches mainly composed of converts from among their members. On the other hand, the member councils of the I.M.C., especially in Europe, included many vigorous and effective missionary societies which were organizationally independent of the Churches and which did not desire close administrative connection with them.

It was of great importance that the powerful voice of Dr Walter Freytag, speaking out of the German context in which missions were organized independently of the Churches, was raised in a definite affirmation of the need for integration. Delaying decision, he said, would be a refusal to grow. If mission is the heart of the Church, the heart cannot be separated from the rest of the Church's life. We are approaching a situation in which the Churches are becoming convinced about the missionary obligation, but are continuing to delegate responsibility for the universal aspect of mission to the missionary societies. There is a very grave spiritual danger in this both for the Churches and for the societies. The Churches' understanding of their mission becomes limited and the societies come to have too narrow an understanding of their work.

The Central Committee of the World Council at its meeting the same summer spent much time on the plan of integration and agreed to commend the plan to its member Churches for study, asking them to answer the following two questions:

(a) Are you in principle in favour of integration provided that a satisfactory plan is evolved?

(b) What comment have you to offer on the details of the proposed plan?

In sending the plan to member Churches the committee tried to allay the fear that integration would alter the character of the W.C.C. as a council of *Churches*. It pointed out to those who were afraid of proselytization by evangelical bodies that the I.M.C. had always worked towards co-operation and unity in mission. It drew attention to the document on "Christian Witness, Proselytism and Religious Liberty in the Setting of the World Council" which had been already commended to the Churches, and argued that the problems of proselytism could be better dealt with in an integrated council than by two separate bodies.

Ghana and the Theological Education Fund

At the end of the same year the I.M.C. held a major international assembly at University College, Accra, Ghana. The consideration of the plan of integration was one of the chief matters on the agenda. Several of the member councils had indicated serious reservations about the plan and many had not yet considered it. It was recognized that a very great deal of further discussion was needed. However, the Assembly decided to "accept in principle" the integration of the two councils and recorded its opinion that the draft plan was a "generally suitable instrument" for this purpose. The plan was sent to the member councils for their study and comment.

During the ensuing four years a vigorous discussion took place among the member Churches and member councils of the two world bodies. These culminated in the integration of the two bodies which was accepted by the Assemblies of both of them held in New Delhi at the end of 1961. Two member councils of the I.M.C. declined to accept the integration. They were the Norwegian Missionary Council and the Congo Protestant Council. It must be noted, however, that the relations between the Congo Council and the World Council of Churches after integration became in practice much more intimate than had been its earlier relationships with the I.M.C.

The accomplishment of administrative integration was an exceedingly important moment in the evolution of missionary thinking in an ecumenical context. However, it is important to recognize that the fundamental debates were continuing both before and after integration on the same basic issues. These issues were vividly expressed by Dr Freytag at the Ghana Assembly. He spoke of the "lost directness" of missions. At an earlier stage missions had understood their task as the sending of the gospel to the nations which had not heard it. In the new situation, where there were Churches in all countries bound together in an ecumenical fellowship, missions could not be conceived in the same terms. The new way to conceive them had not yet been clearly seen. The main thing was to see missions as part of the mission of God. The essential task is being sent to proclaim the gospel outside the Church. It is necessary "to remind every church that it cannot be the Church, in limiting itself within its own area, that it is called to take part in the responsibility of God's outgoing into the whole world, that it has the Gospel because it is meant for the nations of the earth, and that the Church has its life towards that end, the goal of God in the coming again of Christ".[1]

[1] The Ghana Assembly of the I.M.C., p. 146.

Following the lines of Dr Freytag, the Ghana Assembly accepted a statement on "the Christian mission at this hour", which took as its starting-point the phrase "the Christian world mission is Christ's, not ours". The statement affirmed that the distinction between older and younger Churches was no longer valid or helpful because it obscured the fact that every Church, because it is a Church, is equally called to a missionary task. "If they *are* churches, they are all alike called to mission."

The same assembly was the occasion of the launching of a very significant new form of ecumenical missionary action. During the years following the Tambaram Assembly the I.M.C. had given much attention to the training of the ministry in the younger Churches. It had sponsored surveys in several parts of the world, and particularly a series of surveys covering the whole of Africa and Madagascar. These had shown the terrible weakness of the Churches' theological training programmes, and the urgent need for more co-operation. As the result of initiatives taken by Charles Ranson, General Secretary of the I.M.C., John D. Rockefeller, Jr had made an offer of two million dollars to be matched by an equal amount from the mission boards in order to create a fund for the strengthening of theological education in the younger Churches. It was proposed that the fund should "select for individual institutional support those seminaries which on the basis of their strategic location, the excellence of their present work, and their plans for development, offer the greatest possibilities for qualitative growth in the future. It would pursue a policy of concentration by limiting its institutional grants to approximately twenty seminaries throughout the younger church areas, thereby endeavouring to build on strength rather than weakness." The Assembly learned that nine North American mission boards had pledged a total of two million dollars to match the offer of Mr Rockefeller. It was therefore resolved to establish the "Theological Education Fund" with Dr Charles Ranson as its first director. The creation of this fund constituted a new form of co-operative action. The resources of the fund, and in particular the services of its staff, were so wisely deployed over the ensuing years as to bring about a radical change in the quality and strength of the theological education in the younger Churches. The example of "TEF" was later followed by the creation in 1964 of a similar fund for Christian literature.

Kuala Lumpur and Joint Action

The Ghana Assembly had spoken of the missionary obligation resting upon every Church however young or small. While this statement was theologically impeccable it was difficult to make its meaning vivid. Missions still had the appearance of a one-way traffic from the Churches of Europe and North America. On the other hand, the World Council of Churches was creating a network of relationships among Churches in which all felt that they could both give and receive. Such a network corresponded much more closely to the contemporary sense of global unity than did the picture presented by missions. Moreover, the growing work of inter-Church aid in Asia, Africa, and Latin America, especially since the adoption of the "Herrenalb categories", gave increasing vividness to the new picture of ecumenical fellowship. There were some for whom it seemed obvious that such inter-Church aid was the modern equivalent of missions. Since the Church existed in almost every country it could be said that the missionary task in the traditional sense had been completed. The idea that a *foreign* missionary task, as envisaged by Dr Freytag, could still be valid in an age of ecumenical fellowship was difficult to grasp.

It was at this point that the development of regional co-operation in East Asia became important for the whole ecumenical discussion. In December 1949, the I.M.C. and the W.C.C. had jointly sponsored an East Asia Christian Conference at Bangkok, Thailand. Following this Dr R. B. Manikam had been appointed by the two bodies as their joint East Asia Secretary. In July 1955, some of the Churches in the eastern part of the region, with encouragement from the Board of World Mission of the Presbyterian Church in the U.S.A., had come together in Hong Kong to set up the "Asia Council on Ecumenical Mission". In the following year the two world bodies called a consultation in Bangkok to consider the future form of regional development in East Asia, and in March 1957 a representative conference was held at Prapat, Sumatra, which planned the creation of a permanent regional organization.

The East Asia Christian Conference was duly constituted at Kuala Lumpur, in May 1959, forty-eight churches committing themselves to its fellowship. The Kuala Lumpur meeting made plain the fact that the acceptance of missionary responsibility by the younger Churches had passed beyond the stage of theological affirmation to that of practical implementation. A survey embodied in the report of the conference showed that there was already a large number of foreign missionaries sent out by the Asian Churches and serving in countries overseas. The Assembly established machinery for the strengthening of this missionary outreach. It adopted an important statement on "the missionary obligation of the Asian churches" which dealt both with the receiving of missionaries from abroad and with the selection and sending of missionaries from the Asian Churches. In the context of the ecumenical discussion of missions it was a matter of the greatest importance that Kuala Lumpur could demonstrate that the foreign missionary task belongs to younger Churches equally with older and retains its validity in the new context of global ecumenical fellowship.

In another direction also, the Kuala Lumpur Assembly broke new ground. The Willingen Assembly had faced the fact that too much of the strength of missions was absorbed in the support of relatively static younger Churches. The need for a more effective and dynamic partnership between missions and the related younger Churches had been seen. The Kuala Lumpur Assembly saw that, in order to achieve this, the first step was to broaden the relations between them. The umbilical cord which had united young Churches to their parent missions in the earliest days should not remain for ever. The aim should be not simple severance leading to total independence, but rather the development of open and adult relations between all the Churches and missions working in a given area with a view to the accomplishment of their task together. The Kuala Lumpur meeting resolved:

That E.A.C.C. initiate ways of helping Asian churches and mission boards and agencies through national Christian councils and missionary councils to face together their total task with a view to deploying the total resources available in the most strategic way for the fulfilment of the mission. This may involve an increasing shift from the present bilateral relationships to a more ecumenical pattern of relationships.

The staff of the I.M.C. had been struggling to develop some coherent thinking along these lines. The Whitby and Willingen Conferences had seen the need for "internationalizing missions", and the I.M.C. staff had tried to develop this idea. The pamphlet *Out of Every Nation* by R. K. Orchard (1959) sought to give more precise expression to it, and in the staff paper *One Body, One Gospel, One World* (1961) the same idea was put forward under the title of "multi-lateral relationships". Encouraged by the proposals of the E.A.C.C., the I.M.C. staff devoted further time to the development of the idea and, at the next annual staff conference, produced a document entitled *Joint Action for Mission*. These proposals came before the Assembly at New Delhi and were welcomed. The Assembly adopted the following statement on the subject:

It believes that missionary advance in many parts of the world requires a redeployment of the resources available in specific geographical areas. A first necessary step towards this is that churches and related missionary bodies in a given area should together survey the needs and opportunities confronting them and the total resources available to meet them. This process of survey should be followed by a consultation of the churches and mission bodies in that area, aimed at securing real and effective redeployment of resources in the light of the agreed goals. This kind of common action will be impossible unless there is a fresh penitence, reconciliation and commitment on the part of all the bodies concerned. It will also raise in many cases searching issues in the realm of faith and churchmanship. The facing of these issues, both spiritual and confessional, will be a necessary precondition of missionary advance. The committee therefore hopes that the Commission and Division will seek to implement these proposals in consultation with churches, related mission agencies, and national and regional councils, taking due account of the confessional issues which may be involved, and making use of the best material available on questions of missionary strategy.[1]

In view of the fact that the Ghana Assembly had accepted in principle the integration of the two world bodies, and that this integration was likely to take place, the I.M.C. convened a consultation in Oxford in September 1958 which sought to make a restatement of the nature of the missionary task in the new ecumenical context. It was now clear that "foreign missions" could no longer be geographically defined. Europe was as much a mission field as Asia, and the "home base" was in Africa as well as in America. The *differentia of missions* could no longer be stated in geographical terms. Nevertheless, one should not draw from this the conclusion that the whole concept of missions and missionaries should be abandoned in favour of such terms as "inter-Church aid" and "fraternal workers". To abandon the concept of mission would be to abandon the New Testament. There remains a distinctively

[1] New Delhi, pp. 251–2.

missionary task, but it is to be defined essentially in terms of "the crossing of the frontier between faith in Christ as Lord and unbelief". To make clear, and to keep clear, this, the distinctive meaning of the word "missionary", is one of the most important requirements of the present discussion. "He who is sent to make Christ known and obeyed as Lord among those who do not know Him is a missionary whether his journey be long or short. The missionary frontier runs through every land where there are communities living without the knowledge of Christ as Lord."[1] But, the statement continued, it belongs to the essence of the gospel that it concerns the ends of the earth, and therefore it follows that "it is the duty and privilege of every part of the Church everywhere to be involved not only in the missionary task at its own door, but also in some other part of the world-wide task . . . To say that the 'home base' is everywhere is not the obliteration of 'foreign missions' but the universalizing of them."[2]

It has been seen that this thinking was already finding practical expression in East Asia. It also had immediate consequence in the formulation of the tasks of the new Commission on World Mission and Evangelism which was to be created within the integrated World Council of Churches. These tasks were outlined in a paper which was presented to, and accepted by, the Assembly in New Delhi. The first task was formulated as follows:

> To assist churches, missions and other Christian bodies to recognize and draw the practical conclusions from the fact that:
> (i) The Christian mission is one throughout the world, for the Gospel is the same and the need of salvation is the same for all men.
> (ii) This world mission has a base which is world-wide and is not confined to the areas once regarded as constituting "Western Christendom".
> (iii) The mission implies a reaching out both to one's own neighbourhood and to the ends of the earth.

In its statement accepting this task the committee of the Assembly at New Delhi wrote as follows:

> The programme of the new Division is not here fully described. It will provide a new frontier, a new dimension of the World Council. We have made a general outline of its task. We cannot now define all its deeper meanings nor the extent of its activities. Only the experience of living and working together can teach us these. Our temptation will be to think of the Division simply as the continuation of the interests of the International Missionary Council with emphasis on Asia, Africa and South America. We must resist this temptation. This is the Division of the World Mission and Evangelism of the World Council of Churches. We are concerned not with three continents but six.

Integration Achieved at New Delhi

The International Missionary Council and the World Council of Churches became one body at the Assembly in New Delhi in November 1961. The

---

[1] *One Body, One World*, p. 29.   [2] Op. cit., p. 31.

integrated Council had immediately to accept a wide range of responsibilities in the field of missionary study, experiment, and joint action.

1. The Department of Missionary Studies inherited and carried forward work in the four main areas.

(a) The study of the theological basis of missions, begun in connection with the Willingen meeting, had not been completed. In a fresh effort to bring together fundamental thinking and ordinary missionary practice, groups around the world were invited to study a book written for the purpose by Johannes Blauw of the Netherlands on "The Missionary Nature of the Church". The results of these world-wide discussions were reflected on in a book by D. T. Niles entitled *Upon the Earth* (1962).

(b) The study of the Christian encounter with other faiths was the major concern of the Centres for the Study of Non-Christian Religions,[1] and the Department sought to stimulate and co-ordinate their work through contact with, and periodical meetings of, the directors of these centres. An important stage in the whole discussion was reached at the meeting of the directors and others held at Kandy, Ceylon, in 1967 on "Christians in Dialogue with Men of Other Faiths". In the preceding year the Department had also organized, at Brummana, Lebanon, a world consultation on "Christian–Muslim Relations".

(c) One of the biggest and most far-reaching of the projects of the Department of Missionary Studies has been a series of studies in depth of the growth of younger Churches in different selected situations. Originally entitled "Studies in the Life and Growth of Younger Churches", it was later replanned on a "six-continent" basis and renamed "World Studies of Churches in Missions". At the time of writing eight volumes have been published dealing with Churches in Uganda, Zambia, Togo, India, the South Pacific, England, Japan, and Congo-Brazzaville. These studies will in turn provide data for further research on the factors which bear upon the growth of the Church and its witness in its environment.

In addition to these major studies, each of which involved not less than a year of field-work by one or more scholars, there have been other consultations on church growth and related issues. At Mindolo, Zambia, a meeting of leaders of African independent Churches, or scholars who had studied the life of these Churches, and of leaders in several National Christian Councils in Africa was held in 1962 which both opened up valuable contacts between the two groups of Churches and also helped to bring out the lessons to be learned from the experience of the independent Churches. A consultation held at Iberville, Canada, in 1963 dealt with general principles of church growth. And in 1964 a meeting at Yaounde in the Cameroons gathered together the results of a survey conducted by a team during the preceding year on the growth, or absence of growth, of Churches in different parts of West Africa.

[1] See p. 180 above.

(d) The Department also continued and added to the series of research pamphlets on a variety of missionary topics which had been begun by the International Missionary Council.

2. The relations between the Divisions of World Mission and Inter-Church Aid had yet to be worked out in detail. The problems which had arisen in relating these two concerns in their day-to-day working had been among the factors leading to the decision to unite the two world bodies. After New Delhi the two concerns were administered within one structure, which meant that there were much better facilities for mutual consultation both on general policy and on specific projects. The basic problems had not been solved, but a structure had been created in which they could be solved. As a first step the New Delhi Assembly accepted the following statement of the relation:

> The integration of the two world bodies will make for greater co-operation of the two Divisions in their common purpose to express the ecumenical solidarity of the churches through mutual aid in order to strengthen them in their life and mission. Within this common purpose the Division of Inter-Church Aid and Service to Refugees is especially concerned to help the churches to serve the world around them, while the Division of World Mission and Evangelism is especially concerned to further the proclamation to the whole world of the Gospel of Jesus Christ to the end that all men may believe in Him and be saved.

The two Divisions would thus be working within a common field, but each would have a distinct focus of concern. This distinction was of real value in helping the new Division to sharpen its specifically missionary intent, but it left open for discussion very large administrative questions, and these were to be the subject of continuing discussion during the ensuing years.

3. The necessity to work out a new relationship with the Division of Inter-Church Aid forced the new Division constantly to face the following question: Does the conviction that "the home base of mission is everywhere" imply that new ecumenical missionary structures have to be created? Specifically, should the new Division initiate and manage missionary projects of an international and ecumenical character? Or should it concentrate upon stimulating joint action in local situations? There were strong convictions on both sides of this matter. Some feared the creation of a large centralized and expensive bureaucracy and pointed out that it was precisely the fear of this which had led some in the missionary councils to oppose integration with the World Council of Churches. Others urged that the missionary movement could only measure up to the demands of the new age by embarking upon such international and ecumenical action. The New Delhi Assembly approved a statement which authorized the Division to experiment in both directions. It authorized on the one hand: "Study, survey, consultation and the establishment of contacts designed to secure a more effective deployment of resources, more co-ordination of effort, the encouragement of more experiments in "multilateral' action, and more joint action where appropriate, special attention being given to the discovery of, and planning for, those geographical areas where there is no continuing Christian witness" and on the other hand "projects of an

international and interdenominational character initiated by the Commission to meet specific needs".[1]

At the time when these words were written, the Theological Education Fund was the most impressive example of such ecumenical projects. The I.M.C. had, however, also initiated other actions on a smaller scale. These included the Centres for the Study of Non-Christian Religions (to which reference has already been made), the publications of "World Christian Books", the programmes of study and training on the Christian Home and Family Life, and the "Islam in Africa Project". This latter was a particularly significant attempt to strengthen the witness of the Church in those areas of Africa where Islam is advancing by providing specialists, literature, and training courses. The Administrative Committee of the I.M.C. had, in 1959, given careful consideration to the proposal for "an International Fund for Mission". As a result of this, and after much discussion, it was decided to constitute a "Projects Fund" to be financed apart from the administrative budget of the Council, and to support such programmes as those just described, as well as the Department of Missionary Studies, the strengthening of national and regional councils, and the exchange of personnel between Councils and Churches. From a modest beginning this project fund has developed during the years following integration. As a result of continuing discussion with the Division of Inter-Church Aid it was agreed that matters which could properly be described as "projects" should be the responsibility of the latter Division, and that the undertakings sponsored by the Division of World Mission and Evangelism be characterized as "programmes". Among the international and ecumenical missionary programmes which have thus been supported the following may be mentioned in addition to those already referred to:

(*a*) In implementation of the call originally given at Willingen for a new type of non-professional lay missionary the Division collaborated with the Division of Inter-Church Aid in the establishment of a "Secretariat for Laymen Abroad". This did much to stimulate both missions and Churches to provide the means by which laymen going abroad in secular service could play their part in the mission of the Church.

(*b*) In order to complete the series of surveys on the training of the ministry, which the I.M.C. had undertaken, the new Division arranged for comprehensive surveys of the training of the ministry in Latin America and the Caribbean, under the leadership of Wilfred Scopes.

(*c*) In the year 1960 the attention of the I.M.C. had been directed to the need for helping the African Churches to meet the challenge of rapid industrialization. Following the general pattern of the "Islam in Africa" project, the administrative committee, at its meeting in St Andrews in 1960, authorized an "Urban Africa Project" under which provision was made for specialist assistance, travel, and conferences. Following the New Delhi Assembly, and collaboration with the E.A.C.C., the Division sponsored the visit of an international team of specialists to a large number of developing industrial centres

[1] *New Delhi Work Book*, p. 144.

in India. It became plain that there was here an area which called for co-operative international action and, at its meeting in 1964, the executive committee of the Division authorized a programme designed "to involve the total Church in all continents in the ecumenical task of urban industrial evangelism and so to promote greater co-operation and a common understanding of its goals".

(d) From the time of the Edinburgh Conference of 1910 the training of professional missionaries had been an important item on the agenda of ecumenical missionary meetings. The Willingen Conference had given much attention to it, but disappointingly little had been done to implement its findings. The Division sponsored a programme of study and consultation, which was focused in a meeting held in Toronto in August 1963. The implementation of the findings of this conference has been among the continuing tasks of the Division.

(e) There were certain kinds of work in which the responsibility for ecumenical action had been carried for many years by one or two national agencies, especially the specialized agencies of the (then) Division of Foreign Missions of the National Council of Churches in the U.S.A. One of these was Christian literature. The D.F.M.'s Department of Literature and Literacy, together with the Christian Literature Council of the Conference of Missionary Societies in Great Britain, had long carried the burden of literature work in many parts of the world. There was, however, no ecumenical agency dealing with Christian literature from a world base. The New Delhi Assembly recommended that the Division should undertake world-wide consultations with a view to a more effective ecumenical co-ordination of the production of Christian literature. As a result of these consultations, the 1963 Mexico meeting of the Commission authorized the creation of a Christian Literature Fund, analogous in its organization to the Theological Education Fund, with a capital of $3,000,000.

(f) In the field of radio and audio-visual aids the agency of the D.F.M., universally known as R.A.V.E.M.C.O., had for long been serving Churches all over the world. There was also an association of Christian broadcasters, which had its main strength in Europe and owed its beginning largely to the initiative of the B.B.C. The need was felt for the creation of a more effective agency in this field, and in 1962 the Division collaborated with the department of information in sponsoring the appointment of a secretary in the field of radio communication. In this way it proved possible to assist in the creation of an effective World Association of Christian Broadcasters. The Division also took the initiative in organizing a co-ordinating committee for intercontinental broadcasting under the leadership of Dr George W. Carpenter, in order to stimulate and co-ordinate ecumenical support for, and use of, the powerful station "Radio Voice of the Gospel" established by the Lutheran World Federation in Addis Ababa, Ethiopia.

(g) The healing ministry has been from the beginning an integral part of the Church's mission, but the rapid changes characteristic of the post-colonial era, and especially the development of welfare states in the former colonial territories, posed very grave problems for the medical missions. The question had to be asked whether, in a modern secular welfare state, there is any longer justification for the great expense involved in the maintenance of hospitals under Christian auspices. At the request of the Department of World Mission of the Lutheran World Federation, and with their collaboration, the Division organized a consultation in Tubingen, Germany, in 1964. This was intended merely to explore methods of further work, but it issued a brief statement concerning the specifically Christian understanding of the nature of healing which evoked a remarkable response throughout the world, not least in the lands of the older Churches. It became apparent that there was need for ecumenical action to assist the Churches in implementing the new insights given to them regarding the healing ministry in the mission of the Church. As a consequence, the Central Committee at its meeting in Crete 1967 authorized the creation of a Christian Medical Commission related to the Divisions of World Mission and Evangelism and of Inter-Church Aid, Refugee, and World Service.

(h) In addition to these major items, the Programme Fund also includes a small amount available at the discretion of the staff for giving immediate assistance to promising missionary projects of ecumenical significance. The existence of this fund has made possible the initiation and growth of many promising ventures in different parts of the world.

Mexico and Mission to Six Continents

The Division has accepted as a basis of its work the conviction that "the home base of the world mission" is world-wide, and that the "mission field" is also world-wide. The problem has always been to make these abstract statements credible through concrete examples. It has been seen that the development of a vigorous foreign missionary movement by the Asian Churches did much to put substance into the doctrine that the "home base" is indeed not confined to the old "Christendom". It was equally necessary to give substance to the other half of the basic conviction. This could happen only when those who were actively engaged in missionary tasks in Europe and North America could be intimately involved in the work of the Division. The achievement of the meeting of the commission in Mexico City (December 1963) was that this happened on a substantial scale for the first time. By general consent the most significant discussions at the Mexico meeting took place in Sections II and III which dealt respectively with "The Christian Witness to Men in the Secular World" and "The Witness of the Congregation in its Neighbourhood". These discussions, held within the context of a world missionary meeting, made vivid for all the participants the fact that the mission field is indeed in all six continents.

It would, of course, be absurd to suggest that concern with the missionary task in the lands of the "older Churches" was something entirely new in the thinking of the foreign missionary movement. The Jerusalem Conference of

1928 had concerned itself with the rise of secularism as a world-wide movement. Dr J. H. Oldham had become convinced, at least during the early
1930s, that if the missionary movement did not concern itself with the situation in the old "Christendom" it would soon be left in a backwater, and it
was with the cordial approval of his colleagues that he was set free to devote
his immense powers to the issues which led up to, and followed from, the
Oxford Conference on Church, Community and State (1937). But the Mexico
meeting broke new ground in the fact that, for the first time at a world missionary gathering, expert attention was given to the specific problems of
mission in Europe and North America. Men and women engaged in "home
missions" were present in a strength sufficient to ensure that this concern was
at no point overshadowed by that of "foreign missions".

The Mexico meeting gathered together and concentrated the thinking which
had been developed through a variety of study programmes. Reference has
already been made to the continued studies on the theological basis of missions by the Department of Missionary Studies. The Department on Studies
in Evangelism, following the New Delhi Assembly, launched a world-wide
study on "The Missionary Structure of the Congregation", which raised
radical questions concerning the nature of the Church and of evangelism.
And the work of Asian theologians, reflecting on the meaning of events in
that continent, had brought into the main stream of missionary thinking the
conviction that God is somehow at work in the secular events of our time,
beyond the bounds of the Church. These and other streams of thought flowed
together at the Mexico meeting to produce a very vigorous process of thinking
about mission in the context of six continents. If the Tambaram meeting had
placed the Christian mission firmly in a churchly context, and if Willingen
had struggled unsuccessfully to break out of this, Mexico must be regarded
as especially significant for the fact that it conceived the missionary task in the
context of what God is doing in the secular events of our time. "The Pattern
of Christian mission in the secular world", said the report of Section II, "must
therefore be one of constant encounter with the real needs of our age. Its
form must be that of dialogue, using contemporary language and modes of
thought, learning from the scientific and sociological categories, and meeting
people in their own situations."[1] Plainly such language is equally relevant in
Boston or Tokyo. The mission field is everywhere.

The section at Mexico which dealt with the Christian witness to men of
other faiths failed to achieve any significant fresh insights. The study launched
by the (combined) Division of Studies in 1956 on "The Word of God and the
Living Faiths of Men" was still in process. It had been seen to be necessary
that responsibility for this study should be lodged with the study centres
which were actually working in the midst of these living faiths. But there was
little sign at Mexico of the emergence of a clear consensus on this matter.
This is no doubt partly an aspect of the profound crisis of faith in the Western
Churches to which reference was made at the beginning of this chapter. It is
also perhaps a symptom of the fact that the discussion of relations between
the gospel and other religions has not yet taken sufficient account of the

[1] MRCC (Mexico City 1963), p. 121.

insights which are being developed in the encounter of the gospel with the secular world.

The fourth section of the Mexico meeting dealt with "The Witness of the Church across National and Confessional Boundaries". In spite of the hesitations of some members, the section advocated advance in the direction of more international and ecumenical action in the field of mission. Its report was a mandate to the Division to move faster than had yet been thought possible in the direction of joint action both on a world scale and in local situations. The missionary agencies have shown their willingness to move in this direction by putting larger resources at the disposal of the programme fund of the Division, and by underwriting the new funds for Christian literature and for the ministry of healing.

The Church and the Jewish People

Among the programmes for which the International Missionary Conference had at an early stage decided to take responsibility was the work of assisting the Churches in their mission to the Jewish people. A Committee on the Christian Approach to the Jews was formed in 1930 as a sponsored agency of the I.M.C., and it developed a full programme of training consultation and conference. At the Amsterdam Assembly it sponsored a declaration on anti-semitism which was taken up by many of the member Churches. At the New Delhi Assembly, when the two world councils were integrated, the committee was reconstituted as the W.C.C.'s Committee on the Church and the Jewish People. The New Delhi Assembly also issued a statement on anti-semitism which was followed up by a number of member Churches and was warmly welcomed in Jewish circles. Encouraged by this welcome the Committee arranged an international consultation between Christian and Jewish leaders at Bossey in August 1965. The difficulties of the meeting were summed up by one of the Jewish leaders as follows: "Most Christians are unable to engage in dialogue about faith and most Jews are unwilling to do so." The comment aptly indicates the difficulty which the Committee faces. Its purpose has always been both to foster relations of mutual understanding and charity between Christians and Jews and also to help the Churches in their mission to the Jewish people to whom, as to all mankind, the Christian is under an obligation to make known the saving truth of the gospel. It is inevitable that there should be a certain tension between these two elements in the responsibility of the Church towards the Jewish people, and to seek the resolution of it has been the main concern of this committee during the past decade. It is of some significance that whereas in the Roman Catholic Church the concern for relations with the Jewish people is lodged in the Secretariat for Unity, the corresponding concern in the World Council of Churches is expressed through the missionary arm of the Council.

Catholic, Evangelical, and Orthodox

In this, as in other matters, the period under review has seen a radical transformation in the relations between the World Council and the Roman Catholic Church. While the scheme *De missionibus* was still under discussion at the Second Vatican Council, an informal meeting was arranged in Switzerland in May 1965 between representatives of the World Council and the Roman Catholic Church to discuss missionary questions. During a week of very frank and intimate discussion many agreements were registered between the two groups. There was a strong conviction that it is not enough for the Churches to collaborate in service to society since, if collaboration stops short with this, the witness which the Churches give to the world is distorted. Collaboration must, above all, serve to glorify Christ; and therefore, granted the great difficulties involved, every effort must be made to avoid the scandal caused by mutual rivalry and hostility in missionary work. The consultation opened up many lines of study concerning both the substance of the gospel we proclaim and the manner in which it is to be proclaimed. It had some effect upon the final shape of the Vatican Decree *Ad gentes*, and it has laid the foundations for further consultation and collaboration.

It is unfortunately not possible to record similar progress in respect of contact with the missionary work of the Conservative Evangelical agencies. It is well known that these agencies maintain a larger number of foreign missionaries than do the agencies connected with the World Council of Churches. While the Churches with which they are related constitute a very much smaller body than the membership of the World Council, the vigour and volume of their missionary witness constitute a standing challenge to the Churches which collaborate in the ecumenical movement. During the period under review there have been some opportunities for mutually fruitful consultation. It remains true, however, that the Division has not yet been able to do much to fulfil that section of its mandate which requires it "to establish contact with evangelistic groups and movements which are still unrelated to the ecumenical movement". It is to be hoped that the growing strength and maturity of these movements will in due time encourage them to enter more fully into the kind of dialogue with other missionary agencies which can mutually enrich both partners.

During the period when the question of integration was under discussion in the two world councils, there was some anxiety among the Orthodox member Churches of the W.C.C. about the possible consequences of this step. Since the integration took place, Orthodox Churchmen have participated in the work of the Commission and Division of World Mission and Evangelism. The staff have had fruitful contacts with the Greek missionary movement *Porefthendes*, and have been able to render some small assistance to that vigorous movement. There has been a consultation in Aarhus in 1964 with Orthodox theologians on theological questions connected with the missionary task of the Church. The International Review of Missions has also carried valuable articles on the missionary work of the Orthodox

Churches. Much more remains to be done to integrate the missionary witness of the Orthodox Churches more fully in the life of the World Council of Churches.

Urgent New Questions

The questions which were most strenuously discussed during the period of history which we have briefly reviewed were questions concerning the form and structure of missions. The shift from the "three-continent" to the "six-continent" perspective was a matter of structure. The problems posed for missions by the rise of the younger Churches, the end of colonialism, and the development of inter-Church aid on a massive scale were questions about the forms and patterns of missionary action. It would certainly be untrue to say that these problems have been solved; but it can be said that, as a result of the decisions made during this period, a structure has been created within which missions can operate in an ecumenical context. It has been shown that it is not necessary to abandon missionary calling, the calling to take the gospel across the frontier to those who do not have it, in order to be part of the modern ecumenical reality. If one compares the present situation with that at the time of the Ghana Conference, one can perhaps say that the beginnings of an answer have been given by Dr Freytag's question about the "lost directness".

The questions which face the ecumenical movement now are different ones. They are questions about the substance of the gospel itself. The World Council of Churches has a Division whose aim is "to further the proclamation to the whole world of the Gospel of Jesus Christ, to the end that all men believe in Him and be saved". The questions that have now to be answered concern the content of that proclamation itself. What is the relation of this proclamation to the action of God in the secular world, to the service rendered by Christians to their fellow men, and to the life of the Church? There is a crisis of faith in the Church, and upon its outcome will depend the possibility of faithful proclamation. During the years in which drastic changes of structure were being made, those involved largely took the content of the gospel for granted. Today that can no longer be done. The course of the next stage in the world-wide mission of the Church will depend upon the recovery by the Church of clarity regarding the gospel which it has to proclaim.

8
Joint Service
as an Instrument of Renewal

GEOFFREY MURRAY

Introduction

In the epilogue to *A History of the Ecumenical Movement 1517–1948*, Bishop Stephen C. Neill wrote:

> It, [the World Council of Churches] makes possible corporate charitable action on a scale never previously considered possible, and unsurpassed as a means of creating genuine Christian fellowship. It has taken the first steps in corporate witness to the whole body of the churches and to the world (p. 728).

Even in the short time since that judgement was written there have been changes of attitude and outlook. Today those associated with the W.C.C.'s Division of Inter-Church Aid, Refugee, and World Service would shrink from referring to the work in which they are engaged as "charity". Rather, they now speak of the work they do as an endeavour to facilitate the sharing of resources—spiritual, personal, material, and financial—by the ecumenical fellowship to help meet needs on behalf of humanity, and without distinction of creed, caste, race, nationality, or politics. During the 1960s the Churches began to take part in those governmental and intergovernmental programmes known as Development Aid. The role which many Churches played, and are continuing to play in the United Nations' Freedom from Hunger Campaign, World Food Programme, and the Development Decade goes far beyond the accepted limits of "charity".

Nevertheless, Bishop Neill's general statement is still true. Action has been, and is being, taken "on a scale never previously considered possible, and unsurpassed as a means of creating genuine Christian fellowship". This action is what is known as Inter-Church Aid. The first measures tentatively sketched in the Rouse and Neill *History* have gathered an astonishing dynamism and momentum during the past quarter of a century.

They began with one man and a secretary working in a small office in Geneva in the spring of 1945 and gradually evolved to become the largest single Division of the World Council of Churches. In round figures, one person in every four on the headquarters staff of the World Council of Churches in Geneva at the beginning of 1968 was working in the Division of Inter-Church Aid, Refugee, and World Service, and some 200 more were employed by it around the world. Again, the Division raised its own budget and this was, in the mid-1960s, roughly fifty per cent more than the entire general budget of the World Council.

With this money the Division paid its staff, administrative costs, and overhead expenses. It also helped to support other divisions and departments of the World Council, to strengthen various national and regional councils of Churches. It financed certain programmes of its own, such as the Scholarships Programme, the Health Programme, the Literature Programme, and part of the budget of Casa Locarno, the ecumenical rest centre for pastors and church workers and their wives, which it maintained jointly with the Swiss Protestant Churches.

In addition, the Division circulated to the member Churches and their service agencies an annual project list which detailed some 600 projects in about sixty countries which requested support totalling about $20,000,000 a year. In response to these requests, and to emergency appeals which the Division put out from time to time after natural or man-made disasters, roughly $13,000,000 flowed through the Division every year, and these sums were passed on without any deduction whatsoever to the designated recipients.

Two inferences are usually drawn from the figures given in the last paragraph. The first is that the Churches find it easier to act together in relieving human suffering than to act together in any other cause. The second inference is that this joint action creates, as Bishop Neill said in the passage quoted, genuine Christian fellowship. This solidarity of Christian compassion in the face of want and deprivation has taken many forms. Among them are services to tens of thousands of refugees and displaced persons, the provision of theological books, the offering of surgical and medical treatments that could not otherwise be obtained, the means to build churches and parish houses. Also skilled persons are sent to carry out technical services that the Churches have called for. The augmenting of pastors' stipends, funds for the defence of religious liberty and civil rights, the provision of trade training schools, the building of houses for the homeless, the provision of well-boring rigs, the stocking of farms with seeds, animals, and tools, the equipping of hospitals, and a thousand other acts of mercy are regularly undertaken. All this has combined to remove doubts and hesitations about the reality of the Christian fellowship. A not unimportant by-product is that it has persuaded many Churches to enlist in the ecumenical movement.

An attempt will be made in the present chapter to narrate how Inter-Church Aid has grown. But before embarking on the story it is necessary to define what is meant, within the World Council, by "Inter-Church Aid". The present chapter is emphatically not a history of "charity", however conceived, since 1948. The writer is acutely aware of what is being done by denominations, world confessional bodies, mission societies, Roman Catholics, Jews, the Red Cross, inter-governmental and U.N. special agencies, and others. But he has had necessarily to confine himself to the joint service undertaken by the member Churches of the World Council through its Division of Inter-Church Aid, Refugee, and World Service (D.I.C.A.R.W.S.).

Inter-Church Aid Defined

From the beginning the Church has been, or has tried to be, obedient to the command of Jesus to succour those in distress. An early instance of this is cited in Acts 11. 29–30: "Then the disciples, every man according to his ability, determined to send relief unto the brethren which dwelt in Judaea: Which also they did, and sent it to the elders by the hands of Barnabas and Saul." This illustration could be multiplied endlessly. The outcome has been a ministry of service that has spread throughout the world.

But, as the work grew, it was generally marked until recent times by the concern of the Churches for their own people. Church activities of this kind continue and are often international or supranational. Help given by a "mother" Church to a "daughter" Church—by, for example, Methodists in the U.S.A. to Methodists in Ghana, or by Baptists in Britain to Baptists in Pakistan—is right and proper. But this is not Inter-Church Aid as its practitioners have come to understand it. Within the World Council, Inter-Church Aid is interpreted as joint action in service that crosses ecclesiastical and geographical boundaries. In other words, Inter-Church Aid, thus understood, is given when a Church in one part of the world is helped by a Church or Churches of different Christian traditions located elsewhere to carry out the efforts it is making to meet the needs of its neighbours whoever they may be. Inter-Church Aid strives through service to promote the renewal of the Churches.

The core of the work done by the W.C.C.'s Division of Inter-Church Aid, Refugee, and World Service is the co-ordination of inter-Church aid programmes and projects. At the beginning there were those who thought that the way to achieve this was by a pooling of funds. Others believed that inter-Church aid should be effected as a Church-to-Church operation. The genius of the World Council has been to make a circle around the whole network of "service" relationships and in this way give expression to Christian solidarity in helping to meet church, social, and economic needs of almost every kind. A new understanding has emerged that the place where Christ himself is to be served is in the persons of those in need wherever they are and whoever they may be. By serving the whole of mankind in all its diversity, inter-Church aid witnesses both to Christians and others to the oneness of the human family under God.

Inter-Church Aid, in the special ecumenical sense here given to it, has thus established within a relatively few years an entirely new pattern of Christian stewardship and for the dispensing of resources often contributed by those outside the Churches. In one way it has enormously widened ecclesiastical horizons. In another it has dovetailed into a firmly jointed whole a great variety of means for showing the solidarity of Christian compassion in the face of adversity. The conception of "giving" and "receiving" Churches which sometimes carries with it in the "Third World" implications of neo-colonialism and dependence is being phased out by the ecumenical practice. All are together as equals in a common enterprise of service in which they give and share from their own free choice according to their talents, their means, and their opportunities.

Thus, the National Council of the Churches of Christ in the U.S.A. can seek support for its Mississippi Delta Ministry which is helping Negroes and white sympathizers to change the structure of society, in a way that will afford social justice for all. The Mississippi Delta Ministry has attracted workers from overseas as well as contributions from Churches in Africa, Asia, and Europe. Inter-Church Aid includes those who plan, serve, and administer in National and Regional Councils of Churches, and in certain self-governing bodies such as Japan Church World Service, those who give money and material aid, and, no less, those who pray and lend spiritual and moral support. All become partners in a world-wide ministry of mercy.

The role of the Division of Inter-Church Aid, Refugee, and World Service is to foster the renewal of the Churches through service in unity. The Division is charged to ensure that no project admitted to its list for support by members of the World Council is calculated to entice adherents from one Church and enroll them in another.

In reaching this interpretation of Inter-Church Aid, the ecumenical fellowship is indebted incalculably to the late Adolf Keller. The term "Inter-Church Aid" can probably be ascribed to him. It appears in the title of the European Central Bureau for Inter-Church Aid, the body which he was largely instrumental in founding in 1922 and carried on until it was merged in the provisional World Council of Churches in 1944 as an integral part of the Department of Reconstruction and Inter-Church Aid. Dr J. Hutchinson Cockburn, a former Moderator of the Church of Scotland, accepted the post of Senior Secretary of the Department in December 1944. It is at this point that this chapter resumes the history of ecumenical service, begun in the Rouse and Neill book, which is now conceived as the responsibility of a world fellowship of Churches.

The W.C.C. Department of Reconstruction and Inter-Church Aid[1]

Dr Cockburn did not reach Geneva until March 1945, and then only after hammering daily for many weeks on the door of the French authorities in London for permission to travel. The journey from Britain to Switzerland then involved five changes of trains, for bridges and tunnels along the line between Paris and Geneva had been damaged. Flying from Britain to Switzerland appears not to have been possible at that time. These facts serve to indicate something of the conditions of chaos in which the department was to go to work.

In Geneva, Dr Cockburn was installed in an office at the top of a small house in the Champel district which then constituted the headquarters of the World Council. His staff was a shorthand typist who was adept at languages. While the war in Europe dragged on for another two months, Dr Cockburn learned his job, chiefly from various memoranda about countries and their Churches that were put in his hands. One of these memoranda was the mandate for the department. It had been drawn up by W. A. Visser 't Hooft and approved by the Provisional Committee of the World Council of Churches in 1943. It said:

> The paramount principle is that which is implied in the very existence of the World Council, namely, that the task of reconstruction is to be conceived as an ecumenical task in which all the churches participate to the limit of their ability, and that the common objective is to rebuild the whole life of the fellowship of churches which finds expression in the World Council. If this ecumenical principle is taken seriously, this will mean that the churches will agree to co-ordinate their policies and activities in order to make certain that all needy churches receive adequate help, that the churches will not confine

[1] For the following section, the writer has drawn extensively from a Memorandum written by Dr Cockburn and given to the late Dr Leslie E. Cooke, who would have been the author of the present chapter had he not died in February 1967.

their help exclusively to the churches belonging to the same denomination or confession, and that the autonomy and desires of the receiving churches are taken into full consideration.[1]

Cockburn began energetically to recruit staff to carry out the immense task that he saw required to be done. Tremendous though the work before him was, he regarded it as no more than to meet a temporary emergency and looked to its completion within three years, when the First Assembly was to meet in Amsterdam. The first and most urgent need that was seen was to dispense food and clothing. To manage this service of direct material aid a division was created within the Department of Reconstruction and Inter-Church Aid under the direction of S. C. Michelfelder, a Lutheran from the U.S.A.[2] Dr Michelfelder had been sent to Geneva as a special commissioner of the American section of the Lutheran World Convention. He was invited by the World Council of Churches to serve as its material aid secretary in addition to his other responsibilities. The agreement for him to serve in this dual capacity was one of the earliest forms of co-operation between the W.C.C. and what is now the Lutheran World Federation.

A World Council Secretariat for non-Aryan Refugees had been formed as early as February 1939, under the Reverend Adolf Freudenberg, who now became Cockburn's associate. Freudenberg, along with Oliver Béguin, had been giving attention for some time to reconstruction activities. Cockburn soon had a department with eleven divisions. These divisions were: (1) General Support of Churches and Pastors' Salaries; (2) Material Aid; (3) Bibles and Literature; (4) Theological Education and Scholarships; (5) Wooden Churches and Halls; (6) Youth Movements; (7) Refugees; (8) German Churches; (9) German Literature; (10) Finance; and (11) Publicity.

It was accepted in 1945 that each secretary of a departmental division would deal with the matters committed to him in all countries, but it was thought that it would be "valuable" if each made himself an authority on the church life of one country or group of countries. Cockburn therefore made the following allocations. He himself took responsibility for Italy and Greece. Others were allocated for Germany; Scandinavian countries; Rumania, Bulgaria, Yugoslavia, Austria, and Hungary; Holland, Czechoslovakia, Spain, and Portugal; France and Belgium; and Finland and Poland. He began in Europe, for this was the area of greatest immediate damage. Additional expert advice and knowledge were available, when required, from other members of the World Council staff.

Cockburn recruited his divisional secretaries in the U.S.A., Britain, Switzerland and other countries. Among them were those who represented individual Churches, federations of Churches, or National Councils of Churches. Some members of the department were recruited because of their special talents or experience. One was invited to come from the Allied Military

[1] Quoted by Bishop George Bell, *The Kingship of Christ*, p. 38.
[2] The knowledgeable may think this is a reversal of W.C.C. terminology, for its Departments are either autonomous or embraced by "Divisions", but this nomenclature was not adopted until the Second Assembly at Evanston 1954; until then there were divisions within "Departments".

Control in Germany; another was called from a foreign congregation in London. Some persons were appointed to give their energies to a particular country whose language they spoke and wrote. By 1948 Cockburn had built up an organization of sixty-seven persons, including attachés or seconded staff. About twenty had executive status.

The dislocation that prevailed in Europe when the department began added urgency. At that moment there were an estimated 12,500,000 refugees, displaced persons, and uprooted persons in western Europe. There were 10,000 damaged or destroyed church buildings throughout the Continent. More than 3,200 church buildings had been completely demolished. An additional 2,000 pastors' houses, parish halls, and other Church-owned premises had been severely battered by warfare. Many more churches in Britain had been destroyed, in addition to the above. Germany alone had 6,400 ravaged churches. Apart from the spiritual hunger that came from the disruption of church life in so many parishes, physical hunger was also endemic. Food in vast quantities was urgently required for distribution among the starving, as well as an enormous tonnage of clothing, blankets, medicines, beds, and other goods. Telegrams were continually being received that pleaded for the replacement of hospital equipment lost in the bombing, for blankets needed to cover patients in danger of freezing, and of beds, blankets, and mattresses for tuberculous children.

Moreover, it must be stressed that the physical devastation, with its ruined towns, wrecked railways, and shattered factories, and all the chronic shortages of food, clothing, shelter, work, and man-power which accompanied it, was only an outward sign of an inner trauma. There was in Germany the psychological disturbance that came with the realization of defeat and the occupation of the country by the Allies and their soldiers. In France, Denmark, and the Netherlands there was the reverse experience of being "occupied" one day and free the next. Throughout the war years it had been honourable to kill, to lie, to be engaged in sabotage and hate; but after the cease-fire such actions were held once more to be sinful. The tremendous task of renewing the life of the Churches so that they might proclaim the Christian gospel was an "inside" affair. They needed love and friendship.

The Department of Reconstruction and Inter-Church Aid attacked this situation along two lines. First it set up, or, if they already existed, it adopted, corresponding bodies, representative councils or committees in those countries which were able and ready to help the Churches in countries devastated by war. Supporting agencies of this kind were active at first in the U.S.A., Britain, Switzerland, Denmark and Sweden; later in Canada, New Zealand, and Australia. Second, it wrote to, and, where possible, its representatives visited, non-Catholic Churches in European countries and asked them to appoint representatives to meet together, in common council, to discuss their needs. (The Roman Catholic Church was not approached because it had its own plans and organizations.)

The response was most encouraging. Committees of the kind suggested were set up in France, Belgium, Holland, Norway, Germany, Poland, Austria, Czechoslovakia, and Hungary. It was found that in some countries the leaders of a number of Churches had never met for discussion of common needs and purposes. Either at a first meeting or later Cockburn or another member of his staff spent some days in discussion with the committees. Then a report was presented to the department for it to communicate to the supporting agencies so that whatever help was available could be co-ordinated and shipped. Thus was the classic pattern of Inter-Church Aid set and developed.

Assistance was at first tentative, but it quickly mounted as the department was able to gather and validate the needs of the Churches in the war-ruined countries. As early as 15 May 1945 the Central Office for Inter-Church Aid in New York had intimated that it would place $100,000 at the department's disposal. Within a few months the total had grown to $600,000 contributed by Churches in the U.S.A. This was available to buy supplies. Considerable quantities of goods were offered by Churches in Switzerland and Sweden, as well as by others in the U.S.A.

By February 1946 the Provisional Committee of the World Council of Churches had been informed that the World Council Services Committee in the U.S.A. was hoping to raise $9,000,000 over a four-year period. This would be passed to the department or sent directly to needy Churches. The Swiss Reconstruction Committee had raised and spent its first million francs ($233,640) and was appealing for its second million. The British Committee for Reconstruction in Europe also had substantial funds and would spend these as allowed by the regulations controlling the transfer of sterling. In the upshot, the British Committee raised a "Million Pound Fund" (then worth about $4,000,000) at a time when Britain was still enduring severe food rationing and was itself rebuilding war damaged buildings and factories. The Swedish Committee was helping generously its sister Churches in Norway and Finland, and had sent help to Holland and Germany.

The aid given included medicines, food, clothing, footwear, blankets, equipment of various kinds, Bibles, books, libraries in many languages, cattle, seeds, and some thousands of tons of cellulose to enable paper mills to restart and publications to begin. At one point Cockburn telephoned to New York and said that he needed $500,000 in three days for relief work; he got it, and $60,000 in addition. Bishop Berggrav of Norway asked for help to adapt a large fishing boat, with its fish hold made into a church, so that a pastor could sail up the coast beyond the North Cape to offer services of worship, marriage, and baptism to villagers whose churches had been destroyed during the German retreat. Cockburn backed the plan and found supporters in Britain to help pay for it.

Church life had been disrupted and had to be restarted. The "Wooden Churches" division began with a programme to buy 138 barrack huts from the Swiss and Swedish armies and to convert these huts into places of worship, parsonages, and parish centres for those who lacked them. These wooden churches, costing more than $700,000, were allotted to congregations in areas of greatest need: Germany was given forty-four, France forty, Holland thirty-seven, Austria eleven. Two each were sent to Belgium, Hungary, and Poland. They were the direct gift of American Christians, co-operating through Church World Service and Lutheran World Federation, and of British,

H

Canadian, Danish, New Zealand, Swedish, and Swiss church people. Contributions were also received from the Lutheran Church–Missouri Synod which was outside the World Council fellowship.

The department was at pains to encourage and find support for self-help programmes. In Germany, H.E.K.D. (*Hilfswerk der Evangelischen Kirche in Deutschland*—Relief Work of the Protestant Churches in Germany), under the leadership of Dr Eugen Gerstenmaier, quickly became the largest voluntary relief agency in that war-torn country. It channelled the distribution of supplies from abroad and collected goods and money within Germany. Ninety thousand laymen were recruited to administer its programme. Between 1945 and 1950 H.E.K.D. distributed 66,000 tons of goods, clothing, shoes, medicines, raw materials, and books that had been sent to Germany by Churches in twenty-four countries.

In the introduction to a booklet[1] published in 1960, the late Bishop Dr Otto Dibelius, then the Bishop of Berlin and Chairman of the Evangelical Churches in Germany, wrote:

> Every German knows the generosity with which America has assisted the German people to rebuild a new life out of destruction. Our gratitude will never cease, and nowhere is this gratitude felt more strongly than in the Evangelical Churches of Germany. Much aid has come through free-giving in your congregations, but you have also made strong efforts to ensure that the surplus commodities of the U.S.A. did not pass by church institutions. Your giving has been an example of brotherly and personal concern and care … thus establishing a fraternal relationship which until now was unknown between the churches of different countries. This ecumenical fellowship will bear fruit.

Nor were the Orthodox Churches and countries of eastern Europe overlooked. These were the concern, as they continue to be, of the Department. They were helped to restore their church life where this had been disrupted by war. Scholarships were provided for their students. Their priests were helped. Books and periodicals were shipped to their seminaries and theological faculties. Medical treatment was offered to church workers and their families who were sick. In all this, the Orthodox and non-Orthodox were served as equals in the ecumenical fellowship. This loving concern gradually convinced those Orthodox Churches that had refrained from joining the World Council that theological and ecclesiastical hesitations should not keep them out of the ecumenical fellowship, and by 1968 virtually all the Orthodox Churches were members.

Over the years, Orthodox Churchmen have commented on the help given to their people by denominations in other countries and often of radically different Christian tradition from their own. Thus, in 1950, during the meeting of the Central Committee of the W.C.C. at Toronto, Archbishop Strinopoulos Germanos, Metropolitan of Thyateira and at that time one of the Presidents of the World Council, expressed appreciation for the work of the Inter-Church

---

[1] *Dank für Hilfe durch das Amerikanische Volk 1945–1960.* This was published only in German, so that the quotation which follows is an English translation from the original German.

Aid Department among Orthodox clergy and laity in Germany and Greece. Such help, he said, had not been confined to money, but had included essentials needed by chaplains in the camps, down to candles and oil for services. He added that he had been asked by the Ecumenical Patriarch of Constantinople to convey his gratitude to the W.C.C. and Inter-Church Aid. The following year, during the Central Committee meeting at Rolle, Switzerland, Professor H. S. Alivisatos expressed heartiest thanks on behalf of the Greek Churches for allocations to poor clergy, for food and clothing for refugees and the poor, for scholarships, for help with church and religious publications, for a new educational centre for the Church, and for a new printing press. Many others, including Metropolitan James, expressed similar views.

As a footnote to this section, the story of E.C.L.O.F. (The Ecumenical Church Loan Fund) should be remembered. It was established in 1946 to be a supplementary source of funds for Churches wishing to find money to complete their building projects or to buy necessary equipment. In the 1920s, Gustav Hentsch, a Genevan banker, led in founding A.P.I.D.E.P. (*Association Protestante Internationale des Prêts*—International Protestant Loan Association). Hentsch believed that the situation after the Second World War called for a loan organization more broadly based and more flexible than A.P.I.D.E.P. He therefore created E.C.L.O.F. with its central board which allocates capital to national E.C.L.O.F. committees in Europe, Asia, Africa, and Latin America. Money repaid to a national committee stays in that country where it continues to "revolve". The interest charged is nominal. E.C.L.O.F. is an independent body, but the Division, under its various names, is closely associated with it and seeks additions to its capital. A.P.I.D.E.P. and E.C.L.O.F. continued as separate organizations until 1963, when they were brought together in a centralized administration. The capital currently exceeds $700,000 and more than 1,000 loans have been made without any Church defaulting.

Refugee Programme

Arrangements to transfer ecumenical responsibility for refugees and displaced persons to the Department of Reconstruction had been made in July 1945. The mandate of the Refugee Secretariat was:

1. To seek and distribute knowledge on the situation of refugees.
2. To co-ordinate and promote church efforts on their behalf, to help Churches in disaster areas, to help refugees where no Christian organization was available, to minister to their spiritual needs, and to represent the World Council of Churches before intergovernmental and governmental groups interested in refugees.

A Refugee Committee was constituted and had for its chairman the Reverend Henry Carter, a distinguished British Methodist who was honoured by the King of England for his work with refugees.

Broadly, the mandate set out above has continued to govern the work of the World Council of Churches for refugees and displaced persons. Technically, a "refugee" is someone who has fled from his homeland and has no prospect of being readmitted to it; a "displaced person" is someone who has been forced to move to another area but may be repatriated. In popular usage, the two terms are often employed synonymously, but, in fact, they refer to two distinct categories of people. A third category, of whom little was heard outside Western Germany, were those known as "expellees". They included ten million Germans from former German territories that had come under Russian or Polish administration. These people were forced to move and could not be repatriated because they were considered to be Germans moving into another part of Germany. "Expellees" were not "refugees" unless they fled across the right border.

Immediately after the Second World War, U.N.R.R.A. (the United Nations' Relief and Rehabilitation Agency) was charged to meet human need, to foster reconstruction, and to assist governments throughout eastern and western Europe following the devastation caused by the conflict. U.N.R.R.A., which had no mandate to care for the repatriated and displaced persons, was succeeded in 1948 by the I.R.O. (International Refugee Organization), another specialized agency of the United Nations. This, as its name makes clear, had responsibility for refugees. I.R.O. was replaced in 1951 by the United Nations' High Commissioner for Refugees (U.N.H.C.R.) and, for Palestine Arab refugees, by U.N.R.W.A. (United Nations Relief and Works Agency). The U.N.H.C.R. is concerned to provide legal protection for refugees and to assist governments and voluntary agencies to find permanent solutions for refugee problems. Another organization, I.C.E.M. (Intergovernmental Committee for European Migration) is composed of representatives of twenty-seven governments, and serves to facilitate the movement out of Europe of migrants and refugees who would not otherwise be moved. A kindred body was the United States Escapee Programme (U.S.E.P.). This was part of the U.S. State Department and operated among those refugees who had fled from eastern Europe.

The W.C.C. Refugee Programme did not distinguish between refugees, displaced persons, or "escapees" but took "need" as its criterion. It had working relationships with the U.N.H.C.R., U.N.R.R.A., U.S.E.P., and I.C.E.M., and had liaison in Geneva with the National Catholic Welfare Conference, the Lutheran World Federation, and the League of Red Cross Societies, as well as with other bodies that cared for refugees and displaced persons. So far as was practicable, National and Regional Councils of Churches have been encouraged to care for refugees and to integrate them into local communities. But it has always been recognized that to befriend refugees by advising them and trying to find the best solution of their particular problem calls for a great deal of specialized knowledge, especially when the solution is to move them from "countries of first asylum" to countries of resettlement, sometimes halfway around the world.

Legal requirements and intricate knowledge of sources where specialized help can be found, and familiarity with the mandates of intergovernmental, international, governmental, and voluntary agencies all call for unusual attainments and technical skill that National Councils of Churches cannot usually be expected to command. In post-war Europe, staff of the Service to Refugees helped the local Churches to solve refugee problems so vast and complex that they felt they needed help from outside to tackle them. It was not so much that the local Churches lacked skill and knowledge but that they seriously lacked funds and personnel to do all that had to be done if lives were to be saved. Consequently, a centralized service, now known as the Refugee Programme, was set up by the World Council, and this programme has also been, with the full approval of the Churches, an operational one, in the sense of itself carrying out projects for the social integration of refugees unable, for one reason or another, to emigrate from a country of asylum to one of re-settlement. But whenever circumstances have required that services to refugees be operational, the aim has always been to hand over as soon as possible the project to a local Church or ecumenical agency for its mainten-ance. In the operational side of its work, the Division collaborates with organizations engaged in similar activities, including Jewish agencies.

An important step towards the fulfilment of one aspect of the original mandate of the Refugee Secretariat was an agreement entered into in May 1946, with U.N.R.R.A. It was agreed that the Department should operate at first in Germany, Austria, and Italy, and, as developments showed to be desirable and practicable, in Poland, Czechoslovakia, and Hungary. It was expressly stated that the Department's work in Central Europe would not be primarily among Lutheran Displaced Persons of the Latvian and Estonian Churches, who would be the responsibility of Lutheran organizations, but would include Orthodox from eastern countries and Protestants of various denominations from Poland and Czechoslovakia. This apportioning of responsibilities was never regarded as rigid.

The services to be offered by the Department for the rehabilitation of refugees would include the supply and distribution of food, clothing, and medicines, and the provision of facilities and equipment for work among young people, such as the formation of youth clubs associated with Churches; also craft equipment, and supplies and equipment necessary for the main-tenance of divine worship. The Department would draw supplies consigned to it by National Councils or Councils of Churches. U.N.R.R.A. for its part agreed to assist wherever possible in the shipment of supplies to the Depart-ment's field workers. All costs, including those of sea transport, would be borne by the voluntary agencies sending supplies. In the upshot, the Depart-ment recruited many volunteers from all over the world and there was much interchanging of personnel with U.N.R.R.A.

When Cockburn set up the Department of Reconstruction, various church agencies from many countries were working among refugees in Europe. Among these was Church World Service, which was created in 1946 out of various committees to be the service arm of the Federal Council of Churches in the U.S.A. One of the first concerns of Church World Service was the resettlement of the mass of Europe's displaced persons in association with the International Refugee Organization and the United Nations' Relief and Rehabilitation Agency (U.N.R.R.A.). Church World Service soon set up its own displaced persons department, which provided services in Europe in co-operation with the World Council of Churches.

During 1947 the American Christian Committee for Refugees turned over its commitments for assisting refugees and displaced persons to Church World Service, and for the first time there was a joint agency offering refugee and resettlement services on behalf of Protestant and Orthodox Churches in the United States.

Harold E. Fey has noted:

> When Church World Service was launched in 1946, it assumed responsibility for eight material aid centres or warehouses in the United States belonging to the Church Committee on Overseas Relief and Reconstruction. A ninth centre, opened by the Southern Baptists in New Orleans, was also used as a collection point. In 1946, the churches gave through Church World Service 11,069,068 pounds of clothing, medical supplies, food and books, valued at $4.8 million. Church World Service shipped forty-eight car loads of food and 4,000,000 pounds of clothing. This was 88 per cent of all the relief material shipped during the year (although, of course, the armed services supplied relief assistance).[1]

Within a few months of coming into existence, Church World Service had resettled 1,488 refugees in thirty-two cities and 124 communities in the United States. In Europe, it helped the department to serve displaced persons in the camps, and assisted the Y.M.C.A. and Y.W.C.A. to work with war prisoners and to set up summer camps where 41,000 undernourished children were fed.

When Church World Service was reorganized in 1950, it transferred its refugee resettlement field operations to the Department, which by then had been renamed that of Inter-Church Aid and Service to Refugees. When this transfer took place, Church World Service had resettled 51,299 displaced persons, 221 orphans and 7,151 *Volksdeutsche* (ethnic Germans who had been uprooted and were numbered among the "expellees" metioned previously). The handing over did not mean that Church World Service severed its connection with refugee work. On the contrary, it continued this activity through the W.C.C. and in particular maintained an enormous programme for the reception and integration of refugees in the U.S.A. By 1966 Church World Service had resettled in America 147,000 refugees. What is especially significant about the W.C.C.'s Refugee Service in the early post-war period is the way in which it helped in common with the Division of Inter-Church Aid as a whole to renew the life of the Churches in countries that had been at war or had been occupied. A spiritual as well as physical renewal began to reanimate the Churches.

Amsterdam to Evanston

When the World Council of Churches was formally constituted at Amsterdam in 1948, the Department of Reconstruction and Inter-Church Aid had a sizeable operation to report to the First Assembly. Its heaviest expenditure, financed by member Churches in the U.S.A., Britain, Switzerland, Canada,

---

[1] *Co-operation in Compassion* (New York 1966), p. 36.

New Zealand, and Sweden, was $1,088,300 for temporary churches and $900,000 for the salaries of pastors and clergy of different denominations. The balance of its three-year budget of $3,905,500 had gone to the rebuilding of Christian orphanages, hospitals, schools, and homes for the aged.

> All the countries occupied during the war were recipients, without discrimination [Bishop George Bell of Chichester commented], but perhaps the most remarkable example of the "love of the brethren" developed by the World Council was the widespread and generous help given to Germany by the churches, in the U.S.A. most of all, but also by those in Britain and other countries. Those who visited Germany, as I did, in the very early post-war years could not fail to observe both the liberality of the giving and the quality of the personal approach.[1]

The Assembly received the report from its Committee on Christian Reconstruction and Inter-Church Aid. It was recognized that the work in hand could no longer be thought of as temporary. The Assembly authorized the extension of the Department's concern into new regions, particularly the Middle East, where there were 660,000 Arab refugees from Palestine. The task of redesigning the Department was passed to its committee and a cut-back in staff was called for. The proposal was that the general budget of the World Council should be fixed at $756,350, but this was pruned to $300,000. Separately the Department of Reconstruction expected to receive from its supporters for administrative expenses $176,660, out of which it had agreed to contribute $8,000 to the budget of the W.C.C. publicity department. By way of comparison, the general budget of the World Council for 1967 was around $1,000,000, and the separately raised budget—known as the Service Programme—of the Division of Inter-Church Aid, Refugee, and World Service around $1,500,000—almost ten times the figure for 1949.

Dr J. Hutchinson Cockburn came to the end of his term of office at Amsterdam and Dr Robert Mackie, an ecumenical veteran and minister of the Church of Scotland, was appointed to succeed him. Dr Mackie directed this department until the summer of 1955, when be became Chairman of the Administrative Committee on Inter-Church Aid. Dr Elfan Rees, who had been in charge of the Refugee Division of the Department since 1947, continued to direct the refugee work until 1949, when he transferred to the Commission of the Churches on International Affairs, with responsibility for refugee matters. His place as Director of the Refugee Division was taken by Dr Edgar Chandler, from the U.S.A.

In the reorganization of the Department's work that took place after Amsterdam, the main desks became those for refugees; German, Latin, and Orthodox countries; scholarships; health; literature; and publicity. To carry out one directive given at Amsterdam, the welfare of the refugees in the Middle East became a concern of the Department, which responded by calling conferences to make known the needs of Palestinian refugees, and by the channelling of funds to a regional committee that was formed to provide for the welfare of stateless persons in the area.

When the Central Committee of the W.C.C. met at Chichester, England,

[1] *The Kingship of Christ*, p. 110.

in July 1949, the Department was given a new name—that of Inter-Church Aid and Service to Refugees (D.I.C.A.S.R. for short)—to express awareness of a new era that was beginning in its work. The Central Committee reminded the member Churches, in one of the resolutions passed at Chichester, that Inter-Church Aid is a permanent obligation of a World Council of Churches which seeks to be true to its name; that many of the Churches in Europe were desperately in need of assistance; that millions of stateless refugees in Europe had a pressing and incontrovertible claim upon the help of the Churches; and therefore that a fresh approach must be made to their members by the Churches which were able to help for renewed and generous giving on behalf of their fellow-Christians in Europe.

This resolution for the first time recognized inter-Church aid as a "permanent obligation". Reconstruction is a task which is undertaken for a period and comes to an end when it has been accomplished. Inter-Church aid, it was now seen, was a responsibility of the ecumenical life of the Churches. Also, inter-Church aid was related to the permanent spiritual tasks of the Church. The real transition was between a time when an effort was made in a spirit of compassion to restore what had been destroyed to a time of striving to make the Church more effective for the task laid upon it. Chichester recognized that the refugees themselves were in large measure members of Churches and, further, that some of the most acute difficulties of European Churches were occasioned because great numbers of their members were stateless persons, so for an added reason they must be helped.

The report of the Department for 1950 records that 50,206 people, chiefly Orthodox and non-Lutheran displaced persons, had been helped to emigrate to new lands of opportunity. Of this total, 26,791 had gone to the U.S.A. and another 5,000 to South America, Australia, and Canada. The Lutheran World Federation had assisted another 35,000 refugees to migrate. Along with such aid, the Churches maintained a spiritual ministry for members of refugee Churches.

In 1950 also, Congregational–Christian Churches in the U.S.A. had carried out a programme which had led 748 young Christians of thirty-three nationalities to a dozen ecumenical work camps closely related to reconstruction projects and experiments in lay witness and evangelism in several European countries. The camps had been supported by Congregational–Christian, Evangelical and Reformed, Presbyterian and Protestant Episcopal funds totalling $42,200; other camps had been conducted by Brethren, Lutheran, Mennonite, and Quaker bodies. Ecumenical Work Camps developed into an important programme of the W.C.C.'s youth department, and were supported year by year by the member Churches through D.I.C.A.S.R.'s service programme budget.

That same year, 127 theological students from thirteen countries were given scholarships to study for one year in the U.S.A., Britain, Sweden, Switzerland, France, or Germany, through the Department's scholarships programme. Other students were assisted by the Lutheran World Federation and the Swiss Churches. Opportunities to study were arranged directly by British and

German Churches. Also, 132 pastors and church workers had been brought to Casa Locarno in Switzerland for six-week recuperation periods. Another thirty-five church leaders suffering from tuberculosis had been invited to sanatoria in Switzerland for treatment. Medicines otherwise unobtainable had been sent to sick pastors and church leaders in eastern Europe. This had often been the sole means whereby contacts had been possible. Packages of penicillin, insulin, and rare drugs became symbols of Christian solidarity. The scholarships and health programmes cost $80,062 in 1950. This amount was supplemented by other funds provided by church committees in Britain, Scandinavia, Switzerland, and the U.S.A. D.I.C.A.S.R.'s year-end report records that the Inter-Church Aid programme had included ecumenical agencies in Australia, Canada, Denmark, Great Britain, the Netherlands, New Zealand, South Africa, Sweden, Switzerland, and the U.S.A., as well as the Baptist World Alliance and the Lutheran World Federation.

"The first period of Christian reconstruction in Europe is over"—so Dr Mackie began an article in the *Ecumenical Review* in the winter of 1950.[1] This did not mean that the Churches had been able to restore all that had been destroyed by war nor that the physical distress of such countries as Greece and eastern Europe could be passed by, but now minds must reach out into the future. Six months later, in another article headed "A Strategy for Inter-Church Aid in Europe for 1951"[2] Mackie wrote:

> Without an ecumenical perspective it becomes impossible for any church to know how to be wise and fair in assistance. Without an ecumenical pattern of sharing some segment of the total work of the Church, some isolated forgotten community of Christians will not receive the assistance required, and the total life of the Church will thus be weakened. Further, we have to think on a large scale if we are going to secure the loyalty of individual Christians and churches to the task of Inter-Church Aid . . . Flexibility [he concluded] is required if changing needs and fresh opportunities are not to be overlooked.

The need for flexibility, and for immediate access to funds to meet emergencies, was dramatically underscored before the year was out. In December news was received by the International Refugee Organization in Geneva that a camp for 5,500 Russian refugees who had fled from China to the Philippines had been wrecked by a typhoon and that it was necessary to remove the survivors immediately. The situation was made unusually difficult because the disaster came at a moment when the I.R.O. was passing out of existence and it was not known what its successor was to be. Help was therefore sought from the Department. Within forty-eight hours, Edgar Chandler had left by air for the Philippines to make detailed arrangements for the transfer of survivors from the wrecked island and to consult with the Philippines government. The outcome of his flight was that the department was given grants of money to provide immediate emergency aid for all and successfully resettled even 130 "hard-core" refugees on a long-term basis in Church-supported institutions of a dozen countries around the world. The immense skill which Edgar Chandler showed was widely acknowledged. Since then the channelling

---

[1] Vol. ii, no. 2.   [2] *Ecumenical Review*, vol. iii (January 1951).

of ecumenical aid to victims of earthquakes, fires, hurricanes, volcanic eruptions, droughts, floods, and man-made upheavals, has become part of the accustomed responsibilities of Inter-Church Aid.

The year 1951 also marked an important stage in the growing involvement of the Department with Arab refugees in the Middle East. This was the outcome of a conference arranged in Beirut by the Department jointly with the International Missionary Council. Before that time, giving had been generous for Arab refugees, especially from the United States. After the meeting, the flow of gifts increased notably, the sources were enlarged, and regional co-operation was firmly established. In 1952, $40,000 in new grants for this work were received from Australia, Britain, Canada, Germany, New Zealand, and the U.S.A., and these increased the total programme, costing $218,000, of relief and social services sustained by American Churches. By 1954, $2.5 million in cash and kind had been contributed by the Churches for continued succour to Arab refugees, who then numbered some 900,000. A second "Beirut Conference" took place in 1956 and was similarly influential. Both meetings were arranged by Dr Elfan Rees.

By 1952, when the International Refugee Organization closed, to be succeeded by other specialized agencies of the United Nations, two million refugees had been enabled to emigrate, ninety per cent of them to the New World. Four-fifths of these refugee immigrants had been received by Protestant, Roman Catholic, Orthodox, and Jewish bodies that had sponsored them, not all through the W.C.C.

In May 1953, by agreement between the International Missionary Council and the World Council of Churches, the Department became responsible for co-ordinating and commending to the Churches a programme of Emergency Inter-Church Aid and Relief in all countries. Plans were made for adding to the assistance from North American Churches through Church World Service for Korea, Indonesia, India, Pakistan, and Hong Kong by contributions from Australia, Britain, Denmark, Germany, New Zealand, Sweden, and Switzerland.

The conclusion of the truce in Korea in July 1953, which halted the war which had been going on for four years in that country, brought a new challenge to the Churches to send aid to the tens of thousands of war victims and refugees there. Church World Service was already at work. The W.C.C. negotiated an official relationship between D.I.C.A.S.R. and the relief committee of the Korean National Christian Council. An ecumenical staff was recruited to serve in Korea. The department sought support from the member Churches for projects to aid those who had lost limbs, the tubercular, widows, orphans, and others who had suffered in the war. When the executive committee of the W.C.C. met at Bossey, Switzerland, in August 1953, it urged the member Churches to press their governments to participate fully in all intergovernmental relief measures and themselves to support through Christian liberality the relief committee of the National Christian Council of Korea in the work of national reconstruction.

Also in 1953, relief was channelled to flood victims in Britain, Holland, Italy, and Japan, to those who had suffered from earthquakes in Greece and

Cyprus, to those who hungered in India and Pakistan, and to those bereft by fire disasters in Hong Kong and Korea. Thus, when the Second Assembly of the World Council met at Evanston, Illinois, in 1954, the Department, as the ecumenical channel of Inter-Church Aid, was already reaching out far beyond Europe, where it had begun its work.

Evanston to New Delhi

The Second Assembly recognized the Department's ever widening horizons and authorized it to be world-wide in its scope. Robert Mackie was coming to the end of his term as director of this work, and Leslie E. Cooke was appointed to succeed him. Dr Cooke, at the time of his appointment, was general secretary of the Congregational Union of England and Wales. He had been a delegate to the First and Second Assemblies of the World Council and a member of its central and executive committees.

One of the earliest duties of the new director of what became the Division of Inter-Church Aid and Service to Refugees was to work out with the International Missionary Council a clear line of distinction between the projects for which the Division should seek support and those which were the concern of the I.M.C. This demarcation was worked out at two conferences between the Division and the I.M.C., held at Les Rasses in Switzerland and Herrenalb in Germany. Criteria were established which became known as the "Herrenalb categories"[1] and operations continued under them for a decade.

As soon as this had been done, attention was given to building up the Division's annual project list. This list was designed to give details of undertakings for which Churches, Councils of Churches, and ecumenical bodies around the world were seeking support. It was circulated to the members of the World Council and their agencies. It has become an important instrument for communicating needs and for finding funds to meet them. The validating of projects for the list according to agreed ecumenical criteria and the finding of funds to meet these projects were made major concerns of the Division. The first project list was circulated in 1956. It contained 150 projects in forty-five countries and the askings totalled just short of $3,000,000. Today some 600 projects from about eighty countries are listed for the ensuing year, and the askings amount all told to around $25,000,000.

---

[1] Under the Herrenalb agreement, it was laid down that projects from Asia, Africa, and Latin America, submitted through the Division, should be confined to:
1. Needs arising from situations which were strictly of an emergency character created by natural disasters, economic crises, political and social upheavals, and the like.
2. The needs of refugees and displaced persons.
3. The needs of Churches not in regular relation with any missionary society and therefore not normally receiving help from this source.
4. Urgent inter-Church and ecumenical projects, whether designed to strengthen the Churches or the service of the community, in so far as such projects could not be adequately supported either from local sources or through mission boards.
5. Social service or relief projects clearly demanded by the local situation but beyond the resources of the local Churches or the missionary societies co-operating with them.
6. Experiments aimed at ensuring the self-respect of the Church or Christian community where these experiments had been adequately examined and duly commended.

The Herrenalb categories were replaced in 1966 by a new agreement by which the Division of World Mission and Evangelism, the successor to the International Missionary Council, became responsible for long-term programmes and the Division of Inter-Church Aid for projects usually expected to become self-supporting within five years. This agreement opened the way for missionary projects to be included in the Division's project list. The 1967 project list was published by the Division "in collaboration with the Division of World Mission and Evangelism"—an innovation. The project list has been widened to include refugee projects and those world youth projects which are compiled jointly by the World Council's Youth Department and the World Council for Christian Education.

Attention was also given to the development and support of the Division's basic budget, the service programme. Through this, the Division was able to nourish, on behalf of the member Churches, many National and Regional Councils of Churches. It supported various departments and divisions of the World Council in some work not covered by the World Council's general budget. The service programme budget includes the salaries of the Division's staff, administrative and overhead expenses, and the cost of meetings and consultations. Finally, the service programme finds the money to carry on certain programmes which the Churches have decided should be centrally administered. These include health, literature, Casa Locarno, and scholarships.

The change that was coming over inter-Church aid was given considerable impetus by a study of conditions in Asia that was made jointly by Reginald H. Helfferich of Church World Service and Ulrich van Beyma from the Netherlands. Dr van Beyma had joined the Division in November 1954, as secretary for "non-European areas". At about the same time, Church World Service released temporarily Dr Helfferich to be an ambassador of the World Council of Churches to Asia and Africa, with special reference to the U.S.A.'s surplus commodities programme. The survey that Helfferich and van Beyma carried out together in East Asia early in 1955 resulted in Church World Service acting as the agent of the Division for massive feeding programmes that began in Asia and were later extended to Africa, eastern Europe, and Latin America. The Helfferich–van Beyma survey was a key factor in the developing strategy of inter-Church aid. Besides their study, Dr Helfferich and Dr van Beyma created the confidence necessary for Asian projects to be added to the project list.

The most severe demand that had thus far been made on the Service to Refugees came in the autumn of 1956 with the uprising in Hungary. The uprising led to the precipitate flight of about 180,000 new refugees, principally into Austria. At the first news of a threatened emergency, Edgar Chandler, then Director of the Refugee Service, flew to Vienna. After he had consulted with officials of the Austrian Churches and of various international organizations, Chandler began to plan a W.C.C. relief operation with the Director of the Service to Refugees in Austria. On 31 October, the first convoy of two trucks, laden with food, blankets, and medical supplies, went to Hungary. They were received by Lutheran and Reformed parishes in the city of Győr.

All inter-Church aid committees were informed by cable from Geneva that Church supplies were being sent to Hungary, that blankets, clothes, and medicines should be sent direct to *Hilfswerk* in Austria, and that considerable funds would be needed for emergency needs. Five thousand blankets bought in Germany by *Hilfswerk* reached Vienna on 1 November, and funds were pledged by British, United States, and other sources. Next day, Church World Service flew in $16,743 worth of medicines, vitamins, concentrated food, and blankets. Simultaneously, a convoy of nine vehicles, carrying twenty tons of supplies, left Vienna for Hungary. The convoy was stopped at one point by Russian military tanks, but eventually it reached Győr.

By the end of November, 85,000 new refugees had entered Austria and others continued to arrive at the rate of 5,000 a day. The stream continued unabated for many weeks. The Division organized a comprehensive relief, counselling, and welfare service. The Service to Refugees engaged in a massive emigration programme for the Hungarian refugees. For those who could not emigrate, integration projects of many kinds were carried out. Three appeals were made by the Division to the member Churches of the World Council. The first was for $200,000 to cover a unified service by the Division to the Hungarian refugees. The second was for $25,000 as the W.C.C. contribution to the supplies shipped to Hungary by the International Red Cross. The third was for $150,000 as the W.C.C.'s response to the needs of the Hungarian Churches and their social and educational institutions. Ultimately, the response to the Division's appeals reached $734,532.

This total included $249,013 from the U.S.A., $187,000 from Canada, $143,000 from Britain, and contributions from twenty-nine other countries or territories, one of which was the Cook Islands. More than 2,500 pastors and other church workers received emergency outfit allowances valued at the equivalent of one month's salary, and 2,430 retired church workers were given emergency grants amounting to two months' pension. A score of church institutions for the handicapped were enabled to replace damaged equipment. Wrecked church buildings were restored. Rest homes and conference centres were given grants. Raw cotton was shipped and processed for bedding and underclothing for thousands. Paper was provided for 200,000 hymn books and 100,000 Bibles. And more than 26,000 refugees were helped by the Division to emigrate to the U.S.A., Britain, Canada, France, Switzerland, Australia, Germany, and elsewhere.[1]

Through the effort known as World Refugee Year, 1959-60, in which eighty international voluntary agencies joined, the Division received funds that enabled many important projects to be undertaken for the permanent rehabilitation of thousands of people that would not have otherwise been possible. More than $1,780,000 was given by the Churches out of World Refugee Year collections to help the Division and National Councils of Churches to extend their work for refugees. An outline of some of the things accomplished in this way is given in a W.C.C. pamphlet *A Time of Compassion.*

---

[1] W.C.C. pamphlet: *Hungary—Special Report* and the Division's annual report for 1957. For additional information about this ecumenical operation, see Chandler, *The High Tower of Refuge* (London 1959).

An unusual project carried through at this time in partnership with the United Nations' High Commissioner for Refugees was the establishment of Old Believers, a Russian sect which had defied authority since Peter the Great (1672–1725), as a colony in Brazil.

At the time of the Russian Revolution of 1917, some Old Believers fled to China, where they established themselves as self-contained, self-supporting units. But when China became communist after the Second World War, the future of the Old Believers again became precarious. The Division sought for them a country where they could resettle and live in freedom according to their tenets. Brazil was willing to receive them, and so, with the co-operation and assistance of the United Nations' High Commissioner for Refugees, more than one thousand of these Old Believers were sent by ship half-way across the world. They were also provided with materials, seeds, livestock, and tools with which to build and furnish their own villages. At the end of two years, the Old Believers had become self-supporting and they have continued to thrive in Brazil while adhering as firmly as ever to their faith. The success of the venture led to other colonies being established for them in Argentina. A substantial number of Old Believers from China have also been helped to emigrate, as individuals or families, to Australia and New Zealand.

To fulfil the directive given it at Evanston to go out into all the world the Division's "area desks" were increased in number. Already in existence were desks for Europe, for the Orthodox and the Near East, and for "countries outside Europe". By early 1961, new desks had been named for Asia, for Latin America, and for the "study and survey of areas of acute human need". The geographical spread was completed in 1962 when the Africa desk was inaugurated.

Earlier, a Secretary for Migration had been appointed to study the situation occasioned by waves, millions strong, of migratory workers in many part of the world. Out of expert knowledge the secretary has been able to provide the Churches with advice about the spiritual, social, and physical needs of these people and to stimulate measures for their welfare. The first fruits of the work of the Secretary for Migration was the calling of a world conference which met at Leysin, Switzerland, in 1961. There the relationship between the Churches and migrant workers, who included Roman Catholics, Orthodox, Muslims, and others, was more clearly seen.

The Bengal Refugee Service was also set up in 1961 under the direction of Dean Johannes Krohn of Denmark. It was the outcome of a thoroughgoing survey made for Church World Service by a team whose leader was Dean Herbert Stroup of Brooklyn College, New York. The aim was to provide a co-ordinated programme for thousands of displaced persons, including students, from East Pakistan. By the time that the Bengal Refugee Service was wound up in 1965, it had cleared Sealdah Railway Station of 8,000 men, women, and children who had been living in the precincts for more than a decade as squatters, and had established them in three villages, which they had largely built themselves, some twenty miles to the north of Calcutta. Medical services for displaced persons had also been provided and a number of small cottage industries had been launched. The role of the Division in all this was that of seeking funds amounting to roughly $1,000,000 to finance the work from the member Churches of the World Council.

At the final assessment, it was agreed that the Bengal Refugee Service had not fully realized the high hopes with which it had begun, and this was in part attributed to inexperience in setting up such a body. Yet from this partial failure much was learned that was soon to be turned to profit. The willingness of the Anglican, Methodist, Mennonite, and Presbyterian Churches in Calcutta to continue the work begun by the Bengal Refugee Service, with some financial support from outside, meant the growth of inter-Church aid through the active participation of local congregations.

New Delhi and Afterwards

A radical change had thus taken place in the Division when the Third Assembly met at New Delhi towards the end of 1961. Once more, the Assembly changed the name of the Division, this time to Division of Inter-Church Aid, Refugee, and World Service (D.I.C.A.R.W.S., as it became known for short) and furnished it with a new mandate. This said:

> The aim of the division shall be to express the ecumenical solidarity of the churches through mutual aid in order to strengthen them in their life and mission and especially in their service to the world around them (diakonia), and to provide facilities by which the churches may serve men and women in acute human need everywhere, especially orphaned peoples, including refugees of all categories.

To this was added:

> The basic approach of the division to the churches and peoples will be on the basis of areas. The area secretaries will have primary responsibility for the relations of the division with churches and councils in their areas and for relationships with such ecumenical regional organizations as are or may be established . . .

Functional secretaries were to be responsible for refugees, material aid, scholarships, fraternal workers, health, E.C.L.O.F. (the Ecumenical Church Loan Fund), migration, areas of acute human need, and information.

Authority was thus given for the creation of two new "desks" for material aid and fraternal workers. The desk for material aid was not staffed until early in 1967. However, the desk for fraternal workers, to which was added certain responsibilites for teams and personnel, was manned soon after the Third Assembly. It kept the Churches informed of needs and opportunities for personal service abroad.

With its new mandate, "to express the solidarity of the churches . . . especially in their service to the world around them", the Division began to encourage Churches to take social action with a new emphasis, that of engaging in "nation-building" projects and to submit these for inclusion in the yearly project list. This led to requests for support for projects of increased size and complexity and brought problems of its own. Where was the competence to be found that qualified men to advise upon the wisdom and feasibility of such proposals? But need had arisen and ways to meet it were sought. The Rapid Social Change Studies made by the W.C.C. between Evanston and New Delhi helped, and at the Third Assembly authority was given to the Division to take such action as seemed appropriate.

The outcome was that the Central Committee agreed in 1962 to set up a new body, to be known as the Committee of Specialized Assistance to Social Projects (S.A.S.P.). It was to serve, if called upon to do so, the whole World Council and the member Churches and their agencies. Miss Janet Lacey, the Division's Vice-Chairman, was appointed Chairman of S.A.S.P., which set about its work by establishing panels of specialists on press and periodicals, health and medical work, agriculture and rural development, economic development, and urban social work and community development. The duty of these panels was to look at projects which W.C.C. staff had found to present unusual difficulties, and to advise the S.A.S.P. Committee about these. The committee also had power to initiate pilot programmes. A secretariat for S.A.S.P. was provided within the Division which was also responsible for seeking its budget. It was found that the need for such an expert, advisory body was so great that at its first meeting no fewer than eighty projects of unusual difficulty were brought before it! At the Fourth Assembly of the W.C.C. in Uppsala in 1968, S.A.S.P. was dissolved and reconstituted as the Advisory Committee on Technical Services (A.C.T.S.) with a new mandate, staff, and constitution. A.C.T.S. continues to serve the whole World Council, but is administratively located within D.I.C.A.R.W.S.

The end of the seven years' war that had raged in Algeria brought a new challenge in 1962. How best could the Churches help the people of that newly independent, devastated Muslim country. The peace settlement was followed by a mass exodus to France of some 800,000 civil servants, teachers, doctors, accountants, farmers, engineers, pastors, and others with skilled and professional training. The relatively few Churches in Algeria were denuded of their congregations. Even for those Christians who remained in the country it was difficult to provide pastors. The Division met the emergency by calling a conference of interested Churches and agencies, including the Lutheran World Federation, the Mennonites, C.I.M.A.D.E. (*Comité Inter-Mouvements auprès des Evacués*—the ecumenical relief agency of the French Churches), and the Y.M.C.A.s and Y.W.C.A.s.

Because of the impossibility of looking to the weakened indigenous Churches to provide an organization for the carrying out of an inter-Church aid relief programme, it was agreed to create a special agency, the Christian Committee for Service in Algeria (C.C.S.A.). The work which C.I.M.A.D.E. had done throughout the war with courage, persistence, and devotion had given that body an entrée to the new Algerian government. C.I.M.A.D.E. was eager to continue its services to the people of Algeria, and the other Churches and church agencies were equally desirous of supplementing its efforts. The activities of C.I.M.A.D.E.'s teams in Algeria were therefore built into the new organization. Particular responsibilities were allotted to other church bodies, such as the Mennonite Central Committee for a demonstration farm, within the C.C.S.A.'s structure. This structure was rapidly and most imaginatively devised by Heinrich Hellstern, of Swiss H.E.K.S. (*Hilfswerk der Evangelische Kirchen der Schweitz*—the Swiss Protestant Churches' Relief Agency), who was asked to inaugurate the programme. Dr Hellstern served as director of the C.C.S.A. for six months; he then handed over to Pastor Hans Aurbakken, an American Methodist of Norwegian background, who continued as director until the summer of 1966.

Pastor Aurbakken was succeeded by Jacques Blanc, a French pastor, who had been associated with the C.C.S.A. from the beginning. The Division provided a secretariat in Geneva for the C.C.S.A., and sought funds, which reached a total of around $3,000,000 to finance the programme. Church World Service furnished some of C.C.S.A.'s key personnel in the field, much cash, and enormous quantities of food and clothing for the relief service. Other major supporters were Germany, whose contributions from "Bread for the World" were the largest of all, the Christian Aid department of the British Council of Churches, and Inter-Church Aid Committees in Denmark, the Netherlands, Switzerland, and other countries.

From the beginning, the Christian Committee for Service in Algeria determined to ensure that its programme would help the people of Algeria to get on their feet again in the shortest possible time. In the early days, when an emergency situation prevailed, the Algerian government invited the C.C.S.A., the Roman Catholic agencies, and the Red Cross each to take a third of the country for immediate relief work. Operating large-scale school-feeding and milk distribution programmes, distributing blankets and clothing, providing a medical service, and giving help to orphanages and young people, the care of the C.C.S.A. operation soon became a vast reafforestation enterprise. Hundreds of men, teenagers, and even war widows were trained in skills fitting them to earn their own livelinood. At the height of this activity, 90,000 persons were employed. This was made possible by using agricultural commodities from the U.S.A., given by Church World Service on a food-for-work offer. By the time that the reafforestation work was handed over to a government agency in 1965, 22,600,000 fruit and timber trees had been planted and a further 50,000,000 seedlings were being raised in the C.C.S.A.'s nurseries. To some observers the Christian Committee for Service in Algeria seemed to offer a new pattern of ecumenical action. Since 1967, when the five-year programme for which it was set up was phased out, C.C.S.A. has continued to function but with a radically new emphasis in its work. It is still an autonomous body supported by the Churches through D.I.C.A.R.W.S.

The decision to gear the reafforestation activities of the Christian Committee for Service in Algeria to a food-for-work programme was the outcome of lessons learned by experience in many lands. To emergencies created by war, earthquake, famine, and pestilence, the compassionate respond with food, clothing, medicine, and shelter as soon as possible. Here speed saves lives. Repeatedly ecumenical service has temporarily carried out massive feeding programmes for those who were starving. But then what? Endemic need, it is now believed, calls for more than the permanent soup-kitchen and the inexhaustible giving of hand-outs. Indeed, such practices can be shameful and corrupting. This was the lesson taught in Taiwan, where Presbyterians,

Lutherans, and Roman Catholics engaged for a time in the free distribution of food, but turned the responsibility over to the government when abuses crept in which the Churches were powerless to prevent. Similar conclusions were reached in Korea and elsewhere.

The outcome was that alternative methods were sought, and one of these was to invite people to work for the food they were given. In this way, self-respect could be engendered and the possibility of corruption reduced. Similarly, church service agencies in a number of countries began to turn away during the 1960s from the practice of collecting used clothing and shipping it overseas for free distribution to the poor. Old clothes, if given indiscriminately, destroy human dignity. It became clear that Christian compassion to clothe the naked, if it were to be true to itself, must provide people with the means of making new clothes that would enable them to hold their heads high. Not only should whole cloth be provided, but also tailoring, dressmaking, and knitting classes should be formed, equipped, and staffed with competent instructors. All this is indicative of the change in ideas which began to animate Inter-Church Aid during the 1960s.

Yet another instrument for expressing Christian solidarity was found in 1963 when, in response to an offer from the Lutheran World Federation, the Division invited that body to become the agent of the World Council of Churches in administering the Tanganyika Christian Refugee Service. The initiative came from the Lutheran World Federation which made the proposal to the divisional committee of D.I.C.A.R.W.S. The divisional committee sought and obtained the authority of the World Council's Executive Committee for this pioneering venture. The Lutheran World Federation most generously undertook to finance the work which called for a budget by 1967 of $427,800—a sum that was entirely covered by the L.W.F., except for a gift of $14,000 from Britain. The L.W.F. reported regularly to the Divisional Committee on Inter-Church Aid, Refugee and World Service concerning the progress of the operation in Tanzania.

A crucial dilemma that confronted the Division and some of its supporting agencies was resolved by the Central Committee of the World Council when it met at Rochester, New York, in 1963. It must be explained that in the U.S.A. most of the major denominations have their own long-established fund-raising agencies and co-ordinate much of this work in the central department of Church World Service. In other countries, the Churches have organized their inter-Church aid work through national bodies, usually as departments of the National Church Councils. The British Council of Churches has its department of Christian Aid, which stems from work begun in 1942. The Canadian Churches have built up relief and inter-Church aid organizations of their own, and have co-ordinated the work of these in their National Council without creating a distinct national operating agency. The Swiss Protestant Churches are served by H.E.K.S. Similarly, Lutheran Churches have created the Lutheran World Federation/World Service and, in the U.S.A., Lutheran World Relief.

By 1967, L.W.F./World Service had recommended some 200 projects, with requests amounting to about $21,000,000 to potential donor agencies, so that

the younger Churches in Africa, Asia, and Latin America could be strengthened in their community welfare service in the fields of medicine, education,
and agriculture. Also, the world-wide Anglican Communion launched in
1963 its programme of Mutual Responsibility and Interdependence in the
Body of Christ (M.R.I.), and a number of these projects were listed in the
D.I.C.A.R.W.S./D.W.M.E. project list and were supported by Churches
outside the Anglican Communion. After the Second World War, the German
Churches formed the *Hilfswerk* (Relief) organization, which later merged with
the older traditional body known as *Innere Mission,* and then went on to
create the *Brot für die Welt* (Bread for the World) annual fund-raising
campaign of Churches and mission societies which had extraordinary
success.

The German experience was, indeed, altogether exceptional, because up to
1960 the German Churches, although to a yearly diminishing degree, had
received outside support, as earlier passages in this chapter have shown. But
after 1960 the Churches of Germany rapidly became one of the most active
participants in, and generous supporters of, ecumenical service. Since 1957
they have been raising money in *Kirchen helfen Kirchen* (Churches help
Churches) a programme of "classical" inter-Church aid, that gave about
$25,000 a year to projects of this nature on the D.I.C.A.R.W.S./D.W.M.E.
Project List, and to the Division's service programme budget. They had also
programmes for scholarships, migration, and integration, and service overseas. Through "Bread for the World" they were giving about $5,000,000 a
year, from Churches in both Western and Eastern Germany, to church projects in developing countries of feeding, emergency relief, and material aid.
Others were connected with self-help, health, vocational training, community
development, and nation-building, the service of laymen abroad, or structural
research, planning, and preparation for special undertakings. Nor must it be
forgotten that besides these large contributions from Churches in affluent
countries, there is a continual stream of small gifts, no less significant,
for emergencies and projects from congregations in Asia, Africa, and the
Pacific.

By the early 1960s, the West German Government in Bonn was inviting the
Churches in Germany to accept funds for them to carry out or to support
projects overseas. This was part of a pattern that had already been set by the
United States Government with its surplus commodities programme, by
Swiss Aid to Europe and its successor, and by funds made available by the
Swedish and other governments. These States had gone ahead on their own.
But before the German Churches entered into an agreement with their
government to accept state money for use in church projects overseas, they
consulted the World Council. This brought into the open the question
whether such funds could properly be accepted when the needs to be met were
so grave and extensive. Ought monies from Church and State to be kept
separate, even if this meant depriving the needy of aid?

The stand taken by the Division contained four points. It believed that the
use by Churches of funds from governments should be subject to the following
considerations:

1. Projects which fall within its (the Division's) categories and conform to its criteria, or to those of the Committee on Specialized Assistance to Social Projects (S.A.S.P.), might properly use such money.

2. Government aid should not be sought for the normal work of the Churches, for example, in church-building, maintenance of the ministry, and church and mission administration.

3. Government aid should be sought for capital expenditure for projects which will be completed within a specific period of years or which will eventually be self-supporting, or within the resources of the initiating Church or Council to maintain.

4. Government aid should preferably be sought for projects of a pioneering or pilot nature, especially in the fields of social service, leadership training, technical assistance, community and agricultural development, and the permanent rehabilitation or integration of orphaned people.

Before publishing these recommendations, however, the Division turned to the Executive and Central Committee of the W.C.C. for advice. After a long and probing debate, the Central Committee adopted a resolution, of which the following is the substantive part:

> Agreed that the Central Committee instructs the staff to continue the study of this matter, and authorize the Divisional Committee of the Division of Inter-Church Aid, Refugee, and World Service and of the Division of World Mission and Evangelism to deal in the light of this discussion with specific cases on their merits in consultation with the National Christian Council of the country concerned and with the East Asia Christian Conference and All Africa Conference of Churches.[1]

This resolution enabled the German Churches to establish a special bureau, *Evangelische Zentralstelle für Entwicklungshilfe* (Protestant Central Agency for Development Aid), through which funds from the West German government were channelled. Many Churches and Councils of Churches have received generous allocations from the *Zentralstelle* for projects on the Division's project list. The Division's practice has continued to be in line with the Central Committee's resolution. After funds became available from the West Germany government for church projects abroad, a similar source was offered by the Netherlands government. The Fourth Assembly of the W.C.C., held in Sweden in 1968, gave a resounding call to the Churches to become involved in aid to the developing countries of the "Third World". The role of the World Council in general and of D.I.C.A.R.W.S. in particular was still under urgent discussion in the summer of 1969 and had still to be determined. But as this chapter tries to show, inter-Church aid frequently grows into "development aid" and for the time being at least it remained the responsibility of D.I.C.A.R.W.S.

In 1964, the National Council of the Churches of Christ in the U.S.A. requested the Churches of the world, through the World Council, to show

[1] MRCC (Rochester, New York).

ecumenical solidarity with the Churches of America by joining with them in support of the Mississippi Delta Ministry which was designed to serve in an area of grave racial turbulence. The call was for cash and for persons who had experience in areas of tension to take part in the relief, rehabilitation, and reconciliation projects that were being devised by the Mississippi Delta Ministry. The aim was to help to bring about a transformation of society that would ensure social justice for all. This was the first time that the N.C.C.C.U.S.A. had ever turned for support to the other members of the World Council, and it did so because it wished the Church as a whole to share in this ministry. The Division, strongly backed by the Executive Committee of the World Council, responded at once by circulating an emergency appeal to the member Churches, and arranged for the Mississippi Delta Ministry to be included in its project list. The outcome was donations amounting to more than $150,000 from Churches outside the U.S.A. and the finding of a number of persons to work in the project. The Mississippi Delta Ministry has continued to be listed for support year by year by D.I.C.A.R.W.S. At the time of Martin Luther King's assassination in 1968, a collection made by the Division raised some $100,000 additional to the normal response for this project as a memorial to the Negro leader.

That year 1964 also saw the launching of the Ecumenical Programme for Emergency Action in Africa (E.P.E.A.A.). It called for $10,000,000 over five years to finance a programme of urgent nation-building projects and the relief and rehabilitation of refugees throughout the continent. The following year, the All Africa Conference of Churches agreed to be responsible for the general direction and administration of E.P.E.A.A. and created a special agency to do this. This special agency soon had an executive staff comprising the director, the refugee officer, the information officer, and two administrative secretaries.

Of the many emergency appeals after natural disasters that the Division sent to the member Churches and their agencies since New Delhi, three deserve mention. Earthquakes in Iran, 1962, Yugoslavia, 1963, and Turkey, 1966, brought Christian aid for the permanent rehabilitation of people who had suffered grievously in these disasters. The response to the first of these appeals enabled the Christian Council of Iran to rebuild a Muslim village, Esmatabad, that had been wrecked in the catastrophe. Here, 306 houses were put up as well as such community amenities as public baths, an administrative centre, and a water tower. The Armenian Archbishop of Teheran, whose Church is not a member of the Christian Council of Iran, was also enabled to build houses for those of his people who had fled from the earthquakes and resettled in Teheran. After they were housed, a new church was built on a site adjoining their homes. Some restoration work was also done in other villages in the earthquake zone for Muslims and Christians alike, and this included considerable repairs to a mosque.

After the earthquake at Skopje, Yugoslavia, through funds transmitted by Churches through the Division, 125 prefabricated houses were bought and erected in a new suburb. These houses, to each of which the *oikoumene* symbol was attached, have become known as the "Churches' Sector". This work was supervised for the Division by Harald H. Lund, the Church World Service/Lutheran World Relief representative in Yugoslavia. The Serbian Orthodox Church was also enabled to repair churches that had been damaged in the disaster.

For those who had lost their homes in the earthquake in Eastern Anatolia, Turkey, winter shelters were built for about one hundred families as well as two permanent technical schools in the towns of Hinis and Varto. No churches were affected. For each of these emergency appeals the response was more than $700,000.

In the new climate of ecumenism that followed the Second Vatican Council it was suggested that working relations between Roman Catholic agencies and the Division could be extended. Accordingly, an official working party was set up by the Vatican and the World Council and met in Geneva in 1966 and in Rome in 1967. Other meetings were to follow. At the first meeting the news came of the grave threat of impending famine in India. The meeting recommended that synchronized appeals should be made by the Vatican and the Division at the same time as an appeal was put out by the United Nations. This was done. The Division's appeal was for $3,000,000 over a period of three years, to support a co-ordinated programme designed to strike at the causes of hunger in India. Following these appeals, a meeting took place in New Delhi at which it was agreed to set up a new body, Action for Food Production (A.F.P.R.O.), that would co-ordinate the programmes to be carried out by the Roman Catholics and the National Christian Council of India, and would speak with one voice in approaches to government departments. Funds subscribed in response to the Division's appeal were channelled to the experienced Committee on Relief and Gift Supplies (C.O.R.A.G.S.) of the National Christian Council of India. It was later renamed Christian Agency for Social Action (C.A.S.A.).

During 1966, the Service to Refugees, renamed the Refugee Programme, was radically restructured to bring it into still closer accord with emerging needs. A social service officer and a programme officer were appointed to help the assistant director in his work. Negotiations were begun with several National Councils for them to take over refugee responsibilities. In December 1966 Miss Margaret Jaboor retired. She had been with the service to refugees for fifteen years and as director for the last four. When the divisional committee said farewell to her, it was stated that through her work she had directed the resettlement of 300,000 refugees—an "illustrious chapter", it was said, in the story of ecumenical service. But this one figure of 300,000 refugees re-settled in other countries indicates only a part of the work done by the refugee programme over the years.

To fill in the picture, mention must also be made of the aged and handicapped, numbering more than 5,000, who were given lifetime security in Old People's Homes, thanks to the funds provided by Churches, governments, and intergovernmental organizations. Again, integration projects were devised for thousands of individuals in many countries. These projects, also financed at the beginning by Churches, governments, and intergovernmental organizations, enabled the refugees who benefited to become self-supporting.

And behind all these activities has lain the pastoral, education, material, and welfare services of all kinds given by the staff of the refugee programme to tens of thousands of bewildered, friendless, and despairing people in many places.

During 1966, two conferences took place which affected the development of inter-Church aid. The first of these had for its theme "Inter-Church Aid in the Next Ten Years". This world conference was held at Swanwick, England. It was immediately followed by the Church and Society World Conference in Geneva. At both of these the Churches were urged to align themselves more closely to governmental and intergovernmental programmes of development aid. For some years this had been one of the main concerns of the Division's secretariat for the study and survey of areas of acute human need. But to extend this work, expressed largely in the Churches' involvement with the Freedom from Hunger Campaign and the World Food Programme, it was decided to establish an additional, new desk—that for development education.

For ten years, considerable thought had been given to the concept of *diakonia* (service). The report of the W.C.C. Conference on Church and Society at Thessalonica, 1959, said: "God loves not only the Christians but the whole world; and all the revolutions of this world take place in some fashion under God's providence to serve the final goals of the divine will of love." A World Council of Churches' pamphlet[1] comments:

> In a sense, the challenge of the contemporary revolution to the churches' *diakonia* today is to develop new policies, new concepts, new forms of action which will, on the one hand, continue to meet individual, family and wider social needs, and, on the other, to promote social justice on a community or national and ecumenical world basis rather than on a strictly personal one.

The Thessalonica Conference was followed by three consultations arranged by the Division. The first of these was held in Geneva in 1961, and had as its theme "The Role of Institutional Christian Service in Modern Society". The second, which was limited to representatives of Churches in North America and Europe, took place at Mülheim, Germany, in 1962, and was concerned with "The Role of the Churches in Social Service". The third consultation met in Geneva in August 1965, and was called in response to a request of the divisional committee of D.I.C.A.R.W.S. that the staff should prepare a contribution to the World Conference on Church and Society 1966 with regard to the role of the *diakonia* in contemporary society and its future forms of service. Leslie E. Cooke, at that time the Director of the Division, said that the fact that the World Council numbered more than two hundred Churches implied a wholly new relationship between the Churches themselves. Within the World Council, those Churches had equal status; requests for aid and offers of aid had taken on a wholly different connotation. There was no room for paternalistic charity, only for partnership and sharing. Moreover, there was ground for a new solidarity in meeting human need. Ecumenical *diakonia* had thus gained significance.

Other aspects of the new thinking about inter-Church aid were mentioned

---

[1] *The Role of the Diakonia of the Church in Contemporary Society* (1966), p 34.

by Leslie Cooke in the concluding address he gave to the Swanwick Consultation 1966.

> There will be many [Dr Cooke said] who have been generous in their giving for relief who will become hesitant, if not resistant, when they realize that our aim is to change the *status quo*. They will think that the Church has gone leftist, or socialist, or communist . . . There will be those among the rising generation, and in the churches of the developing countries, who are radical, who will say: "At last the churches are with us—they have espoused our cause, they have joined the revolution." Then there will come a moment when to the word "revolution" we will have to add the word "reconciliation", and these heralds of the new dawn will be disappointed and disillusioned as they see that the Church cannot deploy into the long lines to face the enemies of change for violent battle. We shall face grave misunderstanding.
>
> . . . That we are now caught up to go beyond aid to challenge the structures of churches and society, even by aid we give and the purposes to which we give it, is beyond doubt. That there is a price to be paid is also beyond doubt. The only two uncertainties are what the cost will be and whether we are prepared to pay it.
>
> We have to press on beyond co-operation to community . . . The over-whelming compulsion to move from co-operation to community derives from the fact that it is clear that many of the problems which face mankind can be solved only by the building of a world community. Perhaps the most significant contribution the churches can make is in manifesting that they are a world community, that they in fact share a common life in the body of Christ.

Over the years such ecumenical bodies as the East Asia Christian Conference, the All Africa Conference of Churches, and the Near East Council of Churches have been responsible, in one way or another, for inter-Church aid in their region. The East Asia Christian Conference sponsors the Asian Christian Service in Vietnam for which support is sought through the Division. In co-operation with the Asian Churchwomen's Conference, the E.A.C.C. also allocates funds received from the "Fellowship of the Least Coin"; these funds total year by year around $50,000. In January 1965 the All Africa Conference of Churches accepted responsibility for the administering of the Ecumenical Programme for Emergency Action in Africa (E.P.E. A.A.) for which the Division set itself to raise outside Africa $10,000,000 over a five-year period. The All Africa Conference of Churches has set up its own special agency to carry out the E.P.E.A.A.

I.S.A.L. (Church and Society in Latin America) formulated projects which were included in the annual project list of the World Council's Divisions of Inter-Church Aid, Refugee, and World Service and of World Mission and Evangelism. Again, the National Christian Council of India's Christian Agency for Social Action (C.A.S.A.) had its own relief and rehabilitation programmes and also worked out ways in which ecumenical support could be channelled through it to A.F.P.R.O. (Action for Food Production). The Near East Council of Churches had likewise a long-standing programme of Christian service in its area. Many other examples of inter-Church aid in developing areas could be cited.

Somewhat paradoxically, inter-Church aid activities in Europe, where the work had been born, had never been the responsibility of a regional European ecumenical organization, but had been left to the European desk of a division of the World Council of Churches. Should such a regional body be created for some forms of inter-Church aid in Europe? The question became pressing when the World Council of Churches' Divisional Committee on Inter-Church Aid, Refugee, and World Service decided to call a meeting on Inter-Church Aid and appointed a preparatory commission to prepare the agenda. When the preparatory commission met in Geneva in February 1967, it sent an official message to the Presidium of the Conference of European Churches, saying that it regarded the question of a European inter-Church aid organization as a cardinal one, and asked that the Presidium should give careful consideration to it and distinguish between those matters which could and should be carried out by such a body and those better left to the World Council.

During this meeting of the preparatory commission, the news was received of the death in New York of Dr Leslie Cooke, the Director of the Division, and with his passing the story of Inter-Church Aid since the Second World War may appropriately be broken off. Leslie Cooke was a man of unusual vision who was also a man of practical affairs. He coloured indelibly the work of the Division, not only in its structure but also in the quality of its performance. He never forgot, in all the administrative detail with which he was involved, the human touch. Cooke excelled in the interpretation of the inner meaning of Inter-Church Aid, and this had great effect on those churchmen whose commitment to mission might have led them to misunderstand service. His prophetic vision enabled him to seize upon changing needs and situations and to adapt Inter-Church Aid to meet these.

Inevitably, in the years to come Inter-Church Aid will change, since change is a law of life. But whatever the transformations that come about, it is certain that Inter-Church Aid will remain what the smiths who forged it intended—a sharing by Churches and between Churches brought together in the service of their Master, who by his example and commands has charged them to heal, feed, clothe, house, and comfort the distressed and to wash the painful feet of tired men limping along the highways of this troubled world.

9

The Development of
Ecumenical Social Thought
and Action

PAUL ABRECHT

Introduction

A large part of the energy of the ecumenical movement has been directed to the search for a common Christian witness to the problems of modern society. Indeed, for laymen, most of the attraction of the ecumenical movement is in its creativity and vitality in facing social issues and in the challenge they have posed to Churches, too much identified with the political and social system of a particular region or country. The importance of the ecumenical witness on social questions was recognized by most of the early leaders of the World Council of Churches, in particular by Bishop George K. A. Bell of Chichester, Archbishop William Temple, Dr J. H. Oldham, and above all by the first General Secretary, Dr W. A. Visser 't Hooft, who in numerous articles and addresses constantly emphasized the prophetic and reconciling function of the ecumenical movement in relation to social problems. All were keenly aware that the ecumenical movement would have a vital role in the dialogue between the Church and the world, especially where the Churches had allowed themselves to become separated and divided by national and regional interests.

In the beginning, co-operation was hampered by the lack of substantial agreement concerning the theological foundations of Christian action in society and also by disagreements about the method by which Christian thought should proceed in determining the Christian's role in society. It has been well said that, in the first ecumenical discussions of social questions,

> there was no common body of social thought, no common experience in dealing with these issues, not even any agreement as to which issues were of primary importance. There was only a common concern about the urgency of the world's need for social reconstruction . . . and a common conviction that Christians and the Christian churches were called to play a part in that reconstruction.[1]

The search for a common strategy has, moreover, obliged the Churches to make new evaluations of the discoveries of the social and behavioural sciences. As a result, there has developed a new dialectic between theology and Christian doctrine on the one side, and ideology, social experience, and social science on the other. It is this dialectic which has given ecumenical social ethics its particular dynamic. It has also ensured that laymen would find an important role in ecumenical social thinking.

The discovery of the constantly changing interplay between Christian and secular thought has been fundamental to the development of ecumenical social thinking. It accounts for the double-sided character of that thought: on the one hand, the attempt to define the ends and purposes of social institutions and the criteria for judging these; on the other, the investigation of the way in which Christians or Churches in specific situations have met their responsibilities and the analysis they have made of their social problems. The second concern has meant increasing emphasis on the importance of thorough and systematic study of various social problems.

[1] *Statements of the World Council of Churches on Social Questions* (2nd edn, Geneva 1956), p. 6.

Surprisingly there have been only a few substantial studies of the development of World Council social thought.[1] Most of these were written shortly after the Second Assembly in 1954. Since then there has been a great widening of interests and concerns and some of the issues which preoccupied Christian thought up to the 1954 Assembly have receded in importance, while others, particularly the issues of rapid social change in Africa, Asia, and Latin America, have become central themes in ecumenical study and action. In more recent years all the problems of dynamic/affluent and ailing/under-developed societies have been thrust upon the Christian conscience and preoccupy the Churches.

The Social and Theological Dynamics of the First Ecumenical Discussions

It is almost fifty years since Archbishop Nathan Söderblom launched his idea of an Ecumenical Council of Churches "which should be able to speak on behalf of Christendom on the religious, moral and social concerns of men". To Söderblom and to those other international church leaders who collaborated with him in the meeting in Geneva, 2–12 August 1920, to prepare for the Universal Christian Conference on Life and Work in Stockholm, in 1925, the task was an urgent one. They saw the First World War as a great catastrophe for mankind and for Christianity. How otherwise explain the situation of Christian nations which had entered into such a terrible struggle against each other, costing so many millions of lives and the destruction of so many lands? The post-war situation seemed scarcely more promising, as the spirit of vengeance and nationalism prevented co-operation in the rebuilding of destroyed societies and the establishment of world peace. It was apparent also that capitalism had not solved the problems of unemployment, and that industrial disputes and strife would wrack the post-war world even more deeply than the pre-war one.

Despite the sense of ugency and the serious preliminary studies, the great hopes for a bold new Christian programme for world order and social reconstruction were disappointed at Stockholm. Indeed, it is often said that the first efforts (1919–25) to develop a new social teaching in the non-Roman Churches are interesting only because they provided the starting-point for what was later to become a theologically more profound and socially more perceptive movement. The conference showed that the Churches had to do much more serious thinking about both the nature of the problems and the Christian approach to them.

Yet it would be wrong to overlook or underestimate some fundamental achievements of this first effort. Like Roman Catholic social movements in the latter half of the nineteenth century, Protestant, Anglican, and Orthodox

[1] Edward Duff, s.j., *The Social Thought of the World Council of Churches*. London and New York 1956. Also H. ten Dornkaat, *Die ökumenischen Arbeiten zur sozialen Frage*. Zürich 1954. Professor H. D. Wendland also treats some of the systematic theological problems in the development of ecumenical social ethics in his *Die Kirche in der modernen Gesellschaft* (2nd edn, Hamburg 1958).

leaders had committed themselves to a new involvement in the world in the interest of social justice. They perceived that the spirit of pious individualism which predominated at that time was no answer to the problems of industrial revolution and world conflict. They sought to construct a new ecumenical concern based upon the inspiration of various Christian social movements of the day. These were prophetic movements, movements of outrage and protest against social evils, movements of reform and action. It is useful to recall in summary form their basic presuppositions:

1. The rejection of the prevailing static conception of human nature and society, and the refusal to interpret the Christian doctrine of sin and the fall of man as an argument against working for social betterment.

2. The insistence that God is at work in the protest movements within society, and that man must co-operate with him in realizing his will to establish his Kingdom.

3. The rejection of all atomistic and mechanistic conceptions of society such as were dominant in the hey-day of *laissez-faire* capitalism.

4. The insistence that men are largely shaped by their social environment, and the conviction that social structures can be altered in order to promote better conditions of human life.

5. The emphasis on the role of the State and the community in regulating various aspects of social life and in developing new and more just patterns of society.

6. The concern for the solidarity of men and for equality of opportunity as a vital element in the Christian understanding of social reform and social change.

It has been said that the Stockholm Conference of 1925, by endorsing these ideas, gave an ecumenical blessing to the social gospel movements which has already gained momentum in the United States, Great Britain, and many countries of Europe. It would perhaps be more true to say that the Churches incorporated certain insights of these movements into their thinking, while remaining critical of some of the conclusions which the movements themselves drew from these insights.

In later years it has also been said that this was the beginning of an Anglo-Saxon theological domination of ecumenical social ethics, but this overlooks the deep interest in Christian social thought in many European countries at that time (especially Germany, Switzerland, France, and Scandinavia), and the efforts to develop a social ethics combining Christian thought with the insights of the social protest movements and the ideals of socialism. The attraction for Europeans of the American social gospel movement was precisely that it seemed to offer the possibility of a new Christian social concern. A European Christian student leader, writing his doctoral thesis in 1928 on the American social gospel, observed: "In America this ethic constitutes the one most important attempt made to transcend the individualistic notions of the last centuries and arrive at a solidaristic conception of social life."[1]

The appreciation of socialism's contribution to Christian social thought was recognized by European Christian thinkers also. Adolf Harnack, in his classic study of *The Mission and Expansion of Christianity* (London 1908), describing the social expression of Christianity in the first three centuries, concluded:

> The gospel, it has been truly said, is at bottom both individualistic and socialistic. Its tendency towards mutual association, so far from being an accidental phenomenon in its history, is inherent in its character. It spiritualizes the irresistible impulse which draws one man to another, and raises the social connection of human beings from the sphere of a convention to that of a moral obligation. In this way it serves to heighten the worth of man, and essays to recast contemporary society, to transform the socialism which involves a conflict of interests into the socialism which rests upon the consciousness of spiritual unity and a common goal.

The great work of Troeltsch on *The Social Teaching of the Christian Churches* (London 1911) had also opened world Christian thinking to a new concern for society by showing the ethical and sociological pattern of various forms of Christianity and their appeal to particular social classes and groups.

It would be instructive at this point to compare these developments with Roman Catholic social thinking as it developed in the great social encyclicals from *Rerum novarum* (1891) to *Quadragesimo anno* (1931). It might be argued that whereas in later years Roman Catholicism had to overcome an uncompromising rejection of socialism and Marxism, non-Roman social thinkers were obliged to rid themselves of some illusions about man and society which an idealist socialist reading of the Bible had fostered. The economic depression in the western capitalist countries and the rise of the totalitarian political systems in Europe showed the inadequacy of some of the theological and ethical ideas with which the Church was working. A deeper theological basis was needed. This was to be one of the chief contributions of the second major international conference on social questions organized by the Churches—the Conference on Church, Community and State, which met at Oxford in 1937.

New Conceptions of Christian Social Witness
The Oxford Conference of 1937

The 1937 Conference on Church, Community and State was called and prepared for by the Continuation Committee on Life and Work, set up after Stockholm. Like the Stockholm Conference, the Conference of Oxford can be understood only against the background of the economic and political situation and the changing attitudes within the Church regarding its task in society.

---

[1] W. A. Visser 't Hooft, *The Background of the Social Gospel in America*. New York, 1928.

The world economic and social situation had steadily worsened during the 1930s. The effects of the economic depression in the great industrial nations had spread around the whole world, and the social tensions they produced convulsed practically every society. New ideologies offering new solutions to economic order and social justice competed for power, and the battle for supremacy shook the foundations of all the western nations. The trade union movement struggled to gain new power for the workers, and the Churches were called upon to declare where they stood in the midst of industrial strife. The Oxford Conference is noteworthy particularly for what it said about the economic situation and the problem of inequality in the distribution of wealth and income.

It also brought into the open the debate about the theological and biblical basis of Christian social ethics which had been simmering since the 1925 Conference in Stockholm. J. H. Oldham, the chief architect of the Oxford Conference, summarized thus the three theological perspectives presented to the Conference:

> 1. A Christian ethics based on principles derived from New Testament teaching, especially the Sermon on the Mount, representing the position of Stockholm.
>
> 2. A personal ethics of salvation—suspicious of "Christian social programmes" —was held by several continental theologians who maintained that the Christian ethic could not be identified with that of the Sermon on the Mount. Thus Professor Emil Brunner of Zurich argued that "The Christian Church has no right to lay down a social programme, because it is not its business to establish any kind of system. It is doubtful whether we ought to speak of a Christian ethic at all, since an ethic means something which has an independent existence and which once for all lays down rules for the various relations of life."
>
> 3. A Christian ethics of justice derived from the love commandment. This view emphasized the prophetic mission of the Church in relation to the family, the nation, the state, economics and culture. In contrast to the first position, it stressed the reality of evil and the difficulty of direct applications of the love commandment.[1]

There is no evidence that the Oxford Conference formally adopted any one of these interpretations; but it is clear that the third position greatly influenced the conference reports and Christian social thinking in the following years.[2]

The optimism inherent in the view that social and political reform would solve all human ills, or that new social systems would totally eradicate social evils had persisted after the First World War, but it came under challenge in the Oxford Conference, and practically disappeared with the Second World War.

The theological corrective which the Oxford Conference applied to the

---

[1] The Oxford Conference (1937), Official Report, pp. 27–32.

[2] John C. Bennett wrote the preliminary draft for the section on Economic Life in co-operation with J. H. Oldham. The influence of Reinhold Niebuhr is also apparent in the formulation of the theological passages. The book by Archbishop William Temple, *Christianity and Social Order* (London 1942), is one example of writing based on the theological ideas of Oxford.

I

thinking of the 1925 Stockholm Conference is well illustrated in the report on economic life. It is argued that a Christian social ethic cannot be developed directly from the love commandment or the Kingdom of God, since these, because of human sinfulness, are in contradiction with the world. Therefore, "in so far as the Kingdom of God is in conflict with the world and is therefore still to come, the Christian finds himself under the necessity of discovering the best available means of checking human sinfulness and of increasing the possibilities and opportunities of love within a sinful world." The task of the Christian is to make use of the "principle of justice, as the relative expression of the commandment of love in any critique of economic, political and social institutions".

In opposition to some interpretations of Lutheran social ethics, the report emphasized that:

> The laws of justice are not purely negative. They are not merely "dykes against sin". The political and economic structure of society is also the mechanical skeleton which carries the organic element of society. Forms of production and methods of co-operation may serve the cause of human brotherhood by serving and extending the principle of love beyond the sphere of purely personal relations.

The Oxford Report illustrated this by indicating four ways in which the economic order of that day challenged the Christian understanding of man and society:

1. by its enhancement of acquisitiveness;
2. by its inequalities;
3. by the irresponsible possession of economic power;
4. by the frustration of the sense of Christian vocation.

Concerning these problems the report set forth a body of "Christian teaching" representing the "kind of guidance which it is possible to receive from the Christian faith for economic life". What followed constituted the most comprehensive and systematic review ever made by a group of Protestant, Anglican, and Orthodox Churches of the problems of economic life. It was specifically noted that the teaching would apply for about a decade. As matters turned out, the Second World War shortened that period considerably, bringing with it a new concern for social justice and order which was to lead to great economic changes and the rapid development of the modern welfare society and state.

The need for a larger authority for the State in ordering economic life did not lead the participants in the 1937 Conference to overlook the dangers of growing state power. The rise of Nazism and totalitarian communism posed this problem very acutely, and forced participants to a new examination of the power of the State: "Since we believe in the holy God as the source of justice, we do not consider the state as the ultimate source of law but as its guarantor. It is not the lord but the servant of justice. There can be for the Christian no ultimate authority but very God."

The report also declared that, in the present situation, "the widespread tendency of the state to control the totality of human life in all its individual and social aspects, combined with the tendency to attribute absolute value to the state itself", forced the Church to reconsider its relation to the State. The Conference agreed that there are areas where the social activities of Church and State overlap; tensions are therefore unavoidable and solutions will vary in different historical circumstances. The report emphasized that the Church as a Christian community has a responsibility to help its members to interpret their responsibility in relation to the State.

Developments after the Second World War
The Responsible Society

Ecumenical discussion of social questions was interrupted by the Second World War, but Churches in various regions struggled to prepare themselves for the post-war period by their discussions of the conditions of peace and post-war reconstruction. Their debates now focused on the issues of state planning and the welfare society, as alternatives to capitalism and communism, and this came to be the main social issue in the discussions of the First Assembly which constituted the World Council of Churches in Amsterdam in 1948.

In the Assembly report on "The Church and the Disorder of Society", the Churches refused to accept either complete state planning or unqualified freedom in economic affairs. "Coherent and purposeful ordering of society has now become a major necessity. Here governments have responsibilities which they must not shirk. But centres of initiative in economic life must be so encouraged as to avoid placing too great a burden upon centralized judgment and decision." The Assembly stressed that Christians should reject the extreme ideologies of both communism and *laissez-faire* capitalism, and "should seek to draw men away from the false assumption that these extremes are the only alternatives". It could not "resolve the debate between those who feel that the primary solution is to socialize the means of production, and those who fear that such a course will merely lead to new and inordinate combinations of political power, culminating finally in an omni-competent state".

Before the Amsterdam Assembly, J. H. Oldham, W. A. Visser 't Hooft, Reinhold Niebuhr, and M. M. Thomas discussed the best term for identifying the responsibility of the Church in society. Various phrases had been considered: "the open society", "the free society", and "the free and responsible society". Finally "responsible society" was adopted, and it proved to be the key phrase in over a decade of ecumenical social thought. (The term was held to include freedom, responsibility being impossible without freedom to exercise it.)

The definition of the responsible society set forth at Amsterdam is as follows:

> Man is created and called to be a free being, responsible to God and his neighbour. Any tendencies in state and society depriving man of the possibility of acting responsibly are a denial of God's intention for man and his work of

salvation. A responsible society is one where freedom is the freedom of men who acknowledge responsibility to justice and public order, and where those who hold political authority or economic power are responsible for its exercise to God and the people whose welfare is affected by it . . . For a society to be responsible under modern conditions it is required that the people have freedom to control, to criticize, and to change their governments, that power be made responsible by law and tradition, and be distributed as widely as possible through the whole community. It is required that economic justice and provision of equality of opportunity be established for all the members of society.

At the Second Assembly of the World Council of Churches in 1954 the term was broadened and its meaning as a guide for action clarified:

Responsible society is not an alternative social political system, but a criterion by which we judge all existing social orders and at the same time a standard to guide us in the specific choices we have to make. Christians are called to live responsibly, to live in response to God's act of redemption in Christ, in any society, even within the most unfavourable social structures.

In contrast with the earlier Assembly, the Second Assembly (1954) pointed to the great changes in economic and social policy which had come about in many countries in the post-war years:

These developments suggest that disputes about "capitalism" and "socialism" disguise the more important issues in the field of economic and social policy. Each word is applied to many different social forms and economic systems. It is not the case that we have merely a choice between two easily distinguishable types of economic organization . . . . The concrete issues in all countries concern the newly evolving forms of economic organization, and the relative roles of the state, organized groups and private enterprises.

The concept of responsible society helped many Churches in the West in their debates about economic and social policy, especially those in danger of being caught up in the sterile and self-righteous anti-communist crusade which obsessed many western countries in the 1950s. But it found little acceptance among Christians in the Third World who felt the need for concepts which related more closely to the dynamic social conditions in which they lived.

Enlarging the Ecumenical Dialogue

With the formation of the World Council of Churches in 1948 it was possible to launch more continuous systematic study on social questions. Within the Study Department, supervised by Dr Nils Ehrenström of Sweden, an inquiry on "Christian Action in Society" was started, and in August 1949 Paul Abrecht from the U.S.A. was invited to direct this programme.

The organization of an ecumenical programme on this large theme was a challenge. Considering the limited resources of staff and finances available, what should be the structure and the method of such work? What were the critical issues for the Churches, and with what sense of priority should they be considered? Those were real and difficult questions! Attention gradually focused on three issues: (a) the witness of the Church in communist societies;

(*b*) the role of the Church in working for a responsible society; and (*c*) the meaning of work in a technical age.[1]

By 1952 new Christian thinkers were appearing in the ecumenical discussion of these questions. Charles West of the U.S.A. contributed greatly to the discussion of Christianity and Marxism from his experience in China during the triumph of communism, and later from his work in Berlin.[2] Denys Munby, then a young reader in economics at the University of Aberdeen, became known for his writing on economic issues. In 1956 he published *Christianity and Economic Problems*, the first systematic treatise since A. D. Lindsay's *Christianity and Economics*, and the most important book yet written on this theme. Among the theologians, H. D. Wendland of Germany, a veteran of the Oxford Conference, returned to the ecumenical discussion with his contributions on the relation of eschatology and ethics.

A western European group of laymen and theologians, formed in 1951 to reflect from a Christian perspective on the movement for European economic and political integration, became a source of new insights on the meaning of responsible society in Europe. Here European socialists, liberals, and conservatives debated the Christian responsibility for the future of Europe. Members of the group included such laymen as the late John Edwards, Labour M.P. from the United Kingdom, later to become president of the Council of Europe; André Philip, Professor of Economics at the Sorbonne and one of the leaders of the European movement; Max Kohnstamm of Holland, the first secretary of the High Authority for the European Coal and Steel Community; and from Germany, Hermann Ehlers, *Oberkirchenrat* and President of the German *Bundestag*, and Gustav Heinemann, then a strong advocate of a neutral and united Germany, now minister of the interior in the present (1968) German government. The motor of this group was Dr C. L. Patijn of Holland, a leading official of the Dutch Foreign Office, and Chairman of Section III at Amsterdam and Evanston. Other active participants were Jean Rey of Belgium, later to become President of the European Common Market, and Mario Rollier of the Socialist Party of Italy, member of the Milan City Council and nuclear physicist. This lay group opened its discussions to church leaders and theologians from both eastern and western Europe. In 1953 there was a debate in Paris with Bishop Albert Berecsky, and Bishop Janos Peter of Hungary who became foreign minister of Hungary after the uprisings of 1956, participating.

In 1949 and 1952 there were study conferences on social issues in east Asia which opened the door to a new and larger vision of the ecumenical responsibility.

The method of work during these years was non-institutionalized and decentralized, depending much on local initiative. The purpose was to draw in laymen and theologians interested in applying ecumenical criteria to the

---

[1] An inquiry into this last topic started with the publication of a report on the *Work in Modern Society* by J. H. Oldham in 1949, but the resources were lacking to pursue it.

[2] His writings and those of others on this theme appeared in *Background Information on Church and Society*, a mimeographed publication of the Study Department which was started in 1951.

problems of society in particular areas. In this way the staff gained experience and tested the capacity of the ecumenical movement to encourage the new and creative thinking asked for by the First Assembly.

The new structure for the World Council adopted in 1954 provided for a Department on Church and Society within a new Division of Studies. The new Director of the Division, Dr Robert Bilheimer, strongly encouraged the ecumenical study programme on social questions and gave much time to it until he left the World Council staff in 1963. Above all the new department provided the organizational basis and the liberty of action needed for the expansion which began in 1955.

The Ecumenical Witness Against Racism

The Evanston Assembly of 1954 gave its attention primarily to social problems which had preoccupied the ecumenical discussion in the period after the Amsterdam Assembly: the trend towards the "mixed" social planning–private enterprise economies in the West; the function of the Church in relation to communist/non-communist tension; and the problems of the economically underdeveloped regions; but it also attacked the issue of racism.

Many of the Churches affiliated to the World Council of Churches had expressed their opposition to racial and ethnic segregation and discrimination, and the Oxford Conference had made a clear ecumenical critique of racism, but this was the first occasion when the issue was thoroughly debated within the Council. The report received by the Assembly and commended to the Churches for their study and action was unequivocal:

> Racial and ethnic fears, hates and prejudices are more than social problems with whose existence we must reckon; they are sins against God and His commandments that the Gospel alone can cure. To the Church has been committed the preaching of the Gospel. To proclaim the "healing of the nations" through Christ is verily her task . . . As part of its task of challenging the conscience of society, it is the duty of the Church to protest against any law or arrangement that is unjust to any human being or which would make Christian fellowship impossible, or would prevent the Christian from practising his vocation. Some of its members may feel bound to disobey such a law. The Church does not contemplate lightly any breaking of the law, but it recognizes the duty of a Christian to do so when he feels that he has reached that point where the honour and glory of God command him to obey God rather than man. In so doing, the Church must point out the possible consequent necessity for spiritual discipline according to the Gospel.

The Assembly report added:

> The Church of Christ cannot approve of any law which discriminates on grounds of race, which restricts the opportunity of any person to acquire education to prepare himself for his vocation, to procure or to practise employment in his vocation, or in any other way curtails his exercise of the full rights and responsibilities of citizenship and of sharing in the responsibilities and duties of government.[1]

[1] Intergroup Relations—the Church Amid Racial and Ethnic Tensions", *Ecumenical Statements on Race Relations* (Geneva 1965), pp. 17–22.

In a resolution the Second Assembly also declared its conviction that

> any form of segregation based on race, colour, or ethnic origin is contrary to the Gospel, and is incompatible with the Christian doctrine of man and with the nature of the Church of Christ. The Assembly urges the churches within its membership to renounce all forms of segregation, of discrimination, and to work for their abolition within their own life and within society.

These declarations strengthened the position of those struggling against the evils of racism, though they did not move many Churches immediately to bold new action against racism in their own fellowship. So great was the confidence in the prophetic word that the World Council itself acted only relatively slowly to implement a further resolution of the Assembly recommending "that the Central Committee, in consultation with the International Missionary Council, make structural provision for an organisation, preferably a department, giving assistance to the constituent Churches in their efforts to bring the gospel to bear more effectively upon relations between racial and ethnic groups". But increasing racial conflict showed the need for a more active ecumenical role.

The killing of Africans in Sharpeville in South Africa in March 1960, and a request of the Archbishop of Cape Town, led to a meeting on "Church and Apartheid" in South Africa in December 1960. It was attended by a delegation of six leaders from the World Council of Churches. At Cottesloe (near Johannesburg) they met ten representatives from each of the eight Churches in South Africa to consider the Christian witness for racial justice in view of the apartheid policy of that country. The report of the meeting affirmed that no Christian could be excluded from any Church on grounds of race and colour, and it called attention to the injustices and hardships suffered by the African because of the system of communal separation and the restrictions on his participation in the economic and political life of South Africa.[1] The report, though approved by eighty per cent of the participants, was later repudiated by the three Dutch Reformed Churches of South Africa, which also withdrew from the World Council of Churches.[2]

In 1960 the World Council also established a Secretariat on Racial and Ethnic Relations within the Department on Church and Society to strengthen the ecumenical witness in situations of racial and ethnic tensions and to offer assistance to those Churches which were seeking new and creative answers. As the anger and violence created by racism increased, especially in the U.S.A. and Southern Africa, this secretariat endeavoured to arouse greater awareness of the enormous task confronting the Churches. A series of field visits and consultations was organized in many different regions of the world, perhaps the most remarkable being the Ecumenical Consultation on Chris-

[1] *Cottesloe Consultation—The Report of the Consultation Among South African Member Churches of the World Council of Churches, 7–14 December, 1960, Cottesloe, Johannesburg.* Johannesburg 1961. The Consultation was prepared by Dr Robert Bilheimer, who made several visits to South Africa to meet church leaders and to reach agreement on the agenda for the meeting.
[2] See "Message to Christians in South Africa", *The New Delhi Report: Third Assembly of the World Council of Churches, 1961*, p. 322.

tians and Race Relations in Southern Africa, held in Kitwe, Zambia, 25 May–
2 June 1964, under the auspices of the Mindolo Ecumenical Foundation, the
South African Institute of Race Relations, and the World Council of
Churches. The Conference was chaired by Dr Daisuke Kitagawa of the U.S.A.,
who had previously (1960–3) directed the World Council Secretariat on Race
Relations, and was attended by sixty church leaders and laymen from the
countries of Southern Africa. The finding that "the unjust patterns of race
relations now prevailing in most of Southern Africa must be changed" was
detailed in a report of thirty-seven pages.[1] The report provoked new intense
discussion, especially in South Africa where it became one of the principal
issues in a celebrated civil law suit between two Christian leaders who
supported the ecumenical position on racism, and a theologian who opposed
it.[2] (The court made its judgement in favour of the two plaintiffs in the suit
for libel.)

The Kitwe Conference emphasized that the problem of racial justice cannot
be solved without great changes in economic and political structures, and
this was reiterated in the 1966 Conference on Church and Society which
pressed the Churches to become more deeply involved in the world-wide
struggle against racism. The issue was brought to the forefront of the Conference by the sermon of Dr Martin Luther King, who, though prevented
from coming by race riots in Chicago, was seen and heard by millions of
viewers on European television, and by the inability of Bishop Alpheus Zulu
of South Africa, one of the presidents of the Conference, to participate, as
he had been denied a passport by the South African government.

In the Fourth Assembly at Uppsala (1968) the ecumenical consideration
of racism reached a new and sharper focus, reflecting no doubt the increasing
violence of race conflict and the determination of the coloured people,
especially black Americans, to attain full equality of political and social
rights with whites. Two addresses on the theme, "White Racism or World
Community?", by Mr James Baldwin, the distinguished American writer,
and Lord Caradon, delegate of the United Kingdom to the United Nations,
showed the increasing impatience with Christian tolerance or support of
white racism. Mr Baldwin's address expressed this in unmistakable terms:

> At this moment in the world's history it becomes necessary for me, for my own
> survival, not to listen to what you say but to watch very carefully what you do,
> not to read your pronouncements, but to go back to the source and to check it
> out for myself. And if that is so, then it may very well mean that the revolution
> which was begun two thousand years ago by a disreputable Hebrew criminal
> may now have to be begun again by people equally disreputable and equally
> improbable. It has to be admitted that if you are born under the circumstances
> in which most black people in the West are born, that means really black people
> over the entire world, ... and having attained something resembling adult-
> hood, it is perfectly true that one can see that the destruction of the Christian

---

[1] *Christians and Race Relations in Southern Africa.* Geneva 1964.
[2] See "Summary of Judgement in the Supreme Court of South Africa" between Professor A. S. Geyser, C. F. B. Naudé (plaintiffs) and Professor A. D. Pont (defendant),
1 August 1967. Published by the Christian Institute, Johannesburg, 1967.

Church as it is presently constituted may not only be desirable but may be necessary.

A "black caucus" at work in the Fourth Assembly put new force behind the familiar ecumenical declarations of good intentions concerning racism. In every area of ecumenical witness white racism was challenged; and in the election of the new Central Committee a new militant group of black ministers and laymen from the U.S.A. was selected, so insuring that black participation in the World Council would be more than a formality. It is noteworthy that the first decision of the new Central Committee was to endorse the recommendation of the Uppsala Assembly in favour of a World Council programme of study and action on the elimination of racism and to authorize its preparation. It is this new dynamic concern for racial justice together with the urgent demand for Christian involvement in the struggle for freedom and justice in the Third World which more than any other factor accounts for the revolutionary spirit arising within the ecumenical movement in recent years.

The Christian Responsibility for Rapid Social Change in the New Nations

It is a sobering thought that the ecumenical movement discovered the urgent problems of the nations of Africa, Asia, Latin America, and the Middle East only after the process of radical decolonization was well under way. There are institutional reasons which help to explain that fact. The World Council of Churches had very few member Churches from these countries in 1948 and most of the Christian concern for social and political welfare in these lands was expressed through western missionary societies identified with the International Missionary Council until that body merged with the W.C.C. in 1961. Despite the real interest of western Christians, they could not be expected to see the need for revolutionary change as clearly as Christians in the emerging nations.

Nevertheless, as early as 1949 the Churches of Asia had called attention to the confrontation between Christianity and revolutionary social change shaping up there. The Eastern Asia Christian Conference, held in Bangkok in December 1949, the first regional meeting of its kind to be held in Asia, emphasized the challenge to the Church in the social and political life: "The struggle for, and the attainment of, political freedom has awakened the hitherto submerged peoples of East Asia to a new sense of dignity and historical mission. Those are basic elements in the revolutionary ferment which are at work in the contemporary revolts and power-conflicts in Asia."

In 1952 the Study Department of the World Council, taking advantage of the first meeting of the Central Committee of the World Council to be held in Asia, organized in Lucknow an Ecumenical Study Conference for East Asia. The Conference was divided into three sections: Section II dealt with The Responsible Society in East Asia in the light of the World Situation, and Section III, Racial, Class, and Caste Tensions. One of the papers for this meeting was prepared by Professor Egbert de Vries. It was the beginning of the enormous contribution which this renowned specialist on the economics of development was to make to the social thinking of the World Council.[1]

As seen by the Asian Churches the task was to maintain a positive attitude to the social revolution taking place in East Asia as the best answer to the dynamic challenge of communism. The opening paragraphs of the Lucknow report put the issue in this perspective:

> We are concerned with social justice, that is to say with the development of social conditions in which human dignity and freedom can find their expression as befits the nature and destiny of man as a child of God. Communism has awakened and challenged our conscience to see the need for action. It is not, however, primarily the fear of communism but our concern for our brothers for whom Christ died, that should impel us to fulfil our social obligations. But a positive programme for social justice will help to meet the challenge of Communism.

The positive programme proposed by the Lucknow Conference included radical reform of land tenure systems, planned economic development, support of the struggle for freedom and self-determination in East Asia, and new policies by western nations in support of political and economic change in Asia.

The Lucknow meeting had a great influence on the further consideration of Christian action in Asia and on the subsequent decision of the World Council to develop a comprehensive programme in support of Churches facing issues of rapid social change in Africa, Asia, and Latin America. The decision to launch such a programme was taken in July 1955 at the first meeting of the new working committee for the Department on Church and Society, in Davos, Switzerland. It was approved by the Central Committee immediately after.[2]

A strong team of officers and staff was assembled to provide leadership for this inquiry which had as its theme "The Common Christian Responsibility Toward Areas of Rapid Social Change".[3] Professor E. de Vries, as chairman of the working committee, gave constant help, and the staff, now enlarged, included Paul Abrecht and Daisuke Kitagawa with M. M. Thomas as staff consultant for Asia and Dr John Karefa Smart as staff consultant for Africa (1956–7). Over the next five years this group was constantly on the move in Africa, Asia, Latin America, and the Middle East, contacting church and mission leaders, searching for new talent among theologians and laymen, organizing consultations and projects, and pressing the Churches to take up the themes of the rapid social change study. Churches and missions that had previously scarcely heard of the World Council suddenly found themselves plunged into a strenuous ecumenical debate. Sometimes the intrusion of these questions was vigorously opposed in both Church and mission; but

---

[1] Egbert de Vries, "The Churches and the Problems of Social and Economic Development in South and Southeast Asia", *Ecumenical Review*, vol. v (April 1953), pp. 233–43.

[2] See MRCC (Davos 1955).

[3] Two official statements were published on the goals of the programme: *The Common Christian Responsibility Toward Areas of Rapid Social Change* (Geneva 1955) and *Second Statement on the Issues in the Study of Rapid Social Change* (Geneva 1956).

the growing interest in the discovery of new lines of action for the Church in fast-changing societies gradually overcame the hesitations and fears. For many of these Churches the study provided the first opportunity to analyse the role of the Church in their society, and for the World Council it was to lead to a remarkable broadening of social perspective and concern, and a significantly new stage in the development of a truly universal Christian social ethic.

The programme was so constructed that an international series of conferences and publications supported the national and regional programme and vice versa. Over $200,000 was raised to finance this six-year programme (1955–61). Roughly half of this sum was for projects in the new nations and the other half for the international dimension of the inquiry. The results are catalogued in a number of study booklets and pamphlets and in two volumes which summarize the findings of the study.[1]

The development of the World Council's concern for social change seemed at first to require no new theological–ethical categories. But inevitably it became necessary to think in terms of theological perspectives for radical change, and to find a Christian interpretation of the emancipation of the new nations and of their efforts at nation-building.

In contrast with the familiar ecumenical emphasis on gradual social change and reform, the inquiries in the new nations pointed to the rapid breakdown of old social systems and traditions and the need for political and economic systems supporting rapid development. In contrast with western Christian thought which despite all its preoccupation with secularization was based on assumptions of a society still greatly influenced by Christian values and institutions, Christian social thinking in the new nations tended to emphasize the Christian contribution to a pluralistic social ethic which would promote human values in a national perspective. In contrast with the extremely critical attitude manifested toward nationalism in many of the Western Churches, the "younger Churches" stressed the creative role of the new nation-states in the work of development and in creating a new sense of dignity and self-respect. In opposition to the Western Churches, which still placed great confidence in the traditional structures of world political and economic relations, Christians from the new nations pointed to their inherent biases, and challenged the assumption of an "international law" developed by the western powers and imposed on the rest of the world.

This challenge to traditional ecumenical social thinking is well illustrated in the report of the International Ecumenical Study Conference on Social Change, held in Thessalonica, Greece, in July 1959, on the theme "Christian Action in Rapid Social Change; Dilemmas and Opportunities".

> In the earlier years of the ecumenical movement, and particularly at the Oxford Conference of 1937, the subject of nationalism was fully discussed. But in view of the circumstances at that time, attention was concentrated almost exclusively on the nationalist movement in western countries. The specific task in the light of the present situation is to concentrate on a different kind of nationalism in a

[1] Egbert de Vries, *Man in Rapid Social Change* and Paul Abrecht, *The Churches and Rapid Social Change*. New York 1961.

different phase of history in the areas of rapid social change, especially Asia and Africa . . . .

The nationalism of hitherto subject peoples and races gives tangible form to their awakening to a sense of human dignity and their struggle to discover and express their corporate selfhood. This nationalism finds the focus of its unity in the sense of common fate and common fight, that is, in the common determination of peoples to free themselves from alien political domination and racial discrimination.[1]

Similarly in the area of economic development the Thessalonica Conference pointed to the need for a new understanding of world economic justice and welfare.

Our ultimate aim should be a situation where there is no unnecessary poverty among nations, and where each nation by the use of its resources and abilities attacks its own conditions of poverty and contributes to the wellbeing of the whole . . . . Those with greater resources and abilities have the greater obligations. This applies between countries as much as within countries . . . . There is an enormous amount that can and should be done . . . . These responsibilities include not only technical aid and financial help (perhaps as a given proportion of national income), but also a recognition and correction of the ill effects on the poorer countries of western policies on immigration, tariffs and subsidies in foreign trade, stabilization of commodity prices, defence policies, use of surpluses (such as wheat, coal and shipping), and the whole trend of industrial development towards more or less self-sufficiency. Above all, the rich countries need to be aware of the impact of what they do on others. In many cases their contribution to economic development in Africa, Asia and Latin America is totally inadequate . . . .[2]

By 1961, the Churches realized that their social thinking, looked at in the world perspective of social and political change, was in need of a major re-examination, in view of the new problems arising and new ideas about the task of the Church in society. However, the Third Assembly of the World Council of Churches (New Delhi 1961), was unprepared to cope with this new situation. It could only recognize the problem and suggest the need for further ecumenical analysis and consultation, utilizing the insights of Churches and Christians from every continent. It was in recognition of the scope and the urgency of this task that the proposal for a World Conference on Church and Society arose.

The Geneva Conference of 1966

Why was it necessary to wait nearly thirty years after the Oxford Conference for a new World Conference on Church and Society? The answer is that with the formation of the World Council of Churches in 1948, it had been assumed that the Assemblies, meeting at regular intervals of six or seven years would provide the needed opportunity for official World Council action on social

[1] *Dilemmas and Opportunities: Christian Action in Rapid Social Change.* Report of an International Ecumenical Study Conference (Thessalonica 25 July–2 August 1959). Geneva 1959.
[2] Ibid., p. 74.

questions. Indeed the Assemblies of Amsterdam (1948) and Evanston (1954) had contributed significantly to ecumenical reflection. But New Delhi revealed that the amount of time which an Assembly could give to serious consideration of social questions was diminishing; and that the participation of laymen in the discussion of social question was hampered by the predominantly ecclesiastical character and structure of an Assembly. Moreover, the "official" nature of an Assembly inhibited adventurous social thinking; it could only put the seal of World Council approval on ideas already accepted by the Churches, rather than risk new ideas which the Churches had yet to grasp. The search for a way around these obstacles led to the proposal of the staff in 1962 to convene a World Conference on Church and Society, and this was submitted to the Working Committee meeting in 1962.

The Working Committee for Church and Society now included many new faces: M. M. Thomas of India, active in ecumenical social study since 1947, became Chairman, Bishop J. Brooke Mosley of the U.S.A., Vice-Chairman. Other members included Dr Margaret Mead, the noted anthropologist, Professor Mikio Sumiya, an economist from Japan; Bishop Pitirim, the first member from the U.S.S.R.; and Professor Jan M. Lochman of Czechoslovakia. This group, meeting in Paris in July 1962, put forward a plan for a "World Conference on God, Man and Contemporary Society", and their recommendation was approved by the Central Committee a few weeks later.[1]

In structure and organization the World Conference on Church and Society held in Geneva in July 1966 differed from previous world Christian conferences on social questions in two fundamental respects: the majority of the participants were laymen rather than clergy or church officials, and of the 420 participants roughly equal numbers came from the countries of the "third world", from North America, and from western Europe, making it the first large ecumenical conference in which the participants from the western countries were not in a majority. These two features explain the great impact of the Geneva Conference on ecumenical social thought and action.

The Geneva Conference was undoubtedly the most serious attempt on the part of the World Council of Churches to understand the revolutionary realities which shape the modern world. Preparations continued over three years involving the publication of four volumes of essays on the issues of world-wide social change.[2]

The Central Committee further agreed that the Conference should be empowered to speak *to* rather than *for* the Churches and the World Council, thus giving it freedom to explore issues and suggest new approaches. A

---

[1] Subsequently at its meeting in Enugu (1965), the Central Committee reviewed the aims of the Conference and resolved that it should be described as a "World Conference on Church and Society: Christian Response to the Technical and Social Revolutions of our Time". This theme was later abbreviated to "Christians in the Technical and Social Revolutions of our Time".

[2] *Christian Social Ethics in a Changing World*, ed. John C. Bennett. New York 1966.
Responsible Government in a Revolutionary Age, ed. Z. K. Matthews. New York 1966.
Economic Growth in World Perspective, ed. Denys Munby. New York 1966.
Man in Community, ed. Egbert de Vries. New York 1966.

process of selecting participants was devised to correspond with the emphasis on the need for lay experts from the various fields of social life.[1]

The basic work of the Conference was done in four sections on:

I Economic Development in a World Perspective.
II The Nature and Function of the State in a Revolutionary Age.
III Structures of International Co-operation—Living Together in Peace in a Pluralistic World Society.
IV Man and Community in Changing Societies.

In addition there were three Conference working groups on three issues which cut across the concerns of the sections:

1. Theological Issues in Social Ethics.
2. Potentialities of the Contemporary Technological and Scientific Revolution.
3. The Church's Action in Society.

The official report of 162 pages and the conference addresses have been widely studied and discussed. The impact not only on Christian social ethics but on every aspect of the ecumenical movement, whether mission, service, unity, or ministry, has been far-reaching. The Conference has, moreover, produced a chain reaction of follow-up consultations in which Churches and Christian groups around the world have been stimulated to new reflection and consideration on contemporary issues of Church and Society.[2] The theological and intellectual ferment thus created very substantially influenced the thinking of the Fourth Assembly of the World Council meeting at Uppsala in July 1968.

Out of this process of ecumenical inquiry and debate have come many new insights and concerns, radically changing the scope of Christian social thought and action. The resulting debate in the Churches on three concerns of the Geneva Conference deserves special attention because they provide important clues to the future of the ecumenical social thinking.

1. The Christian Responsibility for World Economic and Social Development

The 1966 Conference made the issue of world economic development a major concern of the Churches. The conference report on this theme set before them a new comprehensive understanding of the hopes and concerns of the developing countries, the contributions needed from the "richer" nations, and the changes in world economic and political structures required if world economic growth was to be achieved. The report also recommended a number of practical steps which would involve new commitments on the part of the Churches to world economic and social justice.

The papal encyclical *Populorum progressio*, published early in 1967,

---

[1] World Conference on Church and Society (Geneva 1966), Official Report, pp. 8–9.

[2] For a list of these consultations and an account of the reactions to the World Conference, see *Report to the Uppsala Assembly on the 1966 World Conference on Church and Society and the Subsequent Discussion in the Churches*, by Paul Abrecht (Geneva 1968).

supported similar goals of world development and opened the door to new common Christian action. As a result, a joint Roman Catholic–World Council Exploratory Committee on Society, Development, and Peace was formed. Also a conference on World Co-operation for Development, sponsored by the Pontifical Commission on Justice and Peace and the World Council of Churches, was held in Beirut in April 1968. This was the first major international Christian conference to be so jointly sponsored, organized, and financed.[1] This meeting proposed a larger ecumenical action in favour of world economic co-operation and their proposals were endorsed by the Fourth Assembly at Uppsala.

Stimulated by the challenge of the Geneva Conference and the Beirut meeting, the Uppsala Assembly focused major attention on the issues of development. It is noteworthy that the Assembly's report urges the Churches to go beyond the charitable understanding of "rich" nations helping "poor" nations; it emphasizes the need for fundamental social changes based on a new urgent concern for social justice in a world perspective.

> Effective world development requires radical changes in institutions and structures at three levels: within developing countries, within developed countries, and in the international economy. Precisely because such structural changes have not been promoted, we find that as a community of nations we are unable to do the good we would and efforts for international co-operation tend to be paralysed. At all three levels it is necessary to instil social and economic processes with a new dynamic of human solidarity and justice.[2]

This statement of the Assembly perhaps reflected the address of Professor S. L. Parmar of India who, in speaking to the Assembly on this issue, declared:

> Rightly understood, development is disorder because it changes existing social and economic relationships, breaks up old institutions to create new ones, brings about radical alterations in the values and structures of society. If we engage in development through international co-operation, we must recognize that basic changes become necessary in developing and developed nations as also in the international economy. "Development is the new name for peace." But development is disorder, it is revolution. Can we attempt to understand this apparently paradoxical situation which would imply that disorder and revolution are the new name for peace?[3]

Thus, the Christian discussion of world development, formerly treated almost exclusively in terms of new and expanding forms of aid and trade, has tended more and more to merge with the discussion of revolutionary social

---

[1] *World Development—Challenge to the Churches—Official Report of the Beirut Conference*, edited by Father George Dunne. Geneva 1968.

Several other World Council projects contributed notably to ecumenical thinking on development prior to the Assembly. The work of the Committee on Specialized Assistance to Social Projects (S.A.S.P.) should be mentioned. See especially, *Line and Plummet, The Churches and Development. A report to S.A.S.P.*, by Richard Dickinson (Geneva 1968).

[2] Uppsala Assembly: Report of Section III, on "World Economic and Social Development" (Geneva 1968).

[3] Uppsala Assembly: Professor S. L. Parmar, Statement to the Plenary on the Work of Section III.

change. This is due, no doubt, to the great disappointment with the results of previous efforts of world economic development and the recognition that the familiar patterns of world aid and technical assistance have often increased rather than diminished many of the social problems of the developing nations. There is a widespread desire for new ideas, new techniques, and new initiatives.

The Churches working within the ecumenical movement can make an important contribution in this area—especially in the search for new understanding and new ideas as the basis for new and effective action. It remains to be seen whether, having exposed themselves to a new understanding of human aspirations in the movement for world-wide development, they will discover the imagination, the resources, and the ingenuity to contribute to dynamic action in this field, and give practical expression to their concern for world economic justice. This is perhaps the greatest challenge facing them in the future, and one which will, undoubtedly, test profoundly their ecumenical loyalty and solidarity.

2. *The Revolutionary Transformation of Society*

It is precisely because the call to development is a call to accept and even to initiate revolutionary change that many Christians have become suspicious or even hostile concerning the direction of ecumenical social thought today. Certainly, of all the issues raised by the 1966 Conference none has created more controversy and debate than that on the Church and revolution. The much discussed addresses on this topic by three theologians, Professor H. D. Wendland of Germany, Professor Richard Shaull of the U.S.A., and Archpriest Vitaly Borovoy of the U.S.S.R., brought this issue sharply before the World Conference. Both the message and the report of the Conference reflect one fundamental point of agreement, that the Church must recognize the need for revolutionary change in social and political structures. This view is stated as follows in the conference message:

> As Christians, we are committed to working for the transformation of society. In the past we have usually done this through quiet efforts at social renewal, working in and through the established institutions, according to their rules. Today, a significant number of those who are dedicated to the service of Christ and their neighbour assume a more radical or revolutionary position. They do not deny the value of tradition nor of social order, but they are searching for a new strategy by which to bring about basic changes in society without too much delay. It is possible that the tension between these two positions will have an important place in the life of the Christian community for some time to come. At the present moment, it is important for us to recognize that this radical position has a solid foundation in Christian tradition and should have its rightful place in the life of the Church and in the ongoing discussion of social responsibility.[1]

Around such declarations have arisen demands for a "theology of revolution", now being very widely debated by theologians in many countries.[2]

---

[1] Official Report, Message of the Conference, para. 6, p. 49.

[2] See for example Arthur Rich, in *Kirchenblatt für die Reformierte Schweiz*, no. 17 (25 August 1966). Also Trutz Rendtorff and H. E. Tödt, *Theologie der Revolution* (Frankfurt 1968).

Some commentators have pointed to the ambiguity of the term "revolution", and the different meanings it has for Westerners, who refer to the profound and silent transformation of the structures of industrial society, and for the representatives of the Third World, who mean by it the violent transformations which characterize the post-colonial and pre-industrial period. Professor Roger Mehl of France has observed that what the latter

> asked from the Church was to give them a theology and an ethic which could help them to live in that revolutionary period and to assume often frightening responsibilities in it. They would have liked theologians to start elaborating a theology of revolution—a legitimate claim if one remembers that for centuries theologians have taught nothing but a theology of order and have had a vision of an entirely static human universe. Dangerous claim also if care is not taken ... not to recognize in each of these often ambiguous revolutions the very dynamic of God's Kingdom.[1]

The post-conference discussion on this issue has sought to clarify the meaning of revolutionary change and to provide ethical guide-lines for Christians involved in contemporary revolutionary ferment. An ecumenical consultation of theologians and laymen convened by the Department on Church and Society and the Commission of Faith and Order, 17–23 March 1968 (in Zagorsk, U.S.S.R.), offered its "Reflections on Theology and Revolution" which carry the debate a considerable step further. These may be summarized as follows:

Christian theology warns against sacralizing either the *status quo* or the revolution and should guard against the temptations of false messianism and the fury of self-righteousness. At the same time, theology should free Christians and the Churches for interpretations of creation, providence, and law which have generally exaggerated the importance of order relative to justice, in order to make possible a more dynamic relation between order and justice.

Christians in a revolutionary situation have a moral duty to do all in their power to exercise a ministry of reconciliation to enable the revolutionary change to take place non-violently or, if this is not possible, with a minimum of violence.

Christian theology cannot remove the ambiguity of political ethics in a revolutionary situation. Nevertheless, it should relate the universality of the Church, which includes political opponents, to the Christian's special responsibility as a matter of vocation.

The ecumenical idea of a responsible society still has relevance to the new structures established after the revolutionary overthrow of old ones, when it becomes necessary to make power and technology responsible and to allow for a permanent renewal of structures without the disruption of order.

As already noted, the Uppsala Assembly recognized the need for revolutionary alteration of social and political structures to create the essential conditions of development. In its declaration on the issue of revolution, the Assembly very largely confirmed the conclusions of the Geneva Conference in its own declaration on this problem:

[1] Roger Mehl, article in *Le Monde*, 27 July 1966.

> Revolution is not to be identified with violence . . . . In countries where the ruling groups are oppressive or indifferent to the aspirations of the people, are often supported by foreign interests, and seek to resist all changes by the use of coercive or violent measures, including the "law and order" which may itself be a form of violence, the revolutionary change may take a violent form. Such changes are morally ambiguous. The churches have a special contribution towards the development of effective non-violent strategies of revolution and social change. Nevertheless we are called to participate creatively in the building of political institutions to implement the social changes that are desperately needed.[1]

Undoubtedly many new problems will arise in the future as Christians endeavour to give expression to such concerns, and the Churches will have much further thinking to do on the Christian responsibility in particular revolutionary situations.

3. Co-operation with the Roman Catholic Church in Christian Thought and Action

One of the important discoveries made during the preparation for the World Conference on Church and Society was the convergence at certain points of Roman Catholic and World Council social thinking. The Second Vatican Council had begun its discussion of the Church and human needs at almost the same moment that the Central Committee of the World Council decided to convene the Church and Society Conference. The social encyclicals of Pope John XXIII, *Mater et magistra* (1961) and *Pacem in terris* (1963), showed a new trend in Roman Catholic social thinking which was carried further by the adoption by the Vatican Council of the *Pastoral Constitution on the Church in the Modern World* (1965). Two ecumenical consultations of Roman Catholic and World Council theologians and scholars, in March 1965 and February 1966, revealed wide areas of agreement and encouraged the making of plans for joint programmes of study on theological and practical questions. As the second consultation reported:

> Having considered recent W.C.C. and Roman Catholic documents within the general field of Church and Society, this consultation is firmly convinced that there is no sufficient reason why further work on this theme should be carried on in isolation, but rather that there ought to be consultation (or, as far as their ways of working will allow, collaboration) between the W.C.C. and the Roman Catholic Church . . .[2]

Eight Roman Catholic observers attended the 1966 World Conference on Church and Society.[3] Each observer was a well-known leader in Roman Catholic thinking on social questions. Their participation contributed greatly to the desire on both sides to explore ways of working together. Such co-operation became reality a year later with the establishment in early 1967

---

[1] Report of Section III to the Uppsala Assembly, para. 15.

[2] "Theology and Social Ethics" in *Study Encounter*, vol. ii, no. 2 (1966) p. 98.

[3] Over a score of Roman Catholic priests and laymen attended as guests or as press representatives.

of the Pontifical Commission on Justice and Peace, with Monsignor Joseph Gremillion as secretary.

By June 1967 a joint R.C./W.C.C. Exploratory Committee was formed to search for ways relating the work of the Pontifical Commission and the World Council activities in this area of common concern. This has since become the Exploratory Committee on Society, Development, and Peace, with Monsignor Gremillion and Mr Max Kohnstamm, a layman active in World Council studies on social and international affairs, as co-chairman. In January 1968, the two sides agreed to name as joint secretary to this Exploratory Committee, Father George Dunne, s.j., the first man to serve the Churches in such a larger ecumenical enterprise. The Conference on Development in Beirut (1968) was the first project of the Exploratory Committee, and a major test of the reality of this new co-operative effort. Its success provided a strong indication that this joint work could expand substantially during the coming years. Such wider ecumenical collaboration is likely to influence greatly the shape and direction of ecumenical social thinking in the period ahead.

The Assembly at Uppsala welcomed this collaboration and emphasized "the importance of co-operating at every level with the Roman Catholic Church . . . and indeed with men of good will everywhere". The publication of the latest papal encyclical, *Humanae vitae* shows, however, that fundamental disagreements on certain social issues remain, and it would be wrong to expect that some of these will be quickly or easily overcome. Indeed, it is likely that at many points the Roman Catholic Church, working within long-established structures, will have an uneasy part in the ecumenical dialogue, based as it is on the principles of renewal and self-criticism. Obviously it is not alone in this difficulty.

The Question of Theological Basis

Those who are sceptical about ecumenical social thinking ask: How is it that theologians and laymen are able to come to a relatively large measure of agreement on practical Christian social action in spite of their inability to resolve certain fundamental theological issues of faith and order? This has raised the further question, debated repeatedly in ecumenical circles: How much of a common theological or ecclesiological rationale is necessary before an authentic ecumenical word on social questions can be spoken?

The failure to achieve prior agreement on basic theological or biblical perspectives appears as a serious weakness (and even deception) to those who believe that it is hazardous, if not impossible, to make common Christian declarations on social issues before the theological assumptions underlying them are made explicit. But opposed to that point of view is another which maintains that ecumenical agreement on social questions does not and cannot proceed always from basic theological principles to agreement on practical issues. This viewpoint recognizes that there will probably never be complete agreement on theological debate to be constantly enlivened by new questions. The fact that Churches with different theological outlooks have been able to agree on attitudes or actions in society can be a recognition of a common experience or even of some common theological assumptions which go deeper than the theological differences.

In recent years, the debate about inductive versus deductive social ethics or an ethics of principles versus a contextual ethic has shown how difficult it is to follow one line of reasoning. The World Council has constantly struggled to see the validity of these two perspectives, recognizing, on the one hand, the importance of exploratory work on fundamental theological issues relating to Church and society and at the same time launching inquiries on specific practical concerns. It can easily be demonstrated that ecumenical social thinking has been illuminated by both approaches. Thus, during the years 1948–52, the World Council Study on "The Bible and the Church's Message to the World", directed by the German biblical scholar, Dr Wolfgang Schweitzer, helped to relate biblical exegesis and interpretation to social ethics. And from 1951–4 a substantial study of the main theme of the Second Assembly, "Christ the Hope of the World", involving extensive discussions among thirty-five of the world's foremost theologians, gave much attention to the nature of the Church's witness in society. More recent studies on "The Lordship of Christ over the World and the Church" (concluded in 1958) and on "The Finality of Jesus Christ in an Age of Universal History" (1961–8) provided considerable theological background for the practical work of the World Council in the area of Church and Society.

It is true that there was, often, very little integration or cross-fertilization between these theological studies and the practical inquiries carried on simultaneously. It is also true that laymen have been looking for a more dynamic dialectical relation between the theological reflection and the concrete ethical problems facing them in society than was provided by the theological inquiries.

All these questions were examined at length in the Consultation of theologians and laymen meeting in Russia in March 1968, called to make a theological evaluation of the 1966 Conference. The consultation reviewed the theological method as well as the ecclesiological rationale for ecumenical work on social questions. It observed that various denominations often proceed functionally along similar lines in thinking about the role of the Church in society. It acknowledged that this has made possible the formation of groups or movements within and between the Churches which can engage in social action and study and which in turn have led to the discovery of provisional agreements, bridging differences between Christians and showing the possibility of a larger corporate witness.[1] It urged also that there be more systematic theological study of the ethical issues arising from the practical ecumenical work and welcomed the fact that this particular consultation had been jointly sponsored by the Faith and Order Commission and the Department on Church and Society.

---

[1] See "Ecclesiology and Social Ethics", Section 4 of the report of the Zagorsk Consultation, *Study Encounter* (1968).

Conclusion

Despite the achievements in recent years, ecumenical social thinking remains a precarious enterprise. A substantial number of Christians in our Churches are probably still very much opposed to the directions it takes or would criticize the World Council and other ecumenical bodies for giving too much attention to social issues. Moreover, as the pressures for rapid change in society increase, the polarization of opinion in our Churches on basic social questions will undoubtedly become greater rather than diminish. The continuing division of the Churches on basic issues of theology and ecclesiology also weakens the possibility of a more substantial Christian social witness.

Up to the present, the ecumenical consensus on Christian social responsibility has been limited, experimental, and provisional, and with relatively slight impact on the action of the Churches in society. And no doubt the ecumenical witness will become more difficult in the future. But wherever Christians struggle to maintain the transcendence of the faith to their fellow men, combining the desire for justice with the spirit of compassion, the search for the ecumenical community of ideas and witness will proceed. Possibly the most significant achievement of the ecumenical movement has been its ability to encourage and nourish that dialectic of obedience and unity even in situations where opposing points of view seemed to make real encounter impossible. We can hope for no more and should aspire to no less in the future.

10

Ecumenical Action
in International Affairs

O. FREDERICK NOLDE

The responsibility of the churches to promote international good will is inescapable. Progressive recognition of their imperative involvement in the affairs of nations has sprung from no new or strange faith. The Churches' primary contribution to peace with justice and freedom lies in the steadfast proclamation of the gospel at home and to the uttermost parts of the earth and in the growing solidarity of a Christian fellowship which transcends race, class, and national frontiers. Christian witness to the world of nations is an inevitable projection of Christian faith and experience.[1]

Backgrounds and Origins

At the close of the Second World War—the second within less than half a century and with peace still not secured—Christian leaders felt impelled to look for a new and more direct way to play their responsible part in international affairs. While the particular instrumentality which they conceived had no precedent, the emerging ecumenical movement over a period of some thirty years had been building a solid foundation. Specific Christian concern for peace and justice had been expressed by the Stockholm Conference of 1925, the Oxford Conference of 1937 under the Universal Christian Council for Life and Work, and by the Madras Conference of the International Missionary Council in 1938. These conferences had delineated areas of concern for the Christian witness, but had provided no specialized structure or secretariat for continuing work.

Direct impetus for a new venture came from a war-time agency of the Churches in the United States and Canada—the Commission on a Just and Durable Peace (C.J.D.P.) of the Federal Council of the Churches of Christ in America. It was reinforced by the British Commission on Christian Social Responsibility, led by Archbishop William Temple. Especially in the former, remote from the scene of actual military conflict, were resources available for concentration on post-war planning. The International Round Table at Princeton, N.J., convened in July 1943, by the C.J.D.P., brought together sixty-one Christian leaders from twelve countries in North America, Europe, Asia, and from Australia and New Zealand. One of its purposes was to formulate, in so far as possible, a consensus on the problems of order in the post-war world. The Round Table stimulated an international Christian impact upon the deliberations of the Conference on International Organization at San Francisco in 1945, where the Charter of the United Nations was drafted. It also gave impetus to an organized ecumenical approach to problems of peace, justice, and freedom.

The Commission of the Churches on International Affairs was founded in 1946 at a conference of church leaders in Cambridge, England. The background and intent of the conference were set forth in an explanation signed by Dr Marc Boegner of France, Chairman of the Administrative Committee of the World Council of Churches (in process of formation), and by Bishop

---

[1] While this chapter appears over my name, all my colleagues in the Commission of the Churches on International Affairs have in varying degrees contributed to it. I acknowledge particularly my indebtedness to Dr Richard M. Fagley because, in preparing this review, I have borrowed heavily from his study entitled *The First Twenty Years.—O.F.N.*

James C. Baker of the United States, Chairman of the International Missionary Council:

> As a result of actions taken at Geneva, Switzerland, at the February 1946 meetings of the *ad interim* Committee of the International Missionary Council and the Provisional Committee of the World Council of Churches, the Commision on a Just and Durable Peace of the Federal Council of the Churches of Christ in America was asked to arrange a conference of church leaders to consider the problems of peace and war.

> This was generously undertaken by the officers of the latter Commission. Mr John Foster Dulles and Dr Walter W. Van Kirk, chairman and secretary respectively, made the preparations which resulted in the gathering at Girton College, Cambridge, August 4–7 (1946) of 60 persons coming from 15 countries. The gathering was held under the joint sponsorship of the International Missionary Council and the World Council of Churches and on mandate from those bodies undertook to collaborate with a joint committee of the two in setting up a joint permanent Commission of the Churches on International Affairs to carry forward the type of work to which God's design and man's disorder call the churches.

The composition of the Cambridge Conference appears strange today, but at the time it seemed to be and quite probably was a realistic reflection of the existing situation. Over half the sixty participants were from Anglo-Saxon countries. The conference chairman, the chairman of the drafting committee, and one of the two secretaries were American. Travel difficulties reduced the East European representation to two, the participants from the "younger Churches" to one, and the Orthodox representation to one. These difficulties exaggerated a preponderance which was present even in planning. However, the conference would have been in the circumstances overwhelmingly West European and North American in any case.

Similarly the orientation of the Cambridge Conference was such as would have been expected in the immediate post-war period. There seemed to be no advantage in stating in detail the theological presuppositions; in fact, participants were aware that undue emphasis upon precise theological formulations could rob action of the very considerable unanimity by which it was supported. The difficulties lay rather in ascertaining the hard facts of international life and the responses the Churches were called upon to make to them. There was acute consciousness of the havoc created by war, the new atomic insecurity, and the dangerous signs of tensions among the major powers. Nevertheless, there was a good deal of confidence in regard to the struggle for world order. The issue was the practical one of blocking out the areas for major attention and getting the new organization under way. The emphasis was on action.

The heart of the work of the Cambridge Conference was the "Charter", since called "Aims of the C.C.I.A.", in which the Conference outlined nine functions for the new organization in serving its parent bodies. These aims of the Commission of the Churches on International Affairs stood the test of intervening years. They were only slightly modified at the Third Assembly of the World Council of Churches in New Delhi where the integration of the

International Missionary Council and the World Council took place and again in the new constitution adopted at the Fourth Assembly in 1968. The officers, supported by the Commission, viewed the nine points as a broad definition of areas into which C.C.I.A. was encouraged to move when resources of personnel and budget were available. Their position was that it was better to perform some of the functions reasonably well than to stretch the available resources too thinly.

The first two aims dealt with education and action at the national and denominational level. They reflected the convictions stated in the conclusion of the Cambridge Report, that "witness that is truly ecumenical must spring from local conviction and determination". The C.C.I.A. was encouraged to aid in the formation of national and denominational commissions on international affairs, and to gather, appraise, and disseminate the best available materials on the relations of the Churches to public affairs. Particularly in the early years, the principal officers visited church leaders in a number of countries to stimulate the formation or reorganization of national committees. While only three active national commissions existed when the C.C.I.A. was founded, twenty years later twenty-five national or regional inter-denominational agencies were co-operating with it with varying degrees of competence and effectiveness. While efforts were made to stimulate education in Christian responsibility for international affairs, the C.C.I.A. because of lack of resources attempted no general clearing house function, but was forced to rely upon the action of national and regional groups.

The next three aims dealt with the study function of "selected problems of international justice and world order including economic and social questions". While the C.C.I.A. did not pursue study in the formal sense, by the very nature of its work it was forced to rely upon a variety of study procedures. It was involved in the symposium on international affairs for the First Assembly of the World Council of Churches, as well as in the preparatory work for the Second and Third Assemblies. It conducted various surveys on the requirements of religious liberty leading to the World Council of Churches–International Missionary Council "Declaration on Religious Liberty" of 1948 which was recognized to have played a significant role in the formulation of provisions for religious liberty in the Universal Declaration of Human Rights and in the Covenant of Civil and Political Rights. In 1955 it analysed the status of religious liberty in the face of "dominant forces". It prepared the symposium for its tenth anniversary in 1956 as well as for its twentieth in 1966. Each filled an entire volume of the *Ecumenical Review*. Individual studies produced in books or in articles dealt with the plight of refugees, development strategy, the population problem, power politics, and human rights. One longer range study on the question of an international ethos did not fare very well for a variety of reasons, but it did serve the Commission in its representative work.

The C.C.I.A. was also required to do a very considerable amount of direct study of the background of issues in preparing the representations on the international issues with which it dealt. In many instances these issues were submitted to the W.C.C. Executive and Central Committees for action. This helped to establish in at least some Christian minds that comprehension of the hard political realities was a starting-place for discovering Christian obedience. Experience showed that, while there was need for longer-range study through whatever agency was assigned the task, it would never be met by sacrificing that form of study which is the immediate handmaiden of action.

The next three points in the aims dealt with the realm of action. These provided the main general guide-lines for the C.C.I.A. in the first two decades of its life. The C.C.I.A. was to call attention to urgent international problems and to suggest effective Christian action. It was to advise its parent bodies or speak in its own name on "Christian principles", indicating their bearing on immediate issues. It also represented the parent bodies in relations with international organizations such as the United Nations and its related agencies.

The final point of the aims empowered the Commission to "concert from time to time with other organizations holding similar objectives in the advancement of particular ends". Behind this point, not otherwise reflected in the Cambridge Report, was a considerable discussion of the question of possible collaboration with agencies and leaders of the Roman Catholic Church—a twenty-year forecast of the development of contemporary relationships. In the end, however, it was agreed not to refer specifically to the possibilities of collaboration with the Roman Catholics, taking into account such obstacles as differing stances toward communist societies, matters of religious freedom, and the patterns and forms of Vatican diplomacy.

Operation and Relationships in an Ecumenical Setting

The first battle-line of the World Council of Churches in its offensive against war and injustice is drawn in its far-flung programmes of witness, study, and service, rooted in the faith and commitment of its constituent members. It is against this background that the Commission of the Churches on International Affairs functions as a specialized agency to relate the common ecumenical witness to specific international problems.

The operation of the C.C.I.A. can be most simply described in terms of a two-way line of communication. This involved, on the one hand, contact with Churches and church leaders around the world and, on the other, contacts with intergovernmental bodies.

To serve as a "source of stimulus and knowledge" the C.C.I.A. sought to develop closer relations with Christian groups within the ecumenical fellowship through its commissioners, through national commissions on international affairs, through the constituent Churches and Christian councils, and through special correspondents, as well as through the officially designated representatives of member Churches in World Council Assemblies and meetings of the Central and Executive Committees.

The commissioners, who numbered about fifty, were elected by the parent bodies after careful consultation with church leaders to ensure stature in international affairs and acceptability to Churches at the national level. The large majority were laymen, although place, all too limited, was given to women. Selection was made on the basis of competence in the political and diplomatic fields. Wherever possible commissioners were sought who, in addition to other qualifications, could act as a door into the "corridors of power" and thus facilitate direct representation at highest levels. The continuity of the Commission was relatively high, fourteen of the current commissioners were among the original group. However, the benefits of continuity were diluted by the fact that only a handful were able to attend meetings regularly. Continuity also exacted a price in the age composition of the Commission.

The eminence of the commissioners helped to assure C.C.I.A. access to important information and to expert counsel. But the question remains whether the combined talents of this able group were sufficiently engaged in the formation of policy and whether there was enough dialogue between the officers' groups and the commissioners. In the early years, there was considerable consultation by correspondence. Later, as the officers became more experienced and self-reliant and the commissioners gained greater confidence in their judgement, there was, with a few exceptions, a slackening in the give and take. While there was no doubt that, if commissioners had taken strong exception to positions taken by the officers, they would have been heard from, tacit support, no matter how genuine, was a far cry from the kind of active involvement desirable for such a body.

The importance of ecumenical work at the national level was a constant theme of C.C.I.A. in view of the fact that primary decisions in international affairs are made at that level and most of the Churches are organized along national lines. The arrangement of relationships with regional and national church commissions, however, was a rather curious one in that, while they co-operated on an informal basis with the international C.C.I.A., they remained formal agents of Regional or National Councils. It may well be that the experience of two decades will lead to new forms of collaboration without losing the advantages of that arrangement.

One of the most effective ways in which the Commission maintained roots in the World Council constituency was in meetings of the Council's major organs. It was in assemblies and meetings of the Executive and Central Committees, as well as in meetings of the C.C.I.A. itself or of its Executive Committee, that problems were most sharply seen and positions developed. Contacts in the Churches were also maintained through various mailings to some four hundred churchmen. These included the memoranda prepared by the New York office on selected issues coming before each U.N. General Assembly, and an occasional bulletin of background information and analysis of some current issue prepared by the London office under the title of *C.C.I.A. Brief*. Memoranda also were circulated periodically to solicit information from commissioners and national commissions and to inform them of actions taken.

In an operation of this kind, officers and staff played no small part and no historical sketch would be complete without reference to them. Since the Commission in 1946 had perforce to start on a very modest financial basis—the initial appropriation being $4,000 a year with some additional funds secured from outside sources, it secured the part-time services of two participants in the Cambridge Conference. These were Kenneth Grubb (now Sir Kenneth Grubb), formerly of the Ministry of Information of the United Kingdom and active in Anglican and Latin American affairs, and myself, at that time Dean of the Graduate School of the Lutheran Theological Seminary in Philadelphia and a member of the Commission on a Just and Durable Peace. (I had also served as a consultant at the San Francisco Conference on United Nations Organization.) We were initially designated as director and associate director, but the manner in which the work developed soon led to the titles of chairman and director—Sir Kenneth giving general oversight to organizational matters and I to substantive work, particularly at the United Nations. Professor Frederick van Asbeck of the Netherlands, wise veteran in international relations, had earlier been named president. He served until the W.C.C.'s Second Assembly. Since then the post has remained unfulfilled.

The staffing arrangements were modest for an international agency of the scope proposed in the aims. Starting with secretaries in London and New York, the executive staff, in addition to the two principal officers, grew to four a decade ago and remained at that level, despite explorations seeking additional personnel, particularly from developing countries. The turnover in the staff was small; the average service of the present staff, apart from the chairman and director, has been twelve years. Dr Richard Fagley has been executive secretary, working out of the New York office, since 1951; Dr Elfan Rees has served as representative in Europe since 1952 and earlier was a consultant to the C.C.I.A.; the Reverend A. Dominique Micheli was appointed as secretary in New York in 1955 and now serves as secretary in Geneva; the Reverend Alan Booth served as secretary in London since 1957. The cumulative experience of the officers made possible a continued development of the work.

The founding fathers granted the new agency considerable flexibility and autonomy, subject to prior consultation and subsequent review by the parent bodies. Because of the infrequent stated meetings of the W.C.C. and the I.M.C., the C.C.I.A. and its officers were given the right to speak in their own name so that they might cope with the time-table of events and take advantage of a wider variety of possible resources. This responsibility placed no small burden upon C.C.I.A. officers and staff. It required not only that they ascertain the views predominantly held in the World Council constituency, but that they possess the specialized and technical competence needed to command the respect of the governmental and intergovernmental agencies to whom they communicated the views of the Churches.

There thus developed an "international civil service" of the Churches with a system of staff specialization which gave to each member a major responsibility. The chairman, in the main, was responsible for general administration; the director, in the early years, for work for human rights and later for disarmament and tension points. Rees worked on behalf of refugees; Micheli for human rights; Booth for African problems; Fagley on development and population problems. Other concerns were distributed on an *ad hoc* basis, and each member of the staff played his part in a system of checks and balances for the entire programme. The director's task of co-ordination increased with the expansion of activities. Additional technical and specialized resources of the kind not readily available in ecclesiastical circles were accessible in institutes and foundations. These included the Institute of Strategic Studies, the Institute of Race Relations, and the Overseas Development Institute in London and Carnegie Endowment for International Peace in New York and Geneva. With these the several officers were associated in their personal capacities.

Considerable efforts were made to enlarge the staff to use the potential offered by the regional Christian agencies in Asia and Africa—the East Asia Christian Council and the All African Conference of Churches. Officers met a number of times with agencies of the two bodies to explore the possibilities of establishing regular and significant co-operation. As a result the consultative services were secured of U. Kyaw Than for E.A.C.C. and of Mr Samuel Amissah on behalf of A.A.C.C. In view of the increasing significance of intergovernmental regional associations and programmes, it is important that contacts with regional Christian agencies be strengthened in this field.

C.C.I.A. officers also gave considerable attention to regional manifestations of world problems such as a divided Germany, the tensions of the "cold war", and refugees and migration. Several C.C.I.A. officers participated as members in the discussions of the Committee for Christian Responsibility for European Co-operation and also had contacts with the Christian Peace Conference of Prague. But they did not find it feasible to devote a large portion of staff resources to European developments on the ground that other regions would have to be given attention, and that the limited resources of the C.C.I.A. were more appropriately employed when focused on global problems and institutions. The emergence of a more effective European Council of Churches may open new avenues for co-operation.

A distinctive aspect of C.C.I.A. work in its first twenty years was the attention devoted to relationships with the intergovernmental institutions in the United Nations family of agencies. Several of these came to birth near the time of the Cambridge Conference and the first part of the First General Assembly of the United Nations was held in London just six months before the C.C.I.A.'s founding meeting. The new agencies represented possibilities in the making, a future still malleable and opportunity still bright. They were global in character and offered a chance for concentrated and extended contacts at a minimum of effort with a wide variety of national delegations on issues of ecumenical concern.

The United Nations Charter provided for a consultative relationship with non-governmental organizations and each of the specialized agencies formulated its own plan for observation or representation. The infant C.C.I.A. promptly established such a relationship—formally with ECOSOC, but much broader in practice to include other organs, particularly the General Assembly, and subsequently with F.A.O., U.N.E.S.C.O., the I.L.O., and U.N.I.C.E.F. These relationships provided an important arena for C.C.I.A.

action although in no sense was the total programme operated within the structural limits of inter-governmental organs.

In approaching the substantive issues which have commanded C.C.I.A. attention, one cannot ignore the frequently raised question about the effectiveness of such a Christian witness. The commission and its officers adopted an approach which does not lend itself to a clear-cut answer. They recognized that many forces play upon an international problem or issue and that normally only where a coincidence of interests is achieved can progress towards a solution be advanced. The witness animated by Christian faith and experience must be made without the sure prospect of success. In concert with other constructive forces it may prove effective—whether its effectiveness be identifiable or obscured in history's course. The event and the outcome are in God's hand.

The programme of activities as they evolved came to comprise six major concerns. The following brief account of them should be read with the understanding that the ecumenical constituency is ever enlarging. This was true first within the World Council of Churches whose membership during this period expanded to include Churches in communist countries, particularly Russia, as well as in many developing countries. Secondly, there was growing co-operation with the Roman Catholic Church. In this world Christian setting, now more accurately reflective of the world political scene, action to reconcile peoples and nations had to reckon with the recurring danger of compromising justice in the interest of peace and witness in the interest of unity.

Human Rights—Religious Liberty

When the officers of the newly formed Commission looked about them to ascertain a good place to begin, the answer seemed clearly to lie in the field of human rights in general and the exercise of religious freedom in particular. This was obviously an area in which Christians were vitally concerned, not only for themselves but equally for all men, and in which they could be expected to have special competence.

There was ample precedent for such concern. The Oxford Conference of 1937 and the Madras Conference of 1938 had put forward a number of elements of religious and missionary freedom. The United States National Study Conference early in 1945, supported by joint committees on religious liberty in the United States and Britain, had made the inclusion in the United Nations Charter of a provision for a Commission on Human Rights to devise international standards for basic human rights a main plank in its propositions for improvement of the Dumbarton Oaks proposals. (In fact, it fell to my lot to serve as spokesman for forty-two non-governmental organizations at the 1945 San Francisco Conference on United Nations organization in pressing for this inclusion.) The C.C.I.A.'s founding conference had listed among the six objectives for work by the new body the maintenance of contacts with international agencies, particularly with the United Nations, for the "encouragement of respect for, and observance of, human rights and fundamental freedoms, special attention being given to the problem of religious liberty''.

To an extent unprecedented in history, the opportunities seemed to be at hand to move toward a recognition of international responsibility for the protection of human rights, either by agencies such as the Commission on Human Rights or by international instruments such as Declarations, Covenants, and Conventions. Aware that any formulation accepted would stand little chance of modification or improvement for many decades to come, the C.C.I.A. adopted as a first point in its strategy the objective of seeing to it that the international standards which were being set were acceptable in the light of the Christian conception of man and society. As an initial step, C.C.I.A. officers sent inquiries to commissioners and other church leaders in many countries asking their assistance in identifying the essential elements in religious freedom and the potential support for them in the ecumenical constituency. The immediate result of these inquiries was the adoption in 1948 by the World Council of Churches and by the International Missionary Council of a *Declaration of Religious Liberty*, a document which remains a landmark in the field to this day. Thirteen years later the Third Assembly of the World Council of Churches adopted a second basic instrument, a *Statement on Religious Liberty*. While emphasis in both these documents was laid on religious freedom, concern for related rights and in fact for all fundamental freedoms is clearly expressed.

An immediate practical application of the position expressed in the World Council Declaration came the same year, 1948, at the Paris session of the United Nations General Assembly. There the draft United Nations Declaration on Human Rights, prepared by its Human Rights Commission, came up for consideration and adoption. During the preparatory period C.C.I.A. officers had submitted to the United Nations a "Memorandum on Provisions for Religious Liberty in an International Bill of Rights" and made supporting oral interventions. C.C.I.A. staff followed the detailed work of drafting virtually every minute of the deliberations. The article on religious freedom, as finally adopted in face of strong initial opposition, incorporated the essential points for which the C.C.I.A. had been pressing, namely, freedom to change one's religion or belief, and freedom, either alone or in community with others, and in public or in private, to manifest one's religion or belief in worship, teaching, practice, and observance.

As work continued on the two covenants on human rights—the Covenant on Civil and Political Rights and the Covenant on Economic, Social, and Cultural Rights—C.C.I.A. representation headed by Micheli met periodic challenges to recognition of freedom to change one's religion or belief and to oppose efforts to reduce freedom of manifestation to worship. The current effort to achieve an international Convention on the Elimination of All Forms of Religious Intolerance is highly significant because for the first time in history the four manifestations contained in the Universal Declaration are being elaborated in the form of an internationally binding treaty. In this connection, the Director's statement before the meeting of the W.C.C. Executive Committee at Odessa, U.S.S.R., in 1964, recognizing the right of

K

atheists to be atheists but defending the equal right of all to propagate their faith, underscored the concept of human rights without discrimination. Unhappily, there has not as yet developed a common ethos throughout the world sufficient to sustain, on an inclusive basis, legally binding instruments and the machinery to enforce them. The progress being made on a regional scale in the European Convention on Human Rights is significant in pointing the way.

A further element in the C.C.I.A. human rights strategy involved the efforts to promote the advancement of dependent peoples to independence and to help to bring national constitutions, laws, court decisions, and domestic practice into conformity with emerging international standards. These involved visits to new countries in process of preparing constitutions and laws, and the preparation of detailed information for use by their statesmen and church leaders. Emphasis was placed on education with the clear understanding that laws, whether international or national, are effective only when supported by predominant public opinion. Major and minor violations and curtailments of human rights commanded attention. This included the problems faced by Evangelicals in Spain, Italy, and Colombia to which the Chairman gave particular attention, as well as those faced by Buddhists in Tibet and South Vietnam. It also dealt with difficulties in the Southern Sudan, Indonesia, Greece, Mozambique, Nigeria, Yugoslavia, Israel, Angola, Turkey, Nepal, Rumania, Mexico, Ghana, the U.S.S.R., South Africa, South West Africa, India (the Nagas), and other places. These situations called for a variety of responses ranging from quiet inquiry to public statement and protest. Some of the situations have been frustratingly protracted while in other cases good results came quickly.

In the area of racial and ethnic tensions, the C.C.I.A. responsibility dealt particularly with the international aspects of efforts seeking achievement of human rights without discrimination. The fuller story of action by the W.C.C. is dealt with in the chapter on "The Development of Social Thought and Action". At every point the C.C.I.A. made available to United Nations committees dealing with apartheid and other racial problems, the positions formally taken by World Council organs and conferences held under their auspices. It served in a liaison capacity to enable the W.C.C. to co-operate with the United Nations Trust Fund in the distribution of resources in its humanitarian programme for victims of apartheid. It also supported consideration of South African policies and practices by the International Court of Justice and protested against the procedures for the trials of South West African prisoners.

International Peace and Security

By the time of the W.C.C. First Assembly, and the official establishment of the C.C.I.A., it was clear that political and military issues would form a principal preoccupation of the new agency for a long time to come. The test between the power blocs in the Berlin blockade and airlift formed the backdrop for the Amsterdam Assembly. The following year saw the formation of N.A.T.O., the proclamation of the People's Republic of China, and the end of the United States atomic monopoly. In 1950 the atomic arms race began in earnest. It was a sombre infancy for the new venture.

Most of the C.C.I.A. responses to the international crisis of the early Cold War period were made in relation to particular crises, a programmatic approach which characterized the first two decades of its life. But effort also was made to analyse and speak to the broader aspects of the ideological and power conflict. In 1949 C.C.I.A. sponsored a consultation on "The Ideological Conflict and the International Tensions Involved in It". In 1951 the C.C.I.A. Executive Committee issued a widely quoted summary statement entitled "Christians Stand for Peace", partly to distinguish the C.C.I.A. approach from lines taken by secular agencies serving ideological purposes. The statement stressed both peace and justice, declaring that, "we must neither purchase peace at the price of tyranny nor in the name of justice look on war as a way to justice or as a ground of hope".

In 1949 the Netherlands–Indonesia dispute provided a major challenge. In addition to supporting international efforts to help to resolve the dispute, C.C.I.A. officers secured memoranda on the situation which had been prepared by Christian leaders on either side and arranged for their exchange. When these leaders later met at The Hague Round Table, it was evident that the exchange had contributed to the mutual understanding required for peaceful settlement. The action was a good illustration of the kind of useful approach across lines of division which may be possible when there are strong Christian groups on both sides.

In 1950 the outbreak of the Korean war again launched the world into crisis. Acting on the advice of the C.C.I.A. Executive Committee, the World Council of Churches issued a statement which stressed that it was an on-the-spot United Nations Commission which had identified the aggressor. It supported the United Nations for authorizing a "police measure" and emphasized action for a "just settlement by negotiation and conciliation". This statement received both support and criticism, particularly as the fighting became more intense and protracted. When the conflict was enlarged in November, 1950, representations were made at high levels in the United States and United Kingdom on behalf of policies of moderation and restraint.

Three initiatives of a practical character, advanced by the C.C.I.A. Director, emerged from the efforts to grapple with the issues of the Korean war. The first was the idea of the formation of a United Nations corps of international peace observers to be available for sending to areas of tension to discourage aggression by their presence or to identify the aggressor if aggression occurs. The basic idea was unanimously supported in the establishment of the Peace Observation Commission by the 1950 United Nations General Assembly, and, while the machinery has been used only once (in the Balkan pressures on Greece), it remains a tool of peace available to the United Nations and stands as a precursor of diversified peace-keeping efforts.

The second initiative was a "Plan for Deferred Action on Prisoners of War in Korea". Designed to facilitate a truce without forcible detention or repatriation of prisoners, it was an important contribution to the overcoming of a thorny obstacle in the armistice negotiations.

The third initiative came when misunderstandings between the R.O.K. (South Korea) Government and the United Nations High Command threatened prospects for a truce. Then the C.C.I.A. made its good offices available when the Director flew to Pusan and Seoul for consultations with church leaders and to serve as an intermediary between contending parties within the United Nations forces. This venture was formally recognized by the United States Government, representing the United Nations High Command as "a factor in creating an atmosphere conducive to peace".

The protracted crisis over a divided Germany was the subject of repeated examinations in meetings of the C.C.I.A. Executive and of the Committee on Christian Responsibility for European Co-operation. A more active phase began in 1958 with the tightening of restrictions on religious freedom in East Germany. In 1961 the worsening of the situation by the erection of the Berlin wall prompted the first of a continuing series of C.C.I.A. visits with churchmen and government officials in West and East Berlin. These visits sought both to express concern with the human aspects of the situation, such as the separation of families, and to foster better understanding between church leaders in West and East Germany as a means of contributing indirectly to progress towards a political solution.

In most instances the consultative process between the W.C.C. and C.C.I.A. officers in political crises worked well, enabling responses to be made promptly at both church and political levels. The alert and informed interest of Dr W. A. Visser 't Hooft, General Secretary, and the late Dr Franklin Clark Fry, Chairman of the Central Committee of the World Council of Churches, did much to make this co-operation effective. The sudden "eyeball to eyeball" confrontation between the U.S.A. and the U.S.S.R. over military bases in Cuba in 1962 was initially in this regard an exception due to a somewhat different reading of the portents. As a consequence the statement issued by the officers of the World Council was at variance with the position prepared by the C.C.I.A. for submission to the United Nations Security Council, although the two were eventually reconciled. This crisis of the super-powers, in which the United Nations could play only a limited though useful role, was also a reminder of the need to keep in realistic perspective the United Nations and the realities of the power situation.

The requirements of brevity permit only reference by title to some of the critical situations in which C.C.I.A. officers attempted to make timely and relevant representations. They included: the 1954 Indo-China situation, the conflict and tensions in the Formosa Straits in 1955 and again in 1958, Suez and Hungary in 1956, the 1958 crisis in Lebanon, the tragic events in Tibet the same year, the critical situation in the Congo beginning in 1960, U.S.A.-U.S.S.R. involvement in Cuba, the conflict in Laos as of 1961, the continuing conflict in Algeria, the problems of Angola and Mozambique, and the tensions between the United States and Panama in 1964. Also included were the tensions and conflict in Cyprus that flared in 1964, the "confrontation" of Malaysia by Indonesia, the mounting conflict in Vietnam and various subsequent measures of escalation, United States intervention in the Dominican Republic in 1965, and the fighting between Pakistan and India in 1965 against the background of the long-standing dispute over Kashmir.

In a number of these situations the lack of a strong constituency related to the W.C.C. on one or both sides was a limiting factor both in regard to the securing of balanced information and the taking of effective action. Many problems have not yielded to solution and men have been forced to live with them. World Council and C.C.I.A. concern about Vietnam, expressed at the time of the Geneva Conference in 1954, deepened with the escalation of the conflict after 1962. The W.C.C. Central and Executive Committees and the C.C.I.A. Executive Committee found in the actions of the National Council of Churches in the U.S.A. and of the East Asia Christian Conference strong support for efforts to move the parties in conflict from the battlefield to the conference table. When the official consultations opened at Paris in May 1968, C.C.I.A. officers personally delivered to the chief delegates of the United States and the People's Republic of North Vietnam letters of encouragement to seek a negotiated settlement.

The situation in Nigeria, where Biafra had declared its independence, involved related problems of material help, pastoral care, and political accommodation. While church and mission leaders of D.I.C.A.R.W.S. and A.A.C.C. were active in many ways, C.C.I.A. efforts were directed under the leadership of Alan Booth, whose church and political contacts and attention to preliminary talks in London were followed by further negotiations at Kampala. The approach to the Nigerian conflict was notable for being the first occasion in which the Roman Catholic Church and the World Council issued a joint statement calling for a peaceful settlement.

The representations, with variations adapted to the circumstances, have stressed fundamental themes: the avoidance of unilateral intervention; the avoidance or cessation of violence and recourse to procedures of negotiation and/or mediation; policies of moderation and restraint; the value of a United Nations presence in some form for keeping the peace and United Nations action on behalf of peaceful settlement.

Disarmament

Hand in hand with efforts to bring a moderating influence on specific conflicts and disputes went a very considerable amount of work on the problems of disarmament. No international body, apart from the United Nations General Assembly, received as much C.C.I.A. attention as the committees and conferences on disarmament meeting in Geneva. Following a suggestion made at New Delhi in 1961, two special consultations brought together Christian leaders from communist and non-communist countries to confer with delegates to the disarmament conference from the U.K., U.S.S.R., and the U.S.A., as well as with delegates from several of the non-aligned countries. These discussions contributed to an understanding among Christians from both sides and provided an incentive to government representatives.

It is not possible here to summarize adequately the positions taken in regard to disarmament. An early statement (1949) called for international control of the hydrogen bomb. In succeeding years, emphasis was placed on the political and moral factors affecting a disarmament agreement. The Section on International Affairs at the W.C.C.'s Second Assembly in 1954 stressed the obligation of nations to refrain from the threat or use of weapons of mass destruction against civilians in open cities and underlined the positive uses of atomic power. One of the major C.C.I.A. statements in this field was adopted by its Executive Committee at its 1955 meeting in Davos and subsequently by the Central Committee. It was a pioneer analysis of the relationship between measures to advance peaceful change and settlement and the furtherance of a significant disarmament agreement. *Christians and the Prevention of War in an Atomic Age*, a study completed in 1958, emphasized the restraints which governments must accept and essential positive steps in avoiding the holocaust of nuclear destruction.

Another key statement was adopted by the 1957 C.C.I.A. Executive Committee. This set forth a programme on disarmament, which featured a ban on atomic tests as the first step but related it to a longer-range strategy. Three related principles were emphasized:

1. The main concern must always be the prevention of war itself, for the evil of war is an offence to the spiritual nature of man.

2. The objectives of a strategy to combat the menace of atomic war are interrelated and interdependent, such as ceasing tests, halting production, reducing existing armaments with provision for warning against surprise attacks, the peaceful uses of atomic energy, peaceful settlement, and peaceful change.

3. If persistent efforts bring no sufficient agreements on any of the interrelated objectives, partial agreements should be seriously explored and, if need be, reasonable risks should be taken to advance the objectives which must continue to stand as interdependent.

A decade later this statement continued to provide a framework for various action on the disarmament question. A series of memoranda informed church leaders about scientific data regarding the health hazards of atomic radiation, emphasizing that many peoples, not party to atomic tests, would have to bear the consequences. Convinced that rivalries on earth were too dangerous to project into outer space, C.C.I.A. vigorously supported moves towards its international control. The W.C.C. New Delhi Assembly's Appeal supporting a theme familiar in C.C.I.A. representations, called upon nations to run reasonable risks for peace, in order to break the vicious circle of suspicion. The resumption of tests by the U.S.S.R. in 1961 was regretted, as was the undertaking of tests by France. The W.C.C. and the C.C.I.A. continued to press for the cessation of testing and the former's Executive Committee in a statement at Buenos Aires in 1960 virtually forecast the details of the 1963 Moscow Treaty to ban tests in outer space, in the atmosphere, and under water. The Moscow–Washington agreement on a "hotline" was welcomed. The importance of agreements to halt the proliferation of nuclear arsenals was repeatedly emphasized.

Disarmament is obviously an area where the criterion of Christian witness is patient obedience rather than worldly success. A good excuse can be made for the time and effort devoted to the Geneva negotiations in the hope that a slight nudge in the right direction at the right moment might tip the balance in favour of a step forward.

Refugees and Migrants

The millions of human beings uprooted by the Second World War and its consequences—the refugees and expellees, the stateless and the homeless— challenged the World Council to supplement the work of intergovernmental agencies and to provide a united Christian witness in service to the suffering. The main response was through the service programmes now correlated by the Division of Inter-Church Aid, Refugee, and World Service, but C.C.I.A. was involved at a fairly early stage in issues at intergovernmental levels. While representations to strengthen and extend the international agencies, to broaden their mandate, and to secure more adequate financial support played a considerable part in this work, an even larger role was played by the day-to-day consultations seeking to facilitate co-operation between agencies of the World Council and the United Nations at the field level.

It quickly became clear that the refugee problem was not confined to Europe and that a broad definition of the term was required to cover the human needs involved. In 1949, in response to a Central Committee request to continue its work in this field, C.C.I.A. officers urged the United Nations General Assembly to consider the need for an inclusive definition of the refugee problem and the need for more adequate financial support. They also expressed concern for the Palestine refugee problem. To the Central Committee they reported the need for a "comprehensive plan of action" by the international community both for the stateless refugees and for those who were homeless but not stateless.

The establishment of the Office of the United Nations High Commissioner for Refugees in Geneva at the beginning of 1951 marked a new phase of this consultative work. C.C.I.A. officers supported the formation of a voluntary International Assistance Fund, which in turn made it possible for agencies like the W.C.C. and Inter-Church Aid Division and Lutheran World Relief to extend their humanitarian services. Effective relations with the High Commissioner for Refugees were maintained through three administrations and continue in the fourth as well as with I.C.E.M. and the Council of Europe's Sub-Committee on Refugees.

Improvement in the European situation was accompanied by new refugee problems, in the Near East, and later in Asia and Africa. In 1949 and 1961 C.C.I.A. issued statements of concern for the plight of the Palestinian refugees. C.C.I.A. officers worked with the parent bodies in convening the first Beirut Conference on Palestine Refugees in 1957, This conference asked the C.C.I.A. to seek adequate provision for relief until a permanent solution could be found; stressed, while recognizing the justice of repatriation, the need of funds for resettlement; emphasized the necessity of unfreezing assets and a speedy decision on compensation; and spoke of the need for international guarantees of frontiers and for a reorganization of United Nations agencies in Palestine. A second Beirut Conference in 1956 renewed and reinforced this mandate.

In 1954, after tens of thousands of new homeless from the Korean war had swollen the world's refugee population to an estimated forty million persons, the Commission called for the reunion in freedom of all arbitrarily divided nations, and the repatriation of refugees desiring it. In connection with World Refugee Year (1959–60) Rees, who from the start headed C.C.I.A. work in this field, was elected Chairman of the Executive Committee of the International Committee for the year. He also prepared the special report, *We Strangers and Afraid*, published that year. In more recent years, attention was given to other refugee needs, as in Hong Kong and Rwanda Burundi. The survey on the problems of the 650,000 African refugees, made in 1965 by Sir Hugh Foot (now Lord Caradon) and the late Professor Z. K. Matthews (Ambassador of Botswana to the United Nations and the U.S.A.) focused the attention of the United Nations delegates upon the serious needs to be met there. Support was also given for the extension and broadening of the mandate of the High Commissioner for Refugees, and close contact was maintained in regard to relief projects.

The growth of migration within Europe and outside led to increased attention to this separate but related area. In 1957 a joint study on "The Role of the Churches in Migration" by the C.C.I.A. and the Division of Inter-Church Aid prepared the way for the Conference on Migration held at Leysin, Switzerland in 1961. This was followed by the establishment of the Secretariat on Migration within D.I.C.A.R.W.S.

The work in the field of human rights, like the work on refugee and related problems, was an effort to champion the dignity and worth of the human person. It asserted that Christians have an international interest and obligation, as well as an ecumenical duty in helping to care for human beings uprooted by tyranny, war, or natural calamity. While refugee problems on the whole grew more rapidly than their solution during the two decades, attention in meeting elemental human needs was increasingly centred on anticipatory action as distinct from emergency relief. Prospective food shortages in poor countries stimulated international efforts to secure more adequate food supplies and better nutrition, through F.A.O. and the Freedom from Hunger Campaign.

The Advancement of Dependent Peoples

The most quoted of the C.C.I.A. aims was that which directed it to assist in "acceptance by all nations of the obligation to promote to the utmost the well-being of dependent peoples including their advance toward self-government and the development of their political institutions". One reason this point was cited so frequently was that the constituency of the W.C.C. like that of the United Nations, was divided as to the proper tempo and scope of the decolonization process. Some churchmen, particularly those from Europe, stressed the careful preparation of dependent peoples for self-government or independence. Others, particularly those from the "Younger Churches", chafed with growing impatience against the slow pace of decolonization. However, despite the difference as to application, there was support for the broad Charter principles underlying the Trusteeship Council and the Declaration on Non-Self-Governing Territories.

The result was a rather cautious, quite possibly an over-cautious approach to most of the colonial issues. C.C.I.A. officers informed interested church leaders from time to time of possible contacts with visiting missions of the Trusteeship Council, and called attention to reports on economic, social, and educational conditions in non-self-governing territories. They alerted commissions in countries administering territories to concern expressed in some of the United Nations debates. At one point (1955) certain Central American delegations were persuaded to withdraw a proposal on reports by non-governmental organizations that might have jeopardized the essentially non-political work of the Churches and missions. The welcome increase in progress towards emancipation was tempered by doubts whether there was in a number of cases sufficient preparations to keep them viable. The 1960 United Nations Declaration on Colonialism, which expresses the central convictions of the burgeoning anti-colonial bloc, played an important role in advancing moves towards independence. The W.C.C. and C.C.I.A. officers symbolized their support of this development by formal participation in a number of independence celebrations.

The tendency to make an absolute of self-determination apart from the other considerations which must figure in the responsible society complicated the situation. A frustrating problem, for the C.C.I.A. as well as for the world at large, was to establish a sound view of self-determination. The report of Section IV of the W.C.C.'s Second Assembly had stated that the "legitimate right of the self-determination of peoples must be recognized". But it did not give a clue as to the relationship of this right to other rights, nor to its application to national majorities and national minorities in multi-national societies. A sizeable body of data and considerations, showing the various aspects and complexities of the issues, was brought together, under the title "Notes on Self-Determination", for discussion at the 1956 C.C.I.A. Executive Committee. The discussion tended to recognize that the principle became a concrete right only when certain conditions were present, but it did not go very far in pinning down the conditions.

On certain specific issues the record is clearer. The C.C.I.A. Executive Committee in 1949 supported the reference of the legal status of South West Africa to the International Court. At its 1954 meeting in Chicago, the Commission agreed on "the right and fitness of the people of Cyprus to determine for themselves their future status". The Chairman's and Director's subsequent visit to Cyprus and to the countries most involved, and the interventions to secure on the one hand formal acknowledgment of the right of self-determination, and on the other acceptance of a certain transitional period of self-government, constituted an important chapter in the effort to distinguish between the principle and the right of self-determination. Later actions and interventions supported and encouraged by various W.C.C. bodies were concerned with Angola, Mozambique, Southern Rhodesia, and South West Africa.

In historical perspective, the transition of formerly dependent peoples to independence appears to have been both rapid and relatively peaceful. Nearly one-third of mankind live in countries which have achieved sovereignty within the last twenty years; but the process has raised a host of new problems in regard to economic and social, as well as to political, developments. The 1960 C.C.I.A. Executive Committee recognized that "newly liberated man has many needs, material and spiritual". The result was a correspondingly greater emphasis in C.C.I.A. work beginning in the early 1950s on the sector called "economic and social development".

Economic and Social Development

The undertaking by the United Nations of an expanded programme of technical assistance, and similar enterprises of a bilateral character, convinced the officers that specialized attention should be given to this area. While some effort was made to keep abreast of the more significant trends and events in bilateral and regional programmes, most of the detailed attention was concentrated on the United Nations programmes and those of certain specialized agencies: F.A.O., U.N.E.S.C.O., I.L.O., and U.N.I.C.E.F. As the various interests of the W.C.C. in this field grew, especially those of D.I.C.A.R.W.S., with its projects in areas of acute human need and its Specialized Assistance for Social Projects (S.A.S.P.), the requirements upon C.C.I.A. to facilitate useful contacts were increased.

In addition to the particular issues handled by the officers in their representational work, the Commission and its Executives approved a series of guide-lines on broader policy issues, which sought to make ecumenical concerns relevant without being too specific on the technical aspect which lay outside their competence. In general, these guide-lines stayed ahead of events, possibly though by no means necessarily having some modest influence on them.

The first of these policy guide-lines was a "Statement on Technical Assistant Programmes" approved by the 1951 C.C.I.A. Executive Committee. It put forward seven requirements for effective international development assistance, and some observations on the potential contributions of Christians and Christian agencies. Starting in 1952, the statements approved by the Executive Committee began to develop a major theme of C.C.I.A. representation in this area. They stressed the need for an overall strategy of development, with the United Nations playing a leading role in a longer-range evaluation of programmes, both multilateral and bilateral; consideration of the different sectors of development in their interrelationships; identification of unmet needs and priorities; and provision for more rational assurance for winning this basic war against the ancient enemies of mankind. Elaborated in various ways, this theme was a central testimony in this field.

A statement approved in 1952 provided guide-lines for the relationship to the Food and Agricultural Organization. It stressed requirements for the right use and conservation of both human and natural resources, and offered guidance in regard to such projects as the Freedom from Hunger Campaign and the World Food Programme. The next year the Executive Committee approved certain directions to help to improve the United Nations assistance programme, such as the development of country programming, the resident representatives system, and sustained financial support for a growing United Nations programme.

By 1956 there was obvious need for more ecumenical attention to the population problem and the related question of family planning. It was becoming evident that the impact of successful public health programmes on death rates was not being matched by comparable educational and medical effect on birth rates. C.C.I.A. advanced the position that Christian neglect of the population problem was a contributory factor to neglect at the international level, with possibly fateful consequencies for the development struggle. With the support of his colleagues Richard Fagley began to give specialized attention to the population–parenthood complex of issues and to helping to alert church leaders to the dangers. This led to a number of articles, speeches, and background memoranda, an ecumenical study group on population and responsible parenthood convened at Mansfield College in 1959, a book by Fagley on *The Population Explosion and Christian Responsibility*, a preliminary debate at the 1960 Central Committee, conversations with Roman Catholic scholars, an E.A.C.C. consultation on the Asian Churches and Responsible Parenthood at Bangkok in 1964, and a study on the doctrines and attitudes of major religions for the Second World Population Conference at Belgrade in 1965. During this period a number of communions and councils took a more forthright position on the question of responsible parenthood, a development which had a partial counterpart at the Vatican Council in 1965. The specialized attention given to this set of issues had not been planned or foreseen; but the procedures of C.C.I.A. proved flexible enough to take advantage of the opportunities presented even though at some cost to other concerns, and its work was widely recognized as having been a major factor in the dramatic "break-through" which focused world attention on the problem.

In a 1956 statement approved by the C.C.I.A. Executive Committee, another major theme made its appearance—the concern for strengthening the basis for greater participation by developing countries in international trade as a long-term mainstay for securing the goods and services needed to modernize their economies. A summary entitled "Elements of a Strategy of Development" was given general approval by the Commission at its Bangalore meeting in 1961. Three of its eleven points dealt with the need for positive measures to expand the exports of developing countries, for action to lessen or offset harmful price fluctuations in primary commodities, and for greater trade within the underdeveloped world to promote employment, to meet consumer needs, and to make more effective use of foreign exchange reserves. These points were further developed in a statement on "Trade for Development" which was approved by the 1965 C.C.I.A. Executive Committee to provide guidance for contacts with the new United Nations trade agency—United Nations Conference on Trade and Development (U.N.C.T.A.D.).

Earlier, at Nyborg, Denmark in 1958, officers of C.C.I.A. and the Department on Church and Society had collaborated in advising the Central Committee on a summary statement of development needs. This statement held that the picture would be brighter if countries would contribute at least one per cent of national income to international development. The idea was subsequently incorporated in a unanimous resolution by the United Nations General Assembly, and later by U.N.C.T.A.D. The 1961 Bangalore C.C.I.A. statement, however, had warned that the minimum "one per cent" target might soon become too small, for the costs of a successful struggle would rise with delay in mounting a more adequate international effort.

While C.C.I.A. work in this field remained a rather modest undertaking, concentrated at intergovernmental level in the hope of stimulating a more dynamic and coherent approach to the challenge, there was a gratifying growth of ecumenical concern in the great struggle against world poverty. It received ever-increasing attention in the work of Inter-Church Aid. It was a major topic in the W.C.C. Conference on Church and Society. Possibilities of co-operation with a proposed Vatican agency on world justice and development beckoned. There was also new activity at the national level. The British Council of Churches issued a report on "World Poverty and British Responsibility". Similarly the United States National Council of Churches pressed for a recognition of need and action. Thus voices grew in support of greater efforts than the halfway and half-hearted measures which had characterized the struggle in the past. Stimulated by the C.C.I.A., the W.C.C. Executive and the Central Committees in 1967 called for realistic action to face the growing food gap. But the scope of the challenge, and the threat of catastrophe, continued to mount in Asia, Africa, and Latin America.

The transcendent importance of the war against world poverty fully occupied the very limited resources of C.C.I.A. in the economic field. The idea of enlisting an advisory group of lay experts on problems of international economic co-operation was discussed more than once, but limited resources did not permit action. Consequently, large areas of this concern were touched upon only lightly and in quite general or superficial terms, as for example, the problems of economic collaboration within the western world, the Common Market, and others), and the possibilities of increasing mutual interest and confidence in a divided world through increased trade between the free market economies and the centrally planned economies.

International Law and Institutions

While work on specific issues before the United Nations constituted the largest segment of C.C.I.A. activity during the first two decades, comparatively little attention could be devoted to the longer-range or theoretical aspects of international organizations and their foundations. Even in regard to the question of the development and codification of international law, the officers had to follow evolutions at second hand through commissioners involved in this area.

Attention, however, was devoted to one basic long-range issue. This was the question of an international ethos, needed to undergird international law· and institutions. C.C.I.A. was a co-sponsor of a Conference on the Foundations of International Law in 1950, which attempted to clarify some of the duties and stressed the fact that there was hardly any common ethos binding the large power blocs together. Following the Evanston Assembly, where the International Affairs Section emphasized the need for greater attention to the question of common moral foundations, the C.C.I.A. Executive Committee authorized a study on a Christian Approach to an International Ethos. An able but predominantly European group was enlisted, and some stimulating papers were contributed. The study, however, did not develop beyond the initial phase. The plan was probably over-ambitious with insufficiently clear objectives, and adequate staff and budgetary resources were lacking. The challenge remains to dig more deeply into this basic subject.

Evaluation of the United Nations as a world institution, in addition to what had been said at the Amsterdam, Evanston, and New Delhi Assemblies was attempted on two occasions. The first was the statement *Christians Look at the United Nations*, approved by the 1953 C.C.I.A. Executive Committee. The second was a new statement approved in 1965. Both attempted, in summary fashion, to take stock of the United Nations' values and weaknesses, and emphasized the importance of the practical development of the potentials in the world organization. On the whole, C.C.I.A. has tended to be critical of world government schemes as unrealistic, finding no viable alternative to improvement and reinforcement of the existing body, the United Nations.

Conclusion

Reflecting on the developments over some twenty years one may say that the C.C.I.A. programme was marked by five characteristics:

1. Since international issues are highly complex, the process of relating Christian truth to them requires technical skill and extensive study as well as reliable information. Oversimplification is dangerous. Shibboleths, slogans, and vague peace generalizations often do more harm than good. The agency of the Churches which is assigned responsibility in the field of international affairs should be composed of persons who are not only motivated by Christian faith but who also have the competence to ensure that any proposal advanced will command the respectful consideration of government and intergovernmental officials.

2. Periodic conferences are valuable in shaping policy and in arousing public sentiment; but an effective contribution to peace requires a programme which can function virtually every day of the year. Issues of war and peace do not readily accommodate themselves to the schedule of church conferences and councils.

3. Resolutions or pronouncements indicate the direction which should be followed and may take on general educational value. If they are to become politically influential, they must be explained and registered at the time and place of international political decision. Moreover, they must be kept relevant to the level of immediate negotiation and thus will require adjustment in face of the particular obstacles encountered at any given moment. It is not enough, for example, to say that "nuclear testing should cease". Many a government official would reply, "I agree, but how can we do it?" It is necessary for the representatives of the Churches to get down into the arena where the struggle for peace in any particular form is being waged and to help to break an impasse there or to advance the cause on that front until a new battle line for peace is drawn.

4. While formal responsibility for representation in international affairs perforce rests upon a limited number of technically trained officials, the work of an organization for peace must rely upon the prayers and support of an informed constituency. While some progress in this respect has been made over the last fifteen years, much remains to be done to build a system which can move swiftly as demanded by international events, but will also in fact constitute a witness evangelical in its motivation and democratic in its procedure.

5. The fifth characteristic is barely discernible in formal fashion and is only beginning to emerge—especially from the standpoint of the World Council of Churches and the Roman Catholic Church. The ninth aim in the C.C.I.A. Charter reads: "To concert from time to time with other organizations holding similar objectives in the advancement of particular ends". The adoption and promulgation of the decree *De oecumenismo* by the Roman Catholic Church opened the way for fuller co-operation. The Central Committee of the World Council of Churches formally proposed at Enugu, Nigeria, in January 1965, after prior consultation with the Vatican, that a joint working group be established. It listed among subjects to be considered "practical consideration in the fields of philanthropy, social and international affairs". Cardinal Bea, during his visit to World Council headquarters in February, 1965, formally announced the Vatican's acquiescence in this proposal. A joint working party was established. The World Council of Churches and the Pontifical Commission on Justice and Peace are now formally consulting and acting together. The way is thus being opened to the co-operation of two great Christian communities and, perhaps eventually, to co-operation with all men of good will, whether they profess another faith or a faith other than Christian.

The affirmation contained in the Evanston report on "Christians in the Struggle for World Community" can serve as a continued stimulus to effort and a source of strength in action:

> This troubled world, disfigured and distorted as it is, is God's world. He rules and overrules its tangled history. In praying "Thy will be done on earth as it is

in heaven" we commit ourselves to seek earthly justice, freedom and peace for all men. Here as everywhere Christ is our hope. Our confidence lies not in our own reason or strength, but in the power that comes from God. Impelled by this faith, all our actions will be but humble, grateful, and obedient acknowledgment that He has redeemed the world. The fruit of our efforts rests in His hands. We can therefore live and work as those who know that God reigns, undaunted by all the arrogant pretensions of evil, ready to face situations that seem hopeless and yet to act in them as men whose hope is indestructible.

11

The Orthodox Churches
in the Ecumenical Movement
1948-1968

VASIL T. ISTAVRIDIS

Introduction

Eastern Europe and the Middle East are the geographical areas where Christian Churches known as Orthodox, Greek Orthodox, Eastern Orthodox, or Orthodox Catholic are found. Sometimes they are known by nationality, such as Russian Orthodox. Fifteen of these Churches are described as "autocephalous", meaning self-governing, Churches. Ranking first in honour are the ancient Patriarchates: Constantinople, Alexandria, Antioch, and Jerusalem in that order. The members adhering directly to these patriarchates total fewer than three million. The Russian Orthodox Church has an estimated 50 million members; the Rumanian, 14 million; the Serbian, 8 million; the Greek, 7.5 million; the Bulgarian, 6 million; the Georgian, 1.2 million; the Cyprian, 400,000; the Czecholsovakian, 350,000; the Polish, 350,000; the Albanian, 200,000. Finally, there is the autonomous church or monastery on Mount Sinai, having fewer than 100 members. Churches in Finland, China, Japan, and Macedonia, having a few thousand members each, are termed "autonomous" but not "autocephalous". Three autonomous church administrations are found among the Russians outside Russia. Orthodoxy maintains ecclesiastical provinces in Europe, North and South America, and Australia. These are related to one of the autocephalous Churches or to a Russian jurisdiction in emigration. The above Churches, which constitute what is generally known as Orthodoxy, probably have between eighty and 100 million members.

In addition, Churches which refer to themselves as Oriental Orthodox Churches have histories which go back to the Nestorian and Monophysite controversies over the one or two natures of Christ of the fourth and fifth centuries. The "ancient non-Greek" Orthodox are the Coptic and Ethiopic, the Syrian or Jacobite, the Nestorian, the Armenian Churches of Cilicia and Russia, the Syrian Orthodox of India, and the Maronite of Lebanon. These Churches, which have a total of around 20 million members, are not in communion with the Eastern Orthodox but are generally held to belong to the family of Eastern Churches. They are also referred to as Ancient Oriental, Lesser Eastern, and Pre- or Ante-Chalcedonian Churches. Among the latter the Ethiopian is the only established or state Church.

Developments within the Orthodox Churches between 1948 and 1968 were greatly affected by the Second World War. Dr N. Zernov enumerates the effects of the struggle under five heads, each of which had important consequences which still continue:

1. The re-emergence of the Orthodox Church in Russia and its appearance as an organized and articulate body on the scene of ecumenical relations.

2. The setting up of Communist rule in Rumania, Bulgaria, Yugoslavia, Albania, Poland, and Czechoslovakia.

3. The disappearance of the autonomous Churches of Latvia, Lithuania, and Estonia.

4. The healing in 1945 of the schism between the Bulgarians and the Church of Constantinople which dated from 1872.

5. The coming to the West of a large new contingent of refugees from eastern and central Europe, among whom were many Eastern Christians.

Inter-Church and Inter-Christian Relations

Orthodoxy is not an outsider to the ecumenical movement. In the ecumenical age in which we live, the Eastern Churches, like those in the West, participate in many different forms of relations with other Churches. Some of them are new and others go back to before the present century. Ecclesiastical and theological conversations between Orthodox and Anglicans and between Orthodox and Old Catholics helped the Orthodox to formulate a method of holding conversations with other Churches. They also revealed to the Orthodox their own inner unity and encouraged them to take it more seriously.

The Orthodox Church claims to be the one, holy, Catholic, and Apostolic Church of the Nicene Creed, going back through an unbroken continuity to the years of Jesus Christ and the Apostles. Well known is the ecclesiological principle of Orthodoxy, according to which no communion in the sacraments can be achieved before a full dogmatic union with the other Churches. These positions have not made ecumenical relations impossible; but the understanding between the two cultural and ecclesiastical worlds of East and West has been difficult. In addition, the principle of autocephalicity is often not easy for Western Christians to grasp. It means the independence of each patriarchate or autocephalous Church. This independence, added to the obstacles raised by the conditions under which these Churches live, does not help to promote their sincere wishes for *rapprochement* with other Churches. Nevertheless, some progress has been made towards understanding among the Orthodox Churches themselves and between them and the wider Christian world.

Inter-Orthodox Relations

Eastern Orthodox. The Orthodox Church does not have an external centre of authority, like the office of Pope within the Roman Catholic Church. The Ecumenical Patriarch (Constantinople) is accepted by all Orthodox Churches as *primus inter pares* which gives him the right of initiative in calling pan-Orthodox conferences and in some matters affecting relations with other Churches. In 1948 Athenagoras, the Greek Orthodox Archbishop of America, became the Ecumenical Patriarch. He has been pursuing a policy of closer co-operation within and without Orthodoxy ever since. A special concern of the Ecumenical Patriarch is the problem of the Orthodox Diaspora, which is being gradually solved through the co-operation of ecclesiastical leaders and through the Standing Conference of Canonical Orthodox Bishops in America, founded in 1960, and a similar grouping in France, founded in 1967.

In the year when the present Ecumenical Patriarch was enthroned, when there was great tension between the communist and the capitalist worlds, a celebration was staged in Moscow of the five hundredth anniversary of the autocephalicity of the Orthodox Church of Russia. Officials of the Orthodox Churches which were behind the Iron Curtain were present. The Conference did not claim the authority of a Church Council. Its resolutions criticized the Vatican, the Anglican Church, and the ecumenical movement as represented by the World Council of Churches. The arguments which were used seemed to be influenced by the Russian foreign policy of the Stalin era. It condemned the Roman Catholic and the Anglican Churches, denounced the World Council as "an instrument of American imperialism", and denied any intention to co-operate with these bodies. Nevertheless a great change was imminent.

The difference which can be made by dedicated leadership and the passage of time is indicated by the difference between these actions of 1948 and what happened at the First Pan-Orthodox Conference, called by Patriarch Athenagoras to meet in Rhodes in 1961. The greatest achievement of this conference was the presence in Rhodes of representatives from all Orthodox Churches except the Church of Albania. Other pan-Orthodox conferences followed in Rhodes in 1963 and 1964. The agenda for a future pan-Orthodox pro-Synod was agreed upon and decisions were taken on dialogue with the Churches of Rome, the Anglicans, and the Old Catholics. The attitude towards the ecumenical movement was affirmative and hopeful.

Several festivals or celebrations had brought Orthodox leaders together in the interval. An extended series of visits between Orthodox leaders had helped the ecumenical spirit to grow. An international organization of Orthodox youth movements called Syndesmos, founded in Paris in 1953, had repeatedly convened general assemblies. The constitution of Syndesmos states that its aim is to establish living contact between youth movements and groups, to encourage co-operation, to develop Orthodox unity and mutual aid, and "to assist Orthodox youth in its relations with the non-Orthodox".

Oriental Orthodox Churches   "In the summer of 1948 at Amsterdam at the first Assembly of the World Council of Churches, perhaps for the first time in about a thousand years, a few members of the scattered 'Monophysite' denominations got together", wrote Fr K. M. Simon of the Syrian Orthodox Church in 1951. This took place at a dinner given by his Grace Abuna Theophilos of the Ethiopian Orthodox Church.

> In this meeting, to our great surprise, we discovered that although we were in communion with each other and held the same doctrine, we knew almost next to nothing about each other or even about our common heritage. In our discussions we realized that, while others have progressed in every field, we have been mostly static. This we were convinced was chiefly due to our lack of unity and co-ordination.

Fr Simon then visited Churches of his tradition in Syria, Egypt, and Ethiopia and learned that there was a general willingness to co-operate. So he purposed the holding of a World Conference of the Oriental Orthodox Churches.

The World Conference was held in January 1965 in Addis Ababa upon the invitation of the Emperor Haile Selassie I. Attending were the heads of the Coptic Orthodox, the Syrian Orthodox of Antioch, the Armenian Orthodox of Cilicia, the Syrian Orthodox of India, and the Ethiopian Orthodox Churches. Catholicos Vazken of the Armenian Orthodox Church of Etchmiadzin was present, but did not take part officially. The Conference set up a standing committee of the Oriental Orthodox Churches which met in Addis Ababa later in 1965, in Cairo in 1966, and in Antelias, Lebanon in 1967. It also organized co-operation at the theological education level, with the result that an Armenian theologian and three theologians from the Syrian Orthodox Church of India were appointed to the faculty of the Theological College of the Holy Trinity in Addis Ababa. The Churches represented in the Conference agreed to co-operate in evangelism and in determining their relations with other Churches. The meeting ended with a statement on peace and justice in the world and with a resolution declaring Emperor Haile Selassie as the "Defender of the Faith" because of his work for the unity of these Churches.

In the twenty years following Amsterdam (1948) the growth of ecumenical concern had wrought important changes within the Oriental Orthodox Churches. A division which had sundered the Syrian Orthodox Church in India in 1910 was healed in 1958. The Church in Ethiopia acquired patriarchal status in 1959 from the mother Church in Egypt. The tension between the two Armenian catholicossates—Etchmiadzin in Armenia, U.S.S.R. and Cilicia in Antelias, Lebanon—abated. Primacy of honour has always been recognized by Cilicia as belonging to Etchmiadzin. Vasken I, the Catholicos of Etchmiadzin, visited the World Council of Churches in 1967. He had also visited the Middle East in 1956 and Jerusalem and India in 1963. Emperor Haile Selassie and dignitaries of the Coptic and Ethiopian Churches visited the Syrian Orthodox Church in India at the time of the Third World Assembly of Churches in India in 1961.

Eastern Orthodox Oriental–Orthodox Relations The First Pan-Orthodox Conference, held in Rhodes in 1961, discussed the relations between the two branches of Orthodoxy. It urged the establishment of brotherly attitudes in order to re-establish the union between them. It encouraged visits of professors, students, and church leaders, the study of the history, faith, worship, and organization of Churches on both sides, and collaboration in meetings of an ecumenical character. This work was already under way. Delegates from the different Oriental Orthodox Churches participated in the one thousand nine hundredth anniversary of the coming of St Paul to Greece in 1951 and in the celebrations marking the milennium of Mount Athos in 1963. In 1953 and 1954 theological discussions were held between representatives of the Russian Orthodox Church and the Syrian Orthodox Church of India.

The World Council of Churches helped the representatives of the Eastern Orthodox and the Oriental Orthodox Churches to come together. Because of W.C.C. meetings a small unofficial group from both sides living in Geneva brought together a meeting at Aarhus, Denmark, 11–15 August 1964. After several papers and many conversations, the Conference adjourned with a joint statement which said: "We recognize in each other the one Orthodox faith of the Church. Fifteen centuries of alienation have not led us astray from the faith of our fathers . . . We see the need to move forward together." A similar meeting was held in connection with the Faith and Order meeting held in Bristol, England 25–9 July 1967. So there is growing a belief that the theological differences between these Churches today do not appear to be of such a nature that they cannot be overcome by patient study and the growth of mutual understanding.

The Ecumenical Patriarchate proposed to the Eastern Orthodox Churches in 1965 the establishment of an Inter-Orthodox, Inter-Oriental Orthodox Theological Commission to prepare for an eventual dogmatic union. Earlier the Ecumenical Patriarch had visited the patriarchs of the Syrian Orthodox and the Coptic Orthodox. Other visitors among Orthodox prelates included Iakovos of Melita, now Archbishop of America, to Malabar and Ethiopia; various Orthodox delegates to the Third World Assembly visiting the Syrian Orthodox Church of India; the Catholicos of Etchmiadzin, who made numerous trips outside of Russia and visited almost all Orthodox Patriarchates; the Rumanian Patriarch to Armenia; the Syrian Orthodox Patriarch to the Ecumenical Patriarch; and the Catholicos of Cilicia to Greece. Meanwhile students from the Coptic, the Ethiopian, and the Syrian Churches study theology at schools in Athens, Thessalonika, Halki, Bucharest, and Addis Ababa.

Orthodoxy and Roman Catholicism   In the last two decades the relations between the Orthodox and the Roman Catholic Churches have undergone a great change for the better. Popes John XXIII and Paul VI and Ecumenical Patriarch Athenagoras were major factors in the changing climate. The fact that the Patriarchate of Moscow was represented by observers from the first session of the Second Vatican Council onwards was also important. Tragic events taking place during the Second World War among the Orthodox Churches of the Balkans and Russia unfavourably dominated relations at the beginning of the period. The first major move toward improvement was the 1958 Christmas message of the late Pope John to Patriarch Athenagoras, who responded immediately and affirmatively by sending a New Year's greeting at the beginning of 1959. Relations suffered a temporary setback in 1959 because of a misunderstanding which arose in connection with a meeting of the Central Committee of the World Council of Churches in Rhodes. The misunderstanding arose because of misleading publicity given to an unofficial meeting there between Orthodox delegates and Roman Catholic observers or press representatives. It caused Archbishop Iakovos to declare that the Orthodox had no intention of establishing direct contacts with Rome if the Protestant Churches and the World Council of Churches were not invited to participate. But the matter was cleared up without permanent damage.

The pan-Orthodox Conferences of 1961, 1963, and 1964 discussed the relations of Orthodoxy and the Catholic Church. On the question whether observers should be sent to the Second Vatican Council it was decided that each Orthodox Church should make its own decision. Not all Orthodox responded favourably in the beginning to the invitation of Rome to send observers. At the first and second sessions (1962, 1963) only the Churches of Russia and Georgia sent observers. To the third session observers from Constantinople and Alexandria were added, and in the final session the patriarchates of Serbia and Bulgaria also sent observers. The Secretariat for the Promotion of Christian Unity, established by Pope John and headed by Cardinal Bea, helped immensely to facilitate good relations.

Pope Paul VI continued the efforts of his predecessor. On his visit to Jerusalem in 1964 the meetings between him and the Ecumenical Patriarch and the Patriarch of Jerusalem made history. The mutual lifting in 1965 of the anathemas between Rome and Constantinople, which had stood since 1054, was followed by the visit by Pope Paul to the Ecumenical Patriarchate in Istanbul and the return visit to Rome by Athenagoras in 1967. Roman Catholics were officially invited to come as observers to the Pan-Orthodox Conference in Rhodes, to the Mount Athos celebration of its first thousand years in 1964, and to a commemoration in Thessalonika in 1966 of the work of Cyril and Methodius, apostles to the Slavs. The return from the Western Church of the relics of several saints to churches in Jerusalem, Patras, Crete, and Chios added another evidence of good will. Theologians from the Catholic and Orthodox Churches are meeting in the United States under the auspices of their respective Churches. So the change for the better continues to grow better.

Orthodox–Old Catholic Relations   Orthodoxy had friendly relations with the Old Catholic Church since its formation as an independent Church after 1870. In 1931 a meeting of a Joint Doctrinal Commission of Orthodox and Old Catholics was held in Bonn. A substantial degree of agreement was found to exist. Since the Second World War efforts have been made to revive the work of the Joint Commission. This was discussed at the First Pan-Orthodox Conference at Rhodes, where Old Catholics were present as official observers. Theologians belonging to the Patriarchates of Constantinople, Russia, and Greece have held unofficial conversations with Old Catholic theologians. When Andreas Rinkel, Archbishop of Utrecht, visited the Ecumenical Patriarchate in 1962, it was decided to recreate the Joint Commission. The Archbishop later visited the Church of Russia. The pan-Orthodox commission on the dialogue with Old Catholics met at Belgrade in 1966.

Orthodox–Anglican Relations   In the last two decades work for reunion between these two communions, which began long ago, has been strongly revived. Present relations between the two Churches continue the Orthodox–Anglican discussions held at the 1930 Lambeth Conference and the Joint Doctrinal Commission which met in London a year later. The negative decision on Anglican orders which was taken at the 1948 Moscow Conference, joined in by the Russian, Rumanian, and the Alexandrine delegates, constitute a temporary reversal. But an Anglo-Russian theological conference held in Moscow in 1956 brought the Russian Church to the same level which other Orthodox Churches had reached with reference to the Anglicans.

The visit of Michael Ramsey, Archbishop of Canterbury, to Moscow in 1962 and the return visit to London of Patriarch Alexii in 1964 confirmed these improved relations. Dr Ramsey visited the Ecumenical Patriarch and the Churches of Greece in 1962, Rumania in 1965, and Jerusalem and Belgrade in 1966. He was host to the Patriarch of Rumania in the same year. Anglican observers have been present on invitation at various pan-Orthodox meetings. In the U.S.A. an officially appointed Orthodox Theological Commission meets with a similar group from the Protestant Episcopal Church.

Orthodox–Protestant Relations Between 1948 and 1968 Orthodoxy has met the Protestant world mainly through the ecumenical movement. Formerly tension developed because some Evangelical communities developed missionary work in Orthodox areas, but more recently proselyting seems to have stopped and good will and co-operation are the rule. This has led to better understanding. Greek Orthodoxy was not prepared for the problems which arose when thousands of Greeks spread over Protestant and Catholic areas of Europe in search of work. Generally Protestant and Catholic Churches have adopted a co-operative attitude which has helped workers meet differences in tradition, religion, ethics, and style of living.

In Germany several consultations have been held between Protestant and Orthodox theologians. Theologians of the Orthodox Church of Russia and of the Evangelical Church of Germany met in Arnoldshain, West Germany in 1959; in Zagorsk, Moscow in 1963 and in Hocst, Odenwald, West Germany in 1967. But the Orthodox–Protestant encounter is not limited to theologians. Most of the professors of the Orthodox theological faculties in Athens and Salonika finished their advanced studies in Germany. Since 1946 Orthodox theologians have lectured before German Protestant faculties. Protestant students have studied the Orthodox liturgy at the Ecumenical Institute at Chateau Bossey, Switzerland and at the Orthodox St Serge Institute in Paris. The latter has, with the Russian Student Christian Movement, carried out broad ecumenical activity. There have been many excursions of Protestant and Orthodox students into Egypt, Syria, and Ethiopia and many Orthodox–Protestant youth and student conferences in Germany, France, Belgium, England, Scotland, Greece, and Finland. Professor Leo Zander, Secretary of the Orthodox Student Christian Movement, carried out indefatigable lifelong activity dedicated to the ecumenical approach of the Orthodox Church to the Western Churches.

Ecumenical periodicals render an important service in informing Western Christianity about the Eastern Orthodox Churches. *Irenikon*, published by the Benedictine monks in Chevetogne in Belgium, *Istina*, published by the Dominican order in Paris, *Kyrios*, edited by Professor Meinhood in Kiel, and the *Ostkirchliche Studien*, edited by Professor Stupperich in Münster, give scholarly theological and historical information about Orthodox Churches and their ecumenical relations. They review books and articles and give news about the ecumenical life of the Orthodox Churches.

The W.C.C. department of Faith and Order has brought together Orthodox and Protestant theologians twice: at Athens in 1959 and at Montreal in 1963. The Standing Conference of Orthodox Canonical Bishops in America, which met early in 1967, approved participation in a Orthodox–Lutheran colloquy later that year. The meeting took place in New York, discovered a "basic understanding" on Scripture and tradition, and concluded that "the enormously illuminating and constructive" conversation would "ultimately produce a valuable contribution to ecumenical progress on the American scene". The Bishops' Conference[1] also accepted in "in principle" an invitation to start a similar dialogue with the Presbyterians, but declined because of shortage of Orthodox personnel in the U.S.A. to start an Orthodox–Methodist discussion, even "in principle".

Oriental Orthodox and Western Churches   Contacts have begun to multiply between the Oriental Orthodox Churches and those of the West. At the invitation of Pope Paul VI, the Catholicos of the Syrian Orthodox Church of India attended the Eucharistic Congress held in Bombay in 1964 and met the Pope. Pope Paul exchanged visits with the Armenian Patriarch of Istanbul during his visit in 1967. The Armenian Catholicos Khoren I of Cilicia paid an official visit to Pope Paul in Rome in the same year. In 1965 the Addis Ababa Conference of the Oriental Orthodox Churches noted with approval "the new awareness which the Roman Catholic Church has begun to show" of other Churches, and offered to enter into conversations designed to improve mutual understanding.

Concerning other member Churches of the W.C.C., the conference statement expressed appreciation of the cordial relations with other Churches which the W.C.C. made possible and prayed "that God would open the way for our mutual understanding wherever possible". The statement expressed special interest in dialogue with Anglican and Old Catholic Churches. It asked both Protestants and Catholics to refrain from proselyting "among members of our Churches" and expressed faith "that God who has brought our Churches and the other member Churches of the World Council of Churches together into friendly relation through that Council will help us to grow in fellowship with one another and restore us all into fullness of unity in his own time and in the manner He ordains".

Conclusion   Inter-Orthodox relations have improved immensely, especially during the 1958–68 decade. This has been the work of God. Eastern Orthodoxy has been accused by some of not being able to move fast enough. Admittedly, it does not have a permanent standing office or instrument of pan-Orthodox character, except Syndesmos, the youth organization, which has the blessing of the Ecumenical Patriarchate. On the other hand, the Oriental Orthodox Churches have established "the Standing Committee of the Oriental Orthodox Churches" which does act on their behalf. Since Eastern Orthodoxy maintains old, and has started new, relations or theological contacts with other Churches, and since developments of an ecumenical character are multiplying, the question arises whether Orthodoxy is adequately prepared or has sufficient trained personnel to cope with the demands being made upon it. Without

[1] L.W.F. Press Release, no. 44/67.

criticizing the sincerity of Orthodox intentions, it is obvious that it will take a longer time for their Churches to participate effectively and meet all the demands than the movement of events would make desirable.

Orthodoxy and Wider Ecumenical Manifestations

Introduction

The ecumenical movement, which includes the World Council of Churches, is a wider and richer stream than any council. Movements parallel with, and complementary to, the W.C.C. often originated before 1948 but need to be taken into account. These wider ecumenical manifestations help Orthodox laity, youth, clergy, monks, and others who participate in them to experience and learn about one phase or another of the ecumenical movement. One of the most important of these is missions.

Missions

In modern times, it has been too easy to forget that in times past Orthodox missionaries carried the gospel of Jesus Christ to people in vast areas of what we now know as Christendom. Missionary awareness is not dead within the Eastern Churches, although it has been dormant for too long. Political and other reasons mainly account for this state of affairs, but ecclesiastical reasons also play their part. Protestant missionary expansion within lands to which the gospel was first brought by missionaries of Orthodoxy was viewed by Orthodox leaders as disruptive. In the early years of the ecumenical movement, Orthodox representatives did not fail to protest against proselytism. This led to the formation of a special commission of the W.C.C. Its report, entitled "Christian Witness, Proselytism, and Religious Liberty", was presented to the Third World Assembly of Churches in New Dehli in 1961. This document, in which proselytism is called a corruption of Christian witness, was well accepted by Eastern Orthodox Churches.

New Dehli was also the Assembly at which the International Missionary Council and the World Council of Churches were merged. Orthodoxy's experiences as a result of some Protestant missionary activity had made them miss the very important studies and work done in the field of evangelism by the I.M.C. They concentrated on expressing doubts and concern about the rightness of the proposed merger. When a mandate was given to a joint committee to study the integration of the two councils, the Ecumenical Patriarchate prepared and sent a memorandum to the sister Orthodox Churches. Archbishop Michael of America expressed to the 1957 meeting of the Central Committee of the W.C.C. the reservations which Orthodoxy had on the proposed integration. Later Metropolitan, now Archbishop, Iakovos, presented these reservations at a meeting of the I.M.C. in Ghana, where he was present as an observer. Objections by these and other Orthodox caused the dropping of the theological preamble to the statement of integration and the way for them to participate in its adoption was cleared by the adoption of the statement against proselytizing. The former International Missionary Council became the Commission on World Mission and Evangelism of the World Council of Churches, with a divisional structure within the W.C.C. Participation by the Orthodox in this Commission will hopefully reawaken their missionary zeal.

Oriental Orthodox Churches conducting missionary work include the Church at Malabar, through the Missionary Association of the Servants of the Cross (1924), the Evangelistic Associations of the East (1925), and the Christu Sishya Ashram (1933). The Church of Ethiopia conducts missionary work through its department of mission and some religious associations. The Addis Ababa Conference encouraged member Churches to "examine the experience of the various missionary organizations . . . and see what can be done to co-ordinate our missionary efforts".

In East Africa an African Greek Orthodox Church has developed. It has an estimated membership of 10,000 to 30,000. It represents a merger of Christian groups which originated separately around 1930. The background of these groups was respectively Anglican, Scottish Presbyterian, Pentecostal, and the Society of Friends. Leaders established contact first with the Syrian Orthodox and later with the Greek Orthodox Church. Out of these contacts came the African Greek Orthodox Church. In 1959 the Patriarch of Alexandria appointed a metropolitan to administer the Church.[1]

Within the Orthodox Church of Greece and the Greek Orthodox archdiocese of America there are some projects to help the missionary Churches of Korea as well as these in Uganda. The Fourth General Assembly of Syndesmos (1958) established an international missionary society with headquarters in Athens. Three years later the Fifth Assembly transformed this headquarters into a pan-Orthodox missionary centre with the title *Porefthentes* (Go Ye). Through this centre, through a bulletin with the same title published in Greek and English, through material help to missionary Churches, and by meetings and correspondence, Syndesmos has become a major centre of influence for mission.

Laity

In the Orthodox Church laymen play active roles in church organization, in worship, in service as artists and writers, in philanthropy, in education, including theological education, as monks, and in the mission of the Church. Each baptized member has a special call to verify the genuine church conscience. While one cannot generalize, generally it is true that ecumenical education lags among laity. In villages laymen obtain their information about the ecumenical movement from the priests, the majority of whom take a defensive and rather negative stand. Others are apathetic, but a small minority show a hopeful attitude toward ecumenism. Because of the rising standards of education and Europeanization, "time is working with the ecumenical spirit" in Greece and other Orthodox countries. Since Orthodox monasticism is predominantly of a lay character, the attitude of monks is important. According to Mario Rinvolucri, "with a very few individual exceptions, the

[1] Article by D. E. Wentink, *Ecumenical Review*, vol. xx (January 1968).

monks are emotionally the most anti-ecumenically disposed group in Greek society". The Orthodox Patriarchal Centre at Taizé, France as well as the Orthodox working in the Ecumenical Centre in Geneva may be expected to make the development of good relations between Orthodox monasticism and ecumenism a matter of concern.

The lay element is predominant in the religious movements known as Zoe, Soter, and the movements of Fr Nissiotis (Union of Orthodox Youth) and Fr (now Metropolitan) Kandiotis. So far these movements have not shown a noticeable willingness to co-operate among themselves or with the official Church. Zoe shows signs of developing a more favourable attitude toward ecumenical affairs. It wields considerable influence among the dominant bourgeoisie. The Soter Brotherhood is much more conservative and un-ecumenical. The most ecumenically minded religious movement in Greece is probably that of Fr Nissiotis. Lay professors of theology in the theological schools greatly influence ecumenical education among the Orthodox by their knowledge, their writings, and their teachings. The department of the laity of the World Council of Churches held a consultation on the laity at Beirut, Lebanon in 1967. In such meetings and in other ways the department is of help to the laity of the Eastern Churches.

Youth

The development of associations through which Orthodox youth could work has been an important aspect of ecumenical growth between 1948 and 1968. We have already referred to Syndesmos, the pan-Orthodox youth organiza-tion. Some youth organizations of Protestant origin, such as the Young Men's and the Young Women's Christian Associations, have also contributed. In connection with the World Assemblies of Churches in 1948, 1954, 1961, and 1968 three youth conferences have been held, two in Lebanon and one in Switzerland. The 1955 Consultation in Beirut brought together for the first time leaders responsible for youth work among the Eastern Orthodox, the Oriental Orthodox, the Anglicans, and the Evangelicals. It was the first time in modern centuries for Christians of this whole area to come together and feel their oneness in Christ. Eastern Orthodox were in the majority.

The Assembly of European Youth which was held in Lausanne in 1960 had the support of Syndesmos. The sixty-five page preparatory book of the Assembly was translated into several languages, including Greek and Finnish. Over 100 persons, including forty Greeks, represented Eastern Orthodoxy. Observers included Russians, Yugolavs, Bulgarians, and three Ethiopians. In 1964 a broad range of Middle Eastern countries was again represented in another youth conference in Lebanon. The youth department of the World Council of Churches and the World Student Christian Federation joined resources and appointed Gaby Habib, an Orthodox, to be youth secretary for the Churches of the Middle East. He successfully organized this conference, of which a participant said: "It was the first meeting of its kind to take such a broad range of Middle Eastern countries and to penetrate to the heart of the Christian youth organizations of the region."[1] Strong youth delegations,

[1] Editorial of *The Student World* (1965), quoting Bishop Ignatius Hazim.

Protestant and Orthodox, also took part in the programme celebrating the one thousand nine hundredth anniversary of the arrival of St Paul in Greece. The needs of youth were discussed at the First Pan-Orthodox Conference held in Rhodes in 1961 and in the Conference of Oriental Orthodox Churches held in Addis Ababa in 1965. Orthodox youth often appear earlier in the ecumenical movement than do their elders and sometimes venture beyond the areas of official church co-operation.

Orthodox Religious Education and Bible Societies

From the Protestant world, Eastern Orthodox and Oriental Orthodox Churches have taken the modern idea of the Sunday school. With modifications they have adapted its methods and teaching manuals. In Greece the *Apostolike Diakonia* (Home Missions) of the Church of Greece has finally, after some delay, taken over Sunday school materials and development. The movement has problems in Greece, as it has elsewhere.

The Standing Conference of Canonical Bishops in America has a committee and a programme for united pan-Orthodox action in religious education in America. The Oriental Churches at their Addis Ababa Conference launched a committee of experts to outline a curriculum for Christian education to be used by the Churches. The committee met in 1967 in Antelias for a week and produced the outline for a joint curriculum.

Because proselytism by Protestants was identified with dissemination of the Bible, the Orthodox Churches were at first reluctant to deal with Bible Societies. This reluctance seems to be fading. Eastern Orthodox scholars have participated in translating and editing parts or the whole of the Bible on a regional level. Now members of these Churches buy and distribute scriptures or materials connected with the Bible produced by these societies in local languages. The Rumanian Patriarchate works through a missionary institute and the Serbian Patriarchate is especially active in catechization. A committee of Orthodox biblical scholars, under instructions from the Standing Conference of Orthodox Bishops of America, began planning in 1967 to produce an "American Orthodox" Bible. This will be based on the Revised Standard Version, with some alterations to conform with distinctive Orthodox understandings. The special importance attached to the Septuagint by the Orthodox Church may present the major problems in this enterprise.

Theological Education in the Orthodox Churches

The ecumenical movement is being accepted as the most important feature of ecclesiastical life in the twentieth century, so Orthodox theological schools have taken this into account. Some have added a course on ecumenical significance for theology and church life. The Orthodox Theological Institute of St Sergius is one of the collaborating theological schools in the Roman Catholic Superior Institute of Ecumenical Studies in Paris which was formed in 1967.

Orthodox professors of theology regularly give courses in the Ecumenical Institute at Chateau Bossey in Switzerland. Dr Nikos Nissiotis of the Church of Greece is now director of this institute, which is connected with the World Council of Churches. He was an observer for the W.C.C. at the Second Vatican Council. Orthodox theologians are well represented also in the Ecumenical Institute on Soteriological Studies in Jerusalem. They play significant roles in the Secretariat on Faith and Order of the W.C.C. and in the four-year World Council Study on Patterns of Ministry and Theological Education. They help to advise the administrators of the Theological Education Fund, which is interested in theological schools generally and particularly in some Orthodox theological schools in the Near East and India. Through this fund consultations have been held on church history (1956–9), on ecumenical theology (1960), hermeneutics (1963), patristic studies and practical theology (1967).

The last pan-Orthodox congress on theology was held in Athens in 1936. The 1965 Oriental Orthodox Conference at Addis Ababa urged that a "Common Centre for Advanced Studies and Research" be established, that the writing of theological books and the exchange of students and professors be encouraged. Mixed groups for theological discussions exist in Athens and at the University of Thessalonika. In Great Britain some of the work done by the Anglican and Eastern Churches Association and by the Fellowship of St Alban and St Sergius could be included. The latter group maintain St Basil's House, London, which has a good library, publishes the excellent magazine *Sobornost*, holds conferences, and has Chapters in Britain, Canada, and Australia.

Press, Radio, Television

The Orthodox Churches do not now have a paper exclusively dedicated to the ecumenical movement. Between 1956 and 1962 the liaison office of the Ecumenical Patriarchate at the headquarters of the World Council of Churches published such a paper in Greek each month. The weekly paper *Apostolos Andreas* of the Ecumenical Patriarchate, which continued from 1951 to 1964, published a rich variety of material on the ecumenical movement. A monthly entitled *Orthodoxy* is issued by the autonomous Russian Orthodox Church of America. Other Orthodox periodicals carry ecumenical news and opinions. Some are published by church officials, others by theological schools. The Greek Archbishopric of Crete has its own radio station. The Syrian Orthodox Church is a member of the Near East Council of Churches, which helps to sponsor the radio station at Addis Ababa. In general it must be said that participation in the ministry of communication by the Orthodox Church is in its early stages.

Orthodox Worship

Fr Alexander Schmemann in an article on "Worship and the Ecumenical Encounter" starts with the assertion that the ecumenical encounter of Churches takes place in and through worship.[1] For some, the ecumenical movement moves towards unity through intercommunion by those who

[1] *The Student World*, 51 (1958), pp. 34-5.

accept it as a way towards fuller unity. For the Orthodox, who on ecclesiological grounds reject intercommunion, accepting their Church as the *Una Sancta*, this way is closed. So the most liturgical of all Christian bodies, for which the liturgy is the full and unique expression of Christian fellowship, has to oppose the "liturgical encounter" and to withdraw from all attempt at intercommunion. This tragedy is keenly felt, for nowhere do we realize more what it means to be divided than at the altar, at the table of the Lord.

This does not mean that the Eastern Orthodox do not pray together with their brother Christians. They welcome the presence of fellow-Christians in their worship services, and at the end of each liturgy the *antidoron*, the blessed bread, is given. In Orthodox lands during ecumenical meetings, such as the Central Committee of the W.C.C. at Crete in 1967, non-Orthodox are allowed to preach the sermon and to recite together the Lord's Prayer.

In ecumenical services, Orthodox clergy lead prayers or participate in services in the presence of members of other Churches. Participation in the Week of Prayer for the Unity of the Church is growing from year to year. The Council of Churches of Alexandria, including the Roman Catholic Church, has held every year since 1959 a special service of intercession. What does this mean for co-operation with ecumenical bodies? The Ecumenical Patriarchate issued an encyclical in 1952 on the World Council of Churches. It included the following words, among others:

> (c) It is meet that Orthodox clerics who are delegates [of their Church] should be as careful as possible about services of worship in which they join with the heterodox, as these are contrary to the sacred canons and make less acute the confessional sensitiveness of the Orthodox. They should aim at celebrating, if possible, purely Orthodox liturgical services and rites, that they may thereby manifest, before the eyes of the heterodox, the splendour and majesty of Orthodox adoration.

Again in 1967 an encyclical was sent from the same source to the hierarchs saying: "Intercommunion between the Orthodox Church and other churches does not as yet exist."

Professor Nikos Nissiotis adds an additional illuminating comment.

> From the doctrinal point of view intercommunion is not possible in the Orthodox Church. However some local Orthodox Churches of different jurisdictions do not even have communion with one another if their canonical relationship is broken and if full love and spiritual communion are lacking in either of them. On this basis I would like to modify somewhat the harsh statement that where there is no doctrinal agreement about the Church, its ministry and the significance of the Eucharist there cannot be intercommunion. Instead I would say that, for the Orthodox, love and spiritual communion are equally important when we participate in the same chalice. The Orthodox cannot say that intercommunion is simply the crowning event of a pre-existing, detailed doctrinal agreement (which never existed in a full sense between East and West even before the schism, when intercommunion was nevertheless practised). It is also the God-given means of maintaining unity and of healing divisions, if this unity is at stake or if the appropriate conditions for restoring it exist.
> It might be that the developments in ecumenical relationships and especially

the recognition of the positive signs of the growing fellowship between separated churches could create the basis for the Orthodox to make an exception. However, this exception can only be made by means of the *dispensation (kat' oikonomian)* which is already practised in many other cases, particularly as far as the recognition of baptism is concerned. The *dispensatio* can override the decisions of Canon Law in cases where pastoral care should have priority over the letter of the law. I have concluded by these observations on this crucial problem because again and again the Eastern Church has shown the *kat' oikonomian* to be the expression of the fundamental ecclesiological principle of its own belief and thoughts. It is the love which results from the "unity of the spirit in the bond of peace" for all those who want to keep the unity of the spirit. It manifests the creative spirit of love which breaks through all barriers raised by human failure and shortcomings which divide that which cannot exist as divided, namely communion in the one family of God.[1]

Confessional Bodies, Organic Church Unions, Regional and National Councils

Confessional Bodies Orthodoxy does not regard herself as one of the confessions, but as the true Church, the *Una Sancta* of the Symbol of Faith, and so it is out of place to speak of the efforts spent and the results achieved in the domain of inter-Orthodox relations. However, Orthodoxy is represented at annual meetings in Geneva of representatives of confessional bodies, with representatives of the W.C.C.

Organic Church Unions The relations of the Orthodox Churches to other Churches are almost in their beginnings. A solid step forward is the formation of joint doctrinal commissions of the Orthodox with Anglican, Old Catholic, and Oriental Orthodox Churches.

Regional and National Councils Eastern and Oriental Orthodox Churches participate in these councils. Orthodox Churches and jurisdictions are members of the National Christian Councils of Poland, Czechoslovakia, the United Arab Republic, Great Britain, the United States of America, Canada, and Australia. The Syrian Orthodox Church is a member of the Regional Council of Churches in the Middle East. Orthodox Churches are members of the All-Africa Conference of Churches, of the East Asia Christian Council, and of the European Conference of Churches.

Orthodoxy and the World Council of Churches

Eastern Orthodoxy, without compromising her ecclesiological claims of being the one and true Church of Christ, takes part almost unanimously in the ecumenical movement. Today the following Orthodox Patriarchates, autocephalous or autonomous Churches, are members of the World Council of Churches: (1) Constantinople (2) Alexandria (3) Antioch (4) Jerusalem (5) Russia (6) Serbia (7) Rumania (8) Bulgaria (9) Cyprus (10) Greece (11) Poland

---

[1] N. A. Nissiotis. "Kirche und Welt in Orthodoxer Sicht", *Evangelisches Verlagswerk* Stuttgart 1968.

L

(12) Iberia (Georgia) (13) Czechoslovakia (14) Russian Orthodox of America (15) Archbishopric of the Patriarchate of Antioch in America (16) Rumanian Orthodox Episcopate in America. With the exception of the Orthodox Church of Albania the whole of Eastern Orthodoxy holds membership in the World Council of Churches.

Official co-operation with the ecumenical movement started as long ago as 1920 when the Ecumenical Patriarch, then the Metropolitan of Thyateira, Germanos, sent delegates to the preliminary meeting on Faith and Order which was held in Geneva. Until the year 1937, when it was decided to unite the two movements of Life and Work and Faith and Order in one organization, the World Council of Churches, participation of Orthodox Churches was unanimous, with the exception of the Russian Orthodox Church, which could not get into touch with the ecumenical movement because of political persecution until later. After 1937 co-operation continued with Life and Work, but the Orthodox stand within Faith and Order was not the same.

While the ecumenical movement appeared to be understood and practised only by a handful of clerics and professors of theology, with little impact on the wider membership of the Church, professors of religious philosophy and theology, including the Russians Berdyaev, Bulgakow, Ilmin, and Frank, through their writings had a broad influence on Western Christianity and broadened the understanding of Orthodox thought and literature.

When the World Council of Churches came formally into existence in 1948, it confronted the Orthodox Churches with new problems. The Russian Orthodox Church, which was unable to have contact with the ecumenical movement until after the Second World War, was not prepared for the new event. Consequently the Conference of Orthodox Churches called in Moscow in July of 1948 decided "to decline participation in the ecumenical movement, in its present form". In addition to the Moscow Patriarchate, the Orthodox Churches of Serbia, Rumania, Poland, Albania, Bulgaria, Czechoslovakia, and of Alexandria and Antioch, joined in rejecting membership. Their statement showed lack of knowledge of the nature and work of the World Council of Churches. They accused the W.C.C. of intending to form "an ecumenical church", of projecting social and political activity "which was a diversion of the church's labours towards the taking of human souls . . .", of "losing faith too soon in the possibility of union in one Holy, Catholic and Apostolic Church", and of reducing its statement of purpose "to the simple recognition of Christ as our Lord" which "lowers the Christian faith to such a degree as to be accessible even to the devils". These misunderstandings were cleared up and the position changed radically by 1961 when the Russian Orthodox Church and others entered the World Council of Churches.

The Ecumenical Patriarchate, as we have seen earlier, took a more co-operative attitude in its 1952 encyclical, which approved as "necessary" the participation by the Orthodox Churches in the W.C.C. The practical co-operation as envisaged by the W.C.C. was seen as a "task pleasing to God as an attempt and a manifestation of a noble desire that the churches of Christ should face together the great problems of humanity". It enabled the Orthodox Church "to make known and to impart to the heterodox the riches of her faith, worship and order and her religious and ascetic experience". It would also help Orthodox Churches to learn about new methods and conceptions of church life and activity which would be of great benefit to them. But the Orthodox must avoid discussion of dogmas in the Commission on Faith and Order, must study and act together on problems raised in the W.C.C., and must adopt a reserved attitude towards the worship of the non-Orthodox and celebrate their own worship services.

But the restriction concerning Faith and Order has also been softened. Now delegates of the Ecumenical Patriarchate and the other Orthodox Churches have taken and are taking part in the work of the W.C.C. secretariat of Faith and Order. The way to implement the suggested policy in relation to Faith and Order has been left to the personal discretion of each delegate.

A sign of the change of feelings and the improved relations is seen in the letter of Patriarch Alexii of Moscow to W. A. Visser 't Hooft, the General Secretary of the World Council of Churches, under date of 1 April 1961. It said in part:

> We declare our agreement with the Basis of the World Council of Churches as expressed in paragraph one of its Constitution . . . The Russian Orthodox Church has always attached the utmost importance to the problems of mutual *rapprochement* between all Christians, the deepening of mutual understanding among committed Christians and the strengthening of universal brotherhood, love and peace among the nations on the basis of the Gospel.

The letter said that the Russian Orthodox Church counted on the W.C.C. to strengthen the spirit of ecumenical brotherhood and that that Church

> . . . is fully determined to make her contribution to the great task of Christian unity on the lines of the previous movements of "Faith and Order", "Life and Work" and "International Friendship through the Churches" which now find their common expression in the different forms and aspects of the activities of the World Council of Churches.

When the Russian Orthodox Church entered into membership of the W.C.C. at New Dehli in the same year, the Orthodox Churches of Rumania, Bulgaria, and Poland were also received into membership. The Patriarchate of Jerusalem, whose name appeared in the official documents of the W.C.C. as one of its members, also sent delegates. Following these the Orthodox Churches of Iberia (Georgia), Serbia, and Czechoslovakia came in 1962, 1965, and 1966 respectively into the membership of the W.C.C. To the Second World Assembly of Churches, which was held in the U.S.A. in 1954, came the Orthodox Churches of Constantinople, Antioch, Cyprus, Greece, the autonomous Russian Orthodox Church in America, the Rumanian Episcopate in America, and the Archbishopric of the Church of Antioch in America.

Many factors helped to bring about the remarkable change which took place in the relations of the Russian Orthodox Church and the W.C.C. between 1948 and 1961. One of these was the act of the W.C.C. secretariat in sending to the Moscow Patriarchate all of the publications relating to the Second Assembly of the World Council of Churches in 1954. This opened a correspondence which had constructive results. At Utrecht, Holland in 1958 there was a meeting between the W.C.C. and Russian Orthodox representatives at which many questions were asked and answered. Meetings of the Central Committee of the W.C.C. were opened to observers of the Russian Church, as to others. Finally, an official W.C.C. delegation went in December 1959 to visit the Moscow Patriarchate.

Co-operation between the Eastern Orthodox and the World Council of Churches is indicated by figures showing participation by Orthodox in World Assemblies of Churches. In the First Assembly at Amsterdam, eighty-five seats out of a total of 351 official delegates were assigned to Orthodox but only thirteen seats were filled by participating delegates. A few other Orthodox were present in various capacities. At the Second Assembly (Evanston 1954), out of 502 delegates, thirty Orthodox were present as delegates. At the Third Assembly (New Dehli 1961) out of 600 delegates there were sixty-four Orthodox, but with the admission of the Russian and other Churches the number rose to close on 100. In the Fourth Assembly (Uppsala 1968) the Orthodox had 160 seats assigned out of a total of 800 delegates. While not all were able to attend, the Orthodox delegation was one of the largest in the Assembly. The steady growth in numbers has a psychological effect on the Orthodox, helping them to throw off the inferiority complex implicit in a small representation amidst large delegations of Western Christians. For the first time, at Uppsala, Orthodox participation in a World Council Assembly was numerous, wholehearted, and contributed greatly to the value of the Assembly at all levels.

In the World Council of Churches, the Orthodox delegates seem to have been able to present a common line in dogmatic–ecclesiological matters, with some differences among them on external and social questions. They continue to meet together and to follow a common line in the discussions. Since the New Delhi Assembly, however, the Orthodox have refrained from presenting to the Assembly as a whole separate declarations on points of major difference. Previously on a number of occasions such declarations were made. Now Orthodox delegates are content to make the voice of Orthodoxy heard in discussions within the separate sections, resulting in some influence on the official reports. Orthodox serve as officers in the General Assemblies and give their share of the major addresses. A strong effort is now made by Orthodox leaders to make sure that their delegates are well prepared to participate in the discussions. One of the six Presidents of the W.C.C. at Uppsala was Archbishop Iakovos, Primate of America. Before him Orthodox who had served as presidents were Germanos of Thyateira (1948–51), Athenagoras of Thyateria (1951–4), and Michael of America (1954–8). At Uppsala, the Serbian Orthodox Patriarch was elected to the presidency.

Several developments at New Delhi were the result of the efforts of Orthodox, among others, to influence the World Council of Churches. Perhaps the most important of these was the change in the first article of "Basis" of the constitution of the World Council of Churches. As voted at New Delhi, the "Basis" now includes the trinitarian formula: "The World Council of Churches is a fellowship of churches which confess the Lord

Jesus as God and Saviour according to the Scriptures and therefore seek to fulfil together their common calling to the glory of the one God, Father, Son and Holy Spirit".

Other changes which particularly pleased the Orthodox were the approval of the document opposing proselytism and the New Delhi statement on the unity of the Church, emphasizing unity among "all in each place". Finally, the Orthodox approved the enactment of integration of the International Missionary Council and the World Council of Churches. The vote was taken in a plenary session chaired by Archbishop Iakovos, after several modifications were made in the draft document to meet criticisms, including those of the Orthodox.

In 1955 the Ecumenical Patriarchate established its office for liaison at the headquarters of the World Council of Churches in Geneva. Its first Director was the Bishop of Melita, now Archbishop of America, Iakovos, who grew into one of the leading ecumenicists. His successor since 1959 is Metropolitan Emilianos of Calabria. The office is another sign of continuous interest and co-operation on the part of the Ecumenical Patriarchate. Of similar interest and purpose was the establishment in 1962 of an office of the same nature at W.C.C. headquarters by the Church of Russia, with Proto-Presbyter Vitali Borovoy as its Director. He presently serves also as an Associate Director of the Faith and Order Commission. Other Orthodox officers at the World Council include Fr George Tsetsis, Co-Secretary of the Orthodox Churches in the Division of Inter-Church Aid, Refugee, and World Service, and Professor Nikos Nissiotis, Director of the Ecumenical Institute and Associate General Secretary of the W.C.C.

The holding of ecumenical meetings and conferences in Orthodox territories has aided the growth of knowledge and co-operation. Central Committee meetings of the W.C.C. met in Rhodes in 1959 and in Crete in 1967. Members and staff of this annual meeting total around 200 people. The W.C.C. Executive Committee met at the invitation of the Orthodox Church of Russia in Odessa in 1964; the Working Committee of the Secretariat of Faith and Order met at Zagorsk near Moscow in 1966. We have already mentioned that conferences of youth and laity met in Lebanon in 1955, 1964, and 1967.

It is also important that when the World Council holds meetings and conferences the Orthodox are given opportunities to meet among themselves. Meetings of Eastern Orthodox at such times take place with the representatives of Oriental Orthodox, the Anglican and the Old Catholic Churches. Also the Secretariat on Faith and Order has called unofficial meetings for theological discussion between Orthodox and Protestant (in Greece in 1959 and in Montreal in 1963), and of Eastern Orthodox with Oriental Orthodox (in Denmark 1964 and in England in 1967). All of these contribute to better understanding.

Oriental Orthodox Churches and the W.C.C.

The Church of Ethiopia and the Syrian Orthodox Church of India have been members of the World Council of Churches since its beginning. At the

Second World Assembly the Coptic and the Assyrian Churches entered the Council. At the Third Assembly delegates of the Syrian Orthodox Church of Syria were present. In 1962 at the Central Committee meeting in Paris the Armenian Catholicossates of Etchmiadzin and Cilicia joined the Council.

Notable personalities from the Syrian Orthodox Church of India who work or have worked at the W.C.C. headquarters in Geneva include Fr Paul Verghese, Associate General Secretary 1961-7; C. I. Itty, Associate Executive Secretary in the department of the laity since 1961; and the Reverend J. C. Joseph, Secretary for Scholarships from 1967. Among leaders of these Churches who are well known for their ecumenical work are Bishop Samuel of the Coptic Church, Bishop Karekin Sarkissian of the Armenian Catholicossate of Cilicia, and Bishop K. Philiposa of the Syrian Orthodox Church of India.

Before the 1965 Conference of Addis Ababa closed, it adopted a statement which deserves to be remembered as a keynote to the future. On relations with other member Churches of the W.C.C., it said:

> With the non-Orthodox member churches of the World Council of Churches we have cordial relations through it and we hope and pray that God will open the way for our mutual understanding and co-operation wherever possible . . . We believe that God who has brought our churches and the other member churches of the World Council of Churches together into friendly relations through that council will help us to grow in fellowship with one another and restore us all into fullness of unity in his own time and in the manner he ordains.

On the ecumenical movement, the statement said:

> Before we conclude, we would like to express a genuine appreciation of the whole ecumenical movement such as that made manifest through the World Council of Churches. The new spirit of fellowship, mutual understanding and co-operation fostered by the ecumenical movement has had beneficial effects in the life of all the churches involved. We hope and pray that God will strengthen every effort made for the progress of the ecumenical movement to enable the churches to fulfil their mission through common and concerted efforts in ever greater faithfulness to our common Lord, Jesus Christ.

Evaluation

The ecumenical movement will acquire its full ecumenical form with the eventual and complete participation of the Roman Catholic Church. Meanwhile, the presence of Eastern and Oriental Orthodox Churches within that movement gives it a pan-Christian and not solely a Protestant character, although many of its structures, forms of thought, publications, and officers still belong mainly to the Protestant world. In the ecumenical movement, East and West are finding a common ground and a common language.

Orthodox participation in the W.C.C. has on some occasions been thought of as lacking in balance, in consistency, continuity, and wholeness. To some extent, this is true in comparison with Western Churches. This was probably because of the divided line of action taken by the Orthodox, the unpreparedness of some Orthodox delegates, and their inability to follow the discussions, due to language deficiencies.

The negative attitude against ecumenism taken by conservative Orthodox circles has not helped. The number of well-prepared Orthodox ecumenists, participating in the activities of the Council and working in the ecumenical movement at various levels, is much too small. Since Orthodoxy is now a full partner in the movement, there is a great need to have as many as possible able and well-prepared persons to deal adequately with ecumenical affairs, to work in them and to fill the existing gaps. Orthodox theology should work consistently to prepare these persons.

Participation in the ecumenical movement presents challenges to Orthodoxy. Fr Bobrinskoy says:

> In its confrontation with the churches of Rome and of the Reformation, contemporary Orthodoxy, forced out of its many centuries of isolation, is rediscovering its universal dimensions and is compelled to answer in new terms the question: What is the message of Orthodoxy? It is in terms of plenitude, of experience of trinitarian life, of the divine life radiant in Christians through eucharistic communion that this answer must be built up.

He concludes by saying that the substance of the message of Orthodoxy is inseparable from an attitude of humility and penitence.

My own conclusion is that a process of give and take is in existence between those Churches which participate in the ecumenical movement.

The Orthodox are prepared to learn from others simplicity in personal life, schemes of piety, and Christian life, methods of work, progress in the art of preaching and in the whole field of the expression of Christianity to the world. The Orthodox, meeting the non-Orthodox, are conscious of the enormous progress made by them in theology and especially in some branches of it, such as the comparative study of religions, social Christianity, pastoral psychology, biblical studies, and they try to profit from the work of scholarship carried out by other Churches. The Orthodox know well to what extent others have helped them on the practical level through the many-sided assistance rendered by inter-Church aid, in which Christian love is so abundantly operating.

The presence of Orthodoxy in the ecumenical movement is a witness of Orthodox faith and worship made available for others. She presents to the western world the dimensions and experiences of a Christianity which goes back through an historic continuity and a living tradition to the beginnings of the Faith. The western world has shown a keen interest in the concept of dogma, the liturgical life, the patristic spirit, the religious, mystical, and ascetic concepts of Christian experience, and the work of scholarship to be found in Orthodoxy.

The future lies in the hands of God.

12

The Ecumenical Movement and the Roman Catholic Church

LUKAS VISCHER

Introduction

The Roman Catholic Church underwent great changes in the years dealt with in this volume. The ecumenical movement unexpectedly gained ground. Whereas at the time when the World Council of Churches was founded at Amsterdam the ecumenical movement and the Roman Catholic Church could with some justification be set in contrast, after the pontificate of John XXIII and the Second Vatican Council such a contrast no longer accorded with the facts. The Roman Catholic Church became increasingly influenced by the movement and is now playing an ever more active role within it.

It is obviously impossible to tell the story of this change in a few pages with any adequacy. Twenty years ago it was a simpler story. The Roman Catholic Church stood aside; the official pronouncements and decisions documenting this attitude took little time to summarize. The essentials could be presented by listing the efforts of scattered individual pioneers and small groups overshadowed by this official attitude. Today, however, the subject proves much harder to survey. The ecumenical movement influences the Roman Catholic Church in so many ways that a true picture can be given only by taking account of the entire life of the Church in all its forms. It is no longer possible to limit the theme. Once genuine relationships with the other Churches had been established, everything assumed importance for the Churches' relationships with one another. At the same time the Second Vatican Council shattered the uniformity of the Roman Catholic Church. Many things became fluid. The variety which had indeed always been characteristic of the Roman Catholic Church became more patent, and so our account must cover the new developments in particular sections of the Church.

But the complications do not end there. We are still so close to the events that an objective survey is hardly possible. Many of the cross-connections are not yet clear. All the sources are not yet accessible. How often has the historical pattern been transformed by the discovery of some original documents or letters which put a completely different complexion on certain events! Temporal proximity to events has the advantage of ensuring freshness of recollection, but its drawback is a greater degree of distortion in the picture as a result of personal experience and interests. Most of the accounts appearing today, therefore, present only part of the story. Certain factors are overstressed, others omitted. Everyone tends to give pride of place to what seems to him impressive and significant for the future.

The greatest difficulty, however, is that the change to be described here is still in process. In what direction will the Roman Catholic Church be led? What will the upheaval of recent years mean for the Churches generally? Are they already beginning to absorb the shock? Or is the Second Vatican Council only one of a continuing series of shocks? Will the Council finally go down in history as the beginning of a great renewal or will the future historian see it as the beginning of a decline? Again, what form will the future relationship of the Churches to one another take? Will the Churches successfully develop a viable fellowship? Or will they simply continue their coexistence? These are all still open questions today and the factors affecting future developments are so imponderable that it is impossible to predict the answer to them. Again, our picture of the past will itself inevitably change in accordance with future developments. What has happened will all at once acquire fresh meaning. Every representation of the recent past is fraught with this uncertainty and every interpretation will prove to have been influenced by personal hopes and expectations. The account which follows will be no exception.

From the End of the Second World War to the Death of Pius XII (1945–58)

If we consult the official documents of these years we get the impression, at least at first glance, that the ecumenical movement presented no real problem at all to the Roman Catholic Church of that period. Its response seemed to be settled in advance and the concept of unity underlying its pronouncements so clear and unambiguous that dialogue or even any kind of discussion seemed pointless. This impression is, however, misleading. In reality, the history of those years was marked by considerable tensions. Although official documents and obviously many theologians as well[1] call to mind the concept of unity influenced by the Counter-Reformation and the First Vatican Council, a growing number of theologians were seeking to investigate the questions raised by the ecumenical movement and to offer new answers. In Roman Catholic circles there was a deepening interest in the work of the ecumenical movement and the discussion was marked by increased personal involvement. The official statements of the Magisterium indirectly demonstrate the vigour of this trend. Warnings were felt to be necessary because the Church's official position was in fact being questioned.

The years immediately following the Second World War were notable for an extraordinary movement towards unity. The confessional walls had become transparent as never before. On the non-Roman side the movement led to the founding of the World Council of Churches and, although this was the implementation of an old plan, the energy and enthusiasm with which this was done can be explained only by the mood of those years. Something of this movement to unity was also at work in the Roman Catholic Church. War-time experiences as well as present tasks demanded a coming together of divided Christians. Representatives of different confessions had shared persecution, made common cause on behalf of the Jews, met in concentration camps and in the resistance movement against National Socialism. They had suddenly found themselves in an unexpected solidarity of contemporary witness to the truth.[2]

[1] Cf., for example, E. F. Hanahoe, *Catholic Ecumenism* (Washington 1953); an extremely naive presentation of the ecumenical problem. "All elements are clearly in evidence: the point of departure, the goal to be sought, and the way towards its realisation" (p. 43).

[2] It was certainly no accident that the ecumenical idea gained most ground wherever these experiences had been most deeply felt. When later, at the Second Vatican Council, Dutch, French, and German bishops in particular supported the ecumenical movement of the Church, the comment was made with some justice that the "hand of Hitler" could be seen here.

In these situations many abiding friendships were formed. These friendships ought surely to be maintained. The war had brought with it the transplantation of whole peoples. Even where the war had had no direct influence, the increasing mobility of society led to an ever greater intermingling of the confessions. The number of mixed marriages grew. It was surely essential to establish a new relationship between the confessions. Above all, the Churches were involved in the upheavals which the war brought in its wake not merely in Europe and America but throughout the world. They found themselves faced with gigantic new tasks. Not surprisingly the view gained ground that past confessional conflicts could no longer automatically be regarded as present problems and that by persisting in these conflicts the Churches might be neglecting their proper tasks. All these factors called in question the traditional confessional structure. Although they were not enough to produce a new attitude in the Roman Catholic Church, they did lead to many meetings and to the formation of mixed groups and similar activities in the early postwar years.

But the impetus did not come only from external factors; the development of Roman Catholic theology also played its part. The liturgical movement, stressing what is original and primitive and also pastoral responsibility towards modern man, gave worship a new character and laid the foundation for deeper understanding between the confessions. The new concern for holy Scripture brought into prominence the common authority to which all the divided Churches owed obedience. The outstanding work of Roman Catholics in the field of biblical scholarship almost inevitably made it imperative to re-examine the long-standing controversial question of the relation between Scripture and tradition, an investigation which, at the same time and quite independently, was also being undertaken in the non-Roman Churches.[1]

The greatest stimulus, however, came from the increasingly significant discussion of the nature of the Church. What is the Church? What is the task which Christ has entrusted to the Church? How is the Church to fulfil this task through all its members, both clerical and lay? In both theology and practice these questions began to come to the fore. As the traditional ecclesiology was deepened, so the problem of unity was also seen in a new light. Since ecclesiology had as a result of the ecumenical movement become a major theme in the non-Roman Churches as well, a host of new points of contact resulted. True, the special ecclesiological convictions of the Roman Catholic Church made it a difficult encounter, but the very difficulty forced non-Roman theologians to fresh thinking. Here it proved a happy chance that

---

[1] It was also no accident that the Faith and Order Commission decided after the Third World Conference at Lund (1952) to indicate a study of the problem of tradition. The theme was an obvious choice. A survey of the most important works of both Roman Catholic and other writers in the period 1930–62 may be found in *Schrift und Tradition*, ed. K. E. Skydsgaard and Lukas Vischer (Zürich 1963). Among Roman Catholic theologians particular mention should be made of J. R. Geiselmann, *Lebendiger Glaube aus geheiligter Überlieferung* (Mainz 1942) and *Jesus der Christus* (Stuttgart 1951); later G. H. Tavard, *Holy Writ or Holy Church, The Crisis of Protestant Reformation* (London 1959); and Yves Congar, *La tradition et les traditions* (Paris 1960).

the First Vatican Council had not reached the point of defining a full ecclesiology. Roman Catholic theologians were thus able to deal with this theme more freely and to establish new standpoints.[1]

The decisions of the Magisterium certainly appeared soon to call a halt to this development and, although at first it may still have been reasonable to hope that the Roman Church might play an active part in the ecumenical movement, any such hope seemed in the years that followed doomed to extinction.

The attitude of the Holy See continued to be determined by the conviction that, as the one body of Christ, the Roman Catholic Church could and should fulfil the task committed to that body by its Lord. There can be no denying the achievements accomplished on the basis of this conviction. The pontificate of Pius XII undoubtedly helped to strengthen respect for the Roman Catholic Church and to extend its influence. The Pope's speeches and allocutions contain many proofs of an astonishing awareness of contemporary problems.[2] But this view of Roman Catholic responsibility excluded any genuine understanding of the ecumenical movement and its problems.

Many Roman Catholic theologians had hoped that their Church would be represented at the First Assembly at Amsterdam at least by a few observers. A list of ten possible participants had been drawn up in private conversations. Since at that time it was still possible to assume that the national hierarchies were competent in the matter, it was submitted to Cardinal de Jong of Utrecht. In a *Monitum* of 5 June 1948, however, the Vatican issued a reminder that only the Holy Office could give permission to participate in an international gathering, and it soon afterwards became clear that no official permission would be forthcoming for such participation. Only a few Roman Catholic theologians were able to follow the Assembly's proceedings, unobtrusively (eg. Father C. Boyer). A year and half later the *Instructio Ecclesia catholica* was issued (20 December 1949; published 1 March 1950). Although this text recognized that the movement towards unity was the work of the Holy Spirit in men's hearts, its main thrust was that of warning. References to the encyclicals *Mortalium animos* and *Mystici corporis* recalled the Roman Catholic understanding of unity. The danger of all irenic attitudes was stressed. Roman Catholic teaching had to be presented as a whole and without a watering down of any of its parts.

---

[1] Cf., for example, Yves Congar, "Notes sur les mots 'Confession', 'Eglise', et 'Communion'", *Irenikon* xxii (1950), pp. 3ff; H. de Lubac, *Méditations sur l'Eglise* (Paris 1953); K. Rahner, *Die Freiheit in der Kirche, Lebendiges Zeugnis* (1953), pp. 21ff; M. Villain and J. Baciocchi, *La vocation de l'Eglise* (Paris 1953); detailed bibliography in Ulrich Valeske, *Votum ecclesiae* (Munich 1962). It is significant that Roman Catholic ecumenists relatively seldom dealt with the problem of mission. The divisions of the Church in its missionary outreach had been, for the non-Roman Churches, a primary impetus in the formation of the ecumenical movement, and the call for common witness was one of the major themes from the Edinburgh Missionary Conference onwards. Roman Catholic Christians obviously felt this urgency less; they started rather from the view that the Church by its very nature had to be one.

[2] Cf. *Discorsi e radiomessagi di Sua Santità Pio XII*. 20 vols. Città del Vaticano 1941–59.

Opinons which had been put forward by Roman Catholic ecumenists were condemned as an abandonment of Roman Catholic convictions. Permission from the hierarchy was required for participation in meetings to further the unity of all Christians and precise instructions were given about the authority competent to grant such permission.[1]

More important than this *Instructio* was the encyclical *Humani generis*, which was issued a few months later (12 August 1950).[2] This document was more wide-ranging. It was concerned that the purity of doctrine might be endangered. Even its opening sentences refer to mistaken views which call in question the fundamentals of Catholic doctrine. It was not only outside the Church that these views were to be found but even among Catholic theologians. "Some . . . desirous of novelty and fearing to be considered ignorant of recent scientific findings, tend to withdraw themselves from the Sacred Teaching authority" (para. 11). The encyclical vigorously attacked this tendency. Particular errors were enumerated. They included the idea that dogma is subject to development and has to be constantly reformulated; the relativizing of the concept as distinct from the truth as such; scepticism about the inspiration of Scripture, with a particular reference to Genesis 1-11; and distinguishing between the mystical body of Christ and the Roman Catholic Church. All these views were branded as dangerous and there was an emphatic reminder of the obligatory norms of Catholic doctrine.

This text makes a rather strange impression on anyone re-reading it now, twenty years later. Is it not precisely the ideas which were then rejected which later were to play a decisive role at the Second Vatican Council? Has not almost everything which the encyclical then mentioned only to condemn now been favourably received by the Council? The encyclical was not successful in uprooting and destroying the ideas which it regarded as emerging dangers. In one sense, *Humani generis* already contained the themes of the Second Vatican Council.

In the very same year—the Holy Year—the doctrine of the bodily assumption of Mary was solemnly promulgated (1 November 1950).[3] When the intention of making this definition was announced, many Roman Catholics and non-Roman Catholics advised against it. Their advice went unheeded. The doctrine of the Assumption was defined as binding upon the whole Church. Whereas in previous texts only warnings had been involved, this new step created a new concrete obstacle. For the first time since the First Vatican Council a pope had clearly spoken *ex cathedra*. Quite apart from the fact that a belief had thereby been proclaimed which the vast majority of non-Roman Churches did not share and which even in the view of most Roman Catholic theologians could not be established from holy Scripture and certainly not from Scripture alone, it seemed clear from this act that the Roman Catholic Church was unwilling to take account of the fellowship

---

[1] For the reaction of the W.C.C., see MRCC (Toronto 1950), p. 62.
[2] *Acta Apostolicae Sedis* (*AAS*) (1950), pp. 561-77.
[3] *Munificentissimus Deus*, *AAS* xlii (1950), pp. 753-71.

which had come into being as the result of the ecumenical movement. The disappointment this caused was such that in many places initially promising contacts were broken off. Reactions were frank and explicit[1] and many non-Roman Catholics saw their picture of Rome confirmed.[2] Criticisms now made contained a new element, however. They latched not merely on to doctrinal error but also on to the lack of ecumenical spirit. Increasingly the Roman Catholic Church found itself charged with lacking any interest at all in unity.

The Orthodox Churches also joined in this criticism, indeed they often expressed themselves much more forcibly. Although on the Roman Catholic side the special and substantial relationship to Orthodoxy was stressed with increasing frequency, the estrangement between the Churches was no less great. The Pope's utterances about the Churches of the East could serve only to widen the gulf. For example, the encyclical *Sempiternus rex*, which was addressed to the Eastern Churches on 8 September 1951 on the occasion of the commemoration of Chalcedon, was expressed in terms which could not but wound the Orthodox reader, as had also been the case with the earlier *Orientalis ecclesiae decus* (9 April 1944). "Let those who, because of the iniquity of the times, especially in Eastern lands, are separated from the bosom and unity of the Church, follow the teaching and example of their forefathers and not hesitate to render duly reverent homage to the Primacy of the Roman Pontiff . . . ".[3]

The Roman Catholic Church's attitude to the ecumenical movement placed the World Council of Churches in a particularly difficult position. What was its reaction to be? Was not the ecumenical movement bound to continue to direct itself to the whole of Christendom? All who confessed Jesus Christ as God and Saviour must be led together into one fellowship. Must not everything be done, therefore, to further relationships? There were indeed many who at heart, usually silently but sometimes openly, were glad that the Roman Church stood aside. Many member Churches would have been embarrassed by active co-operation. But the movement had to remain in principle open and to keep the Roman Catholic Church in view. Many leaders of the ecumenical movement openly expressed the hope that

---

[1] One of the most thorough and detailed commentaries was that produced by professors of the Theological Faculty of Heidelberg, *Evangelisches Gutachten zur Dogmatisierung der leiblichen Himmelfahrt Mariens* (Munich 1950).

[2] The Mariological encyclicals of the following years, *Fulgens corona gloriae* (8 September 1953) and *Ad caeli reginam* (11 October 1954), showed that Rome intended to continue steadily along the road once taken.

[3] *Sempiternus rex*, para. 4. On all the papal utterances concerning the Eastern Churches in the years 1850–1950, see P. E. Hermann in the periodical *Periodica de re morali et liturgica* (Rome 1950–1). Relations with the Slav Orthodox Churches were further complicated by the attitude which the Roman Catholic Church adopted towards communism. Many papal statements deal with the persecutions in the East; but the Orthodox Christians are hardly mentioned (cf. encyclical *Orientales Ecclesias* (15 December 1952). The dissolution of the Uniate Churches in the Ukraine (1946) and in Rumania (1948) created a special problem still unresolved to this day. Cf. encyclical *Orientales omnes* (1945), and a text of 17 July 1948.

ultimately even fellowship with the Roman Church might become possible.[1] The rejection was, indeed, so categorical that the World Council of Churches could develop, at least at first, only as a fellowship of non-Roman Churches. If practical co-operation of any kind was to be achieved between Churches, the attitude of the Roman Catholic Church could not be constantly taken into consideration. The essential inconsistencies of this situation frequently showed themselves, in a particularly blatant way at the Amsterdam Assembly,[2] but also on subsequent occasions. In general the World Council adopted a waiting attitude and avoided controversy as well as any special cultivation of contacts with the Roman Catholic Church.

Official statements about the ecumenical movement and negative reactions to signs of renewal in theology were clearly only the outward expression of the spirit which dominated in Rome. Theologians participating in the ecumenical movement found themselves increasingly in trouble. The Holy Office intensified its surveillance and, especially from 1950 onwards, many of them were proceeded against. During these years many of the theologians who had made a decisive contribution to the advance of ecumenical thought were warned, forbidden to publish their works, or forced to give up their work as teachers. To mention only a few who were affected in one or the other way: Yves Congar,[3] Henri de Lubac, Karl Rahner, John Courtney Murray, M. D. Chenu, Pierre Yves Féres. A period of mistrust and suspicion began. In some instances it lasted even into the pontificate of John XXIII. As late as 1962, immediately prior to the opening of the Council, two professors of the Papal Biblical Institute in Rome were temporarily suspended from their chairs.

Although these measures undoubtedly caused much suffering in the lives of many people, they could not halt the ecumenical movement. Even if ecumenical activity had to keep the limits imposed, it nevertheless still continued. A variety of levels must be mentioned here. Firstly, even in these years co-operation in theological study and scholarship was intensified. Existing societies of an academic nature continued their work and others were founded.[4] Of particular significance was the exchange in biblical and patristic studies. But even contacts of an academic nature established between particular Churches were maintained. One important example of this was the *Evangelisch–katholische ökumenische Arbeitskreis* which had been founded in Germany in 1945 with the express approval of the church authorities. Presided over by Bishop Wilhelm Stählin and Archbishop Lorenz Jaeger,

---

[1] Archbishop William Temple said, for example, in his sermon at the opening of the Second World Conference on Faith and Order: "We deeply lament the absence from this collaboration of the great Church of Rome, the Church which more than any other has known how to speak to the nations so that the nations hear" (*Second World Conference on Faith and Order*, ed. Leonard Hodgson (London 1938), p. 20).

[2] Cf. Karl Barth's comments and the ensuing controversy with Jean Daniélou in "Amsterdamer Fragen und Antworten", *Theologische Existenz Heute*, no. 15 (Munich 1949).

[3] Cf. Yves Congar, *Chrétiens en dialogue* (Paris 1964), pp. xlv–lvii.

[4] Societas Veteris Testamenti, 1950; Societas Novi Testamenti; International Patristic Conference, 1952.

it met annually to discuss some important controversial theological subject.[1]

In these years a special part was played by a number of fraternities (for example the *Michaelsbruderschaft*), by certain Anglican orders, and above all by the monastic community at Taizé. Because of their own spiritual interests and aims, these communities had natural points of contact with the Roman Catholic Church and, since they did not represent the Church as such, they enjoyed much more freedom of movement.[2] The Taizé brothers in particular helped to prepare many Roman Catholics and Protestants for the ecumenical discussion. On the Roman Catholic side, special mention must be made of the Istina Centre, directed by Father Christophe Dumont, o.s.p., and the Benedictine Monasteries at Chevetogne and Niederaltaich.

Relations with the World Council were not severed either. Roman Catholic theologians followed its work with the greatest interest. It has often been said that the findings of the World Council were far more carefully studied, analysed, and interpreted on the Roman Catholic side than they were in many member Churches. This work of interpretation did not pass unheeded in the World Council and it is no exaggeration to say that in this quiet and unobtrusive way Roman Catholic theology was a continuing partner in the discussions in the World Council. Except for the Roman Catholic contribution many questions would have been posed differently. In particular, Roman Catholic theologians joined in the discussion of the ecclesiological significance of the World Council of Churches and when the World Council in 1950 was drawing up its statement *The Church, the Churches and the World Council of Churches*, the so-called Toronto statement, a discussion took place in Paris at the Istina Centre with Roman Catholic theologians. This exchange had considerable influence on the drafting of the document.[3]

An important step taken in 1952 was the founding of the *Conférence catholique pour les questions oecuméniques*, the purpose of which was to bring together Roman Catholic ecumenists for regular discussions. The initiative came from the two Dutch priests, Frans Thijssen and Jan Willebrands; the latter became its secretary. The very first theme for discussion obviously bore upon the World Council, namely, the Roman Catholic view of the *vestigia ecclesiae*, a term which had been employed in the Toronto statement. At the end of 1953, Father Willebrands established direct contact with the World Council and from then on the work of the *Conférence* was focused even more closely on the studies being pursued by the World Council. Preparations for the Second Assembly of the World Council of Churches in Evanston (1954) provided an appropriate occasion for a Roman Catholic statement. The *Conférence* produced a detailed study of the Evanston theme, "Christ—the Hope of the World". Father Yves Congar with others played

---

[1] A selection of the addresses given has been collected into a special volume; cf. *Pro Veritate, ein theologischer Dialog* (Münster-Kassel 1963), ed. Edmund Schlink and Hermann Volk.

[2] This freedom led occasionally to serious tensions with the Church to which the community was most closely related.

[3] Among the participants was Father Jérôme Hamer, o.p. He has since then frequently written on the questions raised by the Toronto statement.

a large part in drafting this document. Since it was rather late in arriving, it could only be duplicated and distributed at Evanston, otherwise it would certainly have left an even deeper mark on the discussion and reports.

Contacts with the *Conférence* from the World Council side were primarily in the hands of Pastor Hans-Heinrich Harms who at that time was working in the Division of Studies of the World Council. On several occasions he visited Rome to meet with Roman Catholic theologians. The Evanston Assembly had decided that the central theme for the World Council's study programme should be "The Lordship of Christ over the World and the Church". In 1956 the *Conférence* adopted this theme and after much correspondence it was arranged to hold a joint meeting in Assisi. The meeting was to have been held in 1960 and might well have been the open culmination of a more or less secret dialogue. But the proposed meeting had in the end to be abandoned through a serious deterioration of relations caused by an incident at the Central Committee's meeting in Rhodes, 1959.[1]

The deepening of relationships was the fruit, above all, of the contacts made in connection with the Week of Prayer for Christian Unity. These annual weeks provided an opportunity for representatives of different confessions to meet together in a frank and natural way, to pray together and to reflect upon the significance of the ecumenical movement. Many received the first stimulus towards their "ecumenical conversion" during these Weeks of Prayer.

Prayer for unity still faced one great difficulty at that time. On the Roman Catholic side there was no agreement about the way unity should be prayed for. The formula suggested by Abbé Paul Couturier: "to pray for the unity of the Church of Jesus Christ as He wills and when He wills", was not universally accepted. Indeed, it was vigorously opposed by many who regarded it as a dilution of fundamental convictions and above all, as a source of misunderstandings. Those who opposed it demanded that the specifically Roman Catholic understanding of unity should be clearly stated during these Weeks of Prayer. The chief exponents of this position were the Friars of the Atonement in the United States. Each year they produced material for the Week of Prayer from this standpoint and their literature was widely distributed in many countries. Their line was supported by Father Charles Boyer and the Unitas Centre in Rome which he directed. In numerous articles in his journal *Unitas*, Father Boyer urged the need to insist quite clearly on the principles of unity.[2]

The work done by Abbé Couturier in Lyons, and after his death in 1956 by Father Pierre Michalon, won increasing support in ever widening circles of the Roman Catholic Church. With every year the numbers of those prepared for joint prayer in this sense grew. Abbé Paul Couturier for this reason deserves a special place in the history of the ecumenical movement.[3] It was not surprising that the ceremonies in Lyons following his death

---

[1] See below, p. 326.

[2] Cf., for example, Father C. Boyer, "Le intenzioni della settimana dell'unità", *Unitas* (1960), pp. 97f.

[3] Cf. Maurice Villain, *L'Abbé Paul Couturier* (Louvain 1959)³.

assumed the proportions of a moving demonstration of the growing ecumenical fellowship.

In the following years co-operation with the World Council continued to develop. As early as 1942 the Faith and Order movement had decided to change the timing of the Week of Prayer, which had remained unchanged since 1920, in order to facilitate joint prayer with Roman Catholics. From 1958 onwards the preparation of material for the Week was co-ordinated and from 1960 onwards was discussed together in detail.[1]

The problem of conflicting intentions in such prayer for unity was explicitly and finally resolved after the Second Vatican Council. In 1966 complete agreement was reached between the Roman Catholic Church and the World Council of Churches concerning preparations for the Week of Prayer,[2] and since then the introductory leaflets for the Week of Prayer have been prepared by a mixed group.

All these pointers show how the ecumenical movement, despite all the difficulties, made further progress in the Roman Catholic Church beneath the surface. When John XXIII was elected Pope and shortly afterwards announced the calling of a Roman Catholic Council, the forces were already at hand to give shape to genuine ecumenical intentions, and the voices of theologians who had stood firm for their convictions and who had experienced hard times, now had the more weight just because of this spiritual trial.[3] Many of them played an important part at the Second Vatican Council and were shown marks of esteem which contrasted strangely with their earlier experiences.

The Pontificate of John XXIII and the Beginning of the Second Vatican Council

Pope Pius XII died in October 1958 and at the end of that month Cardinal Angelo Guiseppe Roncalli was elected to succeed him. Within a few months it became clear that this election would mark the beginning of a new era not only for the Roman Catholic Church but also for the ecumenical movement. On 25 January 1959 Pope John XXIII announced, to the surprise of the entire world and even of the circles closest to him, the calling of an "Ecumenical Council". The Pope himself declared that the decision had been a sudden inspiration "like the spontaneous flower of an unexpected springtime".[4] The idea had in fact suggested itself to some of his predecessors.

---

[1] Among these developments must be mentioned, for example, the setting up of the Conference to Promote Prayer for Unity in the United Kingdom. The suggestion of mutual collections, originally made by Oscar Cullmann in 1958, has played in important part in many places; cf. Oscar Cullmann, *Catholics and Protestants, A Proposal for Realizing Christian Solidarity* (London 1960).

[2] Cf. *Prayer for Unity:* The report of the consultation on "The Future of the Week of Prayer for Christian Unity" (Geneva, October 1966) in *One in Christ* (1967), pp. 251ff.

[3] "At the very moment when the Holy See emerged from its semi-absenteeism in ecumenical matters, it found the ground already turned over and sown, covered with a sturdy and already considerable crop."—Yves Congar, *Chrétiens en dialogue* (1964), p. liii.

[4] *Acta et documenta Concilio Oecumenica Vaticano II apparando* (Rome 1960), p. 45.

Pius XI[1] as well as Pius XII had seriously considered calling a Council. Pius XII reflected on the idea in the years 1949 to 1951 and a Commission appointed by him had explored the possibility in detail.[2] One may well wonder what would have emerged from a Council convened at such a time! Historically there is not much point in asking this question, however, because at that time the decision to hold a Council could hardly be taken; the Commission had to come to the conclusion that such an undertaking would involve too many risks.

What distinguished John XXIII's plan from earlier ones was the fact that he made his decision and announced it before giving commissions the task of weighing the pros and cons in detail and of establishing the procedure. This fact was of the greatest significance for the Council's course. The very absence of precise terms of reference at the beginning stirred the imagination and secured the attention of a far greater public. In a sense the charismatic decision was itself an appeal to the charismatic forces in the Church. Theologians and lay people began to speak of the renewal of the Church; the Roman Catholic Church began to live "in outline".

This new attitude was important for the ecumenical movement as well. The announcement did at first give rise to misunderstandings. Because the meaning attached to the term "ecumenical" in official Roman Catholic usage was not widely known, many thought that what was proposed was an inter-confessional assembly or that the real aim of the proposed Council was the reunion of Christendom. This assumption seemed to be justified by many utterances in the early days.[3] It was, however, quickly made clear that what was intended was an assembly of all the Roman Catholic bishops and that the main purpose was the renewal of the Roman Catholic Church. Only indirectly would the work of the Council promote the unity of all Christians. The Pope's own understanding of unity did not greatly differ from the traditional view. Like his predecessors he often spoke of return as the only way to unity.

> May this marvellous spectacle of unity which distinguishes the Catholic Church and which is a luminous example for all, together with her entreaties and prayers by which she implores of God the same unity for all, serve as an incitement to your mind and move it in a salutary manner. We say "your", for we are speaking to those who are separated from this Holy See . . . Note, we beg of you, that when we lovingly invite you to the unity of the Church we are inviting you not to the home of a stranger but to your own, to the Father's house which belongs to all . . .[4]

Although these papal utterances seemed to herald no decisive changes, the

---

[1] "Giovanni Caprile, Pio XI e la ripresa del Concilio Vaticano", *Civiltà Cattolica* (1966), qu. 2785, pp. 27–39.

[2] "Giovanni Caprile, Pio XII e un nuovo progetto di Concilio Ecumenico", *Civiltà Cattolica* (1966), qu. 2787–8, pp. 209–28.

[3] John XXIII declared, for example, on 30 January 1959, with reference to the Churches of the East: "We have no wish to conduct a trial of history. We have no wish to try to show who was right and who was wrong. Responsibility is shared. We simply wish to say: "Let us come together and make an end of divisions."

[4] Encyclical *Ad Petri cathedram* (29 June 1959), *AAS* LI, pp. 498ff.

opening announcement nevertheless continued to exercise great influence. Ideas which hitherto had been considered in relatively limited ecumenical circles were all at once thrown into the public discussion. The dam erected by *Humani generis* began to collapse. The chorus of voices urging that the way to unity should be seen not as a return but rather as the common renewal of all the Churches grew stronger. The Council should open the doors to this process. Polemics should give way to dialogue and the Roman Catholic Church should begin to learn from other Churches in the dialogue and adopt whatever might promote her own renewal. Although the validity of earlier statements was not in doubt, there was a great deal which might be glossed, interpreted, or restated for the sake of truth and for the sake of unity with the separated Churches. Deeper reflection on the tradition could prove important in this connection. Above all, ecclesiology was in need of renewal and enrichment. The Council would be able to contribute much to unity indirectly, by stressing the spiritual and sacramental rather than the juridical and institutional character of the Church, by making room for greater variety in the Church, by reducing in some measure the excessive centralism of recent decades, by redefining the relationship between the hierarchy and the people of God, making much clearer the Church's character as a fellowship, by a deeper understanding of the relationship between the one Church and divided Christendom, and by laying the foundation for serious recognition of the non-Roman Churches as Churches.[1]

Soon the preparations for the Council began to take shape. On 17 May 1959 the Pope nominated a *Commissio antepraeparatoria*, with the task of sounding the views of the bishops, and on 5 June 1960 the Preparatory Commissions were appointed. The same *Motu proprio Superno Dei nutu* also provided for the establishment of a Secretariat for Promoting Christian

---

[1] Countless names would have to be listed in this connection. Obviously we must mention once again men like Yves Congar, Christophe Dumont, and Oliver Rousseau, the pioneers who had for years supported the ecumenical movement. Gustav Weigel, S.J. did great service in the cause of spreading ecumenical thought in the Roman Catholic Church in the United States; cf. *A Catholic Primer on the Ecumenical Movement* (Woodstock Papers I, 1957), but, above all, *Catholic Theology in Dialogue* (New York 1961). George H. Tavard published a new history of the ecumenical movement which enjoyed wide circulation —*Two Centuries of Ecumenism* (London 1960). Karl Rahner wrote on a whole series of problems which were later to assume importance at the Council; cf., for example, Karl Rahner and Joseph Ratzinger, *The Episcopate and the Primacy* (New York 1963). Beside the older generation, however, a younger generation now claimed a hearing. The publication which aroused most interest and was quickly translated into many languages was Hans Küng's *Konzil und Wiedervereinigung, Erneuerung als Ruf zur Einheit*, 1960 (*The Council and Reunion*, London/New York 1961)—a book which, building on ideas long common to the ecumenical movement, outlined a new view of the ecumenical problem. He was one among many. It is only possible here to mention several. Gregory Baum, *That All May Be One* (1958), had even earlier attempted to interpret the view of unity in the papal documents in such a way as to enable the views of Roman Catholic ecumenists to claim the protection of the Church authority. Bernard Lambert, *Le problème oecuménique*, 1962 (*Ecumenism: Theology and History*, London 1966) provided one of the first extensive analyses of the whole ecumenical problem, an attempt which contained a host of new starting-points. Otto B. Roegele, *Was erwarten wir vom Konzil?* (1960), wrote from the standpoint of a layman. On the other hand, of course, there was no lack of conservative presentations.

Unity.[1] Cardinal Augustin Bea was named as its first President and Monsignor Jan Willebrands as its Secretary. The Commission, which was to be responsible for the activity of the Secretariat, was composed of seventeen voting members and nineteen consultants. This was a significant step forward. Although the Secretariat had originally been created simply in order to prepare for the Council, the function it fulfilled went far beyond this, and it later became clear that it not only had an important role to play in the Council itself but would also become a permanent organ even when the Council was over. If the Roman Catholic Church wished to communicate with other Churches officially, a special organ for this purpose was required and the other Churches needed to be clear to whom they should direct their communications. To a limited extent such a channel already existed for the Orthodox Churches. But the Congregation for the Eastern Churches was primarily responsible for the Uniate Churches and was, therefore, not in an advantageous position to encourage any other relationships.

The Secretariat for Christian Unity soon set to work. Its first full meeting took place in November 1960. Its immediate task was to inform non-Roman Catholics about the Council and to make possible their participation in a limited way. The idea soon gained ground that the non-Roman Churches should be invited to be represented at the Council by observers. But the Secretariat also had a role to play in the actual preparation of the Council itself. It had to draw the attention of Commissions to views which were of importance to the ecumenical movement and it produced a number of preparatory texts (on the ecumenical movement, on religious freedom, on prayer, on the Jewish people), and on others.

With the announcement of the Council and the creation of the Secretariat for Unity, there was a gradual change in the attitude of the Roman Catholic Church towards the World Council of Churches. The World Council's own attitude was at first cautious. The Executive Committee, meeting in Geneva in February 1959, shortly after the announcement of the Council, considered the new situation in detail. A brief communiqué summarized the most important results of the discussion. It drew attention firstly to the fact that much depended on the way in which "the Council will be called" and in what spirit "the question of unity will be approached". "The question is: How ecumenical will the Council be in composition and in spirit?" The communiqué next expressed the conviction that real progress on the way to unity could be made "when churches meet together on the basis of mutual respect and with a full commitment on the part of each church to the truth of the Gospel". It added finally that it would be of great gain to the ecumenical movement if "all the churches would join in securing full religious liberty for all people in all lands", a point which was to be frequently repeated in the days to come.

This first comment by the World Council is also significant as the first in a long series. Repeatedly from that time attitudes were articulated towards the developments in the Roman Catholic Church, and anyone reading through these statements will sense a steadily growing World Council involvement in

[1] *AAS* LII (1960), p. 433.

what was occurring. They show that this inner connection was intensified from sheer necessity.

There was a temporary setback in relationships because of an unfortunate incident at the meeting of the Central Committee in Rhodes (August 1959). Roman Catholic theologians, attending the meeting as journalists, met with Orthodox delegates and discussed with them the possibility of bilateral theological discussions. This action was felt on the World Council side to have been a breach of hospitality, especially since a little later a news item broadcast by Vatican Radio left the impression that high authorities in the Vatican had authorized this contact. It took a little time for misunderstandings to be dispelled and for confidence to be restored.

The situation then changed rapidly. The World Council invited the Roman Catholic Church to send observers to the meetings of the Faith and Order Commission and of the Central Committee at St Andrews (August 1960). The invitation was accepted. Father I. Beaupère, Father J. Hamer, and Father B. Leeming attended the meeting of the Faith and Order Commission and Mgr Willebrands and Father Leeming that of the Central Committee. Cardinal Bea attached great importance to putting the World Council in the picture from the very beginning about the creation and work of the Secretariat. Mgr Willebrands visited Geneva a few days after the Pope's decision and on 22 September, i.e., before the first full session of the Secretariat, Cardinal Bea and Dr W. A. Visser't Hooft met in Milan.[1] This meeting provided an opportunity to discuss many points. On the one hand, the sending of Roman Catholic observers to the Third Assembly in New Delhi was discussed, on the other, the way in which non-Roman Catholics might participate in the Vatican Council was considered. The idea of observers was examined, and it was agreed that the Secretariat should draft more detailed proposals. At the same time, plans were made for unofficial meetings about "Renewal of the Church" and "Religious Freedom as an inter-Church problem". These informal meetings would provide an indirect contribution to the preparations for the Council.[2]

Already in these first contacts a problem emerged which would frequently reappear in the years ahead. Was it possible for the World Council as a "fellowship of churches" to enter into a direct relationship with the Roman Catholic Church? Was it qualified to conduct conversations about the sending of observers? Could it agree to being itself represented by observers? Could it adopt a position on what was happening in the Roman Catholic Church? Could it establish a Joint Working Group and initiate a whole programme of joint work? Did it not have to leave all these steps to the individual member Churches? The World Council has no authority over the member Churches. It cannot speak or act for them. Above all, in the matter of achieving church unity they alone are competent to act. On the

[1] Cf. Augustin Kardinal Bea—Willem A. Visser't Hooft, *Friede zwischen Christen* Herder-Bücheri 269, 1966), pp. 14f.

[2] Only the second of these two conferences took place (1–12 May 1961). It was organized by the *Conférence catholique pour les questions oecuméniques* and the World Council of Churches.

other hand, however, could the World Council remain aloof? The Churches had come together and found each other within the Council and had committed themselves to ever greater unity in a provisional fellowship; was the Council not then bound to act in their name within the limits set and to seize the opportunities which presented themselves of developing the ecumenical movement?

This dilemma finds particularly clear expression in the statement issued at the Central Committee's meeting at St Andrews (1960). The statement recalled the limited powers of the World Council, but it also stressed the need to seize the opportunities now offered:

(a) The fact that a dialogue with the Roman Catholic Church becomes possible is to be welcomed.

(b) It is to be hoped, however, that this new development will not mean that the informal discussions which have been going on between Roman Catholic theologians and those of other churches will henceforth be entirely superseded by more official discussions, for at the present stage it is precisely the informal discussions which can best contribute to the removal of misunderstanding.

(c) No church should fear that the W.C.C. will in any way seek to act or speak for its member churches in matters concerning church union. The W.C.C. is, according to its constitution, not authorized to act for the churches in such matters. In these matters each church takes its own decisions in full freedom. This is for us an obvious point. But it must be made because the question is sometimes raised whether the W.C.C. will enter into formal or informal conversations with the Roman Catholic Church about church union. The answer is that this is quite out of the question because of the character of our movement.

(d) The W.C.C. may, however, use such opportunities as may present themselves to make known to the new Secretariat certain basic convictions which have been expressed by the Assembly or Central Committee (e.g. issues of religious liberty, of Christian social action, etc.).

(e) It should be remembered that the creation of the Secretariat does not mean that any of the fundamental differences which exist between the Roman Catholic Church and the churches in the W.C.C. have been solved. The change is a change in procedure and climate. The opportunity for dialogue is to be grasped, but it means that the real problems will come to the fore. Our task in that dialogue will be to represent the insights which God has given us together in the fifty years since our movement was started.[1]

Subsequent statements were progressively less reserved. The need for direct contacts with the Roman Catholic Church was ever more widely recognized. The tension evident in the St Andrews statement, however, continued to accompany the extension of relationships and has not been completely overcome even today.

Relationships were strengthened by the sending of five Roman Catholic observers to the Assembly at New Delhi. No Roman Catholic observers had been present at the Second Assembly at Evanston, any more than at the First Assembly at Amsterdam; indeed, on the very eve of the Evanston Assembly

---

[1] MRCC (St Andrews 16–24 August 1960), p. 105.

the Archbishop of Chicago, Cardinal Stritch, had issued a clear warning against the ecumenical movement in a pastoral letter.[1] Since then the situation had changed. Even so the appointment of the Roman Catholic observers still proved difficult. The Holy Office claimed the right to settle the question and decided that no observers should be sent. The Secretariat for Unity appealed to the Pope and succeeded in having this decision reversed. It was forced, however, to abandon its original list of nominees and to choose theologians who were not among the Secretariat's consultants. The outcome of this dispute made plain the Secretariat's determination to carry out the functions entrusted to it.

The Assembly repeatedly expressed its joy at the presence of the Roman Catholic observers and at the developments in the Roman Catholic Church generally. With regard to the Second Vatican Council, the words which made the deepest impression summed the matter up in this way: "It would undoubtedly mean much for Christendom and the world if it became clear . . . that these councils do not meet against each other and that each does not seek its own advantage but seeks only to serve the Lord Jesus Christ."[2]

Soon after the Assembly, preparations for the Second Vatican Council entered a new phase. On 25 December, 1961 the Pope announced that the Council would meet the following year. The Secretariat, meanwhile, had already prepared a statute dealing with the observers who were to be invited. Negotiations with the Churches could begin. The Secretariat made direct contact with the Patriarch of Constantinople and the other ancient Patriarchs. The invitation was delivered to the Ecumenical Patriarch and, since Athenagoras I had often expressed his interest in the Council, it was generally expected that Orthodoxy would be represented there by observers. But, in fact, after sounding out the views of other Orthodox Churches, the Ecumenical Patriarch felt unable for the present to accept the invitation. Many of the Orthodox were of the opinion that it demeaned Orthodoxy to send mere observers who could have no real part in the proceedings.

The Patriarch of Moscow, to everyone's surprise, finally decided to accept the invitation. Just before the opening of the Council, two observers, Archpriest Vitaly Borovoy and Vladimir Katliarov, arrived in Rome. Evidently misunderstandings had arisen. The Moscow Patriarchate had assumed that Constantinople had already decided in favour of accepting the invitation. The resultant imbalance did not last long. The number of Orthodox observers increased at later sessions. The other Eastern Churches and the Anglican Communion were invited in like manner. Mgr Jan Willebrands paid personal visits to the Patriarchs and to the Archbishop of Canterbury.

Inviting the other Churches presented special problems. As a result of many discussions it had been concluded that it would be better to approach the confessional families rather than the Churches of each country, and the Secretariat set to work on this basis. The positive response of certain Churches was already assured. Contacts with the Lutheran World Federation, for example, had been favourable. On 3 April 1962 Mgr Willebrands was able,

[1] Cf. *Ecumenical Review*, vol. vii (January 1955), p. 169.
[2] Edmund Schlink in *New Delhi Report*, ed. W. A. Visser't Hooft, p. 6.

through the good offices of the World Council of Churches, to outline the plans for the forthcoming Vatican Council to the executive secretaries of the World Confessional Organizations then meeting in Geneva. He asked them to inform him whether they were willing to accept an invitation to send observers. With the exception of the Baptist World Alliance, the Churches accepted this offer. The only individual Churches to receive an invitation to send observers were the Evangelical Church in Germany and, later, the Kyodan (Japan) and the Church of South India. Shortly before the opening of the Council, the number of observers was further increased by several personally invited guests, including in particular Oscar Cullmann and two Taizé brothers.[1]

The invitation to the World Council of Churches was dealt with at the Central Committee at its meeting in Paris (August 1962). Although the invitation was accepted without lengthy discussion, the choice of the observers presented difficulties. It had originally been intended to send two observers, one representing the Eastern tradition and the other the Western. An Orthodox bishop was proposed, but Orthodox delegates raised objections to the World Council's being represented by a bishop. In the end it was decided to appoint only one observer. At subsequent sessions the World Council was able to fill the two to three places offered to it.

These conversations and negotiations could not have produced the results they did had not the preparations for the Council been followed in the Churches with growing interest. The announcement of the Council had aroused the theological and spiritual interest not only of the Roman Catholic Church but of the other Churches as well, particularly the Churches of the West. The General Secretary of the World Council expressed something of the mood of that time when, in his report to the Central Committee in Paris (1962), he raised the serious question as to whether there was to be a genuine dialogue, on the one hand, and on the other hand strongly emphasized the fact that the Vatican Council was the concern of all the Churches: *Nostra res agitur*.[2] The growing interest was initially expressed in a great flood of publications. Many non-Roman Catholic theologians published their views on the forthcoming Council on the Roman Catholic Church and its relationship to other Churches, or on particular aspects of doctrine and practice where more thorough discussion could lead to greater unity. The announcement of the Council gave a fresh stimulus to ecumenical discussion and, to some extent, even provided new themes.[3] The Churches themselves also began to take a more active interest in what was happening. In December 1960 the Archbishop of Canterbury, Dr G. Fisher, visited the Pope; his successor, sometime later, appointed a permanent representative in Rome. The

[1] In all there were about 150 observers who attended the Council for longer or shorter periods or were present at one or other of its sessions. Only a few followed the entire proceedings: cf. *Observateurs-délégués et hôtes du Secrétariat pour l'Unité des Chrétiens au Deuxième Concile du Vatican* (Vatican 1965).

[2] General Secretary's Report, MRCC (Paris 1962), p. 79.

[3] Particularly striking is the number of publications dealing with the history and nature of Councils; cf., for example, *The Councils of the Church, History and Analysis*, ed. H. J. Margull (1966).

330 THE MOVEMENT AND THE ROMAN CATHOLIC CHURCH

Lutheran World Federation gave a group of theologians the task of preparing a volume containing not only detailed information about the Council but also comments on the developments in the Roman Catholic Church.[1] In 1962 Professor Edmund Schlink spent some time in Rome making contacts and keeping the Evangelical Church in Germany fully informed about the work being prepared. Examples of this kind could easily be multiplied.

As relationships continued to improve, preparations for the Council had also advanced. The commissions and secretariats had produced a great many documents. Friends of the ecumenical movement with knowledge of these documents were far from satisfied with their contents. The traditional attitude seemed to have gained the ascendancy despite all the changes. They began to issue warnings against exaggerated hopes, and right up to the opening of the Council remained completely unsure what its outcome would be. The turning-point was the address given by Pope John XXIII at the opening of the Council on 12 October 1962, an event in many respects comparable with the first announcement of the Council. Instead of presenting the assembled bishops with a detailed programme, the Pope limited himself to indicating a few general guide-lines: the Council would be primarily pastoral in character, it would be an expression of love and would, therefore, pronounce no anathemas. He also took the opportunity of asserting that one should distinguish between the *depositum fidei* and its formulation, a hint whose importance can hardly be exaggerated. Was this not the opening of a door? Did it not prevent the Council from merely repeating unaltered the old formulas? Was it not now free, with a freedom hitherto abjured, to seek the formulation demanded by the present age? The whole address, but this hint especially, made clear the Pope's wish that the Council should develop a "personality" of its own. It should not be content merely to safeguard and transmit the received heritage but, as an assembly of this age, was to speak to this age.

It would exceed the purpose and the proportions of this chapter to relate the course of the Council in detail. Even if we restricted our narration to the most important events, it would take us too far.[2] All we can do here is to recall certain steps of decisive importance for the development of the ecumenical movement. This rapid survey will also bring out the unresolved difficulties inherent in the present ecumenical situation.

The First Session made it clear that the Roman Catholic Church's attitude towards the other Churches would change in a far-reaching way. It had been obvious from the outset that the Council would deal with the question of relations with other Churches. The theme of unity had been from the be-

[1] K. E. Skydsgaard, ed., *The Papal Council and the Gospel: Protestant Theologians Evaluate the coming Vatican Council* (Minneapolis 1961); cf. also the later volumes, G. A. Lindbeck, ed., *Dialogue on the Way: Protestants report from Rome on the Vatican Council* (Minneapolis 1964); W. A. Quanbeck ed., *Challenge and Response: Protestant Perspective of the Vatican Council* (Minneapolis 1966).

[2] A great many accounts have appeared, for example:
Antoine Wenger, *Vatican II*, 4 vols. Paris 1962–6.
Robert Rouquette, s.j., *La fin d'une chrétienté*, Chroniques, 2 vols. Paris 1968.
Bernard Lambert, *De Rome à Jérusalem*. Paris 1964.
René Laurentin, *Bilan du Concile*. Paris 1966.

ginning so much to the fore that it was bound to be discussed. What was still quite uncertain was how this would be done. Which view of unity would carry the day? Would the views and proposals of those who had been involved in the ecumenical movement have decisive influence, or would the old traditional view be repeated in different terms? Would the Council deal with the question in a way that would invite controversy and produce upheaval? Or would it adopt some formula easy to accept and therefore of no great consequence?

The debates of the First Session made it clear that the majority of the bishops were not only eager to pose the problem but also ready to tread new paths. The desire to arrive at a new understanding of the separated brethren, the desire for encounter and dialogue was more and more widely shared. True, many were able to express this desire only in inadequate ways. Many started from a view of unity and of the ecumenical movement from which it was difficult to see the need for encounter, dialogue, and joint witness. For many this First Session was an unexpected revelation and experience to assimilate which took time. But at least the proceedings of the First Session soon made it clear that the Council would not be satisfied with a hasty solution.

The way the texts presented to the bishops for discussion were dealt with indicated that this was the case. Two *schemata* on unity had been distributed during the First Session. One was the work of the Theological Commission, the other of the Commission for the Eastern Churches. Neither document was much more than a fresh summary of traditional views. The one spoke of the one Church in such a way that there could hardly be any question of other Churches. The other explained how those Christians separated from Rome, particularly those of the Eastern tradition, could restore unity. A third document, prepared by the Secretariat for Unity, was not brought to the notice of the bishops at all. The Council found itself unable to accept either of the texts and they were referred back. A mixed commission was entrusted with the drafting of a new text. The Secretariat for Unity, which at the very beginning of the Session had been given equal status with the other conciliar Commissions, would play the decisive role in this mixed Commission.

Other texts experienced similar treatment, especially the *schema* on the Sources of Revelation. This text was of great importance for the further course of the Council, since here the question of the relation of Scripture and tradition would be decided. Would the final text be one in which scripturally oriented theological thinking played a greater role? Or would it simply reaffirm the Tridentine position? The first draft did not seem very promising in this respect, but, in a memorable vote on 20 November 1962, it was referred back by the Council by a large majority. Although the requisite two-thirds majority was not obtained, the Pope nevertheless decided that a new *schema* should be drafted.

These decisions were much more important than their description suggests. By rejecting these draft texts the Council had already in principle decided in favour of real relationships with other Churches. True, a great variety of motives played their part in these decisions and the Council was very far from a common mind. While many simply clung to traditional ideas, others believed that the goal might be reached without really radical changes. Only a minority was clear what participation in the ecumenical movement would mean. The future course of the Council could still produce stubborn resistance and disappointing reactions. Yet something like a breakthrough had been achieved. A change had become imperative in the Roman Catholic Church and, consequent on this, in the other Churches as well. *Heil uns, weh uns, der Tauwind weht!*(Nietzsche), as someone exclaimed after the first reports of the First Session.

The presence of the observers had not been without influence on the course so far. The observers had, of course, no possibility of taking any active part in the proceedings. Many of them were instructed by their Churches to exercise the greatest reserve.[1] Yet their very presence had the profound effect of continually pointing to the ecumenical problem. Over and above this, they were able each week to talk informally with members of the Secretariat about the texts being discussed, and many of their comments were passed on to the appropriate commissions. The longer the Council went on, the greater became their freedom of action. Some individual observers produced actual commentaries, and it is possible in some cases to discover traces of these in the conciliar documents. Perhaps even more important were the personal conversations and the meetings in small groups.

The First Session ended without having produced any tangible results. But, in a way far removed from what was originally intended, the Council had become a "spectacle" which drew the attention of the whole world. The very differences which had appeared put the Roman Catholic Church in a new light. The picture which the Roman Catholic Church had presented to non-Roman Catholic Christians began to change and for the first time large numbers began to follow with impartial interest what was happening in the Roman Catholic Church. This change is reflected in the almost unlimited and unqualified sympathy evoked by Pope John XXIII on all sides. The encyclical *Pacem in terris*, although hardly any more remarkable than earlier documents apart from its universal aims, met with a response never given to any papal document. This sympathy deepened still more during the Pope's last illness. John XXIII had become a symbol of agreement, peace, dialogue, and friendship among men. When he died, shortly after Pentecost 1963, he was universally mourned.

The change that had taken place soon made itself felt in the ecumenical movement. An increasing number of Roman Catholics participated in ecumenical meetings. The character of the ecumenical movement began to change. Whereas before at best only a section of the different separated Churches had taken part, now increasingly all traditions were represented. The first example of this on a wider scale was the Fourth World Conference on Faith and Order, held in Montreal (July 1963). Even here, to be sure, the Roman Catholic Church was represented only by observers. But their participation in fact went much further. The themes to be discussed at the Conference had been previously discussed at a special meeting with Roman

[1] Cf., for example, MRCC (Paris 1962), p. 26.

Catholic theologians (18–23 March 1963) at the Ecumenical Institute in Bossey. Papers by Roman Catholic theologians had been distributed to the members of the Conference. As well as the official observers, many guests and journalists attended and took so active a part in the proceedings that the Roman Catholic position was as fully presented as that of any other Church. One of the chief speakers at the conference was a Roman Catholic, Father Raymond Brown. The spirit of fellowship found visible expression in a great public gathering held in the Catholic University of Montreal, with Cardinal Léger of Montreal taking part along with leaders of the Conference.

The work of the Conference produced some remarkable and to some extent unexpected agreements. In particular, the report on the problem of Tradition revealed an important consensus. The report which was agreed upon would have some influence on later discussions at the Second Vatican Council and on the drafting of the Constitution *De divina revelatione*. Certainly the Conference also proved how little the new situation had even then been exhausted either spiritually or intellectually. The President of the Conference, Bishop Oliver S. Tomkins, spoke of "promising chaos",[1] and, while this phrase does not quite do justice to the positive results of the Conference, it surely characterized accurately something of the mood which prevailed in it, as well as that of the whole period between the First and Second Sessions[2] of the Vatican Council.

The comment also sprang from something else which the Conference experienced. Whereas previously the dominant theme of the Faith and Order movement had been ecclesiology in the strict sense, the Montreal delegates suddenly saw this theme in a new light. Was not the search for church unity basically only a secondary question? Should not attention be concentrated mainly on the Church's proving itself to be the Church in the modern world? At least the connection between the concern for unity and this self-authentication of the Church in the world must be demonstrated. And did this not mean tackling new theological themes? The Conference posed this question with great urgency and, while not reaching any firm conclusions, the discussions revealed a whole complex of problems which, in the coming years, and in connection with the Second Vatican Council, would become inescapable.

Shortly after the Faith and Order Conference, the Central Committee held its annual meeting (Rochester, New York, August 1963). After receiving the report on the First Session of the Second Vatican Council, it issued a short statement. This statement first expressed gratitude for what had happened in the Council. It next recalled that Christ was the basis of all genuine ecumenical dialogue, and stressed that the mutual recognition of the divided Churches as Churches was of great importance for the development of the dialogue. Whereas previously it had always been critical problems which had been mentioned (problems hampering relationships, such as, for example, religious

---

[1] Cf. *The Fourth World Conference on Faith and Order* (Montreal 1963), p. 7.

[2] At the Fourth Assembly of the Lutheran World Federation in Helsinki (Summer 1963) and at the Meeting of the Division of World Mission and Evangelism (December 1963) Roman Catholic observers took an active part in the proceedings.

freedom and mixed marriages), now for the first time it spoke also of the need to reach the maximum of agreement in the missionary activity of the Church.[1]

Continuation of the Second Vatican Council under the Pontificate of Paul VI

On 21 June, 1963, after a relatively short conclave, Cardinal Giovanni Battista Montini, Archbishop of Milan, was chosen to succeed Pope John XXIII. A few days later he was enthroned as Pope Paul VI. He at once declared that he intended to continue the Council in the spirit of his predecessor, and it soon became clear that he was determined to introduce reforms. Shortly after his entry to office, addressing the members of the Curia, he announced a thorough reorganization of the central structures. This caused a sensation and had an encouraging effect on the forces seeking a renewal of the Church.[2]

The beginning of his pontificate came, of course, at a time when the character of the Council was bound to change, apart from any change in the supreme leadership of the Church. In its First Session the Council had made its own the widespread demand for renewal, openness, and dialogue. On this basis it had rejected many draft texts. Now it had to work out in detail what it proposed to say affirmatively. Anything radically new was out of the question. Although Pope John XXIII had introduced the distinction between the *depositum fidei* and its formulation and thereby made many new developments possible, this distinction nevertheless rested on the conviction that the Church had at all times preserved the *depositum fidei*, and it followed, therefore, that all the Council's statements had to be shown to be in some way an organic continuation of earlier statements. When the drafting of the texts began, discussion was, therefore, inevitably dominated to a much greater extent by a consideration of the past. Much of the momentum characteristic of the First Session was in consequence lost and many deplored this change. One African bishop, for example, declared after a few weeks of the Second Session that he suddenly found himself, after the invigorating heights of the First Session, back once more in the undergrowth of European history. But this development was undoubtedly inevitable.

In his opening address at the Second Session, Pope Paul VI announced that ecclesiology would be the central theme of the whole Council.[3] This decision had been in the air from the beginning. Already towards the end of the First Session, Cardinal Suenens had pointed out in a widely noted speech that this theme was fundamental to almost all the *schemata* with which the Council would be dealing. This choice of theme in fact was almost inevitable. The First Vatican Council had intended to clarify the doctrine of the Church and a text had even been prepared. Only the premature ending of that Council had prevented its discussion. Was it not essential to

[1] MRCC (Rochester 1963), pp. 32ff.
[2] 21 September 1963; cf. *AAS* LV (1963), pp. 793ff.
[3] *AAS* LV (1963), pp. 841ff.

complete what had been begun? In any event this theme was central to the theological and practical interests of the Roman Catholic Church. Countless questions towards which the Council would have to adopt a position if it was not to disappoint expectations were rooted in ecclesiological assumptions (such as renewal of worship, mission of the laity, missionary activity of the Church). It was, therefore, in this area that the theological orientation had to be found.

At the same time, the Pope's address undoubtedly provided a glimpse of the problems facing the Second Vatican Council. Ecclesiology was not a theme where discussion could move with complete freedom. There were the statements of the First Vatican Council to reckon with and the question arose how those statements were to be related to the new insights into the Church's nature and task in the world today. The discussions of the First Session had projected a new picture of the Church. Three distortions of its nature—legalism, hierarchism, triumphalism—had again and again been condemned. The Church was to be seen, much more than it had ever been seen before, as a fellowship of the Spirit, as the people of God, and as a servant. But what did this "much more" mean? Was it a matter of expanding and developing the statements of the First Vatican Council by these new emphases? Or was a thorough revision absolutely essential? The sharpest debates of the Council centred around this question. Nobody questioned the binding force of the First Vatican Council's doctrinal statements for the Church, but opinion was divided as to how those statements were to be interpreted today. Even the texts finally agreed upon are not fully clear on this point. Old and new stand side by side, often unconnected, and leave unanswered the question whether the new is to be interpreted in terms of the old or vice versa.

There were also obvious ecumenical reasons pressing this theme to the fore. If genuine relationships with other Churches were to be established, was not fresh clarification needed as to the nature of the Church and especially as to the nature of its unity? Hitherto the Roman Catholic Church had stood aside from the ecumenical movement mainly for ecclesiological reasons. Was it not incumbent on her now to explain why participation in that movement was not only possible but even mandatory today? But even here discussion was bound to produce a discordant result. She could not simply abandon the reasons which had held her back from the ecumenical movement, and, since her ecclesiology was developed on the basis of Roman Catholic presuppositions, even the convictions which divided the Roman Catholic Church from other Churches had to be given a fresh lease of life. Therefore the texts finally promulgated have a double tendency. On the one hand, they make it plain that the differences which had in the past prevented agreement, particularly the doctrine of the primacy and universal jurisdiction of the Pope, have not been left behind. On the other hand, they show that today there are far more points of contact between the Churches.

Insights into the nature of the Church, the fruit of the biblical, liturgical, and ecumenical movements of recent decades, have increasingly become the common possession of all Churches. What is the relationship between these

M

two tendencies? What view of the ecumenical movement follows from the tension between them? Is it to be mere openness towards the "separated brethren" or the joint witness of all Christians? Emphasis on the uniqueness and centrality of the Roman Catholic Churches or the fellowship of all Churches? Non-Roman Christians too were thereby presented with a difficult problem. Ought they to heed the warnings of those who were urging that in principle nothing had changed? Or should they take seriously the evidence of change, the new emphases and, above all, the steady spiritual impetus, and cultivate the fellowship? Even today the tension between these various possibilities still exists. Since the Second Vatican Council this is one of the problems with which the ecumenical movement has to live and for which a solution will be found only as it lives with it.

What was the new Pope's role in these debates? Perhaps his position may best be described by saying that on the one hand he seeks to preserve the Church's tradition in all its range and on the other hand is convinced of the need for the Church to break out of its isolation and to present an effective witness in the modern world. This twofold attitude has most clearly emerged in the way he has understood and exercised his office. He brought with him a high view of the papal office. As Archbishop of Milan he had already on occasion spoken vigorously of the significance of the Roman See.[1] He had spent a good deal of his life working in the Vatican in the Secretariat of State. He was well acquainted with the problems of the Curia. He had always been profoundly convinced of Rome's high mission. When, during the Council's proceedings, he saw the papal authority endangered, he frequently and sometimes a little anxiously issued reminders that this authority was not to be diminished. At the same time he sought to give his office a new significance. Whereas earlier popes had represented the Church's centre in a static way, he sought to secure it a hearing in a dynamic way.

Symbolic of the Pope's conception of his office are the journeys which he has undertaken. To the surprise of the bishops, he announced at the close of the Second Session his intention to undertake a pilgrimage to Jerusalem to the sources of the gospel. The unusual character of this proposal exercised a great fascination, and the journey was followed with great interest and sympathy by the entire world. Shortly thereafter he made a second "missionary" journey, this time to India. The occasion was the Eucharistic Congress in Bombay (Autumn 1964). Perhaps even more significant was his visit to the United Nations Organization in New York during the Fourth Session (4 October 1965). Here the mission of the Holy See was fulfilled in a dramatic way: the Pope as the messenger of peace before the nations of the world. His

---

[1] For example, in a pastoral letter to the archdiocese of Milan (Easter 1962) he said: " . . . Rome is the city of the Church; a Council is a phase of the Church's fullness. Rome is the city of Christ; a Council is a period when Christ's mystic presence operates in his Church and in the world. So it seems to us that the Council will give Rome a period of sublime splendour greater than it has ever enjoyed before . . . a charism of prophecy will animate Rome and the human city will be transmuted into a city of God. Rome will become Jerusalem . . ." (*The Mind of Paul VI*, ed. James Walsh, s.j., introduction by Cardinal Bea (London 1964), p. 225; cf. also pp. 223ff, 250).

numerous later efforts to further the peace of the world should also be mentioned in this context.[1]

In August 1964, a little more than a year after entering on his pontificate, Paul VI published his first encyclical *Ecclesiam suam*, a document of programmatic character, which decisively influenced the further course of the Council.[2] In this the Pope expounded his view of the Church and its task in the world. He adopted the concept of dialogue and sketched a picture of the Church turning responsibly with understanding and in service towards the near and the far. The document elicited a mixed response. On the one hand, the Pope's stand in favour of openness and renewal and his consequent encouragement of the best elements in the Vatican Council were welcomed; on the other hand, doubts were raised. On the basis of such a view could there be any real encounter between the Churches? Did it not place the Roman Catholic Church too much in the centre, and around it, in ever descending concentric circles, other Christians, Jews, non-Christian religions, and other men, whether of good will or bad? Was not dialogue here, therefore, a unilateral affair rather than the encounter of equal partners willing to learn from each other?

At the end of the Third Session, three conciliar texts were approved which are particularly important for the ecumenical movement: the Dogmatic Constitution of the Church, the Decree on Ecumenism, and the Decree on the Eastern Catholic Churches. In these texts the Council expressed the essence of its understanding of the ecumenical movement. The texts had been several times discussed and frequently revised during the Second and Third Sessions. The Council had been able to formulate in these documents a series of agreed statements which hardly anyone would have thought possible at the beginning of the Council or even after the Second Session. Taken as a whole, the Decree on Ecumenism presents an understanding of the ecumenical movement which makes encounter with other Churches possible in a way which is convincing. The new attitude can be illustrated by a change which was adopted in the course of the debates. An earlier version of the Decree still spoke of presenting the principles of Roman Catholic ecumenism whereas the final text reads "Roman Catholic principles of ecumenism". This change expresses in the shortest possible way that the Roman Catholic Church does not wish to rival the ecumenical movement but to align itself with it.

Even in the final text it is still possible to discern the different tendencies represented in the Council. Many questions are left open, many expressions can be variously interpreted. Different conclusions may be drawn from it according to the hermeneutical criteria employed. This was indeed the reason why the debates on the Decree continued right to the very last

[1] The series of journeys was continued after the Council. When Florence was overwhelmed by floods in 1966, the Pope visited the city and celebrated the Christmas Mass there. The journey to Fatima in May 1967 aroused mixed feelings because of its political connotations. Shortly afterwards came the visit to the Ecumenical Patriarch in Constantinople (July 1967) and in the following year the visit to Colombia for the Eucharistic Congress being celebrated there.

[2] *AAS* LVI (1964), pp. 609ff.

moment. The opposition tried to secure modifications in the text in the closing days of the session, and even to postpone the promulgation. The Pope himself intervened in this dispute. When the text seemed to have been finalized, he himself presented a list of emendations designed to remove certain obscurities. Some of these restricted the openness of the text. Two other facts cast a certain shadow over the promulgation. Simultaneously with the Decree another text, dealing with the Eastern Catholic Churches in communion with Rome, was also approved. The document as such presented no special difficulties—why should the Roman Catholic Church not express its mind on this important internal problem? But the document also included references to relations with the Orthodox Churches and the question was inevitably raised why these comments were made in this context. Even more distressing was the fact that the Declaration on Religious Freedom should by rights also have been promulgated; but the opposition succeeded in delaying the vote and demanding further revision. Although these events of the final weeks caused considerable sensation, the fact remained that with the promulgation of the Decree the Roman Catholic Church had explicitly and irrevocably committed itself to the ecumenical movement. Compared with this fact, the qualifications and disappointments of the final weeks carried little weight.

The Council's proceedings were, of course, followed closely in the World Council of Churches, and, as the work advanced, the question presented itself with growing urgency: What form would relations between the Roman Catholic Church and the World Council take in the future? Would there be any relations at all? Was not the interest of the Roman Catholic Church directed more to the individual Churches than to the World Council? Was she not more interested in constructing her own network of relationships than in aligning herself with an existing fellowship of Churches? Isolated voices even went so far as to predict the end of the World Council in its present form. The former Archbishop of Canterbury, Dr G. Fisher, proposed, for example, that the Council should be transformed into an organization for inter-Church aid, an organization loose enough to present the Roman Catholic Church with no difficulties in joining its membership. Future development depended, of course, largely on how the Vatican Council would define the ecumenical task of the Roman Catholic Church. If it went no further than an ecumenism centred on the Roman Catholic Church, no genuine relationship with the World Council seemed likely to be possible. But if there were some stress on dialogue, co-operation, and joint witness of all Churches, then such a relationship was almost inevitable.

The drafts of the Constitution *De ecclesia* and the Decree *De oecumenismo* which had been discussed and revised at the Second Session gave rise to fears that a narrow view of ecumenism might win the day at the Council. There was a danger of real tensions emerging. At its meeting in Osades (10–14 February 1964), the Executive Committee of the World Council discussed this situation at length. The brief statement on "Christian Unity", issued as a result of this discussion, betrays something of the anxiety which dominated the meeting. "The real crux of the ecumenical problem remains that of the relationships between the churches. The question is how separated Churches may meet each other in dialogue and co-operation. . . . All are equally bound to confess the truth revealed in Christ. How can they meet together and work towards that full unity which they . . . should manifest?" In answer to this question certain basic principles were recalled which had made the fellowship of the World Council possible and which, in the opinion of the Executive Committee, must also continue to be determinative in the future. Even before the meeting in Odessa, a memorandum had been sent to Cardinal Bea in the name of the Presidents of the World Council containing detailed suggestions for improving the Decree on Ecumenism. This memorandum had later been taken into consideration in the revision of the text.

A few weeks later Cardinal Bea proposed an unofficial meeting between representatives of the Secretariat for Unity and of the World Council. This meeting was held on 15 April 1964 in Milan. The number of participants was limited. Present on the Roman Catholic side, apart from Cardinal Bea, were Bishop Jan Willebrands, Father Jérôme Hamer, and Father Pierre Duprey; and on the World Council side the General Secretary and the two permanent observers at the Vatican Council. The talks cleared the air. The Roman Catholic delegation stressed the importance they attached to good relationships with the World Council. The Roman Catholic Church, though not a member of the World Council and unable in the foreseeable future to become a member, bore a joint responsibility for its life and future development. The idea of appointing permanent representatives in Rome and Geneva was discussed but rejected for the present. Instead it was agreed to remain in close contact by means of regular visits. For the first time the possibility of setting up joint working parties was considered. At that time three different work groups were envisaged, one to consider the principles of future co-operation, the second to study theological questions, and the third to deal with practical matters. But it was agreed that any such step needed careful preparation on both sides and could not be taken before the promulgation of the Decree on Ecumenism.

Discussions were continued in the World Council in the following months. In order to obtain a clearer picture of the attitude of the member Churches, a wider group of leading personalities and a number of observers who had represented their Churches at sessions of the Council were invited to a meeting held at Rummelsberg near Nuremberg on 24–7 July 1964. After a discussion on the general significance of the Council, the results of the Milan talks were reported. The idea of joint working parties found general acceptance, although some doubts were voiced. The Executive Committee, meeting immediately afterwards in the Evangelical Academy at Tutzing near Munich, reached agreement on this plan. The General Secretary was authorized to work out details in further talks. This was done during the Third Session of the Council. The World Council's observers met twice with Bishop Willebrands and other representatives of the Secretariat for Unity. The plan was also presented personally to the Pope.

After the close of the Third Session and the promulgation of the Decree on Ecumenism, the time seemed ripe to implement the plan. The events of the closing weeks of the session had indeed again raised doubts as to whether the establishment of closer relationships should yet be undertaken. It was nevertheless decided to present to the Central Committee at its meeting in Enugu, Nigeria (12–21 January 1965) a more modest plan for discussion. After only brief discussion, it was almost unanimously agreed to propose to the Roman Catholic Church the establishment of a Joint Working Group. This proposal was assured of acceptance in advance. The text presented to the Central Committee had previously been discussed with Bishop Willebrands and he had secured agreement in principle from the highest authorities. The Working Group would have fourteen members—six from the Roman Catholic side and eight from the World Council of Churches. Their task would be to clarify the principles and practical problems of future collaboration.[1] Compared with the original idea this plan had the advantage of leaving open to a far greater degree the future developments; all further co-operation would have to grow from the discussions of the Joint Working Group. A few weeks after the Enugu meeting Cardinal Bea visited the Secretariat of the World Council of Churches in Geneva and conveyed the official answer of the Holy See. The importance of this step was emphasized during a small ceremony in The Ecumenical Centre. Pastor Marc Boegner, a former President of the World Council of Churches, replied to Cardinal Bea.[2] The relationships between Roman Catholic Christendom and the World Council thereby entered at last on a new stage. By the establishment of the Joint Working Group both sides had publicly affirmed their readiness to remain in permanent contact and to deepen the ecumenical fellowship as much as possible. Work could now begin on a more complete manifestation of the ecumenical movement than had hitherto been possible.

This whole development would not have been possible without the simultaneous establishment of contacts at many other levels. The first announcement and still more the impetus of the First Session had already been fruitful in this connection. The longer the Council went on, the more numerous and intensive the contacts became. The message of dialogue had spread so widely that many members of the Roman Catholic Church did not wait for the promulgation of the Decree on Ecumenism but had anticipated the results of the Council by establishing relationships. In many places the hitherto closed confessional borders were being opened up in an astonishing way and the non-Roman Churches found themselves suddenly confronted with a partner they had previously reckoned with at a distance.

Official steps also helped to change the climate. The most important event in this respect was perhaps the meeting between the Ecumenical Patriarch Athenagoras I and Pope Paul VI in Jerusalem (January 1964). After the Pope had announced his intention of visiting Jerusalem, the Ecumenical Patriarch suddenly announced that he too would go to the Holy City. As a result of this meeting, the "journey to the sources" took on a distinctively ecumenical character. The Vatican also showed the importance it attached

[1] MRCC (Geneva 1965), pp. 36ff.
[2] For the text of the speeches see *Rencontre oecuménique à Genève* (Geneva 1965).

to reconcilation with the Eastern Churches in the following years, particularly by such gestures as the return of relics which for one reason or another had been brought from the East to the West (the head of Andrew to Patras 1964, the relics of St Sabas to Jerusalem 1965). Official contacts were also discussed with other Churches; for example, simultaneously with the discussions between the Secretariat and the World Council, discussions were also taking place about the establishment of a mixed commission with the Lutheran World Federation.

At the time of the formation of the Joint Working Group, the Vatican Council had still not ended. Many texts were still not yet at hand, and in many respects it was still not clear what their final form would be. After the postponement of the vote at the end of the Third Session, further developments were awaited with some anxiety. The decision in this matter was especially important for the World Council of Churches. Having indicated in numerous statements how important a clear recognition of the principle of religious liberty was for the co-operation and joint witness of the Churches, a great deal depended on the Council's statement on this matter for the collaboration envisaged between the Roman Catholic Church and the World Council. The Declaration finally adopted rests, especially in its theoretical section, on specifically Roman Catholic premises and cannot in this respect be wholly endorsed by other Churches. But the practical requirements coincide very closely with those found in the statements made by the World Council of Churches, and in this respect it can be said that a common basis has been arrived at. The work of the World Council, and especially the tireless efforts of Dr A. F. Carrillo de Albornoz, doubtless had some share in bringing about this result.[1]

The other texts still to be dealt with had at first glance less to do with the ecumenical movement. They concerned internal problems of renewal and witness in the world. But they were none the less important for future co-operation. For they raised the question of how these texts approached the idea of co-operation and joint witness. Did the Council regard its task as ended with the promulgation of the Decree on Ecumenism? Or did the other texts take the insights of the Decree into account explicitly and carry them further? Was ecumenism only a special self-contained theme? Or would it permeate the life of the Roman Catholic Church in all its forms? The question was not settled with complete clarity during the Fourth Session. Several texts, especially the Decree on the Church's Missionary Activity, and the Pastoral Constitution on the Church in the Modern World, contain explicit references to the need for co-operation with other Christians. Others make no mention of this, and one occasionally has the impression that the Roman Catholic Church is once again preoccupied with its own problems. The general framework established by the Council certainly ensured that all the texts of the Council were increasingly read and interpreted in the light of the ecumenical movement.

---

[1] Cf., for example, *Le Catholicisme et la liberté religieuse* (Paris 1961); on the Council's Declaration, cf. "The Ecumenical and World Significance of the Vatican Declaration on Religious Liberty, *Ecumenical Review*, vol. xviii (1966), pp. 58ff.

The Pastoral Constitution on the Church in the Modern World deserves special mention. In this the Council declared its mind on the great problems of the present time. This text was the only one for which there was no draft in existence prior to the opening of the Council. It was drawn up by various groups during the Council proceedings and this process was doubtless the result of the growing realization that the Church could not remain pre-occupied with itself but had to face up to the problems of our time. Just for this reason, the Constitution was an important contribution to the ecumenical movement. For was this not the point where the divided Churches could most easily co-operate together? Was it not here that the weight of our differences was least in evidence? And might it not be that, when the Churches faced together the questions of the time, they might also be shown even new ways to greater unity? This had again and again been the experience of the ecumenical movement. The Constitution could, therefore, pave the way to a collaboration which might be of the greatest significance for the ecumenical movement. The first thrusts in this direction were already made during the Fourth Session.

Once the Joint Working Group had been established between the Roman Catholic Church and the World Council of Churches, much more intensive relationships would be cultivated. Various questions relative to the Council were discussed at the first sessions of the Joint Working Group. Two special consultations were organized to deal with particular themes. One of these brought together a number of specialists on missionary problems (April 1965). The results of the discussion[1] were in many ways encouraging and the meeting undoubtedly helped indirectly to give the conciliar Decree on the Church's Missionary Activity the strongly ecumenical flavour which characterizes it. The other consultation was concerned with questions of "Church and Society" (March 1965) and provided an opportunity for discussion of the work on the Pastoral Constitution *Gaudium et spes*. The contacts with the various groups responsible for the drafting of the text had been especially close from the beginning. The fact that the World Council had worked in almost all the areas which the Constitution was to deal with made it seem advisable to seek discussion with it. The World Council's observers were given many opportunities to comment on the various draft texts of the document. The consultation in Geneva placed these contacts on a broader footing.[2]

On 8 December 1965 the Council was brought impressively to its close. The final days were marked by two events which were of great consequence for the ecumenical movement. On 4 December the non-Roman Catholic observers were invited to join with the Pope in a service in *San Paolo fuori le mura*. Some of the observers were asked to read the lessons and the prayers. The Pope had thereby given his personal example of common worship. On the last day but one of the Council, an event took place which was of significance especially for relations between the Roman Catholic Church and the Orthodox Church. It was the joint decision to strike from memory the

---

[1] Text obtainable only in duplicated form, W.C.C.
[2] Cf. *Study Encounter*, vol. ii (1966), pp. 75ff.

mutual excommunication of 1054, a step reinforced by solemn ceremonies both in Rome and in Constantinople. While this decision strictly speaking concerned only the relation between the Roman Catholic Church and the Church of Constantinople, it nevertheless had far wider significance. An important step in reconciliation had been taken.[1]

Although the question of the Church's unity had once more dominated the final days, it played hardly any part in the magnificent closing ceremony in St Peter's Square. The ceremony was very much a symbolic presentation of the Roman Catholic Church turning towards the world. The ceremonial, impressive in itself, once again awakened in one's mind with special urgency the question which every observer of the Council could not but ask, especially in these last days. Where had the Council really led? Had it after all been only a matter of renewing the Roman Catholic Church and its witness? Or was it in fact the fellowship and the common witness of all Churches which were the beneficiaries?

From the Second Vatican Council to Uppsala

The end of the Council did not mean the end of the conciliar event. What had been discussed and proposed, formulated and decided, continued to have its effect and had now to pass into the life of the Church. This process of "reception" could lead to extremely varied results. Certainly the texts which had been promulgated contained many formulations and guide-lines. But just because the Council had been concerned not "to close any doors", these texts were in many respects open and could be interpreted in various ways. However, the texts were perhaps not really the most important thing. Much more depended on the way in which the atmosphere of the Council would continue to influence the Roman Catholic Church. After the shocks brought by the Council, would it be possible to restore an order comparable with that of the pre-conciliar period? Or would the questioning and seeking which had marked the sessions of the Council henceforth be a feature of the life of the Church as a whole?

The Council had given rise to a new image of the Church. The very fact that for several years vital questions had been discussed openly before the whole Church, indeed before the whole world, had clearly demonstrated that the Church is most alive when it is moving forward, when it proclaims the gospel while at the same time asking itself questions about the gospel. Had not the Council itself planned with this movement in mind? Had it not continually stressed the Church's readiness for dialogue with the world? The final ceremony on St Peter's Square provided a particularly striking illustration of this aim. On the day after the last texts had been promulgated, the Council briefly addressed various sections and groups (workers, intellectuals, women, etc.) and assured them that the Church recognized its solidarity with them and shared their problems.[2] One by one, representatives of the different sections of the human community received the text of the Declaration. This symbolic action was in one sense a summing up of the Council's

[1] *AAS* LVIII (1966), pp. 40f.   [2] *AAS* LVIII (1966), pp. 5ff.

dominant concern. But could the Church face the problems of the modern world without also continuing its questioning and seeking?

The ferment produced by the Council put the Magisterium in a difficult situation. On the one hand, the Pope had the duty of carrying out the intentions of the Council; on the other hand, included in these intentions was the wish that none of its decisions should hamper a genuine confrontation with the contemporary world. A new exercise of the papal office was needed. The Pope had to become the exponent and symbol of movement. The need for this change was all the greater because of the crisis concerning authority in the Church brought on by the Council. The authority which had been accepted without question before was now being questioned in many quarters, especially among young people. The Pope could no longer count on the unqualified assent of the faithful. To a far greater extent than any of his predecessors he had to appeal to conscience.

The difficulty confronting the Pope is illustrated by the manner in which the decisions of the Council were carried out. On the one hand, Pope Paul arranged for the issue of directives dealing with the implementation of the constitutions and decrees.[1] The Council for the Reform of the Liturgy in particular performed a tremendous task, and the proposals for reshaping the liturgy soon began to be put into operation in most parts of the Church. The Pope also supervised the creation of the new structures demanded by the Council. Even while the Council was still in session, on his own initiative he established two new secretariats—one for relations with other religions and the other for dialogue with atheism. Some time after the close of the Council, the establishment of a Laity Council and a Pontifical Commission for Justice and Peace was announced (6 January 1967).[2] The Council on the Laity was to provide a focus for the work of the laity. The Commission for Justice and Peace was to deal with the questions of development. A few months later came the long-awaited reform of the Curia (18 August 1967),[3] and, although many had hoped for more radical changes, a series of measures was taken which made possible a more effective co-operation within the Curia, a modernizing of its work, its internationalizing and increased mobility.

But it was not only the central government which was reorganized; many of the religious orders also began to make changes. The Pope was above all concerned, however, to continue along the line which had been intimated during the Council through his visit to the United Nations. He repeatedly made new efforts to help to secure peace in the world; his pontificate is so dominated by this concern that some refer to him as the "Pope of Peace". In this connection one of the most important utterances is the encyclical *Populorum progressio* (26 March 1967),[4] in which he summoned the Roman Catholic Church to greater responsibility in the face of the widening gap between rich and poor nations. "Peace, today, means development."

---

[1] Cf. *Motu proprio Finis concilio, AAS* LVIII (1966), pp. 37ff.
[2] *Motu proprio Catholicam Christi Ecclesiam, AAS* LIX (1967), pp. 25ff.
[3] Apostolic Constitution *Regimini Ecclesiae, AAS* LIX (1967), pp. 885ff.
[4] *AAS* LIX (1967), pp. 257ff.

But, on the other hand, the pontificate of Paul VI is marked by a concern lest the movement initiated by the Council should go too far and the Magisterium lose control over it. Again and again he has insisted that the received tradition must be preserved intact. The Council had spoken on particular questions only and it was not in accord with its spirit to want to call everything in question. He frequently appealed for obedience to the Magisterium.[1] Many decisions were obviously affected by this concern. Here must be mentioned, above all, those questions which, although raised by the Council, had been left expressly for the Pope to decide. Almost without exception they have been decided in a conservative sense.

The Apostolic Constitution *Indulgentiarum doctrina* (1 January 1967) repeated with only slight modifications the traditional doctrine of indulgence.[2] Hardly any heed was paid to the views expressed by many speakers at the Council which went much further. The detailed encyclical *Coelibatus sacerdotalis* (24 June 1967), while certainly recognizing the serious pastoral problems arising in connection with celibacy, rejected any change in the existing rules;[3] only new rules regarding the diaconate were conceded. However, the most widespread discussion was provoked by the encyclical *Humanae vitae* on birth-control (25 July 1968).[4] To the surprise of many, it confirmed the utterances which had been made by Pope Pius XII. Dealing as it did with a question which entered deeply into personal life, this encyclical raised in especially wide circles the question of the Pope's authority in the Church.

The tensions found in the Roman Catholic Church after the Council were vividly illustrated in the autumn of 1967 when the Episcopal Synod and the Laity Congress held their meetings simultaneously in Rome. The Pope had already announced during the Council that he would from time to time summon a synod of bishops. The Synod would enable the consultations initiated by the Council to be continued, at least in some measure. The Synod would, to be sure, have only an advisory function. Final decision was to be in the hands of the Pope. In the first session of the Synod, which took place from 29 September to 29 October, the bishops were asked to advise on a number of clearly defined matters (liturgy, canon law, crisis of faith, mixed marriages, seminaries). An opportunity was at hand to examine the state of the Church and carefully to weigh the pros and cons of certain reforms. Some important steps were taken, especially in the field of liturgical renewal. But the Synod was not able to become a focus of the post-conciliar spirit.

At the same time a large congress of lay people met in Rome (11–18 October 1967). There had been similar congresses before. But this congress was in many respects something quite new; it was here that it was made quite clear that the laity were determined to play a vocal and active part in the life of the Church. For the great majority the Council was obviously

[1] General Audience, 12 January 1966; General Audience, 15 December 1965; General Audience, 7 September 1966; Address to Theologians' Congress members, Rome 1 October 1966; General Audience, 5 October 1966.
[2] *AAS* LIX (1967), pp. 5ff.   [3] *AAS* LIX (1967), pp. 657ff.   [4] *AAS* LX (1968), p. 481.

not an end; it was a beginning, and the Congress called for the speedier introduction of many reforms. Since a great many representatives of other Churches were present, the discussions acquired a distinctively ecumenical character.[1] It is perhaps significant that the Pope should have chosen the occasion of his speech to this Congress to recall in urgent terms the place of authority in the Church.[2]

Roman Catholic Participation in the Ecumenical Movement

Similar tensions are also found in the Roman Catholic participation in the ecumenical movement. The impetus given by the Council continued to have great influence. Once the Decree on Ecumenism had been promulgated, meetings, dialogue, and co-operation no longer needed to be confined to special circles. Ecumenism had become the task of the Church as a whole. After the Council, therefore, participation became increasingly the rule. There were, indeed, considerable differences from place to place. In some countries the picture changed rapidly; in others the change was small. Many factors were at work here: the historical circumstances, the attitude of the bishop, the political background, and, finally, the manner in which the non-Roman Churches themselves approached the new possibility of encounter and co-operation. The impetus of the Council, however, also produced results in many places which went beyond what had been formulated in the Decree on Ecumenism. Had not the Council spoken of real encounter? Must not real spiritual fellowship increase? Must not steps be taken to realize these aims without delay? Many individual Christians, many small groups, posed such questions and began to work along these lines. A spontaneous movement began which often found itself in opposition to the explicit instructions of church authorities, by whom it was usually simply tolerated. Joint experiments were undertaken and, with increasing frequency, particular groups were found joining together in communion services.

The Pope himself often acknowledged that the whole Church was committed to the ecumenical movement. For example, in a speech to the members of the Secretariat for Unity: "The ecumenical problem has been raised by Rome in all its urgency, in all its magnitude, and in all its doctrinal and practical aspects. It is not just glanced at occasionally or incidentally. On the contrary! It has become the object of continuing concern, systematic study, and unlimited love. It has become a line which from now on is part of the programme of our apostolic office."[3] Shortly after the end of the Council the Pope announced that the Secretariat for Unity, which had originally been created only for the duration of the Council, was to continue in existence. Its activity had already developed during the Council; subsequently it increased year by year.

One of its most important initial tasks was to draft a document containing directives for the application of the Decree on Ecumenism. Work on this *directorium de re oecumenica* had already begun during the Fourth Session

---

[1] Cf. Report of Congress, *God's People on Man's Journey* (Rome 1968).
[2] *AAS* LIX (1967), pp. 1040ff.   [3] 28 April 1967, *AAS* LIX (1967), pp. 494f.

and the text was eventually published at Pentecost 1967.[1] Among the selected themes it covered were these: it recommended the setting up of ecumenical commissions in each country; directives were issued concerning the recognition of baptisms administered in other Churches; the spirit of ecumenism (*oecumenismus spiritualis*) and, above all, the Week of Prayer for Unity and especially the problems of common worship (*communicatio in spiritualibus*) were discussed. Other questions were to be dealt with in a further document. This *directorium* showed, in the first place, that the Roman Catholic Church was to be introduced to the ecumenical movement in a serious way. The establishment of ecumenical commissions was a particularly significant step and the Secretariat sought to enhance their importance by beginning to hold regular meetings of their secretaries in Rome. At the same time the *directorium* was unquestionably a reminder of the limits which had to be set to participation in the ecumenical movement, limits which had already been and were still being exceeded in certain quarters.

The issue of mixed marriages, though it had an immediate bearing on the ecumenical movement and was considered by many to be the ecumenical issue *par excellence*, was not within the sole competence of the Secretariat for Unity. Towards the end of its Third Session the Council had discussed a proposed revision of the existing regulations, but no decision had been made. The proposals had been passed on to the Pope along with the views of the bishops; the decision was held in abeyance. Opposition to any change in existing rules was obviously strong in many countries, and many bishops warned against any radical departure from the traditional practice. The Holy Office finally published an *Instructio matrimonii sacramentum* (18 March 1966),[2] which, in the case of the recognition of mixed marriages performed in non-Roman Churches, did not even go as far as the original proposals. This was not to say that the matter was now closed. The *instructio* stressed that the new directives had force only *ad experimentum*. Further discussion was, therefore, possible. The problem was discussed with representatives of other Churches on several occasions, in particular at a meeting with the World Council (1–4 March 1967). The Episcopal Synod reconsidered the matter in the autumn of 1967 and, although it was not prepared to make far-reaching changes, further developments are not ruled out.

The Secretariat for Unity was not only in charge of working out directives for ecumenical work; it also had the main responsibility for developing relations with other Churches. In a relatively short time it succeeded in constructing a whole network of new contacts. Special care was devoted to relations with the Orthodox Churches. These had always played a special role in Roman Catholic ecumenical thought and, not surprisingly therefore, especially after the impressive gesture at the close of the Council, reconciliation between East and West was given priority. The Pope himself travelled in July 1967 to Istanbul on a short visit to the Ecumenical Patriarch,[3] and Athenagoras I returned this visit in October of the same year. Both journeys provided an opportunity of emphasizing the common heritage.

---

[1] *AAS* LIX (1967), pp. 574ff.   [2] *AAS* LVIII (1966), pp. 235ff.
[3] Cf. *AAS* LIX (1967), p. 833

The Joint Rome Declaration (28 October 1967) is especially important. Among other things, this Declaration affirms the common conviction that the true dialogue of love, the essential basis of all relationships between them and their Churches, must be rooted in complete obedience to the one Lord and in mutual respect for each other's traditions.[1] Although these gestures in many respects improved the atmosphere between the Churches, no real discussions yet took place. Two pan-Orthodox meetings had some time previously discussed this possibility (Rhodes 1964 and 1965), but had not arrived at any unanimous agreement since the final decision had to be postponed. Even the pan-Orthodox meeting in Geneva (June 1968) produced no essentially different result.[2] The difficulty of actually engaging in the dialogue so frequently proposed is a fresh sign of the West's constant tendency to underestimate the gravity of the difference which divides it from the East.

Initial discussions with the Lutheran World Federation had already been started between the Third and Fourth Sessions of the Council. After two preparatory conferences (August 1965 and April 1966) a mixed group was set up in July 1966. Their main task was to deal with theological questions, particularly with that of "the Gospel and the Church". This group has already held several meetings. Similar contacts have also been established in certain areas. Remarkable results have come in particular from discussions in the United States on the Creed, Baptism, and the Eucharist.[3]

A dialogue with the Anglican Communion was officially announced in March 1966. The Archbishop of Canterbury's meeting with the Pope in Rome (23–4 March 1966) provided the occasion. The joint statement declared that a serious dialogue should be initiated which, based on the Gospel and the ancient common tradition, should lead to the unity for which Christ prayed.[4] A mixed commission was set up to examine the steps to be taken. After three meetings (January 1967, September 1967, and January 1968), it proposed that a permanent commission should be created to deal with all questions of a general character. Special commissions should deal with the most difficult theological problems which divide the two Churches from each other (Church and ministry; authority, its nature, exercise, and implications). This proposal was agreed upon. Closer contacts with the World Methodist Council were established in 1967. A mixed commission was formed and held its first meeting in October 1967. Further contacts of this kind are not impossible in the future.

All these conversations constitute a new element in the ecumenical movement. Encounters at the level of the confessional families had previously been the exception. The World Council of Churches had not been founded as a fellowship of confessional families but primarily as a fellowship of the

---

[1] Cf. *AAS* LIX (1967), p. 1054; quotation on p. 1055.

[2] Discussions on social questions with Russian Orthodox theologians took place in Leningrad in December 1967.

[3] Cf. *The Status of the Nicene Creed as Dogma of the Church* (1965); *One Baptism for the Remission of Sins* (1966); *The Eucharist as Sacrifice* (1967). The results of a Roman Catholic–Reformed dialogue have been published under the title, *Reconsiderations* (New York 1967).

[4] *AAS* LVIII (1966), p. 286.

Churches of the individual countries. The entry of the Roman Catholic Church into the ecumenical movement changed this situation. Being itself a universal fellowship, it saw the confessional families as its natural partners. Although the confessional families were for other reasons becoming more important in the ecumenical movement, this did much to secure increased attention for them. This development was clearly felt at the Fourth Assembly of the World Council of Churches at Uppsala.[1]

Relations with the World Council of Churches

But what of the contacts which had already been established earlier with the World Council? Bilateral relations with the individual confessions were in many respects more in accord with Roman Catholic thinking than co-operation with, or even membership in, a fellowship of Churches. It is not surprising, therefore, that the Roman Catholic Church, and the Pope especially, at first attached more importance to these relationships. Even at the national level, contacts were often sought primarily with the individual Churches. There were sound reasons for this. If the Churches wished to draw nearer together, they had to face and overcome in direct conversations the barriers dividing them, and the various bilateral discussions had in fact already led to notable steps towards reconciliation. But must not encounter and co-operation still be sought at another level? Must not all Churches, even though they are still divided, form a provisional fellowship with one another? The goal of the ecumenical movement is the unity and common witness of the whole people of God. Is not this goal most likely to be reached if all the Churches remain in permanent contact, if they live together and, anticipating the ultimate fellowship as far as possible, bear common witness? Relationships with the World Council were, therefore, of the greatest importance, and, to the extent that co-operation developed at all levels, the ques.ion regarding the co-operation of the Roman Catholic Church in the National Christian Councils naturally also arose.

The Joint Working Group of the Roman Catholic Church and the World Council of Churches (established in 1965; see above, p. 340), from its inception held two meetings every year, each meeting lasting several days. So far it has twice presented a report to the Holy See and to the Central Committee of the W.C.C., together with proposals and recommendations concerning the form of the relationship and of co-operation (February 1966 and August 1967).[2] Both reports were approved.

The task of the group was first to clarify general questions. How did each side understand the ecumenical movement? Had the Vatican Council expressed a view which differed from that of the Churches bound together in the World Council of Churches—which would inevitably entail a different form of ecumenical work? Or could the Roman Catholic Church declare its fundamental agreement with the view of the World Council of Churches?

[1] *The Uppsala Report*, p. 225.

[2] The first report has been published in *Ecumenical Review*, vol. xviii (1966), pp. 243ff (see also MRCC (Geneva 1966), pp. 47ff). The second report has been published in MRCC (Heraklion 1967), pp. 140ff (cf. also pp. 53ff).

The question soon became even more pointed. Was it conceivable that the Roman Catholic Church might become a member of the World Council? The Joint Working Group has not yet ended its discussions on this matter. So far it has reached only a number of provisional conclusions. Its second report stresses that at all events there can be only one ecumenical movement and that both the Roman Catholic Church and the World Council of Churches are committed to serve this one movement. Membership of the World Council of Churches is, therefore, not excluded in principle. The report expressly emphasizes that the present structures cannot be regarded as final. However, obstacles which stand in the way of a more complete manifestation of the one ecumenical movement may not be underestimated either. They can be overcome only gradually. Indeed, it is possible, since the relationships are still so new, that they have not yet been seen in their full extent. The Joint Working Group, therefore, recommends that the common work should proceed step by step.[1]

The conversations are not confined to such general questions, however. The Joint Working Group has been no less concerned with tasks which even now can be undertaken together. The range and importance of these tasks increases with each meeting. Its first report consisted for the most part of a list of the areas in which contacts should be sought. Many of these plans were translated into action in the months which followed. New groups came onto being to deal with particular aspects of co-operation. The second repor if the Joint Working Group contained a survey of these groups; six different areas were mentioned. There are the theological and liturgical questions. A special commission examined the problem of the "Catholicity and Apostolicity" of the Church. Conversations about joint services at ecumenical gatherings,[2] and above all about the joint planning of the Week of Prayer were held; contacts were made with the Consilium for the Reform of the Liturgy. Co-operation over missionary problems was only slowly developed, despite the fact that the Conciliar Decree had stressed the ecumenical task; even today it is still embryonic. Far more advanced are the contacts in matters concerning the service and task of the laity in the Church. Various meetings in this regard have taken place;[3] the Laity Congress in Rome, in particular, afforded an opportunity for a fruitful exchange.

Furthest developed, however, is co-operation in the field of social ethics. The World Conference on Church and Society in Geneva (1966) was not only a powerful stimulus to the member Churches of the World Council but also to the development of relationships with the Roman Catholic Church. Roman Catholic theologians played an important part in the Conference. The creation of the Pontifical Commission for Justice and Peace the following year provided the opportunity to extend co-operation. A joint Secretariat was set up in Geneva and in the spring of 1968 a large joint conference on the

[1] On this discussion cf. *Ecumenist*, vol. iv. 3 (1966); *Ecumenical Review*, vol. xx (1968), pp. 205–44.

[2] *Ecumenical Review*, vol. xviii (1966), pp. 252ff.

[3] Cf. *Laity Formation*, Proceedings of the Ecumenical Consultation Gazzada (Rome 1966); Report of the Women's International Ecumenical Conference (Taizé 1967).

Church's responsibility in the problems of development was held at Beirut.[1] The Assembly in Uppsala attached great importance to this co-operation.

Useful contacts were also established in the field of inter-church aid. A number of consultations led to closer collaboration between Roman Catholic aid organizations, Caritas in particular, and the World Council of Churches. In February 1966 the World Council and the Roman Catholic Church made a joint appeal in view of the threatened famine in India. It proved far more difficult to reach a common witness in international affairs. In this sphere the traditions and structures of the Roman Catholic Church are least favourable to co-operation. Nevertheless, in the spring of 1968, a joint declaration on the increasingly critical situation in Nigeria was issued. Last to be mentioned is the fact that the Joint Working Group continued—either itself or through special groups—to study problems which constitute special hindrances to the ecumenical movement, such as mixed marriages and proselytism.

Developing Roman Catholic relations with other international Christian organizations must also be referred to in this context. Of particular importance is the co-operation with the United Bible Societies. This arose naturally out of the Vatican Council. The fresh emphasis on the importance of the Bible in the life of the Church, and, above all, the decision to give more place to the vernacular in the liturgy, made it necessary to increase the production of biblical translations and the number of its editions. The Constitution on Revelation had, in this connection, expressly encouraged "co-operation with the separated brethren" in producing such translations (para. 22). This co-operation grew rapidly. Following extended discussions full agreement was reached on the principles of translation and editing. Joint translations and editions of the Bible are already in preparation in many countries.

The 1968 Uppsala Assembly of the W.C.C. signified another important step forward in the development of relationships. The question of mutual relationships was, as it had already been at the meetings of the Central Committee, one of the dominant themes of the Fourth Assembly. The Roman Catholic Church sent fourteen observers, and in addition several guests and consultants attended. A great number of Catholic journalists followed the proceedings. The Pope as well as Cardinal Bea sent official messages. Two speakers—Father Roberto Tucci and Lady Barbara Jackson —addressed the Assembly. Shortly before the Assembly opened, the Vatican had given permission for Roman Catholic theologians to become full members of the Faith and Order Commission. The Assembly made use of this opportunity by appointing nine Roman Catholics to the Commission. The Roman Catholic Church is, therefore, like the member Churches of the World Council, now represented in the Faith and Order movement.

On many occasions the hope was voiced that relations might develop in other directions too, and the question of membership was again and again raised, especially in private discussions. Father Roberto Tucci had explicitly taken it up in his address to the Assembly and, though not concealing the

[1] *World Development, Challenge to the Churches.* Geneva 1968.

difficulties, he had made it quite clear that Roman Catholic ecclesiology did not make membership impossible. The Assembly itself spoke vigorously on the subject. Not only did it approve the previous work of the Joint Working Group, but it also made it absolutely clear that from the side of the World Council of Churches there was, in principle, no obstacle to the membership of the Roman Catholic Church in the Council. The Assembly also, for the first time, expressed the desire that a complete manifestation of the one ecumenical movement might actually be realized. The realization of this desire may still take a long time, but at least the task has now been made explicit.[1]

Increasingly, of course, the question arises: What significance is to be attributed to the expansion of relations between the Churches? How do all the bilateral relationships contribute to the renewal of the people of God? How would this renewal be furthered, supposing we were successful in creating a fellowship of the majority of the now divided Churches? The decisive question is whether Christianity can stand the test in the present world. The urgency of this question becomes increasingly obvious, and more and more people are asking with a certain uneasiness whether ecumenical relationships are at bottom simply a new form of the Church's self-preoccupation. This doubt surfaced at the Fourth World Conference on Faith and Order and, in a more reticent way, at the Second Vatican Council. It was posed, above all, at the World Conference on Church and Society, emphatically and unequivocally. The future of the ecumenical movement lies, therefore, not—or, at least, not exclusively—in the further development of relationships but in the places where the Church authenticates itself.

[1] Cf. *The Uppsala Report*, p. 178.

13

The Ecumenical Movement
in the Churches and at
the Parish Level

HANS JOCHEN MARGULL

The One People of God in Each Place

In the ordinary daily life of the Churches and local parishes the ecumenical movement has only just begun. Apart from a few and important exceptions, ecumenicity on the denominational and local level lags far behind the bold and lofty thrusts of the world ecumenical conferences. Sometimes one even gets the impression that the waves that rushed forward at the conferences set up a backwash at the local level. At any rate it is noticeable that on the whole the ecumenical movement in the Churches and parishes advances much more slowly and ponderously than at the great world-wide or regional gatherings. It is easier to adopt certain principles than to carry them out. However, no one would underestimate what has been accomplished, especially during the last few years.

The Churches have not only become aware of one another; they have also drawn closer to each other. This is clearly shown by the exchange of visits between church representatives, by the intercession, the mutual help, by some very promising consultations to prepare the way for church unions and some actual mergers, by the growing number of theological conversations, the agreements about many joint projects, the exchange of statements and information, and by many of the events described in the preceding pages. Even in cases where, owing to the formation and development of the World Council of Churches and to the break-through of ecumenism in the Roman Catholic Church, the tendency is rather to wait, or even to start anti-ecumenical campaigns or attempts to divide Churches (as in Korea), the question of the One Lord of the world and the Church cannot be ignored for very long, as the consequence of the question of the One Church in the world.

The word "ecumenical", which was hardly known a generation ago, is no longer strange; it has become more and more meaningful. One can see how the names of the places where the Assemblies of the World Council of Churches have been held have become as familiar in sermons and in Christian education as the work of the Second Vatican Council. One frequently hears people speak of the situation "before Amsterdam", or about the main theme at "Evanston", or about the basis of the World Council "since New Delhi", or about the emphases of "Uppsala". Sometimes one can even notice how in theological thinking there is a tendency to divide newer church history and the history of theology into periods marked by the Assemblies of the W.C.C. and the Second Vatican Council. In the Churches and at the parish level, therefore, we really have moved forward since 1948.

The gap between the ecumenical movement at its conferences and in the places where it has to be lived out day by day may be considerable; but it cannot be so large that there is no longer any connection between a world conference and a local Church. On the one hand, the insights and challenges of the conferences are dependent on what is alive to a certain extent in the Churches and at the parish level. On the other hand, ever since the ecumenical movement started, it has been realized that "the universal must be local to be real".[1] At its conferences, therefore, attention was constantly drawn to

[1] Montreal, p. 81.

355

the importance of the local Church for the witness, service, and unity of the Church nevertheless. A growing ecumenical questioning both in and of the local Churches, especially during the last few years, was needed before a World Conference on Faith and Order like the one at Montreal could decide to have a whole section on the ecumenical importance of the local congregation.

This section had as its theme "All in each place: the process of growing together". The unity formula of New Delhi was taken up and used in the formulation of this theme. This formula has an interesting history, which it is not without importance to mention here. The formula goes back to Lesslie Newbigin, Bishop in the Church of South India, formerly in Madurai, now in Madras. Its *Sitz im Leben* arises from situations on which the Bishop reported in 1958 and 1959. When he visited local Churches in South India the Hindus and Muslims in the place used to crowd around out of curiosity when the local congregation gathered in front of the church building to welcome their bishop. He then felt that it was incumbent upon him to say something to these people who surrounded the Christian congregation. And it became clear to him that what he said would be understood if the local congregation surrounded by non-Christians was a genuine Church of Jesus Christ.

In 1958 Bishop Newbigin became General Secretary of the International Missionary Council. In the same year, in preparation for the integration of the World Council of Churches and the International Missionary Council, he published a book entitled *One Body, One Gospel, One World*, from which we quote:

> For myself, I do not believe that we can be content with anything less than a form of unity which enables *all who confess Christ as Lord to be recognizably one family in each place and in all places,* united in the visible bonds of word, sacrament, ministry and congregational fellowship, and in the invisible bond which the Spirit Himself creates through these means, one family offering to all men everywhere the secret of reconciliation with God the Father. I believe that missionary obedience in our day requires of us that we should treat the issue of such visible churchly unit as an issue not for tomorrow but for today.[1]

Thus the expression concerning the unity of all Christians "in each place" was coined. The Faith and Order Commission took it up at its meeting at St Andrews, Scotland, in 1960, and passed it on to the discussion at the World Council's Assembly at New Delhi. Here it was explained that as God's will and God's gift unity must become visible among "all in each place".[2] The place, the local stage for separated Christians and Churches was thus indicated as the platform for the gift and the task of unity. Consequently the local congregation gained high attention in the ecumenical discussion. In the conclusions of the report of Section V at Montreal we read:

> We acknowledge that many of God's gifts to his whole Church cannot be shared by us in our local churches until we recognize ourselves as the one people

---

[1] Lesslie Newbigin, op. cit., pp. 55–6.
[2] *New Delhi Report*, ed. W. A. Visser 't Hooft (London 1962), p. 116.

of God in each place, and are prepared to embody this fact in new and bold ventures of living faith today.[1]

We now turn our attention to ecumenical events which took place at the level of the Churches (denominations) and local parishes after 1948. These events are so numerous that only a few examples of them can be mentioned in this limited space; and they are of so many different kinds that a selection is justifiable only if attention is also drawn to the references to the subject in the other chapters of this book.

Meetings

There were meetings and visits not only between Pope Paul VI and the Ecumenical Patriarch of Constantinople, Athenagoras, whose historic meeting in the Holy Land in 1964 and in Istanbul and Rome in 1967 have attracted world-wide attention and aroused strong ecumenial hopes within Christendom. Important visits were paid not only to the Holy See, for instance by Bishop Otto Dibelius of Berlin, by the Very Reverend Dr A. C. Craig in his capacity as Moderator of the Church of Scotland, by the Archbishop of Canterbury, and by Metropolitan Nikodim of the Russian Orthodox Church. Equally important for the ecumenical movement were the contacts between representatives of individual Churches and local congregations, which aroused much less attention, but the number of which has meanwhile become too numerous to count or to estimate.

Many visits take place on the occasion of the conferences of the World Council of Churches. A large number of the delegates to its Assemblies, its Central Committee meetings, and its Commission meetings, pay visits to other Churches in the country or area where the meeting takes place, also stopping on their journeys to visit local congregations, church conferences, and theological seminaries. And as there are few areas where the World Council of Churches has not held any conferences, or which were not accessible on the way to its conferences, there are now very few Churches which have not received visits from representatives of another Church that plays an active part in the ecumenical movement. Every such visit has been a manifestation of the ecumenical movement, has helped to broaden the horizon of the Churches, and has often also deepened the problem of divided church traditions. Each has thereby raised the question of direct co-operation, and has strengthened the hope of unity in the mission and life of the Churches. Not infrequently permanent contacts have been formed. Even more often further visits have been arranged between Churches and churchmen of different countries and continents.

One outcome of such visits is, for instance, a passage which has been inserted into the Deed of Appointment of pastors belonging to the Evangelical Church in Germany when they serve abroad:

We expect you to maintain the link between your Church and the Evangelical

---

[1] *Fourth World Conference on Faith and Order*, p. 90 (para. 190).

Church in Germany and *to support and promote the contacts with the Christian Churches belonging to the World Council of Churches.*[1]

Visits take place not only between Christians living in fairly close proximity to each other but also over great geographical distances. Since 1948 not a single summer has passed in which groups of church people from North America (beginning with students, then extended to include older people) have not visited Europe, Latin America, and finally even Asia, Africa, and Australia. Some times they came for short visits, sometimes they stayed longer. In a large number of cases they met together with congregations or church groups for conferences. In quite a number of cases these visits were returned. The United Church of Christ in Japan had to appoint a full-time person to look after the visitors, who came mainly from North America and Australia. In the summer time a group of about twenty pastors came regularly from North America to assist Japanese pastors in the evangelism of remote districts in the North of Japan. Within Europe, since the beginning of the 1950s a great deal of inter-Church visiting has been going on. Many theological seminaries sent their students for one or two weeks to seminaries abroad. The exchange started within western Europe, but it soon extended so as to include eastern Europe.

A similar movement goes on between the different Lay Institutes. So many ecumenical guests attended the German Protestant Kirchentag that it was obliged to make arrangements for a programme in English. Characteristic of the nature of these contacts was a visit paid by sixty members of the Anglican Church of St Helen's, Kensington (London) in 1965 to attend the consecration of the Lutheran Church of St Andreas at Hildesheim (Germany). The church at Hildesheim, which was nearly 600 years old, was destroyed in 1945 by British bombs. Twenty years later it was rebuilt, and the church leaders of the Kensington church and of the Hildesheim church entered the new building together. The liturgy was celebrated partly in English and partly in German. The sermons were preached by the local Bishop and by the Provost of the Anglican Cathedral of Coventry. The presence of the Provost illustrated the contact made with Coventry in the previous years, when young Christians from Germany helped to rebuild Coventry Cathedral. Like Coventry Cathedral, the old church at Hildesheim was to be a place of reconciliation.

Equally characteristic of the new ecumenical movement was the presence of Protestant and Roman Catholic clergy at the consecration of the first Russian Orthodox Cathedral in the traditionally Lutheran city of Hamburg that same year. In fact, since the formation of the World Council of Churches and still more since the Second Vatican Council, it has become customary for clergy from Churches of different traditions to attend consecration services of Churches and of priests, ordinations, and induction services. The enthronement of the Anglican Archbishop of Sydney in 1966 was attended

---

[1] This phrase was included in the Deed of Appointment read at the introduction of the Pastor of the German-speaking Protestant Church in Tokyo-Yokohama on 24 October 1965.

not only by representatives of the Methodist, Presbyterian, Congregationalist, Baptist, and Greek Orthodox Churches, and of the Salvation Army, but also by the Roman Catholic Archbishop of Sydney; the two Archbishops sat facing each other in the chancel of the Cathedral. Furthermore the sermon of the Archbishop who was being enthroned was concerned with the responsibility of the Australian Church for the people in Asia and the Pacific. Even in Columbia (South America) where in the 1950s the small Protestant groups were often suppressed by force, in 1965 a Roman Catholic priest representing the archdiocese of Bogota was able to attend the ordination of the first native Anglican clergyman. This was an exceptional case then; such events increase in number every year.

Particularly important were the meetings of Protestant and Anglican Church leaders and theologians with representatives of the Orthodox Church and (somewhat later) of the Lutheran Churches and of the Union of the Evangelical Christian Baptists of U.S.S.R. Equally important were the return visits in western Europe and North America. After the Russian Revolution the Church of England continued to maintain contact with the Moscow Patriarchate. In September 1943 the Patriarchate was legalized by the Soviet Government, and in the same month the Archbishop of York went to Moscow. As soon as the war was over, Patriarch Alexis sent Metropolitan Nikolai to London as his representative. In 1952 Pastor Martin Niemöller, who was then President of one of the "Landeskirchen" in Western Germany and a member of the Executive Committee of the W.C.C., visited Moscow. More church delegations followed between 1950 and 1955.

In 1956 a delegation from the National Council of Churches of Christ in the U.S.A., led by Dr Eugene Carson Blake, who was then its President, paid a visit to Moscow which was to have far-reaching consequences. One of the members of this delegation was the late Dr Franklin Clark Fry of New York, then Chairman of the W.C.C. Central Committee. A delegation from the Moscow Patriarchate and other Russian Churches paid a return visit to the United States. In 1958 conversations were opened between the Moscow Patriarchate and the World Council of Churches which led in 1961 to the Russian Orthodox Church becoming a member of the W.C.C. This event opened the way for a large number of visits from the Western Churches to Russia during the next few years. Hardly ever had any ecumenical event been followed with such close attention as the reports on the meeting with the Churches in the Soviet Union. It evoked such keen interest that during the last few years whole groups of church members from the West have been to Russia to visit the Churches there.

At these meetings theological conversations played an important role. The Russo-American meetings were concerned mainly with situation analyses and the question of the Church's task in the world today. The communiqué after the mutual visits between Moscow and New York summed up the conversations as follows: "In the first centuries when the relations between the peoples were just as confused as they are today, it was said that the Christians held the world together. God grant that we may play the same role!"[1] Questions relating to the history of dogma, church order, and liturgical problems, were on the agendas of the different Anglican–Orthodox conferences.

Fundamental problems which divide the Russian Orthodox Church from the Reformation Churches were discussed at the conference of theologians of the Moscow Patriarchate and of the Evangelical Church in Germany. The first of these conferences was held in 1959 at Arnoldshain, near Frankfurt; the second in 1963 at Zagorsk Monastery, near Moscow; and the third in 1967 at Höchst, near Darmstadt. For the first and most important conversation the Orthodox theologians had prepared a questionnaire, containing questions about the Lutheran concept of Scripture and tradition, faith and works (both the traditional concept and the concept held today). As a result the problem of tradition and the question of justification by faith became central in the conversations. Like many of the theological meetings held during recent years between representatives of different church traditions in all kinds of places, the outcome of this meeting was surprising.

The outcome was the possibility of a free and promising theological conversation between Lutherans and Orthodox, and in this case between Germans and Russians. In the discussion itself joint statements were reached like the following:

> In the theology of both churches, tradition is extremely important; consequently the contrast between the Orthodox principle of "Scripture and Tradition" and the Protestant principle of "Scripture alone" is not apposite. We receive justification through grace in faith in the redemption through our Lord Jesus Christ. There is no justification on the basis of good works. This excludes the misconception that in Orthodox theology good works are a necessary prerequisite for justification, or that Protestant theology rejects the New Testament's teaching about judging men by their works. The Reformation experience of justification by faith has its counterpart, to a large extent, in Orthodox liturgy and asceticism.[2]

Conversations like these revealed the new possibility and readiness for dialogue also in many other places, such as the many recent interconfessional conversations in America.

In this connection mention must be made of one result of many years of contact in France, which were not without tension. During the Week of Prayer for Christian Unity in 1966, for the first time a joint version of the Lord's Prayer was used, which had been worked out by a commission of Lutheran, Reformed, Roman Catholic, and Orthodox theologians. It has received the approval of the Pope also for the French-speaking Catholics in Belgium, Switzerland, Canada, and the African countries. Since Easter 1966 this approved version has been compulsory for use at Catholic Mass.

The exchange of students between different countries, Churches, and

---

[1] *News* from the National Council of the Churches of Christ in the U.S.A., New York (13 June 1956); also *Journal of the Moscow Patriarchate*, No. 8 (1956), pp. 24ff.

[2] The conversation between Protestants and Orthodox at Arnoldshain (*Ökumenische Rundschau* 9 (1960), pp. 26ff); see "Tradition und Glaubensgerechtigkeit", *Arnoldshain Conversation 1959* (Witten/Ruhr 1961).

continents, especially since the Second World War, has borne rich ecumenical fruit. In many cases this exchange was arranged through the scholarship programme of the World Council of Churches; in many other cases it was due to the private initiative of theological seminaries, Churches, and congregations. As a result thousands of theological students received the opportunity of getting to know other Churches and their history, other situations and their problems, and of obtaining theological knowledge which was beyond their reach in their own countries. Many of the men who later on took part in theological conversations between representatives of different Churches, or who have been entrusted by their own Church with responsibility for ecumenical contacts and for promoting the ecumenical cause in the local Churches, or who have translated important literature or even founded ecumenical centres, or who became leaders of local, regional, or world-wide Christian movements and Councils, were once holders of ecumenical scholarships.

The Student Christian Movement, which in many cases has been the historic source of the ecumenial movement, has done a great deal also since 1948 to promote meetings between Christians and Churches. Only two facts can be mentioned here. They were extraordinary, but their exceptional character is an indication of developments which have been going on during the last few years in the life of all the Student Christian Movements. In 1965 a joint Student Conference was held in Göttingen, Germany, for Protestant and Catholic students, critically followed by the Churches. It was expected of this meeting that Protestant and Catholic students would deliberate together about one of their joint problems, namely the rapidly increasing specialization in university studies. It was also expected that in the discussion on this problem the common Christian life of Protestants and Catholics would find its expression. Both these expectations were fulfilled. Finally, it became an actual fact, experienced and confirmed, that the groups of Protestant and Catholic students at the universities have the task of learning to think together and for one another.

On the other side of the Atlantic in the U.S.A., the University Christian Movement was founded in 1966 by the ecumenical union of groups of Protestant, Anglican, Roman Catholic, and Orthodox student associations which had hitherto been separate. This merger on the national level is so far unique. It brought hope of a more intensive encounter and co-operation between Christian students on the local level everywhere.

Different in kind were the encounters in ecumenical work camps and meetings between campers and Christians in the places where the camps were held. It is usually not realized that the history of ecumenical work camps goes back to an experiment made by the International Fellowship of Reconciliation in 1920. In that year young people of different nationalities came together on the site of the German and French battle of Verdun in order to overcome their estrangement and to promote reconciliation and peace. In 1947 the Congregational Christian Service Committee in the U.S.A. arranged a work camp for a group of young American and French Christians at Le-Chambon-sur-Lignon in France. The concept of reconciliation was now joined by another concept: that of service. A year later six camps of this kind were held in western Europe. In 1949 sixteen were held in Europe and Asia, including three camps in Japan, two in Korea, and two in the Philippines. A camp at Nagasaki undertook the task of rebuilding a Christian school destroyed by the atom bomb. A camp in Quezon City (Philippines) helped with an anti-malarial campaign.

In 1950 work camps (which had arisen as a result of free ecumenical contacts) were taken into the programme of the Youth Department of the World Council of Churches. The financial responsibility for them, which existed in spite of the considerable amounts paid by the campers themselves for their travel and living expenses, was assumed by the Division of Inter-Church Aid, Refugee, and World Service of the W.C.C. The number of camps increased. In 1954 there were thirty-four; in 1957 there were forty; in 1961 there were fifty-three. Since 1950 ecumenical work camps have been held in no fewer than fifty-one countries in Asia, Africa, the Middle East, North America, South America, and Europe, and every year not less than 1,000 young people from over fifty different countries and from many different Churches belonging to the World Council have attended these camps. It should be borne in mind that these figures refer only to camps organized in connection with the Youth Department of the World Council. They do not include the large number of camps organized locally, nationally, or denominationally by church associations and Y.M.C.A.s and Y.W.C.A.s for youth or by national Youth Councils.

Most of the camps were attended by an average of twenty young Christians from different countries and different Churches. They usually lasted three to four weeks for building churches, kindergartens, youth centres, hospitals, homes, schools, camps for refugees, or for rebuilding houses destroyed by war or catastrophe. Since 1962, however, the Youth Department of the W.C.C. has also organized camps of longer duration, which provide an opportunity for young people (especially from America and Europe) to give a year's service in co-operation with young Christians of the same age in Asia and Africa. In 1962–3 a camp helped to remove the damage done by the flooding of the River Tana in Kenya. In 1963–4 an ecumenical work camp of this kind was held at Chiengmai, Thailand, which helped to build a conference centre for the young people there. In 1964–5 a group of twenty-two volunteers co-operated in a development programme of Indonesian Inter-Church Aid on the island of Bali. In 1965–6 one camp built an orphanage and an agricultural training centre in Korea.

At these camps, and also at the shorter camps, the campers worked six hours a day simply doing physical work, and then had three or four hours for worship, Bible study, and discussion. "A project of this kind", said the appeal to this ecumenical commitment, "offers everyone a unity of living, working, worship, and fellowship, which has become rare in modern society." The gain for the ecumenical movement was tremendous. At these camps most of the participants for the first time encountered people from other congregations and Churches. They sang hymns that they had never heard. They attended services with which they were not familiar. They worked, talked, slept, ate, and prayed together with people of whose existence they had previously had no conception (or a most inadequate one). Religious, national, and racial prejudices were broken down. It no longer mattered what colour a person was, nor what kind of passport he carried. Superficial differences between Churches became obsolete.

Admittedly, now and again there was a dangerous tendency to ignore important differences. But the faith shared by all was expressed in the hymn, "In Christ there is no East nor West", which was sung with enthusiasm again and again. As a result the local Churches discovered that the Christian Church is far wider than they had hitherto experienced. They often came together for the first time with other local Churches, either in preparing for the camp or through the contacts made by the campers. The campers themselves took back reports to their own countries, the most striking point being the change in the personality of the campers themselves as a result of their experiences of an ecumenical work camp. The ecumenical movement found important expression in the camps, which proved to be a permanent instrument for the renewal of the Churches and for promoting their efforts for unity.

Churches for Others

The ecumenical movement was also going on in the Lay Institutes, a considerable number of which (like the Ecumenical Foundation at Mindolo, Zambia) had been founded as ecumenical projects. It is probable that they have promoted ecumenical contacts more than almost any other organizations. They arranged meetings between people from all over the world, and they opened their doors to Christians who had no opportunity to attend theological conferences, for example, or theological discussion groups, people who could not take part in ecumenical work camps or similar projects. They were opened in many parts of the world, and during the last few years an increasing number of them have been created for people who usually represent the local congregation, although this does not imply that pastors and young people have no share in their work. Here, as in the ecumenical work camps, the encounter did not take place merely for the sake of encounter, but in order to answer the question what it means to be a Christian in a world which has become both larger and smaller, more united and at the same time more divided, more mature and at the same time more dangerous. The Lay Institutes, rightly called "centres of renewal", place themselves at the service of Christians from different Churches, so as to encourage them to undertake service both inside and outside their own local congregations. The lay movement also grew stronger and spread more widely in the ecumenical movement.

What was happening in many places and at countless meetings, which usually discussed very concrete questions of daily life, found expression in a statement made by the Department on the Laity in 1956 to the Central Committee of the World Council of Churches. Speaking of the new insights that had been gained, the statement said "that the whole Church shares Christ's ministry in the world and that the effective exercise of this ministry must largely be by Church members when they are dispersed in the life of the world".[1]

The ecumenical question involved on the one hand the concept of the Church itself, on the other hand the relevance of church traditions outside the walls of the Church. The statement continues:

> As was said in Evanston: "The real battles of faith today are being fought in factories, shops, offices and farms, in political parties and government agencies, in countless homes, in the press, radio and television, in the relationship of nations. Very often it is said that the Church should 'go into these spheres', but the fact is that the Church *is* already in these spheres in the persons of its laity." There is nothing new in this conception, for our Lord said, "Ye are the salt of the earth . . .", but it is a truth which has been obscured over many periods of the Church's life.[2]

It was a joint ecumenical task to bring this truth to light in the Lay Institutes. How seriously this task was taken is shown by the following sentences in the statement:

> None of us fully understands, in our complex modern world, what this ministry of the laity really is. God reveals it to those who listen; every situation in His world can speak to us. But it is becoming clear that one of the main tasks of the Church, when it assembles its scattered members, is to listen to them speaking of their trials and difficulties, hopes and fears, opportunities and needs, and even simply about the facts of life in the world. The assembled Church cannot become a teaching Church until it listens. We urgently need a Church that will teach out of the experience of listening.

It is sentences like these which have given rise to the question (which has come to the fore in the ecumenical movement especially during the last few years) whether the Church is not called to live for others, namely for people which do not yet belong to it, or no longer belong to it; the question whether, by courageously shouldering this task, the Church may be able to achieve unity in a way that is not possible merely by discussing doctrinal matters. We describe below the attempts made to formulate this question; its importance was shown by the fact that for years the publications concerning the question of the laity, and that of the Church in the world today, were the most widely read of any of the periodical literature published in Geneva. The efforts within the World Council to stimulate the broad mass of church members to think in ecumenical dimensions proved more successful here than anywhere else.

A great many lay movements have sprung up transcending the boundaries of local Churches. They were a response to the increasing need to break down parochial barriers in an increasingly homogeneous world. But they arose also from the increasing recognition of the fact that it is hardly ever possible for a single Church, or a single congregation, to deal single-handedly with the situations that arise today. Lastly, they were an attempt to express as far as possible the unity given in the One Lord Jesus Christ.

[1] MRCC (Galyatetö, Hungary, 1956), p. 26.
[2] Quoted from *The Evanston Report*, p. 168.

One striking example of these lay movements is the "Fellowship of the Least Coin", an association of Christian women, located mainly in East Asia. Founded in 1956 by Mrs Shanti R. Solomon, a modest member of the United Church of North India, it became the most striking expression of the wide and deep ecumenical concern found among Christian women in many Churches. Speaking at a meeting of the Asian Church Women's Conference, which spontaneously and wholeheartedly followed her example, she said: "We Asians always want to interpret spiritual feelings through concrete actions, to connect prayer with action. Every woman can put a least coin aside as a token that she has prayed for specific concerns". In a few years an association had grown up which spread far beyond Asia, and which she herself defined as follows: "It joins together women and many denominations and nations through the common acts of prayer and of giving the least coins of their countries to a common fund for special missions projects."

During the ten years since the association was founded its members have collected 223,775 dollars. The amazing thing was that this money did not remain entirely in Asia. It has been used to support ninety-one projects in all six continents. Thus the women of Asia helped with the Child Care Programme of the East Harlem Protestant Parish in New York, with youth conferences in Asia, with a hospital for Indians in Argentina, with evangelism in Spain. Their money was spent on medicines and treatment for sufferers from tuberculosis in India, to support the Protestant Medical Centre at Kimpese (in the Congo), and finally they sent a cheque to people in a place called Strike City in Mississippi where racial tensions are very strong. The oppressed congregations in this poor little town sent a reply. At the third Asian Church Women's Conference in Tokyo in 1966, a carved wooden Nativity scene was on view; it was a gift from Strike City thousands of miles away, and a token of its gratitude.

The help to the people in Strike City was sent through the so-called "Delta Ministry" of the National Council of the Churches of Christ in the United States of America. The name of this ministry was derived from the fifteen counties in the Delta of the Mississippi. The ministry itself was an attempt to improve the situation of the coloured people in this region. It would have been reasonable to expect that the appeal to support this ministry would have been sent only to rich American Churches. However, the request for co-operation was sent out through the member Churches of the National Council of Churches (U.S.A.) to all the Churches belonging to the World Council of Churches. The racial struggle in the 1950s and 1960s, which in the U.S.A. itself had become an ecumenical concern of the Churches, was thus through this request brought to the attention of the Churches all over the world. In 1966, 480,000 dollars were allocated to the Delta Ministry; of this sum 384,000 dollars were to be contributed by America itself and 96,000 dollars were expected from non-American sources. Thus for the first time in the history of Inter-Church Aid, funds flowed into the U.S.A., whose Churches had always been "giving" Churches since the Second World War, financially never "receiving" Churches.

In this connection mention must at least be made of the fact that in the

Churches and local congregations the ecumenical movement has found its most direct, obvious, and perhaps also its most lasting expression both in the giving Churches and in the receiving Churches, in the many forms of help, both large and small, that have been given by one Church to another, by one local congregation to another, by individuals to individuals, more and more transcending the barriers of denomination, confession, nation, and race.

The aims of the Delta Ministry revealed the tasks which confront the Churches everywhere today, where they seek to give service to men. This ministry began by giving direct help to people who could not help themselves, and who needed to be helped in a way that would enable them to help themselves. Its first concern was for reconciliation between the white and the coloured congregations, and for the promotion of human dignity among the members of both groups. Its ultimate aim was to develop a peaceful community of people co-operating in a region in which fate had brought them together, These aims were rooted in the Christian gospel of love for one's neighbour and the forgiveness of sins. At the same time, however, it became clear that the gospel was being preached in normal sermons and in all forms of proclamation, and thus the being of the Church as the Church of the loving, forgiving Lord, had to be lived out in pursuance of these aims.

The ecumenical fellowship between the Churches in the U.S.A., and especially the readiness of many local congregations to participate in such fellowship, had to pass the hard test of the racial struggle. At the same time this highly complex and often extremely confusing struggle brought a deeper experience and understanding of the ecumenical relationship between the Churches and congregations in many places. A new feature of the ecumenical movement in America found expression in the demonstration marches for which Dr Martin Luther King, Jr had set the example. His martyrdom in 1968 only intensified the struggle. These marches brought together people from South and North, from widely differing church traditions, not only Christians but also Jews and humanists, and pointed the way to co-operation in faith and action between Protestants and Catholics which sometimes far transcended the achievements arrived at hitherto by the ecumenical movement. Just as it was in the concentration camps during the Second World War, so now it was, especially in the prisons, that people who had not really taken one another seriously as Christians, and had often mistrusted each other, were reminded of the one baptism into the death and resurrection of the one Lord of the world and of the Church.

Events in many coloured congregations revealed perspectives about the Church in the past and in the future, which were of deep ecumenical importance. The racial struggle in America revealed with fresh clarity that in emergency situations those separated Churches are brought together which are open to that which is human. The decision to take action in face of the racial challenge raised the question whether it was possible for Churches with different traditions to co-operate. The response to this question then deepened the fellowship between the Churches, even if that response could not be unconditional. Thereby it was discovered that emergency situations can be tackled by Churches and local congregations only in an ecumenical way.

The meetings, ecumenical and public, which were held as part of the struggle led to a kind of liturgy both new and appropriate to the situation. Hymns in the form of the traditional spirituals were sung about the recent events. Equally spontaneous were the prayers for the freedom movement and for its enemies. The sermon was followed by discussion on future action and the recruitment of persons prepared to undertake it. The collection was devoted to the current tasks of the congregation (a congregation composed for the first time of many Churches). A report on this says that furthermore "it is really non-essential whether the leadership is in the hands of an ordained minister or of a non-ordained person". The determination to find a solution for the situation, and the confidence that the right solution would be found, produced new charismatic leaders. And the action itself gave rise to the faith that one was called to co-operate in God's work in order to let the world be reconciled with him, by forcing the world out of its bastions into the open where it could receive the freedom and justice ordained by him.

This faith gave rise to a renewed sense of social responsibility due to the belief that the Church is the people of God. The new ecumenical fellowship made Christians realize that they have a task for the world, which is God's own world. In some important places in the South of the U.S.A. one idea was thoroughly understood. It was an idea that was born among Christian students in Eastern Germany in relation to the question whether coexistence is possible between the Church and an atheist–socialist social order, or with the world at all. The idea was given the name "pro-existence". Through the ecumenical discussion it reached Christians engaged in the racial struggle in America. They then began to see and to say that a Church of Jesus Christ cannot be anything but a fellowship for pro-existence, following the pattern of Jesus Christ who lived and died for all men. Having arrived at this understanding of what the Church is, and having stood up for their convictions courageously again and again, these Christians then appealed to the Church all over the world to take a stand against all forms of injustice, and especially racial injustice, and urged it to repent wherever it accepted or even promoted any kind of discrimination. The ecumenical intention inherent in this appeal found simultaneous expression in the request to make intercession, to give help, to be prepared to suffer with others. This appeal did not fall on deaf ears, as is shown by the response to it all over the world, including that of the Fellowship of the Least Coin.

The above, very provisional summary of the ecumenical importance of church action in the racial struggle in America was based on a paper drafted under the leadership of the Reverend Andrew Young, a colleague of Martin Luther King, in connection with the study on Structures for Missionary Congregations.[1] The theme of this study arose from the intensive ecumenical discussion about evangelism since Amsterdam (1948) which produced both many insights due to fresh encounters with the world and the realization

[1] "Missionary Presence in the Racial Revolution", in *Planning for Mission*, ed. Thomas Wieser (N.C.C.U.S.A., New York 1966), pp. 164ff.

N

that in many cases the local Churches, owing to their introspective structure, are incapable of carrying out the evangelism that is required today. By raising the question what form a local Church ought to assume, this discussion again brought up some of the problems and findings of the discussion on the role of the laity in a rapidly changing world. The study was launched at the Third Assembly of the World Council of Churches in 1961, at the time of the integration of the World Council and the International Missionary Council, that is, just at the moment when Churches and local congregations had to face the question of how the Church and the missions should come together in the daily life of a local parish.

The response to this study was amazing. An unprecedented number of study groups for this and related questions was discovered. They showed the strength of the view, held especially by young pastors and committed lay Christians, that the local Church cannot become related again to its environment unless it transforms its own self-concept, and its own form. Also the study was in accordance with the conviction of many people that ultimately the problems both of the renewal of the Church and of evangelism can be solved only through ecumenical co-operation. But the discussion raised the question whether there can be any attempt at unity without new efforts to evangelize and to renew the Church beginning with drastic changes at the local level.

Working groups had been formed in many parts of the world to undertake this study. Their wide exploration of immediate and long-range needs for new forms and structures of Churches, particularly in their localities, eventually led them both to identify and to interpret what already was happening with certain groups of Christians, certain congregations, and certain church associations. Basically, then, all they were required to do was, in certain prominent parts of recent church history, to describe the way in which pioneers were walking already and to which the Churches would be led, each in its own place all over the world, when the time came. Side by side with some local Churches which took up the racial struggle in America, with the Industrial Missions in Great Britain or in India and Japan, and with many achievements of the Lay Institutes, special attention was drawn to the Port Harcourt project in Biafra, East Nigeria and to the Church of the Saviour in Washington, U.S.A.

In Port Harcourt the Church had to discover how to serve in a large town which had sprung up like a mushroom during the last few years in the marshland at the delta of the River Niger.[1] The attempt to carry out this task clearly showed that local Churches, in a place of this kind which is undergoing rapid industrialization and urbanization, cannot venture to evangelize unless their evangelism forms the kernel of a far-reaching concern for man living in an unfamiliar environment which presents many new dangers, and unless the whole effort is ecumenical from the outset. The need to promote ecumenical co-operation was evident owing to the fact that, as already pointed out in 1925 at the Stockholm Conference, the world is too strong for a divided Church. It was also evident that the people converted to the one Christ were

[1] The Port Harcourt Project (*Monthly Letter about Evangelism*, Geneva April–May 1965).

not destined to be just members of a large number of different separate Churches. So the work was begun by an ecumenical team, consisting mainly of members of Churches which were negotiating about a united Church of Nigeria. Church union on the local level was to be promoted. The team consisted of pastors and laymen, missionaries and social workers. It worked on the pattern of the Group Ministry in the East Harlem Protestant Parish, New York. The work undertaken in the young city aimed at showing the local Churches, whose people only a short time previously had been living in little towns and villages how they must meet the new situation in the light of witness, service, and unity. As in many other places, the team and some local Churches in Port Harcourt learned that witness has to be made within and in the face of the social tensions of our time. They realized that service must take many different forms in the actual local situation. They understood that unity must be envisaged as a form of Church highly differentiated, yet coherent.

When the Church of the Saviour was founded in Washington in 1946, it boldly announced that it was an ecumenical Church. The formulation was as follows:

> An ecumenical Church is one whose heart is heavy because of a divided Christendom. It will pray and work for the healing of its divisions. Its only weapon is love. It will at all times consciously feel itself a part of the World Church and give its first loyalty to the world Christian fellowship. It will be openminded and sympathetic. This is different from tolerance. This spirit is born, not of indifference, but of deep conviction. An ecumenical church gives unqualified corporate allegiance to Jesus Christ.[1]

The importance of this Church, however, lay in the strict commitment of its members, in the elimination of the traditional distinction between pastors and laity, and in a unique form of Christian service which led especially in the U.S.A. and in Australia to the coffee-house movement. Assuming as a matter of course that a local Church exists to serve people, and that this is the only way of convincingly presenting the message, this Washington Church with great personal sacrifice bought a shop in a busy street in Washington and turned it into a café, so as to provide people with a place where they could meet, ask questions, air their grievances, have conversation, and receive help. Groups of church members waited at the tables in the evenings. This service was itself a witness and led to witness. It also became a witness to many local Churches of different denominations which sent their people to Washington from all over the United States in order to see and to ask advice, so that they could do the same. Many Christian coffee houses were then opened in other places, run by different local Churches or by Christians from different denominations together. The ecumenical character of this work attracted wide notice. But it has not yet received ecclesiological recognition; the question whether this kind of coffee house is a new type of Church has still to be answered.

---

[1] E. O'Connor, *Call to Commitment*. New York 1963.

Ecumenical Pioneers

In 1966 and 1967 an unexpectedly large number of people in Indonesia made inquiries about the Christian faith. Churches and congregations reacted not only by increasing evangelism; they sought, wherever possible, a wide ecumenical evangelism. So, in the market place at Bandung, in Java, great services were held daily, led by evangelists and pastors of different Protestant Churches. Joint campaigns of this kind are no longer unusual in many parts of the world. Regional and local Christian Councils (and also well-known evangelists) usually succeed in bringing Churches together for joint evangelism campaigns. The great ecumenical step towards joint baptism, however, hardly occurred. It became possible in Karobatakland, North Sumatra, a remote, ethnically homogenous area where different forms of denominations were still unknown. Here, on 19 June 1966 in a village called Tigalinga, nearly 2,000 people were baptized by fifteen pastors belonging to six different denominations. The baptized people were then integrated into one single Church called the Karobatak Church. The pastors came from the Batak Church, the Simalungun Church, the Niass Church (which are Lutheran in trend), from the Protestant Church in western Indonesia (which is Reformed in tendency), from the Methodist Church in Sumatra, and from the small Karobatak Church itself. These Churches had previously conducted a joint mission campaign lasting several months, on the lines of the Joint Action for Mission programme advocated by the Division of World Mission and Evangelism of the W.C.C. since 1962. Without being particularly well known there, this programme attained its goal in the baptism at Tigalinga.

The rise of new towns has opened the way to further ecumenical action in some cases, even if only on a small scale. For instance, in 1965 in the new industrial town of Churchill, in Victoria, Australia, the Anglican, Presbyterian, and Methodist Churches and the Church of Christ started joint parish work, with the aim of setting up a single Church in the town. In 1966 in the new town of Livingston, near Edinburgh, Scotland, a pastor of the Church of Scotland and a priest of the Scottish Episcopal Church were ordained together for their work in that town. Later a Congregational clergyman joined their team. They co-operate in the work among youth, men, and women and in the Church's relations with the town. The church building of the Church of Scotland, which was still unfinished, was placed at the disposal of the Episcopal congregation, and the hope was expressed that an ecumenical centre will be built, which can be used also by other Churches. Similar decisions were taken in view of the future work and life of Churches in some inner cities where the rapid social change is recognized by many Churches.

In the inner city situations, the East Harlem Protestant Parish in New York became the pattern for the union of local Churches with similar traditions. This parish was created in 1948 in recognition of the irrelevance of maintaining traditional Sunday congregations in an extreme inner city situation. It was a union of four congregations, and adopted new, comprehensive working methods based on the group ministry. In a few years it had become an ecumenically integrated congregation. Similar parishes exist in Chicago and elsewhere.

Following this example, a Presbyterian Church and a Methodist Church in the centre of Sydney have decided to merge, thus providing a starting-point for a larger "United Church of the City of Sydney". Even in the prosperous suburbs of the American towns where after the Second World War a very large number of new churches of widely differing denominations were built, perhaps too many in the view of an ecumenical observer, and therefore had to be filled with people, mergers have been effected between two or three denominations, especially during recent years. At least in some places, for instance in Trenton, a suburb of Detroit, the United Presbyterian Church and the United Church of Christ united in 1966. More important than this, however, was a joint project undertaken by the Lutheran Church in America, the Methodist Church, the Reformed Church in America, the United Church of Christ, and the United Presbyterian Church, to undertake service to the people living in a new residential area in Orange County, north of the city of New York, in the hope that it would develop into a single Church. Here the tradition of the federated Churches and the "community" Churches is followed with a new ecumenical consciousness.

In many places for many years local Churches have placed their church premises at the disposal of other denominations. Many Protestant Churches in Germany offered hospitality to Roman Catholic congregations which, owing to the stream of refugees after the war, found themselves in places where no Roman Catholic church existed. Similar hospitality was extended to Orthodox congregations in many towns in western Europe, the last example being in Birmingham, England in 1965. In 1965 a Roman Catholic Church in Saxony, a traditionally Lutheran area of Eastern Germany, offered hospitality to the Lutheran congregation of Deutzen, when their old church building was pulled down owing to the extension of the coal-mining industry. In Islamabad, the new capital of Pakistan, when a site was made available for building a church, the Protestants and Roman Catholics agreed in 1967 to co-operate in building one single church with two separate chapels underground for Sunday services, the main church however being available for use on festival occasions by all the Christians in the country. In 1967 a permanent arrangement was made between the Protestants and Catholics in the industrial centre of Hoogvliet near Rotterdam to share their church buildings. In this case, as a Roman Catholic church could not be built for financial reasons, the Reformed Church invited the Catholic congregation to use its premises, which made it unnecessary for the Catholics to build a church of their own.

Nevertheless, ecumenical co-operation of this kind is still very unusual. This is shown by an appeal made by the Dutch Ecumenical Council to the Churches of Holland, to regard themselves in future wherever possible as "churches in the process of becoming united", and to act accordingly. The Churches in one place should regard themselves (and each other) as the Church of that place, and thus gradually develop a common life. As had been recognized in the ecumenical movement at all levels, this is the first step, and certainly an extremely important one, towards ecumenism on the local level. To quote a phrase of W. A. Visser 't Hooft, if this step were taken the Churches would go a long way towards being "unitable".[1] In order to take it hundreds of thousands of local Churches all over the world must show greater readiness to live in the light of the promise that there shall be one Church and one World, through faith in the future of him who came.

At its meeting in Geneva in February 1966 the Central Committee of the W.C.C. issued a statement "On the Ecumenical Way" which read as follows:

> Walking in the ecumenical way requires of local congregations:
>
> (a) That Church members be now prepared for a wider and deeper unity with Christians of other Communions;
>
> (b) That both in public and in private, specific intercessions be offered for other churches, and not only general prayers for unity;
>
> (c) That religious education be given an ecumenical dimension both in experience and in word;
>
> (d) That the reading of the Scriptures be faithfully practised by Church members, as the necessary inspiration of the ecumenical way;
>
> (e) That in preaching, the scriptural vision of the one people of God united under the cross of Christ should be insistently proclaimed;
>
> (f) That congregations and their members bear a costly part in the mission of the Church and be given a vision of the significance of the churches' task as "mission in six continents";
>
> (g) That a generous response be made to the claims of human need in a world in which men are hungry both for bread and for knowledge;
>
> (h) That Christian citizens actively seek to secure human dignity and rights for all men and that they diligently exercise a responsible citizenship wherever they may live.[2]

The draft had contained another sentence, which was not included in the statement:

> We welcome the obedience in which local groups of Christians are led to make ecumenical experiments both towards each other and in common action to the community. Such obedience helps to make clear the ecumenical way and to revitalize the movement.[3]

---

[1] W. A. Visser 't Hooft, "The Una Sancta and the Local Church", *Ecumenical R eview*, vol. 13 (October 1960), p. 12.

[2] "On the Ecumenical Way", *Ecumenical Review*, vol. 18 (1966), p. 228.

[3] MRCC (Geneva 1966), pp. 91f.

14

Signs of Radicalism
in the Ecumenical Movement

DAVID L. EDWARDS

Introduction

Some Christians have been convinced that desirable changes in the Churches would come from listening to the swiftly changing world and from serving it, in order to hear and serve the revolutionary God revealed in Jesus Christ. This conviction holds that mankind matters more than the institutional Church, and the future more than the past; and it constitutes radicalism in the ecumenical movement. *Oikoumene* meant in Greek "the inhabited earth"; "ecumenical" means more than "inter-Church".

The pioneers of the modern ecumenical movement, properly subordinating ecclesiastical questions to the Kingdom of God, believed that the Churches could be united by their work in the world, by their commitment to evangelism, or by working out a "social gospel" based on a liberal theology, through hospitals, colleges, schools, clubs for the unemployed, and organizations for peace and temperance. When the dismantling of the colonial empires destroyed the old simplicity in the missionary enterprise, and when the social gospel seemed powerless to heal the deep tragedies of the nations, the Churches began to acknowledge that the ecumenical movement must be more costly. If the Christian mission was to be discharged in the world, if the gospel was to be proclaimed meaningfully and practised relevantly, if the Church was to be a model for society, there must be changes in the Churches. To Churches as to individuals the word had been spoken: they must die before rising. Christians began to pay this cost of discipleship afresh under Hitler, and it was in the prayer of discipleship that the World Council of Churches was constituted.[1]

Since 1948, however, the extent of the changes required has been seen more clearly. It is the task of this chapter to describe some experiments through which some Christians have risen to this challenge. These Christians have shown a new courage and a new flexibility, and they have glimpsed, beyond their continuing divisions and problems, a new hope and a new unity for the Church serving the Kingdom.

The word "radical" when transferred from left-wing politics to religion is, however, ambiguous. Many "radicals" have responded to the challenge of the modern world by abandoning belief in any God distinguishable from man and the universe. Their faith has been in the actual or potential lordship of man, who stands on his own. Some such radicals have called themselves Christians. To them the death of Jesus without any miracle to save him has been a specially effective demonstration of the fact that there is no God, but they have been greatly moved by the personal freedom and the outgoing love which they have seen in Jesus. A religious emotion based on the "death of God" was expounded in the United States during the later 1960s by some radicals who wished to say that Christian theologians could and should be atheists.

We may agree that this "death of God" theology has been a valuable reminder that the liberal theologians of a past era addressed themselves to some important questions. How could minds shaped by an age of science

[1] W. A. Visser 't Hooft, *The Renewal of the Church*. London 1956.

get into any relationship with dogmas inherited from a vanished age of faith? How could a "natural" theology based on a contemplation of nature and history, including mankind's religious experience, get into any relationship with the specifically Christian commitment and obedience to the transcendent God as Lord and Father? These questions were not answered by orthodox or neo-orthodox theologians such as Karl Barth who gloried in the discontinuity between science and faith, between the God of nature and the God of revelation; and it was inevitable that the questions should be raised again when the historical circumstances favouring a conservative theology (the Churches' resistance to Hitler, etc.) had passed. Many competent Christian theologians have wrestled with these questions since 1948, and no lack of sympathy with their struggles is implied if we exclude the "death of God" from the scope of this chapter.[1]

Many Christians who have maintained a faith which others could recognize as faith in God through Jesus Christ have been unwilling to go regularly to any local Church. Already before 1948 this attitude was very common, for example among the millions who had lapsed from attendance at public worship while preserving nominal connections with the national Churches in Europe. Something of the same attitude was also found among many in Asia who respected the teachings of Jesus Christ, but refused to be baptized because they had been born into a non-Christian national religion. Since 1948 the total number of such churchless Christians has probably not varied greatly, but their attitude has been voiced more freely.

Since 1948 belief in a Christianity outside the historic denominations has indeed been expressed with a vigour which has earned the use of the term "radical". A phrase of Dietrich Bonhoeffer's has been used, and often misused, in this context: the phrase translated as "religionless Christianity". However, many of these churchless Christians have developed in such a way as to place them outside the ecumenical movement, for they have abandoned the vision and the struggle of the whole Church taking the whole gospel to the whole world. Religious broadcasts, and perhaps some fairly haphazard religious readings, have been their only contacts with articulate belief. Their warnings against the complacency of the Churches have grown less urgent as they have themselves become more completely absorbed in their own jobs and homes.

The only Christians who come within the scope of this chapter are, therefore, those believers in God through Christ who have seriously sought and persistently supported the emergence of new forms of Christian fellowship, or the renewal of the old forms, for the sake of the service of God in the world. Ecclesiastical traditions have been attacked or ignored when they seemed to be irrelevant to the life and work of Christians in an age of swift change. On the other hand, some movement or group has been valued, for these rebels have been sure that they have needed a fellowship if they were to be Christians at all, and they have hoped that this fellowship would deepen the authenticity of their faith. Such convictions have connected this kind of

---

[1] I offered discussions of theological radicalism in Chapter 1 of *The Honest to God Debate* which I edited (London 1963) and in *Religion and Change* (London 1969).

protest with the ecumenical movement, in previous periods as in our own. For example, the Mukyokai (no-Church) movement in Japan, consisting largely of Bible study groups and independent students of the Bible, has been continuous since the work of the independent evangelist Kanzo Uchimura at the beginning of the century. Without full-time organizers, this movement has been given some cohesion by occasional rallies and by literature. It is believed to include some twenty to fifty thousand Japanese, many of whom are also members of normal congregations.[1]

The form of Christian radicalism which has been most useful to ecumenical progress has, however, been the form taken by protest when it has worked within the Churches out of love for the Church. Such radicals have been convinced that, under the power of the Holy Spirit, the denominations as they naturally were should and could be loved into renewal. Dietrich Bonhoeffer, for one, never separated himself from the devotion and discipleship of the Church, the Communion of Saints about which he wrote profoundly as a young man.

Radically minded churchmen of this breed have, of course, not found it easy to remain loyal to the Churches. When American sociologists analysed mercilessly the sentimental and escapist shallowness of the piety of the suburban Churches, when a Canadian journalist hit at those who slumbered in comfortable pews instead of addressing themselves to the great challenges of the twentieth century, when British paperbacks or German broadcasts discussed at length what was wrong with the remnants of European Christendom, when Marxists declared that the religion of the Churches was opium administered to the workers by capitalists and landowners, when Afro-Asian nationalists denounced the "white man's religion" controlled by missionaries, these Christians have recognized the force and the justice in such attacks. They, too, have known how tragically often the Churches have backed a sinful *status quo* and how tragically often the renewal of the Church has degenerated into tricks to fill unchanged churches.

If these churchmen have not yielded to despair about the Church, it has been because of inspiration drawn from unusual movements or groups or prophets. But they have cared about their fellow-Christians in those comfortable pews, and any insights which they have gained have been related to the question of the future of the Church. Thus they have not abandoned the rediscovery of the missionary urgency of the gospel of God, or the rediscovery of the People of God, made in earlier periods of ecumenism. Nor have they forgotten that the most testing challenge to Christian radicalism comes from the new age announced in the Bible, not from the new events announced in the newspapers. "We have no intention of becoming a sect or a para-church", wrote one industrial chaplain. "Neither are we concerned to find a theology for industry, but rather to relate Christian theology to the community in which we live."[2] Such radicals have carried the misery of the Church, "God's frozen people", in their minds and hearts because they have

---

[1] Emil Brunner paid a tribute to the Mukyokai in *Religion and Culture: Essays in Honour of Paul Tillich* (New York 1958), pp. 287–90.

[2] Leonard Dryden in *Theology* (London December 1966), p. 531.

been convinced that the People of God is not dead, that the Church's real grandeur is hidden in the invincible purpose of God for all men.[1]

The Sign of Taizé: Religious Communities

The cry of these radicals in the ecumenical movement has been for action. The pace of the official inter-Church encounters has seemed too slow for a revolutionary world, and for a revolutionary God. But the most useful of these radicals have not forgotten the true nature of Christian action. Their small actions have been contributed as prophetic signs, pointing to the character of the activity of God. They opened the Bible, they found there the great Sign of Jesus Christ, and they prayed. They asked for strength from the one source beyond human resources; and when their actions ended in failure they knew that the God on whom they relied could still show his power as King, if necessary by the resurrection of the dead.

It seems right to mention first the prophetic sign of Taizé.[2] When Roger Schutz, a Reformed theologian, came to this half-abandoned French village in August 1940, he found an empty house and a plea from the old peasant woman who gave him a meal: "Buy this house, stay here, we are so lonely, so isolated." In that house Schutz cared for refugees. Then he had to take refuge himself, back in the Switzerland where he had been born; but when he returned to Taizé it was with the nucleus of a community in which seven brothers took life vows at Easter 1948. The brethren were under a rule modelled on the monastic (or coenobetic) tradition of the Catholic Church. More than four centuries after Luther's attack on monastic vows, the first Taizé brothers said their regular "offices" together in the cathedral of St Peter in Geneva, where Calvin (who also condemned the monastic life) had preached.

Back in France, the community has continued to be a sign of Christian care for the world's needs. It has raised the efficiency of farming in its district, and has founded a co-operative instead of growing rich. The brothers have given the skills learned in their former professions to help their neighbours in Burgundy, and have been sent to industrial France and to other nations. Notably since 1958 they have gone to Latin America, in "Operation Hope" which has concentrated on agricultural co-operatives and the distribution of the New Testament in a translation approved by the Catholic hierarchy. Taizé has also welcomed many thousands of students and other young people.

The brothers' life of prayer, sustaining this service to others, has not been a mere imitation of the ancient monastic centres such as Cluny and Cîteaux, although both historic sites lie near Taizé in Burgundy. When the *Office de Taizé* was published in 1962, its careful balance of old and new aroused the attention of many who were concerned for the renewal of Christian worship around the world. Nor has the life of Taizé been the product of a mere

---

[1] Mark Gibbs and T. Ralph Morton have written two popular books: *God's Frozen People* (London 1964) and *God's Lively People* (London 1969). Collin Williams has summed up "new directions" in thinking about *The Church* (New York 1969).

[2] For this section, see Bibliography, p. 449 below.

enthusiasm. The writings of Roger Schutz have been valued widely as the writings of a master of the spiritual life, while another able theologian in the community, Max Thurian, has made a fresh approach to some of the most difficult problems in the Catholic–Protestant dialogue from a biblical basis: celibacy, confession, confirmation, inter-Communion, the Eucharist, and devotion to the Blessed Virgin Mary. Taizé has maintained the theological review *Verbum Caro*, and has included an Orthodox centre as a witness to the relevance of the Eastern tradition.

This establishment by Protestants of a community both charitable and liturgical has challenged both Protestants and Catholics to reconsider their past rejection of each other. Here a comparison may be made between Taizé and older communities which have lived under a religious rule within Churches of the Reformation. Almost exactly a century before the arrival of Roger Schutz in Taizé, Marion Hughes took her religious vows for life in Oxford, and since then many monastic communities for men and women have been founded in the Anglican Communion. These communities have been centres of prayer for Christian unity, and the humble French Catholic priest, Paul Couturier, who was the founder of the Week of Prayer for Unity in its contemporary form, found a quick understanding among the religious of the Church of England during his visits to that island. Anglican monks and nuns have had a special interest in developing contacts with the Roman Catholics to whose examples they have been indebted in the life of the spirit, and they have done other ecumenical work.

Among Lutherans also, there has been a revival of *Life Together* (the title of a little book by the young Dietrich Bonhoeffer). Communities of deaconesses in Germany began in 1836 and have combined a life of common prayer with their charitable and pastoral work in the parishes; by 1968 there were about 40,000 deaconesses based on almost 120 houses. The Sisterhood of Mary at Darmstadt, founded by Mother Basilea (Klara Schlink) in 1947, has concentrated on a deep prayer life. This community has reached out to the Jews in penitence for the recent past, emphasizing that Israel has its own place in the hope of the coming of the Kingdom of God. Deaconesses and some small communities of women vowed to the life of prayer have also arisen in the Churches of Sweden and Denmark.

If the question is asked why Taizé has developed its extraordinary influence on the ecumenical movement, one answer is that its roots in Calvin's Geneva have made its closeness to Rome interesting and even astonishing. Its only precedents were women's communities. A community of deaconesses was founded in Reuilly near Paris in 1841, and others followed. In 1923 a community of Veilleurs (Watchmen) was founded by the French pastor Wilfred Monod, modelled on the Franciscan third order but with no mother house. At the retreat house at Pomeyrol in the South of France, in 1950 four sisters pledged themselves for life in poverty, chastity, and obedience. Another house of prayer was founded in 1936 at Grandchamp near Neuchâtel in Switzerland, and the sisters in it formed a community with life vows under Geneviève Micheli in 1952; next year they adopted the rule of Taizé. But the brothers of Taizé were more consciously ecumenical than those women aspired to be; for it was no accident that the new community of men who were Swiss and Reformed was placed in the middle of a Catholic (or ex-Catholic) France. Couturier had spoken of an "invisible monastery" in the ecumenism of prayer; Schutz founded a community which was to be international and interdenominational because it was to be a visible sign of unity.

At Taizé the opportunities for extensive fellowship with Catholics did not come quickly, although the community was allowed to use the parish church for some of its worship; and many Protestants were suspicious of a compromise with a Catholicism which seemed superstitious and reactionary. The change came when Roger Schutz was received in audience by Pope John XXIII in 1958. After that meeting it was "spring" at Taizé as part of the "spring" of the Catholic Church (as the Pope himself said), and the community was asked to send its own observers to the Second Vatican Council. Members of Catholic religious orders have shared in the life and work of Taizé and have used it for their own conferences.

The first large-scale meeting of Catholic and Protestant leaders in France took place at Taizé, four hundred years after the disastrous Colloquies of Poissy. In 1962 Christian young people from Germany built the large Church of Reconciliation in order to welcome the mainly Catholic crowds. Catholic and Orthodox chapels were built in the crypt. A large conference centre also became necessary. In the twenty-fifth year after Schutz's arrival in the village, 200,000 people came to see the sign at Taizé. The radical courage of one Protestant theologian, and of the brothers who had joined him, had come at the right time.

What of the future? Taizé stresses that its experiments have all been "provisional". Although Protestants from many nations have admired this community, and have even contributed recruits to it, at present it seems likely that less traditional forms of community life will appeal more. The Taizé brothers take the traditional vows of lifelong poverty, chastity, and obedience (slightly modified in that some use of personal possessions is allowed, and obedience is to the community rather than to the Prior alone). Some modern communities have shown that these vows have not been necessary to their purposes.

A number of ashrams in India and Ceylon have adapted Hindu models for a life of devout simplicity and they have found that this life speaks to their neighbours.[1] Perhaps the most notable example has been Joytiniketan, founded by Murray Rogers. St Julian's Community in Sussex, founded by Florence Allshorn, has adapted the model of the English country house. It grew from a concern for the spiritual refreshment of missionaries on furlough, and has been remarkable for its courage in getting away from the retreat house atmosphere in its hospitality to many guests. It now has a daughter house in Kenya.[2]

The Iona Community in Scotland, founded in 1938, has completed the

[1] Bishop A. J. Appasamy described twenty-five ashrams founded after 1921 (when an experiment was begun at Tiruppattur near Madras) in *Frontier* (London, Winter 1961), pp. 281–5.

[2] Margaret Potts, *St Julian's*. London, 1968.

buildings on the hallowed island of Iona where its worship and conferences are maintained each summer. It has also expanded the work of its members in Glasgow, in the "church-extension charges" of the new housing areas, and in other parishes. This fellowship of ministers and laymen lives under a simple discipline covering prayer and expenditure, and this has been an indispensable element in its contribution to the renewal of the (Presbyterian) Church of Scotland. But the inspiration of its founder, George (now Lord) MacLeod, has made the community evangelistic and political rather than "Catholicizing" and theological as Taizé is.[1]

Whether or not the traditional monastic vows will be regarded as essential, the sign of Taizé seems likely to remind many Christians that the spirit of discipline founded on worship is essential if Christians are to live in what the Taizé brothers call "the joy, simplicity and pity of the Gospel". To give two examples: it is through this spirit that Christian laymen serving abroad can be envoys of the Church in its ecumenical mission, and Christian laymen staying at home can be stewards responsible to God for the faithful use of their time, talents, and money.[2]

Even in its narrower sense of inter-Church relations, the ecumenical movement seems bound to involve a radical courage in the life of the spirit if it is to involve more than theological conversations and paper schemes. Specialist agents of this movement such as the staffs of Councils of Churches will be seen to resemble the members of a religious order more closely than the members of a civil service. Missionaries sent from one Church to the assistance of another will be understood mainly as ecumenical workers, and in their training and support it will not be forgotten that when Count Zinzendorf in 1732 launched the modern Protestant missionary movement into the world (with a strong emphasis on Christian reunion), it was from the base of the Moravian religious community at Herrnhut.

The Sign of Pentecostalism

There seems to be no connection between the "Calvinist monks" of Taizé and a movement which has rejected Catholic forms of prayer and belief and which has criticized the ecumenical movement for including non-fundamentalist theologians. However, a connection exists, for both the Taizé brothers and the Pentecostals have combined a conservative theology with radical experiments in fellowship.[3]

When the Pentecostal movement began in the U.S.A. and Wales as this century began, it was a movement within a number of denominations for a

[1] George F. MacLeod, *Only One Way Left* (Glasgow 1956) and T. Ralph Morton, *The Iona Community Story* (London 1957).

[2] The concern of the ecumenical movement in these areas is reflected in the reports on *Laymen Abroad* in the *International Review of Missions* (October 1967), pp. 444–58, and on *Christian Stewardship and Ecumenical Confrontation* (New York 1961).

[3] In this section I am indebted to Dr W. J. Hollenweger, whose *Enthusiastisches Christentum* (Zürich 1969) is now the standard work. An English translation is in preparation. See also his article on "The Pentecostal Movement and the World Council of Churches" in the *Ecumenical Review* (July 1966), pp. 310–20.

revival of the simplicity and fervour of the Acts of the Apostles; it was in that sense ecumenical. Today Pentecostalism has largely, although not entirely, become a family of new denominations, and its greatest strength lies in the warmth of its worship. Its lay members communicate spontaneously among themselves and with their pastor on the basis of the Bible; it is in that sense a liturgical movement. Pentecostalism, like the Taizé community, longs to see all Christians united in a more joyous and courageous fellowship of the Spirit. While Pentecostalism may seem to be an emotionalism appealing to the ignorant, in fact the nearest secular parallel is the jam session of a jazz band. Here, too, there is an underlying pattern which may be varied by the members of the band according to their own understanding of it. Here, too, we find the expression of a disinherited subculture which is now being accepted by more sophisticated people as a valuable way of making music. And here, too, there is a communal vitality which many need in the modern world.

The growth of Pentecostalism in this period has been phenomenal. Its best-known manifestations, "speaking in tongues" (glossolalia), "divine healing", and prophecy, are parts of a charismatic revival which has affected many in the traditional Churches in the U.S.A. and Europe. In Italy Pentecostals outnumber all other Protestants, and their small communities survive and spread in Russia and China. In Africa and Latin America Pentecostals form a "new tribe" which often has a quicker appeal than any other form of the Christian mission. In Brazil and Chile, it is estimated that Pentecostals constitute a fifth of the voters. Here is "soul-saving", but here also is one expression of a whole people in crisis, one factor highly relevant to social change.

Although suspicion has been dominant on both sides, consultations have taken place between leaders of Pentecostalism and of the official ecumenical movement, recognizing that "whereas Catholicism and Protestantism have laid immense stress upon what is given and unalterable, the type of Christian faith which I have called Pentecostal has laid its stress on that which is to be known and recognized in present experience, the power of the ever living Spirit of God".[1] Small Pentecostal Churches have joined the World Council of Churches, and some of its leaders have taken part in its meetings.

Some attempts have also begun to bring into the ecumenical dialogue the Africans, estimated to number around seven millions, who have expressed their Christian faith enthusiastically through "independent" or "prophetic" Churches. These religious movements, using African, not European, forms of worship, and charismatic, not bureaucratic, forms of fellowship, are similar to the Pentecostals in their warmth and simplicity. There were about six thousand of them in Africa by 1968, and it was an open question whether the older Churches in that continent—Churches which had doubled in size every ten years—would absorb such a ferment of enthusiasm.[2]

---

[1] Lesslie Newbigin, The Household of God (London 1953), p. 98.

[2] Victor Hayward, African Independent Church Movements (London 1963), and David B. Barrett, Schism and Renewal in Africa (Nairobi 1968).

Bad Boll and Bangalore: Lay Institutes and Study Centres

In the centres of Christian renewal which are to be mentioned now, the work has been formed not around the traditional order of common prayer, and not around the free worship of Spirit-filled groups of believers, but around the contemporary disorder of life in the world.[1] The laymen who have gone to the Evangelical Academies in Germany—about 40,000 a year—have gone in order to discuss their own problems freely with each other and with theologians whose thought is relevant to these problems, so that, when they return to their jobs and their homes, they may live with a fresh insight into their secular responsibilities. In these Evangelical Academies the laity come together, but only in order that they may scatter.

The Evangelical Academies were born as a result of the ruin of Germany in the 1940s. Until Hitler fell, the ruin was moral: too many Germans allowed themselves to be corrupted by Nazism. In 1945 almost all the institutions of the country were, like many of its physical assets, destroyed or despised. The universities, for example, which had always been isolated from the life of ordinary men, had compromised themselves by subordinating their liberal values to the ideology of Nazi power. Amid the ruins of a nation the Churches were left standing, if not completely in either a physical or a moral sense, at least enough to be spiritual centres of the national reconstruction. Two Protestant theologians, Helmut Thielicke and Eberhard Müller, supported by Bishop Wurm, therefore invited lawyers and industrialists to talk freely about their problems in this tragic crisis. In September 1945, 150 came to a hotel in the health resort of Bad Boll. Other groups were invited to later conferences, until twenty-three years later the Evangelical Academy at Bad Boll had enough work to keep a permanent staff of 130 (not including domestic help) busy with from 350 to 400 conferences a year, on a budget equivalent to almost one and a half million United States dollars.

Bad Boll has remained the largest, but other academies have sprung up in Germany, analysing and meeting people's spiritual and intellectual needs. Both the authorities of the Federal (Western) Republic and the Churches have been willing to support them despite their high cost in man-power and money. The Federal Republic has subsidized the discussions as part of its drive for adult education, and employers have encouraged people to attend in working time. The Churches have benefited from the arrangement by which the State collects a "church tax" from all citizens except the minority which has deliberately opted out of all church connections. So far the Churches have been willing to use part of these resources in equipping the academies, although probably most people who use them have not been, and have never become, active members of a parish congregation. In December 1945, Bad Boll convened a conference of industrial workers by relying on recommendations from parish Churches. The group did not represent the workers, and this method of invitation was not repeated. Worship in the chapels is voluntary and often poorly attended, but the conference day usually includes corporate study of the Bible. The Christian theologians and sociologists on

[1] See Bibliography, p. 449 below.

the staff contribute to each course, and they are listened to because of their knowledge of the subject under discussion and because they are familiar with the techniques of free group work.

The academies have varied in emphasis and method. Those at Arnoldshain and Loccum owe their foundations more clearly than Bad Boll to the initiatives of the Churches in their areas. Loccum, with its staff of forty, runs in addition to conferences retreats for church people and week-long courses for workers under twenty-five. The approach of Bad Boll to a group through problems arising in that group's common job has been adopted by other academies with various modifications. The Tutzing Academy by its lake specializes in cultural themes, while the Friedewald Academy in its castle specializes in courses for politicians and trade unionists. For years the Hamburg Academy owned no house, but sponsored many study groups.

Both the "pastoral" desire to serve the visible Churches and the "frontier" desire to serve laymen who are probably alienated from these Churches are present in the German academy movement. Some confusion of aim has been inevitable. However, all the academies are convinced that the Church's traditional pattern of work through parish Churches is not sufficient by itself, for "the world has become different".[1] It would not be enough to minister to people on a residential basis, even if there were enough ministers. Laymen must be helped to relate the Christian faith to their places of work and to the political and other questions which dominate modern life. This idea has made the academy movement a sign to Christians, although not a panacea to solve all the problems of the Churches.

The idea was in the air, apart from the particular circumstances which produced the first Bad Boll conference in 1945. As long back as 1915 Manfred Bjorkquist began the foundation of Sigtuna above Lake Mälar in Sweden. That foundation enabled students and industrialists to meet industrial workers at a time when social divisions went deep; and the discussions of life's problems in a free and open, basically Christian context at Sigtuna have been continuous since 1918. Sigtuna now includes a boarding school, a people's college for adult education, a large library, the Cultural Institute of the Church of Sweden, and the Scandinavian Ecumenical Institute; and it is famous for its encouragement of drama and experimental worship. There are other lay training centres in the Swedish dioceses.[2]

In England, another country with an established Church but a largely unchurched population, no Bad Boll or Sigtuna has happened. But J. H. Oldham took the lead in the Christian Frontier Council, a body of thirty to forty prominent laymen in London with its organ the *Christian Newsletter* (latterly called *Frontier*). Under Anglican auspices St George's College, Windsor, has run short courses for lay leaders and clergy, and William Temple College, Rugby, has specialized in lectures to (and discussions by) industrialists and trade unionists, and in theological training for men and women in one or two-year courses. At Dunblane in Scotland an ecumenical centre for lay training (Scottish Churches' House) was opened in 1961.

---

[1] Eberhard Müller, *Die Welt ist anders geworden.* Hamburg 1953.
[2] Olov Hartman, *The Sigtuna Foundation.* London 1955

In the Netherlands the involvement of the Church in the world has been studied more systematically, partly, it would seem, because of many Dutchmen's continuing zeal in theology, but also because this country went through the experience of occupation in the war. At the world-famous Kerk en Wereld Institute (on the estate known as De Horst at Driebergen near Utrecht) the programme has included courses of three or four years for training lay workers for the parishes and schools, as well as short conferences. At Oud Poelgeest near Leiden the laymen's conferences last for a week or a week-end, with special emphasis on international meetings and cultural activities. The Catholic Church has established a centre at De Dreef, where the emphasis is on adjusting rural Catholics to urbanization, and other centres have been thrown up by the ferment of the 1960s in Dutch Catholicism.

The most influential Dutch Reformed pioneer was Hendrik Kraemer, who like Dietrich Bonhoeffer saw in a Nazi prison that the Church must change radically if it was to take part in the life of the post-war world. Kraemer was called to be the first Director of the Ecumenical Institute founded by the World Council of Churches (thanks to the generosity of John D. Rockefeller, Jr) in the Château de Bossey near Geneva in 1946. Also on the staff was Suzanne de Diétrich, the French leader in study groups for biblical theology.

Under that great leadership, and under the next two directors, H. H. Wolf and Nikos Nissiotis, the institute at Bossey has held many international meetings for different professions and around different concerns of the contemporary world. In the winters it has also arranged a Graduate School where theological students could acquaint themselves with the work and thinking of the World Council of Churches and the wider ecumenical movement, and go back to their Churches enlightened and disturbed. Despite the difficulties which are inevitable when busy men have to organize internationally and when participants face many problems of language and idiom, Bossey has been a home of creative dialogue and study. Being stimulated by lay pressures, some of its thinking has been radical.

Although mention must be made of the beautiful centre at Boldern on the lake near Zürich, and of one of the French centres in an industrial area at Glay, the lay institutes of Europe have now become too numerous to list.

Lay institutes have spread outside Europe. Academies have been founded with German support in Japan, at Oiso near Tokyo and at Kyoto, and in Korea at Seoul. The Ecumenical Christian Centre at Bangalore and the Ecumenical Institute at Calcutta were conceived as Indian versions of Bossey, while the Ecumenical Centre at Sukabumi serves Indonesia. The Mindolo Foundation in Zambia, including the Dag Hammarskjöld Memorial Library as a Swedish gift, and the Limuru Conference Centre in Kenya were the first in a growing number of institutes where Christian participation in the new African nations could be studied and served. In South Africa, Wilgerspuit and other centres have battled for interracial co-operation and other forms of Christian action. Sometimes a council has been supplied with the resources to sponsor such lay training, as the Christian Council of Kenya did between the Mau Mau emergency and the first years of independence, publishing a brave journal of political and social comment, *Rock*. At other times a Council of Churches has given autonomy to a lay fellowship which could include many non-churchmen in its concern for special problems. A successful example has been "Australian Frontier", under the leadership of Sir James Darling and of Peter Mathews (formerly Director at Mindolo).

Such academies or training programmes have needed to be supplemented by more systematic investigations of the social and spiritual conditions of an era in close collaboration with non-Christians, leading to small consultations and to publications. Since many areas have not been too well served by Christian scholars in the universities, a world-wide chain of "study centres" has been forged since 1957. Eighteen such centres could be counted in 1968, and more were planned (such as an Institute for the Study of Man and Society in Canberra, Australia). Major contributions to research and reflection have been made in India by the Christian Institute for the Study of Religion and Society at Bangalore under the outstanding leadership of Paul Devanandan and M. M. Thomas, and in Latin America by the River Plate Christian Study Centre which has sponsored research in Montevideo under Julio de Santa Ana and in Buenos Aires under Leopoldo Niilus.

Other centres have studied the religion and culture of the Muslims (at Algiers and at the Henry Martyn Institute which has recently moved to Lucknow in India), the Buddhists (at Colombo), the Sikhs (at Batala), the Chinese (at Tao Fong Shan near Hong Kong), the Japanese (at Kyoto), the animists (at Manila), and a new socialist society (at Havana in Cuba). Other study programmes have been conducted, notably the studies of Islam directed by Kenneth Cragg for the Near East Christian Council; and the Councils of Churches in the western countries have also sponsored "working parties"— notably in London and New York—which have produced some expert reports on current political problems.

But an estimate of the world-wide influence of the academy movement must partly depend on a judgement about the willingness of North American Christians to renew their vast "lay training" programmes, stressing the techniques used and the insights gained in Germany. One of the problems here is that so many elements have been combined in the network of lay institutes and study centres. In 1948 the American Committee for the World Council of Churches published a brochure in which Walter M. Horton urged that many more centres of "re-Christianization" should be formed in America as in Europe. He included five elements in his plea:

(*a*) a sociological institute to make a national or regional survey;

(*b*) a study circle, to think out the cultural problems revealed by the survey, in the light of the affirmations of Christian faith and the principles of Christian ethics (these first two elements demand the services of a university faculty);

(*c*) a community of some sort, with a permanent leader and at least semi-permanent fraternal members, where new patterns of Christian culture can actually be tried out and launched (this and the following elements demand a rural retreat);

(*d*) an adult education programme (conferences, courses, laymen's training schools) which conveys the inspiration of the community to the nation or region, by personal contact and free persuasion;

(*e*) an ecumenical bureau.[1]

Since then, a number of books have tried to sort out the elements in such a plea which are most relevant to the American scene, and in each case they have concentrated on Horton's element (*d*)—on the idea of an academy. However, American Protestantism through twenty years seems to have agreed that academies are not for import. Instead, the lay movement which Professor Horton advocated has spread in a less organized way.

Mainly it has spread through small groups in the local Churches and projects sponsored by the national, state, or area Councils of Churches, but there have been symbolic centres. The United Church of Canada has developed four lay leadership centres. In the United States, where conference centres for youth work have a long history, many experiments have been made, although few have secured wide or long-term influence. The best-known new centres have been Pendle Hill near Philadelphia (Quaker), Kirkridge in Pennsylvania under John Oliver Nelson, and Packard Manse in Massachusetts under Paul Chapman. Such centres have conducted seminars on a very wide variety of subjects in lay people's minds, and the relevance of a renewed Christianity to the secular world has emerged through this "problem-centred" free discussion.

Paris and Sheffield: Industrial Mission

Some of these lay institutes have considered carefully problems of life in industry, and other centres, including some local Churches, have been placed in the industrial world in more than a geographical sense.[2] Examples in England are the Luton Industrial College under the Methodist Bill Gowland and the new Anglican Cathedral at Coventry which has an Industrial Chaplain on its staff and a large programme to train youth in civic responsibility. In France the Mission Populaire Evangelique (founded in 1871 as a piece of inter-Church aid by an Englishman, Robert McAll) has developed centres where agnostics can meet Christians in order to talk and work together on the problems of the industrial neighbourhood and the world.

Perhaps the most influential example has been given by the Gossner Haus at Mainz-Kostel in West Germany, under Horst Symanowski. There the Christian witness is thoroughly adjusted to the surrounding factories. Symanowski invites agnostic workers to help his sermon preparation, and has run courses for young pastors about industry; but first he himself worked for six months of each of five years as a labourer in a cement factory.

It is, however, futile to expect workers to visit such buildings unless

---

[1] Walter M. Horton, *Centres of New Life in European Christendom* (New York 1948), pp. 21–2.
[2] In this section I am indebted to the Reverend Richard Taylor. See Bibliography, p. 506 below.

Christians witness within industry. Since the Church and the proletariat have been divorced for a long time, some bold experiments have had to struggle to express a quiet Christian presence.

The two most famous of these experiments both had their origins during the war of 1939–45. Many Catholics then discovered France as a "missionary country" (*pays de mission*). They saw that the mission to the dechristianized countryside demanded new work by new teams (*équipes*) of priests with a new training in the Mission de France. And they saw that the industrial areas presented an even worse problem. Some priests, therefore, entered the lives of the anti-clerical (and often Communist) workers by doing full-time manual jobs in their midst, by joining their trade unions, and by living anonymously in the style of the proletariat. By the mid-1950s this courageous mission included about a hundred "worker priests". They knew no precedent except the priests who during the war had gone to Germany among the deported labourers.

In England, on the other hand, the complete identification of the priest with the worker has not seemed necessary, although there have been some worker priests in the Church of England. Because anti-clericalism has been less fierce in England, it has been possible to ask management and workers to receive full-time industrial chaplains, and by the mid-1960s there were about seventy of these. During the war some munition factories had appointed chaplains. Among these was E. R. Wickham, who later began the Sheffield Industrial Mission in the steel works in 1944.

Such missions on the shop floor were daring departures from the normal work of a clergyman, and the priests both in France and in England have known agonizing problems. In Paris worker priests felt obliged in conscience to identify themselves with the left-wing politics of the working class. Some of them took part in strikes and anti-N.A.T.O. riots. Many of them grew increasingly estranged from the devotional and other habits of the normal bourgeois clergy. A best-seller was written about them: *Les Saints vont en enfer* (*The Saints Go to Hell*), by Georges Cesbron. Punishment came in 1954 when the Vatican, after various warnings, ended the permission to priests to do full-time industrial work. Some of the worker priests loyally submitted to this tragedy, and eventually permission came from Rome for the Mission Ouvrière to be resumed under new conditions designed to preserve the worker priests' devotional life and to shield them from publicity. Others, however, left the priesthood rather than leave the class whose sufferings and dreams they had come to share.

In Sheffield "Ted" Wickham showed that an industrial chaplain could become a useful friend and an acceptable critic with a bold analysis, both theological and sociological. This required not only pastoral skill but also an ability to speak a rough, everyday language and a dialetical method based on an understanding of the real issues which men faced at their work. Although many small groups met for discussion with the chaplains, the chief aim was not to "win souls" or to "build congregations" in the old sense. In 1965–6, after Wickham's departure to be Bishop of Middleton, most of the clergy in the Sheffield Industrial Mission resigned because they believed that the policy of continuous experiment, and of service to industry, had been abandoned in favour of a more traditional view of evangelism. Many laymen also protested that the basis had been changed. However, the mission continued in Sheffield, and elsewhere in England Wickham's ideas had won such influence that this crisis was not a disastrous blow.

Such problems remind us of the debt owed to the church leaders who originally conceived these visions, Cardinal Suhard of Paris and Bishop Hunter of Sheffield. While experience has been gained at great human cost, tensions and dilemmas are bound to continue. A great gap continues to divide the urban, industrial masses from the traditional parishes. Another gap exists within industry, between the managers and the men (and women) who contribute their labour, but who feel alienated because they do not participate responsibly either in the work or in the surrounding society. Christians who enter these gaps must meet the cross. Quick campaigns are worse than useless. Hymns in canteens would be impertinent. Long-term commitment is essential; but the industrial mission has to be at least as flexible as the changes taking place in the community.

Since its beginning in 1956, the Detroit Industrial Mission has inspired many other industrial and urban missions in North America. Detroit has shown how an experiment which breaks loose from the conventional patterns of church life can change gear every few years. At first the ministers involved were learners. Slowly they acquired the knowledge which equipped them as counsellors, slowly they gathered groups for discussion, and slowly these groups discussed the social goals of an industrial society. By 1968 the thrust had become an emphasis on the participation of all workers in their work. The mission now spoke of the need for a fourth industrial revolution, where the focus would be on people, not on the methods of the previous three revolutions: manufacturing by hired "hands", assembly line production, and cybernetic control mechanisms.[1]

A conference in 1966 at Kyoto, Japan, brought together experienced industrial missioners from the advanced industrial countries of Japan and Australia and from nations where centuries-old traditions were being eroded (India, Korea, the Philippines, Taiwan, Thailand). The involvement of the Churches included community service among workers and their families, educational courses for labour unions, study programmes for executives, and, in Australia, visitation by chaplains.[2]

In Asia, as in Europe, by 1968 denominational differences were seen as obstacles to a Christian presence among the machines, and all over the world there was a search by Christians and others for a goal better than the old forms of capitalism and communism. Pioneering missionaries such as the ecumenical teams at Nairobi in Kenya or at Port Harcourt in Nigeria had in many places helped to urge the Churches to relate to urban life; but everything done was inadequate now that the same questions were being pressed in Africa as in the North American "secular city".

[1] See *Church in Metropolis*, (New York 1968), pp. 11–14. The story of *The Detroit Industrial Mission* (New York 1969) has been told by one of its leaders, Scott Paradise.
[2] *God's People in Asian Industrial Society*. Kyoto 1967.

Signs of Political Mission

Radically minded Christians have responded to the political drama of this period in two ways. First, they have attempted to rescue some of the miserable people who have been its victims. Second, they have attempted to influence the actual process of change, so that change may be for the sake of greater justice in society. Among all the groups which have worked in either or both of these directions, only a few, all coming from continental Europe, can be discussed here. There is not space enough even for movements as active as Christian Action in London or the Oxford Committee for Famine Relief, both of which had their origins in co-operation between Anglicans and Roman Catholics during the 1940s.[1]

C.I.M.A.D.E. (*Comité Inter-Mouvements auprès des Evacués*) began in 1939 when young French Protestants responded to the needs of refugees from Alsace. During the war it helped Jews and others to escape from an occupied France. Afterwards it met urgent needs in a ruined France, but also sent "teams" to work among refugees and young people in Germany.[2] The end of the 1940s did not, however, bring an end to the calls on C.I.M.A.D.E.'s compassion. Within France, old people, the chronic unemployed, discharged prisoners, foreign students, and migrant workers have been among the up-rooted people to whom C.I.M.A.D.E.'s workers have given friendship and some security. Through the long agony of the French defeat in North Africa teams from C.I.M.A.D.E. won the confidence of Muslims by their relief and educational work, so that an independent Algeria has continued to welcome their many activities.

C.I.M.A.D.E. describes itself as "the Church on the spot, a presence in new and difficult situations needing rapid relief or new ways of Christian witness". Mainly Protestant, it has collaborated closely with Roman Catholics and has included Orthodox colleagues. Two-thirds French, it has drawn many volunteers and also financial help from Christians in other countries. Its teams have been committed to put themselves at the service of those who suffer, regardless of religion, race, nationality, or politics. But after twenty-five years one of its leaders said:

> We must not come to the wrong conclusion that C.I.M.A.D.E. is powerful, important, admirable. The daily struggle for, and with, people in a labyrinth of problems . . . weakness, doubts and defeats, slow maturing of ideas, patient plodding . . . this is C.I.M.A.D.E.; but all this takes on a new meaning through the joy that springs from the commitment of a Christian in the fellowship of the Church.[3]

The Sjaloom movement in the Netherlands has been even more radically ecumenical than C.I.M.A.D.E. in France, although much smaller. For years Catholic and Protestant young people, laity and clergy, had been co-operating

---

[1] The founder of Christian Action has told his own story: L. John Collins, *Faith under Fire* (London 1966). "Oxfam" is not exclusively Christian.

[2] Jeanne Merle d'Aubigné, *Les Clandestins de Dieu*. Paris 1968.

[3] Pierre Buogener, address distributed by C.I.M.A.D.E., 1965.

in projects related to the renewal of the Church ("the small *oikoumene*") and the peace and development of the world ("the large *oikoumene*"). In 1963 most of the members of the group which had planned an Ecumenical Youth Congress on the needs of the world, with the theme "Five Loaves and Two Fishes", resolved to stay together in a movement to which they gave the Hebrew name for a healthy, prosperous peace based on justice.

This Sjaloom movement was soon criticized because it expressed its unity in *agape* meals (with bread and wine) which ignored the Catholic–Protestant divisions, but it has concentrated on social and political questions. Its members have, for example, taxed themselves voluntarily in order to protest against the inadequacy of government aid for the underdeveloped countries. Within five years the nucleus consisted of about thirty people, at work in almost as many professions, but a far wider circle had been touched by the monthly magazine *Sjaloom*, by other publications, and by local discussions.[1]

Agape is the name of a centre built in North Italy after the war by international youth teams in order to provide a meeting place for young people concerned for the renewal of the Church or the world (or preferably both). Its leader, the Waldensian pastor Tullio Vinay, then moved with a team to the Sicilian village of Riesi, in order that the presence of a team of Christians might bring hope and help in a scene of poverty and apathy. In Riesi, as at Agape, the work around Tullio Vinay has aroused the interest and respect of Christians and non-Christians in many nations, as a sign of a new desire in the Churches in western Europe to identify themselves with the young and the poor in their own nations and in the world.[2]

The Christian Peace Conference held its first Assembly in Prague in 1958. It originated in the desire of Protestant Christians in eastern Europe to find in the conditions of their socialist countries a way in which Christians might address themselves to public world affairs as Christians and not merely as loyal citizens of their countries.[3] The theme of "peace", already familiar for political reasons, provided an acceptable basis, and the support of the Russian Church provided financial help for an international operation. But in securing participation from other parts of the world, the Conference had the assets that its full-time secretariat was largely Czech, and its moving spirit Professor Josef Hromadka of the Comenius Theological Faculty.

Although most of the leaders steadily maintained that they sought western colleagues in their movement, although the integrity of Dr Hromadka and many of his associates was recognized in the West, and although the representative quality of western participation steadily improved, the West was never present at Prague in the person of churchmen who could match in rank the eastern leaders. Moreover, although western and especially American and N.A.T.O. policies have been rigorously and even stridently criticized, criticism

---

[1] For the story of Sjaloom, see *De Tafel van één* (Utrecht 1967) and *Shalom* (London 1969).

[2] Two books by Tullio Vinay are: *Agape: ein Wagnis der Hoffnuag für unsere Zeit* (Wuppertal-Barmen 1960) and *Reisi: Geschichte eines Christlichen Abenteuers* (Stuttgart 1964).

[3] In this section I am indebted to Canon David Paton.

of eastern and especially Russian policies has been expressed, if at all, in very subdued tones. None the less, there has been steady progress, and the third All-Christian Peace Assembly in March–April 1968 was marked by a much stronger and more representative western participation among the 500 delegates, by much more genuine dialogue, by a considerable decrease in crudely political speeches, and by a more open attitude all round.

The 1968 Assembly met in Prague a few months before the intervention by the Red Army in Czechoslovakia's liberalization. But it was preoccupied with the issue of international economic justice between the rich North and the poor South, rather than with the East–West "cold war". Chinese Christians were last present in 1961 when they spoke bitterly of the *pax Russo-Americana*. The Asians, Africans, and Latin Americans later took up this theme in a less polemical way. A feature of 1968 was the lack of interest of the Third World in the German question, and their tendency, notably in the Indian delegation, to call in question the decisiveness of the distinction between capitalist and socialist.

The Prague movement, as the Conference has aptly been called, had thus become a world movement within ten years, and from one point of view it could be regarded as the eastern European form of the ecumenical movement —that part where the discussion was conducted according to socialist rules, as in the East Asia Christian Conference the rules were Asian. At the same time, Prague must be affected by arguments between Communists and by developments in the eastern European countries. By 1968 some of those who started it were felt by impatient younger people to have accepted too many assumptions of the Stalinist period, and there were reminders that the anti-official "underground" churches (in Russia specially) were worthy of respect in working out the harsh problems of twentieth-century Christianity.[1]

If it could survive the political tensions, it might turn out that the Prague movement was essential to the healthy functioning of the World Council of Churches not only because of its eastern European character, but also because it focused the revolutionary thrust of the 1966 Church and Society Conference at Geneva. In 1968 Professor Hromadka recalled that "ten years ago, we met in order to tackle a simple programme to work for disarmament, to call for the destruction of atomic and hydrogen weapons, and to deliberate about peaceful coexistence between the so-called West and the so-called East". And he added that although the "cold war" had diminished in Europe, the contradiction between the socialist and capitalist systems, illustrated by the Vietnam war, had deepened until "we are confronted by a much more dangerous international crisis than has occurred since the end of the Second World War".[2] Yet we may conclude that the Prague movement has remained a sign of hope, for by 1968 there was some prospect not only of socialist criticisms of capitalism but also of radical criticisms within an acceptance of Communist-led revolutions.

The more basic themes of dialogue between Christians and Marxists also

---

[1] Michael Bordeaux has done his best to report from outside the Soviet Union on *Opium of the People* (London 1965) and *Religious Ferment in Russia* (London 1968).

[2] J. L. Hromadka, *Save Man: Peace is Possible* (Prague 1968), pp. 1, 4.

began to emerge during the 1960s—and not only in Prague. Outside China and Russia, official Communist pressure against the Churches has slackened off. Some Marxists such as Togliatti in Italy, Machovec in Czechoslovakia, and Garaudy in France have been saying that, if the future cannot be built without the Communists, neither can it be built without the Christians. Some scientific students of socialist societies have observed, and have respected, the strong survival of religious feelings after any revolution so far achieved. On the Marxist side, therefore, there has been some willingness to accept, and even to invite, the collaboration of religious believers in the struggles for "justice and peace" and (more rarely) some willingness to listen to the theologians' own explanations of religious belief.

On the Christian side of this dialogue, there has also been a much more active sympathy with the Communists. Pastors such as Dr Hromadka himself, Johannes Hamel in East Germany, and Bishop K. H. Ting in China have urged their fellow-churchmen to stay and accept the Communist regimes established in their countries, without forsaking belief in God as the ultimate transcendence and in Christ as the deepest liberator. Only after that acceptance could there be a gospel for atheists. Outside the Communist countries, Protestant theologians such as Helmut Gollwitzer and Georges Casalis have urged that, in a world where oppression is often a reality and religion an illusion, Karl Marx must be acknowledged as a prophet of Israel. A theology of the "just revolution" has been attempted by analogy with the "just war" approved by Augustine and Aquinas.

Although a decree from Rome in 1949 had excommunicated all Communists and had warned all those co-operating with Communists, some gestures by Pope John and the Second Vatican Council have been interpreted as softening this condemnation without changing the doctrinal attitude to Marxist atheism. Bishops have spoken up for the workers and the peasants, and have authorised some gestures such as the sale of church lands at a loss or a reduction in expensive buildings. Numbers of Roman Catholics have identified themselves with the exploited in less official, and even rebellious, ways which Communists could applaud. The best known among these was Camilo Torres, the former priest and university lecturer who was killed among the guerillas fighting the government of Colombia in 1966. Thus collaboration and dialogue with Marxists have been made possible, where before there were only anathemas.[1]

The Sign of the Kirchentag: Lay Movements

Although these lay institutes and industrial and political missions have exercised an influence, sometimes intense, on those who have taken part in their work, a radical ecumenism could not be content with the awakening of a fraction of the laity. If it is true that all Christians should contribute to the renewal of the Church and to the betterment of human life in society, means

[1] The Christian–Marxist dialogue was summarized in *Study Encounter*, vol. iv, no. 1 (Geneva 1968). See also Roger Garaudy, *De L'Anathème au Dialogue* (Paris 1965), translated as *From Anathema to Dialogue* (New York 1966).

must be found to bring their responsibilities and opportunities home to the millions.

In Germany the Bad Boll Academy has recognized the problem of linking its conferences with the whole of society, and has had the resources to prepare and carry out not only courses for parish ministers but also courses in the areas where lay people live and work, thus making an impact on a total community. But the chief instrument of the wider lay awakening has been the Kirchentag. The enterprise which now brings together some 40,000 Germans and about a thousand international visitors for four days of intensive education and argument after extensive preparation has owed its existence to the courage of one man, Reinold von Thadden-Trieglaff. This German aristocrat was a leader among Christian students and in the Confessing Church in Germany.[1] While close to death as a result of his treatment as a prisoner in Russia, he kept the vision of a popular lay movement which would bring a Christian understanding into the life of Germany. He drew some of his inspiration from (comparatively smaller) pre-war rallies of Protestants and Catholics, but the post-war difficulties and the suspicions of many church leaders were so great that he often wondered whether anyone would listen.

In the event, more than 25,000 people attended the whole programme of lectures and study circles, recitals and plays, exhibitions and sectional gatherings, in the first Kirchentag which was held at Essen, the centre of the Ruhr industrial belt, in August 1950; and about 200,000 came to the closing assembly. The Kirchentag crossed the political barriers dividing Germany at Berlin next year, and again at Leipzig in 1954, when over 600,000 were at the closing assembly. Combining Bible study with current problems of secular life, it has been in some sense a Protestant parliament, but it has been more also. The small groups into which it has been divided, and the regional and local meetings which have prepared for its great rallies, have given many lay people some experience of a personal participation in Christian thinking, and have encouraged them to speak their own minds. Collaboration with Catholics has also grown.

The massive efficiency and success of the Kirchentag have attracted many ecumenical visitors. Dr von Thadden-Trieglaff stressed from the first that it was to be more than a German affair. The Kirchentag has also inspired some modest imitations: the Kerk Dagen in regions of the Netherlands, the Rassemblement Protestant in France, and Kirk Week in Scotland. Nor should it be forgotten that the Maraman Conventions of the Mar Thoma Church in South India, which have continued to attract and educate great numbers, were already flourishing long before 1950. However, experience has suggested that outside Germany only occasional Catholic congresses and conservative Evangelical crusades are likely to bring great numbers together at a central rally.

The outstanding success in mass evangelism has been scored by the crusades of Billy Graham. These crusades resemble the Kirchentag in some ways. They are organized and financed on an independent basis, and they show that

[1] Werner Hühne, *Thadden-Trieglaff, Ein Ceben unter uns* (Stuttgart 1959), translated as *A Man to be Reckoned With*, with additional material by Mark Gibbs (London 1962).

dramatically big events still appeal, but they rely heavily on the good will of the local Churches and they make no attempt to found a new denomination (indeed, Dr Graham has often demonstrated his support of the World Council of Churches). There has been some strong teaching on specific moral issues: Dr Graham often denounces sexual laxity, warns against the danger of nuclear war, and refuses to hold racially segregated meetings. However, these Evangelical crusades have avoided the practical, controversial discussion of contemporary problems—the discussion which has been the hallmark of the Kirchentag.

The main answer to the problem of the diffusion of the radical emphasis in the ecumenical movement must, it would seem, lie in the books, periodicals, and broadcasts which supplement and influence the normal lay training of programmes of the Churches. The emphasis on ecumenism and the emphasis on radicalism, and the emphasis on the two together, have been strong at many levels of Christian writings, from the academic to the popular, during 1948-68. Journals such as *The Christian Century* in Chicago, *Christianity and Crisis* in New York, *New Christian* in London, *Réforme* in Paris, the German *Evangelische Kommentare*, and the Roman Catholic *Herder Correspondence* and *Concilium*, would provide a wealth of material, and a list of other relevant publications would seem endless. The present volume which the reader holds is only a drop in the ocean of literature which has collected the fresh experience and thoughts of Christians around the world, and the present chapter is only a brief, quiet reference to the storm of criticism which has been unleashed by writers against conventional churchgoers.

Many have purchased such books and periodicals. Less thoughtful, but even more widely read, has been the increasing volume of reportage in the newspapers and magazines with a mass circulation. But it has been through broadcasting that most have been reached.

The Sign of Addis Ababa: Broadcasting

The rapid development of means of communication during the period under review has, indeed, left the Churches stunned and exhilarated.[1] Scientific forecast has outstripped science fiction, so that Marshall McLuhan's "global village" seems about to become a reality. With satellite communication direct to the remotest corner of the world, everyone will be forced to know everyone else's business. The Churches find themselves like blundering amateurs in a highly technical world, with budgets inadequate to match the astronomical figures which only governments and vast monopolies can supply. At the same time they are exhilarated by the thought that for the first time in history it is possible to take literally the commission recorded in Matthew 28.19: "Go therefore and make disciples of all nations". This challenge has called for new structures, and because these have arisen at a time when denominationalism has been under fire, they are structures which do not depend upon the old denominational structures—apart from a few exceptions such as Vatican Radio.

[1] In this section I am indebted to the Reverend E. H. Robertson.

The advent of radio had already set a pattern for these new structures; for the pioneers of missionary radio, almost entirely from the U.S.A. and operating principally in Latin America, were from various denominations. This whole world of missionary radio, including now a TV station, has grown enormously since the Second World War, with radio stations in every Latin American country and studios in Africa, Asia, and Latin America. The transmitters have increased in strength and now pour out programmes from Quito, Manila, Monte Carlo, Monrovia, the Maldive Islands, and soon the Seychelles, to mention only the international transmitters. They all have vast follow-through operations and seek to build up the Churches overseas. They help the governments in their educational projects; but the intention is to preach the gospel, and on this basis they raise their money from Evangelical bodies, usually such as are not associated with the World Council of Churches.

Meanwhile, other structures have developed, more closely associated with the Churches of the ecumenical movement and arising partly from secular organizations. In Britain the B.B.C., largely under the direction of its first Director General, John (now Lord) Reith, evolved a Religious Broadcasting Department as part of a public corporation. That department, made up mostly of ordained ministers of various denominations including Roman Catholics and Protestants, now numbers more than thirty executives. They are responsible to the B.B.C., which pays them, and not directly to the Churches. This pattern of a religious broadcasting department within a public corporation (or a commercial radio or TV system) has become the accepted pattern in most of Europe and the Commonwealth.[1]

There are, however, other patterns. The Netherlands has developed a "pillar system" of its own. While operating like the other public corporations by means of licence fees, this has given the public an opportunity to choose its own corporation and has allowed for the ownership of programme companies by church groups. But the greater alternative was that pioneered by the U.S.A., which began with denominational structures and eventually led to co-operative ventures. Although the separate denominations still produce programmes and provide much of the money, local Councils of Churches advise local radio stations about their religious content, and the Churches' relation to the major networks is partially co-ordinated by a Broadcasting and Films Commission of the National Council of Churches. In overseas work the American Churches have also co-operated in this and related fields through R.A.V.E.M.C.O.

The Lutheran World Federation has also taken a considerable share in the use of radio for missionary work. The building of the international transmitter at Addis Ababa, "Radio Voice of the Gospel" (R.V.O.G.), was on Lutheran initiative. It has become ecumenical through co-operation with the N.E.C.C., E.A.C.C., A.A.C.C., and the Division of World Mission and

---

[1] For the reflections of the head of religious broadcasting at the B.B.C., 1955–63, see Roy McKay, *Take Care of the Sense* (London 1964). Arrangements for religious broadcasting were surveyed in the European Broadcasting Union's *Review* for December 1966 (E.B.U., Geneva).

Evangelism of the W.C.C. A similar transmitter has more recently been erected in Manila. The principle behind these transmitters has been that programmes should be produced in the countries for which they are intended and the transmitter used to send them back. By producing a balanced and responsible programme, including news and music, the aim has been to set an example of responsible broadcasting for the building up, rather than the exploiting, of the nations. The partner to the Lutheran World Federation in this work has been the Co-ordinating Committee for Christian Broadcasting. In 1968 this body united with the World Association for Christian Broadcasting, another product of the period under review, to form the World Association for Christian Communication.

The Churches thus find themselves within a communications revolution. They can try to build their own radio stations and thereby have a share in the world of broadcasting, bidding on the open market but in danger of confining their influence to a ghetto of religious people. They can recognize that they are at present privileged because they are invited to take a share in secular radio and TV, and they can take up this opportunity within whichever structure their country provides. The Churches can also encourage their members within broadcasting organizations, not in order to make it easy for a Church to gain time on the air, but in order to influence effectively the policy of those organizations as they affect the lives of the people. The only choice not left open to the Churches is evasion. The Churches are within the broadcasting industry, whether they like it or not, and they have responsibilities within it which they dare not neglect. Those responsibilities seem to be:

1. *A pastoral ministry to those engaged full-time in the industry whether as producers of religious or of secular programmes*

The conscience of the programme director needs the nurture of the Christian Church. The loneliness of men in the great industries of radio and television, making decisions which influence the lives of millions, must be recognized as clearly as that of political leaders.

2. *A prophetic ministry to the mass media in relation to what they are doing to people*

When due allowance is made for the dangers of uniformed protests, there remains an abiding need to study the effect of the mass media upon our culture and to see that as prophets the Churches warn the centres of power about the consequences of certain decisions and attitudes taken.

3. *A teaching ministry which includes the gospel in the things that are being taught*

If broadcasting develops, as seems most likely, there will be a greater freedom of choice among different programmes. The Churches must see to it that it is possible to choose the gospel.

4. *A recognized place in the world*

At a time when the structures of the Churches are under radical reappraisal, the broadcasting media must make the disarray evident. Already televised discussions of theological problems have brought distress to many conservative believers and stimulus to many confused seekers; already broadcasts of worship in the patterns of many denominational traditions have constituted an ecumenical movement in themselves; and already many people have found their faith sustained through TV and radio, not through local Churches. It is therefore essential that Christians should decide what really constitutes the essence without which there is no Church, if they are to be exposed in the open communications of a global village.[1]

The Sign of Strasbourg: Students

In our "global village" students and other young people have, of course sensed most quickly the revolutionary drama of our time. This changing mood can be seen in the World Student Christian Federation. The W.S.C.F. has grown to unite Student Christian Movements in about eighty countries, and obviously so many students have not all moved at one pace. But the intellectual vitality of the W.S.C.F., expressed through conferences and the journal *Student World*, has been impressive, and its leadership has been small enough to make its story coherent. And during this period the W.S.C.F. has handled more and more money, mainly in its "Ecumenical Assistance Programme", has sponsored "Frontier Study and Service Projects" for young graduates to work among the world's students, and has arranged much leadership training. Such things have made its life more than a succession of meetings.

The story begins with a task which was "not so much one of reconstruction as a struggle against threatening chaos".[2] These were grim days; but in the late 1940s the Federation struggled with a confidence born in the Bible study which had been filled with fresh meaning and excitement for many groups in the European Resistance. The struggle was to build on this biblical basis a stronger and more comprehensive understanding of *The Task of the Christian in the University*, the title of a W.S.C.F. "Grey Book" by John Coleman.

Co-operation among Christians in the universities and colleges was one clear aim in this period. In the United States, the United Student Christian Council, formed in 1944, encouraged contacts and co-operative projects although the bulk of "religious activity" on the campus was organized by the now flourishing Churches. In Germany the student parishes (*studentengemeinde*) gathered Evangelical students in fellowships under pastors appointed by the Churches. In Asia the S.C.M.s were the main representatives of Protestant Christianity among students, and the task was to train their leadership. The W.S.C.F. itself provided this training and acted as a channel for the generosity of American and other Christians towards the students in

---

[1] A good beginning to the necessary discussion about these responsibilities was made in the document on "The Church and the Media of Mass Communication" presented by the W.C.C. communications department to the Uppsala Assembly of the W.C.C.

[2] *Unto a Lively Hope*, a report on the W.S.C.F. 1946–9 (Geneva 1949), p. 12.

physical or mental need, first in war-destroyed Europe, and then in Asia, Africa, and Latin America.

But what was to be the aim of the work? It took some time for the S.C.M. to see what could replace, or supplement, the old call to missionary work overseas. This answer was already clear to some leaders in 1949:

> We must see the significance of vocation not so much in mere personal, social and even ecclesiastical terms, but first of all in terms of God's work of bringing history to its consummation and of the re-creation of the whole universe. This divine plan is the only movement or process in the universe to which every individual must say his Yes or No.[1]

In such words may be read the basic theology of a radical ecumenism. However, in the 1950s, while the post-war reconstruction slowly proceeded, problems of personal life seemed to most students more urgent than the large and probably insoluble problems of the world; and Christian students shared this attitude. "The prevailing temper of our S.C.M. has become more conservative", the Canadians reported in 1952, adding: "There is a danger of a superficial orthodoxy which is simply not interested in asking questions."[2] In the U.S.A. it became customary for their more public-spirited elders to lament the "silent generation" then at college, interested only in "fraternities, football, and fornication". The Churches built centres for recreation and pastoral care on the edge of the campus, and welcomed considerable numbers of students to worship services which contributed to the peace and pleasure of the weekend.

This safe period in student Christianity ended towards 1960—partly as a consequence of the spread of S.C.M.s in the 1950s. The first W.S.C.F. secretary was appointed for Latin America (Valdo Galland, later General Secretary). African activity grew in higher education as well as in the schools, and the work in Asia was expanded. Because it was more global than ever before, the Federation listened more and more attentively to the post-colonial world's angry and eager talk, even when western Europe and North America had grown bored with politics. In 1952 M. M. Thomas of India collaborated with Davis McCaughey to write a W.S.C.F. "Grey Book" on *The Christian in the World Struggle*. It was a call to Christians to take part in the social revolution, sometimes with a No but often with a Yes and always with a conviction that God's purposes for his world (not merely for the Church) could be discerned and obeyed.[3]

In 1956 the General Committee of the Federation, meeting in the Evangelical Academy at Tutzing with strong delegations from the younger S.C.M.s, took two decisions which together summed up one period and inaugurated another. First, the Federation's aims were revised. The new words declared the intention to lead students to live as disciples of Jesus

---

[1] *Unto a Lively Hope*, p. 67.

[2] *Witnessing in the University Communities*, a report on the W.S.C.F. 1949–52 (Geneva 1952), p. 4.

[3] *Witnessing to Jesus Christ the Reconciler*, a report on the W.S.C.F. 1953–6 (Geneva 1956) and Philippe Maury, *Politics and Evangelism* (New York 1959).

o

Christ "within the life and mission of the Church". Second, a new programme of conferences and publications was inaugurated on "the Life and Mission of the Church". The leaders of the Federation at this juncture (notably D. T. Niles, the Chairman from Ceylon, and Philippe Maury, the General Secretary from France) believed that an "ecumenical consensus" had emerged about the revealed nature of the gospel and the missionary nature of the Church. The programme was designed in order to educate students in this theological consensus, and in order to train them for the mission to the world. But as the project developed, the cries of a revolutionary world almost drowned the dynamic simplicity of this original massege, and the ecumenism which had emerged in the Federation countless words later was no longer neo-orthodox: it was radical.

At Strasbourg in 1960 the Federation held a world "teaching conference". Some of the Church's ablest speakers—Barth, Niles, Visser 't Hooft, and Newbigin were four of the galaxy—did their best to pass on the vision. But at Christmas 1958 a preparatory conference in Rangoon had already indicated another trend; for young Asians, afire with the promise of a new world, had their own sharp questions for the missionary Church. As Davis McCaughey wrote, "Rangoon marked an important step away from high biblicism or high churchmanship into a high view of God's dealings with the world: high worldmanship."[1] So at Strasbourg the eloquent theologians might have some radical ideas to propound, but the audience was restless. There seemed to be too much speaking about the life of the Church; what students wanted was action in their world. And there seemed to be too much mission; what students wanted was a welcome to this world.

Subsequent conferences attempted to see what the right actions would be within a setting of acceptance. How could Christian students serve the revolution in Asia, Africa, and Latin America? How could they serve in a western world which was being united by an economic progress which brought secularization? The building of new nations seemed to these students a cause more sacred than the expansion of the more narrowly Christian work which the missionaries had led. The new secular city in Europe or America seemed a place of life and hope while the Christian denominations argued about the past. A European conference at Graz in Austria in 1962 took as its theme "Who is Man? The Presence of Jesus Christ in our World". The basic thought was that Europe was bored with religion (and perhaps North America also, although the churchgoing there made this conclusion less plausible), so Christianity must be shown as a humanism, as "proexistence", and one of Christianity's few permanent assets was the example of the humanity of the Son of Man. It was by meeting the revolution in the world that a new generation would meet Jesus Christ.

When the General Committee of the Federation met in Argentina in 1964, at Embalse Rio Tercero, it approved a statement on "The Christian Community in the Academic World". The statement recognized the diversity both in higher education and in Christian theology around the world, but it

[1] *Students and the Life and Mission of the Church*, a report on the W.S.C.F. 1956–64 (Geneva 1964), p. 6.

clarified some basic convictions about the style of approach which was right for Christian students. It was a humble approach.

> Presence for us means engagement, involvement in the concrete structures of our society. . . . First we have to be there before we can see our task clearly. . . . We have no Christian philosophy of education and no ideology about the academic world. We are partners in the ongoing discussion about them.

But it was also an approach of Christian hope.

> For us, to be present in the name of Christ spells death to the *status quo*, both in society and in the Christian community: we will not tire of pleading and working for the restoration of normal manhood as we see it in Jesus. . . . From what happened to the Lord, we know what resistance and opposition to expect. And as for our weak faith, our poverty of understanding of what we believe, we trust that while present we will be given new words or an authentic silence.

Some characteristics of the Christian community in the university were listed by the 1964 document: openness to persons and groups, diversity, experimentation, unity among Christian students, and an understanding with the Churches. The Federation then called for many consultations about an "ecumenical strategy" in the academic world, but it emphasized a new meaning of ecumenism. "By this we mean the discovery which the churches participating in the ecumenical adventures are beginning to make: that the basic ecumenical concern is the relationship between the Church and the world."[1]

It was in the United States that the new emphasis on Christian presence within the secular world came to its sharpest focus. There, students had the opportunity not only to discuss the world but also to transform a significant part of it, and Christian students had a cause which they could serve with enthusiasm. In 1959 the United Student Christian Council became the National Student Christian Federation, a body with a greater identity. The N.S.C.F. encouraged a new generation in American religion, tougher and outward-looking, and the movement to assert the civil rights of America's own coloured people gave a cutting edge to it. There was a cause both worldly and humanitarian, which had Negro ministers already prominent in the leadership and which could arouse many consciences in the white Churches. There was a cause which was momentous in itself and which connected with the response of Christians to the whole Afro-Asian revolt. There was a cause which demanded political action and physical risk in demonstrations, but which also asked individuals to co-operate as friends, "black and white together", and to think strenuously; and here was a cause which, if served worthily, would overcome.

More than 3,500 students went to a conference at Athens, Ohio, in December 1959, many of them after preparation in study groups which were international, interdenominational, and interracial. There they discussed the Christian world mission, and in the new year many of them were involved in civil rights demonstrations which included "sit-ins" (when Negro and white

---

[1] See also Martin Conway, *The Undivided Vision: Students Explore a Worldly Christianity* (London 1966).

students would sit until they were served in segregated restaurants—or thrown out). When James Lawson was expelled from Vanderbilt Divinity School for his part in these demonstrations, the right to take part in civil disobedience and passive resistance in order to uphold God's law of human equality was affirmed in a statement issued rapidly by the N.S.C.F. As the civil rights movement gathered strength, more and more Christian students took part in its protests. The activism of the Student Non-Violent Co-ordinating Committee spilled over into international work camps and into the Peace Corps as part of the idealism of John Kennedy's presidency.

Those Kennedy years ended in blood; but as the United States got more deeply involved in the horror and futility of the Vietnam war and in the riots of the cities at home, the non-violent philosophy learned in the civil rights struggle combined with the new wave of sympathy with coloured mankind's grievances to feed an anti-war and anti-poverty campaign led passionately and effectively by students and their teachers and by clergymen. In 1966 such pressure transformed the N.S.C.F. into the more integrated University Christian Movement, including many Roman Catholics. Organizational difficulties soon seemed to be frustrating that particular adventure, but it was clear that many Christian students were still radical in politics and religion. When Martin Luther King was murdered in 1968, he became the triumphant martyr of a "Freedom Movement" which had begun in civil rights, but which would not now rest content until peace and justice had come nearer to the whole world. Here, as students struggled for the future of the world, was a working embodiment of the "secular" gospel of which the theologians were speaking. The world was now so powerful that it had "come of age"; but those who would serve God in it must accept both the action and the suffering to which Christians had been called by one who was now the most influential theologian of them all: Dietrich Bonhoeffer, martyred twenty-three years before Martin Luther King.[1]

Outside the United States the involvement of Christian students in the political life of the world has been on a smaller scale, but in almost every country during the 1960s student protests made the headlines and attracted the (often influential) participation of young Christians. The Uniao Christa de Estudantes do Brasil, for example, adopted in 1961 the position that "the contemporaneity of Christianity is on the Left", and since then it has been strengthened in its revolutionary work by a covenant with the New England S.C.M. Already in the late 1950s the Federation Française des Associations Chrétiennes des Etudiants had declared its solidarity with all Frenchmen who refused to take part in the war in Algeria, and in the winter of 1960-1 its Executive Committee condemned "conscious or unconscious apoliticism as a sin in the light of the Incarnation", asking all members if the time had not come to join the ranks of the Communists or the Socialists. Both in Brazil and in France these militant students cheerfully defied the caution of the church leaders, and did it before "protest" became the student posture.

Other radically political moves involving young Christians included the

---

[1] See the lively magazine of the U.C.M., *Motive*, founded by the Methodists but dominated by a radical ecumenism treating secular subjects.

efforts of Australian students to question the "white Australia" immigration laws; the 1968 student riots which attacked the conservatism of West Germany and France; the anti-militarization demonstrations in Japan; and the anti-apartheid demonstrations throughout the western world. In 1964 the Student Christian Association of South Africa, arguing that the W.S.C.F. had become a political organization, left the world body, only to find, a few months later, that it must split up itself on the racial issue.[1]

The Sign of Lausanne: Youth

The World Student Christian Federation has become a political organization (if not in the sense alleged from South Africa) partly because the students in its membership have *not* been really typical of young Christians. The circles organized by chaplains appointed by the Churches, or the Christian or Scripture Unions which are linked in the International Fellowship of Evangelical Students, have probably been more typical of students with an interest in Christianity (a minority of all students), while of course most young people have not been in higher education. By 1968 over half of mankind was under twenty years of age. So we have to look beyond the colleges in order to ask: Do new ideas about Christianity appeal to the new generation?

> Our experience at Martin Luther King's talk was very good [was one entry in a diary kept by three young Roman Catholics and three young Lutherans as part of a small project of ecumenical education in Chicago in 1966]. Here is an issue we can confront together and not piddle around with or get bogged down with doctrine. That's what I want to see the Church do—face the problems of the world together.

Another of these young people wrote:

> My Church is two churches. One is the surface; the other is the depth. The depth is coming to the fore as people realize that God, man, love, life, Christ cannot be defined. The truth can only be plumbed when he realizes that the important questions are mysteries. But most of us want to define God!

An adult summed up their experience:

> The young people involved in this project discovered that to have new life in Christ and to be open to his new creation requires death ... perhaps the death of one's own traditions and one's own identification as a Lutheran or Roman Catholic. . . . Is not this the meaning of reformation?[2]

It is impossible to say how widespread are the concerns and convictions indicated by those three excerpts from one experiment in Chicago. However, the Youth Department of the World Council of Churches has often pointed to these as the themes which are vital to the new generation.[3] Apart from its sponsorship of ecumenical work camps, the Youth Department has made no

[1] *Reflections on Protest*, ed. Bruce Douglass (Richmond, Virginia 1967).

[2] *Wine in Separate Cups* (Chicago 1967), pp. 62. 87, 120.

[3] As in its document on "Youth in God's World" for the Uppsala Assembly of the W.C.C. See also *The New Creation and the New Generation*, ed. Albert H. van den Heuvel (New York 1965).

attempt to be an executive body with an ambitious budget; but its staff and publications (especially the imaginative magazine *Risk*) have probably encouraged many leaders of young people's groups. These leaders would recognize the words from Chicago as echoes of the thoughts of their own more sensitive and articulate young friends. Enough confidence may have been gained in this period to justify a great multiplication of ecumenical educational projects and of ecumenical teams of young people in longer-term social service over the next twenty years.

The work of the Y.M.C.A. and Y.W.C.A. has indeed already given some indication of what a truly ecumenical programme for youth might look like. These bodies were pioneers in what the *History of the Ecumenical Movement, 1517–1948*, rather unhappily called "diffused ecumenicity". In the last twenty years their work has grown in two main directions. By providing clubs and hostels for the social, cultural, and physical development of young people in every nation where they were allowed to do so, and by arranging some colleges and courses to train young people as workers and citizens, the Ys have quietly practised the gospel which the more sophisticated W.S.C.F. began to preach in the 1960s: the gospel of "cohumanity" with a humble serving "presence" among those unrelated to the active life of the Churches. Non-Christians have therefore trusted the Ys as they have trusted few other Christian organizations.[1] And by earning the good will of many churchmen for this practical service to young people, the Ys have secured an important basis for the participation of Christians in common prayer, Bible study, and work.

At the Centennial World Conference in Paris in 1955 there was a growing awareness of the need to pay fresh attention to the Christian basis and ecumenical opportunities of the Ys as lay movements, and a world-wide discussion began.[2] A consultation at St Cergue in Switzerland in 1962, with both Orthodox and Roman Catholic participation, affirmed about the Ys: "As world movements they are not organically related to any Church or confession." Locally "each Association must be challenged to scrutinize its own practices and programme to see whether unconsciously it may be treating persons of another confession as guests rather than full members".[3] This ecumenical policy of both movements received a clear emphasis in statements by their World Councils in the years 1963–5.

The work in predominantly Orthodox communities has always been conducted in harmony with the principles of the Orthodox Church, since the days of John R. Mott;[4] and the World Conference of Young Adults at Beirut in 1964, for example, showed this policy in action. An international meeting of Y leaders of the Roman Catholic confession was held in Geneva in 1961. Bishops in Canada and the U.S.A. approved the full participation of Roman Catholics in the Ys where appropriate conditions obtained locally. In other

[1] *An Open Door*, a report on a consultation at Kandy on the talk of the Ys in countries where dominant faith is non-Christian (Geneva 1967).
[2] *The Y.M.C.A., the Church and Christian Unity* (Geneva 1957) supplements the *History of the World Alliance of Y.M.C.A.'s* by C. P. Shedd and others (London 1955).
[2] *Report of the Consultation on Ecumenical Policy and Practice for Lay Christian Movements* (Geneva 1962), pp. 28–9.
[4] See Paul B. Anderson, *Orthodoxy and the Y.M.C.A.* (Geneva 1963).

areas such as Latin America and the Philippines, where large numbers of Roman Catholics had already availed themselves of the facilities and fellowship of the Ys, this participation has begun to be blessed by the ecclesiastical authorities. Such developments show how much has changed since 1920, when the Holy Office in Rome denounced the Y.M.C.A.

A detailed commentary on the problems of the Churches has, however, not been forthcoming from the Ys, either from their local units, which have been mostly absorbed in their own social work, or at the world level, where a certain suspicion of theology has been natural (although the work of the world conference centre at Castle Mainau has been an exception). The 1952 World Conference of Christian Youth at Travancore, India, was also quiet in its criticisms. In order to provide a forum for plainer speaking, an Ecumenical Youth Assembly for Europe was sponsored by the World Council of Churches at Lausanne in Switzerland in July 1960.

Some 1,700 young people and their leaders, delegated and prepared by their Churches, came to Lausanne from almost every country in Europe. Their enthusiasm was a tonic to those grown weary in the service of the ecumenical movement. It was also a rebuke; for these young Europeans were hurt and angry to discover that they knew so little about other Churches and nations, that they were unable to agree about so many ecclesiastical, political, and personal questions, and that they were forbidden to receive Holy Communion together.

Most of the young people did share in an open Communion outside the conference programme. All of them accepted some radical findings which urgently pleaded for a movement of "aid and reparation" from Europe to the poorer continents, and a movement of Christian renewal and reunion within Europe. This message stated:

> The ecumenical movement is not a liberation from the bounds of the local Church, but a calling to a more conscious participation in the life of the Church. We are agreed that we are more than ever committed to our local Church. But we belong to them now as people who know that in our local Church the whole Church is supposed to be there for the whole world in its need. We belong to our local churches henceforth as restless and impatient members called to critical participation. . . . We are going home as Christians who have experienced what it means not to be able to become one at the Lord's Table, and who do not want to shrug off this pain and no longer want to conceal this guilt from themselves.

Although several Churches have made progress towards intercommunion and reunion since 1960, the radical attacks on outworn conventions which stimulated the Lausanne Assembly would not have been entirely answered even if all barriers at the Lord's Table were to come down. For the Christian mission was seen at Lausanne to demand new methods.

These young Europeans said:

> We go home with the knowledge that mission is not advertisement but service, a real entering into the need of other people, and the struggle with their need in practical help, prayer, and witness in daily life. We go home with the know-

ledge that mission of this kind is perhaps more a concern of lay people than of pastors, because they are closer to the everyday life of their fellow men; and that the fulfilment of mission is thus our concern, particularly in regard to our contemporaries. We go home with the urgent question as to whether the mission of the local Church is not best fulfilled by small, flexible, closely-knit communities of people living or working together, communities which by their presence in the everyday world of today, by the manner of their life together, and by the fact of their being unconditionally at the disposal of their fellow men, create trust and bear witness to the reality of Christ's presence.

In other words, the Lausanne Youth Assembly, like the simultaneous Strasbourg Conference of the W.S.C.F., saw the beginnings of a radical re-interpretation of the ecumenical task. More than thirty years after the First World Conference on Faith and Order (Lausanne 1927), a new generation in the Christian Church responded to speakers such as the Dutch theologian, J. C. Hoekendijk, who asked:

> Are there no revolutionaries here? People who do not want to improve or to modify the structures and institutions of our Christian life but who are ready to break out of these prisons. . . . ? Is there any chance for you to avoid one of the major ecumenical sins, that is to be churchy? [1]

Other continental Youth Assemblies (for North America at Ann Arbor in 1961, for Africa at Nairobi in 1962, and for Asia at Damaguete City at the turn of 1964–5) saw further beginnings. Asian youth, for example, stirred to the protest of T. B. Simatupang, the lay Chairman of the National Council of Churches in Indonesia:

> What is going on often gives the impression as being not much more than just a repetition of the endless dialogues between the different denominations among the Western churches. Sometimes I wonder whether what we need in facing the call to unity, service and witness now is not a kind of revolution. . . . [2]

And this would certainly be thought an understatement by the ardent revo-lutionaries in movements such as the Union Latinoamerican de Juventudes Evangelicas.

The Radical Renewal of the Church

What would this revolution for the sake of mission bring to the Churches of Europe or Asia or anywhere? The World Council of Churches has produced many exhortations and hints at its meetings, and the European and North American working groups set up by the Council to study "the missionary structure of the congregation" produced in 1967 reports which excited a widespread discussion. These reports virtually confessed that the problem of the renewal of the local Church in its parish had proved too big.

Readers who noted how few parish ministers had served in these high-powered groups could not be surprised by this failure. Readers in Asia and Africa, where habits of communal worship have often survived, and Christians

---

[1] A report of the Assembly was in *Youth* (W.C.C., Geneva) for October 1960.
[2] *Christ the Life* (Colombo 1965), p. 71.

under communism, who are usually allowed *only* their communal worship, have been disappointed by the apparent irrelevance of the reports to their situations. The academic flavour was pronounced: "to speak of God's action in the contemporary world is to raise the problem of *Christus extra muros ecclesiae* . . ." So too was the bureaucratic style: "The world provides the agenda . . ."

But what emerged from the reports, despite these limitations, was an emphasis on new congregations, meeting around the needs of particular parts of the secular world. These new "zones" were the natural units of working or social life, and often they were unrelated to the parochial boundaries which divided residential neighbourhoods. The para-parochial congregations related to the new "zones" would find their validity from that participation in the divine purpose which the reports insisted on Latinizing as *missio Dei*. And they would soon learn that "in *Mission* every denominational difference is irrelevant".[1]

The European group pleaded that some "theological competence" was now needed by all and spent most of its energy working towards a new theology of the mission, but it hinted at the practical implications. It could point to several of the "signs" mentioned in this chapter together with the *Aktion Sühnezeichen* (Action Reconciliation) movement of young Christians in Germany (contributing labour to new buildings at Taizé, Coventry Cathedral, and elsewhere)[2] and the world-wide movement of Telephone Samaritans founded by a London priest to help those tempted to despair or suicide.[3] The North American group decided to get at the theory through the practice, and gave most of its energy to evaluations of its members' participation in "task forces". The projects described included involvement in the Freedom Movement and in new fellowships for artists, scientists, and young adults in San Francisco, in concern for the schools of Vermont and the gaols of Los Angeles, work for the underprivileged of Chicago and San Francisco, the study and action of the Metropolitan Association of Philadelphia, and experiments in training ministers.

The reports thus indicated a new energy among Christians who turned to the world in order to serve it as the students and young people in Strasbourg and Lausanne had recommended. Another sign of the times was a survey by the W.C.C. of the development of the ordained ministry in western Europe. Of the 52,400 ordained ministers of the member-Churches of the World Council in this area, 6,800 were in specialist ministries, such as education, evangelism, administration, hospitals, armed forces, retreat houses, and religious communities. Most of these specialists were carrying on work long recognized by the Churches; the chaplain was a familiar enough figure. But observing the 1960s one could say that some notice had been taken of the fact that the greater diversification of modern urban life demanded more chaplaincies if the church structures were to be relevant. The possibility had been faced that many more ordained ministers would work mainly in secular employment and only part-time as professional clergymen; and, whether or

---

[1] *The Church for Others* (Geneva 1967), pp. 11, 20, 35.
[2] Ansgar Skriver, *Aktion Sühnezeichen*. Stuttgart 1962.
[3] Chad Varah, *The Samaritans*. London 1965.

not many non-parochial congregations were on the horizon, more emphasis had been placed on the life and work of the laity as 99.9 per cent of Christian witness and service. It had been agreed, even if the agreement had not been worked out in practice, that the Church must scatter to do its work in the world, but also that somehow it must continue to be the Church in the world, for many pressures in the world were liable to destroy Christian faith and life.

By 1968 many hopes of a radical renewal in the parishes in order that the laity might be equipped for this daily task had been disappointed. Many of the Bible study groups and house churches and many of the experiments in youth work which had been inspired in the war-time or post-war atmosphere had been ended. Albert van den Heuvel complained in 1963:

> When we look back at the period since 1945, we see the renewal movement imprisoned in carefully defined and tentative experiments which were never allowed to become a strategy. We see courageous new initiatives domesticated, and others stopped because they were dangerous; some were institutionalized, and only a handful are still swimming against the stream of easy restoration. . . . The result is an ever increasing and ever continuing exodus of our best laymen and pastors, and the growing sense of conservatism among many who despair of total renewal. There is a terrific frustration among those who stayed and who still feel God is in the structure of the Church.[1]

But, as the previous chapter in this volume shows and as Albert van den Heuvel has urged with equal eloquence elsewhere, despair would not do justice to the whole picture. By 1968 there were some signs that some of the themes of "renewal" were stirring the parishes. It was clear that, if renewal came, it would be through congregations meeting their Lord in worship which would offer the common life of the Body of Christ; meeting themselves in discussions which might replace many sermons, and in house churches; and meeting their neighbours in action teams, in open groups, in humble service, in new church buildings which would not be used only for worship, in worship which would have meaning for modern men.[2] It was no accident that some of the Churches' most effective in work for a neighbourhood sprang out of the commitment of a team of ordained and lay Christians to that neighbourhood and to each other. So the Christian community bred a larger community, when the inner team of Christians had a radically ecumenical concern for the world.

The dramatic and unexpected changes in Roman Catholicism during this period suggested that a radical renewal might not be an impossibility within official structures and traditional patterns. For Roman Catholic ecumenism has not been confined to the new spirit of prayer, courtesy, and co-operation with other Christians at the official level. As Roman Catholics have questioned traditional customs and teachings for the sake of a more effective mission in the modern world, there has been an ecumenism of *aggiornamento* (updating). The priesthood and the religious orders have been examined afresh. The liturgy has been reformed and put into the local language in order to make it

---

[1] Albert H. van den Heuvel, *The Humiliation of the Church* (Philadelphia 1966), pp. 52–3.

[2] J. G. Davies, *Worship and Mission*. London 1966.

more clearly the offering of the people. A new emphasis has been placed on the layman's responsibility and initiative, especially in Roman Catholic movements of students and young people. Within the Eastern Orthodox tradition also, especially among more than three million Orthodox in the U.S.A., some similar stirrings and changes have begun. [1]

No one in our period was able to say definitely exactly what changes would finally result in the Churches. Exciting words such as "radicalism", "renewal", "revolution", and "reformation" have been used without agreement as to their content, despite many attempts at definitions. In a period which future generations might regard as the eve of a new reformation, all that had been gained was a vision; and the "signs" would have to multiply if the Churches were to be changed and if the world was to be served in the name of Christ. But precisely here, in the 1960s, lay the challenge. Hoekendijk at Lausanne told the young people about some of the groups formed in Europe's new missionary era. He added:

> When we try to define the character of these groups we can combine the key words of the Iona Community, *commitment*, and of Taizé, *disponibilité* (being disposable). There is no mystery at all in starting these groups. Each one of us could do it. Just find one other partner and try to explore what life in *commitment* and *disponibilité* actually means. Before long you will have a house Church around you, I can assure you. . . . When do you begin to think of the partner with whom to start this group?

---

[1] Some Christian groups in revolt against normal church life, but given a sense of direction by political protest, have arisen informally in the United States and are described in *The Underground Church*, ed. Malcolm Boyd (New York 1969).

15
Uppsala and Afterwards

EUGENE CARSON BLAKE

INTRODUCTION

The Fourth Assembly of the World Council of Churches opened with worship of God in the Cathedral of Uppsala, Sweden, on 4 July 1968. The year 1968 had been marked by "the excitement of new scientific discoveries, the protest of student revolts, the shock of assassinations, the clash of wars".[1] It will not be possible to assess the accomplishments of the Assembly, its limitations, or its implications for the future, without careful attention to what was going on in the world in 1968 as the delegates of the Churches gathered in Uppsala.

Every report received, document approved, and programme envisaged was affected by the state of the world even more than by the state of the Church. Technology had caught up with and passed the vision and programme of the ecumenical movement. The members of the Assembly knew that the world had become one technologically. The world, for better or for worse, was now a neighbourhood, made so by instant communication, rapid mobility, economic interdependence, and mutual political involvement. But these world neighbours were clearly not yet a community. Men's attitudes towards each other in 1968 remained limited by the old and familiar smaller unities of race, nation, confession, ideology, class, and even of tribe and family. Whether consciously or not, each member of the Assembly knew in his depths that radical change, creative and destructive, was the mark of the times forcing all to re-examine the foundations, to dream new dreams, to build new structures in order to be relevant to the ultimate fears and hopes of man.

The question faced by the Assembly, a question too great to find a cosy place on the docket, was whether the world community demanded by the world's new technological interdependence could and would be established in time to prevent that nuclear self-destruction imminent since Hiroshima. And a secondary question was faced by the Assembly. Did the faith in God revealed in Jesus Christ which had drawn the Churches together in the World Council of Churches have power enough to contribute to the human necessity of 1968?

The conservatism of the Uppsala Assembly was marked by its worship of a God still believed to be very much alive, and by its continued dependence upon the Scriptures. These two convictions were summed up in its biblical theme "Behold, I make all things new" (Rev. 21. 5). This theme of the Uppsala Assembly was more than a motto. Its meaning was seriously expounded in the opening sermon, and exegetically examined in the main theme address. But even more than this, the present activity of the living God in anticipation of his plan of cosmic salvation for his world was assumed and acted upon by most of the delegates to the Fourth Assembly. This was not an easy faith to hold to in 1968. There in the pulpit at the opening service was a substitute preacher because Martin Luther King, who had been invited to preach because he was reckoned to be the Christian leader most "with it" in 1968, had fallen to an assassin's bullet.

[1] This statement was part of the concluding message of the Fourth Assembly; see Uppsala, p. 5.

413

One could have asked whether God's design was still relevant after this kind of disorder in 1968. One could have lost nerve in a revolutionary, reactionary, divided, and materialistic world wondering whether Jesus Christ still signified either hope or light. Yet despite world-wide fear, despair, and cynicism, the Uppsala Assembly revealed that the gospel of Jesus Christ is still revolutionary when it is heeded, still powerful to convert men and nations, and is still the only reason that the Church and the Churches are important.

But the Uppsala Assembly was not conservative in the bad sense which many "progressive" critics predicted it would be. It did not reject the findings of the 1966 Church and Society Conference. On the contrary, it approved a message which read in part:

> All men have become neighbours to one another. Torn by our diversities and tensions, we do not yet know how to live together. *But God makes new.* Christ wants his Church to foreshadow a renewed human community. Therefore, we Christians will manifest our unity in Christ by entering into full fellowship with those of other races, classes, age, religious and political convictions, in the place where we live.

The Fourth Assembly did not limit its radical newness to the approval of messages and resolutions, but responded positively and enthusiastically to the several new programmes of action, described below, which had been proposed to it by the staff with the approval of the retiring Central Committee.

Again, the Uppsala Assembly did not bog down or retreat, as had been widely predicted, because of the presence in its membership of many more representatives of the Orthodox Churches than had been present in any previous Assembly. The Orthodox members of the Assembly did not in fact become a bloc either politically or theologically any more than, for example, were the Anglican members or the representatives of the American Churches. It was to be expected that Orthodoxy would have its own theological traditions and convictions. The Orthodox members were there to reflect and express them. The fact that so many Protestant progressives feared the influence of the greater numbers of Orthodox is an indication of how important Orthodox–Protestant dialogue has become. Such dialogue must be mutually corrective as the concluding message put it: "We reaffirm our covenant to support and correct one another." This covenant was honoured at Uppsala. For the first time in a major ecumenical meeting fully attended by the Eastern Churches, their representatives at no place found themselves forced by conscience or theological conviction to make a separate Orthodox statement on the subject at issue. This was a tribute not only to the members and leadership of the Assembly itself but also to the preparations for the Assembly which had provided for full Orthodox participation from the very beginning. The Uppsala Assembly was clearly the most ecumenical assembly of the World Council of Churches because of this large and effective Orthodox presence.

Nor did the Fourth Assembly waver or hesitate to approve dynamic new relationships with the Roman Catholic Church which since New Delhi had affected the World Council of Churches in almost every part of its life and programme. It had been widely predicted that sharp criticisms would be voiced or deep hesitations expressed about this new intimate collaboration with Rome especially from minority Protestant Churches in the Latin countries and from some of the Orthodox Churches in eastern Europe. This did not occur either in the Policy Reference Committee or in plenary session of the Assembly.

This fact should not be cited to prove that no such concern is felt by these or other Churches. We know that the effects of nine centuries of polemics, East and West, do not disappear in five years. We know that the vexing problems of Uniate Churches have hardly begun to be discussed in the new post-Vatican Council II atmosphere. Nor is it to be expected that nearly five hundred years of ecclesiastical war in the West, hot and cold, can be forgotten especially in areas where there has been as yet little change in attitude or practice arising out of the ecumenical movement. But the point is that very important reports of the Joint Working Group were received and approved[1] anew, programmes of collaboration were recommended, and even the ultimate question of Roman Catholic membership was not shirked.[2]

Thus a rather strong case for the success of the Uppsala Assembly can be made on a purely negative basis. What the prophets of gloom predicted did not happen.

The Fourth Assembly of the World Council of Churches was the largest and most complete gathering of representatives of Christian Churches in over nine hundred years. And due to the missionary expansion of the nineteenth century, it may be said that this Assembly was the most widely representative world gathering of Christian Churches ever held.

Note who were there: 704 delegates from 235 member Churches. Delegated observers (a new category established for the first time at Uppsala) from 29 non-member Churches including 14 from the Roman Catholic Church, 4 from the Lutheran Church Missouri Synod, and 3 from the Seventh Day Adventist Church. There were also delegated observers from 7 associate member Churches, too small to be included in full World Council membership. Add to these 12 fraternal delegates from Christian Councils and from world Christian organizations. Also there were present 15 observers from 14 non-member Churches even though they were not officially delegated by them. Guests, advisers and youth participants, all invited by the Executive Committee, increased the total. 330 of staff, regular and co-opted, were included in the official Assembly roster. Of the 750 press representatives it must be admitted that several hundred were there for personal interest as much as for the stories they contracted to write, this despite strenuous efforts to limit press applicants to those who were bona fide press men and women. Add to all these several hundreds of visitors who had no official status in the Assembly but came to Uppsala anyway. The accomplishments of the Assembly must be assessed, therefore, in the light of who were there. Only

[1] See Uppsala, pp. 177–9   [2] See ibid., p. 178.

those who had illusions about what could happen at such an Assembly came away disillusioned.

No assembly which was representative of any "establishment" could expect to meet in 1968 without criticisms and demonstrations by youth and student groups. Youth was visibly present and clearly critical of what went on at the Uppsala Assembly. Around 150 youth participants had been invited to the Assembly by the Executive Committee according to a plan approved by the Central Committee which provided for their nomination by youth bodies in the various nations and regions, and 127 arrived. Considerable subsidy for their travel and entertainment had been provided in the Assembly budget. In addition to these official participants youth was present in the persons of 345 stewards (mostly from Sweden) who provided domestic and technical services for the delegates and staff and at the same time entered fully into youth discussions of the ecumenical issues in the late night hours. Furthermore, the Swedish Student Christian Movement under the title Club '68 brought many other students to Uppsala and provided the best place for dialogue between youth and establishment. The Swedish students from the beginning with their march from Stockholm to Uppsala made it clear, however, that they were marching in support of the World Council of Churches.

The official youth participants met in a special pre-Assembly conference of their own arranged for them by the World Council Youth Department. The general distrust of "establishment", including their own, made hard going of the first day of their own meeting. They insisted on voting about their own programme. Some were not sure that they wanted to hear the distinguished leaders who were available to address them. A small minority, chiefly continental European, apparently came with the intention of disruption. The whole group were clearly dissatisfied with their place in the Assembly itself. They did not like it that they had no votes in the Assembly even though it was clearly explained to them that they had been invited, as were the advisers (who had no votes), because the Central Committee felt that their corrective and creative presence was needed.

Youth participants made it clear that constitutional requirements for limiting votes to those who were appointed as delegates by the Churches was not and would not be satisfactory to them so long as the Churches failed to appoint a higher percentage of young delegates. On the other hand, the great majority of the youth participants decided against any revolutionary policity of disruption of the Assembly in favour of participating in sections, committees, and plenary sessions. Their presence and applause at the plenary sessions did make a contribution to the whole atmosphere of the Assembly, a contribution welcomed by some of the delegates. It was less happily received by others. It was reported that there was good and useful participation by many of the youth participants in many sections, sub-sections, and committees although the excellence of youth participation varied as did that of the delegates themselves. The final resolutions of the youth participants were heard by the Assembly in plenary session on the last day. They were received with thanks but were not discussed. Generally speaking the concrete proposals of the youth participants on the subjects before the Assembly were neither better not more "radical" than the proposals officially before the Assembly backed by the authority of the central and other "establishment" departmental and divisional committees. One method of youth participation that had some effect was provided through "Hot News", an every-other-day publication highly critical of all that went on, although some older participants noted that "Hot News" avoided any sharp criticism or even discussion of unresolved differences or even questionable activities of the youth themselves.

The final effort of youth, which centred in a twenty-four hour vigil in the cathedral beginning on the last night before the closing service, resulted in their unplanned participation in that service. These young people insisted upon this participation even though permission was asked only a few hours before the service was due to begin. The closing service itself was simple and impressive; a real part of its excellence was provided by the solemn marching of the young people carrying placards upon which were quotations from some of the most important actions taken by the Assembly and calling for the personal dedication of the worshippers to carry them out by costly self-dedication. This visible participation was briefly but eloquently underlined by a youth leader who was invited to make the only address at the closing service.

The Uppsala Assembly marked an end to an era of the ecumenical movement. It also marked a new beginning.

The name of Archbishop Nathan Söderblom was often referred to by speakers. His continuing influence as the founder of the "Life and Work" movement, which held an influential conference in Stockholm, Sweden in 1925, in part determined the emphasis on Christian service to humanity which will likely be what is most remembered as characteristic of the Uppsala Assembly. The reports of Uppsala Sections III and IV particularly, along with major programmes which were approved, were in the "Life and Work" tradition. Nevertheless, it would be wrong to say that Faith and Order contribution or the missionary tradition of the former International Missionary Council were eclipsed by this emphasis. Sections V and VI provided a new emphasis upon renewal in worship and in personal commitment. The emphases in Sections I and II on unity and mission respectively revealed that the World Council of Churches enters its new era with the same creative tensions between Unity, Mission, and Renewal that have marked and characterized its life from the beginning.

Although it must be said, therefore, that all of the past continues to make its contribution to the new era which began with Uppsala and that there was no radical break with that past, nevertheless it is evident that it is indeed a new era which began at Uppsala. The Structure Committee report which will be discussed below provides for a thorough examination and reorganization of the function and structure of the World Council of Churches, including the structure and function of the Fifth Assembly. There will never be another assembly in the pattern of the first four assemblies.

Furthermore, the elections at Uppsala put into responsible leadership for the next period a new generation of leadership. By 1968 the founding veterans of 1948 had mostly given place to a younger generation of ecclesiastical leaders. The elections at Uppsala hastened this process by choosing a Central Committee which in turn elected officers and an Executive Committee which have a very small carry-over of persons who have had previous experience in the central life of the World Council. Even the six presidents, who have always been the father figures in the organization, contain only four real veterans, W. A. Visser 't Hooft, Honorary President, Bishop Hanns Lilje, Ernest Payne, and D. T. Niles. With the exception of John Coventry Smith, the others have never served before, even on the Central Committee.

The new Executive Committee, which includes the Presidents, is more representative of Asia and Africa than formerly. It consists of an entirely new membership with the exception of Juan Faune of the Philippines and Metropolitan Nikodim of the Russian Orthodox Church. One of the new Vice-Chairmen, Miss Pauline Webb, has not served before on the Central Committee. The other Vice-Chairman, Metropolitan Meliton, has not been a member until now of the Executive Committee.

After each assembly, it has taken a little time for the new committees to become acquainted and to become effective groups. After the Fourth Assembly, it is clear that, however influential the experienced members may be, the new leadership elected at Uppsala will be responsible for a new and exciting and more ecumenical era in the life of the Council.

THE SECTION REPORTS

The Uppsala Assembly was divided into six sections. Approximately half of its sixteen days was spent in the Sections, discussing, amending, and rewriting draft statements on major ecumenical concerns which had been prepared by representative committees of ecclesiastics and experts assisted by the staff. Each draft was approximately 2,500 words in length. They had been put into print and widely distributed for study months before the Assembly. Each Section was asked to consider the draft, to amend or rewrite it if desired, and if possible to indicate how its concerns could best be related to the Churches. It was suggested that the maximum length of the final report of a Section should be 3,500 words.

As usual, there was a great deal of complaint about the procedure of attempting to do such important work in such large and varied groups in so short a time. In Uppsala this was aggravated by the fact that the overall time of the Assembly had been shortened by twenty-four hours due to date problems of the university on the one hand and the Lambeth Conference on the other. While the procedures of work of the Sections at Uppsala were sharply criticized by most of the delegates, it is not clear that the alternative suggestions which were offered for future assemblies would in fact work out any better. Some of these suggestions had been tried before. Others had been examined and rejected for what appeared to be good reasons. When the structure of the next assembly has been determined, careful attention must be given to finding a way to retain the value of generalized intellectual and spiritual discussion in an assembly, not allowing it to become simply an administrative and programme body, nor asking it to do more than it reasonably can be expected to accomplish, nor changing it into an educational training school for church representatives by self-styled experts.

The Section documents are not supposed to be authoritative dogma for the Church. They were not even offered to the Assembly for its adoption on behalf of the World Council of Churches as if it were a Church or the Church. "The substance of each of the Section reports, which are discussed below, was approved and commended to the churches for study and appropriate action."

This does not, however, lessen their importance for the future of the ecumenical movement. In general they reveal how much consensus has been reached on the most important areas of life and thought confronting all the Churches. They indicate directions for further study and action. Some contain seed thoughts or new insights that may determine the shape that the renewal and obedience of the Churches must take.

Section I: *The Holy Spirit and the Catholicity of the Church*

Perhaps the best way to assess the value of the report of Section I at the Fourth Assembly is to note first the issues that stand out in theoretical and practical discussion of church unity in 1968 and then to examine the document to see what light, if any, it throws upon each of them.

Is there an irreconcilable difference between evangelical Protestant understanding of Faith and Church and Catholic understanding whether Orthodox, Anglican, or Roman?

This is obviously the most fundamental question that faces the ecumenical movement in the whole area of church unity. At the Amsterdam Assembly in 1948 it was stated:

> Yet from among these shades of meaning, we would draw special attention to a difference to which, by many paths, we are constantly brought back. Historically it has been loosely described as the difference between "Catholic" and "Protestant",[1] although we have learned to mistrust any over-simple formula to describe it. The essence of our situation is that, from each side of the division, we see the Christian faith and life as a self-consistent whole, but our two conceptions of the whole are inconsistent with each other.[2]

Does this Amsterdam comment still hold true, twenty years later, after the massive entrance of the Oriental Churches into the life of the World Council, after Vatican Council II, and after two decades of faith and order work, highlighted at Lund (1952) and Montreal (1963)?

Section I at Uppsala tackles this basic question, first of all by its title and second by the general structure of the whole report. To put together in the title the Holy Spirit on the one hand and Catholicity of the Church on the

---

[1] Clearly "Catholic" is not used here to mean Roman Catholic, and "Protestant" in most of Europe is better rendered "Evangelical".

[2] Amsterdam, p. 52.

other is itself to come to grips with this central question. The ethos of evangelical Christianity has always depended upon a belief that God the Holy Spirit was not confined in his action to the visible structures of the established Catholic Church. Martin Luther could not have taken his stand without the confidence that the Holy Spirit was his guide to the understanding of the Word contained in the Scriptures. John Calvin developed his ecclesiology and his sacramental theology on a high doctrine of the Holy Spirit. And the farther to the left you go in Protestant theology, the more is ecclesiastical authority directly understood to be dependent upon whether or not the Holy Spirit is actively present with Christ's people guiding and inspiring. The Pentecostal Churches with whom the World Council is seeking closer relations and better understanding are clearly at this theological pole.

The very word Catholic, however carefully you define it, has for nearly 500 years caught up connotations which contradict this evangelical understanding of the Holy Spirit at almost every crucial point. For example, to the average Evangelical the Catholic position on the efficacy of the sacraments seems to be a precise attack upon their understanding of God's activity in the Church and in the world.

That this is still a central issue in the ecumenical movement became evident during the preparations for Section I at the Central Committee meeting in Crete in 1967. There was a considerable group of Evangelicals who did not want to use the word Catholic or Catholicity even in the title of the Section, not because of what the word denoted, but because of the connotations of the 500 years' ecclesiastical cold war in the West.

Despite these reservations, it was decided not only to keep Catholic in the title but also to draft the document itself in such a way that the issue could not be dodged. Paragraphs 14 and 15 of the draft document that was submitted to the Section on Uppsala[1] and which do not appear in the final Uppsala document, recognize the depth of the theological disagreement in terms little advanced beyond Amsterdam. For example, in paragraph 15, we read: "While some of us consider it both possible and necessary for the divided churches to come together at the same table, as the direct implication of God's reconciliation in Christ, to others such a step is both impermissible and dangerous."

This division is nowhere spelled out so clearly in the final document except perhaps by implication from its description of the remaining task. "We must continue to seek the union of all Christians in a common profession of faith in the observance of Baptism and the Eucharist, and in recognition of a ministry for the whole Church."[2]

It must be admitted that the strength of the final draft of Section I is not in a startling new insight or conclusion about how evangelical and Catholic can be truly united, but rather in its spelling out of the commonly accepted assumptions of the gospel which demand that Holy Spirit and Catholic must no longer be used in opposition to each other.

[1] *Drafts for Sections* (Uppsala 1968), p. 11.
[2] Uppsala, p. 17, para. I, 17.

Does the gospel permit Christians to concern
themselves with questions of ecclesiastical unity
when it is the unity and reconciliation of mankind
which is alone relevant in 1968?

It was to answer this question fully that the Uppsala document was chiefly changed from that which the Section received from the preparatory committee and the Faith and Order Commission. Although the draft document did begin in its preface with an attempt to set ecclesiastical unity in the world of 1968 by making such statements as: "Within the Church we long for unity in faith, order and common life. Within human society we seek for all men the realization of justice and integrity, freedom and joy",[1] and "How can that universal community express the wholeness of the life and truth of Christ, the Lord of *all* men?"[2]

The Church and Society Conference of 1966 is referred to in paragraph 4 and in paragraph 5 of the preparatory document. An attempt was made to break out of the ecclesiastical ghetto by including these sentences:

> The oneness of the *world* is an inescapable fact; the oneness of *humanity* is an essential aspiration. As the Spirit of God has drawn the churches towards a stronger fellowship with each other, the belief is also awakening that God in his inscrutable ways is working out His purposes in contemporary history.[3]

The final report of Section I at Uppsala did not find God's ways quite so inscrutable, as is illustrated by these quotations. It said:

> ... we are confronted with the fact that the basis of our endeavour for unity [clearly in the context, church unity] is being widely questioned. It seems to many, inside and outside the Church, that the struggle for Christian unity in its present form is irrelevant to the immediate crisis of our times. The Church, they say, should seek its unity through solidarity with those forces in modern life, such as the struggle for social equality, and should give up its concern with patching up its own internal disputes.[4]

In response to this challenge, the report reads:

> In the agonising arena of contemporary history—and very often among the members of the Churches—we see the work of demonic forces that battle against the rights and liberties of man, but we also see the activity of the life-giving Spirit of God. We have come to view this world of men as the place where God is already at work to make all things new, and where he summons us to work with him.[5]

The unity and Catholicity of the Church is thus squarely set in God's activity in history.

> The purpose of Christ is to bring people of all times, of all races, of all places, of all conditions, into an organic and living unity in Christ by the Holy Spirit under the universal fatherhood of God.[6]

[1] *Drafts for Sections* (Uppsala 1968), p. 7, para. 1.
[2] Ibid., pp. 7–8, para. 3 (italics added).
[3] Ibid., p. 8, para 5 (italics added).
[4] Uppsala, p. 12, para. 3.   [5] Ibid., p. 12, para. 4.   [6] Ibid., p. 13, para. 6.

In a list of "confusions" caused by Christians misusing their freedom under the Spirit, there are included examples,

> ... wherever Christian communities allow their membership to be determined by discrimination based on race, wealth, social class or education; ... [and] allow cultural, ethnic, or political allegiances to prevent the organic union of churches which confess the same faith in the same region; ... [or] permit loyalty to their own nation to hinder or destroy their desire for mutual fellowship with Christians of another nation.[1]

This kind of statement is not unusual in ecumenical documents, but it is unusual in a document on the unity of the Church. Faith and Order is by this report pushed or drawn into the arena of Church and Society and International Affairs. Furthermore, as was indicated above, these theologians do not think that God's ways in history are inscrutable. They call racial discrimination demonic, and civil rights movements a part of the Spirit's activity in the world. If church unity is sought in this new context, no one ought to fault the continuing effort by the World Council of Churches in this area of ecclesiastical activity.

*Is there an irreconcilable conflict between
continuity of the Church with the past and
its renewal for the present and the future?*

The answer of the report of Section I to this question is a resounding "No". The report recognized both as necessities.

> The Church is faced by the twin demands of continuity in the one Holy Spirit, and of renewal in response to the call of the Spirit amid the changes of human history.[2]

The Holy Spirit is not to be thought of, as so often we have done, as being confined on the one hand to new insight or changed understandings or practices; on the other hand, his action is not to be discussed only in the vitalization of ancient traditions and practices. Both renewal and continuity are functions of the Holy Spirit in the Church and in the world.

This double action of the Holy Spirit is outlined in four statements which emphasize a unity and continuity broader and deeper than dogmatic formulation or organizational arrangements or programmatic functions.

> The Church is revealed as one body of Christ, the one people of God in every age, and so its continuity is made *actual* in the "faith once given to the saints" embodied in the Scriptures, confessed in the Church and proclaimed to the world; in the liturgical life of the Church, its worship and sacraments; in the continuous succession of apostolic ministry of Word and Sacrament; in constantly preparing the people of God to go into the world and meet human needs; in the unbroken witness of the lives of prophets, martyrs and saints.[3]

This refusal to tear apart tradition and renewal is perhaps the greatest contribution of the report and gives a sure foundation for the ongoing dialogue and active collaboration within the ecumenical movement.

[1] Uppsala, pp. 14–15, para. 10.   [2] Ibid., p. 16, para. 15.
[3] Ibid., p. 16, para. 14 (italics added).

At the world level, to what may we look forward
or for what should we work?

This has been a question that has haunted ecumenists from the beginning and has grown sharper since the New Delhi statement, which envisioned the unity of "all in each place", and since Vatican Council II, which revealed that the Holy Spirit was beginning to move the Roman Catholic Church to an alternative conception of unity to that of return. Perhaps the most startling sentences of this report, and hardly noticed, read:

> The ecumenical movement helps to enlarge this experience of universality, and its regional councils and its World Council may be regarded as a transitional opportunity for eventually actualizing a truly universal, ecumenical, conciliar form of common life and witness. The members of the World Council of Churches, committed to each other, should work for the time when a genuinely universal council may once more speak for all Christians, and lead the way into the future.[1]

Here the next stage, "a genuinely universal council", is for the first time seriously articulated by the official representatives of the Churches in an Assembly. Note the points: (i) No final structure of universal unity is envisioned. (ii) But the World Council is seen as an instrument of transition to the next stage of world unity—a central and crucial instrument for that transition. (iii) The next stage is flatly stated to be a truly universal council able to speak for all Christians. Here is a pattern that clearly implies a universal council with the kind of authority of the seven ancient ecumenical Councils of the Church.

If this vision finds approval in the Churches, it will become the most important guiding action for the future of the ecumenical movement. Here is not the place to discuss the relationships between present world confessional families and the World Council of Churches; but it does definitely project the guide-lines for ecumenical work in the next period.

In conclusion one can say that the report of Section I at Uppsala may, through its influence on the Churches, the regional and confessional bodies, and upon the World Council of Churches, contribute greatly to the unity of the one pilgrim people of God. A position has been taken which cannot be ignored in the future; it must be adopted or amended.

Section II: Renewal in Mission

The preparation for the section work of the Uppsala Assembly included a wide circulation of the Section drafts for study and response in the Churches before the Assembly. This had never been done before. Of the six drafts, that on "Renewal in Mission" stirred up more controversy than any other and revealed deeper issues of understanding and conviction as well. In Scandinavia the original draft was so badly received that an entirely new draft was prepared and proposed as a substitute starting-point for the discussion in Section II. Parties and blocs began to form even before the

---

[1] Uppsala, p. 17, para. 19.

Assembly convened, and there were moments in its sessions when communication, let alone agreement, seemed impossible.

In view of the fundamental importance of the subject matter and the ecclesiastical–political implications of the controversy, it is surprising that the Section was able in its limited time to put together a report that was generally acceptable to its members and to the Assembly. An analysis of the issues which tended to divide the Section and the Assembly into partisan blocs reveals that there is a great deal of creative work based upon mutual communication still to be done.

Perhaps the chief underlying reason for the controversy was that sociologists do not write like theologians, and theologians do not write like sociologists. Since the 1961 integration of the International Missionary Council and the World Council of Churches, one of the most important developments has been the gradual development of "mission on six continents" as the ethos of the W.C.C. Division of World Mission and Evangelism. This has brought together in the World Council mission administrators whose work is oriented sociologically to mission in what once was "Christendom" and others whose whole work has been in the areas of the younger mission-founded Churches. This is the reason that the study on the missionary structure of the congregation found such wide acceptance. Former "foreign" mission people and "home" mission people thoroughly agreed that a new acceptance of mission was required in the parish-congregations of the Churches everywhere. The representatives of the "younger" Churches, third or fourth generation Christians, found themselves facing the same problems. How can an organized parish be (not merely support) a missionary movement?

Most serious home mission administrators had sought and found help from sociologists and sociological thinkers as they had been struggling with evangelism in the increasingly secular societies from which converts must come if there were to be any conversions. The first draft of Section II seemed to many "foreign" missionary society leaders as a capitulation to a secular, if not secularized, description of the mission of the Church and even a betrayal of the gospel. Anyone who knew the people responsible for the draft knew that they were not betrayers of the gospel even though their language seemed strange and new. On the other hand, those responsible for the draft felt that the theological language insisted upon by some of the missions people was in effect obscurantist to anyone not already inside the Church.

In addition to this, however, it should be noted that real theological differences among the membership of the Churches, still unresolved, found their focus here. "Pietists" understand conversion and evangelism in highly individualistic terms and expect that the resultant Christians will be obviously "not of the world". Many other Christians see conversion in the context of "this world" conforming much more to the ways of the world in an external sense, but, on the other hand, attacking society's structures and values much more radically than does the average pietist. All Churches have within their membership both kinds of members. Their styles of life[1] are different and each remains sharply critical of the other.

[1] See Section VI below.

Another sharp contrast among twentieth-century Christians (as old, however, as the New Testament) is between those who see salvation in other-worldly terms primarily, and those who believe that other-worldliness is an escape. Furthermore, there are some Christians who believe that "proclamation" of the gospel is usually triumphalist and self-defeating, while there are others who believe that "dialogue" with non-Christians is engaged in only by Christians who have already lost their faith. Clearly these attitudes towards other Christians and their ideas are unfair to the other Christians, but it is also clear that these "parties" do represent real theological differences that could not be resolved in this report.

With this analysis as a background, it is encouraging to see how many important things about the mission of the Church the Uppsala Assembly was able to say. First, it was agreed that there must be an ethical and social content to conversion.

> Our part in evangelism might be described as bringing about the occasions for men's reponse to Jesus Christ. Often the turning point does not appear as a religious choice at all. Yet it is a new birth. . . . For we have to be torn out of the restricted and perverted life of "the old man"! We have to "put on the new man" and this change is always embodied in some actual change of attitude and relationship. For there is no turning to God which does not bring a man face to face with his fellow men in a new way. The new life frees men for community, enabling them to break through racial, national, religious and other barriers that divide the unity of mankind.[1]

Again the report states the first criterion for priorities of missionary programmes as a positive reply to this question: "Do they place the Church alongside the poor, the defenceless, the abused, the forgotten, the bored?"[2]

Second, it is agreed in the report that all the structures of the Church from local to world level must be examined to see whether they enable the Church and its members to be a mission, or obstruct them from it. The question is not "Have we the right structures for mission?" but "Are we totally structured for mission?"[3] The call is made for a total restructuring of the Church at all levels aimed at its renewal for the function of mission.

Third, despite a great deal of dispute as to whether mission is properly aimed at baptisms and new church members on the one hand, or at "new men" who might very well not make any open "religious" shift on the other hand, the report was able to say:

> Mission bears fruit as people find their true life in the Body of Christ, in the Church's life of Word and Sacrament, fellowship in the Spirit and existence for others. There the signs of the new humanity are experienced and the People of God reach out in solidarity with the whole of mankind in service and witness. The growth of the Church, therefore, both inward and outward, is of urgent importance.[4]

Here as elsewhere the report was able to escape the horns of a dilemma by stating concretely and positively that the mission of Jesus Christ includes both purposes and that you dare not choose between them.

[1] Uppsala, p. 28, para. I, 4.   [2] Ibid., p. 32, para. II, 3.
[3] See ibid., p. 33, para. III, 1.   [4] Ibid., p. 29, para. I, 5.

Fourthly, the report eloquently states the dependence of mission upon a biblical foundation. Missionary education "needs to be rooted in a Biblical understanding of mission, so that people share the encouragement and insights which Bible study can give. If a congregation is engaged in mission, it needs Biblical nurture; if it is opposed or persecuted, it needs Biblical encouragement; if it fails in missionary calling, it needs Biblical vision."[2] The distinction sometimes made between Bible-believing Christians and ecumenical Christians is given no encouragement in this report.

Finally, the report makes it clear that truly ecumenical mission is a necessity.

> There is but one mission on all six continents. This makes it now imperative that Christians engage effectively in joint planning and action in both local and international situations. Only ecumenical co-operation can be adequate for the immensity of our task. . . . Present structures obviously do not provide adequate vehicles for developing joint strategy. We must determine to find ways in which joint action can become operative . . . we find it impossible to envisage any situation where it would not be more effective to act together across all frontiers rather than going it alone.[1]

The report of Section II of the Uppsala Assembly must be seen as an interim report. Until theological divergence is bridged, until mutual confidence is increased, until resources are redeployed, until societies and Churches seriously build ecumenical structures through which to do their work, until the Church recaptures her nerve and is able to proclaim her faith in terms that are understandable and persuasive to outsiders, mission will remain the most controversial area of the Churches' life. More dialogue with the world and more effective proclamation of the good news are equally needed.

Section III: World Economic and Social Development

It was widely predicted before the Uppsala Assembly that the delegates of the Churches would reject, or at least emasculate the findings of the 1966 Church and Society Conference. This did not happen for two reasons: first, the 1966 report was subjected to widespread study and criticism; before Uppsala clarifications and amendments were made carefully and after mature consultation and consideration. Second, the representatives of the Churches in the Assembly were clearly conscious of the bankruptcy of the *status quo* in 1968, and were therefore ready to support the concrete programmes proposed in the area of the development and to approve their theoretical and theological foundations.

> If our false security in the old and our fear of revolutionary change tempt us to defend the *status quo* or to patch it up with half-hearted measures, we may all perish. The death of the old may cause pain to some, but failure to build up a new world community may bring death to all.[2]

It is difficult to summarize the most important insights in this report since it is a closely written document which needs to be read in full for full

---

[1] Uppsala, pp. 35–6, para. III, 3.   [2] Ibid., p. 45, para. 4.

understanding. Here it may be valuable to emphasize the theoretical points made in this report as a background for the later description of the practical programmes also approved in the area of development by the Uppsala Assembly.[1]

(a) Christians in the twentieth century must learn to recognize the moral issues in the economic life of the world as they came to see those issues in the nineteenth century in the life of individual nations.[2]

(b) Neo-isolationism is gaining ground in both developed and developing nations because they earlier supposed that world development could be accomplished without "radical changes in institutions and structures at three levels: within developing countries, within developed countries, and in the international economy".[3] These changes will not come without a new instillation of a morality which includes total human solidarity and world-wide justice.[4]

(c) Although development has usually been chiefly thought of in economic terms, not only must new morality be introduced into the world's thought,[5] but also new political insights must become a part of man's concern. These political insights must include at least two recognitions of reality: (i) "The new technological possibilities turn what were dreams into realities."[6] This is to say that modern technology is a new fact. (ii) But there is another fact, not so new, which must equally be reckoned with: " . . . the creation of *political* instruments of development becomes important. Since mankind is politically organized in nation-states, these instruments have to be related to the politics of sovereign nations."[7] In a world which is becoming unified technically at an amazing pace, the political instrumentalities to cope with that new fact must be developed, and Churches must be concerned even politically (in this sense) or they will be irrelevant to the real solutions of the development problems. "No structures—ecclesiastical, industrial, governmental or international—lie outside the scope of the churches' task . . . "[8]

(d) Public opinion must be persuaded to support changes in both developed and developing nations. Not only must the Churches work at this programme of education, but "students and the intelligentsia can play a crucial role in the shaping of public opinion". "Powerful political lobbies are essential to create the necessary conditions" of commitment to development.[9]

(e) "The central issue in development is the criteria of the human. We reject a definition of development which makes man the object of the operation of mechanical forces . . . "[10] The humanization of modern technological life must be a chief concern of the Churches in both developed and developing nations. It must not be taken for granted that modernization, as such, is good for men. A variety of cultures, a distribution of power, non-

---

[1] See below, p. 457.   [2] See Uppsala, p. 45, para. 3.   [3] Ibid., p. 46, para. 11.
[4] See ibid., p. 47, para. 12.   [5] See above, p. 414.   [6] Uppsala, p. 45, para. 1.
[7] Ibid., p. 47, para. 14 (italics added).   [8] Ibid., p. 52, para. 35.
[9] Ibid., p. 49, para. 19.   [10] Ibid., p. 49, para. 20.

discrimination with respect to colour or age or sex, must be included in the Churches' concerns.[1]

(f) The production and distribution of food must in these next years be a technical preoccupation of all who are interested in development. The population explosion lays impossible burdens upon nations which are attempting to develop technologically. Means of population control must be sought and implemented even though Christians are divided on the question of what are the moral means for family planning.[2]

The Uppsala Assembly will likely be remembered longest for its emphasis on development. Progress was made both in the theoretical understanding of the problems and Christians' responsibility to work at their solutions. The report of Section III will remain for many years as the charter of the newest task of all the Churches and of the ecumenical movement itself.

Section IV: Towards Justice and Peace in International Affairs

A study of the drafts for the Sections and the reports for Committees of the Assembly revealed, some months before the representatives of the Churches arrived in Uppsala, a remarkable theological convergence of many of these documents. They all pointed towards a new emphasis at this time on the human, whether they concerned Christology or education, development or international affairs. As will be noted later, the study programme of the World Council for the next years has been built upon this convergence of theological emphasis and direction.

Few people would, however, have expected that one of the important theological statements of the Assembly would be found in Section IV, since many people have taken it for granted that in the area of international affairs the ecumenical movement was more skilful diplomatically than theologically. Nevertheless, the theological base for this Section's report was important not only because of its inherent worth, but also because of its crucial relevance to the main question facing man today, namely, whether he can survive.

The report begins by stating succinctly the faith in God's promise contained in the theme of the Assembly "Behold, I make [am making] all things new." "This word includes the certainty that in Christ the new reconciled creation has already dawned. The Church lives in this certainty and presses on towards this hope."[3]

The effect in political affairs of this basic certainty is to substitute a Christian hope for worldly uncertainty and a Christian sober humility for worldly romanticism and utopianism. "We are directed away from anxiety, resignation, self-assertion and oppression by guilt towards openness and solidarity with all men, towards the venture of trust and the readiness to sacrifice for constructive solutions."[4] Since "the aim of our political thinking and acting is to benefit and to help men"[5] we are led to co-operate with non-Christians who have the same aim of human service. " . . . our particular

---

[1] Uppsala, pp. 49–50, paras. 20–3.   [2] See ibid., p. 50, paras. 24 and 25.
[3] Ibid., p. 60, para. 1.   [4] Ibid., pp. 60–1, para. 2.   [5] Ibid., p. 61, para. 2.

contribution will be made not only in the sober realization that all we do remains inadequate and limited, but also in our unshakable hope . . ."[1]

Specific Christian witness and work in international affairs depends upon insights which come from the Word of God. They are listed as follows: (a) The unity of creation and the unity of all men in Christ. (b) Because of Christ's own sacrifice, Christians are challenged not only to ask sacrifices of others, but to make them ourselves. (c) Christians must always identify themselves with the poor and oppressed in their struggle for justice. (d) We must seek change and not resist it. (e) Christian peace is built upon love of enemies. (f) Reconcilation is based upon the reconciling work of God in the world.[2]

The Church must make a costly witness:

> It must speak out where no one else dares to, or where truth is not respected, where human lives or human dignity are endangered, and where opportunities for a better future are neglected. . . . The ecumenical fellowship can help them [the Churches] to stand by their convictions and not simply to reflect the predominant opinions in their own country.[3]

With this as a theological basis, the report proceeds to analyse the major tasks in international affairs.

The first of these is the prevention of disastrous wars, large or small. The points made are that the prevention of nuclear war is the first duty of all governments. This must be done by moving "away from the balance of terror towards disarmament".[4] There are three aspects of this problem. The relationships between the nuclear powers, primarily the U.S.A. and the U.S.S.R., but including China, Great Britain, and France, the relationships to the non-nuclear powers and their relationship to each other to make for peace, and finally, methods of change without increasing the threat of nuclear destruction.[5] "Since smaller nations are expected to accept the discipline of nuclear abstinence, the nuclear powers should accept the discipline of phased disarmament in all categories of weapons."[6] Christian pacifists and non-pacifists must work together to control the use of weapons of any sort. "Wars by proxy through the competitive delivery of armaments" create "an international scandal which governments must no longer tolerate or permit."[7]

The next major task of the Churches is the protection of individuals and groups. Human rights must be supported everywhere, both by encouraging regional and national protection of fundamental liberties, and also by strengthening the efforts of the United Nations in winning universal sanction for these liberties. Protection of conscience and religious liberty, freedom of expression—all aiming at human dignity is the work of the Churches.[8]

In this effort, the Churches must recognize that minorities of all kinds must be protected from the tyranny of the majority and that the majority must not be prevented from governing by unreasonable demands of

---

[1] Uppsala, p. 61, para. 3.   [2] Ibid., p. 61, paras. 4–9.   [3] Ibid., p. 62, para. 10.
[4] Ibid., p. 62, para. 11.   [5] Ibid., p. 62, para. I, 12.   [6] Ibid., p. 63, para. I, 13.
[7] Ibid., p. 63, para. I, 15.   [8] Ibid., pp. 63–4, para. II. A.

minorities.[1] Racism is recognized as an underlying danger to peace and justice and deserves constant attention to its root causes to avoid widespread violence or war. Racism is particularly dangerous because it is linked with economic exploitation; it is based upon false myths, generalizations, and stereotypes, and it produces counter-racism.[2]

Other minority groups that require the continued attention of the Churches are refugees, displaced persons, and migrants. The long-term effort must be to eliminate the conditions that create these tragic groups of men. In the meantime, they must remain in the special care of the Churches.[3]

In addition to a briefer treatment of the relationship of economic justice to world order and peace,[4] more fully treated in Section II of the Assembly, the report of Section IV includes a requirement that Christians give full support to the importance of international and multilateral structures if they are to contribute to world peace. Nationalism must give way to regionalism since nations are too small to survive in complete independence from each other. But regions must also be comprehended in world community if political arrangements are to keep pace with the growing technological unity of the planet. The United Nations, the rule of law both to restrain disorder and to create new order must be supported by the Churches.[5]

It is finally noted that the growth of the ecumenical movement gives new possibilities for "concerted contributions to international relations".[6] Such Christian co-operation should, however, include "more serious efforts at dialogue with the adherents of other religions and all men of good-will".[7]

In a world which is threatened with ultimate disaster through nuclear war, the report of Section IV was remarkably strong both in its overall Christian basis, in its analysis of the concrete issues, and in its suggestions of programmes and positions that Christians must take on the basis of their faith and hope.

Section V: Worship

At Uppsala for the first time in a World Council Assembly, a Section was devoted to the study of Worship. This does not mean that there had been no previous attention given to the subject by the World Council of Churches, or by other instrumentalities of the ecumenical movement. Faith and Order had produced a useful volume called "Ways of Worship" in preparation for its conference in Lund in 1952. Liturgical scholars from many Churches had found themselves often in more ecumenical agreement about worship than the actual practices of their Churches would have led anyone to expect. But the fact is that World Council Assemblies had not before studied worship together and there was much hope that this section would mark a new beginning in mutual understanding and mutual help in the renewal of worship in the Churches. It may be that the beginning made in the work of

---

[1] Uppsala, p. 65, para. II. B.
[3] Ibid., pp. 66–7, para. II. D, 29.
[5] Ibid., pp. 69–70, paras. IV. B, 37–41.
[7] Ibid., p. 71, para. V, 42.

[2] Ibid., pp. 65–6, para. II. C.
[4] Ibid., pp. 67–9, paras. III, 30–3.
[6] Ibid., p. 70, para. V, 42.

Section V and the increased and fruitful attention of the Assembly to its own worship, already referred to, will be one of the most memorable contributions of Uppsala.

The practice of worship in the various families of Churches in the membership of the World Council of Churches indicates more concretely than anything else the wide divergence of ethos of these divided Churches. One thing all of them have in common is that their people resist change in their accustomed form of worship, especially if it appears that the suggested change comes out of the other traditions. Although, as noted above, liturgical scholars have found much in common in their basic criticism of all the actual practices of worship, the practices themselves do not change easily except by accretion or elimination.

Accepting this as the ecclesiastical background for the work of Section V, the problem is complicated by today's process of secularization which affects the worship of all the Churches. More and more it appears that modern man feels himself to be in a strange and alien atmosphere when he enters any church from his familiar world of office, factory, laboratory, theatre, home, or athletic stadium. Unless he has strong childhood memories which the worship recalls, he is apt to find Christian worship meaningless and boring, no matter whether it be that of Salvation Army, Pentecostal, Methodist, Anglicans, Lutheran, Orthodox, or Roman Catholic. Section V had to develop its report, then, against the two strong realities of 1968: great diversity of practice in worship among the Churches and the alienation of modern man from all worship.

The report begins by recognizing two attitudes towards worship among its own members: some who find joy in the old forms of worship and others "who do not find the old forms helpful and who are glad that there is now a radical questioning of all traditions".[1] A further complication was also recognized at the outset, that members of the so-called younger Churches in Asia and Africa feel frustrated at the alien cultural forms (especially music and art) in which Christian worship has been brought to them and their Churches, along with the gospel itself.

Again it is noted that part of the anxiety about formal worship in the Churches arises out of a breakdown of personal and private prayer discipline which in turn arises from the crisis of faith. Without argument the Section rejected the radical suggestion of many progressives who are saying that God is praised only when he is served in the person of the neighbour in the world.[2] While rejecting this radical position, the report recognizes the need for "a study of fundamental Christian faith in order to deal more profoundly with the crisis of worship".[3]

With all of these complications and difficulties it is interesting to see how much it was possible to say together and to note how basic are the agreements.

"Worship needs no more justification than does love." So the report begins. The mystery of human life and being is accepted by all as the pro-

---

[1] Uppsala, p. 78, para. 1.   [2] Ibid., p. 78, para. 3.   [3] Ibid., p. 78, para. 3.

P

found basis for worship. Those who believe in the being of God believe that he gathers his people for worship and elicits their response.[1]

Christian worship is centred in Jesus Christ. Its form is not as important as that Jesus be there enabling the worshipper to "share in the joy, the peace, and the love of God". "Worship is a privilege more than a problem."[2]

Because of its christocentric nature, Christian worship is ethical and social in nature and can never be true worship unless it is oriented towards the social injustices and divisions of mankind. Arrogant sectarianism, narrow nationalism, racism, war or oppression, poverty or wealth are the demonic forces to which Christian worship is opposed in a battle in which Jesus Christ has already won the final victory.[3] Here the report lays its foundation for the embarrassing questions which it asks the representatives of all Churches and traditions to ask themselves.

> We are bound to ask the churches; whether there should not be changes in language, music, vestments, ceremonies, to make worship more intelligible; whether fresh categories of people (industrial workers, students, scientists, journalists, etc.) should not find a place in the churches' prayers; whether lay people should not be encouraged to take a greater share in public worship; whether our forms of worship should not avoid unnecessary repetition, and leave room for silence; whether biblical and liturgical texts should not be so chosen that people are helped to worship with understanding; whether meetings of Christians for prayer in the Eucharist (Holy Communion, the Lord's Supper) should be confined to church buildings or to traditional hours?[4]

The form of these questions implies a positive answer. And it should be noted that the questions are aimed at the several traditions of worship, evangelical and catholic.

But the Section was able to do more together than to ask questions. It was agreed that "proclamation of the Word is essential".[5] This is not understood, however, as an unqualified support of the sermon as traditionally prepared and preached.[6] New forms are suggested for experiment in proclamation.

Because of the basic theological agreement as to the significance of baptism (considered as a part of worship), the Section was able to urge on all the Churches "their mutual recognition of the one baptism", and their continued effort to establish agreement as to the liturgical elements to be included by all so that the mutual recognition would be easier for all. The report further urges that baptism take place normatively in the presence of a worshipping congregation, and that Churches should be more careful as to those for whom they authorize baptism in order to avoid allowing baptism to be a social custom only.[7]

Again, the report accepts as fact that the Eucharist including Communion is at the heart of Christian worship.[8] On this basis the report urges:

---

[1] Uppsala, pp. 78-9, para. 5   [2] Ibid., pp. 78-9, para. 5.   [3] Ibid., p. 79, para. 7.
[4] Ibid., p. 81, para. 24.   [5] Ibid., p. 81, para. 26.   [6] See ibid., p. 81, para. 27
[7] See ibid., p. 82, para. 30.   [8] See ibid., p. 82, para. 31

(a) that all churches consider seriously the desirability of adopting the early Christian tradition of celebrating the Eucharist every Sunday; (b) that they consider the desirability of new styles of celebration of the Eucharist; (c) that all Christians present at the Eucharistic service should normally take part in holy communion; and (d) that every church should examine its reasons for its present disciplines about participation in holy communion, remembering Christ's prayer for unity and his command to be reconciled.[1]

Again it should be noted that these urgings upon the Churches are directed to all the Churches and that some are more difficult for Orthodox or Catholic Churches and others more difficult for Evangelicals.

The final section of the report is aimed at the practical task of helping people to worship God. It makes four points: (a) worship is dependent upon symbols that are cognitively and emotionally understood. There is need, therefore, to examine our use of symbols to see whether they continue to perform this function; (b) all Christians should be open to learn from the practices of worship of other Christians—uniformity and freedom, the universal and the local, continuity and change are all valuable; (c) segregation by race or class must be rejected in Christian worship; and (d) God, through the Holy Spirit, is the one who alone can quicken our worship and make it alive. We need to pray to be enabled to pray.[2]

If the Churches take seriously the questions, suggestions, and exhortations of this report, their unity and renewal will be furthered at the most fundamental levels of their life; a good beginning has been made by the Assembly.

Section VI: Towards New Styles of Living

There had been two hopes often expressed in the preparation time for the Assembly with regard to the task of Section VI. One of these was that this Section might make a practical ethical contribution in the area of dispute between contextual ethics and moral principles. The other hope was that the Section would help Christians everywhere to make a sharp distinction between ethics of the gospel on the one hand, and cultural mores blessed by the varied Christian communities on the other.

It must be admitted that the Section failed in its report to solve these important problems, or to give clear direction as to their solution. Perhaps this was too much to expect. On the positive side it can be said that there is little phariseeism in the report and many creative hints and suggestions which, if followed, would renew the life of individual Christians and of communities of Christians.

The report begins well with a call to Christians "to leave familiar territory and venture out towards unknown horizons".[3] The basis of this challenge is history's reminder that Christians have at different times and in different places been a conserving force or a renewing force. In our time of radical change the position is clearly taken that Christians today ought to choose the latter role.

[1] Uppsala, p. 82, para. 32.   [2] See ibid., pp. 82-3, paras. 33-9.
[3] Ibid., p. 87, para. 1.

The rest of the opening section does not adequately follow up the beginning. In these "theological passages" there is too great a preoccupation with trying to say the "right" thing biblically and theologically. Furthermore, there is a tendency to avoid the hard questions posed by an examination of what Christian communities really are in favour of a discussion of subjective attitudes about them both positive and negative. The positive descriptions breathe a sense of unreality, as, for example, the sentence "As we wait upon God, day after day, praying and reflecting upon his revelation in Jesus Christ, and actively involved in the secular world, we can be . . . examples of that love for one another by which men recognize disciples of Christ".[1] No one can fault the vision here of the Church as it ought to be or even might become. But there is introduced a sense of unreality when the report continues: "As we share our possessions and break together the bread of Holy Communion, our life becomes an offering to God."[2] The fact is that we are not sharing our goods like those of the way described in the Book of Acts and we are scandalously divided at the communion table.

The report[3] then describes in sharp and accurate terms the typical view of the Church held by those outside the Church, but the effect is to cancel out the ideal of the Church described in the preceding paragraph. Nor does the last paragraph of the introduction successfully resolve the issue; its only contribution is to remind us that the novel or new is not always God's action and that the Christian must feel himself part of the whole Church and of all of humanity.[4]

With this disappointing introduction, the report goes on to say some very important things about various aspects of the new styles of Christian life as they are made concrete by the major issues before man in 1968—namely, the attitude of and towards youth, the issue of the rich and poor, and finally, the issues of sexual relations.

In general the report comes out in favour of earlier and more active participation of youth in our whole society and particularly in the Church. The ground for this is laid in a fact of 1968 that, due to longer life, three or four generations of men are living at the same time in large numbers. The problem is that the old are often retired from most areas of life before they are ready to quit, the young are kept from full participation in the decisions that affect them until they are no longer young, and the middle-aged are overburdened by caring for too many human beings who really should not be "cared for", but should be fully involved in the caring process.[5]

The problem of the old is analysed, but no solution is offered.[6] The concrete suggestion[7] is that the Church as community should be a locus of communication and reconciliation. The Churches themselves and the World Council of Churches must be sure to include youth in their decisive assemblies. The old are already there in positions of power and authority.

The problem of rich and poor is examined next, and very fruitfully, because the consideration begins with the question of power concentrated

---

[1] Uppsala, pp. 87–8, para. 2.   [2] Ibid., p. 88, para. 2.   [3] See ibid., p. 88, para. 3.
[4] See ibid., p. 88, para. 4.   [5] Ibid., pp. 88–9, paras. 5–7, 9.
[6] See ibid., p. 89, para. 8.   [7] See ibid., p. 89, para. 9.

in the hands of the few rather than with money as such. Money, as the saying goes, is important only for what it can buy. That buying power may be directed by the governments of wealthy nations towards armaments, roads, schools, theatres, or factories. Rich men can also choose what they will buy. Those who are poor have no choice but to buy food, clothes, and shelter. It is recognized that money may bring as much boredom as it does happiness, as leisure time is increased collectively or individually.[1]

Power in our world is largely in the hands of "middle class people" whether in socialist or other countries. Middle class people tend to be conservative and to devote themselves to the preservation of the *status quo* with only such slight changes as the power of the two-thirds of mankind who are poor makes necessary.[2]

The divisions of the world are seen along three lines chiefly: colour, wealth, and knowledge.[3] Lack of education or being black makes it hard to shift from poor to rich; but if one is rich one can make a life transcending colour and one can buy education.

The positive conclusion of the report is that any Christian style of life must be fully involved in the suffering of all who are deprived and must be fully dedicated to equity and justice.[4]

Concrete suggestions are made for life patterns of Christian behaviour whether the Christian is one of the privileged or the underprivileged. These include political, protest, and career actions which should all be the vocation of the new styles of Christian life.[5]

The report looks at the moral issues of sex in terms of creative partnership between men and women. It welcomes the process by which women in many societies are no longer merely the agents of man's creativity, but are becoming collaborators.[6] Sex is seen not simply as a natural physical relationship but as a creative component adding to the zest for human community and activity. Women must have full rights as persons if life is to be full.

The positive values of chastity and celibacy are asserted, although the report says flatly: "There is an essential link between healthy sexuality and personal fulfilment."[7]

Responsible parenthood and family planning are supported in general terms which would imply the use of adequate techniques of birth control so long as such programmes do not become substitutes for a positive attack on the increase of economic development, especially in the areas of food production.[8]

The fact that traditional patterns of family life are under pressure in all societies due to urbanization and modern industrial practices is recognized. No solution is offered, but a request for study of such a wide variety of problems as "polygamy, marriage and celibacy, birth control, divorce, abortion and also of homosexuality".[9]

In conclusion, the report grapples in general terms with the crucial problem

---

[1] See Uppsala, p. 90, para. 11.   [2] See ibid., p. 90, paras. 11 and 12.
[3] See ibid., pp. 89–90, para. 10.   [4] See ibid., pp. 90–1, paras. 14–15.
[5] See ibid., p. 91, para. 16.   [6] See ibid., p. 92, para. 18.
[7] Ibid., p. 92, para. 19   [8] Ibid., p. 92, para. 20.   [9] Ibid., p. 93, para. 22.

of how does a Christian truly make his ethical decisions. The report makes it clear that social and cultural differences make a single style of Christian life impossible and even wrong. But are there rules or standards or principles? In answer, the report does not choose an antinomian contextualism, but it does emphasize that morals are attached to varied mores which are produced by people in various environments.[1] But how do we hear the command of God?

> The command of God is holy, just and good. Human rules, which grasp and express this command, can guide us in discerning the will of God and in making our decisions. But when rules become detached from the Spirit they can make us blind to the recklessness of the Gospel and to those signs of the times by which God is speaking to us.[2]

Having refused finally to choose between contextualism and "rules", the report concludes by pressing eloquently for the position that individual moral choices can be made only in community. We all need each other. We all can help each other as we can all drag each other down. This becomes a strong argument for true Christian communities held together by biblical insight and the communion table.[3] The report concludes with a plea for personal commitment which produces new styles of life which cannot be produced by documents.[4]

DECISIONS FOR THE FUTURE

Some friends of the ecumenical movement had decided even before Uppsala that the great days of the World Council of Churches were in its past. They believed that the increasing size of the organization of the World Council and the transition of its leadership from Student Christian Movement types to ecclesiastical "leaders of Churches" types must inevitably produce a kind of Council unable to keep pace with, let alone lead, the ecumenical movement. I shall not attempt here to make a judgement as to whether they are right or wrong. That judgement will have to be made in some future volume of ecumenical history.

The programme actions taken at the Uppsala Assembly were, however, new and radical enough to indicate that the committees and staff who had prepared these recommendations were envisioning a World Council which, both in the short and long range, would continue to press forward witn the ecumenical movement rather than to settle down into organizational ease. It will be impossible within the length of this chapter to comment upon all the programmes and organizational decisions taken at Uppsala. A selection of these will be made below on the basis of their relevance to the major question just posed: "Can the World Council move fast enough to retain its central place in the ecumenical movement?" Obviously, final judgement must be reserved until it is seen how effectively the committees and staff carry out the Uppsala decisions.

In the twenty years since the founding of the World Council of Churches

[1] See Uppsala, p. 93, para. 24.   [2] Ibid., p. 93, para. 25.   [3] Ibid., p. 94, para. 27.
[4] See ibid., p. 94, para. 28.

the most fundamental structural decisions were made at the Evanston Assembly in 1954. Amsterdam in 1948 provided for essential ecumenical functions to continue under the auspices of the newly established Council. The present basic structure of the World Council of Churches was approved at Evanston. The Programme and Finance Committee that reported to the New Delhi (Third) Assembly decided that it would be better to delay any major changes in World Council structure until after integration with the International Missionary Council had taken place. Some at the New Delhi Assembly were disappointed at this decision and pressed for a new structure committee immediately to work out the implications of integration in the period between New Delhi and Uppsala. This did not happen.

The first years were full of necessary adjustments on the basis of the simply enlarged Evanston structure. These years were also taken up with the reception into membership of the last of the Orthodox Churches and with watching with increasing interest the implications for the World Council of Vatican Council II. Add to this the retirement of the first General Secretary in 1966, his pre-occupation with the matters referred to above, and the fact that he had intended to retire at least a year earlier than he did, and the reluctance of the new General Secretary to allow basic structural changes to be decided upon before he had the opportunity to be fully involved in the discussions, and it is easy to see why the report of the Structure Committee, authorized at New Delhi in 1961, established at Enugu in 1965, was a transitional document leaving the most important decisions about the basic structure and functioning of the World Council until after Uppsala. The above analysis is intended as a criticism of no one, least of all of the members of the Structure Committee itself or its distinguished chairmen.

The report of the Structure Committee approved at Uppsala consisted of three parts. The first part recorded what had happened since New Delhi and the minor structural changes that had been made by the Central Committee during the seven-year period. Part two consisted of recommendations for immediate actions to be put into effect at Uppsala for the three-year period during which there would be a basic study of changes now needed in the structure of the World Council as recommended in part three. The new Central Committee was authorized and instructed to undertake a comprehensive structure study during the three years 1969-71, and to implement its decisions beginning 1 January 1972 in so far as the Constitution would permit the Central Committee so to act.[1]

New Programmes Approved

A cursory examination of Section II of the Structure Committee report plus the implementing actions taken in various committees for the immediate future will reveal that there is no tendency upon the part of the World Council of Churches to mark time during the next three years. Despite real financial restrictions under the general budget, the following new programmes, to start at once, were approved by the Assembly:

[1] See Uppsala, p. 183, para. 4(d).

(a) The appointment of a new Associate General Secretary to be responsible for relations with National and Regional Christian Councils of Churches. The Reverend Victor Hayward is already appointed to study these relationships full-time and to prepare for a consultation within a three-year period looking towards closer and more satisfactory mutual relationships among the councils. The expectation that this office will be partly supported by a number of the National Councils symbolizes the conception that this new Associate General Secretary will represent the National and Regional Councils to the World Council, as well as represent the World Council to them.[1] This appointment is new and arose from the conviction that these council relationships are central to world-wide ecumenical progress. Despite much good work done in the General Secretariat from New Delhi onwards, experience had revealed that adequate progress would not be made without the full-time attention of a staff member at the highest level in the General Secretariat.

(b) Arising out of the three-year study on education, jointly conducted by the Division of Ecumenical Action and the World Council of Christian Education, there was approved a new programme consisting of at least three executive staff within the Division of Ecumenical Action, designed to serve not only that division but also the other divisions and departments. This will for the first time put the World Council squarely into the technical problems of education. Until Uppsala the World Council had stayed out of the field partly because of the existence of the World Council of Christian Education. The work together during the three years preceding the Fourth Assembly had indicated from both sides the real possibility of merging the W.C.C.E. into the World Council of Churches. It was thought, necessary however, to create a new educational staff in the World Council itself in order that such a uniting of the two world bodies would not be a mere take-over by the W.C.C. of the present ethos and functions of the World Council of Christian Education. This new department is expected to secure persons competent in general education, Christian nurture, and theological education (broadly interpreted as education for ministry, both ordained and lay). This programme was approved at Uppsala to begin when financial support could be secured from new educational sources within the member Churches. Investigation of these financial possibilities was already well begun before the Assembly and considerable interest has been shown by Churches in the U.S.A., Canada, Britain, and the continent to establish the programme, looking forward to the possible merger referred to above. The new Structure Committee will conduct or co-ordinate such merger discussions which are scheduled to begin in 1968.

(c) A new post of Senior Press Officer was established, the decision becoming operative on 1 October 1968, in order to make viable the enlarged Department of Communication which had been created by the Central Committee in 1967. This new central department includes the former departments of Information, Publication, and Translation. In view of the increasing im-

[1] See Uppsala, p. 181, para. C. (c) 2.

portance to the ecumenical movement of communication, this new staff post is significant as a pledge of better and increased communication by the World Council of Churches.

(*d*) Due to the financial stringency affecting the general budget, a race relations secretariat had not been proposed to the Assembly at Uppsala. Events in 1968 and the obvious long-range importance of racial equality and justice to the whole programme of the Council, persuaded the Assembly to direct the Central Committee to act positively in the field of race relations. The newly elected Central Committee took action even at Uppsala to carry out this directive. It is expected that a programme on race, administratively located within the Department of Church and Society, but also related directly to the General Secretariat, will be under way early in 1969.

(*e*) A further growth made possible by the Uppsala Assembly was an enlarged and renewed Commission of the Churches on International Affairs (C.C.I.A.). An examination of this Commission had begun with actions taken by the Central Committee at Enugu in 1965, and at Geneva in 1966. A consultation on the C.C.I.A. with world-wide representation had been held at The Hague in April 1967. The General Secretary-elect began to work on this before he took office. The concrete result of the Hague consultation was a new constitution for the C.C.I.A., which came to the Assembly from the Central Committee (Heraklion and Uppsala) through the Structure Committee. This instrument makes it possible to envisage a larger and more representative staff, closer relations with world confessional families and with national and regional councils, and more intimacy of relationship with the other units of the World Council itself. A new Director, who it is hoped may begin work by 1 July 1969, will have the opportunity and responsibility to lead the newly elected Commission to develop the new possibilities provided for in the revised constitution approved by the Assembly. Although there have been inevitably sharp criticisms of the C.C.I.A., careful examination of the record revealed how well the ecumenical movement had been served for over twenty years under the leadership of the Chairman and Director, Sir Kenneth Grubb and Dr O. Frederick Nolde, respectively.

Studies in the World Council of Churches

Considerable unrest had been developing in the constituency of the Council, especially in Europe, at the long delay in filling the post of Director of the Division of Studies since the resignation of Dr Robert Bilheimer in 1963. This unrest increased with the election of the new General Secretary in 1966, who was relatively unknown to the continental constituency and without the personal competence in academic theology of his predecessor. In part the unrest was not justified under either regime. All of the study of the World Council of Churches had never been within the Division of Studies. The Ecumenical Institute and the Division of World Misson and Evangelism had been carrying on studies at a very high level since New Delhi. And despite the lack of a permanent director in the Division of Studies, the work of Faith and Order, Church and Society, and the Department of Missionary Studies had expanded and deepened during these years.

Nevertheless, the unrest about "study" and the fear that the World Council would become more activist and less intellectual increased during 1966 and 1967. The climax came when, due to financial limitations, the Executive Committee meeting at Windsor in February 1967 decided that the two vacancies, then foreseen, of the Directors of the Division of Ecumenical Action and of the Division of Studies could not both be filled before Uppsala. This was even more alarming to some when, in January 1968, it was the Director of the Division of Ecumenical Action, the Reverend Ernst Lange, who was appointed, and the post of the Director of the Division of Studies remained in the hands of an acting director. Mr Lange was asked to replace Mr Hayward, who had been acting director of studies, because Mr Hayward was overburdened with Assembly preparations of which he had been in charge from the beginning.

A most creative series of events and actions, under Professor Lange's staff leadership, made it possible to bring to the Uppsala Assembly a recommendation on World Council study that had the approval of staff, Executive Committee, and Central Committee. The Assembly warmly approved the actions taken and the recommendations made for the study work of the Council for the three-year period during which the new Structure Committee will examine and determine how the World Council should be organized more permanently to perform its study functions along with its other functions and responsibilities.

This interim programme for World Council study includes:

(a) The appointment of "a highly qualified full-time co-ordinator for a minimum period of three years to act as a research consultant or study adviser".[1] It is understood that this three-year project must be supported outside the budget and that its programme will be integrated into the new structure of the Council when it is effected in 1972.

(b) There will be "an *ad hoc* consultative committee to advise the co-ordinator for the studies on man". The concept of "studies on man" referred to in this action had grown out of careful examination of the Work Book prepared for the Assembly. This examination had revealed that in the various departmental recommendations for study there was a remarkable convergence on this theme. The Study on Man as approved at Uppsala is not a separate unified study project in addition to the studies approved for the various units of the Council, but rather a plan to unify and accent the whole study programme of the Council.

(c) In view of the above, the Division of Studies will be suspended for the three-year period, the Director of Church and Society being added to the staff executive group in which the Director of Faith and Order had already been sitting. The Department of Missionary Studies is temporarily attached administratively to the Division of World Mission and Evangelism.

[1] Uppsala, p. 203, para. B. (c).

(*d*) The new Structure Committee is instructed "to give careful attention to the future development of ecumenical study".

In view of the unrest referred to above, and the shortness of time available to create the plan for study, the ecumenical movement is greatly in debt to Ernst Lange for his inspiring and inspired leadership in the first six months of his service to the World Council of Churches.

The Other Major Divisions

A careful study of the Assembly actions bearing upon the work of the Divisions of Ecumenical Action, World Mission and Evangelism, and Inter-Church Aid will reveal that in each of these divisions under the distinguished new Directors (Mr Philip Potter, Mrs Browne-Mayers, and Mr Lange) thorough internal reorganization is already under way in looking to creative new programmes and co-ordinated activities. Due to space limitations these cannot be discussed in this chapter.[1]

Roman Catholic Relationships

Between 1961 and 1968, as has been recounted in this volume, ecumenical developments in the Roman Catholic Church in connection with Vatican Council II had completely transformed the relationships of that Church, not only with the member Churches and the world confessional bodies but also with the World Council of Churches which remains their overall ecumenical instrument. The Uppsala Assembly approved the two official reports of the Joint Working Group of the World Council of Churches and the Roman Catholic Church.

The story revealed in these two reports, now approved by the highest authority of both the Roman Catholic Church and the World Council of Churches, is one of almost unbelievable progress and development in a very short time. Consultation and co-operation has rapidly developed in all the major areas of work of the World Council: mission, service, international affairs, youth activity, faith and order, and development activity. The ecumenical story revealed in these two reports is not finished; it has hardly begun. The recognition and approval of "more dynamic" relationships between the World Council of Churches and the Roman Catholic Church suggests that the next five years will be as excitingly new as the last. This is not to conceal or cover up the ever present difficulties of learning to work together, or to say that no setbacks will take place. The reports assume that there is only one ecumenical movement and that it is the common task of all Churches and Councils to co-operate in that one movement. This is a revolution which we have witnessed in our time.

The question of membership of the Roman Catholic Church in the World Council of Churches could not be avoided, although the question has so many theoretical and practical problems connected with it that the official

---

[1] See Uppsala, pp. 228–66.

reports made it clear that concentration on membership at this time would be premature.

In approving the official reports of the Joint Working Group, however, the Uppsala Assembly took action which expresses succinctly the World Council's attitude towards such membership in terms which have been well received by Roman Catholic ecumenists. The report of Reference Committee 1 as approved by the Assembly states:

> The Assembly encourages the Joint Working Group to continue to give attention to the question of the membership of the Roman Catholic Church in the World Council of Churches. Membership depends upon the initiative of individual churches willing to accept the basis. The World Council reaffirms its eagerness to extend its membership to include all those Christian Churches at present outside its fellowship.[1]

In the same report there is an additional statement which emphasizes the adherence of the Assembly to the ecumenical stance of the World Council of Churches within the one ecumenical movement. "In the World Council of Churches, separate churches have been drawn into a Koinonia by common acceptance of its Basis and by a covenant to fulfil their common calling together. The Assembly affirms its belief that this Koinonia is essential to the one ecumenical movement and that it must be more fully manifested."[2] It should be remembered that the discussion of "membership" has been equally of interest to Roman Catholic ecumenists and officials. It is clear that this will continue to be discussed while we shall continue to collaborate more and more dynamically. The fact that Roman Catholic members were elected to the Faith and Order Commission, with the approval of their Church, makes it clear that the new relationships are truly dynamic.

The area of collaboration and joint activity most rapidly developing between the Roman Catholic Church and the World Council of Churches is in the area of the programme in Church and Society, Development and Peace. This collaboration is with the Pontifical Commission on Justice and Peace appointed by Pope Paul VI in January 1967. The new commission, determined to be ecumenical from the beginning, is now fully committed to working with the World Council on a joint programme *ad experimentum* for the years 1969–71. In January 1968 a first staff member was employed jointly for six months to mount a world consultation on economic strategy for peace which was held in Beirut in April of the same year. Father George Dunne, S.J. was appointed by Cardinal Roy, Chairman of the Pontifical Commission, and by the General Secretary of the World Council of Churches under the authority of the Executive Committee. His office is in the Ecumenical Centre in Geneva. The Uppsala Assembly approved the continuance and development of this joint project.[3] In September 1968 the announcement was made by Cardinal Roy and the W.C.C. General Secretary that Father Dunne's appointment was continued for three years.

The joint project is planned to be an all-out educational campaign among

[1] Uppsala, p. 178, para. I. (iii).   [2] Ibid., p. 179, para. I. (viii).
[3] See ibid., p. 179, para. II. (ii).

the constituencies of all the Churches to change the minds of their ordinary members as to their Christian responsibility for world development in the broadest sense. Based generally upon the common thinking in the report of the World Council's 1966 Church and Society Conference and in the papal encyclical *Populorum progressio*, economic, political, spiritual, and moral considerations will be combined to mobilize Christians everywhere to help overcome the growing gap between the rich and the poor nations. This increase of justice is understood to be the only adequate basis for the long-range establishment of world peace.

In the exploratory period in the spring of 1968 the Beirut Conference was held. During the same period plans were formed for a political and theological process of world consultation on the same high level. In the meantime a programme of education of the Churches has been projected to spend over a million and a half dollars during the three years. It is expected that resources for this programme will be provided by several foundations and some individuals. Enough of this support had already been promised to enable Father Dunne's staff to be expanded in the autumn of 1968 so that the programme will be fully under way early in 1969. The joint effort will be supervised by a strengthened joint committee under the co-chairmanship of Mr Max Kohnstamm for the World Council of Churches and Mgr Joseph Gremillion for the Pontifical Commission for Justice and Peace.

Long before the Uppsala Assembly it had been hoped that the Fourth Assembly would make its greatest contribution in the area of development. No one could have believed that, in addition to the ideas conceived and the purposes approved, it would be possible to plan so important a concrete effort ready to be implemented so quickly. And no one would have supposed that such a programme could be mounted jointly with the Roman Catholic Church. Yet within two years of the date of its appointment the Pontifical Commission was able not only to organize itself to do its task but also to join to create the first common world-wide programme with the World Council of Churches. The World Council of Churches proved its own flexibility by making its full contribution to the exploration and planning. The future of wide ecumenical co-operation will depend heavily upon the success of this first great effort together.

Next Steps

What of the future? This is a book of history rather than one of prophecy. It is best therefore to point towards the future by examining part III of the report of the Structure Committee referred to above[1] in which the Uppsala Assembly directed the Central Committee to restructure the World Council in the light of the functions that the ecumenical movement now requires of it. It is important to note that the new Committee on Structure, which began its work in December 1968, was not asked merely to tinker with organizational procedures in order to produce organizational efficiency even though that is doubtless useful and necessary. The report begins: "After twenty years of

[1] See p. 437 above.

life together the member churches need to review their understanding of the significance of the World Council of Churches and the meaning of their membership in it."[1] The report then goes on to suggest the major considerations that should be in mind for the future. These are:

1. The effect of the World Council's growth away from the North Atlantic region which gave it birth "towards the Third World".
2. The fact that Orthodox Churches now play a larger role in its life.
3. The ramifying partnership with the Roman Catholic Church since Vatican Council II and with other non-member Churches.[2]

Furthermore, the new Structure Committee is reminded that

> They need to consider what are the specific ways in which the World Council functions; how its life can be renewed from fresh springs of life in the churches and in the world; how the influence of official leaders of the churches (who are mostly clerical) can best be balanced with men and women, especially younger men and women, whose primary field of Christian service is in the world.[3]

The new Committee is warned against supposing that all programmes and functions must necessarily be continued, and it is directed to attempt to see "how the World Council of Churches can be both faithful and flexible in its response to the calling of God".[4]

It is recognized further that it will not be easy for a structure committee to "grapple with questions of worship and spiritual life or with our differing assumptions about the way in which Christians live together in the Church".

> Nevertheless, it should ask itself whether, in the life of the Council, its Assembly, its committees and its headquarters, there are unexamined ways of doing things or leaving them undone, which render the Council a place in which Orthodox Christians, Christians from the people's democracies, and Christians from the third world of Asia and Africa, Latin America and the Pacific, do not easily feel at home, and whether there are implications in this for the structure of the World Council.[5]

The Committee is further instructed to take into its consideration the implications of the regional Councils of Churches on the one hand and of the existence of the world confessional families on the other. A warning is noted about the cost and complexities that can arise out of Roman Catholic co-operation and the cultivation of new relationships with other non-member Churches.[6]

An examination of the Assembly and of all the committee structure is also called for. The two most important questions that need to be considered are

> (a) The relations between church representation and legislative authority and responsibility and between ecclesiastical control and lay professional expertise and insight. . . . (e) . . . how the committees needed can in practice secure an attendance more fully representative geographically and confessionally and also of the varied energies and enthusiasms, with experience and insight, within the churches.[7]

[1] Uppsala, p. 376, para. 58.   [2] See ibid., p. 376, para. 59.
[3] Ibid., p. 376, para. 60.   [4] Ibid., p. 376, para. 61.
[5] Ibid., p. 377, para. 63.   [6] Ibid., p. 377, paras. 64, 65.   [7] Ibid., p. 378, para. 67.

Conclusion

If a study of the structure of the World Council of Churches, conceived of in such terms as the above, can be completed and implemented in the next three years, it is likely to be the best hope and promise for the future of the ecumenical movement at least as far as the World Council can serve the movement. Effective programmes carried on by viable structures built upon a discernment of the right functions and priorities which in turn arise out of the enduring truth of the Christian faith are the essence of the World Council. New and younger leadership is now established in the Central and Executive Committees. Since January 1967 new directors are in charge or are soon coming to take charge of almost all the major programmes and service units of the Council. It is a new era.

The attitude of the world towards the World Council of Churches remains as ambivalent as its attitude toward the Churches themselves. Hope and fear, criticism and appreciation, longing for faith and a retreat towards nihilism— all are compounded to make up this attitude.

Positive and effective action, in identification with the poor and the exploited, based upon strong intellectual and spiritual insights from the Christian faith can alone answer the widespread criticism of Christianity. The World Council of Churches is in a position to provide the ecumenical leadership that the years ahead demand. Some will pray fervently that the promises of the Uppsala Assembly will be fulfilled.

Bibliography

ANS J. VAN DER BENT

The bibliography of this book has been compiled in a way similar to the bibliography of the first volume of the *History of the Ecumenical Movement*. It is a selective bibliography referring the reader only to major documentary sources and important ecumenical books and pamphlets published during the last twenty years.

Purposely no attempt has been made to compile a comprehensive and systematic bibliography covering all ecumenical literature since the Amsterdam Assembly, 1948. Such a bibliography would make up a thick volume of several hundred pages and would still not be complete. Fortunately, a number of useful ecumenical bibliographies have been published and are still relatively up to date. The following bibliographies can be consulted by those readers who wish to refer to more detailed bibliographical information:

Paul A. Crow, *The Ecumenical Movement in Bibliographical Outline*. New York, U.S.A., 1965.

J. F. Lescrauwaet, M.S.C., *Critical Bibliography of Ecumenical Literature*. Nymegen, Bestel Centrale V.S.K.B., 1965.

International Ecumenical Bibliography. Mainz, Matthias—Grünewald-Verlag; München, Chr. Kaiser Verlag, vol. i, 1962–3, published in 1967.
A second volume covering the years 1964–5 will be issued in the course of the year 1969. Thereafter annual volumes are planned.

Some bibliographies dealing with special subjects should be mentioned also:

Ulrich Valeske, *Votum Ecclesiae*. München, Claudius Verlag, 1962.
Part II represents an extensive interconfessional ecclesiological bibliography.

Laici in Ecclesia: An ecumenical bibliography on the role of the laity in the life and mission of the church. Geneva, Department of the Laity of the World Council of Churches, 1961.

An excellent service is rendered by the Missionary Research Library, New York, Broadway at 120th Street 10027, U.S.A., which publishes regularly selected lists of books and detailed bibliographies in some special fields of missions.

Finally, the reader might want to consult the *International Review of Missions* and the *Ecumenical Review*, both published by W.C.C. in Geneva, which carry in each number a well-selected bibliography of current publications. Also the catalogues of the Publication Department of the World Council of Churches, 150 Route de Ferney, 1211 Geneva 20, should be consulted; these give a complete list of books and pamphlets still for sale.

All these and other bibliographical sources together provide the student with a more or less complete view of the ecumenical literature over the last twenty years. This bibliography, therefore, contains no general bibliography, no lists of ecumenical periodicals, *Festschriften*, doctoral dissertations, or ecumenical memoirs and biographies. Each chapter is documented only by a choice of the most significant works on the subject and a selection of the most important official World Council of Churches documents. For the chapter on the *Roman Catholic Church and the Ecumenical Movement* only a few major Catholic evaluations and Protestant, Anglican, and Orthodox reactions to Vatican II are indicated. No official sources are listed.

In case an English work has been translated into French or German, the title of the French or German translation has been added to the bibliographical description of the book in English. When a book was written originally in French or German, the English version has been given first with the indication that the work was translated from the French or German. Only in an exceptional case has a book not written in either English, French, or German been added to the bibliography.

Finally, the reader should bear in mind that numerous World Council of Churches and other ecumenical publications exist only in type-written or mimeographed form. All these papers, minutes, reports, etc. can be consulted in the Archives of the Library of the World Council of Churches in Geneva. This Ecumenical Library now also houses the complete records of the International Missionary Council from 1910 to 1961 and continues to collect extensively materials prepared by national and regional Councils of Churches and other ecumenical organizations in six continents.

ANS J. VAN DER BENT
Librarian, World Council of Churches

CHAPTER 1

The General Ecumenical Development since 1948

GENERAL SURVEYS

ALTHAUS, Hans-Ludwig, *Oekumenische Dokumente, Quellenstücke über die Einheit der Kirche*. 251pp. Göttingen, Vandenhoeck & Ruprecht, 1962.

BELL, G. K. A., ed., *Documents on Christian Unity*. 4 vols. London, Oxford University Press, 1920–57.

BENZ, Ernst, *Kirchengeschichte in ökumenischer Sicht*. 147pp. (Oekumenische Studien, 3. Leiden, Brill, 1961.

BILHEIMER, Robert S., *The Quest for Christian Unity*. 181pp. New York, Association Press, 1952.

BOYER, Charles, *Christian Unity and the Ecumenical Movement*. 131pp. (Faith and fact books, 138). London, Burns & Oates, 1962. Translated from the Italian *Unità cristiana e movimento ecumenico*.

CONORD, Paul, *Brève histoire de l'oecuménisme*. 233pp. Paris, Collection "Les Bergers et les Mages", 1958.

GOLTERMAN, W. F., *Eenheid in de chaos der Kerken*. 207pp. (Volksuniversiteits Bibliotheek, 68.) Haarlem, De Erven F. Bohn, 1962.

GOODALL, Norman, *The Ecumenical Movement: What it is and what it does*. 2nd edn. 257pp. London, New York, Oxford University Press, 1964.

HOPE, Norman V., *One Christ, One World, One Church: A short introduction to the ecumenical movement*. 96pp. Philadelphia, The Church Historical Society, 1953.

HORNIG, Ernst, *Der Weg der Weltchristenheit. Eine Einführung in die ökumenische Bewegung, ihre Geschichte und Probleme*. 2. Aufl. 338pp. Stuttgart, Evangelisches Verlagswerk, 1958.

KINDER, Ernst, *Die ökumenische Bewegung, 1948–1961*. 135pp. (Kirchengeschicht-liche Quellenhefte, 12/13.) Gladbeck, Schriftenmissions-Verlag, 1963.

MCNEILL, John T., *Unitive Protestantism; The ecumenical spirit and its persistent expression*. 352pp. Richmond, Virginia, John Knox Press, 1964.

MICHALON, Pierre, *L'Unité des chrétiens*. 127pp. Paris, Arthème Fayard, 1965. German translation *Der Sinn für den anderen. Auf dem Weg zur Einheit der Christen*.

NELSON, John Robert, *Overcoming Christian Divisions*. Rev. edn. 126pp. (1958 edn. entitled: *One Lord, One Church*.) New York, Association Press, 1962. German translation *Die Einheit der Kirche in Welt und Gemeinde*.

NUTTALL, Geoffrey F., and CHADWICK, Owen, ed., *From Uniformity to Unity, 1662–1962*. 423pp. London, S.P.C.K., 1962.

O'BRIEN, John A., *Steps to Christian Unity*. 321pp. Garden City, New York, Doubleday & Company, 1964.

RENKEWITZ, Heinz, *Die Kirchen auf dem Wege zur Einheit*. 189pp. (Evang. Enzyklo-pädie.) Gütersloh, Gütersloher Verlagshaus Gerd Mohn, 1964.

ROUSE, Ruth, and NEILL, Stephen C., ed., *A History of the Ecumenical Movement, 1517–1948*. 2nd edn. with revised bibliography. 838pp. London, S.P.C.K., 1967. German translation *Geschichte der ökumenischen Bewegung, 1517–1948*. 2 vols.

SLACK, Kenneth, *The Ecumenical Movement*. 44pp. London, Edinburgh House Press, 1960.

452 BIBLIOGRAPHY

Weltkirchen-Lexicon. Handbuch der Oekumene; im Auftrag des Deutschen Evangelischen Kirchentages, hrsg. von F. H. Littell und H. H. Walz. 1756pp. Stuttgart, Kreuz Verlag, 1960.

WINTERHAGER, Jürgen Wilhelm, *Kirchen-Unionen des zwanzigsten Jahrhunderts.* 253pp. Zürich, Gotthelf-Verlag, 1961.

INTERPRETATIVE INTRODUCTIONS

BAROT, Madeleine, *Le mouvement oecuménique.* 128pp. (Que sais-je?, 841.) Paris, Presses Universitaires de France, 1967.

BLAKEMORE, W. B., ed., *The Challenge of Christian Unity.* 144pp. St Louis, Bethany Press, 1963.

BOEGNER, Marc, *L'exigence oecuménique. Souvenirs et perspectives.* 366pp. Paris, Ed. Albin Michel, 1968.

BRADSHAW, Marion J., *Free Churches and Christian Unity: Critical view of the ecumenical movement and the World Council of Churches.* 225pp. Boston, Beacon Press, 1954.

BRIDSTON, Keith R., and WAGONER, Walter D., *Unity in mid-career, an ecumenical critique.* 211pp. New York, London, Macmillan, 1963.

BROMILEY, G. W., *The Unity and Disunity of the Church.* 104pp. Grand Rapids, Mich., Eerdmans, 1958.

BRUCE, Michael, *Barriers to Unity.* 112pp. London, Faith Press, 1959.

CAVERT, Samuel McCrea, *On the Road to Christian Unity: An appraisal of the ecumenical movement.* 192pp. New York, Harper, 1961.

FLETCHER, Grace N., *The Whole World's in his Hand.* 219pp. New York, Dutton, 1962.

HENDERSON, Ian, *Power without Glory: A study in ecumenical politics.* 184pp. London, Hutchinson, 1967.

HORTON, Walter M., *Christian Theology: An ecumenical approach.* Rev. edn. 320pp. New York, Harper, 1958.

JENTSCH, Werner, *Vielfalt und Einfalt. Eine ökumenische Besinnung.* 222pp. Kassel, Eichenkreuzverlag, 1966.

KEAN, Charles D., *The Road to Reunion.* 145pp. Greenwich, Conn., Seabury Press, 1958.

LAMBERT, Bernard, *Ecumenism: Theology and history.* 533pp. London, Burns and Oates, 1966. Translated from the French *Le problème oecuménique.* German translation *Das ökumenische Problem.*

LAWRENCE, John, *The Hard Facts of Unity.* 127pp. London, S.C.M. Press, 1961.

MACKAY, John A., *Ecumenics: The Science of the Church Universal.* 294pp. Englewoods Cliff, N.J., Prentice-Hall, 1964.

MARXSEN, Willi, *Einheit der Kirche?* 148pp. Ringvorlesungen der Evang.-Theologischen Fakultät der Westfälischen Wilhelms-Universität Münster. In Verbindung mit Kurt Aland, Wilhelm Anz, Ernst Kinder, Helmut Kittel, Heinz-Dietrich Wendland und Siegfried Hebart. Witten, Luther Verlag, 1964.

MASCALL, Eric L., *The Recovery of Unity: A theological approach.* 242pp. New York, Longmans, Green, 1958.

MEINHOLD, Peter, *Die Kirchen auf neuen Wegen. Wie sie heute aufeinander blicken.* 172pp. Freiburg, Herder, 1964.

MEINHOLD, Peter, *Oekumenische Kirchenkunde.* 652pp. Stuttgart, Kreuz-Verlag 1962.

MICHAEL, J. P., *Christen glauben eine Kirche*. 239pp. Recklinghausen, Paulus Verlag, 1962.

MUDGE, Lewis S., *One Church: Catholic and Reformed*. 96pp. Philadelphia, Westminster, 1963.

NEWBIGIN, Bp J. E. Lesslie, *The Reunion of the Church: A defense of the South India scheme*. Rev. edn. 192pp. London, S.C.M. Press, 1960.

NEILL, Stephen, *The Church and Christian Union*. 423pp. (The Bampton Lectures, 1964.) London, Oxford University Press, 1968.

NEUMANN, Johannes, *Auf Hoffnung hin; eine Sammlung ökumenischer Gedanken*. 284pp. Meitingen bei Augsburg, Kyrios-Verlag, 1964.

NICHOLLS, William, *Ecumenism and catholicity*. 159pp. London, S.C.M. Press, 1952.

Un nouvel age oecuménique. Etude du Centre international d'information et de documentation sur l'Eglise conciliaire. 394pp. (L'Eglise en son temps—études, 10.) Paris, Editions du Centurion, 1966.

OUTLER, Albert C., *The Christian Tradition and the Unity we Seek. Given as Richard Lectures at the University of Virginia in Charlottesville*. 165pp. New York, Oxford University Press, 1957.

PIPER, Otto A., *Protestantism in an Ecumenical Age: Its root, its task*. 254pp. Philadelphia, Fortress Press, 1965.

RISTON, Helmut, and BURGERT, Helmuth, ed., *Konfession und Oekumene. Aspekte—Probleme—Aufgaben*. 588pp. Berlin, Evang. Verlagsanstalt, 1965.

ROBINSON, William, *The Shattered Cross: The many churches and the one church*. 92pp. Birmingham, Berean Press, 1955.

SARTORY, Thomas, *Ecumenical Movement and the Unity of the Church*. 290pp. Oxford, Blackwell, 1963. Translated from the German *Die ökumenische Bewegung und die Einheit der Kirche: ein Beitrag im Dienste einer ökumenischen Ekklesiologie*.

SCHLINK, Edmund, *The Coming Christ and the Coming Church*. 333pp. Edinburgh, Oliver & Boyd, 1967. Translated from the German *Der kommende Christus und die kirchlichen Traditionen*.

SCHUTZ, Roger, *Unity: Man's tomorrow*. 94pp. London, Faith Press, 1962. Translated from the French *L'unité, espérance de vie*. German translation *Einheit und Zukunft. Die Christenheit im technischen Zeitalter*.

SPINKA, Matthew, *The Quest for Church Unity*. 85pp. New York, Macmillan, 1960.

TAVARD, George, *Two centuries of ecumenism*. 239pp. Notre Dame, Fides, 1960. Translated from the French *Petite histoire du mouvement oecuménique*. German translation *Geschichte der ökumenischen Bewegung*.

THILS, Gustave, *Histoire doctrinale du mouvement oecuménique*. Nouvelle édition. 340pp. Louvain, E. Warny, 1962.

THURIAN, Max: *Visible Unity and Tradition*. 137pp. London, Darton, Longman and Todd, 1964. Translated from the French *L'unité visible des chrétiens et la tradition*. German translation *Sichtbare Einheit*.

TOMKINS, Oliver, *A Time for Unity*. 127pp. London, S.C.M. Press, 1964.

TORRANCE, T. F., *Conflict and agreement in the Church*. 2 vols. 331pp. and 213pp. London, Lutterworth Press, 1959–60.

VILLAIN, Maurice, *Unity: A history and some reflections*. 3rd rev. and augmented edn. 381pp. London, Harvill, 1963. Translated from the French *Introduction à l'oecuménisme*.

VISSER 'T HOOFT, W. A., *The meaning of ecumenical*. 28pp. London, S.C.M. Press, 1953.

VISSER 'T HOOFT, W. A., *Hauptschriften*. 2 vols.—1. *Die ganze Kirche für die ganze Welt;* 2. *Oekumenischer Aufbruch*. Berling, Kreuz Verlag, 1967.

VISSER 'T HOOFT, Willem A., *Oekumenische Bilanz*. Reden und Aufsätze aus zwei
   Jahrzehnten. Mit Vorwort von Hanfried Krüger. 168pp. Stuttgart, Evang.
   Missionsverlag, 1966.
VISSER 'T HOOFT, W. A., *The Pressure of our Common Calling*. 90pp. Garden City,
   New York, Doubleday, 1959. French translation *Les exigences de notre vocation
   commune*. German translation *Unter dem einen Ruf*.

CHAPTER 2

The Life and Activities of the World Council of Churches

ASSEMBLIES

First Assembly: Amsterdam 1948

The First Assembly of the World Council of Churches, 1948. 271pp. Ed. W. A. Visser
   't Hooft. London, S.C.M. Press, 1949.
KENNEDY, James W., *Venture of Faith: The birth of the World Council of Churches*.
   120pp. New York, Morehouse-Gorham Co., 1948.
Man's Disorder and God's Design. The Amsterdam Assembly series. 4 vols.—1. *The
   Universal Church in God's Design*. 217pp.; 2. *The Church's Witness to God's
   Design*. 226 pp.; 3. *The Church and the Disorder of Society*. 205pp.; 4. *The Church
   and the International Disorder*. 232pp. New York, Harper, 1949.

Second Assembly: Evanston 1954

*Assembly work book. Prepared for the Second Assembly of the World Council of
   Churches at Evanston, 1954*. 108pp. Geneva, W.C.C., 1954.
*The Christian Hope and the Task of the Church. Six ecumenical surveys and the report
   of the assembly prepared by the Advisory Commission on the main theme*. 405pp.
   New York, Harper, 1954.
"Evanston Main Theme" in *Ecumenical Review*, vol. vi, no. 4, pp. 431–65. Geneva,
   W.C.C., July 1954.
The Evanston Report: The Second Assembly of the World Council of Churches, 1954.
   360pp. London, S.C.M. Press, 1955.
*Evanston Speaks: Reports from the Second Assembly of the World Council of
   Churches, 1954*. 71pp. Geneva, W.C.C., 1954.
*The First Six Years 1948–1954. A report of the Central Committee of the World
   Council of Churches on the activities of the departments and secretariats of the
   Council*. 149pp. Geneva, W.C.C., 1954. French translation *Les six premières
   années 1948–1954*. German translation *Die ersten sechs Jahre 1948–1954*.
HERKLOTS, Hugh G. G., *Looking at Evanston. A study of the Second Assembly of
   the World Council of Churches*. Evanston, 1954. 114pp. London, S.C.M. Press,
   1954.
KENNEDY, James W., *Evanston Scrapbook. An account of the Second Assembly of the
   World Council of Churches, held in Evanston, 1954*. 124pp. Lebanon, Pa., Sowers
   Printing Co., 1954.
MARSH, John, *The Significance of Evanston*. 72pp. London, Independent Press, 1954.

NICHOLS, James H., *Evanston: An interpretation.* 155pp. New York, Harper, 1954.

Response to Evanston. A survey of the comments sent in by the member Churches on the report of the Second Assembly of the World Council of Churches at Evanston, 1954. 87pp. Geneva, W.C.C., 1957.

Third Assembly: New Delhi 1961

Constitution and Rules of the World Council of Churches. As adopted by the Assembly at Amsterdam, 1948, amended at Evanston, 1954 and further amended at New Delhi, 1961. 20pp. Geneva, W.C.C., 1961.

Evanston to New Delhi, 1954–1961. Report of the Central Committee to the Third Assembly of the World Council of Churches. 288pp. Geneva, W.C.C., 1961.

Jesus Christ, the Light of the World. World Council of Churches. Third Assembly, New Delhi, 1961. 76pp. Geneva, W.C.C., 1961.

KENNEDY, James W., *No Darkness At All.* 122pp. St Louis, Bethany Press, 1962.

The New Delhi Report: The Third Assembly of the World Council of Churches, 1961. 448pp. London, S.C.M. Press, 1962.

New Delhi Speaks: About christian witness, service and unity. The message, appeal, and section reports of the Third Assembly in New Delhi, 1961, ed. W. A. Visser 't Hooft. 124pp. New York, Association Press, 1962.

SLACK, Kenneth, *Despatch from New Delhi.* 111pp. London, S.C.M. Press, 1962.

The Work Book for the Assembly Committee. Prepared for the Third Assembly of the World Council of Churches. 188pp. Geneva, W.C.C., 1961.

Fourth Assembly: Uppsala 1968

All things new. Fourth Assembly Uppsala 1968. 48pp. Geneva, W.C.C., 1967.

Drafts for sections prepared for the Fourth Assembly of the World Council of Churches, Uppsala, 1968. 136pp. Geneva, W.C.C., 1968.

FEY, Harold E., *Life: new style. How the hope for a new style of life for humanity was advanced by the Fourth Assembly of the World Council of Churches meeting in Uppsala, Sweden, July 4 to 20, 1968.* 128pp. Cincinnati, Forward Movement Publications, 1968.

FRIELING, Reinhard, *Uppsala 1968: Erneuerung der Welt?* 105pp. Göttingen, Vandenhoeck and Ruprecht, 1968.

New Delhi to Uppsala, 1961–1968. Report of the Central Committee to the Fourth Assembly of the World Council of Churches. 220pp. Geneva, W.C.C., 1968.

PERCHENET, Annie, *Chrétiens ensemble. Journal d'Upsal, juillet 1968.* 206pp. Paris, Desclée, 1968.

SCHELZ, Sepp, *Weltkirche in Aktion. Ein Bericht über die Weltkirchenkonferenz in Uppsala 1968.* 157pp. München, Siebenstern Taschenbuch Verlag, 1968.

SLACK, Kenneth, *Uppsala Report. The story of the World Council of Churches Fourth Assembly, Uppsala, Sweden, 4–19 July 1968.* 88pp. London, S.C.M. Press, 1968.

Unity of mankind. Speeches from the Fourth Assembly of the World Council of Churches, Uppsala 1968, ed. Albert H. van den Heuvel. 142pp. Geneva, W.C.C., 1969.

The Uppsala Report 1968, Official report of the Fourth Assembly of the World Council of Churches, Uppsala July 4–20, 1968, ed. Norman Goodall. 513pp. Geneva, W.C.C., 1968. German version *Bericht aus Uppsala 68.* French version *Rapport d'Upsal 68.*

WENGER, Antoine, *Upsal, le défi du siècle aux Eglises.* 384pp. Paris, Editions du Centurion, 1968.

Workbook for the Assembly Committees. Prepared for the Fourth Assembly of the World Council of Churches, Uppsala, 1968. 200pp. Geneva, W.C.C., 1968.

Central Committees

Minutes and Reports of the .... *Meeting of the Central Committee of the World Council of Churches* .... Geneva, W.C.C., 1949–67.

1949	2nd	Meeting	Chichester	127pp.
1950	3rd	,,	Toronto	133pp.
1951	4th	,,	Rolle	138pp.
1952/53	5th	,,	Lucknow	140pp.
1954	6th	,,	Chicago	56pp.
1954	7th	,,	Evanston	37pp.
1955	8th	,,	Davos	146pp.
1956	9th	,,	Galyatetö	128pp.
1957	10th	,,	New Haven	136pp.
1958	11th	,,	Nyborg Strand	133pp.
1959	12th	,,	Rhodes	208pp.
1960	13th	,,	St Andrews	218pp.
1961	14th and 15th	,,	New Delhi	59pp.
1962	16th	,,	Paris	153pp.
1963	17th	,,	Rochester	142pp.
1965	18th	,,	Enugu	167pp.
1966	19th	,,	Geneva	151pp.
1967	20th	,,	Heraklion	270pp.

Executive Committees

Minutes of meetings of the Executive Committee of the World Council of Churches (mimeographed, in Archives of W.C.C. Library).

1949, Feb.	Bossey	1959, Feb.	Geneva
1949, July	Chichester	1959, Aug.	Kifissia
1950, Feb.	Bossey	1960, Feb.	Buenos Aires
1950, July	Toronto	1960, Aug.	St Andrews
1951, Jan.	Bièvres	1961, Feb.	Geneva
1951, Aug.	Rolle	1961, June	Bossey
1952, Feb.	London	1961, Nov.	New Delhi
1952, Aug.	Nykøbing	1961, Dec.	New Delhi
1952, Dec.–		1962, March	Geneva
1953, Jan.	Lucknow	1962, Aug.	Paris
1953, Aug.	Bossey	1963, Feb.	Geneva
1954, Feb.	Königstein im Taunus	1963, Aug.	Rochester
1954, Aug.	Chicago	1964, Feb.	Odessa
1955, Feb.	Geneva	1964, July	Tutzing
1955, July/Aug.	Davos	1965, Jan.	Enugu
1956, Feb.	Gilbulla	1965, July	Geneva
1956, July	Vienna	1966, Aug.	Geneva
1957, Feb.	Geneva	1966, Feb.	Geneva
1957, July	Greenwich	1967, Feb.	Windsor
1958, Feb.	London	1967, Aug.	Heraklion
1958, Aug.	Nyborg Strand	1968, Feb.	Geneva

BOOKS ABOUT THE WORLD COUNCIL OF CHURCHES

BELL, George Kennedy Allen, *The Kingship of Christ. The story of the World Council of Churches*. 183pp. Harmondsworth, Penguin Books, 1954. German translation *Die Königsherrschaft Jesu Christi; Die Geschichte des Oekumenischen Rates der Kirchen*.

DUFF, Edward, S.J., *The Social Thought of the World Council of Churches*. 339pp. New York, Association Press, 1956.

GAINES, David P., *The World Council of Churches: A study of its background and history*. 1302 pp. Peterborough, Richard R. Smith, 1966.

GOODALL, Norman, *The Ecumenical Movement: What it is and what it does*. 2nd edn. 257pp. London, New York, Oxford University Press, 1964.

GRANT, John Webster, *The Ship under the Cross*. 106pp. Toronto, The Ryerson Press, 1960.

Index to Ecumenical Statements and World Council of Churches Official Reports. 119pp. Trilingual. Geneva, W.C.C., 1968.

KRÜGER, Hanfried, *Oekumenische Bewegung, 1955–1958* (Sonderdruck aus *Kirchliches Jahrbuch für die evangelische Kirche in Deutschland*. 1958. Gütersloh, Gerd Mohn), pp. 310–78. Also surveys for the years 1959, 1960–1, 1962, 1963–4.

MACY, Paul Griswold, *If it be of God: The story of the World Council of Churches*. 192pp. St Louis, Mo., Bethany Press, 1960.

NEILL, Stephen C., *Men of Unity*. 192pp. London, S.C.M. Press, 1960. (American edn. with title: *Brothers of Faith*. Nashville, Abingdon Press, 1960.) German translation *Männer der Einheit; ökumenische Bewegung von Edinburgh bis Neu-Delhi*.

THEURER, Wolfdieter, *Die trinitarische Basis des ORK*. 285pp. Frankfurt/M., Verlag Gerhard Kaffke, 1967.

CHAPTER 3

Out of All Continents and Nations
A review of regional developments in the
ecumenical movement

ASIA

ASSEMBLIES

With the exception of Asia and North America no specific studies have been made concerning regional developments in other continents. The sources for the study of ecumenical regionalism remain the reports and minutes of various assemblies and committees of regional ecumenical organizations as well as some articles published in their periodicals.

Bangkok 1949

The Christian Prospect in Eastern Asia. Papers and minutes of the E.A.C.C. Bangkok, December 3–11 1949. 156pp. New York, published for the International Missionary Council and the World Council of Churches by Friendship Press, 1950.

Prapat 1957

The Common Evangelistic Task of the Churches in East Asia. Papers and minutes of the E.A.C.C. Prapat, Indonesia, March 17–26, 1957. 167pp.

Kuala Lumpur 1959

Witnesses Together, being the Official Report of the Inaugural Assembly of the E.A.C.C., held at Kuala Lumpur, Malaya, May 14–24, 1959. 179pp. Ed. by U Kyaw Than. Rangoon, E.A.C.C., 1959.

Bangkok 1964

The Christian Community within the Human Community. Containing statements from the Bangkok Assembly of the E.A.C.C., Feb. 25–March 5, 1964. 84pp. Bangalore, India 1964.

Bangkok 1968
In Christ All Things Hold Together. Statements and findings of the Fourth Assembly of the E.A.C.C. 60pp. Bangkok 1968.

OTHER CONFERENCES

The Asian Churches and Responsible Parenthood. Bangkok, Thailand, E.A.C.C. Consultation 1964. 100pp. E.A.C.C. 1964.
Christ—the Hope of Asia. Papers and minutes of the ecumenical study conference for East Asia, Lucknow, India, December 27–30, 1952. 102pp. Madras, The Christian Literature Society, 1953.
Church's Witness in relation to religion, society, international affairs and religious liberty. Programme for 1964–68. 129pp. Bangkok, E.A.C.C., 1964.
Confessing the Faith in Asia Today. The First Faith and Order meeting in Hongkong, 1966. 116pp. Redfern, Epworth Press, 1967.
Consultation Digest. First Asian Consultation on Inter-Church Aid held under the joint auspices of D.I.C.A.R.W.S.–E.A.C.C. at Hongkong, Oct. 17–23, 1963. 118pp. Geneva, W.C.C., 1964.
Consultation on the Place of Education in the Mission of the Church. Singapore, E.A.C.C., April 4–8, 1961. 59pp. Wellawatte, Wesley Press, 1961.
Consultations on New Patterns of Christian Service, 1960–62:
New Forms of Christian Service and Participation. Nasrapur, October 1960 (Kottayam 1960).
New Forms of Christian Service in the Philippines. Quezon City, 1–4 April 1961 (Manila 1961).
Towards the New Form of Service in Japan. Atami, Japan, 29–31 March 1961 (Tokyo 1961).
New Forms of Christian Service and Participation in Korea. Onyang, Korea (Bangalore 1961).
Christian Service in the Revolution. Sukabumi, Indonesia, 14–18 November 1962. (Bangalore 1963).
East Asia Christian Conference. Minutes of the meeting of the enlarged Continuation Committee of the E.A.C.C., held at Bangalore, India, 7–12 November 1961. 135pp. Jaffna, St Joseph's Catholic Press, 1962.

East Asia Christian Conference. Report of Situation Conferences, convened by the E.A.C.C., February–March 1963. 56pp. Bangkok, E.A.C.C., 1963.

East Asia Christian Conference. Summary Reports of E.A.C.C. Committees (1959–64). 55pp. Bangkok, Rajadaromp Printery and Typefoundry, 1964.

East Asia Christian Literature Conference, Minutes of the . . . Tomlinson Hall, Singapore, December 7–11 1951. Sponsored by the International Missionary Council and the World Council of Churches. 48pp. Mysore City, Wesley Press, 1952.

God's People in Asian Industrial Society. The report of the E.A.C.C. on Christians in industry and lay training, ed. Robert M. Fukada. 198pp. Kyoto, Doshisha University School of Theology, 1967.

Men and Women in Home, Church and Community in Asia. Papers and statements of an Asian consultation on "The Christian home in a changing society". 114pp. Rangoon, Burma, 1963.

The Mission of the Church and the Cultural Minorities. Sagada, Philippines, Oct. 26 to Nov. 4, 1963. 27pp. E.A.C.C., Committee on Church and Society, 1964.

ROSE, Douglas A., *Seed of the Lotus: A diary of the Asian Christian Youth Assembly 1964/1965.* 68pp.

Structures for a Missionary Congregation. The shape of the Christian community in Asia today. 124pp. Singapore, E.A.C.C., 1964.

Towards Kuala Lumpur, 1959. Papers prepared for the Inaugural Assembly of the East Asia Christian Conference, ed. U Kyaw Than. Rangoon, E.A.C.C., 1959.

The Witness of the Churches in the midst of Social Change: A survey of ecumenical social thought. Papers for preparatory reading for the assembly of the East Asia Christian Conference, Port Dickson, Malaya, May 14–24 1959. 146pp. Rangoon, E.A.C.C., 1959.

Church and Society, 1960—. Official periodical of the East Asia Christian Conference.

A Decisive Hour for the Christian Mission. The East Asia Christian Conference and the John R. Mott memorial lectures. Norman Goodall, James Edward Lesslie Newbigin, Willem Adolf Visser 't Hooft, Daniel Thambirajah Niles. 96pp. London, S.C.M. Press, 1960.

MANIKAM, Rajah B., ed., *Christianity and the Asian Revolution.* 293pp. Madras, Joint East Asia Secretariat of the I.M.C. and W.C.C., 1954.

South East Asia Journal of Theology, 1959—. Contains several official papers published by E.A.C.C.

WEBER, Hans-Ruedi: *Asia and the Ecumenical Movement 1895–1961.* 319pp. London, S.C.M. Press, 1966.

AFRICA

ASSEMBLIES

Ibadan 1958

The Church in Changing Africa. Report of the All Africa Church Conference, held at Ibadan, Nigeria, January 10–19, 1958. 106pp. New York, I.M.C., 1958. French translation *Ibadan, Conférence des Eglises d'Afrique, 1958.*

Kampala 1963

Drumbeats from Kampala. Report of the First Assembly of the All Africa Conference of Churches held at Kampala, April 20 to April 30, 1963. 77pp. London, U.S.C.L., Lutterworth Press, 1963. French translation *La Conférence de Kampala.*

OTHER CONFERENCES

Africa in Transition: The Challenge and the Christian Response. 95pp. Published by All Africa Churches Conferences in collaboration with the Dept on Church and Society, Division of Studies, World Council of Churches, Geneva, W.C.C., 1962. French translation *L'Afrique en devenir.*

Africa Seminar on the Christian Home and Family Life, held at Mindolo Ecumenical Centre, Kitwe, N. Rhodesia, 17 Feb. to 10 April, 1963. Sponsored by the A.A.C.C. in collaboration with the W.C.C. 72pp. Geneva, W.C.C., 1963. French translation *Séminaire panafricain sur le foyer chrétien et la vie de famille.*

Approved programme. Ecumenical programme for emergency action in Africa. 78pp. Geneva, W.C.C., D.I.C.A.R.W.S., 1965.

Christian Education in Africa. Report of a conference held at Salisbury, Southern Rhodesia, 29 December 1962 to 10 January 1963. 120pp. London, Oxford University Press, 1963. French translation *L'Education chrétienne en Afrique.*

Christian Women of Africa Share in Responsibility. Report of the Consultation on the Responsibility of Christian Women in Africa today, held at Makerere University, Kampala, Uganda, April 11–19th, 1963. 45pp. Geneva, W.C.C. and the Department on Co-operation of Men and Women in Church, Family, and Society, 1963. French translation *Les femmes chrétiennes d'Afrique assument leur part de responsabilité.*

Consultation Digest. A summary of reports and addresses. A.A.C.C. Inter-Church Aid Consultation. Sponsored jointly by the A.A.C.C., D.I.C.A.R.W.S., and C.C.I.A. 116pp. Geneva, W.C.C., 1965.

The Urban Africa Consultation, held in Nairobi, Kenya, March 1961. Sponsored by the A.A.C.C. in conjunction with the I.M.C. 55pp. New York, Commission on World Mission and Evangelism, 1962.

A.A.C.C. Bulletin, 1963–1967. English and French editions.

BEETHAM, T. A., *Christianity and the New Africa.* 206pp. London, Pall Mall Press, 1967.

L'oecuménisme en Afrique. Ecumenism in Africa. 169pp. Roma, C.I.P.A., 1966

LATIN AMERICA

CONGRESSES AND ASSEMBLIES

Congress on Christian Work in Latin America, Panama, 1916. 3 vols. New York, Missionary Education Movement, C.C.L.A., 1917.

Christian Work in South America. Report of the Montevideo Congress, 1925. Robert E. Speer and other editors. 2 vols. New York, C.C.L.A., 1925.

Hacia la renovacion religiosa en Hispano-América. Report of the Congreso Evangélico Hispano-americano, Havana, 1929. 213pp. Mexico, C.U.P.S.A., 1930.

El cristianismo en la América Latina. Report of the First Latin American Evangelical Conference in Buenos Aires, 1949. 103pp. Buenos Aires, La Awrora, 1949.

Cristo la Esperanza para América Latina. Segunda Conferencia Evangelica Latinoamerica. 176pp. Lima, 1961.

OTHER CONFERENCES AND LITERATURE

America hoy; accion de Dios y responsabilidad del hombre: II consulta latinoamericana de Iglesia y Sociedad. 132pp. Montevideo, I.S.A.L., 1966.

Christians and Social Change in Latin America. Findings of the first Latin American Evangelical Consultation on Church and Society, 23rd to 27th July 1961. 22pp. Huampani, Peru. Geneva, W.C.C., 1961. Translated from the Spanish *Encuentro y desafio.*

CONSIDINE, John J., ed., *The Church in the New Latin America.* 240pp. Notre Dame, Fides Publishers, 1964.

Cristianismo y sociedad, 1963—. Montevideo, I.S.A.L. The Official Latin American Church and Society journal.

The Listening Isles. Records of the Caribbean Consultation, San German, Puerto Rico, May 17–24, 1957. New York, I.M.C., 1958.

MACKAY, John A., *The Latin American Churches and the Ecumenical Movement.* 34pp. New York, N.C.C.C.U.S.A., the Committee on Co-operation in Latin America, Division of Foreign Missions, 1963.

N.C.C.C.U.S.A. Committee on Co-operation in Latin America. Study Conferences, Buck Hill Falls, 10–12 November 1957, 6–8 November 1958, 12–14 November 1959, 20–2 November 1960, 5–7 November 1961. Each Conference issued several short reports.

OBERMÜLLER, Rudolf., *Evangelism in Latin America: An ecumenical survey.* 32pp. (World evangelism today, 2). Published for the W.C.C. by U.S.C.L., London, Lutterworth Press, 1957.

Raise a Signal: God's Action and the Church's Task in Latin America Today. A Symposium compiled by Hyla S. Converse. 126pp. New York, Friendship Press, 1961.

SINCLAIR, John H., *Protestantism in Latin America: A bibliographical guide.* 213pp. Austin, Texas, Hispanic American Institute, 1967.

PACIFIC

Beyond the reef. Records of the Conference of Churches and Missions in the Pacific. Malua Theological College, Western Samoa, April 22–May 4, 1961. 114pp. London, I.M.C., 1961. French translation *La route du soleil.*

EUROPE

Konferenz Europäischer Kirchen. Ein Bericht über die Tagung in Liselund, Dänemark vom 27–31 Mai 1957. Den Haag, Konferenz Europäischer Kirchen, 1957.

Nyborg I

Die europäische Christenheit in der heutigen säkularisierten Welt. Konferenz europäischer Kirchen, Nyborg-Dänemark, 6–9 Januar 1959. 141pp. Vorträge und Berichte. Zürich, Frankfurt/M., Gotthelf-Verlag, 1960.

Nyborg II

Der Dienst der Kirche in einer sich veränderten Welt. Konferenz europäischer Kirchen, 3–8 Okt. 1960. 114pp. Zürich, Gotthelf-Verlag, 1961.

Nyborg III

Die Kirche in Europa und die Krise des modernen Menschen. Konferenz Europäischer Kirchen, 1–5 Okt. 1962. 160pp. Zürich, Gotthelf-Verlag, 1963.

Nyborg IV

Zusammen leben als Kontinente und Generationen. Konferenz Europäischer Kirchen vom 5–9 Okt. 1964. 224pp. Zürich, Gotthelf-Verlag, 1965.

Nyborg V

To serve and to reconcile. The task of the European Churches today. Preparatory document for the "Nyborg V" Assembly of the C.E.C., 1967. 38pp.

DE-LA-NOY, Michael, *A Task for the Churches in Europe: To serve and reconcile. A report of the "Nyborg V" Assembly in Pförtschach, 1967.* 48pp. Geneva, C.E.C., 1968. German report by Schulz, Otmar. *Die Aufgabe der europäischen Kirchen: Dienen und Versöhnen.* More complete than English edn.

NEAR EAST

The Christian Faith in the Contemporary Middle Eastern World. Asmara Study Conference, April 1–9, 1959. New York, 1959.

N.E.C.C. Study Programme in Islam. Operation reach. 1st–5th series, 1957/58–1961/62. Beirut, 1957–1962. 24 fasc.

News Bulletin of the N.E.C.C. Beirut, 1945—.

Survey of the Training of the Ministry in the Middle East. Report of a survey of theological education in Iran, the Arabian-Persian Gulf, Jordan, Lebanon, Syria, and Egypt, undertaken in September to November, 1961 by Douglas Webster and K. L. Nasir. 63pp. Geneva, Commission on World Mission and Evangelism, 1962.

CHAPTER 4

National Councils of Churches

The basic sources for studying the history of national developments within the ecumenical movement remain the minutes of committees and reports of conferences and consultations of the various national councils, which frequently exist only in mimeographed form. The W.C.C. Library has a special collection of these stenciled documents.

GENERAL WORKS

Directory of Christian Councils. 1959. 214pp. Mimeographed. London, Joint Committee of the W.C.C. and I.M.C. Supplement 1960.

MACCRACKEN, James, *Church World Service Support of National Christian Councils.* 81pp. Mimeographed. 1968.

De oecumenische situatie in de verschillende landen. J. Hamer, T. F. Stransky, L. G. M. Alting van Geusau (and others). 184pp. Hilversum, Antwerpen, Paul Brand, 1965.

La situation oecuménique dans le monde. Etudes du Centre international d'Information et de documentation sur l'Eglise conciliare. 254pp. Paris, Editions du Centurion, 1967.

NATIONAL COUNCIL OF THE CHURCHES OF CHRIST IN THE U.S.A.

CAVERT, Samuel McCrea, *The American Churches in the Ecumenical Movement, 1900–1968.* 288pp. New York, Association Press, 1968.

Christian Faith in Action. Commemorative volume; the founding of the National Council of Churches of Christ in the U.S.A. 272pp. New York, N.C.C.C.U.S.A., 1951.

The Churches Working Together for a Christian America. 32pp. New York, N.C.C.C.U.S.A., 1962.

The Ecclesiological Significance of Councils of Churches. 26pp. New York, N.C.C.C. U.S.A., 1963.

KNAPP, Forrest L., *Church Co-operation; Deadend street or highway to unity?* 249pp. New York, Doubleday, 1966.

MACFARLAND, Charles S., *Christian Unity in the Making. The first twenty-five years of the Federal Council of the Churches of Christ in America, 1905–1930.* 376pp. New York, Federal Council of the Churches of Christ, 1948.

National Council of the Churches of Christ in the U.S.A. *Biennial and Triennial Reports. Annual Division Reports.* New York, National Council of Churches, 1952–.

ROSS, Roy G., *The Ecumenical Movement and the Local Church. A statement of imperative and suggested plans, as approved by the General Board, March 2, 1962.* 16pp. New York, N.C.C.C.U.S.A., 1962.

RYCROFT, W. Stanley, *The Ecumenical Witness of the United Presbyterian Church in the U.S.A.* 332pp. Published by the Board of Christian Education of the United Presbyterian Church in the U.S.A., 1968.

SANDERSON, Ross W., *Church Co-operation in the United States. The nation-wide backgrounds and ecumenical significance of state and local Councils of Churches in their historical perspective.* 272pp. Hartford, Conn., Association of Council Secretaries, 1960.

CANADIAN COUNCIL OF CHURCHES

Canadian Council of Churches. *Record of proceedings, 13th, St Catharines, Ontario, Nov. 3–7, 1960.* Also later biennial assemblies.

GALLAGHER, W. J., *The Canadian Council of Churches.* Mimeographed, n.d.

GRANT, John Webster, *The Canadian Experience of Church Union,* 106pp. (Ecumenical Studies in History, 8). London, Lutterworth Press, 1967.

GRANT, John Webster, *The Churches and the Canadian Experience; A Faith and Order study of the Christian tradition.* Foreword by David W. Hay. 161pp. Toronto, Ryerson, 1963.

WILSON, Douglas J., *The Church Grows in Canada.* 224pp. Published by the Committee on Missionary Education, Canadian Council of Churches. Toronto, New York, Friendship Press, 1966.

Q

BRITISH COUNCIL OF CHURCHES

CAIRD, George B., *Making it Visible*. 29pp. (The unity we seek, 2). London, B.C.C., 1964.

DAVIES, Rupert E., *In All Places and All Ages*. 37pp. (The unity we seek, 5). London, B.C.C., 1964.

First Ecumenical Work-Book. Programme suggestions for local councils of churches, united Christian youth groups, ecumenical fellowships and parishes and congregations. 34pp. London, B.C.C., 1960.

SLACK, Kenneth, *Growing Together Locally. Some suggestions as to how the ecumenical movement can be made a reality wherever Christians of different traditions are found together*. 40pp. London, B.C.C., 1958.

Unity Begins at Home. A report from the First British Conference on Faith and Order, Nottingham, 1964. 95pp. London, S.C.M. Press, 1964.

NATIONAL CHRISTIAN COUNCIL OF INDIA

BAAGO, K., *A History of the National Christian Council of India, 1914-1964*. 89pp. Nagpur, The National Christian Council. Christian Council Lodge, 1965.

Ecumenical Development among Christian Youth in India. Work of the Central Youth Committee. 12pp. National Christian Council of India, 1963.

KELLOCK, James, *Breakthrough for Church Union in North India and Pakistan*. 146pp. Madras, Christian Literature Society, 1965.

National Christian Council of India. *Worship and the Church's Mission and Unity. A report of the third Indian Conference on Worship held under the auspices of the National Christian Council of India and the East Asia Theological Commission of the World Council of Churches at Bangalore, May 26-30, 1960*. 65pp.

SADIQ, John W., *Adventure in Christian Fellowship. The story of the Life and Work of the National Christian Council of India*. 46pp. Delhi, I.S.P.C.K., 1966.

NATIONAL COUNCIL OF CHURCHES IN NEW ZEALAND

One Lord, one World. Being the official report of the Third New Zealand Ecumenical Youth Conference, held at Lower Hutt, December 27, 1960-January 4, 1961. 64pp. Christchurch, H. F. Cross, 1961.

Towards the One Church. Questions and answers by the Churches. 49pp. Christchurch, National Council of Churches in New Zealand, 1954.

WATSON, Nigel M., *A report of the Third New Zealand Faith and Order Conference, held at Massey University College of the Manawan, February 4-11, 1964*. 68pp. Christchurch, National Council of Churches in New Zealand, 1964.

OTHER COUNTRIES

BROWN, Basil H. M., ed., *The New Dimensions of Mission for South Africa Today. Reports and addresses of a National Conference held in Johannesburg, May 1964*. 89pp. Cape Town, Christian Council of South Africa, 1964.

BRUNOTTE, Heinz, *Die Evangelische Kirche in Deutschland. Geschichte, Organisation und Gestalt der EKD*. 208pp. Gütersloh, Gütersloher Verlagshaus Gerd Mohn, 1964.

The Burma Directory of Christian Service. Agencies affiliated to or in co-operation with, the Burma Christian Council (1956–1957). 84pp. Rangoon, St Gabriel's Church, 1958.

The Church and the Problems of the Town. Tanganyika rapid social change study, commission "C", sponsored by the Christian Council of Tanganyika and the East Africa Urban Consultation, 14–21 May 1964. 109pp. Dar-es-Salaam, Tanganyika, 1964.

Die Evangelische Kirche im ökumenischen Spannungsfeld. Synode der Evangelischen Kirche in Deutschland, Berlin Spandau/Potsdam-Babelsberg, 1966. Herausgegeben von Wilhelm Gundert. 79pp. Witten, Luther-Verlag, 1966.

DUYVENDAK, J. H., *Memorandum on the History of the Ecumenical Movement in the Netherlands.* 68pp. Geneva, W.C.C., 1950.

Fellowship of Service. Life and work of Protestant Churches in Czechoslovakia. 120pp. Prague, Ecumenical Council of Churches in Czechoslovakia, 1961.

GOWING, Peter C., *Islands under the Cross. The story of the Church in the Philippines.* 286pp. Manila, National Council of Churches in the Philippines, 1967.

Où en est l'oecuménisme? Suède, Espagne, Belgique. 56pp. Lyou, "Unite Chrétienne", 1961.

PORKSEN, Martin, *Uebermorgen; die Hoffnung der indonesischen Christenheit.* 167pp. Wuppertal-Barmen, Verlag der Rheinischen Mission, 1965.

Projects in Church Unity. Studies prepared for Australian Churches with suggestions for group discussion and action. 32pp. Sydney, Australian Council of Churches, n.d.

SOBREPENA, Enrique S., *That They may be One. A brief account of the United Church Movement in the Philippines.* 177pp. Manila, United Church of Christ in the Philippines, 1964.

TIPPETT, A. R., *Solomon Islands Christianity Obstruction.* 407pp. (World studies of churches in mission). London, Lutterworth Press, 1967.

Towards a Better Life. An appraisal of Christian rural work, undertaken by a conference held at the Conference Centre of the Institute of Administration, Zaria, Nigeria, 1966, with a view to determining more clearly the role of the Church in rural development. 65pp. Ibadan, Christian Council of Nigeria, Daystar Press, 1966.

Unser Weg. Vom Leben der Mitgliedskirchen des Polnischen Oekumenischen Rates. 223pp. Warsau, der Polnische Oekumenische Rat, 1966.

VISCHER, Lukas, *Der Schweizerische Evangelische Kirchenbund, Bund oder Kirche?* 58pp. Zürich, EVZ-Verlag, 1962. French translation *La Fédération des Eglises protestantes de la Suisse, Fédération ou église?*

We Were Brought Together. Report of the National Conference of Australian Churches held at Melbourne University, 1960, ed. David M. Taylor. 181pp. Sydney, Australian Council for the World Council of Churches, 1960.

WELCH, F. G., *Towards an African Church.* 128pp. Nairobi, Christian Council of Kenya, 1962.

466

CHAPTER 5

Confessional Families and the Ecumenical Movement

GENERAL WORKS ABOUT CONFESSIONALISM, CREEDS AND HISTORY OF DENOMINATIONS

Creeds of the Churches. Ed. J. H. Leith. 589pp. New York, Doubleday, 1963.
The Faith of Christendom. A source-book of creeds and confessions. Selected, edited, and introduced by B. A. Gerrish. 371pp. New York, World Publishing Co., 1963.
GRUNDER, J., *Lexikon der christlichen Kirchen und Sekten; unter Berücksichtigung der Missionsgesellschaftlichen und zwischenkirchlichen Organisationen*. 2 vols. Wien, Herder, 1961.
Die Kirchen der Welt. Hrsg. von F. Sigg, H. H. Harms und H. H. Wolf. Reihe A: Selbstdarstellungen der Kirchen. Reihe B: Ergänzungsbände. Stuttgart, Evangelisches Verlagswerk, 1959.
MEAD, Frank S., *Handbook of Denominations in the United States*. 2nd. rev. edn. 272pp. New York, Abingdon, 1961.
MEINHOLD, P., *Oekumenische Kirchenkunde. Lebensformen der Christenheit heute*. 652pp. Stuttgart, Kreuz Verlag, 1962.
"Und ihr Netz zerriss"; die Grosskirchen in Selbstdarstellungen. Hrsg. von H. Lamparter. 456pp. Stuttgart, Quell-Verlag der Evang. Gesellschaft, 1957.
Weltkirchen-Lexikon. Handbuch der Oekumene; im Auftrag des Deutschen Evangelischen Kirchentages. Hrsg. von F. H. Littell und H. H. Walz. 1756pp. Stuttgart, Kreuz Verlag, 1960.
World Christian Handbook. 5th edn. 1968. 378pp. Ed. H. W. Coxill and K. Grubb. London, Lutterworth Press, 1967.

WORKS ON THE HISTORY AND THEOLOGY OF VARIOUS DENOMINATIONS

ARMSTRONG, A., *Rediscovering Eastern Christendom. Essays in commemoration o, Dom Bede Winslow*. Ed. A. H. Armstrong and E. F. B. Fry. 166pp. London, Darton, Longman & Todd, 1963.
ATIYA, Aziz S., *A History of Eastern Christianity*. 468pp. London, Methuen, 1968.
ATTWATER, Donald, *The Christian Churches of the East*. 2 vols. London, Chapman, 1961.
BAYNE, Stephen F., *An Anglican Turning Point; Documents and intepretations*. 317pp. Austin, Texas, Church Historical Society, 1964.
Bekenntnisschriften und Kirchenordnungen der nach Gottes Wort reformierten Kirche; 3. Aufl. Hrsg. von W. Niesel. 358pp. Zürich, EVZ-Verlag, 1958.
BENZ, Ernst, *The Eastern Orthodox Church: Its thought and life*. 230pp. New York, Doubleday, 1963. Translated from the German *Geist und Leben der Ostkirche*.
The Book of Concord: The confessions of the Evangelical Lutheran Church. Ed. Th. G. Tappert. 717pp. Philadelphia, Mühlenberg Press, 1959.
CASTLE, E. B., *Approach to Quakerism*. 178pp. London, Bannisdale Press, 1961.
DAVIES, H., *The English Free Churches*. 2nd edn. 216pp. London, Oxford University Press, 1963.
DAVIES, Rupert E., *Methodism*. 224pp. Harmondsworth, Penguin Books, 1963.

EMPIE, Paul C., and McCORD, James I., ed., *Marburg revisited: A re-examination of Lutheran and Reformed traditions*. 193pp. Minneapolis, Augsburg Publishing House, 1966.

GRUNDMANN, Siegfried: *Der Lutherische Weltbund. Grundfragen—Herkunft— Aufbau*. 586pp. Köln, Böhlau, 1957.

HARMON, Nolan B., *Understanding the Methodist Church*. 191pp. Nashville, Methodist Publishing House, 1955.

The History of American Methodism, ed. Emory S. Bucke. 3 vols. New York, Abingdon, 1964.

HORTON, Douglas, *The United Church of Christ; Its origins, organization and role in the world today*. 287pp. Edinburgh, New York, Thomas Nelson, 1962.

LORD, F. Townley, *Baptist World Fellowship: A short history of the Baptist World Alliance*. 185pp. London, Carey Kingsgate Press, 1955.

LOUKES, Harold, *The Quaker Contribution*. 528pp. London, S.C.M. Press, 1965.

LUCCOCK, Halford E., and HUTCHINSON, Paul, *The Story of Methodism*. 528pp. New York, Abingdon, 1949.

The Lutheran Churches of the World, ed. Abdel Ross Wentz. 443pp. Geneva, L.W.F., 1952.

Lutheran Directory, 1963. Part I: *Lutheran Churches of the World*. Part II: *Lutheran World Federation*. Berlin, Lutherisches Verlagshaus, 1963. Supplement 1968. Also German translation.

MEYENDORFF, Jean, *The Orthodox Church: Its past and its role in the world today*. 244pp. New York, Pantheon, 1962. Translated from the French *L'Eglise orthodoxe hier et aujourd'hui*. German translation *Die orthodoxe Kirche gestern und heute*.

MEYENDORFF, Jean, *Orthodoxy and Catholicity*. 180pp. New York, Sheed and Ward, 1966. Translated from the French *Orthodoxie et catholicité*.

MOSS, C. B., *The Old Catholic Movement: Its origins and history*. 2nd edn. 362pp. London, S.P.C.K., 1964.

"The Nature of the L.W.F. Documents", in *Lutheran World* (Geneva), vol. ii, no. 2 (April 1964), pp. 161–215.

NEILL, Stephen C., *Anglicanism. An explanation, in the light of history and theology, of the nature and working of the Anglican Communion, its relationship with other Christian groups and its part in the movement for Christian unity*. 466pp. London, Penguin, 1958.

NIESEL, Wilhelm, *Reformed symbolics*. 400pp. Edinburgh, Oliver and Boyd, 1964. Translated from the German.

PAYNE, Ernest A., *The Baptist Union; A short history*. 317pp. London, Carey Kingsgate Press, 1959.

RACK, Henry D., *The Future of John Wesley's Methodism*. 80pp. (Ecumenical studies in history, 2). London, Lutterworth Press, 1965.

ROBINSON, William, *What Churches of Christ stand for*. 4th edn. 112pp. Birmingham, Berean Press, 1959.

ROUTLEY, Erik, *The Story of Congregationalism*. 177pp. London, Independent Press, 1961.

SANDALL, Robert, and WIGGINS, Arch, *The History of the Salvation Army*. 4 vols. London, Thomas Nelson, 1964.

SCHLINK, E., *Theology of the Lutheran Confessions*. 353pp. Philadelphia, Muhlenberg Press, 1961. Translated from the German *Theologie der lutherischen Bekenntnisschriften*.

SMITH, C. Henry, *The Story of the Mennonites*. 4th edn. revised and enlarged by Cornelis Krahn. 856pp. Newton, Kansas, 1957.

TORBET, Robert G., *A History of the Baptists*. 540pp. Philadelphia, Judson Press, 1955.

TRUEBLOOD, David E., *The People Called Quakers*. 298pp. New York, Harper, 1966.

VAJTA, Vilmos, ed., *Church in Fellowship: Pulpit and altar fellowship among Lutherans*. 279pp. Minneapolis, Augsburg Press, 1963. Translated from the German *Kirche und Abendmahl*.

VAJTA, Vilmos and WEISSGERBER, Hans, ed., *The Church and the Confessions. The role of the confessions in the life and doctrine of the Lutheran Churches*. 218pp. Philadelphia, Fortress Press, 1963. Translated from the German *Das Bekenntnis im Leben der Kirche*.

WARE, Timothy, *The Orthodox Church*. 352pp. Harmondsworth, Penguin Books, 1963.

We believe. A digest of Salvationist doctrine. 39pp. London, Salvationist Publishing and Supplies, 1963.

WENGER, J. C., *The Mennonite Church in America*. 384pp. Scottdale, Herald Press, 1966.

The World Alliance of Reformed Churches. 104pp. Geneva, World Presbyterian Alliance, 1964.

World Lutheranism Today (Welt-Luthertum von heute). A tribute to Anders Nygren. 438pp. Oxford, Blackwell; Rock Island, Ill., Augustana Book Concern, 1950.

WORKS ON THE APPROACH OF DENOMINATIONS AND OF CONFESSIONAL BODIES TO THE ECUMENICAL MOVEMENT AND TO PROBLEMS OF CHURCH UNION

Anglican Initiatives in Christian Unity: Lectures delivered in Lambeth Palace Library, ed. E. G. W. Bill. 168pp. London, S.P.C.K., 1967.

Baptists and Unity. 60pp. London, Baptist Union of Great Britain and Ireland, 1967.

Baptists for Unity. 34pp. Coventry, Reynolds Press. 1968.

The Church for Others and the Church for the World: A quest for structures for missionary congregations. Final report of the Western European Working Group and North American Working Group of the Department on Studies in Evangelism. 135pp. Geneva, W.C.C., 1967.

"Confessional loyalty at all costs?" *Risk*, vol. ii, no. 4, 1966. 102pp. Geneva, W.C.C.

"Consultation on Church Union Negotiations. Bossey, April 9–15, 1967", *Midstream*, vol. vi, no. 3, Spring 1968. Indianapolis, Council on Christian Unity.

DAMMERS, A. H., *A.D. 1980: A study in Christian unity, mission and renewal*. 125pp. London, Lutterworth Press, 1966.

ESTEP, William R., *Baptists and Christian Unity*. 200pp. Nashville, Broadman Press, 1967.

FORSYTH, P. T., *Congregationalism and Reunion*. 78pp. London, Independent Press, 1952.

GARRISON, Winfred E., *Christian Unity and Disciples of Christ*. 286pp. St Louis, Bethany Press, 1955.

GASSMANN, Gunther, *Das historische Bischofsamt und die Einheit der Kirche in der neueren anglikanischen Theologie*. 283pp. Göttingen, Vandenhoeck und Ruprecht, 1964.

HOLLIS, Michael, *Mission, Unity and Truth: A study of confessional families and the churches in Asia*. 138pp. London, Lutterworth, 1967.

JOHN, Glynmor, *Congregationalism in an Ecumenical Era*. 23pp. London, Independent Press, 1967.

KIK, J. Marcellus, *Ecumenism and the Evangelical.* 152pp. Philadelphia, Presbyterian and Reformed Publishing Co., 1958.

LAMPE, G. W. H., *An Anglican Approach to Intercommunication and Reunion.* 20pp. London, S.P.C.K., 1962.

PACKER, J. I., *All in Each Place; Towards reunion in England. Ten Anglican essays with some Free Church comments.* 237pp. Appleford, Abingdon, Berks., Marcham Manor Press, 1965.

PATON, David, *Anglicans and Unity.* 115pp. (Starbooks on reunion, 2). London, Mowbray, 1962.

PERCHENET, A., *Renouveau communautaire et unité chrétienne: Regards sur les communautés anglicanes et protestantes.* 480pp. Paris, Mame, 1967.

ROBERTS-THOMSON, E., *With Hands Outstretched. Baptists and the ecumenical movement.* 128pp. London, Marshall Morgan and Scott, 1967.

ROUTLEY, Erik, *Congregationalists and Unity.* 94pp. London, Mowbray, 1962.

RYCROFT, W. Stanley, *The Ecumenical Witness of the United Presbyterian Church in the U.S.A.* 332pp. Published for the Commission on Ecumenical Missions and Relations by the Board of Christian Education of the United Presbyterian Church in the U.S.A., 1968.

SANSBURY, Kenneth, *Truth, Unity and Concord: Anglican faith in ecumenical setting.* 262pp. London, Mowbray, 1967.

SHORT, Howard E., *Christian Unity is Our Business: Disciples of Christ within the ecumenical fellowship.* 59pp. St Louis, Bethany Press, 1953.

"World Confessionalism and the Ecumenical Movement", *Lutheran World* (January 1963), vol. x, no. 1. 4 articles.

YODER, John H., *The Ecumenical Movement and the Faithful Church.* 44pp. Scottdale, Mennonite Publishing House, 1958.

Minutes of the Meetings of Representatives of World Confessional Groups, held in Geneva, 1957— (mimeographed, in Archives of W.C.C. Library).

International Meetings of World Confessional Bodies

Anglican Congresses

Minneapolis 1957
Toronto 1962
Lambeth Conferences 1948, 1958, 1968

Assembly of the International Congregational Council

7th, St Andrews, Scotland 1953
8th, Hartford, Conn. 1958
9th, Rotterdam 1962
10th, Swansea, Wales 1966

Assembly of the Lutheran World Federation

2nd, Hanover, Germany 1952
3rd, Minneapolis, Minn. 1957
4th, Helsinki 1963

Baptist World Congress

8th, Cleveland, Ohio 1950
9th, London 1955
10th, Rio de Janeiro 1960
11th, Miami Beach, Florida 1965

General Council of the Alliance of the Reformed Churches Holding the Presbyterian Order

17th, Princeton, N.J. 1954
18th, Sao Paulo, Brazil 1959
19th, Frankfurt/Main 1964

World Conference of Friends

3rd, Oxford, England 1952
4th, Greensboro, North Carolina 1967

World Methodist Conference

8th, Oxford 1951
9th, Lake Junaluska, North Carolina 1956
10th, Oslo 1961
11th, London 1966

World Convention of the Disciples of Christ

1955 Toronto
1960 Edinburgh
1965 San Juan, Puerto Rico

CHAPTER 6

Faith and Order 1948—1968

GENERAL WORKS

DeGroot, Alfred T., ed., *Check list Faith and Order Commission official, numbered publications, series I, 1910–1948; series II, 1948 to date 1962.* Ed. A. T. D. with the special assistance of the Reverend Dr Floyd W. Tomkins. Geneva, W.C.C., 1963.

Skoglund, John E., *Fifty Years of Faith and Order. An interpretation of the Faith and Order Movement.* 159pp. St Louis, Bethany Press, 1964.

Vischer, Lukas, ed., *A Documentary History of the Faith and Order Movement.* 246pp. St Louis, Bethany Press, 1963. German edition *Die Einheit der Kirche.* French edition *Foi et constitution.*

LUND 1952

BAILLIE, Donald, ed., *Intercommunion: The report of the theological commission*. 406pp. London, S.C.M. Press, 1952.

FLEW, R. Newton, ed., *The Nature of the Church. Papers presented to the theological commission*. 347pp. London, S.C.M. Press, 1952.

KENNEDY, James W., *He that Gathereth. A first-hand account of the third world conference on Faith and Order, held at Lund, Sweden, August 15-28, 1952*. 112pp. New York, W.C.C., 1952.

TOMKINS, Oliver Stratford, *The Church in the purpose of God. An introduction to the work of the commission on Faith and Order of the World Council of Churches, in preparation for the third world conference on Faith and Order to be held at Lund, Sweden, in 1952*. 118pp. (Faith and Order papers, 3). London, S.C.M. Press, 1950.

TOMKINS, Oliver Stratford, ed., *The Third World Conference on Faith and Order held at Lund, August 15th to 28th, 1952*. 380pp. London, S.C.M. Press, 1953. French translation *Rapport de la troisième conférence mondiale de "Foi et Constitution"*. German translation *Lund; dritte Weltkonferenz der Kirchen für Glauben und Kirchenverfassung*.

Ways of worship. The report of a theological commission on Faith and Order. 362pp. Ed. Pehr Edwall, Eric Hayman, William D. Maxwell. London, S.C.M. Press, 1951.

MONTREAL 1963

MINEAR, Paul S., ed., *Faith and Order findings. The final report of the theological commissions to the fourth world conference on Faith and Order, Montreal 1963*. 31pp., 62pp., 63pp., 64pp. (Faith and Order papers, 37-40: Institutionalism; Christ and the Church; Worship; Tradition and traditions, printed in one volume.) London, S.C.M. Press, 1963.

The Old and the New in the Church. Report on tradition and traditions, report on institutionalism and unity presented to the commission 1961. 96pp. (Faith and Order papers, 34). London, S.C.M. Press, 1961.

One Lord, One Baptism: Report on the Divine Trinity and the unity of the Church and report on the meaning of Baptism, by the theological commission on Christ and the Church. 79pp. (Faith and Order papers, 29). London, S.C.M. Press, 1960. French translation *Un seul Seigneur, un seul baptême*.

RODGER, Patrick C., and VISCHER, Lukas, ed., *The Fourth World Conference on Faith and Order, Montreal, 1963*. 126pp. (Faith and Order papers, 42). London, S.C.M. Press, 1964. French translation *4e Conférence mondiale de Foi et Constitution*. German translation *Montreal 1963. Bericht*.

OTHER CONFERENCES

Confessing the Faith in Asia Today. Statement issued by the consultation convened by the East Asia Christian Conference and held in Hongkong, October 26-November 3, 1966. 116pp. Redfern, Epworth Press, 1967. And in *South East Asia Journal of Theology*. October 1966-January 1967.

MINEAR, Paul S., ed., *The Nature of the Unity we Seek. Official report of the North American Conference on Faith and Order, September 3-10, 1957, Oberlin, Ohio*. 304pp. St Louis, Bethany Press, 1958.

Minutes of the meetings of the Faith and Order Commission and Working Committee held at the University of Aarhus, Denmark, 15-27 August 1964. 104pp. (Faith and Order papers, 44). Geneva, W.C.C., 1965.

NELSON, J. Robert., ed., *Christian unity in North America: A symposium.* 208pp. St Louis, Bethany Press, 1958.

New directions in Faith and Order, Bristol, 1967: Reports, minutes, documents. 183pp. (Faith and Order papers, 50). Geneva, W.C.C., 1968. German translation *Bristol 1967.* French translation *Nouveauté dans l'oecuménisme.*

Unity Begins at Home: A report from the first British Conference on Faith and Order, Nottingham, 1964. 95pp. (S.C.M. Press Broadsheet). London, S.C.M. Press, 1964.

WATSON, Nigel M., *Massey 1964. A report on the third New Zealand Faith and Order Conference, 1964.* 68pp. Christchurch, National Council of Churches in New Zealand, 1964.

SECRETARIAT ON FAITH AND ORDER

Concerning the Ordination of Women. 72pp. (World Council Studies, 1). Department on Faith and Order. Geneva, W.C.C., 1964. French translation *De l'ordination des femmes.* German translation *Zur Frage der Ordination der Frau.*

The Deaconess. 86pp. (World Council Studies, 4). Geneva, W.C.C., 1966. French translation *La diaconesse.* German translation *Die Diakonisse.*

An Ecumenical Exercise. The Southern Baptist Convention, the Seventh-Day Adventist Church, the Kimbanquist Church in the Congo, the Pentecostal Movement in Europe, ed. M. B. Handspicker and Lukas Vischer. 46pp. (Faith and Order papers, 49). Geneva, W.C.C., 1967.

The Ministry of Deacons. 86pp. (World Council Studies, 2). Geneva, W.C.C., 1965. French translation *Le ministère des diacres.* German translation *Das Amt der Diakone.*

ECUMENICAL THEOLOGY

Biblical Authority for Today. A World Council of Churches symposium on "the biblical authority for the churches social and political message today". Ed. Alan Richardson and W. Schweitzer. 347pp. London, S.C.M. Press, 1951.

EHRENSTROM, Nils, and MUELDER, Walter G., ed., *Institutionalism and Church Unity. Symposium prepared by the Study Commission on Institutionalism, Commission on Faith and Order, World Council of Churches.* 378pp. London, S.C.M. Press, 1963.

JENKINS, Daniel, *Tradition, Freedom, and the Spirit.* 195pp. Philadelphia, Westminster Press, 1951.

LASH, Nicholas, ed., *Doctrinal Development and Christian Unity.* 223pp. London, Sheed and Ward, 1967.

SCHLINK, Edmund, *The Coming Christ and the Coming Church.* 33pp. Edinburgh, Oliver and Boyd, 1967. Translated from the German *Der kommende Christus und die kirchlichen Traditionen.*

SWIDLER, Leonard J., ed., *Scripture and Ecumenism: Protestant, Catholic, Orthodox, and Jewish.* 197 pp. Pittsburgh, Pa., Duquesne University Press, 1965.

THURIAN, Max, *Visible Unity and Tradition.* 137pp. Baltimore, Helicon Press, 1962. Translated from *L'Unité visible des chrétiens et la tradition.* German translation *Sichtbare Einheit.*

TOMKINS, Oliver Stratford, *A Time for Unity*. 127pp. London, S.C.M. Press, 1964.
VISSER 'T HOOFT, Willem Adolf, *The Pressure of our Common Calling*. 192pp. London, S.C.M. Press, 1959. French translation *Les exigences de notre vocation commune*. German translation *Unter dem einen Ruf*.

PRAYER FOR CHRISTIAN UNITY

AUBERT, Roger, *Unité; la semaine de prière pour l'unité chrétienne*. Edition remaniée. 94pp. Bruxelles, Editions Pro Apostolis, 1959.
Christen beten gemeinsam. Herausgegeben vom Arbeitskreis "Gemeinsames Beten". 163pp. Bonn, Witten, Luther-Verlag, 1968.
HURLEY, Michael, *Praying for Christian Unity. A handbook of studies, meditations and prayer*. Foreword by the Bishop of Down and Connor. 240pp. Dublin, The Furrow Trust Gill and Son, 1963.
"*Prayer for Unity*. The report of the Consultation on the future of the week of prayer for Christian Unity, Geneva, 16–20 October 1966." Published in *One in Christ*, vol. iii, no. 3, 1967. pp. 251–304.

ECUMENICAL ECCLESIOLOGY

BERKHOF, Hendrik, *Die Katholizität der Kirche*. 112pp. Zürich, EVZ-Verlag, 1964. Translated from the Dutch *De Katholiciteit der Kerk*.
The Church, the Churches and the World Council of Churches. The Ecclesiological significance of the World Council of Churches. 16pp. New York, W.C.C., 1950.
HAMER, Jerome, *The Church is a Communion*. 240pp. London, Geoffrey Chapman, 1964. Translated from the French *L'Eglise est une communion*.
MINEAR, Paul, *Images of the Church in the New Testament*. 294pp. London, Lutterworth, 1961.
NEWBIGIN, Lesslie, *The Household of God. Lectures on the nature of the Church*. 160pp. London, S.C.M. Press, 1964. French translation *L'Eglise, peuple des croyants, corps du Christ, temple de l'Esprit*. German translation *Von der Spaltung zur Einheit*.
NEWBIGIN, Lesslie, *One Body, One Gospel, One World: The Christian mission today*. 56pp. London, I.M.C., 1958.
WEISSGERBER, Hans, *Die Frage nach der wahren Kirche. Einer Untersuchung zu den ekklesiologischen Problemen der ökumenischen Bewegung*. 391pp. Essen, Ludgerus-Verlag Hubert Wingen, 1963.

SACRAMENTS AND INTERCOMMUNION

ALLMEN, Jean-Jacques von, *Essai sur le repas du Seigneur*. 124pp. (Cahiers théologiques, 55). Neuchâtel, Delachaux et Niestlé, 1966.
BLENKIN, Hugh, *Immortal Sacrifice. A study, in the cause of Christian unity of the relation between the Sacrifice of Christ and the Holy Communion Service*. 101pp. London, Darton, Longman & Todd, 1964.
GILMORE, A., *Baptism and Christian Unity*. 108pp. London, Lutterworth Press, 1966.
HURLEY, Michael, *Church and Eucharist*. 298pp. Dublin and Melbourne, Gill and Son, 1966.
Intercommunion Today, being the report of the Archbishops' Commission on Intercommunion. 174pp. London, Church Information Office, 1968.

474 BIBLIOGRAPHY

LAUBENTHAL, Allan R., *The Eucharist as Sacrifice in the Faith and Order Movement. Dissertation.* 93pp. Roma, Pontificia Studiorum Universitas A. S. Thoma Aq. in Urbe, 1968.

McDONNELL, Kilian, *John Calvin, the Church, and the Eucharist.* 410pp. Princeton, New Jersey, Princeton University Press, 1967.

MARSHALL, Romey P., *Liturgy and Christian Unity.* 186pp. Englewood Cliffs, N.J. Prentice-Hall, 1965.

The Sacraments, an Ecumenical Dilemma. 178pp. (Concilium, 24). New York, Paulist Press, 1967.

SIMPSON, E. P. Y., *Ordination and Christian Unity.* 184pp. Valley Forge, The Judson Press, 1966.

STEADY, Leo J., *Intercommunion in the Faith and Order Movement 1927–1952. A dissertation submitted to the Faculty of Theology of the University of Ottawa in partial fulfilment of the requirements for the degree of Doctor of Theology.* 367pp. Ottawa 1964.

SWIDLER, Leonard, ed., *Ecumenism, the Spirit and worship.* 258pp. Louvain, Ed. E. Nauwelaerts, 1967.

THURIAN, Max, *The Eucharistic Memorial.* 2 vols. (Ecumenical studies in worship, 7–8). London, Lutterworth Press, 1960–1961. Translated from the French *L'Eucharistie.* German translation *Eucharistie.*

VISCHER, Lukas, "Questions on the Eucharist, its past and future celebration", in *Studia Liturgica* (Rotterdam), vol. v, no. 2. Summer 1966. pp. 65–86.

CHURCH UNION

Anglican Initiatives in Christian Unity: Lectures delivered in Lambeth Palace Library. ed. E. G. W. Bill. 168pp. London, S.P.C.K., 1967.

Auf dem Weg. Lutherisch-reformierte Kirchengemeinschaft. Berichte und Texte zusammengestellt und herausgegeben vom Sekretariat für Glauben und Kirchenverfassung. 124pp. (Polis, 33). Zürich, EVZ-Verlag, 1967.

Autorität und geistliche Vollmacht; Bericht über eine theologische Konferenz zwischen Vertretern der Kirche von England und der Evangelischen Kirche in Deutschland. Herausgegeben von Wolfgang Schweitzer und Claus Kemper. 81pp. Stuttgart, Evang. Missionsverlag, 1965. (Beihefte zur Ökumenischen Rundschau, 1). English edn *Authority and the Church*, ed. R. R. Williams. 92pp. London, S.P.C.K., 1965.

BECKWITH, R. T., *Priesthood and Sacraments. A study in the Anglican-Methodist report.* 128pp. (Latimer Monographs, 1). Appleford, Marcham Manor Press, 1964.

BLAKE, Eugene Carson, *A Proposal toward the Reunion of Christ's Church.* 16pp. Philadelphia, General Assembly Office of the United Presbyterian Church in the U.S.A., 1961.

BROWN, Robert McAfee, *The Challenge to Reunion. The Blake proposal under scrutiny.* 292pp. New York, McGraw-Hill Co., 1963.

BURBIDGE, John, *One in Hope and Doctrine: A study in the theology of church union.* 101pp. Toronto, The Ryerson Press, 1968.

COCU, *The official reports of the first four meetings of the consultation.* 96pp. Cincinnati, Forward Movement Publications, 1966.

Consultation on Church Union. Principles of Church Union; guidelines for structure, and study guide. 144pp. Cincinnati, Forward Movement Publications, 1967.

Conversations between the Church of England and the Methodist Church. A report to the Archbishops of Canterbury and York and the Conference of the Methodist Church. 63pp. Church Information Office and Epworth Press, 1963.

CROW, Paul A., *A Bibliography of the Consultation on Church Union.* 23pp. mimeographed. Lexington, Kentucky, Consultation on Church Union, 1967.

Digest of the Proceedings of the Consultation on Church Union for 1962 and 1963, 1964, 1965, 1966, 1967. 5 vols. Fanwood, New Jersey, C.O.C.U., 1963-7.

GRANT, J. Webster, *The Canadian Experience of Church Union.* 106pp. (Ecumenical studies in History, 8). London, Lutterworth Press, 1967.

KEMP, Eric W., *The Anglican-Methodist Conversations: A comment from within.* 45pp. London, New York, Oxford University Press, 1964.

NEILL, Stephen, *The Church and Christian Union. The Bampton lectures 1964.* 448pp. London, Oxford University Press, 1967.

NEILL, Stephen, *Towards Church Union, 1937-1952. A Survey of approaches to closer union among the churches.* 96pp. (Faith and Order Papers, 11). Published on behalf of the Faith and Order Commission of the W.C.C. London, S.C.M. Press, 1952.

FISHER, Geoffrey Francis, *The Anglican-Methodist Conversations and Problems of Church Unity. Some personal reflections.* 44pp. London, Oxford University Press, 1964.

HUNT, George L., and CROW, Paul A., *Where we are in Church Union.* 126pp. New York, Association Press, 1965.

LEE, Robert, *The Social Sources of Church Unity. An interpretation of unitive movements in American protestantism.* 238pp. New York, Abingdon, 1960.

NELSON, Robert J., *Church Union in Focus.* 87pp. Boston, Philadelphia, United Church Press, 1968.

PACKER, J. I., *The Church of England and the Methodist Church. A consideration of the report; conversations between the Church of England and the Methodist Church; ten essays.* 63pp. Appleford, Marcham Manor Press, 1963.

Principles of Church Union, adopted by the consultation at its meeting in Dallas, 1966. 96pp. Cincinnati, Forward Movement Publications, 1966.

Survey of Church Union Negotiations. 18pp. (Faith and Order papers, 11b). Geneva, W.C.C., 1955.

Survey of Church Union Negotiations, 1957-1959. 32pp. (Faith and Order papers, 28). Geneva, W.C.C., 1960.

Survey of Church Union Negotiations, 1959-1961, Lukas Vischer. 31pp. (Faith and Order papers, 35). Geneva, W.C.C., 1962.

Survey of Church Union Negotiations, 1961-1963, Meredith B. Handspicker. 40pp. (Faith and Order papers, 43). Geneva, W.C.C., 1964.

Survey of Church Union Negotiations, 1963-1965, Meredith B. Handspicker. 43pp. (Faith and Order papers, 47). Geneva, W.C.C., 1966.

Survey of Church Union Negotiations, 1965-1967, Gerald F. Moede. 32pp. (Faith and Order papers, 52). Geneva, W.C.C., 1968.

"Unofficial consultation between theologians of Eastern Orthodox and Oriental Orthodox Churches, August 11-15, 1964. Papers and minutes", ed. John S. Romanides, Paul Verghese, N. A. Nissiotis, *The Greek Orthodox Theological Review,* vol. x, no. 2, Winter 1964-5. 168pp.

Versöhnung. Das deutsch-russische Gespräch über das christliche Verständnis der Versöhnung zwischen Vertretern der Evangelischen Kirche in Deutschland und der Russischen Orthodoxen Kirche. Hrsg. vom Aussenamt der Evang. Kirche in Deutschland. 197pp. Witten, Luther Verlag, 1967.

WINTERHAGER, Jürgen Wilhelm, *Kirchen-Unionen des zwanzigsten Jahrhunderts.* 253pp. Zürich, Gotthelf-Verlag, 1961.

Wort und Abendmahl. Bericht über die zweite Konferenz zwischen Vertretern der

Kirche von England und der Evangelischen Kirche in Deutschland. Herausgegeben von Ronald R. Williams. 110pp. (Beihefte zur Ökumenischen Rundschau, 5). Stuttgart, Evang. Missionsverlag, 1967.

CHURCH OF SOUTH INDIA

Church of South India. Commission on Integration and Joint Action. 1963 renewal and advance. 209pp. Madras, published for the Synod of the Church of South-India by the Christian Literature Society, 1963.

The Constitution of the Church of South India. With amendments up to 31 December 1951 together with the Basis of Union as adopted by the Governing Bodies of the Uniting Churches in India and elsewhere. 97pp. Madras, Christian Literature Society for India, 1952.

The C.S.I.–Lutheran Theological Conversations 1948–1959. A selection of the papers read together with the Agreed Statements. 196pp. Madras, Christian Literature Society, 1964.

Empty Shoes: A study of the Church of South India. 153pp. New York, The National Council Protestant Episcopal Church, 1956.

GIBBARD, Mark, *Unity is not enough: Reflections after a visit to the Church of South India.* 145pp. London, Mowbray, 1965.

GRAMBERG, Th. B. W. G., *Oecume in India en Ceylon; op weg naar Gods ene kerk.* 366pp. 's-Gravenhage, Boekencentrum, 1962.

HOLLIS, Michael, *Paternalism and the Church: A study of South India Church history.* 144pp. London, Oxford University Press, 1962.

HOLLIS, Michael, *The Significance of South India.* 82pp. (Ecumenical Studies in History, 5). London, Lutterworth Press, 1966.

The Holy Spirit and the Life in Christ. Papers submitted to the joint theological commission of the Church of South India and the Lutheran Churches, July 1953. 52pp. Madras, Christian Literature Society, 1953.

LA CROCE, Jacobus F., *The Catholicity of the Church of South India. A comparison of its formularies with those of the Anglican Church on the doctrines of the Church and the Ministry. Exerpta ex dissertatione ad Lauream in Facultate Theologica Pontificiae Universitatis Gregorianae.* 110pp. Roma 1965.

NEWBIGIN, James Edwards Lesslie, *The Reunion of the Church. A defence of the South Indian Scheme.* Revised edn. 192pp. London, S.C.M. Press, 1960.

NEWBIGIN, James Edwards Lesslie, *A South India Diary.* 125pp. London, S.C.M. Press, 1951. French translation *Journées indiennes.* German translation *Südindisches Tagebuch.*

RAWLINSON, A. E. J., *The Church of South India.* 128pp. London, Hodder and Stoughton, 1951.

Report on South India. Being the report of the delegation to the Church of South India with certain recommendations and theological comments. 84pp. New York, Joint Commission on Ecumenical Relations, 1957.

The Sacraments. The meeting of the Joint Theological Commission of the Church of South India and the Federation of Evangelical Lutheran Churches in India, March 1955. 166pp. Madras, Christian Literature Society, 1956.

Unity in Faith and Life. The Joint Theological Commission of the Church of South India and the Federation of Evangelical Lutheran Churches in India, Bangalore 1954. 105pp. Madras, Christian Literature Society, 1955.

WAGNER, Herwig, *Erstgestalten einer einheimischen Theologie in Südindien; ein Kapitel indischer Theologiegeschichte als kritischer Beitrag zur Definition von "einheimischer Theologie".* 306pp. München, Chr. Kaiser, 1963.

NORTH INDIA AND PAKISTAN

KELLOCK, James, *Breakthrough for Church Union in North India and Pakistan.* 146pp. Madras, Christian Literature Society, 1965.
Plan of Church Union in North India and Pakistan. Prepared by the Negotiating Committee for Church Union in North India and Pakistan, as revised in April 1957. 3rd edn. 64pp. Madras, Christian Literature Society, 1957.

CEYLON

BOISVERT, Robert G., *The Scheme of Church Union in Ceylon and the Problem it Presents to the Anglican Communion.* Pars dissertationis. 160pp. Rome, Catholic Book Agency, 1964.
GRAMBERG, Th. B., *Oecumene in India en Ceylon; op weg naar Gods ene kerk.* 366pp. 's Gravenhage, Boekencentrum, 1962.
Proposed Scheme of Church Union in Ceylon. Prepared by the Negotiating Committee for Church Union in Ceylon, June 1955. 3rd edn. 111pp. Madras, Christian Literature Society, 1955.

CHAPTER 7

Mission in Six Continents

GENERAL WORKS

The Encyclopedia of modern christian missions. The agencies. A publication of the Faculty of Gordon Divinity School. Ed. Rurton L. Goddard. 743pp. Camden, New Jersey, Thomas Nelson and Sons, 1967.
HOGG, William Richey, *Ecumenical Foundations. A history of the International Missionary Council and its nineteenth-century background.* 466pp. New York, Harper, 1952. German translation *Mission und Oekumene.*
Index to International Review of Missions, 1912–1966. 82pp. Geneva, W.C.C., 1968.
LATOURETTE, Kenneth Scott, *Christianity in a Revolutionary Age. A history of Christianity in the nineteenth and twentieth centuries.* vols. iii and v. New York, Harper and Row, 1961–2.
Zur Sendung der Kirche. Material der ökumenischen Bewegung. Hrsg. von H. J. Margull. 378pp. München, Kaiser Verlag, 1963.

INTERNATIONAL MISSIONARY COUNCIL

Minutes of the Committee of the I.M.C. London, I.M.C. 1948–58:
1948 Oegstgeest
1950 Whitby
1952 Willingen
1954 New York
1958 Ghana

Willingen 1952

GOODALL, Norman, ed., *Missions under the cross. Addresses delivered at the enlarged meeting of the Committee of the International Missionary Council at Willingen, in Germany, 1952, with statements issued by the meeting.* 264pp. London, I.M.C., 1953.

Ghana 1957–8

ORCHARD, Ronald Kenneth, *The Ghana Assembly of the International Missionary Council, 28 December 1957–8 January 1958.* Selected papers, with an essay on the role of the I.M.C. 240pp. London, Edinburgh House Press, 1958.

INTEGRATION I.M.C.—W.C.C. NEW DELHI, 1961

Minutes of the Assembly of the I.M.C., November 17–18, 1961 and of the first meeting of the Commission on World Mission and Evangelism of the W.C.C., December 7–8, 1961 at New Delhi. 93pp. Geneva, W.C.C., 1962.

PAYNE, Ernest A., and MOSES, David G., *Why integration? An explanation of the proposal before the World Council of Churches and the International Missionary Council.* 80pp. London, Edinburgh House Press, 1957.

Report to the final Assembly of the I.M.C. and the third Assembly of the W.C.C., New Delhi 1961. 48pp. Lausanne, Impr. La Concorde, 1961. French translation *Conseil international des missions. Rapport présenté . . .* German translation *Internationaler Missionsrat. Bericht an die . . .*

MEXICO CITY 1963

LATHAM, Robert O., *God for All Men. The meeting of the Commission on World Mission and Evangelism of the W.C.C. at Mexico City, December 8th to 19th, 1963.* 84pp. London, Edinburgh House Press, 1964.

Minutes of the second meeting of the Commission on World Mission and Evangelism, Mexico City, December 8th–19th, 1963. 135pp. Geneva, W.C.C., 1964.

NEWBIGIN, Lesslie, *Gottes Mission und unsere Aufgabe. Treffpunkt 1963 Mexiko.* 31pp. (Weltmission heute, 23). Stuttgart, Evang. Missionsverlag, 1963.

ORCHARD, Ronald Kenneth, *Witness in Six Continents. Records of the meeting of the Commission on World Mission and Evangelism of the World Council of Churches, held in Mexico City, December 8th to 19th, 1963.* 200pp. London, Edinburgh House Press, 1964.

D.W.M.E.

The Christian Ministry in Latin America and the Caribbean. Report of a survey of theological education in the Evangelical Churches undertaken February–May 1961 on behalf of the I.M.C., now the Commission on World Mission and Evangelism of the W.C.C. by Bp Foster Stockwell . . ., ed. Wilfred Scopes. 264pp. Geneva, D.W.M.E., 1962.

HAYWARD, Victor E. W., ed., *African Independent Church Movements.* 94pp. (C.W.M.E. Research pamphlets, 11). Published for the W.C.C. Commission on World Mission and Evangelism. London, Edinburgh House Press, 1963.

The Healing Church. The Tübingen consultation 1964. 55pp. (World Council Studies

3). Geneva, W.C.C., 1965. Franch translation *Eglise et guérison.* German translation *Auftrag zu heilen.*

LOEFFLER, Paul, ed., *Secular man and Christian Mission. A discussion through correspondence.* 48pp. (C.W.M.E. Study pamphlets, 3). Geneva, W.C.C., Commission on World Mission and Evangelism. New York, Friendship Press, 1968.

PATON, David M., ed., *New Forms of Ministry.* 102pp. London, published for the W.C.C. Commission on World Mission and Evangelism by Edinburgh House Press, 1965.

EVANGELISM

The Church for Others and the Church for the World. A quest for structures for missionary congregations. Final report of the Western European Working Group and North American Working Group of the Department on Studies in Evangelism. 135pp. Geneva, W.C.C., 1967. German translation *Die Kirche für andere.*

Planning for Mission. Working papers on the new quest for missionary communities. 230pp. New York, U.S. Conference for the W.C.C., 1966. French adaptation *Vers une Eglise pour les autres.* German adaptation *Mission als Strukturprinzip.*

ECUMENICAL ASPECTS OF MISSIONS

ANDERSON, Gerald H., ed., *The Theology of the Christian Mission.* 341pp. New York, McGraw-Hill, 1961.

BATES, M. Searle, and PAUCK, Wilhelm, *The Prospects of Christianity throughout the World.* 286pp. New York, Charles Scribner's Sons, 1964.

BEAVER, R. Perce, *Ecumenical Beginnings in Protestant World Mission.* 366pp. New York, T. Nelson, 1962.

BECKMANN, Joachim, *Mission und Diakonie in ökumenischer Verantwortung. Synode der Evangelischen Kirche in Deutschland, Bethel, 1963.* Herausgegeben im Auftrag der Synode von Joachim Beckmann. 77pp. Witten, Luther-Verlag, 1963.

BLAUW, Johannes, *The Missionary Nature of the Church. A survey of the biblical theology of mission.* 182pp. New York, McGraw-Hill, 1962.

BRENNECKE, Gerhard, *Weltmission in ökumenischer Zeit.* Herausgegeben von G.B. und 28 Mitarbeitern. 336pp. Stuttgart, Evang. Missionsverlag, 1961.

BRIDSTON, Keith, *Mission, Myth and Reality.* 128pp. New York, Friendship Press, 1965.

CATE, William B., *The Ecumenical Scandal on Main Street.* 126pp. New York, Association Press, 1965.

HANDY, Robert T., *We Witness Together: A history of co-operative home missions.* 273pp. New York, Friendship Press, 1956.

History's Lessons for Tomorrow's Mission. 300pp. Geneva, W.S.C.F., 1960.

HOGG, William Richey, *One World, One Mission.* 165pp. New York, Friendship Press, 1960.

KARLSTRÖM, Nils, *Oekumene in Mission und Kirche. Entwicklungslinien der heutigen ökumenischen Bewegung.* 280pp. München, Claudius Verlag, 1962. Translated from *Mission och ekumenik.*

KLAPPERT, Erich, *Dialog mit Rom. Zusammenarbeit und Zukunft der Mission auf ökumenischer Basis, 450 Jahre nach Luther.* 280pp. Wuppertal, Aussaat Verlag, 1967.

LEE, Robert, *Stranger in the Land. A Study of the Church in Japan.* 216pp. (World Studies of Churches in mission). London, Lutterworth Press, 1967.

LE GUILLOU, M-J., *Mission et unité. Les exigences de la communion*. 2 vols. (Unam Santcam, 33–34). Paris, Editions du Cerf, 1960.

MARGULL, H. J., *Hope in Action: the Church's Task in the World*. 298pp. Philadelphia, Muhlenberg Press, 1962. Translated from *Theologie der missionarischen Verkündigung*.

MEYER, Heinrich, *Mission in ökumenischer Verantwortung; Referat auf der Synode der Evangelischen Kirche in Deutschland, im März 1963 in Bethel*. 24pp. (Christus und die Welt, 15). Bad Salzuflen, MBK-Verlag, Verlag für Missions- und Biblekunde, 1963.

NEILL, Stephen Charles, *The Unfinished Task*. 228pp. London, Edinburgh House Press, 1957. German translation *Mission zwischen Kolonialismus und Oekumene*.

NEWBIGIN, Lesslie, *One Body, one Gospel, one World. The Christian Mission today*. 58pp. London, International Missionary Council, 1958.

NEWBIGIN, Lesslie, *The Relevance of Trinitarian Doctrine*. 78pp. Published for the World Council of Churches, Commission on World Mission and Evangelism. London, Edinburgh House Press, 1963.

NILES, Daniel Thambyrajah, *Upon the Earth: the mission of God and the Missionary enterprise of the churches*. 270pp. London, Lutterworth Press, 1962. French translation *Sur la terre*. German translation *Feuer auf Erden*.

ORCHARD, Ronald K., *Out of every nation. A discussion of the internationalizing of missions*. 78pp. (I.M.C. Research Pamphlets, 7). London, S.C.M. Press, 1959.

PORTMANN, John R., *The Concepts of Mission and Unity in the World Council of Churches. A study of the official documents of the Central Committee from its inception to the New Delhi Assembly, 1961*. 134pp. Pars dissentationis ad lauream in Facultate S. Theologiae apud Pontificiam Universitatem S. Thomae de Urbe, Rome. Catholic Book Agency, 1966.

SUNDKLER, Bengt, *The World of Mission*. 318pp. London, Lutterworth Press, 1965.

TIPPETT, A. R., *Solomon Islands Christianity. A study in growth and obstruction*. 407pp. (World Studies of Churches in Mission). London, Lutterworth Press, 1967.

VAN DUSEN, Henry P., *One Great Ground of Hope. Christian missions and Christian unity*. 206pp. Philadelphia, Westminster Press, 1961.

VICEDOM, Georg, *Mission im ökumenischen Zeitalter*. 208pp. (Evangelische Enzyklopädie, 17/18). Gütersloh, Gütersloher Verlagshaus Gerd Mohn, 1967.

WARREN, Max, *The Missionary Movement from Britain in Modern History*. 192pp. London, S.C.M. Press, 1965.

CHAPTER 8

Joint Service as an Instrument of Renewal

D.I.C.A.R.W.S.—OFFICIAL REPORTS

Division of Inter-Church Aid, Refugee and World Service. Consultation Digest. Geneva, W.C.C., 1956–67.
Les Rasses 1956
Eastbourne 1957
Evian 1958
Berlin 1960
Nyborg 1962

Hong Kong 1963

Consultation Digest. A summary of reports and addresses. First Asian consultation on Inter-Church Aid, held under the joint auspices of D.I.C.A.R.W.S.–E.A.C.C., at Hong Kong, October 17–23, 1963. 117pp. mimeographed. Geneva, W.C.C., 1964.

Enugu 1965

Consultation Digest. A summary of reports and addresses. All Africa Conference of Churches, Inter-Church Aid Consultation, Enugu, Eastern Nigeria, January 4–9, 1965. 116pp. Geneva, W.C.C., 1965. French translation *Consultation en abrégé.*

Swanwick 1966

Digest of the 1966 World Consultation on Inter-Church Aid, at Swanwick, Great Britain. 136pp. Geneva, W.C.C., D.I.C.A.R.W.S., 1966. French translation *Colloque de Swanwick.* German translation *Swanwick Konsultation.*

Belgrade 1967

Digest of the European consultation on Inter-Church Aid, at Belgrade, Yugoslavia, December 4–9, 1967. 99pp. mimeographed. Geneva, W.C.C.–D.I.C.A.R.W.S., 1968.

Inter-Church Aid. Year and Report. Geneva, W.C.C.–D.I.C.A.R.W.S., 1953.
    1953: (*a*) *Year and Report 1953;* (*b*) Statistical Summaries; (*c*) The Service to Refugees; (*d*) Greece, 1953. 1954: *Year and Report 1954.* 1955: *Pain and Promise.* 1956: *Inter-Church Aid in 1956.* 1957: *Inter-Church Aid 1957.* 1958: *Inter-Church Aid 1958.* 1959: *Inter-Church Aid 1959.* 1960: *Across My Desk.* 1961: *Inter-Church Aid in 1961.* 1962: *Many Churches, One Service.* 1963: *Service in Unity.* 1964: *Rooted in Love.* 1965: *To Live in Hope.* 1966: *A World of Difference* (also in German). 1967: *From One to Another* (also in French and German).
Service Programme and List of Projects. 8 vols. Geneva, W.C.C.–D.I.C.A.R.W.S., 1961–8.

FIRST PERIOD OF INTER-CHURCH AID

RYBERG, James A., ed., *Church-aided Projects. A visitor's guide to Church-aided projects in Europe.* 40pp. Geneva, W.C.C., Department of Inter-Church Aid, 1950.
RYBERG, James A., ed., *Europe's Homeless. The plight of refugees—Europe's homeless—an international problem.* 48pp. Geneva, W.C.C., Department of Inter-Church Aid, 1951.
RYBERG, James A., ed., *Fellowship in christian sharing. The story of Inter-Church Aid.* 40pp. Geneva, W.C.C., Department of Inter-Church Aid, 1951.
VISSER 'T HOOFT, Willem Adolf, *La reconstruction des Eglises en Europe.* 13pp. Lausanne, Impr. La Concorde, 1944.

D.I.C.A.R.W.S.

COOKE, Leslie E., *The Church is There.* 59pp. Greenwich, Conn., The Seabury Press, 1957.

COOKE, Leslie, *Entwicklungshilfe der Mitgliedskirchen des Oekumenischen Rates der Kirchen.* 44pp. Stuttgart, Kreuz-Verlag; Mainz, Matthias-Grünewald, 1966. (Sonderdruck aus Entwicklungspolitik; Handbuch und Lexicon, pp. 879–922).

COOKE, Leslie E., *The World Council of Churches and the Division of Inter-Church Aid, Refugee, and World Service. An address given by L.E.C. at the opening session of the Asian Consultation on Inter-Church Aid, Hong Kong, October 17–23, 1963.* 16pp. (Extr. from *Ecumenical Review,* vol. 16, no. 2, January 1964). Geneva, W.C.C., 1964.

D.I.C.A.R.W.S. in Action and Study. The report of the Division on Inter-Church Aid, Refugee, and World Service to the Central Committee of the World Council of Churches at its meeting in Geneva, Switzerland, February 1966. 12pp. Geneva, W.C.C.–D.I.C.A.R.W.S. 1966. French translation *Action et étude.* German translation *Studium und Aktion.*

In the service of mankind. A manual of inter-church aid. Geneva, W.C.C.–D.I.C.A.R.W.S., 1963.

Inter-Church Aid Directory. 48pp. Geneva, W.C.C., 1965.

MACKIE, Robert C., *Inter-Church Aid and Service to Refugees Today. The director's report—Division of Inter-Church Aid and Service to Refugees.* 16pp. Geneva, W.C.C., 1955.

MATTHEWS, Z. K., *Africa Survey Report. Together with "Ferment in Africa", an article by Sir Hugh Foot; an account of a visit to Africa by Sir Hugh Foot and Dr Z. K. Matthews on behalf of the Division of Inter-Church Aid, Refugee, and World Service.* 96pp. Geneva, W.C.C.–D.I.C.A.R.W.S., 1964.

MATTHEWS, Z. K., *Africa Surveys I and II. Survey I: Report by Z. K. Matthews together with "Ferment in Africa", an article by Sir Hugh Foot. Survey II: Report by Jean Fisher, Frank Hutchison, James Lawson.* 119pp. Geneva, W.C.C.–D.I.C.A.R.W.S., 1964–5.

MURRAY, Geoffrey, *Number one, Sophocles Street.* 40pp. Geneva, W.C.C.–D.I.C.A.R.W.S., 1963. German translation: *Das Haus in der Sophokles-Strasse.*

The Role of the Churches in Social Service: An international perspective. Reporting a consultation held at Mülheim, Germany, July 16–20, 1962. 106pp. Auspices: W.C.C. and D.I.C.A.R.W.S. New York, National Council of Churches, 1963.

The Role of the diakonia of the Church in Contemporary Society. Report to the World Conference on Church and Society 1966: Christians in the Technical and Social Revolution of our time. 63pp. Geneva, W.C.C., 1966. French translation *L'Eglise dans son rôle diaconal.* German translation *Die Diakonie der Kirche in der gegenwärtigen Gesellschaft.*

A Statement of the Aim, Functions, Facilities and Procedures of its Programme and Project Listening. 18pp. Geneva, W.C.C.–D.I.C.A.R.W.S., 1964.

THOMPSON, Betty, *Turning world.* 128pp. New York, Friendship Press, 1960.

World Council of Churches and All Africa Conference of Churches. Approved programme. Ecumenical programme for emergency action in Africa. 78pp. Geneva, W.C.C.–D.I.C.A.R.W.S., 1965.

REFUGEES

Report from Hamburg. A survey of the German refugee problem in 1949. 32pp. Geneva, World Council of Churches, Refugee Division, 1949. German translation *Hamburger Bericht.*

Report from Salzburg. Conference in Salzburg on Austria's refugee problems. January 17–19, 1950. 42pp. Geneva, World Council of Churches, Service to Refugees, 1950. German translation: *Salzburger Bericht.*

Hungary, special report. 30pp. Geneva, W.C.C., 1957.
Report from Beirut. A report of a conference on Arab refugee problems, Beirut, Lebanon, May 4–8, 1951. Jointly convened by I.M.C. and the Department of Inter-Church Aid and Service to Refugees of the W.C.C. 56pp. Geneva, W.C.C., 1951.
Second report from Beirut. Report of a conference on the problem of Arab refugees from Palestine, held at Beirut, Lebanon, May 21–25, 1956. 61pp. Geneva, W.C.C., 1956.
A Time of Compassion. A report on the Churches' contribution to world refugee year. 34pp. Geneva, W.C.C., 1961.

MIGRATION

In a Strange Land. A report of a world conference on problems of international migration and the responsibility of the Churches, held at Leysin, Switzerland, June 11–16, 1961. 96pp. Geneva, W.C.C.–D.I.C.A.R.W.S., 1961.
Migrant workers: a test case of human relationship. Consultation on migrant workers in Western Europe. Bossey, May 29–June 4, 1965. Ecumenical Institute of Bossey, Churches Committee on Migrant Workers in Western Europe. 55pp. Geneva, Churches Committee on Migrant Workers in Western Europe, 1965. French translation *Les migrations de travailleurs.* German translation *Ausländische Arbeitnehmer.*
Within Thy Gates. A report of the conference on migrant workers in Western Europe, held at Arnoldshain, Western Germany, June 10–15, 1963. 96pp. Geneva, W.C.C. Secretariat for Migration, 1964. French translation *L'Etranger qui est dans tes portes.* German translation *Fremde unter uns.*

CHURCH WORLD SERVICE

CHAKERIAN, Charles G., *From Rescue to Child Welfare.* 92pp. New York, Church World Service, 1968.
Community compassion. The story of C.R.O.P. 32pp. Elkhart, Indiana, C.R.O.P., 1967.
FEY, Harold E., *Co-operation in compassion. The story of Church World Service.* 175pp. New York, Friendship Press, 1966.
GOODALL, Norman, *Christian Ambassador. A life of A. Livingstone Warnshuis.* 174pp. (Pertinent as a biography of a founder of Church World Service). New York, Channel Press; London, Edinburgh House Press, 1963.
GRODKA, Sonia, and HENNES, Gerhard, *Homeless No More. A discussion on integration between sponsor and refugee.* 126pp. New York, Church World Service, 1960.
HACKSHAW, James, *Social and Economic Planning in the Leeward and Windward Islands.* 36pp. New York, Church World Service, 1967.
LANDIS, Benson Y., and Jacquet, Constant H. Jr, *Immigration Programs and Policies of Churches of the United States.* 71pp. New York, N.C.C.C.U.S.A., 1957.
MACCRACKEN, James, *Church World Service support of National Christian Councils.* 81pp. mimeographed. 1968.
MOOMAW, I. W., *Crusade against Hunger.* 199pp. (esp. C.W.S. ref. on page 197). New York, Harper and Row, 1966.
MOOMAW, I. W., *The Challenge of Hunger.* 222pp. (esp. C.W.S. ref. on pages 51, 54 and 133). New York and London, Frederick A. Praeger, 1966.

MYERS, Melvin B., and ABBOTT, John W., *Resource Guide on World Hunger.* 207pp. New York, Church World Service, 1968.

STANLEY, Frances, *The New World Refugee: The Cuban exodus.* 64pp. New York, Church World Service, 1967.

STEVENSON, Russell, *A More Excellent Way.* 16pp. New York, Church World Service, 1959.

The Wanted Child. Report of 1967 family planning survey of five islands in the Caribbean. 58pp. New York, Church World Service, 1967.

Witness for Immigration. Report of the consultation on immigration policy in the U.S. Washington, D.C., 13–14 April 1961. 112pp. New York, National Council of Churches, 1961.

CHAPTER 9

The Development of Ecumenical Social Thought and Action

DEPARTMENT ON CHURCH AND SOCIETY

Africa in Transition: The challenge and the Christian response. 95pp. Published by All Africa Churches Conference in collaboration with the Department on Church and Society, Division of Studies, World Council of Churches. Geneva, W.C.C., 1965. French translation *L'Afrique en devenir.*

Christian Action in Society: An ecumenical inquiry. 19pp. Geneva, W.C.C. Study Department, 1949. French translation *L'Action chrétienne dans la vie sociale.*

Main Ecumenical Statements on Principles concerning Religious Freedom. 47pp. mimeographed. Geneva, W.C.C., Secretariat on Religious Liberty, 1965.

The Meaning of Work. 20pp. (Christian action in society, 2). Geneva, W.C.C., Study Department, 1950.

Statements of the World Council of Churches on Social Questions. With a preface on the development of ecumenical social thinking. 2nd edn. 72pp. Geneva, W.C.C., Department on Church and Society, 1956.

TURNBULL, John W., *Ecumenical Documents on Church and Society, 1925–1953.* 172pp. Geneva, W.C.C., 1954.

RAPID SOCIAL CHANGE

ABRECHT, Paul, *The Churches and Rapid Social Change.* 216pp. New York, Doubleday, 1961.

The Common Christian Responsibility toward Areas of Rapid Social Change. 2nd statement. 39pp. Geneva, W.C.C., Department on Church and Society, 1956. French translation *La responsabilité commune des chrétiens à l'égard des sociétés en pleine évolution.* German translation *Die gemeinsame christliche Verantwortung gegenüber Gebieten raschen sozialen Umbruchs.*

Dilemmas and Opportunities; Christian action in rapid social change. Report of an international ecumenical study conference, Thessalonica, Greece, July 25–August 2, 1959. 104pp. Geneva, World Council of Churches, 1959. French translation _Dilemmes et possibilités._ German translation *Aufgaben und Möglichkeiten.*

SCHWEITZER, Wolfgang, *Christians in Changing Societies.* 80pp. (World christian books, 58). London, Lutterworth Press, 1967. Translated from the German *Christen im raschen sozialen Umbruch heute.*

VRIES, Egbert de, *Man In Rapid Social Change.* 240pp. Garden City, New York, Doubleday, 1961.

RESPONSIBLE SOCIETY

The Arnoldshain report 1956. A regional conference on the responsible society in national and international affairs. 30pp. Geneva, W.C.C., Division of Studies, 1956. German translation *Der Arnoldshain Bericht 1956.*

MUELDER, Walter G., *The Idea of the Responsible Society.* 26pp. Boston, Boston University Press, 1955.

The Responsible Society. 24pp. (Christian Action in Society, 1). Geneva, W.C.C., Study Department, 1949.

Social Questions—the Responsible Society in a World Perspective. An ecumenical survey prepared under the auspices of the World Council of Churches. 68pp. (Evanston surveys, 3). London, S.C.M. Press, 1954. French translation *Questions sociales.* German translation *Soziale Fragen.*

WORLD CONFERENCE ON CHURCH AND SOCIETY, GENEVA, 1966

Christian Social Ethics in a Changing World: An ecumenical theological inquiry, ed. John C. Bennett. 381pp. (Church and Society, 1). London, S.C.M. Press, New York, Association Press, 1966. French translation *L'éthique sociale chrétienne dans un monde en transformation.*

Responsible Government in a Revolutionary Age, ed. Z. K. Matthews. 381pp. (Church and Society, 2). New York, Association Press: London, S.C.M. Press, 1966. French translation *La responsabilité des gouvernements à une époque révolutionnaire.*

Economic Growth in World Perspective, ed. Denys Munby. 380pp. (Church and Society, 3). New York, Association Press: London, S.C.M. Press, 1966. French translation *Le développement économique dans une perspective mondiale.*

Man in Community: Christian concern for the human in changing society, ed. Egbert de Vries. 382pp. (Church and Society, 4). New York, Association Press: London, S.C.M. Press, 1966. French translation *L'individu et le groupe.* German translation of the Church and Society series *Kirche als Faktor einer kommenden Weltgemeinschaft.*

EDWARDS, David L., *Christian in a New World.* 77pp. London, S.C.M. Press, 1966.

Kirche und Gesellschaft. Berichte und Vorträge nach der Konferenz, A. Lavanchy, A. Rich, H. Rieben, W. A. Visser 't Hooft. 70pp. (Polis, 29). Zürich, EVZ Verlag, 1967.

MOSLEY, J. Brooke, *Christians in the Technical and Social Revolutions of Our Time. Suggestions for study and action.* 141pp. (A Forward Movement miniature book). Cincinnati, Ohio, Forward Movement Publications, 1956. German translation *Christen leben in der technischen und gesellschaftlichen Revolution unserer Zeit.*

RAMSEY, Paul, *Who Speaks for the Church? A critique of the 1966 conference on Church and Society.* 189pp. Nashville, Tenn., Abingdon Press, 1967.

RENDTORFF, Trutz, und TÖDT, Heinz E., *Theologie der Revolution: Analysen und Materialen.* 165pp. Frankfurt am Main, Suhrkamp Verlag, 1968.

TÖDT, Heinz Eduard, "Bedeutung und Mängel der Genfer Weltkirchenkonferenz", in *Zeitschrift für evangelische Ethik*, Jg. 11, 1967: 1, pp. 2–19.

TÖDT, Heinz Eduard, "Theologie der Revolution". "Revolution als sozialethisches Konzept und seine theologischen Grenzen", in *Oekumenische Rundschau*, Jg. 17, 1968: 1, pp. 1–22.

World Conference on Church and Society, Geneva, July 12–26, 1966. Christians in the Technical and Social Revolutions of Our Time. The official report with a description of the conference by M. M. Thomas and Paul Abrecht. 232pp. Geneva, W.C.C., 1967. French translation *Conférence mondiale Eglise et Société, 1966*. German translation *Appell an die Kirchen der Welt*.

CHURCH AND SOCIETY IN LATIN AMERICA

America hoy; accion de Dios y responsabilidad del hombre. II consulta latinoamericana de Iglesia y Sociedad. 132pp. Montevideo, "Iglesia y Sociedad en América Latina", 1966.

Christians and Social Change in Latin America. Findings of the first Latin American Evangelical Consultation on Church and Society, 23rd to 27th July, 1961 at Huampani, Peru. 22pp. Geneva, W.C.C., 1961. Translated from the Spanish *Encuentro y desafio*.

Hombre, ideologia y revolucion en america latina. 133pp. Montevideo, "Iglesia y Sociedad en América Latina", 1965.

La responsabilidad social del cristiano. Guia de Estudios. 140pp. Montevideo, "Iglesia y Sociedad en América Latina", 1964.

RACE PROBLEMS

BECKMANN, Klaus-Martin, ed., *Die Kirche und die Rassenfrage*. Beiträge von E. C. Blake, W. A. Visser 't Hooft and others. 147pp. ("Kirche im Volk", 34). Berlin, Kreuz-Verlag, 1967.

Christians and Race Relations in Southern Africa: Report on an ecumenical consultation on Christian practice and desirable action in social change and race relations in Southern Africa, held at Kitwe, Zambia, May 25–June 2, 1964. 37pp. Geneva, W.C.C., Department on Church and Society, 1964.

Ecumenical Statements on Race Relations: Development of ecumenical thought on race relations 1937–1964. 47pp. Geneva, W.C.C., 1965.

Intergroup Relations: The Church amid racial and ethic tensions. An ecumenical survey prepared under the auspices of the World Council of Churches. 54pp. (Evanston surveys, 5). London, S.C.M. Press, 1954. French translation *Relations entre groupes humains*. German translation *Gemeinschaftsprobleme*.

Mission in South Africa, April–December 1960. Prepared by the W.C.C. delegation to the consultation in December 1960, F. C. Fry, W. A. Visser 't Hooft, R. S. Bilheimer, etc. 36pp. Geneva, W.C.C., 1961. French translation *Mission en Afrique du Sud*. German translation *Der Auftrag in Südafrika*.

VISSER 'T HOOFT, Willem Adolf, *The Ecumenical Movement and the Racial Problem*. 70pp. (The race question and modern thought). Paris, U.N.E.S.C.O., 1954. French translation *Le mouvement oecuménique et la question raciale*.

SOCIOLOGICAL ASPECTS OF THE ECUMENICAL MOVEMENT

BARNES, Roswell P., *Under Orders: The Churches and public affairs.* 138pp. Garden City, N.Y., Doubleday, 1961.

COLE, Patricia Ann, *The Function of the Church as Critic of Society Exemplified in the Area of United States International Policy.* Boston 1963.

DICKINSON, Richard, *Line and Plummet: The Churches and development.* 112pp. Geneva, W.C.C., 1968. French translation *La règle et le niveau.* German translation *Richtschnur und Waage.*

DOORNKAAT, Hans ten, *Die oekumenischen Arbeiten zur sozialen Frage.* 274pp. Zürich, Gotthelf-Verlag, 1954.

DUFF, Edward, *The Social Thought of the World Council of Churches.* 339pp. London, Longmans, Green and Co., 1956.

GREET, Kenneth, and REARDON, Martin, *Social questions.* 58pp. (Star books on reunion). London, Mowbray, 1964.

HASE, Hans Christoph von, *Diakonie als ökumenische Aufgabe.* 2 vols. Berlin, Christlicher Zeitschriftenverlag, 1961-3.

MEHL, Roger, *Traité de sociologie du protestantisme.* 283pp. (Bibliothèque théologique). Neuchâtel, Delachaux et Niestlé, 1965.

Methodism and society. 4 vols. New York, Nashville, Abingdon Press, 1960-2.

MOBERG, David O., *The Church as a Social Institution. The sociology of American religion.* 569pp. Englewood Cliffs, N.J. Prentice-Hall, 1964.

NELSON, Claud D., *Religion and Society: The ecumenical impact.* 181pp. New York, Sheed and Ward, 1966.

ROSE, Stephen C., ed., "The development apocalypse" or "Will internationa injustice kill the ecumenical movement". *Risk,* vol. iii, nos. 1 and 2, 1967. 152pp

CHRISTIAN SOCIAL THEOLOGY

BARRY, F. R., *Christian ethics and secular society.* 287pp. London, Hodder and Stoughton, 1966.

COX, Harvey, *The secular city; secularization and urbanization in theological perspective.* 276pp. London, S.C.M. Press, 1965. German translation *Stadt ohne Gott?*

DUNNE, George H., ed., *Poverty in plenty.* New York, P. J. Kennedy and Sons, 1964.

Evangelisches Soziallexikon. Im Auftrag des Deutschen Evangelischen Kirchentages. Hrsg. von Friedrich Karrenberg. 1400pp. Berlin, Kreuz-Verlag, 1965.

FAGLEY, Richard M., *The Population Explosion and Christian Responsibility.* 260pp. New York, Oxford University Press, 1960. German translation *Zu viel Menschen.*

SCHALLER, Lyle E., *The Churches' War on Poverty.* 160pp. Nashville, Tenn., Abingdon Press, 1967.

WALTHER, Christian, *Theologie und Gesellschaft. Ortsbestimmung der evangelischen Sozialethik.* 204pp. Zürich, Zwingli Verlag, 1967.

WENDLAND, Heinz-Dietrich, *Einführung in die Sozialethik.* 144pp. (Sammlung Göschen, 1203). Berlin, Walter de Gruyter, 1963.

WENDLAND, Heinz-Dietrich, *Die Kirche in der revolutionären Gesellschaft. Sozialethische Aufsätze und Reden.* 259pp. Gütersloh, Gütersloher Verlagshaus Gerd Mohn, 1967.

WENDLAND, Heinz-Dietrich, *Person und Gesellschaft in evangelischer Sicht.* 219pp. Köln, J. P. Bachem, 1965.

R.C. CHURCH AND SOCIAL QUESTIONS

BIGO, Pierre, *La doctrine sociale de l'église. Recherche et dialogue.* 548pp. Paris, P.U.F., 1966.

CALVEZ, Jean Yves, and PERRIN, Jacques, *The Church and Social Justice. The social teaching of the popes from Leo XIII to Pius XII (1878–1958).* 466pp. London, Burns and Oates, 1961. Translated from *Eglise et société économique.* German translation *Kirche und Wirtschafts-Gesellschaft.*

The documents of Vatican II. Edited by Walter M. Abbott. 794pp. London, Dublin, G. Chapman, 1966. (See mainly the pastoral constitution on the church in the modern world, *Gaudium et spes*, pp. 199–308).

John XXIII, Encyclical letter of His Holiness John XXIII . . . on establishing universal peace in truth, justice, charity and liberty. Pacem in terris. 47pp. Vatican, Vatican Polyglot Press, 1963.

John XXIII, Encyclical letter of His Holiness John XXIII . . . on recent developments of the social question in the light of christian teaching. Mater et magistra. 61pp. Vaticano, Tipografia poliglotta vaticana, 1961.

Paul VI, Encyclical letter of His Holiness Paul VI . . ., on the development of peoples Populorum progressio. 62pp. Vatican Polyglot Press, 1967.

EXPLORATORY COMMITTEE ON SOCIETY, DEVELOPMENT AND PEACE

World Development: The challenge to the Churches. The Conference on World Co-operation for development, Beirut, Lebanon, April 21–27, 1968. Sponsored by the Exploratory Committee on Society, Development and Peace. The Official report . . . 65pp., Geneva, W.C.C., 1968. French translation *Les Eglises face au problème du développement.* German translation *Weltentwicklung.*

CHAPTER 10

Ecumenical Action in International Affairs

The most important documents of the C.C.I.A. are printed in the Minutes of the Central Committee and Executive Committee meetings and in the volumes of W.C.C. Assemblies. For more information see Chapter 2. See also the Minutes of I.M.C. meetings in Chapter 7.

C.C.I.A. Brief. London. Commission of the Churches on International Affairs. 1959—. Irregular.

Commission of the Churches on International Affairs. Memorandum. C.C.I.A. and the session of the general assembly (UNO). New York, C.C.I.A., 1952–66.

Commission of the Churches on International Affairs. Memorandum on Selected Actions. United Nations General Assembly. Session. New York, C.C.I.A., 1952–67.

Commission of the Churches on International Affairs. Report. Annual. Geneva, W.C.C., 1946–67.

For the tenth anniversary of the C.C.I.A. *Ecumenical Review*, July 1956. Entire number.

For the twentieth anniversary of the C.C.I.A. *Ecumenical Review*, April 1967. Entire number.

THOMPSON, Betty, *Commission of the Churches on International Affairs, 1946-1956. A joint agency of the World Council of Churches and the International Missionary Council.* Prepared by the Information Department of the W.C.C., Geneva, W.C.C., 1956.

RELIGIOUS LIBERTY AND HUMAN RIGHTS

CARRILLO DE ALBORNOZ, A. F., *Religious Liberty.* 209pp. New York, Sheed and Ward, 1967. Translated from the Spanish *La libertad religiosa y el Concilio Vaticano II.* French translation *Le Concile et la liberté religieuse.*

CARRILLO DE ALBORNOZ, A. F., *Religious Liberty in the World: A general review of the world situation in 1965.* 42pp. Geneva, W.C.C., Secretariat on Religious Liberty, 1966.

Ecumenical Statements on Race Relations, 1937-1964. 47pp. Geneva, W.C.C., 1965.

KELSEY, George D., *Racism and the christian understanding of man.* 178pp. New York, Charles Scribner's Sons, 1965.

La liberté religieuse: exigence spirituelle et problème politique, E. Schillebeeckx, A. F. Carrillo de Albornoz, etc. En annexe: Documents du Conseil oecuménique des Eglises. 224pp. (L'Eglise en son temps). Paris, Editions du Centurion, 1965.

Main Ecumenical Statements on Principles concerning Religious Freedom. 47pp. mimeographed. Geneva, Secretariat on Religious Liberty, 1965.

MURRAY, John Courtney, ed., *Religious Liberty: An end and a beginning. The declaration on religious freedom: an ecumenical discussion.* 192pp. New York, The Macmillan Company, 1966.

NOLDE, O. Frederick, *Free and Equal: Human rights in ecumenical perspective.* With reflections on the origin of the Universal Declaration of Human Rights by Charles H. Malik. 88pp. Geneva, W.C.C., 1968.

WEIL, Gordon L., *The European Convention on Human Rights. Background, development and prospects.* 260pp. Leyden, Sythoff, 1963.

WOGAMAN, Philip, *Protestant Faith and Religious Liberty.* 254pp. Nashville, Abingdon Press, 1967.

INTERNATIONAL PEACE AND SECURITY

BAINTON, Roland Herbert, *Christian Attitudes towards War and Peace; A historical survey and critical re-evaluation.* 299pp. London, Hodder and Stoughton, 1961.

BOOTH, Alan R., *Not only Peace: Christian realism and the conflicts of the twentieth century.* 141pp. London, S.C.M. Press, 1967.

The Christian Faith and War in the Nuclear Age. 108pp. New York, Nashville, Abingdon Press, 1963.

Christians and the Prevention of War in an Atomic Age. A theological discussion. A provisional study document on ... Mimeographed. Geneva, W.C.C., Division of Studies, 1958. French translation *Les chrétiens et la prévention de la guerre au siècle de l'atôme.* German translation *Christen und die Verhütung des Krieges im Atomzeitalter.*

COMBLIN, Joseph, *Théologie de la paix.* 2 vols. (Encyclopédie universitaire). Paris, Editions Universitaires, 1960.

DIRKS, Walter, ed., *Friede im Atomzeitalter.* 94pp. Mainz, Matthias-Grünewald-Verlag, 1967. Translated from the Dutch *Met Pacem in terris onder weg.*

FLANNERY, Harry W., ed., *Pattern for Peace: Catholic statements on international order*. 411pp. Westminster, Maryland, Newman Press, 1962.

HORMANN, Karl, *Peace and Modern War in the Judgment of the Church*. 162pp. Westminster, Newman Press, 1966. Translated from the German *Friede und moderner Krieg im Urteil der Kirche*.

MILFORD, T. R., *The Valley of Decision: The Christian dilemma in the nuclear age*. 50pp. London, B.C.C., 1961.?

REGAMEY, P., *Non-violence and the Christian Conscience*. 172pp. London, Darton, Longman and Todd, 1966. Translated from the French *Non-violence et conscience chrétienne*.

TAYLOR, Thomas M., and BILHEIMER, Robert S., ed., *Christians and the Prevention of War in an Atomic Age: A theological discussion*. 46pp. London, S.C.M. Press, 1961.

MIGRATION AND REFUGEES
see also chapter 8 (I.C.A.)

BOUSCAREN, Anthony T., *International Migrations since 1945*. 176pp. New York, F. A. Praeger, 1963.

REES, Elfan, *We Strangers and Afraid: The Refugee story today*. 72pp. New York, Carnegie Endowment for International Peace, 1959.

THOMAS, Brinley, *International Migration and Economic Development*. A trend report and bibliography. 85pp. Paris, U.N.E.S.C.O., 1961.

ADVANCEMENT OF DEPENDENT PEOPLES

BIRMINGHAM, Walter, and FORD, A. G., ed., *Planning and Growth in Rich and Poor Countries*. 267pp. London, Allen and Unwin, 1966.

Dictionnaire des sciences économiques. 2 vols. Paris, P.U.F., 1958.

Entwicklungspolitik. Handbuch und Lexikon. Im Auftrag von Bernhard Haussler und Hans Hermann Walz. Hrsg. von H. Besters und Ernst E. Boesch. 1770pp., parallel columns. Berlin, Kreuz-Verlag, 1966.

FAGLEY, Richard M., *The Population Explosion and Christian Responsibility*. 260pp. New York, Oxford University Press, 1960. German translation *Zu viel Menschen*.

International Encyclopedia of the Social Sciences. 17 vols. London, Collier-Macmillan Ltd, 1957.

LACY, Creighton, ed., *Christianity amid Rising Men and Nations*. 192pp. New York, Association Press, 1965.

LEBRET, L. J., *Dynamique concrète du développement*. 550pp. (Développement et civilisations). Publié avec le concours du C.N.R.S. Paris, Les Editions ouvrières, 1961.

MOOMAW, I. W., *Crusade against Hunger. The dramatic story of the world-wide anti-poverty crusades of the churches*. 199pp. New York, Harper and Row, 1966.

Le Tiers-monde, l'occident et l'Église, B. Atangana, G. de Bernis, etc. 325pp. (Parole et mission, 13). Paris, Les Editions du Cerf, 1967.

TURIN, Laurent, *Combat pour le développement*. 311pp. (Développement et civilisations). Paris, les Editions ouvrières, 1965.

WARD, Barbara, *The Rich Nations and the Poor Nations*. 159pp. New York, W. W. Norton and Co, 1962: London, Hamish Hamilton, 1962.

WARD, Barbara, *Spaceship Earth*. 152pp. New York, Columbia University Press, 1966: London, Hamish Hamilton, 1966.

WARD, Richard J., ed., *The Challenge of Development. Theory and practice.* 500pp. Chicago, Adling Publishing Co., 1967.

Weltarmut. Eine kirkliche Denkschrift. Herausgegeben, einegeleitet und kommentiert von Klaus-Martin Beckmann und Klaus Lefringhausen. 95pp. Stuttgart, Kreuz Verlag, 1967.

World Poverty and British Responsibility. 80pp. Published for the British Council of Churches. London, S.C.M. Press, 1966.

INTERNATIONAL LAW

BENNETT, John C., *Christians and the State.* 302pp. New York, Charles Scribner's Sons, 1958.

BENNETT, John C., *Foreign Policy in Christian Persepctive.* 160pp. New York, Charles Scribner's Sons, 1966.

Christians in the Struggle for World Community. Report of the section on international affairs received by the second assembly of the W.C.C., Evanston, 1954, remitted to delegates to the ninth general assembly of the United Nations by the Presidents during the second assembly. 16pp. New York, W.C.C., 1954.

DEWART, Leslie, *Christianity and Revolution: The lesson of Cuba.* 320pp. New York, Herder and Herder, 1963.

ELERT, Werner, *Law and Gospel.* 53pp. (Facet books. Social ethics series, 16). Philadelphia, Fortress Press, 1967.

Evangelisches Staatslexikon. Hrsg. von H. Kunst und S. Grundmann in Verbindung mit W. Schneemelcher und R. Herzog. 2688pp., parallel columns. Berlin, Kreuz-Verlag, 1966.

HUEGLI, Albert G., ed., *Church and State under God.* 516pp. St Louis, Missouri, Concordia Publishing House, 1964.

International Affairs: Christians in the struggle for world community. An ecumenical survey prepared under the auspices of the W.C.C. 54pp. (Evanston surveys, 4). London, S.C.M. Press, 1954. French translation *Affaires internationales.* German translation *Internationale Angelegenheiten.*

JAMES, Walter, *The Christian in Politics.* 217pp. London, Oxford University Press, 1962.

KRAMER, Leonard J., *Man amid Change in World Affairs.* 175pp. New York, Friendship Press, 1964.

MCDONAGH, Edna, *The Declaration on Religious Freedom of Vatican Council II. The text with commentary in the context of the church–state discussion.* 155pp. London, Darton, Longman and Todd, 1967.

SANDERS, Thomas G., *Protestant Concepts of Church and State: Historical background and approaches for the future.* 388pp. (Anchor book). New York, Doubleday, 1964.

SCHREY, Heinz-Horst, and HERMANN, Hans, and WHITEHOUSE, W. A., *The Biblical Doctrine of Justice and Law.* 208pp. (Ecumenical biblical studies, 3). London, S.C.M. Press, 1955. Translated from the German *Gerechtigkeit in biblischer Sicht.*

SMITH, Elwyn, *Church–State Relations in Ecumenical Perspective.* 280pp. (Duquesne ecumenical books). Pittsburgh, Pa., Duquesne University Press, 1966.

The Treysa Conference on "the biblical doctrine of law and justice". Report of a conference arranged by the Study Department of the World Council of Churches, held at Treysa, Germany, August 2nd to 7th, 1950. 60pp. Geneva, W.C.C., 1951. Translated from the German *Die Treysa-Konferenz 1950.*

CHAPTER 11

The Orthodox Churches in the Ecumenical Movement

ORTHODOXY IN DIALOGUE WITH OTHER DENOMINATIONS

The Dialogue of East and West in Christendom. Lectures delivered at a conference arranged by the Fellowship of St Alban and St Sergius in Oxford, March 10, 1962. Foreword by A. M. Allchin. 47pp. London, published for the Fellowship of St Alban and St Sergius by the Faith Press, 1963.

EVERY, George, *Misunderstandings between East and West*. 70pp. (Ecumenical Studies in History, 4). Richmond, Va., John Knox Press, 1966.

GILL, Joseph, and FLOOD, Edmund, *The Orthodox: Their relations with Rome*. 58pp. (Where we stand). London, Darton, Longman and Todd, 1964.

GILL, Joseph, *The Orthodox and the Ecumenical Movements*. London, The Mouth, 1962.

ISTAVRIDIS, Vasil T., *The Ecumenical Patriarchate and the World Council of Churches*. 18pp. Brookline, Mass., 1963. In *The Greek-Orthodox Theological Review*, vol. 9, no. 1, Summer 1963, pp. 9–28.

ISTAVRIDIS, Vasil T., *Die griechisch-orthodoxe Bibliographie zur ökumenischen Bewegung*. Würzburg, Augustinus Verlag, 1961.

ISTAVRIDIS, Vasil T., "The Orthodox World", in *The Layman in Christian History*, ed. S. C. Neill and H. R. Weber, pp. 276–97. London, S.C.M. Press, 1963.

ISTAVRIDIS, Vasil T., *Orthodoxy and Anglicanism*. 185pp. Translated from the Greek. London, S.P.C.K., 1966.

Major Portions of the Proceedings of the Conference of Heads and Representatives of the Autocephalous Orthodox Churches, Moscow, 8–18 July 1948. 250pp. Paris, Y.M.C.A. Press, 1952.

MAXIMOS IV, Patriarch of Antioch, Alexandria and Jerusalem: *The Eastern Churches and Catholic Unity*. 236pp. Edinburgh/London, Nelson, 1963.

Die Moskauer Konferenz vom Juli 1948. Herausgegeben vom Kirchlichen Aussenamt der E.K.D. 79pp. Witten, Luther-Verlag, 1949? (Dokumente der orthodoxen Kirchen zur ökumenischen Frage, 1).

Orthodoxy. A Faith and Order Dialogue. 80pp. (Faith and Order papers, 30). Geneva, W.C.C., 1960.

SAVRAMIS, Demosthenes, *Oekumenische Probleme in der neugriechischen Theologie*. 118pp. (Oekumenische Studien, 6). Leiden/Köln, Brill, 1964.

SLENCZKA, Reinhard, *Ostkirche und Oekumene. Die Einheit der Kirche als dogmatisches Problem in der neueren ostkirchlichen Theologie*. 316pp. (Forschungen zur systematischen und ökumenischen Theologie, Bd. 9). Göttingen, Vandenhoeck & Ruprecht, 1962.

STAWROWSKY, Alexis, *Essai de théologie irénique: L'Orthodoxie et le Catholicisme*. 266pp. Paris, Sedim, 1966.

STUPPERICH, Robert, *Die Russische Orthodoxe Kirche in Lehre und Leben*. 312pp. (Studienausschuss der EKU für Fragen der Orthodoxen Kirche, Schriftenreihe, 2). Witten, Luther-Verlag, 1966.

Toward a Protestant understanding of Orthodoxy. 23pp. (Resources for ecumenical encounter, 2). New York, Commission on ecumenical mission and relations, 1966.

Versöhnung. Das deutsch-russische Gespräch über das christliche Verständnis der Versöhnung zwischen Vertretern der Evangelischen Kirche in Deutschland und der

Russischen Orthodoxen Kirche. Hrsg. vom Aussenamt der Evangelische Kirche in Deutschland. 197pp. Witten, Luther Verlag, 1967.

VRIES, Wilhelm de, *Orthodoxie et catholicisme*. 183pp. Paris, Desclée, 1967. Translated from the German *Orthodoxie und Katholizismus*.

WADDAMS, Herbert, *Meeting the Orthodox Churches*. 128pp. London, S.C.M. Press, 1964.

ZERNOV, Nicolas, *Orthodox Encounter: The Christian East and the ecumenical movement*. 200pp. London, J. Clarke, 1961.

STUDIES ON ORTHODOXY

ATIYA, Aziz S., *A History of Eastern Christianity*. 486pp. London, Methuen, 1968.

ATTWATER, D., *The Christian Churches of the East*. 3rd rev. edn. 2 vols. London, Chapman, 1961.

BARSOTTI, Divo, *Christianisme russe*. Traduit de l'italien par Ch. Roux de Bézieux et Y. Mourbarac. 196pp. Tournai, Paris, Casterman, 1963.

BENZ, Ernst, *The Eastern Orthodox Church: Its thought and life*. 230pp. New York, Doubleday, 1963. Translated from the German *Geist und Leben der Ostkirche*.

BENZ, Ernst, *Die russische Kirche und das abendländische Christentum*. 186pp. München, Nymphenburger Verlagshandlung, 1966. Chapter II, pp. 39–73: "Die gegenwärtige Stellung der östlich-orthodoxen Kirche in der Oekumene".

BOGOLEPOV, Alexander A., *Toward an American Orthodox Church. The establishment of an Autocephalous Orthodox Church*. 124pp. New York, Morehouse-Barlow, 1963.

BRATSIOTIS, Panagiotis, *Von der griechischen Orthodoxie*. 156pp. Würzburg, Echter-Verlag, 1966.

CLEMENT, Olivier, *L'Eglise orthodoxe*. 128pp. (Que sais-je? 949). Paris, P.U.F., 1961.

CONSTANTELOS, Demetrios J., *The Greek Orthodox Church: Faith, history and practice*. 127pp. New York, The Seabury Press, 1967.

DALMAIS, Irénée-Henri, *The Eastern Liturgies*. 144pp. London, Burns and Oates, 1960. Translated from the French *Les liturgies d'Orient*. German translation *Die Liturgie der Ostkirchen*.

ETTELDORF, Raymond, *The Soul of Greece*. 235pp. Westminster, Maryland, Newman Press, 1963.

EVDOKIMOV, Paul, *L'Orthodoxie; la foi et la vie des Eglises d'Orient*. 352pp. (Bibliothèque théologique). Neuchâtel, Delachaux et Niestlé, 1959.

LE GUILLOU, M.-J., *L'esprit de l'orthodoxie grecque et russe*. Préface par R. P. Dumont. 127pp. (Encyclopédie du catholique au XXe siècle "Je sais—je crois", 13e partie: Frères séparés). Paris, A. Fayard, 1961.

LOSSKY, Vladimir, *A l'image et à la ressemblance de Dieu*. 225pp. Paris, Aubier-Montaigne, 1967.

LOSSKY, Vladimir, *The Vision of God*. 139pp. Westminster, Faith Press, 1963. French translation *Vision de Dieu*. German translation *Schau Gottes*.

MEYENDORFF, Jean, *The Orthodox Church: Its past and its role in the world today*. Translated from the French by John Caphin with additions made by the author for this new English edition. 245pp. London, Darton, Longman & Todd, 1963. Translated from the original *L'Eglise orthodoxe; hier et aujourd-hui*. German translation *Die Orthodoxe Kirche gestern und heute*.

MEYENDORFF, Jean, *Orthodoxy and Catholicity*. 180pp. New York, Sheed and Ward, 1966. Translated from the French *Orthodoxie et catholicité*.

ONASCH, Konrad, *Einführung in die Konfessionskunde der orthodoxen Kirchen.* 291pp. (Sammlung Göschen, 1197/1197a). Berlin, Walter de Gruyter, 1962.

Orthodoxy 1964: a pan-orthodox symposium, Athens. 444pp. The Brotherhood of theologians "Zoe", 1964.

PHILIPPOU, A. J., *The Orthodox Ethos. Essays in honour of the centenary of the Greek Orthodox Archdiocese of North and South America.* 288pp. Oxford, England, Holywell Press, 1964.

POSPISCHIL, Viktor, *Der Patriarch in der Serbisch-orthodoxen Kirche.* 271pp. Wien, Herder Verlag, 1966.

La primauté de Pierre dans l'Eglise orthodoxe, N. Afanassieff, N. Koulomzine, J. Meyendorff, A. Schmemann. 152pp. Neuchâtel, Paris, Editions Delachaux & Niestlé, 1960. German translation *Der Primat des Petrus in der orthodoxen Kirche.* Zürich, EVZ, 1961.

RINVOLUCRI, Mario, *Anatomy of a Church: Greek orthodoxy today.* 192pp. London, Burns & Oates, 1966.

SARTORIUS, Bernard, *L'Eglise orthodoxe.* 350pp. (Les Grandes religions du monde, 10). Genève, le Cercle du Bibliophile, 1968.

SCHMEMANN, Alexander, *The Historical Road of Eastern Orthodoxy.* Translated by Lydia W. Kesich. 359pp. London, Harvill Press, 1963.

SCHMEMANN, Alexander, *Sacraments and Orthodoxy.* 124pp. New York, Herder and Herder, 1965.

ZANANIRI, Gaston, *Catholicisme oriental.* 266pp. Paris, Editions SPES, 1966.

ZANANIRI, Gaston, *Pape et patriarches.* Préface du T. R. P. Dumont. 221pp. Paris, Nouvelle Editions Latines, 1961.

ZERNOV, Nicolas, *Eastern Christendom. A study of the origin and development of the Eastern Orthodox Church.* 326pp. (The Weidenfeld and Nicolson History of Religion). London, Weidenfeld & Nicolson, 1961.

ORIENTAL ORTHODOX CHURCHES

CHAKMAKJIAN, Hagop A., *Armenian Christology and Evangelization of Islam.* 146pp. Leiden, E. J. Brill, 1965.

HANNA, Shenouda, *What are the Copts.* 110pp. Cairo, C. Tsoumas, 1958.

KAWERAV, Peter, *Die jakobitische Kirche im Zeitalter der syrischen Renaissance.* 153pp. Berlin, Akademie-Verlag, 1960.

LEPISA, Titus, *The Cult of Saints in the Ethiopian Church.* 55pp. Roma, Universitas gregoriana, 1963.

MATHEW, C.-P., and THOMAS, M. M., *The Indian Churches of Saint Thomas.* 168pp. Delhi, I.S.P.C.K., 1967.

SARKISSIAN, Karekin, *The Council of Chalcedon and the Armenian Church.* 264pp. London, S.P.C.K., 1965.

"Unofficial consultation between theologians of Eastern Orthodox and Oriental Orthodox Churches, August 11–15, 1964. Papers and minutes", ed. John S. Romanides, Paul Verghese, Nikos A. Nissiotis, *The Greek Orthodox Theological Review,* vol. x, no. 2, Winter 1964–5, 168pp.

CHAPTER 12

The Ecumenical Movement and the Roman Catholic Church

ROMAN CATHOLIC APPROACHES TO THE ECUMENICAL MOVEMENT

At-one-ment: Studies on Christian unity. Washington, D.C., Friars of the Atonement, 1959—. Annual volumes.

BAUM, Gregory, *The Quest for Christian Unity.* 285pp. London, Sheed and Ward, 1963.

BEA, Augustinus, Cardinal, *The Unity of Christians*, ed. Bernard Leeming. Introduction by Gerald P. O'Hara. 231pp. London, Chapman, 1963. Translated from Italian *L'Unione dei Cristiani; problemi e principi, ostacli e mezzi, realizzazioni e prospettive.* French translation *Pour l'unité des chrétiens; problèmes et principes, obstacles et moyens, réalisations et perspectives.* German translation *Die Einheit der Christen. Probleme und Prinzipien, Hindernisse und Mittel, Verwirklichungen und Aussichten.*

BEA, Augustinus, *The Way to Unity after the Council.* 256pp. London, Geoffrey Chapman, 1967. Translated from the Italian *Il cammino all'unione dopo il Concilio.* French translation *Le chemin de l'unité.* German translation *Der Weg zur Einheit nach dem Konzil.*

BIOT, François, *De la polémique au dialogue.* 2 vols. Paris, Editions du Cerf, 1963. Contents: vol. 1: *L'église face aux chrétiens séparés.* 140pp. vol. 2: *Les chrétiens séparés face à l'église.* 135 pp.

BOELENS, Wim L., *Die Arnoldshainer Abendmahlsthesen. Die Suche nach einem Abendmahlskonsens in der Evangelischen Kirche in Deutschland 1947–1957 und eine Würdigung aus katholischer Sicht.* 393pp. Assen, Van Gorcum, 1964.

BOILLAT, Fernand, *L'oecuménisme catholique.* 83pp. St Maurice, Editions St Augustin, 1964.

BOYER, Charles, *Christian unity.* 131pp. (Twentieth century Encyclopedia of Catholicism, v. 138). New York, Hawthorn, 1962.

CRANNY, Titus, ed., *The Episcopate and Christian Unity. A symposium conducted by the Graymoor Friars Saint Pius X Seminary, September 1–4, 1964.* 158pp. Garrison, N.Y., Chair of Unity Apostolate Graymoor, 1965.

HAMER, Jerome, *The Church is a Communion.* 240pp. London, Geoffrey Chapman, 1964. Translated from the French *L'Eglise est une communion.*

HASTINGS, Adrian, *One and Apostolic.* 200pp. London, Darton, Longman & Todd, 1963.

HEUFELDER, Emmanuel Maria, *In the Hope of his Coming. Studies in christian unity.* 261pp. Indiana, Fides, 1964.

IOANNIS XXIII, *Pope John and christian unity.* Compiled and edited by Titus Cranny. 95pp. Graymoore, Garrison, Chair of Unity Apostolate, 1962.

LAMARQUE, Alfred, *Vers l'unité? Catholiques et protestants.* 335pp. Paris, Editions du Cerf, 1963.

LAMBERT, Bernard, *Ecumenism: Theology and history.* 533pp. London, Burns and Oates, 1966. Translated from the French *Le problème oecuménique.* German translation *Das ökumenische Problem.*

R

LEEMING, Bernard, *The Church and the Churches; A study of ecumenism.* 340pp. London, Darton, Longman and Todd, 1960.

LEFEBVRE, Georges, *L'Unité mystère de vie.* 107pp. Paris, Bruges, Desclée de Brouwer, 1964.

MARSHALL, Romey P., *Liturgy and Christian Unity.* 186pp. Englewood Cliffs, N.J., Prentice-Hall, 1965.

MOOY, Suitberto, *Problemas ecumenicos; na igreja e nas igrejas.* 255pp. Sao Paulo. Editora Herder, 1963.

O'BRIEN, John A., *Steps to Christian Unity.* 321pp. Garden City, New York, Doubleday, 1964.

Problems before Unity, J. G. M. Willebrands, Shawn G. Sheehan, Paul Mailleux. Foreword by Augustine Cardinal Bea. 149pp. Dublin, Helicon, 1962.

ST JOHN, Henry, *Essays in Christian Unity 1928–1954.* 144pp. London, Blackfriars, 1955.

SARTORY, Thomas, *The Oecumenical Movement and the Unity of the Church*, tr. Hilda C. Graef. 290pp. Oxford, Blackwell, 1963. Translated from the German *Die ökumenische Bewegung und die Einheit der Kirche; ein Beitrag im Dienste einer ökumenischen Ekklesiologie.*

SCHÜTTE, Heinz, *Um die Wiedervereinigung im Glauben. Vierte, wieder stark erweiterte Auflage, 1961.* 228pp. Essen, Fredebeul & Koenen, 1961.

SWIDLER, Leonard, *Ecumenism; The Spirit and Worship.* 258pp. Louvain, ed. E. Nauwelaerts, Duquesne University Press, 1967.

TAVARD, George, *The Church Tomorrow.* 190pp. London, Darton, Longman & Todd, 1965.

TAYLOR, Michael J., *The Protestant Liturgical Renewal; A catholic viewpoint.* 336pp. Westminster, Maryland, Newman Press, 1963.

VALESKE, Ulrich, *Votum Ecclesiae. I. Teil: Das Ringen um die Kirche in der neuen röm. kath. Theologie. Dargestellt auf dem Hintergrund der evangelischen und ökumenischen parallell Entwicklung. II. Teil: Interkonfessionelle ekklesiologische Bibliographie.* 210pp. München, Claudius, 1962.

VILLAIN, Maurice, *Unity: A history and some reflections.* Translated by J. R. Foster from the third revised and augmented edition. 381pp. London, Harvill, 1963. Translated from the French *Introduction à l'oecuménisme.*

WACKER, Paulus, *Theologie als ökumenischer Dialog. Herman Schell und die ökumenische Situation der Gegenwart.* 571pp. München, Wien, Verlag Ferdinand Schöningh, 1964.

WILLEBRANDS, J. G. ed., *Problems before Unity.* 149pp. Baltimore, Helicon Press, 1962.

ROMAN CATHOLIC—PROTESTANT, ANGLICAN, ORTHODOX DIALOGUE

ASMUSSEN, Hans, and STÄHLIN, Wilhelm, ed., *Die Katholizität der Kirche. Beiträge zum Gespräch zwischen der evangelischen und der römisch-katholischen Kirche.* 390pp. Stuttgart, Evang. Verlagswerk, 1957.

ASMUSSEN, Hans, and SARTORY, Thomas, *Lutheran–Catholic dialogue.* Baltimore, Helicon Press, 1960.

BEVAN, R. J. W., ed., *The Churches and Christian Unity.* 263pp. London, Oxford University Press, 1963.

BOSC, Jean, *Geeint durch das, was trennt. Ein katholisch-protestantisches Gespräch.* Mit einem Geleitwort von Albert Brandenburg. 163pp. Graz-Wien, Köln, Styria, 1963.

BROWN, Robert M., and WEIGEL, Gustave, *An American Dialogue. A Protestant looks at catholicism and a Catholic looks at protestantism.* Foreword by Willy Herberg. 216pp. Garden City, New York, Doubleday, 1960.

BRUNE, Friedrich, *Die Begegnung der evangelischen und katholischen Gemeinden im Alltag.* 68pp. Witten, Luther-Verlag, 1962.

CALLAHAN, Daniel, ed., *Christianity Divided; Protestant and Roman Catholic theological issues.* 335pp. New York, Sheed and Ward, 1961.

The Catholic Protestant Dialogue, Jean Bosc, Jean Guitton, Jean Daniélou. 138pp. Baltimore, Helicon Press, 1960. Translated from the French *Le dialogue catholique-protestant.*

CONGAR, Yves Marie Joseph, *Dialogue between Christians: Catholic contribution to ecumenism.* 472pp. Westminster, Maryland. Newman Press, 1966. Translated from the French *Chrétiens en dialogue; contributions catholiques à l'oecuménisme.*

CULLMANN, Oscar, *Message to Catholics and Protestants.* 57pp. Grand Rapids, Eerdmans, 1959. Translated from the German *Katholiken und Protestanten. Ein Vorschlag zur Verwirklichung christlicher Solidarität.*

Do we know the others? Ecumenical theology. 180pp. New York, Paulist Press, 1966.

Ecumenical dialogue in Europe. The ecumenical conversations at Les Dombes (1937–1955) inspired by the Abbé Couturier. Introduced by Patrick C. Rodger. 83pp. London, Lutterworth Press, 1966.

EMPIE, Paul, and BAUM, William W., ed., *Lutherans and Catholics in dialogue. II: One Baptism for the Remission of Sins.* 87pp. New York, National Committee of the Lutheran World Federation, Bishop's Commission for Ecumenical Affairs, 1966.

GARRETT, James Leo, *Baptists and Roman Catholicism.* 45pp. Nashville, Tennessee, Broadway Press, 1965.

GRANT, Frederick C., *Rome and Reunion.* 196pp. New York, Oxford University Press, 1965.

GREENSPUN, William B., and NORGREN, William A., *Living room dialogues.* 255pp. N.C.C.C.U.S.A., Glen Rock, Paulist Press, 1965.

L'infaillibilité de l'église: journées oecuméniques de Chevetogne, 25–29 Septembre 1961, O. Rousseau, J. J. von Allmen, B.-D. Dupuy, etc. 268pp. Chevetogne, Editions de Chevetogne, 1963.

KING, Betty, and JULIANA, Lorraine, *The wall between us. A Protestant–Catholic dialogue.* 173pp. Milwaukee, The Bruce Publishing Co., 1964.

KLEIN, Laurentius, und MEINHOLD, Peter, *Ueber Wesen und Gestalt der Kirche; ein katholisch-evangelischer Briefwechsel.* 124pp. Freiburg, Basel und Wien, Herder-Bücherei, 1963.

MILLER, Samuel H., and WRIGHT, Ernest G., *Ecumenical Dialogue at Harvard: The Roman Catholic–Protestant colloquium.* 385pp. Cambridge, Mass., Belknap Press of Harvard University Press, 1964.

PELIKAN, Jaroslav J., *Obedient Rebels; Catholic substance and Protestant principle in Luther's reformation.* 212pp. New York, Harper, 1964.

Reconsiderations. Roman Catholic–Presbyterian and Reformed conversation of the Bishop's Committee for Ecumenical and Inter-religious Affairs and the North American Area of the World Alliance of Reformed Churches. 158pp. New York, World Horizons, 1967.

Rencontre oecuménique à Genève. 124pp. Genève Editions Labor et Fides. Paris, Librairie Protestante, 1965.

SWIDLER, Leonard, ed., *Dialogue for Reunion: The Catholic premises.* 88pp. New York, Herder and Herder, 1962.

TAVARD, George, *La poursuite de la catholicité; étude sur la pensée anglicane.* 247pp. Paris, Editions du Cerf, 1965.

WEIGEL, Gustave, *Catholic theology in Dialogue*. 126pp. New York, Harper, 1961.

ZANANIRI, Gaston, *Catholicisme oriental*. 266pp. Paris, Editions SPES, 1966.

ZANDER, Leo A., *Einheit ohne Vereinigung; ökumenische Betrachtungen eines russischen Orthodoxen. Aus dem Russischen von Reinhard Slenczka*. Mit einem Geleitwort von E. Schlink. Stuttgart, Evangelisches Verlagswerk, 1959.

ROMAN CATHOLIC REACTIONS TO VATICAN II

BAUMANN, Richard, *Vom Konzil zur Einheit*. 2 vols. Vol. 1 *Auch wir sind Kirche*. 211pp. Vol. 2 *Hoffnung aus Sankt Paul*. 292pp. Essen, Verlag Hans Driewer, 1965.

HÄRING, Bernhard, *The Johannine Council: Witness to unity*. 155pp. New York, Herder and Herder, 1964.

JAEGER, Lorenz, *The Ecumenical Council, the Church and Christendom*. 194pp. London, Geoffrey Chapman, 1961. Translation from the German *Das ökumenische Konzil, die Kirche und die Christenheit*.

KÜNG, Hans, *The Council and Reunion*. Translated by Cecil Hastings. 307pp. (Stagbooks). London, New York, Sheed and Ward, 1961. Translated from the German *Konzil und Wiedervereinigung: Erneuerung als Ruf in die Einheit*. French translation *Concile et retour à l'unité; se renouveler pour susciter l'unité*.

KÜNG, Hans, *The Living Church: Reflections on the Second Vatican Council*. Translated by Cecily Hastings and N. D. Smith. 421pp. London, New York, Sheed and Ward, 1963. Translated from the German *Strukturen der Kirche*. French translation *Structures de l'Église*.

VILLAIN, Maurice, *Vatican II et le dialogue oecuménique*. 236pp. Tournai, Casterman, 1966.

PROTESTANT, ANGLICAN AND ORTHODOX REACTIONS TO VATICAN II

Die Autorität der Freiheit. Gegenwart des Konzils und Zukunft der Kirche im ökumenischen Disput. 3 vols. Herausgegeben von Johann Christoph Hampe. München, Kösel-Verlag, 1967.

BARTH, Karl, *Ad Limina Apostolorum*. 66pp. Zürich, EVZ-Verlag, 1967.

BERKOUWER, G. C., *The Second Vatican Council and the New Catholicism*. 264pp. Translated by Lewis B. Smedes. Grand Rapids, Michigan, Eerdmans, 1965. Translated from the Dutch *Vatikaans concilie en nieuwe theologie*.

Challenge ... and Response: A protestant perspective of the Vatican Council, ed. Warren A. Quanbeck in consultation with Friedrich Wilhelm Kantzenbach and Vilmos Vajta. 226pp. Minneapolis, Augsburg Publishing House, 1952.

HAMPE, Johann Christoph, *Ende der Gegenreformation? Das Konzil Dokumente und Deutung*. 445pp. Stuttgart u. Berlin, Kreuz-Verlag, 1964; Mainz, Matthias-Grünewald-Verlag, 1964.

HORTON, Douglas, *Toward an undivided Church*. 96pp. New York, Association Press, 1967.

HORTON, Douglas, *Vatican Diary. A Protestant observes the third session of Vatican Council II*. 4 vols. Philadelphia, Boston, United Church Press, 1966.

KARRER, Otto, *Das Zweite Vatikanische Konzil. Reflexionen zu seiner geschichtlichen und geistlichen Wirklichkeit*. 275pp. München, Kösel-Verlag, 1966.

LINDBECK, George A., *Dialogue on the way; Protestants report from Rome on the Vatican Council*. 270pp. Minneapolis, Augsburg Publishing House, 1965. French translation *Le dialogue est ouvert. Le Concile vu par les observateurs luthériens. Les trois première sessions du Concile Vatican II.* German translation *Dialog unterwegs; eine evangelische Bestandesaufnahme zum Konzil.*

MEINHOLD, Peter, *Die Kirchen auf neuen Wegen. Wie sie heute aufeinander blicken.* 172pp. Freiburg, Herder, 1964.

MILLER, John H., *Vatican II an interfaith appraisal. International theological conference, 1966.* 656pp. Notre Dame and London, University of Notre Dame, 1966.

NEUMANN, Johannes, *Auf Hoffnung hin; eine Sammlung oekumenischer Gedanken.* 284pp. Meitingen bei Augsburg, Kyrios-Verlag, 1964.

OUTLER, Albert C., *Methodist Observer at Vatican II.* 189pp. New York, Newman Press, 1967.

The Papal Council and the Gospel. Protestant theologians evaluate the coming Vatican Council, ed. K. E. Skydsgaard. 213pp. Minneapolis, Augsburg Publishing House, 1961. German translation *Konzil und Evangelism.*

PAWLEY, Bernard C., *The Second Vatican Council: Studies by eight Anglican observers.* 262pp. London, Oxford University Press, 1967.

Points de vue de théologiens protestants: Etudes sur les décrets du Concile Vatican II, J. BOSC, G. Casalis, H. Roux. 269pp. Paris, Editions du Cerf, 1967.

ROUX, Hébert, *Détresse et promesse de Vatican II: Réflexions et expériences d'un observateur au concile.* 205pp. Paris, Editions du Seuil, 1967.

SCHLINK, Edmund, *After the Council: The meaning of Vatican II for protestantism and the ecumenical dialogue.* Philadelphia, Fortress Press, 1968. Translated from the German *Nach dem Konzil.*

STUBER, Stanley, and NELSON, Claude D., *Implementing Vatican II in your community. Dialogue and action manual based on the sixteen documents of the Second Vatican Council.* 239pp. New York, Association Press.

SUBILLA, Vittorio, *La nuova cattolicità del Cattolicesimo.* Una valutazione protestante del Concilio Vaticano II. 309pp. Torino, Editrice Claudiana, 1967.

SUBILIA, Vittorio, *The Problem of Catholicism.* 190pp. London, S.C.M. Press, 1964. Translated from the Italian *Il problema del cattolicesimo.*

VINAY, Valdo, *Rom und die anderen. Das Verhältnis der römischen Kirche zur nichtrömischen Christenheit an Hand der Konstitution "De Ecclesia" und des Dekrets "De Oecumenismo".* 41pp. Göttingen, Vandenhoeck & Ruprecht, 1965.

VISCHER, Lukas, *Ueberlegungen nach dem Vatikanischen Konzil.* 79pp. Zürich, EVZ-Verlag, 1966.

JOINT WORKING GROUP BETWEEN THE ROMAN CATHOLIC CHURCH AND THE WORLD COUNCIL OF CHURCHES

"First Official Report", in *Ecumenical Review,* vol. xviii, no. 2, April 1966, pp. 243–55. See also *Minutes of the Central Committee, Geneva, February 1966,* pp. 47–51.

"Second Official Report", in *Ecumenical Review,* vol. xix, no. 4, October 1967, pp. 461–9. See also *Minutes of the Central Committee, Heraklion, August 1967,* pp. 53–5.

"On the Ecumenical Dialogue. A Working Paper", in *Ecumenical Review,* vol. xix, no. 4, October 1967, pp. 469–73.

500

CHAPTER 13

The Ecumenical Movement in the Churches and at the Parish Level

ECUMENISM AT LOCAL LEVEL

Agenda for the Churches. A report on the "People Next Door" programme, Kenneth Sansbury, Robert Latham, Pauline Webb. With appendixes by Vere Ducker. 71pp. London, S.C.M. Press, 1968.

BENIGNUS, Emma, *All in Each Place: A guide to local ecumenism*. 127pp. Cincinnati, a Forward Movement Publication, 1966.

BLAKEMORE, William Barnett, *The Challenge of Christian Unity*. 144pp. (The William Henry Hoover Lectures on Christian unity, 1963). St Louis, Missouri, Bethany Press, 1963.

BRENNECKE, Ursula, *Gelebte Verantwortung: Ein ökumenischer Rundblick in die Frauenarbeit der Kirchen*. 239pp. Berlin, Evangelische Verlagsanstalt, 1966.

BRUNE, Friedrich, *Die Begegnung der evangelischen und katholischen Gemeinden im Alltag*. 68pp. Witten, Luther-Verlag, 1962.

DAVIES, Rupert E., *In All Places and All Ages*. 37pp. (The unity we seek, 5). London, B.C.C., 1964.

First ecumenical workbook. Programme suggestions for local Councils of Churches, united Christian youth groups, ecumenical fellowships, and parishes and congregations. London, B.C.C., 1960.

FRANZMANN, Martin H., and LUEKING, F. D., *Grace under Pressure: The way of weakness in ecumenical relations*. 105pp. St Louis, Concordia Publishing House, 1966.

GOODALL, Norman, *The Local Church: Its resources and responsibilities*. 63pp. London, Hodder and Stoughton, 1966.

GREENSPOON, William B., and NORGREN, William A., ed., *Living Room Dialogues*. 255pp. Glen Rock, Paulist Press, 1965.

GREENSPOON, William B., and WEDEL, Cynthia C., *Second Living Room Dialogues*. 270pp. Glen Rock, Paulist Press, 1967.

HORNIG, Ernst, *Die Bedeutung der ökumenischen Bewegung für die Ortsgemeinde. Herrn Generalsekretär Dr W. A. Visser 't Hooft zum 65. Geburtstag*. 24pp. Sonderdruck aus Pastoralblätter 5/6 1965 im Kreuz-Verlag, Berlin.

HOSKINS, Fred, *Servants of the Eternal Christ; Local ecumenicity. A study book for local Churches. In preparation for the 1963 General Assembly of the National Council of Churches*. 48pp. New York, The Office of publication and distribution, National Council of Churches, 1962.

Interim Guidelines for Ecumenical Activities in the Archdiocese of Boston. 24pp. Boston, Archdiocesan Ecumenical Commission, 1967.

KEABLE, Gladys, *Squares in Circles; Reshaping the local Church*. 135pp. London, Darton, Longman and Todd, 1965.

LEE, Robert, *Church Co-operation of the Local Level through Comity*. With a foreword by Meryl Ruoss. 15pp. New York, Protestant Council of the City of New York, Department of Church Planning and Research, 1954.

Oekumene am Ort; Gedanken, Berichte und Vorschläge zur ökumenischen Arbeit in den Ortsgemeinden. Zusammengestellt von Ludwig Rott mit Beiträgen von

Nevill B. Cryer, Walter Fritz, etc. 44pp. (Oekumenische Arbeitshefte, 5). Kassel, Werkbrüder-Verlag, 1963.

PRICE, Hetley, and WAKEFIELD, Gordon S., *Unity at the Local Level*. 58pp. (Star books on reunion). Oxford, Mowbray, 1964.

ROSS, Roy G., *The Ecumenical Movement and the Local Church. A statement of imperative and suggested plans, as approved by the General Board, March 2, 1962*. 16pp. New York, N.C.C.C.U.S.A., 1962.

SANDERSON, Ross W., *Church Co-operation in the United States. The nation-wide backgrounds and ecumenical significance of state and local Councils of Churches in their historical perspectives*. 272pp. New York, Association of Council Secretaries, 1960.

SILLS, Horace S., ed., *Grassroots ecumenicity: Case studies in local Church consolidation*. 140pp. Philadelphia, United Church Press, 1967.

SLACK, Kenneth, *Growing Together Locally. Some suggestions as to how the ecumenical movement can be made a reality wherever Christians of different traditions are found together*. 40pp. London, B.C.C., 1958.

SLUSSER, Gerald H., *The Local Church in Transition; Theology, education, and ministry*. 204pp. Philadelphia, Westminster, 1964.

WIESER, Thomas, "A new ecumenical discussion on the congregation", in *Ecumenical Review*, vol. xvi (1963–4), no. 2, pp. 153–7.

WILLIAMS, Colin W., *For the World: A study book for local Churches. In preparation for the 1966 general assembly*. 64pp. New York, The National Council of Churches, 1965.

LAITY

BLISS, Kathleen, *We the People: A book about laity*. 139pp. London, S.C.M. Press, 1963.

CHENU, M. D., *Peuple de Dieu dans le monde*. 159pp. (Foi vivante, 35). Paris, Editions du Cerf, 1966.

CONGAR, Yves M. J., *Lay People in the Church: A study for a theology of laity*. 447pp. London, Bloomsbury Publishing Co., 1957. Translated from the French *Jalons pour une théologie du laicat*. German translation *Der Laie*.

GIBBS, Mark, and MORTON, T. Ralph, *God's Frozen People; A book for and about ordinary Christians*. 190pp. London, Collins, 1965.

God's People in Asian Industrial Society. The report of the East Asia Christian Conference on Christians in Industry and Lay Training. 198pp. Kyoto, Doshisha University School of Theology, 1967.

GRIMES, Howard, *The Rebirth of the Laity*. New York, Abingdon, 1962.

GRUPP, Kenneth G., *A Layman looks at the Church*. 190pp. London, Hodder and Stoughton, 1964.

KRAEMER, Hendrik, *A Theology of the Laity*. 192pp. London, Lutterworth, 1958.

Laici in Ecclesia. An ecumenical bibliography on the role of the laity in the life and mission of the Church. 107pp. Geneva, W.C.C., Department on the Laity, 1961.

The Laity: The Christian in his Vocation. An ecumenical survey prepared under the auspices of the W.C.C. 58pp. (Evanston surveys, 6). London, S.C.M. Press, 1954. French translation *Les laïcs*. German translation *Laienarbeit*.

Laity formation. Proceedings of the Ecumenical Consultation Gazzada (Italy), September 7–10, 1965; jointly sponsored by the Department on the Laity of the W.C.C. and the Permanent Committee for International Congresses of the Lay Apostolate. 94pp. Rome, Arti Grafiche Scalia, 1966.

Layman's Church, J. A. T. Robinson and others. 99pp. London, Lutterworth Press, 1963.

LÖFFLER, Paul, *The layman abroad in the mission of the church. A decade of discussion and experiment.* 96pp. (C.W.M.E., research pamphlets, no. 10). London, Edinburgh House Press, published for the W.C.C. Committee on World Mission and Evangelism, 1962.

ROLLET, Henri, *Les laïcs d'après le Concile.* 304pp. Paris, Editions de Gigord, 1965.

THURIAN, Max, *Consecration of the Layman; New approaches to the sacrament of confirmation.* 118pp. Baltimore, Dublin, Helicon Press, 1963. Translated from the French *La confirmation.*

WEBER, Hans-Ruedi, *The Militant Ministry: People and pastors of the early Church and today.* 108pp. Philadelphia, Board of Publication of the Lutheran Church in America, 1963.

WENTZ, Frederick K., *The Layman's Role Today.* 229pp. Garden City, N.Y., Doubleday, 1963.

STRUCTURES FOR MISSIONARY CONGREGATIONS

BRIDSTON, Keith, *Mission, Myth and Reality.* 128pp. New York, Friendship Press, 1965.

The Church for Others and the Church for the World: A quest for structures for missionary congregations. Final report of the Western European Working Group of the Department on Studies in Evangelism. 35pp. Geneva, W.C.C., 1967. German translation *Die Kirche für andere.*

GARDNER, E. Clinton, *The Church as a Prophetic Community.* 254pp. Philadelphia, The Westminster Press, 1967.

HILLMAN, Eugene, *The Church as Mission.* 144pp. London, Sheed and Ward, 1966.

MARGULL, Hans Jochen, *Mission als Strukturprinzip; ein Arbeitsbuch zur Frage missionarischer Gemeinden.* 246pp. Genf, Ö.R.K., 1965.

METZ, Donald L., *New congregations: Security and mission in conflict.* 170pp. Philadelphia, Westminster Press, 1967.

O'CONNOR, Elisabeth, *Call to Commitment.* 205pp. New York, Harper, 1963.

Structures for a Missionary Congregation. 123pp. Singapore, E.A.C.C., 1964.

WEBBER, George W., *The Congregation in Mission; Emerging structures for the Church in an urban society.* 208pp. New York, Abingdon Press, 1964.

WIESER, Thomas, ed., *Planning for Mission: Working papers on the new quest for missionary communities.* 230pp. New York, U.S. Conference for the W.C.C. 1966.

WILLIAMS, Colin W., *What in the World?* 105pp. New York, N.C.C.C.U.S.A., 1964.

WILLIAMS, Colin W., *Where in the World? Changing form of the church's witness.* 116pp. New York, N.C.C.C.U.S.A., 1963. German translation *Gemeinden für andere.*

HOUSE CHURCHES

"The Church in the House", in *Laity* (W.C.C.), no. 3, April 1957.

Die Gemeinde im Haus; Berichte über eine wiederentdeckte Lebensform der Kirche; mit Beiträgen von W. D. Cattanach, A. Klamer, Hilda Lehotsky, etc. 40pp. (Oekumenische Arbeitshefte, 3). Frankfurt a.M., Arbeitsgemeinschaft christlicher Kirchen in Deutschland, Ökumenische Zentrale, 1961.

HIRATA, Satoshi, "House Churches in Osaka", in *Laity* (W.C.C.), no. 18, 1964, pp. 45–8.

KLESSMANN, Ernst, *Die Hausgemeinde.* 56pp. (Handbücherei für Gemeindearbeit, 8). Gütersloher Verlagshaus Gerd Mohn, 1960.

MORTON, T. Ralph, "The House Church in Scotland", in *Frontier* (London, vol. 5, Spring 1962), pp. 342–4.

ORR, David C., *The House Church. An Iona Community Pamphlet.* Glasgow, Iona Community Publishing Department.

PERRY, John D., *The Coffee House Ministry.* 127pp. Richmond, Va., John Knox Press, 1966.

SOUTHCOTT, Ernest W., *The House Church.* 14pp. (Evangelism Broad Sheets, no. 1). London, B.C.C., n.d.

THOMAS, Donald F., *Manual for the Church in the Home. Procedures for the creation of small groups as outposts of the gathered Church.* 39pp. Valley Forge, Pa., American Baptist Home Mission Societies, Division of Evangelism. 1961.

TEAM MINISTRIES

BEESON, Trevor, ed., *Partnership in Ministry.* 148pp. London, A. R. Mowbray, 1964.

BUSIA, K. A., *Urban Churches in Britain: A question of relevance.* 173pp. (World studies of churches in mission). London, Lutterworth Press, 1966.

HUGHES, Robert, *Team Ministry.* For the team at St Mary's, Woolwich, Nicolas Stacey, Robert Hughes, and others. 16pp. Copies may be obtained from Mitre House, 177 Regent Street, London W.1.

JUDY, Marvin T., *The Co-operative Parish in Non-metropolitan Areas.* 208pp. Nashville, Abingdon Press, 1967.

JUDY, Marvin T., *The Larger Parish and Group Ministry.* Nashville, Abingdon Press, 1959.

KENRICK, Bruce, *Come Out the Wilderness.* 254pp. London, Collins, 1963.

O'CONNOR, Elisabeth, *Journey Inward, Journey Outward.* 175pp. New York, Harper, 1968.

Partners in Ministry. Being the report of the commission on the development and payment of the clergy. 112pp. Westminster, Church Information Office, 1967.

PAUL, Leslie, *The Deployment and Payment of the Clergy.* 311pp. Westminster, Church Information Office, 1964.

SMITH, Arthur C., *Team and Group Ministry.* 111pp. Westminster, Church Information Office, 1965.

VINAY, Tullio, *Agape: ein Wagnis der Hoffnung für unsere Zeit.* 64pp. Wuppertal-Barmen, John. Kiefel Verlag, 1966.

VINAY, Tullio, und VINAY, Gio, *Riesi; Geschichte eines christlichen Abenteuers.* Herausgegeben und bearbeitet von Reinhard W. Schmidt. 221pp. Stuttgart, Kreuz-Verlag, 1964.

CHAPTER 14

Signs of Radicalism in the Ecumenical Movement

CRITICISM OF THE ESTABLISHED CHURCH AND OF TRADITIONAL CHRISTIAN THEOLOGY

ADOLFS, Robert, *The Grave of God: Has the Church a future?* 157pp. New York
Harper, 1967. Translated from the Dutch *Het graf van God.*

BERGER, Peter L., *The Noise of Solemn Assemblies.* 189pp. Garden City, Doubleday,
1961.

BERTON, Pierre, *The Comfortable Pew: A critical look at Christianity and the religious establishment in the new age.* 158pp. Toronto, McClelland and Stewart,
1965.

BROCKWAY, Allan R., *The Secular Saint.* 238pp. Garden City, New York, Doubleday, 1968.

CALLAHAN, Daniel, *Honesty in the Church.* 188pp. London, Constable, 1965.

COX, Harvey, *The Secular City: Secularization and urbanization in theological
perspective.* 276pp. London, S.C.M. Press, 1965.

EAGLETON, Terence, *The New Left Church.* 180pp. London, Sheed and Ward, 1966.

EDWARDS, David L., ed., *The Honest to God Debate.* 287pp. London, S.C.M. Press,
1963.

FOSTER, John, *Requiem for a Parish: An inquiry into customary practices and procedures in the contemporary parish.* 155pp. Westminster, Maryland, Newman Press,
1962.

GILKEY, Langdon, *How the Church Can Minister to the World without Losing Itself.*
151pp. New York, Harper, 1964.

HOEKENDIJK, J. C., *The Church Inside Out.* 212pp. Philadelphia, Westminster Press,
1966. Translated from the Dutch *De Kerk binnenste buiten.*

KEABLE, Gladys, *Squares in Circles: Reshaping the local Church.* 135pp. London,
Darton, Longman and Todd, 1965.

LOHSE, Jens M., *Kirche ohne Kontakte? Beziehungsformen in einem Industrieraum.*
212pp. Stuttgart, Kreuz Verlag, 1967.

MARTY, Martin E., ed., *Death and Birth of the Parish.* Martin E. Marty, editor and
author with Paul R. Biegner, Roy Blumhorst and Kenneth R. Young. 163pp.
St Louis, Concordia, 1964.

MARTY, Martin E., *The New Shape of American Religion.* 180pp. New York,
Harper, 1959.

MATTHES, Joachim, *Die Emigration der Kirche aus der Gesellschaft.* 113pp. Hamburg, Furche-Verlag, 1964.

METZ, Donald L., *New Congregations: Security and mission in conflict.* 170pp.
Philadelphia, Westminster, 1967.

PIKE, James A., *If This be Heresy.* 205pp. New York, Harper, 1967.

ROBINSON, John A. T., *Honest to God.* 143pp. London, S.C.M. Press, 1963.

ROBINSON, John A. T., *The New Reformation?* 142pp. London, S.C.M. Press, 1965.

ROSE, Stephen C., *The Grassroots Church: A manifesto for Protestant renewal.*
Introduction by Harvey Cox. 174pp. New York, Holt, Rinehart and Winston,
1966.

SCHULTZ, Hans Juergen, ed., *Kritik an der Kirche.* 335pp. Stuttgart, Kreuz Verlag,
1960.

STAMMLER, Eberhard, *Churchless Protestants*. 223pp. Philadelphia, Westminster, 1964. Translated from the German *Protestanten ohne Kirche*.

THIELICKE, Helmut, *The Trouble with the Church: A call for renewal*, translated and edited by John W. Doberstein. 136pp. New York, Harper, 1965. Translated from the German *Leiden an der Kirche*.

Who's Killing the Church? ed. Stephen C. Rose. 141pp. Chicago, Renewal Magazine, 1966.

WINTER, Gibson, *The new creation as metropolis*. 152pp. New York, London, Macmillan, 1963.

WINTER, Gibson, *The suburban captivity of the churches: An analysis of Protestant responsibility in the expanding metropolis*. 216pp. New York, Doubleday, 1961.

WORLD STUDENT CHRISTIAN FEDERATION

Students and the Life and Mission of the Church. A report on the World Student Christian Federation, 1956–1964. 108pp. Geneva, W.S.C.F., 1965.

Unto a Lively Hope. A report on the life of the World's Student Christian Federation and related National Student Christian Movements during the years 1946–1949. 127pp. Geneva, W.S.C.F., 1950.

Witnessing in the University Communities. A report of the World's Student Christian Federation and related National Student Christian Movements during the years 1949 to 1952. 88pp. Geneva, W.S.C.F., 1953.

Witnessing to Jesus Christ the Reconciler. A report on the life of the W.S.C.F. and related national S.C.M.s during the years 1953–1956. 142pp. Geneva, W.S.C.F., 1957.

WORLD ALLIANCE OF Y.M.C.A.s AND WORLD Y.W.C.A.

ANDERSON, Paul B., *A Study of Orthodoxy and the Y.M.C.A.* Geneva, World Alliance of Y.M.C.A.s, 1963.

And Now—Tomorrow. Report of the World Y.M.C.A. Conferences, Paris, France, August 1955. Geneva, World Alliance of Y.M.C.A.s, 1955.

Basic Issues in Y.M.C.A. Ecumenical Policy and Practice. Geneva, World Alliance of Y.M.C.A.s, 1962.

Called to New Things: Report of the 3rd meeting of the World Council of Y.M.C.A.s, Geneva, Switzerland, July 1961. Geneva, World Alliance of Y.M.C.A.s, 1961.

History of the World's Alliance of Y.M.C.A.s, C. P. Shedd and other contributors. London, S.P.C.K., 1955.

Into All the World. Report of the 2nd meeting of the World Council of Y.M.C.A.s, Kassell, Germany, July 1957. Geneva, World Alliance of Y.M.C.A.s, 1957.

Meeting of Y.M.C.A. Leaders of Roman Catholic Confession, Geneva, July 1961. Geneva, World Alliance of Y.M.C.A.s, 1961.

Report of the Consultation on Ecumenical Policy and Practice for Lay Christian Movements, St Cergue, Switzerland, July 1962. Geneva, World Alliance of Y.M.C.A.s and World Y.W.C.A., 1962.

Varieties of Service but the Same Lord. Report of 4th meeting of the World Council of Y.M.C.A.s, Tozanso, Japan, August 1965. Geneva, World Alliance of Y.M.C.A.s, 1965.

WORLD COUNCIL OF CHURCHES YOUTH DEPARTMENT AND ECUMENICAL YOUTH CONFERENCES

Christ the Life. The report of the Asian Christian Youth Assembly, ed. Soritúa A. E. Nabadan. 130pp. Silliman University, Dumaguete City, 1965.

Ecumenical Youth Assembly in Europe, Lausanne, 1960, ed. Rod French. 91pp. (Youth no. 2, October 1960). Geneva, W.C.C., Youth Department, 1960.

Footprints in Travancore. Report of the Third World Conference of Christian Youth, December 11–26, 1952. 95pp. Coonoor, Nilgiris, India Sunday School Union, 1953.

HEUVEL, Albert H. van den, ed., *The New Creation and the New Generation: A forum for youth workers*. 128pp. New York, Friendship Press, 1965.

North American Youth Assembly, Ann Arbor, 1961, ed. Rod French. 50pp. (Youth no. 4, November 1961). Geneva, W.C.C., Youth Department, 1961.

Risk. Published by the Youth Department of the World Council of Churches, vol. 1, 1965—.

INDUSTRIAL MISSION

EDWARDS, David L., ed., *Priests and Workers: An Anglo-French Discussion*. 160pp. London, S.C.M. Press, 1961.

Priest and worker. The Autobiography of Henry Perrin. 247pp. London, Macmillan, 1965. Translated from the French *Itinéraire de Henri Perrin*.

ROWE, John, *Priests and Workers: A refounder*. 78pp. London, Darton, Longman and Todd, 1965.

SIEFER, Gregor, *The Church and Industrial Society*. 355pp. London, Darton, Longman and Todd, 1964. Translated from the German *Die Mission der Arbeiterpriester*.

SYMANOWSKI, Horst, *The Christian Witness in an Industrial Society*. 160pp. Philadelphia, Westminster Press, 1964. Translated from the German *Gegen die Weltfremdheit*.

TAYLOR, Richard, *Christians in an Industrial Society*. 128pp. London, S.C.M. Press, 1961.

VELTEN, Georges, *Mission in Industrial France*. London, S.C.M. Press, 1968.

WICKHAM, E. R., *Church and People in an Industrial City*. 292pp. London, Lutterworth Press, 1957.

WINTER, Gibson, *The New Creation as Metropolis*. 152pp. New York, Macmillan, 1963.

EVANGELICAL ACADEMIES AND LAY TRAINING CENTRES

Centres of Renewal for Study and Lay Training. 64pp. Geneva, W.C.C., Dept. on the Laity, 1964.

Directory of Lay Training Centres. 2 vols. Geneva, W.C.C., Dept. on the Laity, 1962–3.

DOEHRING, Johannes, ed., *Die Gemeinde in der modernen Gesellschaft*. Loccum, Evangelical Academy Loccum, 1960.

Evangelical Academies in the German Federal Republic. 77pp. Publilhed by the Directors' Association of the Evangelical Academies in Germany, Inc., 1966. Translated from the German *Evangelische Akademien in der Bundersrepublik Deutschland*.

FRAKES, Margaret, *Bridges to Understanding: The "Academy Movement" in Europe and North America.* 134pp. Philadelphia, Muhlenberg Press, 1960.
GABLE, Lee J., *Church and World Encounter: The Evangelical Academies in Germany and their meaning for the ecumenical Church.* 111pp. Philadelphia, United Church Press, 1964.
HARTMAN, Olov, *The Sigtuna Foundation.* 54pp. London, S.C.M. Press, 1955.
KOLLER, Martin, ed., *A New Road in Germany: Evangelical academy.* Hamburg, Furche Verlag, 1956.
Signs of Renewal: The life of the lay institute in Europe, ed. Hans-Ruedi Weber. 63pp. Geneva, W.C.C., Dept. on the Laity, 1956. German translation *Zeichen des Aufbruchs.*
WEBER, Hans-Ruedi, *Salty Christians: A handbook for leaders of lay training courses.* 43pp. Geneva, W.C.C., Dept. on the Laity, 1962.

IONA COMMUNITY

MACLEOD, George F., *Only One Way Left.* Glasgow, Iona Community, 1956.
MORTON, T. Ralph, *The Community of Faith.* U.S. edn. with added chapters by Alexander Miller and John O. Nelson. New York, Association Press, 1954. English edn. *The Household of Faith* (1951).
MORTON, T. Ralph, *The Iona Community Story.* 96pp. London, Lutterworth Press, 1957.

ORDERS

BRUMMET, Jacob, *Die Kirche ist immer jung.* München, J. Pfeiffer, 1960.
Frauen entdecken ihren Auftrag. Weibliche Diakonie im Wandel eines Jahrhunderts. Dargestellt von Hermann Schauer. 252 pp. Göttingen, Vandenhoeck und Ruprecht, 1960.
PERCHENET,. Annie, *Renouveau communautaire et unité chrétienne. Regards sur les communautés anglicanes et protestantes.* 479pp. Paris, Mame, 1967.
PRÄGER, Lydia, *Frei für Gott und die Menschen. Evangelische Bruder- und Schwesternschaften der Gegenwart in Selbstdarstellungen.* 591pp. Stuttgart, Quell-Verlag der Evang. Gesellschaft, 1964.
WYON, Olive, *Living springs: New religious movements in Western Europe,* 28pp. London, S.C.M. Press, 1963.

TAIZÉ

The Eucharistic liturgy of Taizé. With an introductory essay by Max Thurian. 85pp. London, Faith Press, 1962. Translated from the French *Eucharistie à Taizé.*
HEIJKE, John, *An Ecumenical Light on the Renewal of Religious Community Life, Taizé.* 203pp. Pittsburgh, Pa., Duquesne University Press, 1967.
PAUPERT, Jean-Marie, *Taizé et l'Église de demain.* 268pp. (Le Signe, grandes études oecuméniques). Paris, Fayard, 1967.
The Rule of Taizé in French and English. 78pp. Taizé, Presses de Taizé, 1961.
"Taizé, 25 ans de communauté, 25 ans d'oecuménisme", in *Fêtes et saisons,* no. 191. January 1965. 28pp.

GRANDCHAMP

Communauté de Grandchamp. 16pp. Lausanne, Imprimerie Centrale, 1959.

SJALOOM MOVEMENT

De tafel van één. Leren rekennen met een nieuwe wereld. Een documentaire van de sjaloomgroep. 204pp. Utrecht, Ambo, 1967.
Sjaloom (Den Haag), vol. 1, 1964—.

AKTION SÜHNEZEICHEN

Skriver, Ansgar, *Aktion Sühnezeichen. Brücken über Blut und Asche.* 150pp. Stuttgart, Kreuz-Verlag, 1962.

ALL CHRISTIAN PEACE ASSEMBLY

Prague 1–4 June 1958

Task and Witness. Christian Peace Conference. 87pp. Prague, Ecumenical Institute of the Comenius Faculty, 1958.

Prague 1960

The Only Future. Documents of the Third Session of the Christian Peace Conference 134pp. Prague, 1960.

Prague 13–18 June 1961

... And on earth peace. Documents of the First All Christian Peace Assembly, Prague, 1962. 190pp.

Prague 28 June–3 July 1964

Documents and Informations from the Second All Christian Peace Assembly. Prague. International Secretariat of the Christian Peace Conference, 1965. 147pp. 48pp.

Christian Peace Conference. Published by the International Secretariat of the Christian Peace Conference. Praha 1, Jungmannova 9. Bi-monthly.
Hudak, Adalbert, *Die Prager Friedenskonferenz; Kirche und kommunistischer Totalstaat in der Begegnung.* 47pp. München, Bergstadt-Verlag Wilh. Gottl. Korn, 1964.

Bibliography of the Ecumenical Movement and the World Council of Churches 1968-1985

This is an updated bibliography, and includes the major publications on ecumenical developments since 1968, dealing with the life and activities of the World Council of Churches, regional developments in the ecumenical movement, and current concerns of the Orthodox Churches and the Roman Catholic Church in the area of ecumenism.

But the bibliography, like the previous bibliography covering the years 1948-68, is necessarily selective. There are a great many books and pamphlets — not to mention articles in periodicals — and a wealth of stencilled and off-set literature and archival material not included here. Nor does it list translations of the reports of assemblies and major conferences and other official publications.

For more detailed bibliographical information readers should consult the *Classified Catalogue of the Ecumenical Movement*, 1972, 2 volumes; 1981 First Supplement (Boston: G.K. Hall and Co.); *The International Ecumenical Bibliography*, 1962-77 (München: Chr. Kaiser Verlag; Mainz: Matthias-Grünewald-Verlag); the *Répertoire Bibliographique des Institutions Chrétiennes*, 1968- (Strasbourg: CERDIC-Publications). These reference works also contain extensive bibliographical information on other ecumenical subjects and concerns not covered in this bibliography.

Geneva, July 1986   Ans J. van der Bent

General Surveys

THE GENERAL ECUMENICAL DEVELOPMENT SINCE 1968

Bloch-Hoell, Nils E. *Okumenikk. Fakta og Meniger*. Oslo: Gyldendal Norsk Forlag, 1976. 167pp.

Congar, Yves. *Essais oecuméniques: Le mouvement, les hommes, les problèmes*. Paris: Le Centurion, 1984. 316pp.

Crow, Paul A. *Christian Unity: Matrix for Mission*. New York: Friendship Press, 1982. 119pp.

Davies, Rupert E. *The Church in Our Times*. An Ecumenical History from a British Perspective. London: Epworth, 1979. 132pp.

Desseaux, Jacques Elisée. *Vingt siècles d'histoire œcuménique*. Paris: Ed. du Cerf, 1983. 110pp.

Dias, Patrick V. *Vielfalt der Kirche in der Vielfalt der Jünger, Zeugen und Diener*. Freiburg: Herder, 1968. 407pp. (Ökumenische Forschungen, Ekklesiologische Abteilung, 2).

Ecumene. By Cesare Vasoli, Hans Küng, Carlo Molari and others. Roma: Jouvence, 1983. 112pp. (La Nuova Critica, XVII Serie).

Ecumenical Methodology. Documentation and Report. Ed. by Peder Hoejen. Geneva: LWF, 1978. 129pp.

Ecumenismo anni '80. Verona: Il Segno Editrice, 1984. 420pp.

Ecumenismo oggi. Bilancio e prospettive. Asti: Ed. L.D.C., 1976. 416pp.

Fahlbusch, Erwin. *Kirchenkunde der Gegenwart.* Stuttgart: Kohlhammer, 1979. 288pp.

Fiolet, Herman A. *De Kerk op de kruispunten van de geschiedenis: Onmacht en Uitdaging.* Baarn: Ten Have, 1982. 142pp. (Oekumene, 3).

Fox, Helmut. *Ökumene, Hoffnung oder Illusion?* Eine Katholische Bilanz. Trier: Spee-Verlag, 1974. 168pp.

Frost, Francis. *Œcuménisme.* Paris: Letouzey et Ané, 1984. 99pp.

Für Willem A. Visser 't Hooft zum 80. Geburtstag. Mit Beiträgen von Nikos A. Nissiotis, Lukas Vischer, Heinrich Stirnimann, Vitali Borovoy and others. In: Reformatio, 1980. 106pp.

Gleixner, Christine. *Ökumene heute.* Eine Orientierungshilfe. Wien: Verlag Herold, 1980. 232pp.

Goodall, Norman. *Ecumenical Progress. A Decade of Change in the Ecumenical Movement, 1961-1971.* London: Oxford University Press, 1972. 173pp.

Heel de kerk. Een oekumenisch werkboek. Door A Houtepen, P. van Leeuwen, J. Roes, J. Roos, A van de Weijer. Ingeleid door N.K. van den Akker. Hilversum: Gooi en Sticht, 1977. 208pp.

Huelin, Gordon. *The Church and the Churches.* London: Sheldon Press, 1970. 87pp.

Une introduction à l'œcuménisme. Paris: Secrétariat national pour l'unité des chrétiens, 1982. 43pp.

Die Kirche im Gespräch der Kirchen. Ökumenische Themen, ausgewählt und eingeleitet vom Ökumenischen Institut Berlin. Berlin: Evangelische Verlagsanstalt, 1975. 286pp.

Kirchen auf gemeinsamen Wegen. Ed. by Johannes J. Degenhardt, Heinrich Tenhumberg, Hans Thimme. Bielefeld: Luther Verlag, 1977, 200pp.

Krüger, Hanfried. *Ökumenische Bewegung 1965-1968.* Stuttgart: Evang. Missionverlag, 1970. 172pp. (Ökumenische Rundschau, Beihefte, 12-13)

Krüger, Hanfried. *Ökumenische Bewegung 1969-1972.* Stuttgart: Evang. Missionverlag, 1973. 193pp. (Ökumenische Rundschau, Beihefte, 28).

Krüger, Hanfried. *Ökumenische Bewegung 1973-1974.* Stuttgart: Evang. Missionsverlag, 1975. (Ökumenische Rundschau, Beihefte, 29).

Lehmann, Wolfgang. *Kirche im Schmelzprozess. Berichte über zehn Frankfurter Gespräche.* Wuppertal: Verlag R. Brockhaus, 1969. 151pp.

Macquarrie, John. *Christian Unity and Christian Diversity.* London: SCM Press, 1975. 118pp.

Minus, Paul M. *The Catholic Rediscovery of Protestantism. A History of Roman Catholic Ecumenical Pioneering.* New York: Paulist Press, 1976. 261pp.

Müller-Römheld, Walter. *Zueinander — Miteinander. Kirchliche Zusammenarbeit im 20. Jahrhundert.* Frankfurt am Main: Lembeck Verlag, 1971. 196pp.

Neill, Stephen. *The Church and Christian Union.* London: Oxford University Press, 1968. 423pp.

Neuner, Peter. *Kleines Handbuch der Ökumene.* Düsseldorf: Patmos Verlag, 1984. 184pp.

Oecumene. Utrecht: Ambo, 1968. 144pp.

L'œcuménisme. Ambilly: Le Monde religieux, 1975. 276pp.

L'œcuménisme. Pierre Struve, René Beaupère, Maurice Ferrier-Welti. Tours: Mame, 1968. 166pp. (Eglises en dialogue, 7).

L'œcuménisme. Unité chrétienne et identité confessionnelle. Paris: Beauchesne, 1985. 123pp.

Ökumenische Gestalten. Brückenbauer der Einen Kirche. Hrsg. von Günther Gloede. Berlin: Evangelische Verlagsanstalt, 1974. 373pp.

Ökumenische Spannungen. Philip Potter, Konrad Raiser, Ian M. Fraser and others. Göttingen: Vandenhoeck & Ruprecht, 1974. 80pp. (Wissenschaft und Praxis in Kirche und Gesellschaft, Heft 4, April 1974).

Orientierung Ökumene. Ein Handbuch. Im Auftrag der Theologischen Studienabteilung beim Bund der Evangelischen Kirchen in der DDR, hrsg. von Hans-Martin Moderow und Matthias Sens. Berlin: Evangelische Verlagsanstalt, 1979. 342pp.

Our Common History as Christians. Essays in Honour of Albert C. Outler. Ed. by John Deschner, Leroy T. Howe, and Klaus Penzel. New York: Oxford University Press, 1975. 298pp.

Powers, Edward A. *In Essentials, Unity*. An Ecumenical Sampler. New York: Friendship Press, 1982. 119pp.

Rusch, William G. *Ecumenism — A Movement Toward Church Unity*. Philadelphia: Fortress Press, 1985. 133pp.

Schütte, Heinz. *Ziel-Kirchengemeinschaft: Zur ökumenischen Orientierung*. Paderborn: Verlag Bonifatius, 1985. 207pp.

Theologie in Entstehen. Beiträge zum ökumenischen Gespräch im Spannungsfeld kirchlicher Situationen. Hrsg. von Lukas Vischer. München: Kaiser, 1976. 144pp.

Theologischer Konsens und Kirchenspaltung. Hrsg. von Peter Lengsfeld und Heinz-Günther Stobbe. Stuttgart: Kohlhammer, 1981. 174pp.

Torrance, Thomas F. *Theology in Reconciliation*. Essays Towards Evangelical and Catholic Unity in East and West. Grand Rapids: Wm. B. Eerdmans, 1976. 302pp.

Towards Christian Unity. A Symposium. Ed. by Bernhard Leeming. London: Geoffrey Chapman, 1968. 167pp.

Unity: The Next Step? Ed. by Peter Morgan. With contributions by David L. Edwards, Michael Turnbull and others. London: SPCK, 1972. 91pp.

Vismann, Dieter. *Ökumene*. Hannover: Lutherhaus Verlag, 1980. 140pp.

Voies vers l'unité. Colloque organisé à l'occasion de l'éméritat de Mgr Gustave Thils. Louvain-la-Neuve, 27-28 avril 1979. Louvain-la-Neuve: Faculté de Théologie, 1981. 102pp.

Wainwright, Geoffrey. *The Ecumenical Movement. Crisis and Opportunity for the Church*. Grand Rapids: Wm. B. Eerdmans, 1983. 263pp.

Weinberg, Karl. *Ende der Konfessionen. Eins in Christus*. München: Profil Verlag, 1985. 110pp.

Welche Ökumene meinen wir? Eine Bilanz der Ökumene seit Nairobi. Mit Beiträgen von Richard Boeckler, Johannes Brosseder, Reinhard Frieling, Peter Lengsfeld, Harding Meyer, Otmar Schultz and others. Frankfurt am Main: Lembeck Verlag, 1978. 120pp. (Ökumenische Rundschau, Beihefte, 32).

Whale, J.S. *Christian Reunion. Historic Divisions Reconsidered*. London: Lutterworth Press, 1971. 141pp.

What Unity Implies. Six Essays after Uppsala. Ed. by Reinhard Groscurth. Geneva. WCC, 1969. 135pp. (World Council of Churches Studies, 7).

INTERPRETATIVE INTRODUCTIONS

Against the World for the World. The Hartford Appeal and the Future of American Religion. Ed. by Peter L. Berger and Richard J. Neuhaus. New York: Seabury Press, 1976. 164pp.

Beaupère René. *La trame de l'œcuménisme*. Paris: Editions œcuméniques, 1970. 5 vols.

Begegnung. Beiträge zu einer Hermeneutik des theologischen Gesprächs. Festschrift für Heinrich Fries. Hrsg. von Max Seckler, Otto Pesch, Johannes Brosseder, Wolfhart Pannenberg. Wien: Verlag Styria, 1972. 839pp.

Bent, Ans J. van der. *God So Loves the World. The Immaturity of World Christianity*. Maryknoll: Orbis Books, 1979. 150pp.

Bent, Ans J. van der. *Incarnation and New Creation. The Ecumenical Movement at the Crossroads*. Madras: Christian Literature Society, 1985. 171pp.

Bent, Ans J. van der. *Major Studies and Themes in the Ecumenical Movement*. Geneva: WCC, 1980.

Bent, Ans J. van der. *Theology — Miserable and Wonderful*. Some Personal Reflections in European and Asian Contexts. Madras: Christian Literature Society, 1982. 170pp.

Bent, Ans J. van der. *Vital Ecumenical Concerns. A Collection of Sixteen Historical, Analytical and Documentary Surveys*. Geneva: WCC, 1986, 333pp.

Biehler, Ekkehard. *Der Umbruch theologischen Denkens in der Ökumene zwischen New-Delhi und Uppsala*. Berlin: Kirchliche Hochschule, 1974. 201pp.

Boegner, Marc. *The Long Road to Unity*. Memories and Anticipations. London: Collins, 1970. 416pp.

Boss, Gerhard. *Ökumene — Fragen und Antworten*. Anregungen zum ökumenischen Gespräch. Düsseldorf: Verlag Haus Altenberg, 1970. 179pp.

Boyd, Robin. *Ecumenism, Threat or Promise?* Dublin: Irish School of Ecumenics, 1981. 15pp.

Brown, Robert McAfee. *Frontiers for the Church Today*. New York: Oxford University Press, 1973. 149pp.

Brunner, Peter. *Bemühungen um die einigende Wahrheit*. Aufsätze. Göttingen: Vandenhoeck und Ruprecht, 1977. 292pp.

Chenu, Bruno; Neusch, Marcel. *Au pays de la théologie. A la découverte des hommes et des courants*. Paris: Le Centurion, 1979. 199pp.

Congar, Yves. *Une passion: l'unité*. Réflections et souvenirs, 1929-1973. Paris: Ed. du Cerf, 1974. 117pp.

Contemporary Christian Trends. Perspectives on the Present. Ed. By William M. Pinson. Waco: Texas Word Books, 1972. 217pp.

Coventry, John. *Reconciling*. London: SCM Press, 1985. 136pp.

Desseaux, Jacques Elisée. *Dialogues théologiques et accords œcuméniques*. Paris: Ed. du Cerf, 1982. 199pp.

Directions. Theology in a Changing Church. Dublin: APCK, 1970. 255pp.

Duchrow, Ulrich. *Conflict over the Ecumenical Movement. Confessing Christ Today in the Universal Church*. Geneva: WCC, 1981. 443pp.

Fiolet, Herman A. *Ecumenical Breakthrough. An Integration of the Catholic and the Reformed Faith*. Pittsburgh, PA: Duquesne University Press, 1969. 475pp.

Fries, Heinrich. *Ökumene statt Konfessionen? Das Ringen der Kirche um Einheit*. Frankfurt am Main: J. Knecht, 1977. 168pp.

The Future of Ecumenism. Ed. by Hans Küng. New York: Paulist Press, 1969. (Concilium, 44)

Göllner, Reinhard. *Der Beitrag des Romanwerks Gertrud von le Forts zum ökumenischen Gespräch.* Paderborn: Verlag Bonifatius, 1973. 154pp.

Goodall, Norman. *Second Fiddle. Recollections and Reflections.* London: SPCK, 1979. 168pp.

Herbst, Karl. *Jenseits aller Ansprüche. Neue ökumenische Perspektiven.* Mit Nachworten von Anton Antweiler und Norbert Greinacher. München: J. Pfeiffer, 1972. 232pp.

Huber, Wolfgang. *Der Streit um die Wahrheit und die Fähigkeit zum Frieden.* Vier Kapitel ökumenischer Theologie. München: Kaiser, 1980. 147pp.

Jungclaussen, Emmanuel. *Die grössere Ökumene. Gespräch um Friedrich Heiler.* Regensburg: Verlag Friedrich Pustet, 1970. 101pp.

Krüger, Hanfried. *Ökumenischer Katechismus.* Eine kurze Einführung in Wesen, Werden und Wirken der Ökumeme. Frankfurt: Evangelisches Verlagswerk, 1985. 92pp.

May, John. *Sprache der Ökumene — Sprache der Einheit.* Die Einheit der Menschheit: zukünftige Grundlage der theologischen Ethik der Katholischen Kirche und des Oekumenischen Rates der Kirchen. Bonn: Linguistica Biblica, 1976. 521pp.

Metz, Johann Baptist. *Reform und Gegenreformation heute. Zwei Thesen zur ökumenischen Situation der Kirchen.* Mainz: Matthias-Grünewald Verlag, 1969. 44pp.

Newbigin, Lesslie. *The Other Side of 1984.* Questions for the Churches. Geneva: WCC, 1983. 75pp. (Risk Book Series, No. 18).

Newbigin, Leslie. *Unfinished Agenda. An Autobiography.* London: SPCK, 1985. 263pp.

No Man is Alien. Essays on the Unity of Mankind in Honour of Willem Adolf Visser 't Hooft. Ed. by J. Robert Nelson. Leiden: Brill, 1971. 334pp.

Oecumenica. An Annual Symposium of Ecumenical Research. Ed. by Friedrich Wilhelm Kantzenbach and Vilmos Vajta. Neuchâtel: Delachaux et Niestlé, 1968, 1970, 1971, 1972.

Ökumene: Möglichkeiten und Grenzen heute. Oscar Cullmann zum achtzigsten Geburtstag, 1982. Hrsg. von Karlfried Froehlich. Tübingen: Mohr, 1982. 173pp.

Oekumene verändert die Kirchen. Beiträge von Helmut Hild, Christian Hübener und André Appel. Göttingen: Vandenhoeck und Ruprecht, 1976. 50pp.

Ökumenische Theologie. Ein Arbeitsbuch. Hrsg. von Peter Lengsfeld. Stuttgart: Kohlhammer, 1980. 508pp.

Pluralisme et œcuménisme en recherches théologiques. Mélanges offerts au R.P. Dockx, O.P. par Y. Congar, N. Zernov et al. Gembloux: Duculot, 1976. 314pp.

Post-Ecumenical Christianity. Ed. by Hans Küng. New York: Herder and Herder, 1970. 160pp. (Concilium, 54).

Potter, Philip A. *Life in All its Fulness.* Geneva: WCC, 1981. 173pp.

Richter, Hans-Friedemann. *Die Kommende Ökumene. Theologische Untersuchungen.* Zum 25.jährigen Bestehen des Ökumenischen Seminars an der Kirchlichen Hochschule Berlin. Festschrift für Jürgen W. Winterhager. Wuppertal: Verlag Rolf Brockhaus, 1972. 288pp.

Roux, Hébert. *De la désunion vers la communion.* Un itinéraire pastoral et œcuménique. Paris: Le Centurion, 1978. 311pp.

Scheele, Paul-Werner. *Alle eins: Theologische Beiträge II.* Paderborn: Verlag Bonifatius, 1979. 269pp.

Schmidt-Clausen, Kurt. *Reformation als ökumenisches Ereignis*. Reden und Aufsätze zu Themen der ökumenischen Bewegung. Berlin: Lutherisches Verlagshaus, 1970. 331pp.

Schrey, Heinz-Horst. *Christliche Daseinsgestaltung*. *Ökumenische Stellungnahmen zu Fragen der Gegenwart*. Bremen: C. Schünemann, 1971. 617pp.

Stobbe, Heinz Günther. *Hermeneutik — ein ökumenisches Problem*. Eine Kritik der katholischen Gadamer-Rezeption. Zürich: Benziger, 1981. 178pp.

Till, Barry. *The Churches Search for Unity*. Harmondsworth, Middlesex: Penguin Books, 1972. 556pp.

Unterwegs zur Einheit. Festschrift für Heinrich Stirnimann. Hrsg. von Johannes Brantschen und Pietro Selvatico. Freiburg: Universitätsverlag, 1980. 942pp.

Until He Comes. A Study in the Progress Toward Christian Unity. Ed. by Nicolas Lash. Dayton, Ohio: Pflaum Press, 1968. 223pp.

Vischer, Lukas. *Ökumenische Skizzen*. Zwölf Beiträge. Frankfurt am Main: Lembeck Verlag, 1972. 246pp.

Visser 't Hooft, Willem Adolf. *Has the Ecumenical Movement a Future?* Belfast: Christian Journals Limited, 1974. 97pp.

Visser 't Hooft, Willem Adolf. *Memoirs*. London: SCM press, 1973. 379pp.

Voices of Unity. Essays in Honour of Willem Adolf Visser 't Hooft on the Occasion of His 80th Birthday. Ed. by Ans J. van der Bent. Geneva: WCC, 1981. 101pp.

Zukunft der Ökumene. Drei Vorträge von Heinrich Stirnimann, Willem Adolf Visser 't Hooft, Hans Jochen Margull. Freiburg: Universitätsverlag, 1974. 42pp. (Ökumenische Beihefte, 7).

Die Zukunft des Ökumenismus. Mit Beiträgen von Per Lonning, Georges Casalis, Bernhard Hering und einer Einleitung von Günther Gassmann. Frankfurt am Main: Otto Lembeck, 1972. 109pp. (Ökumenische Perspektiven, 1).

Books about the World Council of Churches

Bent, Ans J. van der. *Six Hundred Ecumenical Consultations, 1948-1982*. Geneva: WCC, 1983. 246pp.

Bent, Ans J. van der. *The Utopia of World Community*. An Interpretation of the World Council of Churches for Outsiders. London: SCM Press, 1973. 150pp.

Bent, Ans J. van der. *What in the World is the World Council of Churches?* With an Interview with Philip Potter. Geneva: WCC, 1978. 4th printing, 1983. 90pp.

Bock, Paul. *In Search of a Responsible World Society*. The Social Teachings of the World Council of Churches. Philadelphia: Westminster Press, 1974. 251pp.

Bouman, Johan. *Der Glaube an das Menschenmögliche*. Der Ökumenische Rat der Kirchen und der Friede. Giessen: Brunnen Verlag, 1984. 69pp.

Brash, Alan A. *The World Council of Churches*. Geneva: WCC, 1978. 34pp.

Chappuis, Jean-Marc. *Divisions des chrétiens ou service de l'unité? Jalons pour interpréter l'action du Conseil œcuménique des Eglises*. Genève: Labor et Fides, 1979. 57pp.

Chenu, Bruno. *La signification ecclésiologique du Conseil œcuménique des Eglises, 1945-1963*. Thèse de doctorat en théologie. Paris: Beauchesne, 1972. 418pp.

Constitution and Rules of the World Council of Churches as Approved by the Vth
Assembly at Nairobi and Amended by the Central Committee at Geneva, 28 July to 6
August 1977. Geneva: WCC, 1977. 32pp.

Faith and Faithfulness. Essays on Contemporary Ecumenical Themes. A Tribute to
Philip A. Potter. Ed. by Pauline Webb. Geneva: WCC, 1984. 128pp.

Fuerth, Patrick W. *The Concept of Catholicity in the Documents of the World Council of
Churches 1948-1968*. A Historical Study with Systematic-Theological Reflections.
Roma: Editrice Anselmiana, 1973. 291pp.

García Hernando, Julián. *El Consejo Ecuménico de las Iglesias. Ante la Asamblea de
Vancouver 1983*. Madrid: Centro Ecuménico "Misionarias de la Unidad", 1982.
64pp.

Handbook of Member Churches of the World Council of Churches. Ed. by Ans J. van der
Bent. Geneva: WCC, 1982. 1985 (revised edition). 281pp.

Howell, Leon. *Acting in Faith. The World Council of Churches since 1975*. Geneva,
WCC, 1982. 120pp.

The Human Face of the World Council of Churches. London: The Methodist Church
Overseas Division, 1981. 32pp.

Payne, Ernest A. *The World Council of Churches, 1948-1969*. London: The Baptist
Union of Great Britain and Ireland, 1970. 20pp.

Rowe, Richard C. *Bible Study in the World Council of Churches*. Geneva: WCC, 1969.
81pp. (CWME Research Pamphlets, 16).

Runia, K. *De Wereldraad in Discussie*. Met reacties van E. Flesseman-van Leer, H.
Berkhof, A.H. van den Heuvel. Kampen: J.H. Kok, 1978. 184pp.

Schrotenboer, Paul G. *The Social Teaching of the World Council of Churches*. Grand
Rapids: Reformed Ecumenical Synod, 1978. 31pp.

Visser 't Hooft, Willem Adolf. *The Genesis and Formation of the World Council of
Churches*. Geneva: WCC, 1982. 130pp.

Wegener-Feuter, Hildburg. *Kirche und Ökumene*. Das Kirchenbild des Ökumenischen
Rates der Kirchen nach den Vollversammlungsdokumenten von 1948-1968.
Göttingen: Vandenhoek und Ruprecht, 1979. 306pp.

The World Council of Churches and the Churches. By Anna Marie Aagaard, Johannes
M. Aagaard and others. Aarhus: IDOC, 1969. 94pp.

The Life and Activities of the World Council of Churches

Fifth Assembly: Nairobi 1975

Breaking Barriers, Nairobi 1975. The Official Report of the Fifth Assembly of the
World Council of Churches, Nairobi, 23 November-10 December 1975. Ed. by
David M. Paton. London: SPCK; Grand Rapids: Wm. B. Eerdmans, 1976. 411pp.

Dat was Nairobi. H.A.M. Fiolet, Hendrik Greven, A.H. van den Heuvel, H.M. de
Lange, D.C. Mulder. 's-Gravenhage: Boekencentrum, 1976. 112pp.

Eenheid door bevrijding: Jesus Christus bevrijdt en verenigt. A.H. van den Heuvel, H.
Berkhof, H.A. Fiolet and others. Kampen: Kok, 1975. 109pp.

Jesus Christ Frees and Unites. World Council of Churches, Fifth Assembly Jakarta,
1975. New York: Friendship Press, 1974. 48pp.

BIBLIOGRAPHY

Jesus Christ Frees and Unites. Bible Studies Prepared for the Fifth Assembly of the World Council of Churches, Nairobi 1975. 37pp.

Jesus Christ Frees and Unites. Dossiers. 5th Assembly World Council of Churches, Nairobi 1975. Geneva: WCC, 1974. 6 vols.

Leitourgia. A Worship Book for the Fifth Assembly of the World Council of Churches. Geneva: WCC, 1975 (Risk, Vol. 11, No. 2-3, 1975). 96pp.

Ökumene im Spiegel von Nairobi '75. Hrsg. von Peter Beyerhaus und Ulrich Betz. Bad Liebenzell: Verlag der Liebenzeller Mission, 1976. 376pp.

Orthodox Contributions to Nairobi. Papers Compiled and Presented by the Orthodox Task Force of the WCC. Geneva: WCC, 1975. 35pp.

Runia, K. *Nairobi in Perspektief*. Kampen: Kok, 1976. 106pp.

Scheele, Paul-Werner. *Nairobi, Genf, Rom*. Die Weltchristenheit vor und nach der 5. Vollversammlung des Ökumenischen Rates der Kirchen. Paderborn: Verlag-Bonifacius, 1976. 198pp.

Slack, Kenneth. *Nairobi Narrative*. The Story of the Fifth Assembly of the World Council of Churches 1975. London: SCM Press, 1976. 90pp.

Uppsala to Nairobi 1968-1975. Report of the Central Committee to the Fifth Assembly of the World Council of Churches. Ed. by David E. Johnson. London: SPCK, 1975. 256pp.

Vischer, Lukas. *Veränderung der Welt — Bekehrung der Kirchen*. Denkanstösse der Fünften Vollversammlung des Ökumenischen Rates der Kirchen in Nairobi. Frankfurt: Lembeck, 1976. 111pp.

Welche Ökumene meinen wir? Eine Bilanz der Ökumene seit Nairobi. Mit Beiträgen von Richard Boeckler, Johannes Brosseder, Reinhard Frieling, Peter Lengsfeld, Harding Meyer, Otmar Schultz, and others. Frankfurt: Lembeck, 1978 (Ökumenische Rundschau, Beihefte, 32). 120pp.

Workbook for the Fifth Assembly of the World Council of Churches. Nairobi, Kenya, 23 November-10 December 1975. Geneva: WCC, 1975. 176pp.

Sixth Assembly: Vancouver 1983

An African Call for Life. Contribution to the World Council of Churches Sixth Assembly Theme "Jesus Christ — the Life of the World". Ed. by Masamba ma Mpolo, Reginald Stober, Evelyn V. Appiah. Geneva: WCC, 1983, 152pp.

Assembly Assembling. Towards the Sixth Assembly of the World Council of Churches, Vancouver 1983. Geneva: WCC, 1981. 15pp.

Assembly Directory. Sixth Assembly of the World Council of Churches, Vancouver 1983. Vancouver: WCC Assembly, 1983. 28pp.

Booth, Rodney M. *The Winds of God*. The Canadian Church faces the 1980s. Geneva: WCC, 1982. 128pp. (Risk Book Series, No. 16).

Christians for Peace and Justice. Contribution of the Christian Peace Conference to the Sixth Assembly of the World Council of Churches in Vancouver. Prague: CPC, 1983. 45pp.

Conway, Martin. *Look – Listen – Care*. London: British Council of Churches, 1983. 62pp.

Driemaal de basis, en eenmaal de top. Over het thema van Vancouver. Amsterdam: Allerwegen, 1983. 52pp.

The Feast of Life. The Eucharist at the Sixth Assembly of the World Council of Churches, Vancouver 1983. La fête de la vie... Das Fest des Lebens... Geneva: WCC, 1983. 40pp.

Fiolet, Herman A.M. *Vanuit Vancouver*. Impressies en rapporten van de zesde assemblee van de Wereldraad van Kerken, gehouden te Vancouver in de periode 24 juli-10 augustus 1983. Amersfoort: De Horstink, 1983. 139pp.

García Hernando, Julián. *El Consejo Ecuménico de las Iglesias*. Ante la Asamblea de Vancouver 1983. Madrid: Centro Ecuménico "Misioneras de la Unidad", 1982. 64pp.

Gathered for Life. Official Report, Sixth Assembly of the World Council of Churches, Vancouver, Canada, 24 July-10 August 1983. Ed. by David Gill. Geneva: WCC; Grand Rapids: Eerdmans, 1983. 355pp.

Gerechtigheid, eenheid en vrede. De oecumenische agenda van de Wereldraadbijeenkomst te Vancouver 1983. Een bundel studies onder redactie van Anton Houtepen. Amersfoort: De Horstink, 1982. 150pp.

Images of Life. An Invitation to Bible Study. Geneva: WCC, 1982. Pagination varies.

Issues. Discussion Papers on Issues Arising Out of the Life and Work of the World Council of Churches in Preparation for its Sixth Assembly, Vancouver, Canada, 24 July-10 August 1983. Geneva: WCC, 1982. Pagination varies.

Jesus Christ — the Life of the World. An Orthodox Contribution to the Vancouver Theme. Ed. by Ion Bria. Geneva: WCC, 1982. 121pp.

Jesus Christ — the Life of the World. Jésus-Christ, vie du monde. Jesus Christus, das Leben der Welt. Jesucristo, vida del mundo. A Worship Book for the Sixth Assembly... Geneva: WCC, 1983. 166pp.

Jesus Christ With People in Asia. Report of the Asian Consultation in Singapore, 5-11 July, 1982 on the Theme "Jesus Christ — the Life of the World". Singapore: Asia Task Force of the WCC Office, 1983. 73pp.

Long, Charles Henry. *Vancouver Voices*. The Sixth Assembly of the World Council of Churches. A Personal Report. Cincinnati: Forward Movement Publications, 1983. 119pp.

The Lord of Life. Theological Explorations of the Theme "Jesus Christ — the Life of the World". Ed. by William H. Lazareth. Geneva: WCC, 1983. 164pp.

Lorenz Günter. *Vancouver — erlebt und notiert*. Eindrücke von der sechsten Weltkirchenkonferenz. Berlin: Evangelische Verlagsanstalt, 1984. 135pp.

The Meaning of Life. A Multifaith Consultation in Preparation for the Sixth Assembly of the World Council of Churches. Mauritius, 25 January-3 February 1983. Geneva: WCC, 1983. 20pp.

Nairobi to Vancouver, 1975-83. Report of the Central Committee to the Sixth Assembly of the World Council of Churches. Geneva: WCC, 1983. 238pp.

No Longer Strangers. A Resource of Women and Worship. Ed. by Iben Gjerding and Katherine Kinnamon. Geneva: WCC, 1983. 80pp.

Ökumenische Impressionen Vancouver 1983. Mit Beiträgen von Gerhard E. Stoll, Dieter Trautwein and others. Hrsg. von Konrad Raiser. Frankfurt: Lembeck, 1983. 134pp.

Poulton John. *The Feast of Life*. A Theological Reflection on the Theme "Jesus Christ — the Life of the World". Geneva: WCC, 1982. 78pp. (Risk Book Series, 14).

Struggle Against Death. WCC Vancouver Assembly 1983. Co-Ordinators of the Study Programme: Paulos Gregorios, M.J. Joseph, K.M. George. Kottayam: The Editorial Board for the Study Programme, 1982. 167pp.

Who's Who. Revised Edition November 1983. Geneva: WCC, 1983. No pagination.

Work Book Vancouver 83. Work Book for the Sixth Assembly of the World Council of Churches, Vancouver, Canada, 24 July-10 August 1983. 119pp.

Central Committees

Minutes and Reports of the ... meeting of the Central Committee of the World Council of Churches, Geneva, WCC, 1968-85:

1968	21st meeting	Uppsala, Sweden	22pp.
1968	22nd meeting	Uppsala, Sweden	13pp.
1969	23rd meeting	Canterbury, Great Britain	296pp.
1971	24th meeting	Addis Abeba, Ethiopia	313pp.
1972	25th meeting	Utrecht, The Netherlands	274pp.
1973	26th meeting	Geneva, Switzerland	260pp.
1974	27th meeting	Berlin (West)	87pp.
1975	28th meeting	Nairobi, Kenya	35pp.
1976	29th meeting	Geneva, Switzerland	114pp.
1977	30th meeting	Geneva, Switzerland	123pp.
1979	31st meeting	Kingston, Jamaica	171pp.
1980	32nd meeting	Geneva, Switzerland	175pp.
1981	33rd meeting	Dresden, German Democratic Republic	163pp.
1982	34th meeting	Geneva, Switzerland	153pp.
1983	35th meeting	Vancouver, Canada	42pp.
1984	36th meeting	Geneva, Switzerland	195pp.
1985	37th meeting	Buenos Aires, Argentina	128pp.

Executive Committees

Minutes of meetings of the Executive Committee of the World Council of Churches (mimeographed, in archives of WCC library), 1969-86.

1969, Jan.	Tulsa, OK, USA
1969, Aug.	Canterbury, England
1970, Febr.	Geneva, Switzerland
1970, Aug./Sept.	Arnoldshain, Federal Republic of Germany
1971, Jan.	Addis Abeba, Ethiopia
1971, Sept.	Sofia, Bulgaria
1972, Febr.	Auckland, New Zealand
1972, Aug.	Utrecht, The Netherlands
1973, Jan.	Bangalore, India
1973, Aug.	Geneva, Switzerland
1974, Febr.	Bad Saarow, German Democratic Republic
1974, Aug.	Berlin (West)
1975, Apr.	Geneva, Switzerland
1975, Nov.	Nairobi, Kenya
1976, Mar.	Geneva, Switzerland
1976, Aug.	Geneva, Switzerland
1977, Febr.	Geneva, Switzerland
1977, July	Geneva, Switzerland
1978, Febr.	Zurich, Switzerland
1978, Sept.	Helsinki, Finland
1978, Dec.	Kingston, Jamaica
1979, Sept.	Bossey, Switzerland

1980, Febr.	Liebfrauenberg, Woerth, France
1980, Aug.	Geneva, Switzerland
1981, Febr.	Geneva, Switzerland
1981, Aug.	Dresden, German Democratic Republic
1982, Febr.	Geneva, Switzerland
1982, July	Geneva, Switzerland
1983, Febr./Mar.	Geneva, Switzerland
1983, July	Vancouver, BC, Canada
1984, Febr.	Geneva, Switzerland
1984, July	Geneva, Switzerland
1985, Febr.	Geneva, Switzerland
1985, July	Buenos Aires, Argentina

Conferences and Official Publications
of the Sub-Units of the World Council of Churches

UNIT I

Faith and Order

Faith and Order. Louvain 1971. Study Reports and Documents. Geneva: WCC, 1971. 264pp. (Faith and Order Paper, No. 59).

Uniting in Hope. Reports and Documents from the Meeting of the Faith and Order Commission. 23 July-5 August 1974, University of Ghana, Legon. Geneva: WCC, 1975. 144pp. (Faith and Order Paper, No. 72).

Sharing in One Hope. Reports and Documents from the Meeting of the Faith and Order Commission, 15-30 August 1978, Bangalore, India. Geneva: WCC, 1978. 290pp. (Faith and Order Paper, No. 92).

Towards Visible Unity. Commission on Faith and Order, Lima 1982. Vol. I: Minutes and Addresses; Vol. II: Study Papers and Reports. Ed. by Michael Kinnamon. Geneva: WCC, 1982. 2 vols. (Faith and Order Paper, Nos. 112 and 113).

Faith and Renewal. Reports and Documents of the Commission on Faith and Order, Stavanger, Norway, 13-25 August 1985. Ed. by Thomas F. Best. Geneva: WCC, 1986. 256pp. (Faith and Order Paper, No. 131).

And Do Not Hinder Them. An Ecumenical Plea for the Admission of Children to the Eucharist. Ed. by Geiko Müller-Fahrenholz. Geneva: WCC, 1982. 81pp. (Faith and Order Paper, No. 109).

Apostolic Faith Today. A Handbook for Study. Ed. by Hans-Georg Link. Geneva: WCC, 1985. 280pp. (Faith and Order Paper, No. 124).

Baptism and Eucharist. Ecumenical Conversion in Celebration. Ed. by Max Thurian and Geoffrey Wainwright. Geneva: WCC; Grand Rapids: Eerdmans, 1983. 258pp. (Faith and Order Paper, No. 117).

Baptism, Eucharist and Ministry. Geneva: WCC, 1982. 33pp. (Faith and Order Paper, No. 111).

The Bible: Its Authority and Interpretation in the Ecumenical Movement. Ed. by Ellen Flesseman-van-Leer. Geneva: WCC, 1980. 79pp. (Faith and Order Paper, No. 99).

Called to be One in Christ. United Churches and the Ecumenical Movement. Ed. by Michael Kinnamon and Thomas F. Best. Geneva: WCC, 1985. 77pp. (Faith and Order Paper, No. 127).

Church and State. Opening a New Ecumenical Discussion. A Colloquium Held at the Ecumenical Institute Bossey, 19-25 August 1976. Geneva: WCC, 1976. 181pp. (Faith and Order Paper, No. 85).

Churches Respond to BEM. Official Responses to the "Baptism, Eucharist and Ministry" Text, Vol 1. Ed. by Max Thurian. Geneva: WCC, 1986. 129pp. (Faith and Order Paper, No. 129).

Confessing our Faith Around the World, I. With a Foreword by C.S. Song. Geneva: WCC, 1980. 84pp. (Faith and Order Paper, No. 104).

Confessing Our Faith Around the World, II. Ed. by Hans-Georg Link. Geneva: WCC, 1983. 100pp. (Faith and Order Paper, No. 120).

Confessing Our Faith Around the World, III. The Caribbean and Central America. Ed. by Hans-George Link. Geneva: WCC, 1984. 110pp. (Faith and Order Paper, No. 123).

Confessing Our Faith Around the World, IV. South America. Ed. by Hans-Georg Link. Geneva: WCC, 1985. 111pp. (Faith and Order Paper, No. 126).

Councils, Conciliarity and a Genuinely Universal Council. Geneva: WCC, 1974. 24pp. (Faith and Order Paper, No. 70).

Ecumenical Exercise II. The Church of God, the Russian Old Ritualists, the Church of the Nazarene. Ed. by Gerald F. Moede. Geneva: WCC, 1971. 50pp. (Faith and Order Paper, No. 58).

Ecumenical Exercise III. The Church of the Lord, the Assemblies of the Brethren, the African Brotherhood Church. Ed. by Gerald F. Moede. Geneva: WCC, 1972. 41pp. (Faith and Order Paper, No. 61).

Ecumenical Exercise IV. The Wesleyan Church. The Christ Apostolic Church. Mennonites. Ed. by Robert Welsh. Geneva: WCC, 1976. 32pp. (Faith and Order Paper, No. 79).

Ecumenical Exercise V. The Presbyterian Church in Mizoram. The Gypsy Evangelical Church. The Churches of Christ. Ed. by Stephen Cranford. Geneva: WCC, 1979. 24pp. (Faith and Order Paper, No. 94).

Ecumenical Perspectives on Baptism, Eucharist and Ministry. Ed. by Max Thurian. Geneva: WCC, 1983. 246pp. (Faith and Order Paper, No. 116).

Ehrenström, Nils and Gassmann, Günther. *Confessions in Dialogue*. A Survey of Bilateral Conversations Among World Confessional Families 1962-1971. Geneva: WCC, 1972. 166pp. (Faith and Order Paper, No. 63).

Ehrenström, Nils and Gassmann, Günther. *Confessions in Dialogue*. A Survey of Bilateral Conversations Among World Confessional Families 1959-1974. Geneva: WCC, 1975. 266pp. (Faith and Order Paper, No. 74).

Ehrenström, Nils. *Mutual Recognition of Baptism in Inter-Church Agreements*. Geneva: WCC, 1978. (Faith and Order Paper, No. 90).

Episkopé and Episcopate in Ecumenical Perspective. Geneva: WCC, 1980. 59pp. (Faith and Order Paper, No. 102).

Fourth Forum on Bilateral Conversations. Report. Geneva: WCC, 1985. 20pp. (Faith and Order Paper, No. 125).

Giving Account of the Hope Today. Geneva: WCC, 1976. 54pp. (Faith and Order Paper, No. 81).

Giving Account of the Hope Together. Geneva: WCC, 1978. 135pp. (Faith and Order Paper, No. 86).

Growing Towards Consensus and Commitment. Report of the Fourth International Consultation of United and Uniting Churches, Colombo, Sri Lanka, 1980. Geneva: WCC, 1981. 82pp. (Faith and Order Paper, No. 110).

Growth in Agreement. Reports and Agreed Statements of Ecumenical Conversations on a World Level. Ed. by Harding Meyer and Lukas Vischer. Geneva: WCC, 1984. 514pp. (Faith and Order Paper, No. 108).

How Can Unity be Achieved?. Ecumenical Case Studies: Ghana, Korea, Rumania, Switzerland, Uruguay. Ed. by Robert Welsh. Geneva: WCC, 1975. 35pp. (Faith and Order Paper, No. 75).

How Does the Church Teach Authoritatively Today? Geneva: WCC, 17pp. (Faith and Order Paper, No. 91).

Lausanne 77. Fifty Years of Faith and Order. Geneva: WCC, 1977. 82pp. (Faith and Order Paper, No. 82).

Lazareth, William H. *Growing Together in Baptism, Eucharist and Ministry.* A Study Guide. Geneva: WCC, 1982. 107pp. (Faith and Order Paper, No. 114).

Louisville: Consultation on Baptism. Geneva: WCC, 1980. 108pp. (Faith and Order Paper, No. 97).

Müller-Fahrenholz, Geiko. *Partners in Life. The Handicapped and the Church.* Geneva: WCC, 1979. 184pp. (Faith and Order Paper, No. 89).

Müller-Fahrenholz, Geiko. *Unity in Today's World.* The Faith and Order Studies on: "Unity of the Church — Unity of Humankind". Geneva: WCC, 1978. 240pp. (Faith and Order Paper, No. 88).

One Baptism, one Eucharist and a Mutually Recognized Ministry. Three Agreed Statements. Geneva: WCC, 1975. 65pp. (Faith and Order Paper, No. 73).

Ordination of Women in Ecumenical Perspective. Workbook for the Church's Future. Ed. by Constance F. Parvey. Geneva: WCC, 1980. 96pp. (Faith and Order Paper, No. 105).

The Orthodox Church and the Churches of the Reformation. A Survey of Orthodox-Protestant Dialogues. Geneva: WCC, 1975. 101pp. (Faith and Order Paper, No. 76).

Orthodox Perspectives on Baptism, Eucharist, and Ministry. Ed. by Gennadios Limouris and Nomikos M. Vaporis. Brookline, Mass.: Holy Cross Orthodox Press, 1985. 168pp. (Faith and Order Paper, No. 128).

The Roots of Our Common Faith. Faith in Scriptures and in the Early Church. Ed. by Hans-Georg Link. Geneva: WCC, 1984. 135pp. (Faith and Order Paper, No. 119).

Spirit of God, Spirit of Christ. Ecumenical Reflections on the Filioque Controversy. Ed. by Lukas Vischer. Geneva: WCC, 1981. 186pp. (Faith and Order Paper, No. 103).

Survey of Church Union Negotiations 1967-1969. Geneva: WCC, 1970. 34pp. (Faith and Order Paper, No. 56).

Survey of Church Union Negotiations 1969-1971. Geneva: WCC, 1972. 20pp. (Faith and Order Paper, No. 64).

Survey of Church Union Negotiations 1971-1973. Geneva: WCC, 1974. 22pp. (Faith and Order Paper, No. 68).

Survey of Church Union Negotiations 1973-1975. Geneva: WCC, 1976. 42pp. (Faith and Order Paper, No. 78).

Survey of Church Union Negotiations 1975-1977. Geneva: WCC, 1978. 30pp. (Faith and Order Paper, No. 87).

Survey of Church Union Negotiations 1977-1979. Ed. by A.H. Harry Oussoren. Geneva: WCC, 1980. 30pp. (Faith and Order Paper, No. 101).

Survey of Church Union Negotiations 1979-1981. Ed. by Michael Kinnamon. Geneva: WCC, 1982. 32pp. (Faith and Order Paper, No. 115).

Survey of Church Union Negotiations 1981-1982. Ed. by Thomas F. Best. Geneva: WCC, 1984. 16pp. (Faith and Order Paper, No. 122).

The Three Reports of the Forum on Bilateral Conversations. Geneva: WCC, 1981. 52pp. (Faith and Order Paper, No. 107).

Towards a Confession of the Common Faith. Geneva: WCC, 1980. 13pp. (Faith and Order Paper, No. 100).

Towards an Ecumenical Consensus on Baptism, the Eucharist and the Ministry. Geneva: WCC, 1977. 31pp. (Faith and Order Paper, No. 84).

Unity In Each Place — In All Places. United Churches and the Christian World Communions. Ed. by Michael Kinnamon. Geneva: WCC, 1983. 135pp. (Faith and Order Paper, No. 118).

Vischer, Lukas. *Intercession.* Geneva: WCC, 1980. 66pp. (Faith and Order Paper, No. 95).

What kind of Unity? Geneva: WCC, 1974. 131pp. (Faith and Order Paper, No. 69).

What Unity Requires. Papers and Report on the Unity of the Church. Geneva: WCC, 1976. 74pp. (Faith and Order Paper, No. 77).

World Mission and Evangelism

Salvation Today and Contemporary Experience. A Collection of Texts for Critical Study and Reflection. Geneva: WCC, 1972. 110pp.

Bangkok Assembly 1973. Minutes and Reports of the Assembly of the Commission on World Mission and Evangelism, 31 December, 1972 and 9-12 January 1973. Geneva: WCC, 1973. 118pp.

Beyerhaus, Peter. *Bangkok 1973. The Beginning or End of the World Mission?* Grand Rapids: Zondervan, 1973. 192pp.

The Evangelical Response to Bangkok. Ed. by Ralph Winter. South Pasadena, CA: William Carey, 1973. 153pp.

From Mexico City to Bangkok. Report of the Commission on World Mission and Evangelism 1963-1972. Geneva: WCC, 1973. 94pp.

Sovik, Arne. *Salvation Today.* Minneapolis, Minnesota: Augsburg Publishing House, 1973. 112pp.

Webb, Pauline. *Salvation Today.* London: SCM Press, 1974. 117pp.

Gort, Jerald D. *World Missionary Conference Melbourne, May 1980.* An Historical and Missiological Interpretation. Amsterdam: Free University, Department of Missiology, 1980. 30pp.

Newbigin, Lesslie. *Sign of the Kingdom* Grand Rapids: Eerdmans, 1980. 70pp.

Your Kingdom Come. Mission Perspectives. Report of the World Conference on Mission and Evangelism at Melbourne, Australia, 12-25 May 1980. Geneva: WCC, 1980. 283pp.

Witnessing to the Kingdom. Melbourne and Beyond. Ed. by Gerald H. Anderson. Maryknoll, NY: Orbis Books, 1982. 170pp.

Banana, Canaan. *The Gospel According to the Ghetto*. Salisbury: Mambo Press, 1980. 88pp.

Can Churches be Compared? Reflections on Fifteen Study Projects. Ed. by Steven G. Mackie. Geneva: WCC, 1970. 101pp. (CWME Research Pamphlets, No. 17).

Castro, Emilio. *Freedom in Mission. The Perspective of the Kingdom of God*. An Ecumenical Inquiry. Geneva: WCC, 1985. 348pp.

Castro, Emilio. *Sent Free. Mission and Unity in the Perspective of the Kingdom*. Geneva: WCC, 1985. 102pp. (Risk Book Series, No. 23).

The Christian Community in Mission — in a Near and Global Context. A European Seminar on Education for Mission, Aarhus, Denmark, May 1977. Geneva: WCC, 1978. 40pp.

Crossing Boundaries. Stories from the Frontier Intership in Mission Programme. Compiled by Kathleen Todd. Geneva: WCC, 1985. 108pp. (WCC Mission Series, No. 5).

Directory of Study Centres. Geneva: WCC, 1982. 83pp.

Edinburgh to Melbourne. Geneva: WCC, 1978. In: *International Review of Mission*, Vol. 67, No. 27, pp.249-396.

Eve of the Storm, The Great Debate in Mission. Ed. by Donald McGavran. Waco, Texas: World Books, 1972. 299pp.

Go Forth in Peace A Pastoral and Missionary Guidebook. Reports and Documents from the Orthodox Missionary Consultations 1974-1980. Ed. by Ion Bria. Geneva: WCC, 1982. 54pp.

Hallencreutz, Carl F. *New Approaches to Men of Other Faiths, 1938-1968*. A Theological Discussion. Geneva: WCC, 1970. 95pp. (Research Pamphlet, No. 18).

Howell, Leon. *People are the Subject*. Stories of Urban Rural Mission. Geneva: WCC, 1980. 80pp.

McGavran, Donald. *The Conciliar-Evangelical Debate*. The Crucial Documents, 1964-1976. South Pasadena, CA: William Carey, 1977. 397pp.

Martyria — Mission. The Witness of the Orthodox Churches Today. Ed. by Ion Bria. Geneva: WCC, 1980. 255pp.

Mission and Evangelism. An Ecumenical Affirmation. Geneva: WCC, 1982. 24pp.

Mission and Evangelism. An Ecumenical Affirmation. A Study Guide Compiled by Jean Stromberg. Geneva: WCC, 1983. 84pp.

Mission and Justice. Urban and Industrial Mission at Work. Geneva: WCC, 1977. 70pp.

Orthodox Consultation on Confessing Christ Through Liturgical Life of the Church Today. Report of the Orthodox Consultation at Etchmiadzine, Armenia, 16-21 September 1975. Geneva: WCC, 1975. 31pp.

The Role of the Study Centres. Consultation Report, Singapore, 2-8 December 1980. Geneva: WCC, 1981. 25pp.

Sharing One Bread, Sharing One Mission. The Eucharist as Missionary Event. Ed. by Jean Stromberg. Geneva: WCC, 1983. 79pp. (WCC Mission Series, No. 3).

Struggle to be Human. Stories of Urban-Industrial Mission. Ed. by Bobbi Wells Hargleroad. Geneva: WCC, 1972. 78pp.

Urban Rural Mission. Africa Urban Rural Mission Consultation, Nairobi, Kenya, 3-8 October 1979. Geneva: WCC, 1979. 69pp.

The Witness of St Methodius. Orthodox Mission in the 9th century. Ed. by Ion Bria. Geneva: WCC, 1985. 43pp.

What is CWME? A Brief History of the Commission on World Mission and Evangelism. Geneva: WCC, 1984. 25pp.

Church and Society

From Here to Where? Technology, Faith and the Future of Man. Report on an Exploratory Conference, Geneva, 28 June-4 July 1970. Ed. by David Gill. Geneva: WCC, 1970. 111pp.

Report of an Ecumenical Consultation on Global Environment, Economic Growth and Social Justice. Cardiff, 3-8 September 1972. Geneva: WCC, 1972. 34pp. *Anticipation*, No. 13.

Report of an Ecumenical Conference on the Scientific, Technological and Social Revolutions in Asian Perspective. Kuala Lumpur, Malaysia, 19-23 April 1973. Geneva: WCC, 1973. 36pp. *Anticipation*, No. 14.

The Technological Future of the Industrialized Nations and the Quality of Life. Report from a North American — European Conference, Pont-à-Mousson, France, 27 May-2 June 1973. Geneva: WCC, 1973. 49pp. *Anticipation*, No. 15.

Science and Technology for Human Development. The Ambiguous Future and the Christian Hope. Selected Preparatory Papers for the 1974 World Conference in Bucharest, Romania. Geneva: WCC, 1974. 61pp. *Anticipation*, No. 17.

Science and Technology for Human Development. The Ambiguous Future and the Christian Hope. Report of the 1974 World Conference in Bucharest, Romania. Geneva: WCC, 1974. 43pp. *Anticipation*, No. 19.

Faith, Science and the Future. Preparatory Readings for a World Conference, Cambridge, Mass., 12-24 July 1979. Ed. by Paul Abrecht, Charles Birch, John Francis. Geneva: WCC, 1978. 236pp.

Faith and Science in an Unjust World. Report of the WCC Conference on Faith, Science and the Future, Cambridge, Mass., 12-24 July 1979. Vol. 1: Plenary Presentations. Ed. by Roger L. Shinn. Geneva: WCC, 1980. 392pp.

Faith and Science in an Unjust World. Report of the WCC Conference on Faith, Science and the Future, Cambridge, Mass., 12-24 July 1979. Vol. 2: Reports and Recommendations. Ed. by Paul Abrecht. Geneva: WCC, 1980. 214pp.

Burning Issues. Papers from the Consultation in Cambridge, 20-26 1977. Papers from the Consultation in Zürich, 11-16 July 1977. Geneva: WCC, 1979. 79pp. *Anticipation*, No. 25.

Burning Issues. The New International Economic Order, Transnational Corporations and World Disarmament. Ed. by Paulos Gregorios. Kottayam: Sophia Centre Publications, 1977. 98pp.

Church and Society. Ecumenical Perspectives. Essays in Honour of Paul Abrecht. Geneva: WCC, 1985. 163pp.

Church and Society. Three Reports of the Working Committee on Church and Society in Nemi, Italy 20-26 June, 1971. Geneva: WCC, 1971. 24pp.

The Churches and the Nuclear Debate. Geneva: WCC, 1977. 50pp. *Anticipation*, No. 24.

Energy for My Neighbour. An Action Programme of the WCC. Geneva: WCC, 1978. 32pp.

Energy for My Neighbour. Perspectives from Asia. Towards More Just and More Sustainable Policies of Energy Development. Ed. by Janos Pasztor. Geneva: WCC, 1981. 158pp.

Energy for My Neighbour. Report of the Latin American Regional Consultation, Held in Lima, Peru 26-31 October, 1981. Geneva: WCC, 1982. 52pp.

Facing up to Nuclear Power. Geneva: WCC, 1975. 43pp. *Anticipation*, No. 20.

Facing up to Nuclear Power. A Contribution to the Debate on the Risks and Potentialities of the Large-Scale Use of Nuclear Energy. Ed. by John Francis and Paul Abrecht. Edinburgh: Saint Andrew Press, 1976. 244pp.

Genetics and the Quality of Life. Ed. by Charles Birch and Paul Abrecht. Elmsford: Pergamon Press, 1975. 232pp.

MacClure, Michael F. *The Contribution of the World Council of Churches to an Ethic and a Just, Participatory and Sustainable Society*. Banyo, Australia: The Pius XII Provincial Seminary, 1982. 278pp.

Manipulating Life. Ethical Issues in Genetic Engineering. Geneva: WCC, 1982. 36pp.

Paulos Gregorios. *The Human Presence*. An Orthodox View of Nature. Geneva: WCC, 1978. 104pp.

Report on Nuclear Energy. Geneva: WCC, 1975. 47pp. *Anticipation*, No. 21.

Science and Our Future. Ed. by Paulos Gregorios. Madras: Christian Literature Society, 1978. 131pp.

Science Education and Ethical Values. Introducing Ethics and Religion into the Science Classroom and Laboratory. Ed. by Bert Musschenga and David Gosling. Geneva: WCC, 1985. 115pp.

Thomas, M.M. *Religion and the Revolt of the Oppressed*. Delhi: ISPCK, 1981. 69pp.

Dialogue with People of Living Faiths and Ideologies

Dialogue Between Men of Living Faiths. The Ajaltoun Memorandum. Geneva: WCC, 1970. 10pp.

Dialogue between Men of Living Faiths. Papers Presented at a Consultation Held at Ajaltoun, Lebanon, March 1970. Ed. by Stanley J. Samartha. Geneva: WCC, 1971. 127pp.

Christian-Muslim Dialogue. Papers Presented at the Broumana Consultation 12-18 July 1972. Ed. by S.J. Samartha and J.B. Taylor. Geneva: WCC, 1973. 167pp.

Towards World Community. Resources and Responsibilities for Living Together. Memorandum, Multi-Lateral Dialogue, Colombo, 17-26 April 1974. Geneva: WCC, 1974. 23pp.

Primal World Views. Christian Dialogue with Traditional Thought Forms. Ed. by J.B. Taylor. Ibadan: Daystar Press, 1976. 131pp.

Faith in the Midst of Faiths. Reflections on Dialogue in Community. Consultation at Chiang Mai, 1977. Geneva: WCC, 1977. 198pp.

Inside Out, a Style for Dialogue Where We Have Come From (Chiang Mai, 1977). Geneva: WCC, 1977. 77pp.

Religious Experience in Humanity's Relation with Nature. A Consultation, Yaoundé, Cameroon, 1978. Geneva: WCC, 1979. 37pp.

Christian Presence and Witness in Relation to Muslim Neighbours. A Conference, Mombasa, Kenya, 1979. Geneva: WCC, 1981. 88pp.

Ariarajah, S. Wesley. *The Bible and People of Other Faiths*. Geneva: WCC, 1985. 71pp. (Risk Book Series, No. 26).

Christian-Jewish Relations in Ecumenical Perspective with Special Emphasis on Africa. Ed. by F. von Hammerstein. Geneva: WCC, 1978. 146pp.

Christians Meeting Muslims. WCC Papers on Ten Years of Christian-Muslim Dialogue. Geneva: WCC, 1977. 155pp.

Churches Among Ideologies. Report of a Consultation and Recommendations to Fellow Christians, 15-22 December 1981, Grand Saconnex, Switzerland. Geneva: WCC, 1982. 60pp.

Cracknell, Kenneth. *Why Dialogue?* A First British Comment on the WCC Guidelines. London: British Council of Churches, 1982. 80pp.

Dialogue in Community. Essays in Honour of Stanley J. Samartha. Ed. by Constantine D. Jathanna. Balmatta, Bangalore, India: Karnataka Theological Research Institute, 1982. 259pp.

Ecumenical Considerations on Jewish-Christian Dialogue. Geneva: WCC, 1983. 11pp.

Faith and Ideologies. An Ecumenical Discussion. Cartigny, Geneva, May 1975. Geneva: WCC, 1975. 13pp.

Guidelines on Dialogue with People of Living Faiths and Ideologies. Geneva: WCC, 1979. 23pp.

Hallencreutz, Carl F. *Dialogue and Community*. Ecumenical Issues in Inter-Religious Relationships. Geneva: WCC, 1977. 109pp.

Jewish-Christian Dialogue. Six Years of Christian-Jewish Consultations. The Quest for World Community. Geneva: WCC, 1975. 72pp.

Living Faiths and the Ecumenical Movement. Ed. by Stanley J. Samartha. Geneva: WCC, 1971. 183pp.

Living Faiths and Ultimate Goals. A Continuing Dialogue. Ed. by Stanley J. Samartha. Geneva: WCC, 1974. 120pp.

Man in Nature: Guest or Engineer? A Preliminary Enquiry by Christians and Buddhists into the Religious Dimensions in Humanity's Relation to Nature. Ed. by Stanley J. Samartha and Lynn de Silva. Colombo: Ecumenical Institute for Study and Dialogue, 1979. 106pp.

The Meaning of Life. A Multifaith Consultation in Preparation for the Sixth Assembly of the WCC at Vancouver 1983; Mauritius, 15 January-3 February 1983. Geneva: WCC, 1983. 20pp.

Mulder, D.C. *Ontmoeting van gelovigen*. Over de dialoog tussen aanhangers van verschillende religies. Baarn: Bosch en Keuning, 1977. 100pp.

Religious Resources for a Just Society. A Hindu — Christian Dialogue at Rajpur, North India, 30 May-6 June 1981. Geneva: WCC, 1981. 22pp.

Samartha, Stanley J. *Courage for Dialogue*. Ecumenical Issues in Inter-Religious Relationships. Geneva: WCC, 1981. 157pp.

Towards World Community. The Colombo Papers. Ed. by Stanley J. Samartha. Geneva: WCC, 1975. 165pp.

UNIT II

Commission on the Churches' Participation in Development

Building a Fellowship of Commitment. Report of the CCPD Network Meeting, Crete, 1980. Ed. by Wolfgang Schmidt. Geneva: WCC, 1980. 126pp.

Caribbean Ecumenical Consultation for Development, Chaguaramas, Trinidad, November 1971. *Called To Be*. Official Report. Bridgetown: CADEC, 1971. 80pp.

Churches and the Transnational Corporations: an Ecumenical Programme. Geneva: WCC, 1983. 145pp.

Comprehensiveness in the Churches' Participation in Development: the Challenge of the Eighties. Report of a CCPD Consultation, Crêt-Bérard, Switzerland, 28-31 January 1981. Geneva: WCC, 1981 67pp.

Creative Commitment: the Response of the Churches in Indonesia to the Development Challenge. Ed. by Wolfgang Schmidt. Geneva: WCC, 1979. 137pp.

Dejung, Karl-Heinz. *Die ökumenische Bewegung im Entwicklungskonflikt 1910-1968.* Stuttgart: Ernst Klett, 1973. 494pp.

Dickinson, Richard D.N. *Poor, Yet Making Many Rich: the Poor as Agents of Creative Justice.* Geneva: WCC, 1983. 219pp.

Dickinson, Richard D.N. *To Set at Liberty the Oppressed.* Towards an Understanding of Christian Responsibilities of Development/Liberation. Geneva: WCC, 1975. 193pp.

Ecumenical Development Cooperative Society. *A Model for Action in Development Cooperation.* Comp. and ed. by Fred Bronkema. New York: EDCS, 1979. 16pp.

Ecumenical Perspectives on Political Ethics. The Report of a Consultation, Cyprus, 18-25 October 1981. Geneva: WCC, 28pp.

Elliott, Charles. *Patterns of Poverty in the Third World.* A Study of Social and Economic Stratification. Assisted by Françoise de Morsier. London: Praeger, 1975. 416pp.

Gallis, Marion. *Trade for Justice: Myth or Mandate?* Geneva: WCC, 1972. 146pp.

Gruber, Pamela H. *Fetters of Injustice.* Report of an Ecumenical Consultation on Ecumenical Assistance to Development Projects, Montreux, 26-31 January 1970. Geneva: WCC, 1970. 164pp.

Hürni, Bettina S. *Development Work of the World Council of Churches.* Geneva: Médecine et hygiène, 1974. 318pp.

The International Financial System: an Ecumenical Critique. Report of the Meeting of the Advisory Group on Economic Matters, Geneva, 1-4 November 1984. Ed. by Reginald Green. Geneva: WCC, 1985. 88pp.

Just Development for Fullness of Life: a Responsible Christian Participation. Orthodox Consultation in Kiev, 22-30 June 1982. Geneva: WCC, 1983. 138pp.

Justice and Development. Asia Forum on: CCA-WCC-CCPD, Singapore, 26-30 November 1984. Ed. by Yong-Bock Kim. Seoul: Yang Seo Press, 1985. 333pp.

Learning in the Struggle. The Report of an Interregional Consultation on Education for Development: Action for Justice, Cuba, 4-16 November 1979. Ed. by Reinhild Traitler. Geneva. WCC, 1980. 75pp.

Millwood, David. *The Poverty Makers.* Geneva: WCC, 1977. 69pp.

Minutes of the First Exploratory Consultation on Transnational Corporations, Cartigny, 26-28 January 1977. Geneva: WCC, 1977. Pagination varies.

Perspectives on Political Ethics: an Ecumenical Enquiry. Ed. by Koson Srisang. Geneva: WCC, 1983. 193pp.

Pury, Pascal de. *People's Technologies and People's Participation.* Geneva: WCC, 1983. 164pp.

Report of the Commission on the Churches' Participation in Development 1970-1976. Geneva: WCC, 1977. 70pp.

Rudersdorf, Karl Heinrich. *Das Entwicklungskonzept des Weltkirchenrates.* Entstehung und Entwicklung des Konzepts der Entwicklungsforderung im Weltrat der Kirchen. Saarbrücken: Verlag der SSIP-Schriften, 1975. 355pp.

Santa Ana, Julio de. *Good News to the Poor.* The Challenge of the Poor in the History of the Church. Geneva: WCC, 1977. 124pp.

Separation Without Hope? Essays on the Relation Between the Church and the Poor During the Industrial Revolution and the Western Colonial Expansion. Ed. by Julio de Santa Ana. Maryknoll: Orbis Books, 1980. 192pp.

Towards a Church of the Poor. The Work of an Ecumenical Group on the Church and the Poor. Geneva: WCC, 1979. 210pp.

Sartorius, Peter. *Churches in Rural Development.* Guidelines for Action. Geneva: WCC, 1975. 157pp.

Signs of Hope and Justice. Ed. by Jether Pereira Ramalho. Geneva: WCC, 1980. 134pp.

To Break the Chains of Oppression. Results of an Ecumenical Study Process on Domination and Dependence. Geneva: WCC, 1975. 113pp.

Towards a Church in Solidarity with the Poor. Ed. by IDOC International. Rome: IDOC, 1980. 99p.

Traitler, Reinhild. *Leaping Over the Wall.* An Assessment of Ten Years' Development Education. Geneva: WCC, 1982. 83pp.

World Hunger, a Christian Reappraisal. Report of the Fourth Meeting of the Advisory Group on Economic Matters, Held in Washington, 5-8 October 1981. Ed. by Diogo de Gaspar, Caesar Espiritu and Reginald Green. Geneva: WCC, 1982. 63pp.

Numerous numbers of *CCPD Documents* deal with specific concerns and problems

Churches in International Affairs

Barnaby, Frank. *Nuclear Proliferation and the South African Threat.* Geneva: WCC, 1977. 22pp.

Before It's Too Late: the Challenge of Nuclear Disarmament. The Complete Record of the Public Hearing on Nuclear Weapons and Disarmament, Amsterdam, 1981. Ed. by Paul Abrecht and Ninan Koshy. Geneva: WCC, 1983. 391pp.

Churches as Peacemakers? An Analysis of Recent Church Statements on Peace, Disarmament and War. By Friedhelm Sölms and Marc Reuver. Rome: IDOC, 1985. 85pp.

The Churches in International Affairs. Reports, 1970-1973, 1974-1978, 1979-1982. Geneva: CCIA, 1974, 1979, 1983.

Derr, Thomas Sieger. *The Political Thought of the Ecumenical Movement, 1900-1939.* Ann Arbor, Michigan: University Microfilms, 1972. 758pp.

Evans, Archibald A. *Workers' Rights Are Human Rights.* A Guide on International Labour Standards. Rome: IDOC, 1981. 112pp.

Fonseca, Glenda Da. *How to File Complaints of Human Rights Violations.* A Practical Guide to Intergovernmental Procedures. Geneva: WCC, 1975. 152pp.

Grubb, Kenneth. *Crypts of Power: an Autobiography.* London: Hodder & Stoughton, 1971. 253pp.

Hamelink, Cees. Towards a New International Information Order. *CCIA Background Information*, 1978, No. 7.

Hudson, Darril. *The World Council of Churches in International Affairs.* Leighton Buzzard: Faith Press, 1977. 336pp.

Hudson, Darril. *The Ecumenical Movement in World Affairs.* London: Weidenfeld & Nicolson, 1969. 286pp.

Human Rights: a Challenge to Theology. Ed. by Marc Reuver. Rome: IDOC; Geneva: WCC, 1983. 174pp.

Human Rights and Christian Responsibility. Report of the Consultation in St Pölten, Austria, 21-26 October 1974. Geneva: WCC, 1974. 68pp.

Militarism and Human Rights. Reports and Papers of a Workshop at Glion, Switzerland, 10-14 November 1981. *CCIA Background Information*, 1982, No. 3.

Nolde, O. Frederick. *The Churches and the Nations*. Philadelphia: Fortress Press, 1970, 184pp.

Peace and Disarmament. Documents of the WCC presented by the Commission of the Churches on International Affairs, and of the Roman Catholic Church Presented by the Pontifical Commission Iustitia et Pax. Geneva: WCC, 1982. 254pp.

Regehr, Ernie. *Militarism and the World Military Order*. A Study Guide for Churches. Geneva: WCC, 1980. 69pp.

Religious Freedom. Main Statements by the World Council of Churches, 1948-1975. Geneva: WCC, 1976. 75pp.

Report of the Conference on Disarmament, Glion, Switzerland, 9-15 April 1978. Geneva: WCC, 1978. *CCIA Background Information*, 1978, No. 4. 29pp.

Report of the Consultation on Militarism, Glion, Switzerland, 13-18 November 1977. Geneva: WCC, 1977. *CCIA Background Information*, 1977, No. 2. 22pp.

Report of the Hague Consultation on the CCIA, 12-17 April 1967. Geneva: WCC, 1967. 46pp.

The Security Trap: Arms Race, Militarism and Disarmament. A Concern for Christians. Ed. by José-Antonio Viera Gallo. Rome: IDOC, 1979. 291pp. Revised ed. 1982, 291pp.

Violence, Nonviolence and Civil Conflict. Geneva: WCC, 1983. 32pp.

WCC Statements on Nuclear Weapons and Disarmament, 1948-1981. Prepared for the Public Hearing at Amsterdam, 23-27 November 1981. Geneva: WCC, 1981. 56pp.

Weingärtner, Erich. Human Rights on the Ecumenical Agenda. Report and Assessment. *CCIA Background Information*, 1983, No. 3.

Zalaquett, Jose. The Human Rights Issue and the Human Rights Movement: Characterization, Evaluation, Propositions. *CCIA Background Information*, 1981, No. 3.

Many numbers of *CCIA Background Information* (1975-) deal with specific concerns in various countries and regions.

Programme to Combat Racism

Aboriginal Issues. Racism in Australia. Geneva: WCC, 1971. 29pp.

Adler, Elisabeth. *A Small Beginning*. An Assessment of the First Five Years of the Programme To Combat Racism. Geneva: WCC, 1974. 102pp.

Austin, George. *World Council of Churches' Programme to Combat Racism*. London: Institute for the Study of Conflict, 1979. 30pp. (Conflict Studies, No. 105).

Bank Loans to South Africa Mid-1982 to End 1984. Prepared by Eva Militz. Geneva: WCC, 1985. 124pp.

Bassarak, Gerhard; Günter Wirth. *Herausforderung des Gewissens*. Über den Ökumenischen Beitrag zum Kampf gegen den Rassismus. Berlin: Union Verlag, 1977. 77pp.

Breaking Down the Walls. World Council of Churches Statements and Actions on Racism 1948-1985. Ed. by Ans J. van der Bent. Geneva: WCC, 1986. 107pp.

Challenge to the Churches. Official Report of the Joint AACC/PCR — WCC Consultation on the Church and the Liberation of South Africa. Nairobi: AACC, 1976. 61pp.

Christian Response to Race and Minority Issues in Asia. Proceedings and Findings of a Regional Consultation, 24-29 March 1980, New Delhi. Hong Kong: CCA-URM, 1980. 124pp.

Church Investments Corporations and Southern Africa. New York: Friendship Press, 1973. 242pp.

The Churches' Involvement in Southern Africa. Geneva: WCC, 1982. 76pp.

Churches Responding to Racism in the 1980s. Noordwijkerhout, Netherlands, 16-21 June 1980. Geneva: WCC, 1980. 88pp. (PCR Information, No. 9).

Cunene Dam Scheme and the Struggle for the Liberation of Southern Africa. Geneva: WCC, 1971. 47pp.

Downing, John. *Now You Do Know.* An Independent Report on Racial Oppression in Britain. London: WOW Campaigns, 1980. 80pp.

Ecumenical Involvement in Southern Africa. Geneva: CETIM, 1975. 173pp.

Fuchs, Erika. *Antirassismus-Programm 1969-1979.* Eine Dokumentation. Hrsg. von Peter Karner. Wien: Evangelischer Oberkirchenrat H.B., 1979. 260pp. (Aktuelle Reihe, N. 16).

Fuelling Apartheid. Shell and the Military. Geneva: WCC, 1984. Pagination varies.

Heuvel, Albert van den. *Shalom and Combat.* A Personal Struggle Against Racism. Geneva: WCC, 1979. 53pp. (Risk Book Series, No. 5).

Justice for Aboriginal Australians. Report of the WCC Team Visit to the Aborigines, 15 June-3 July 1981. Sydney: Australian Council of Churches, 1981. 91pp.

Die Kirchen im Kampf gegen den Rassismus. Eine Materialsammlung, zusammengestellt vom Kirchlichen Aussenamt der EKD. Verantwortlich Lothar Coenen. Frankfurt: Lembeck, 1980. 104pp.

Luckhardt, Ken. *Working for Freedom.* Black Trade Union Development in South Africa Throughout the 1970s. Geneva: WCC, 1981. 118pp.

Meyers-Herwartz, Christel. *Die Rezeption des Antirassismus-programms in der EKD.* Stuttgart: Kohlhammer, 1979. 378pp.

Muntendam, J.W. Th. *De bestrijding van het racisme en de oecumene.* Utrecht: Interuniversiteit Instituut voor Missiologie en Oecumenica, 1973. 76pp.

Payne, Ernest A.. *Violence, Non-Violence and Human Rights.* London: The Baptist Union of Great Britain and Ireland, 1971. 15pp. (Living Issues, No. 15).

Racism in Children's and School Textbooks. A Report. Evangelische Akademie Arnoldshain, 13-18 Oktober 1978. Geneva: WCC, 1979, 28pp.

Racism in Theology and Theology Against Racism. Geneva: WCC, 1975. 21pp.

Richardson, Neville. *The World Council of Churches and Race Relations: 1960 to 1969.* Bern: H. Lang, 1977. 78pp. (Studien zur interkulturellen Geschichte des Christentums, N. 9).

Rogers, Barbara. *Race: No Peace Without Justice.* Churches Confront the Mounting Racism of the 1980s. Geneva: WCC, 1980. 132pp.

Sansbury, Kenneth. *Combating Racism.* London: British Council of Churches, 1975. 78pp.

Schmidt, Robert Frederick. *The Legitimacy of Revolution.* The World Council of Churches' Grants to Liberation Movements in Southern Africa, 1983. 347pp.

Sjollema, Baldwin. *Isolating Apartheid.* Western Collaboration with Southern Africa. Geneva: WCC, 1982. 136pp.

The Slant of the Pen. Racism in Children's Books. Ed. by Roy Preiswerk. Geneva: WCC, 1980. 151pp.

Time to Withdraw. Investments in Southern Africa. Geneva: WCC, 1972. 27pp.

Verkuyl, J. *Bestrijding van het racisme en de kerken in Nederland.* Kampen: Kok, 1972. 72pp.

Vincent, John J. *The Race Race*. London: Notting Hill, 1969. London: SCM Press, 1970. 116pp.

Walther, Christian. *Rassismus*. Berlin: Lutherisches Verlagshaus, 1971. 101pp. (Kirchliche Aspekte Heute, Nr. 6).

Weisse, Wolfram. *Südafrika und das Antirassismusprogramm*. Kirchen im Spannungsfeld einer Rassengesellschaft. Bern: H. Lang. Frankfurt: lang, 1975. 465pp. (Studien zur interkulturellen Geschichte des Christentums, 1).

Wie lange noch? Apartheid als Herausforderung für Südafrikas Christen und Kirchen: Dokumente 1970 bis 1980. Hrsg. und eingeleitet von Elisabeth Adler. Berlin: Union Verlag, 1982. 255pp.

Williamson, Roger. *Alternative Strategies?* Reactions in the Two Germanies to the World Council of Churches' Programme to Combat Racism, 1969-75. Dissertation, Birminghham, 1980. 250pp.

The World Council of Churches and Bank Loans to Apartheid. Geneva: WCC, 1977. 95pp.

Many numbers of *PCR Information* deal with specific concerns, problems and conflicts.

Commission on Inter-Church Aid, Refugee and World Service

Asia Country Papers. Geneva: WCC, 1975. 112pp.

Bouman, Pieter. *Tears and Rejoicing*. The Story of European Inter-Church Aid 1922-1956. 1983. 473pp.

Bouwen, Frans. *An Ecumenical Concern*. The Participation of Refugees. Geneva: WCC, 1982. 79pp.

The Churches and the World Refugee Crisis. Geneva: WCC, 1981. 18pp.

The Churches in Eastern Europe and the Ecumenical Sharing of Resources. Report of the Consultation on the Ecumenical Sharing of Resources with the Churches in Eastern Europe, Sofia, 24-26 May, 1982. Geneva: WCC, 1983. 56pp.

Contemporary Understandings of Diakonia. Report of a Consultation. Geneva, Switzerland, 22-26 November 1982. Geneva: WCC, 1983. 67pp.

Cooke, Leslie E. *Bread and Laughter*. Geneva: WCC, 1968. 280pp.

Early, Tracy. *Simply Sharing*. A Personal Survey of How Well the Ecumenical Movement Shares its Resources. Geneva: WCC, 1980. 84pp. (Risk Book Series, No. 8).

Ecumenical Church Loan Fund. *Consultations of National ECLOF Committee Chairmen, September 1979*. Geneva: WCC, 1979. 68pp.

Ecumenical Church Loan Fund. *Lending a Hand*. Geneva: WCC, 1983. 16pp.

Empty Hands. An Agenda for the Churches: a Study Guide on the Ecumenical Sharing of Resources for Use by Churches, Local Congregations and Other Groups. Geneva: WCC, 1980. 50pp.

Fryer, Jonathan. *Food for Thought*. The Use and Abuse of Food Aid in the Fight Against World Hunger. Geneva: WCC, 1982. 54pp.

Government Funding. Report of the Consultation Held at Aurora Conference Centre. Toronto, Canada, 8-10 February 1983. Geneva: WCC, 1983. 68pp.

Hennes, Gerhard G. *Alone, You Get Nowhere*. An Attempt at Assessing the Involvement of Personnel in the Sudan Relief and Rehabilitation Programme 1972-75. Geneva: WCC, 1977. 114pp.

King, Michael Christopher. *The Palestinians and the Churches* Geneva: WCC, 1981.

Newby, Donald O. *Toward a New Process for Mission and Service*. A Report on the Project List Review for the Commission on Interchurch Aid, Refugee and World

Service, New Windsor, Maryland, 24-28 April 1979, and the Commission on World
    Mission and Evangelism, Wuppertal, 14-22 May, 1979. Geneva: WCC, 1979. 48pp.
The Orthodox Approach to Diaconia. Consultation on Church and Service: Orthodox
    Academy of Crete, 20-25 November, 1978. Geneva: WCC, 1980. 64pp.
Palestine Refugees-Aid with Justice. The Report of the Consultation on the Palestine
    Refugee Problem. Geneva: WCC, 1970. 100pp.
Partners. A World Council of Churches' Contribution for the International Year of
    Disabled Persons, 1981. Geneva: WCC, 1981. 20pp.
Partners in the Family of God. The Church Includes Persons with Disabilities. Geneva:
    WCC, 1981. 92pp.
Programme Unit on Justice and Service. Ecumenical Consultation on Indochina: Hong
    Kong, 17-21 April 1978. Geneva: WCC, 1978. 79pp.
Refugees, a Global Concern. Geneva: WCC, 1977. 92pp.
Report of a Consultation with Agencies for Service and Development and Mission
    Boards on the Resource Sharing System, Geneva, 10-11 October 1983. Geneva:
    WCC, 1984. 26pp.
Report of the Middle East Consultation on Inter-Church Aid, Salamis, Cyprus, 12-14
    November 1972. Geneva: WCC, 1972. 95pp.
Resource Sharing System. Progress Reports, Decisions and Recommendations. Geneva:
    WCC, 1983. 49pp.
Reuschle, Helmut. *Material Resources in Asia.* A Survey Report. Geneva: WCC, 1978,
    219pp.
Schot, Willem J. *Do We Project Ourselves in Projects?* An Examination of the Project
    System in Relation to Service, Mission and Development. Geneva: WCC, 1979.
    28pp.
Towards a New System for Sharing. Report of the Consultation Held at Glion,
    Switzerland on 3-6 February, Geneva: WCC, 1983. 40pp.
Towards an Ecumenical Commitment for Resource Sharing. Geneva: WCC, 1984. 16pp.
Unity in Service with the Palestinians. Consultation on Service to Palestine Refugees.
    Beirut: MECC, 1980. 116pp.

Christian Medical Commission

Caribbean Regional Conference on the Churches' Role in Health and Wholeness. Port of
    Spain, Trinidad, 12-16 March 1979. Geneva: WCC, 1979. 51p.
Cottingham, Jane. *Bottle Babies.* A Guide to the Baby Foods Issue. Geneva: WCC,
    1976. 47pp.
The Future Role of the Church in Health Care Programmes in Ghana. Proceedings of a
    Workshop. The Ghana Institute of Public Administration, Greenhill, Ghana, 17-23
    August 1975. Compiled from notes supplied by Mary Zosso. 1975. 38pp.
Genetics and the Quality of Life. Ed. by Charles Birch and Paul Abrecht. Rushcutters
    Bay, N.S.W.: Pergamon Press, 1975. 232pp.
Genetics and the Quality of Life. Report of a Consultation of Church and Society/
    Christian Medical Commission, Zürich June 1973. Geneva: WCC, 1975. 26pp.
Health, the Human Factor. Readings in Health, Development and Community Participa-
    tion. Guest ed. Susan B. Rifkin. Geneva: WCC, 1980. 124p.
Hellberg, J.H. *Community, Health and the Church.* Geneva: WCC, 1971. 74pp.
Kingma, Stuart J. *Survey of Church and Mission Health Programmes in Sierra Leone
    and Workshop, 6-31 May 1975.* Geneva: WCC, 1975. 35pp.

MacGilvray, James C. *The Quest for Health and Wholeness.* Tübingen: German Institute for Medical Missions, 1981. 118pp.
Pacific Regional Consultation on the Christian Understanding of Health, Healing and Wholeness. Madang, Papua New Guinea, 23-29 October 1981. Geneva: WCC, 1982. 80pp.
The Principles and Practice of Primary Health Care. Geneva: WCC, 1979. 112pp.
The Search for a Christian Understanding of Health, Healing and Wholeness. A Summary Report on the Study Programme of the Christian Medical Commission of the World Council of Churches 1976-1982. Geneva: WCC, 1982. 41pp.
Seminar on the Healing Ministry of the Church. Ecumenical Institute Bossey, 25 June-7 July 1979. Geneva: WCC, 1979. 74pp.
The Third Conference for Coordinators of Church-Related Health Work in Africa. Mombasa, Kenya, 18-21 February 1975. Geneva: WCC, 1975. 29pp.

UNIT III

Education

Christians and Education in a Multi-Faith World. Considerations on Christian Participation in Education in a Multi-Faith Environment. Geneva: WCC, 1982. 43pp.
Encuentro. New Perspectives for Christian Education. Geneva: WCC, 1971. 183pp.
Freire, Paulo. *Pedagogy in Process.* The Letters to Guinea-Bissau. New York, Seabury Press, 1978. 178pp.
Freire, Paulo. *Education for Critical Consciousness.* New York, Seabury Press, 1973. 164pp.
Seeing Education Whole. Geneva: WCC, 1970. 126pp.
Tradition and Renewal in Orthodox Education. Report of the Consultation on "Tradition and Renewal in Orthodox Education" held in the Neamt Monastery, Romania, 6-12 September 1976. Ed. by Maurice Assad, 1977. 130pp.
World Council of Churches. *Ecumenical Scholarship Programme.* Geneva: WCC, 1980. 23pp.
World Council of Churches. Office of Education. *Learning Community.* A Consultation on Evaluating the Sunday School Contribution to Church Education in Europe Today, Glion-sur-Montreux, Switzerland, 24-28 September 1973. Geneva: WCC, 1973. 129pp.
When I'm Grown Up I'm Going to Change Things. Children at the 6th Assembly, World Council of Churches, Vancouver 1983. Geneva: WCC, 1985. 41pp.

Women in Church and Society

Bam, Brigalia, ed. *New Perspectives for Third World Women.* Madras: The Christian Literature Society, 1979. 42pp.
Bam, Brigalia. *What is Ordination Coming To?* Report of a Consultation on the Ordination of Women Held in Cartigny, Geneva, Switzerland, 21-26 September 1970. Geneva: WCC, 1971. 86pp.
By Our Lives. Stories of Women — Today and in the Bible. Geneva: WCC, 1985. 57pp.
A Caring Community. A Consultation of the World Council of Churches, Sao Paulo, Brazil, 23-29 November 1981. Geneva: WCC, 1982. 8pp.

Choose Life — Work for Peace. Report of an International Workshop, the Sub-Unit on Women in Church and Society, 27 November-7 December 1981, Nassau, Bahamas. Geneva: WCC, 1982. 40pp.

The Church and the Aging in a Changing World. Geneva: WCC, 1983. 198pp.

The Community of Women and Men in the Church. Report of the Asian Consultation Held at the United Theological College, Bangalore, 11-15 August 1978. Geneva: WCC, 1978. 105pp.

Community of Women and Men in the Church. New York, National Council of Churches, Commission on Faith and Order, 1981. 27pp.

Consultation of European Christian Women. Brussels, 19 January-4 February 1978. Geneva: WCC, 1978. 63pp.

Davies, Margaret and Davies, Rupert. *Circles of Community.* A Study Guide. Towards a Renewed Community of Women and Men in Church and Society, Based on a World Council of Churches Consultation, Sheffield, 1981. London, British Council of Churches, 1982. 15pp.

Family Power. A Report on a Consultation of an International Ad Hoc Advisory Committee of the Office of Family Ministries, Assembled at Salina Bay, Malta, 25 April-3 May 1973. Geneva: WCC, 1973. 57pp.

Family Profiles. Stories of Families in Transition. Ed. by Masamba Ma Mpolo. Geneva: WCC, 1984. 96pp.

Half the World's People. A Report of the Consultation of Church Women Executives. Glion, Switzerland, January 1977. Geneva: WCC, 1978. 64pp.

Hahn, Elisabeth. *Partnership.* Geneva: WCC, 1954. 72pp.

Herzel, Susannah. *A Voice for Women.* The Women's Department of the World Council of Churches. Geneva: WCC, 1981. 197pp.

In God's Image. Reflections on Identity, Human Wholeness and the Authority of Scripture. Ed. by Janet Crawford and Michael Kinnamon. Geneva: WCC, 1983. 108pp.

Middle East Council of Churches Consultation. *The Community of Women and Men in the Church.* Beirut, Lebanon, 22-26 January 1980. Geneva: WCC, 1981. 87pp.

Orthodox Women, the Role and Participation in the Orthodox Church. Report on the Consultation of Orthodox Women, 11-17 September 1976. Agapia, Romania. Geneva: WCC, 1977. 55pp.

Report of Conference on Women, Human Rights and Mission. Venice, Italy, 24-30 June 1979. Geneva: WCC, 1979. 64pp.

Report of the Fourth Seminar on Marriage and Family Life. New Caledonia, 18 January-8 February 1975. Geneva: WCC, 1975. 40pp.

Report on the Consultation "Pastoral Care and Those Confronted With Abortion". Monbachtal, Federal Republic of Germany, 6-11 October 1974. Geneva: WCC. 1974. Pagination varies.

Sexism in the 1970s. Discrimination Against Women. A Report of a World Council of Churches Consultation West Berlin 1974. Geneva: WCC, 1975. 150pp.

Study on the Community of Women and Men in the Church. Geneva: WCC, 1979. 39pp.

Thompson, Betty. *A Chance to Change.* Women and Men in the Church. Geneva: WCC, 1982. 121pp.

Towards Self-Reliance I. A Handbook on Rural Development. Geneva: WCC, 1980. 54pp.

Towards Self-Reliance II. A Handbook on Rural Development. Report of Asian Regional Workshop for Rural Women, 28 April-8 May 1980. Tagaytay City, Philippines. Geneva: WCC, 1981. 54pp.

Ujamaa Safari. An Impression of the World Assembly on the Family, Familia 74, Tanzania, June 1974. Geneva: WCC, 1974. 49pp. (Risk. Vol. 10, No. 4, 1974).

We Listened Long, Before We Spoke. Women Theological Students. A Consultation of the Sub-unit on Women in Church and Society of the World Council of Churches. Geneva: WCC, 1979. 56pp.

WCC, Community of Women and Men in the Church. *A Space to Grow In.* European Regional Consultation, Bad Segeberg, FRG, 20-24 June 1980. Geneva: WCC, 1981. 32pp.

WCC, Community of Women and Men in the Church. *Theological Anthropology, Towards a Theology of Human Wholeness.* The Benedictine Abbey at Niederaltaich, FRG, September 1980. Geneva: WCC, 1981. 53pp.

WCC, The Office of Family Education. *The Multicultural Context of Family Education, Challenges of the Eighties.* Report of Advisory Group Meeting, Alexandria, Egypt, 10-16 November 1980. Geneva: WCC, 1981. 177pp.

WCC, The Office of Family Education. *Marriage and Family Education in Theological Perspective.* Pastoral and Practical Implications. Report of a Consultation, Milan, Italy, 2-7 November 1979. Geneva: WCC, 1980. 109pp.

WCC, Office of Family Education. *Oaxtepec, Mexico, January 1980.* Geneva: WCC, 1980. 151pp.

WCC, Office of Family Education. *The Pan African Ecumenical Consultation on Christian Family and Family Life Education.* Yaounde, 17-23 April 1983. Geneva: WCC, 1983. 93pp.

WCC, Office of Family Education. *Participation in Change.* A Group Process of Action, Reflection in Family Education. Geneva. WCC, 1981. 65pp.

WCC, Office of Family Education. *Report of a Consultation on Humanity and Wholeness of Persons with Disabilities.* São Paulo, Brazil, 23-30 November 1981. Geneva: WCC, 1982. 142pp.

Renewal and Congregational Life

The Church is Charismatic. Ed. by Arnold Bittlinger. Geneva: WCC, 1981. 241pp.

Lange, Ernst. *Leben im Wandel.* Überlegungen zu einer zeitgemässen Moral. Gelnhausen, Burckhardthaus-Verlag, 1971. 111pp.

A Spirituality for Our Times. Report of a Consultation, Annecy, France, 3-8 December 1984. Geneva: WCC, 1985. 23pp.

Vision '83. Geneva: WCC, 1983. 24pp.

Voices of Solidarity. A Story of Christian Lay Centres, Academies and Movements for Social Concerns. Geneva: WCC, 1981. 56pp.

Youth

Bent, Ans J. van der. *From Generation to Generation.* The Story of Youth in the World Council of Churches. Geneva: WCC, 1986. 136pp.

Christian Youth in a Troubled Society. Ayia Napa, Cyprus, 13-20 July 1978. Geneva: WCC, 1978. 75pp.

First Interregional Ecumenical Youth Encounter. Human Rights, Peoples' Rights, Panama, August 1980. Berlin: Ecumenical Youth Council in Europe, 1981. 92pp.

Macbay, Joanne. *Youth Participation in the World Council of Churches Assemblies.* 1982. 47pp.

Pacific Conference of Churches. *The Dancing Convention. Youths of the 80s.* Suva: Lotu
Pasifika Productions, 1980. 45pp.

Programme on Theological Education

Directory. Theological Schools in Africa, Asia, the Caribbean, Latin America and the
South Pacific, June 1970. Bromley, Kent: TEF, 1970. 58pp.

Directory. Theological Schools and Related Institutions in Africa, Asia, the Caribbean,
Latin America and the South Pacific. Bromley, Kent: TEF, 1974. 227pp.

*Ecumenical Responses to Theological Education in Africa, Asia, Near East, the South
Pacific, Latin America and the Caribbean.* London, 1976. 64pp.

Fleming, Bruce C.E. *Contextualization of Theology.* An Evangelical Assessment.
Pasadena: William Carey Library, 1980. 147pp.

Fleming, Bruce. *Global Solidarity in Theological Education.* Report of the US-Canadian
Consultation Held at Trinity College, University of Toronto, 12-15 July 1981.
Geneva: WCC, 1981. 140pp.

Kinsler, F. Ross. *The Extension Movement in Theological Education.* A Call to the
Renewal of the Ministry. Pasadena: William Carey Library, 1981. 294pp.

Lienemann-Perrin, Christian. *Training for a Relevant Ministry.* Madras: The Christian
Literature Society and Geneva: WCC, 1981. 252pp.

Learning in Context. The Search for Innovative Patterns in Theological Education.
Bromley: New Life Press, 1973. 195pp.

Ministerial Formation. Report, Tagaytay City, Manila, Philippines, 7-10 July 1979.
Geneva: WCC, 1979. 109pp.

Ministry by the People. Theological Education by Extension. Geneva: WCC, 1983,
332pp.

Ministry in Context. The Third Mandate Programme of the Theological Education Fund,
1970-77. Ed. by the TEF Staff. Bromley, Kent, 1972. 108pp.

Ministry with the Poor. Geneva: WCC, 1977. 80pp.

Orthodox Theological Education for the Life and Witness of the Church. Report on the
Consultation at Basel, Switzerland, 4-8 July, 1978. Geneva: WCC, 1978. 117pp.

Theological Education in Europe. Report of the Consultation Held in Herrnhut, GDR, 8-
14 October 1980. Geneva: WCC, 1981. 129pp.

Zorn, Herbert M. *Viability in Context.* A Study of the Financial Viability of Theological
Education in the Third World, Seedbed or Sheltered Garden? Bromley, Kent, 1975.
108pp.

Biblical Studies

Communicating Across Cultural Barriers. A Dynamic Equivalent Approach to the Use
of Radio and Other Media in Biblical Evangelism. Ed. by Charles T. Hein. Nairobi:
1977. 139pp.

Schrotenboer, Paul G. *The Bible in the World Council of Churches.* 1977. 20pp.

Weber, Hans-Ruedi. *Experiments with Bible Study.* Geneva: WCC, 1981. 319pp.

Weber, Hans-Ruedi. *Immanuel: The coming of Jesus in Art and the Bible.* Geneva:
WCC, 1984. 122pp.

Weber, Hans-Ruedi. *Jesus and the Children.* Biblical Resources for Study and Preaching. Geneva: WCC, 1979. 95pp.

Weber, Hans-Ruedi. *The Cross.* Tradition and Interpretation. London: 1979. 162pp.

Weber, Hans-Ruedi. *On a Friday Noon.* Meditations under the Cross. Geneva: WCC,
1979. 94pp.

Regional Ecumenical Developments

AFRICA

All Africa Conference of Churches. *Directory of AACC Member Churches.* Kenya: 1981. 224pp.

All Africa Conference of Churches. *Fourth General Assembly.* Nairobi, Kenya, 2-12 August 1981. Nairobi: AACC, 1981. 20pp.

All Africa Conference of Churches. Lusaka 1974. *The Struggle Continues.* Nairobi: AACC, 1974. 20pp.

All Africa Conference of Churches. *The Hard Road to Peace.* A Report of the Churches in Their Part in the Reconciliation in the Sudan and an Appeal. Nairobi: AACC, 1972. 28pp.

All Africa Conference of Churches. *Follow Me — Feed my Lambs.* Fourth Assembly, Nairobi, Kenya, 2-12 August 1981. Nairobi: AACC, 1982. 124pp.

Challenge to the Churches. WCC Consultation of the Church and the Liberation of South Africa. Nairobi: AACC, 1976. 61pp.

Drumbeats from Kampala. Report of the First Assembly of the All Africa Conference of Churches Held at Kampala, 20-30 April 1963. London, United Society for Christian Literature. Lutterworth Press, 1963. 77pp.

M'Passou, Denis. *Mindolo, a Story of the Eumenical Movement in Africa.* To Mark the 25th Anniversary of Mindolo Ecumenical Foundation. Kabulong Lusaka: Multimedia Publications, 1983. 118pp.

Mugambi, Jesse. *Ecumenical Initiatives in Eastern Africa.* Final Report of the Joint Research Project of the All African Conference of Churches and the Association of Member Episcopal Conferences of Eastern Africa 1976-1981. Co-authored by Jesse Murgambi and others and ed. by Brian Hearne. Nairobi: AACC, 1982. 188pp.

The Nuclear Conspiracy. Nairobi, AACC, 1977. 116pp.

Rafransoa, Maxime. *Eglise d'Afrique, qui es-tu?* Lausanne: Editions du Soc, 1983. 77pp.

Report of a Consultation for Directors of Lay Centres in Africa. Sponsored by All African Conference of Churches and the Mindolo Ecumenical Foundation, 19-23 May 1970. 97pp.

Report of Regional Consultation on Community of Men and Women in the Church Study. Nairobi: AACC, 1981. Pagination varies.

Salvation — Development — Liberation. Nairobi: AACC, 1972. 41pp.

The Struggle Continues. Official Report Third Assembly All Africa Conference of Churches Lusaka-Zambia, 12-24 May 1974. Nairobi: AACC, 1975. 132pp.

Together in One Place. The Story of PACLA (Pan African Christian Leadership Assembly), 9-19 December 1976. Ed. by Michael Cassidy and Gottfried Osei-Mensah. Nairobi: Evangelical Publishing House, 1978. 301pp.

Vers l'autonomie. CETA 1975-78. Nairobi: La conférence des Eglises de toute l'Afrique, 1975. 33pp.

ASIA

Achutegui, Pedro S. de, ed. *Towards a "Dialogue of Life"*. Ecumenism in the Asian Context. First Asian Congress of Jesuit Ecumenists, Manila 18-23 June 1975. Manila: Loyola School of Theology, 1976. 337pp.

Asia Youth Assembly, Delhi 1984. *Out of Control*. Official Report. Ed. by Chris Tremewan. Singapore: CCA, 1985. 208pp.

Asian Christian Leaders in China. Impressions and Reflections of a Visit to China, 1-14 June 1983. Singapore: CCA, 1983. 72pp.

Asian Christian Peace Conference, 9-14 January 1975. Kottayam, India. 84pp.

The Asian Christian Peace Conference. Theological Consultation on the Theological Basis for Cooperation with the Living Faiths for Peace with Justice. Colombo, Sri Lanka, 23-26 October 1980. Christian Peace Conference, 1980. 54pp.

Asian Realities and Christian Response: the Search for a New Community. Record and Proceedings, Asia Regional Consultation, 11-20 November 1979. Dhyana Pura, Bali, Indonesia. Sponsored by the CCA and the WCC, 1980. 106pp.

Asian Theological Reflections on Suffering and Hope. Ed. by Yap Kim Hao. Singapore: CCA, 1977. 80pp.

Asians and Blacks. Bangkok, Thailand: EACC, 1973. 81pp.

Asian's Struggle for Full Humanity: Towards a Relevant Theology. Papers from the Asian Theological Conference, 7-20 January 1979, Wennappuwa, Sri Lanka. Ed. by Virginia Fabella. Maryknoll, Orbis Books, 1980. 202pp.

Breaking Through Oppressions. An Asian Minority Women's Consultation Report. Race and Minority Women's Consultation Osaka, Japan, 13-18 October 1983. Hong Kong: CCA, 1983. 67pp.

Captives on the Land. Report of a Consultation on Land, Colombo, February 1976. Tokyo: CCA, 1977. 69pp.

CCA Consultation with Church Leaders from China. Hong Kong, 23-26 March 1981. Singapore: CCA, 1981. 80pp.

Christian Action in the Asian Struggle. Ed. by M.M. Thomas, Emilio Castro, Willem Adolf Visser 't Hooft and others. Singapore: CCA, 1973. 100pp.

Christian Conference of Asia. The First Christian Conference of Asia Urban Rural Mission Committee Meeting, Hong Kong, 30 August-5 September 1974. 74pp.

Christian Conference of Asia. Fifth Assembly, 6-12 June 1973. Singapore: CCA, 1973. 112pp.

Christian Conference of Asia. *Minutes*, Sixth Assembly, 31 May-9 June 1977. Penang, Singapore: CCA, 1977. 149pp.

Christian Conference of Asia. *Sixth Assembly*, 31 May-9 June 1977. Singapore: CCA, 1977. 75pp.

Christian Conference of Asia. *A Call to Vulnerable Discipleship*. CCA Seventh Assembly, 1981. Singapore: CCA, 1982. 114pp.

Christian Conference of Asia. *From Penang to Bangalore*. A Programme Report of the Work of the Christian Conference of Asia for the Years 1977 to 1981, Written as Preparation for the Seventh Assembly, Bangalore, India, May 1981. Singapore: CCA, 1981. 84pp.

Christian Conference of Asia. *Seventh Assembly*, Bangalore, India, 18-28 May 1981. Singapore: CCA, 1981. 124pp.

Christian Conference of Asia. *From Bangalore to Seoul*. Eighth Assembly. A Programme Report of the Work of the CCA for the Years 1981-85. Singapore: CCA, 1985. 142pp.

Christian Conference of Asia. *Minutes*. Eighth Assembly, Seoul, 26 June-2 July 1985. Singapore: CCA, 1985. 144pp.

Christian Conference of Asia. *Communicators Consultation*, 23-29 June 1975. Singapore: CCA, 1975. 66pp.

Christian Conference of Asia. *Minutes*, National Reports, Biblical Reflections, Twelfth Committee Meeting, Singapore, 7-9 September 1981. Singapore: CCA, 1981. 123pp.

Christian Conference of Asia. *Spirituality for Combat*. Published by the CCA Urban Rural Mission. Hongkong: CCA, 1983. 63pp.

Christian Response to Race and Minority Issues in Asia. Proceedings and Findings of a Regional Consultation Organized by the Christian Conference of Asia in Cooperation with the World Council of Churches, 24-29 March 1980. Hong Kong: CCA, 124pp.

Christianity in Asia. Ed. by T.K. Thomas. Singapore: CCA, 1979. 112pp.

The Church and Education in Asia. Ed. by Rob Evans, Tosh Arai. Singapore: CCA, 1980. 113pp.

Daniel, Kiran and Jin, Lee Soo, eds. *Asian Women Confront, Challenge, Change*. Singapore: CCA, 1977. 66pp.

East Asia Christian Conference. *Fifth Assembly*, Singapore, 6-12 June 1973. Singapore, CCA, 1973. 46pp.

East Asian Christian Conference. *1971 Reports of Urban Industrial Mission Projects in the East Asia Christian Conference Area*. Tokyo: EACC, 1972. 83pp.

Ecumenical Communication in Asia. Ed. by T.K. Thomas. Singapore: CCA, 1981. 71pp.

An Ecounter with Education for Liberation and Community. Ed. by John C. England. Singapore: CCA, 1975. 101pp.

Escape from Domination. A Consultation Report on the Patterns of Domination and People's Movements in Asia. Tokyo: CCA, 1980. 110pp.

Glimpses of Asian Youth in Life, Strife and Developments. Singapore: CCA, 1973. 74pp.

Guidelines for Development. Ed. by Harvey L. Perkins. Singapore: CCA, 1980. 95pp.

Handbook of the Association for Theological Education in South East Asia and the South East Asia Graduate School of Theology. Singapore: CCA, 1982. 65pp.

Health in the Development of Nations. Asian Ecumenical Conference on the Role of Health in the Development of Nations, 7-13 December 1972. Bangkok: 1973. 91pp.

Heiwa, Life for the People. Report of the Asia Heiwa Conference, Okinawa, Japan 19-23 February 1985. Kowloon: CCA, 1985. 172pp.

The Human and the Holy. Asian Perspectives in Christian Theology. Ed. by Emerito P. Nacpil and Douglas J. Elwood. Maryknoll, Orbis Books, 1980. 367pp.

In Clenched Fists of Struggle. Report of the Workshop on the Impact of TNCs in Asia. Hong Kong: CCA, 1981. 172pp.

Inheritors of the Earth. Report of the People's Forum on People, Land and Justice. Ed. by Alison O'Grady. Hong Kong: CCA, 1981. 114pp.

Islam's Challenge for Asian Churches. Papers from a Consultation on "The Challenge of Islam for Asian Churches". Ed. by Yap Kim Hao. Singapore: CCA, 1980. 50pp.

Jesus Christ with People in Asia. Report of the Asian Consultation in Singapore, 5-11 July 1982. Singapore: Asia Task Force of the WCC Office, 1983. 73pp.

Judiciary under Siege. Report of the Consultation on Asian Lawyers for Justice and Human Rights. Hong Kong: CCA, 1984. 136pp.

Justice and Development. Singapore, 26-30 November 1984. Ed. by Yong-Bock Kim. Seoul, Yang Seo Press, 1985. 333pp.

Living in Faith. Report of Asia Youth Resource Conference I, Kabanjahe, North Sumatra, Indonesia, 26 November-10 December 1979. Singapore: CCA, 1980. 115pp.

Minangkabau. Story of the People vs TNCs in Asia. Hong Kong: CCA, 1981. 154pp.

Minjung Theology: People as the Subjects of History. Ed. by Kim Yong Bock. Singapore: CCA, 1981. 196pp.

Mission in Asia Today. Papers from Hong Kong, 1975. Singapore: CCA, 1976. 103pp.

Models of Christian Education in Asia. Singapore: CCA, 1977. 55pp.

No Place in the Inn. Voices of Minority Peoples in Asia. Tokyo: CCA, 1979. 130pp.

O'Grady, Ron. *Christian Art in Asia.* Report of a Consultation Held at Dhyana Pura, Bali, Indonesia, 24-30 August 1978. Singapore: CCA, 1979. 47pp.

O'Grady, Ron. *Singapore to Penang.* The Christian Conference of Asia from 1973 to 1977. Singapore: CCA, 1977. 62pp.

People Against Domination. A Consultation Report on People's Movements and Structures of Domination in Asia, Kuala Lumpur, Malaysia, 24-28 February 1981. Tokyo: CCA, 1981. 197pp.

People Toiling under Pharaoh. Report of the Action-Research Process on Economic Justice in Asia. Ed. by Kim Yong Bock and Pharis J. Harvey. Tokyo: CCA, 1976. 282pp.

Proclaiming Christ in Solidarity with the Poor. Hong Kong: CCA, 1983. 83pp.

Profit at Gunpoint. Militarization and Economic Domination, a Christian Response. Fourth Asia Youth Resource Conference, Mindanao, Philippines, 15-30 Maz, 1983. Singapore: CCA, 1984. 186pp.

Race and Minority Women's Consultation, Korean Christian Centre, Osaka, Japan, 13-18 October, 1983. 67pp.

Rajendra, Cecil. *Refugees and Other Despairs.* Singapore: Choice Books, 1980. 91pp.

Religion and Asian Politics. An Islamic Perspective. Report of the Consultation on Religion and Asian Politics. Hong Kong, 19-22 November 1984. Kowloon: CCA, 1985. 138pp.

Report of an Asian Ecumenical Consultation on Development. Priorities and Guidelines. Singapore: CCA, 1974. 97pp.

Rifkin, Susan B. *Community Health in Asia.* Report on Two Workshops. Singapore: CCA, 1977. 149pp.

Rural Youth in Asia. Report of the Christian Conference of Asia Rural Youth Study Group, Sibu, Malaysia, 1976. Singapore: CCA, 1977. 51pp.

Set Free to Struggle for Freedom. Ed. by Barbara Weatherspoon. Hong Kong: CCA, 1985. 115pp.

Struggle With People is Living in Christ. Ed. by George Mathew. Hong Kong: CCA, 1981. 157pp

Tarakwon '83: Asian Ecumenical Youth Leaders' Seminar and Minutes of the Third Meeting of the Christian Conference of Asia Youth Programme Committee, Tarakwon, Korea, 19-26 April 1983. Singapore: CCA, 1984. 130pp.

Theology and Ideology in Asian People's Struggle. Ed. by George Ninan. Hong Kong: CCA, 1985. 82pp.

There Is No End. Check list of EACC-CCA Publications and Other Related Asian Ecumenical Documents 1948-1981. Comp. by Dorothy M. Harvey. Singapore: CCA, 1982. 104pp.

Thomas, T.K. ed. *Testimony Amid Asian Suffering.* Singapore: CCA, 1977. 102pp.

Towards an Asian Sense of Science and Technology. Papers of a Consultation on "the Future — Science, Faith and Justice in Asia", Manila, Philippines, 18-22 December 1983. Ed. by Lourdino A. Yuzon. Singapore: CCA, 1984. 197pp.

Towards the Sovereignty of the People. A Search for an Alternative Form of Democratic Politics in Asia. A Christian Discussion. Singapore: CCA, 1983. 193pp.

Varieties of Witness. Ed. by Preman Niles and T.K. Thomas. Singapore: CCA, 1980. 139pp.

Witnessing to the Kingdom. Ed. by Preman Niles and T.K. Thomas. Singapore: CCA, 1979. 76pp.

Women in Asia: Status and Image. Ed. by Mary John Mananzan. Singapore: CCA, 1979. 51pp.

CARIBBEAN

Caribbean Christian Challenge. The Report of the Ecumenical Team from the Caribbean who Visited Britain in the Autumn of 1981. London: BCC, 1981. 71pp.

Caribbean Conference of Churches. *CCC-CADEC: Report of the Third Biennial Local-isation Meeting,* Grenada, May 1981: "Towards More Effective Management". Barbados: CADEC, 1981. 68pp.

Caribbean Conference of Churches. *The CCC Communications Cluster.* The Second Assembly, Georgetown, Guyana, 16-23 November 1977. Kingston: CCC, 1977. 40pp.

Caribbean Conference of Churches. *Common Ground.* Some Discussion Notes for the Second General Assembly, Georgetown, Guyana, 16-23 November 1977. Kingston: CCC, 1977. 56pp.

Caribbean Conference of Churches *Report.* Continuation Committee Held in Port-au-Prince, Haiti, 5-11 June 1974. Trinidad: CCC, 1974. 33pp.

Caribbean Conference of Churches. *Report of the Caribbean Ecumenical Programme.* Consultation on Personnel in Mission, Trinidad, 15-18 December 1981. Ed. by M. Ramcharan. Trinidad: CCC, 1981. 37pp.

Caribbean Conference of Churches. *Report* of the Inaugural Assembly Held in Kingston, Jamaica, 13-16 November 1973. Kingston: CCC, 1973. 143pp.

Caribbean Conference of Churches. *The Right Hand of God.* Inaugural Assembly, 1973. CCC Assembly. Kingston: CCC, 1976. 24pp.

Caribbean Conference of Churches. *Workers Together With Christ.* Report of the Second General Assembly, Georgetown, Guyana, 16-23 November 1977. Georgetown: CCC, 1978. 102pp.

Caribbean Ecumenical Consultation for Development. Chaguaramas, Trinidad, November 1971. *Called to be.* Official Report of the Consultation. Bridgetown, Barbados, West India: CADEC, 1971. 80pp.

Caribbean Ecumenical Consultation for Development. Chaguaramas, Trinidad, November 1971. *Called to be.* Second Version. 1973, 59pp.

Caribbean Regional Conference on the Churches' Role in Health and Wholeness. Port of Spain, Trinidad, 12-16 March 1979. Geneva: WCC, 1979. 51pp.

Caribbean Women in Communication for Development. Report of Workshop, Mona Campus, Jamaica, 13-15 June 1975. Ed. by Marlene Cuthbert. Barbados: Cedar Press, 1975. 61pp.

Consultation on Church-Communications-Development. Held at Codrington College, Barbados, 3-8 January 1972. Geneva: SODEPAX, 1972. 59pp.

Davis, Kortright. *Mission for Caribbean Change.* Caribbean Development as Theological Enterprise. Frankfurt: Lang, 1982. 259pp. (Studien zur interkulturellen Geschichte des Christentums, Nr. 28).

The First Ten Years. CCC/CADEC/ARC. A Synopsis of the Movement 1967-77. Specially Prepared to Commemorate the Second General Assembly of the CCC, Held in Georgetown, Guyana, 16-23 November 1977. Barbados: CADEC, CCC, 1977. 18pp.

Handbook of Churches in the Caribbean. Specially Prepared for the Inaugural Assembly of the Caribbean Conference of Churches, 13-16 November 1973. Ed. by Joan A. Brathwaite, Bridgetown: Barbados, CADEC, 1973. 234pp.

Handbook of Churches in the Caribbean. Comp. by Lisa Bessil-Watson. Bridgetown: CEDAR Press, 1982. 134pp.

In Search of Partnership. Report of the First CCC Consortium Held at Mt St Benedict, Trinidad, 24-26 February 1977. Bridgetown, Barbados: CADEC, 1977.

Troubling of the Waters. A Collection of Papers and Responses Presented at Two Conferences on Creative Theological Reflection Held in Jamaica on 3-4 May and in Trinidad on 28-30 May 1973. Ed. by Idris Hadrid. San Fernando, Trinidad, Rahaman, 1973. 207pp.

Out of the Depths. A Collection of Papers Presented at Four Missiology Conferences Held in Antigua, Guyana, Jamaica and Trinidad in 1975. Ed. by Idris Hamid. San Fernando, Trinidad: St Andrew's Theological College, 1977. 261pp.

With Eyes Wide Open. A Collection of Papers by Caribbean Scholars on Caribbean Christian Concerns. Ed. by David I. Mitchell. Published by CADEC to Commemorate the Inaugural Assembly of the CCC, Jamaica, November 1973. Bridgetown, Barbados: CADEC, 1973. 202pp.

EUROPE

Alive to the World in the Power of the Holy Spirit. Theological Preparatory Document for Conference of European Churches, Eighth Assembly in Crete, 25-28 October 1979. Geneva: CEC, 1979. 90pp.

Christen und Europa. Der Beitrag der christlichen Kirchen zur europäischen Integration. Andernach: Pontes 1977. 99pp.

The Churches and Islam in Europe (II). Geneva: CEC, 1982. 76pp.

Churches in Conciliar Fellowship? A Discussion Amongst European Churches on Unity and Cooperation. Report of a Consultation at Sofia-Bulgaria, 3-8 October 1977. Geneva: CEC, 1978. 116pp. (CEC, Occasional Paper, No. 10).

The Churches of Europe and the Churches of Other Continents. Report of a Consultation Held at Basle, Switzerland, 27-30 November 1976. Geneva: CEC, 1968. 90pp.

The Common Christian Roots of the European Nations. An International Colloquium in the Vatican (Rome, 1981). Florence: Le Monnier, 1982. 300pp.

The Communion of the Holy Spirit Today: Trinity, Church, Creation. Report of the Study Consultation of the Conference of European Churches, 24-28 March 1981, Cardiff, Great Britain. Geneva: CEC, 1981. 90pp.

Conference of European Churches. *Directory of Theological Training Institutions in Europe (non-Roman Catholic).* Annuaire des établissements d'enseignement théologique en Europe (non catholiques romains). Verzeichnis theologischer Ausbildungsstätten in Europa. (nichtrömisch-katholisch). Geneva: CEC, 1970. 57pp.

Conference of European Churches. *Dossier On Danger.* European Churches React to International Tension. Geneva: CEC, 1980. 108pp.

Conference of European Churches. *This Happened at Nyborg VI.* The Report of the Sixth Assembly of the Conference of European Churches, 26 April-3 May 1971. Geneva: CEC, 1971. 268pp.

Conference of European Churches. *To Be One "That the World May Believe".* Report of the European Ecumenical Encounter CCEE-CEC, Chantilly, France, 10-13 April 1978. Conference of European Churches and Consilium Conferentiarum Episcopalium Europae. Geneva: CEC, 1978. 111pp.

Conference of European Churches. *Why is it? What is it? Who is it?* Geneva: CEC, 1971. Pagination varies.

Conference of European Churches. Assembly *Nyborg VI to Nyborg VII*, reports to the Assembly: Nyborg VII Assembly, 16-23 September 1974, Engelberg, Switzerland. Geneva: CEC, 1974. 63pp.

Conference of European Churches. *From Engelberg to Crete, Reports to the Assembly.* Eighth Assembly, 18-25 October 1979, Crete, Greece. Geneva: CEC, 1980. 119pp.

Conference of European Churches. *Unity in the Spirit, Diversity in the Churches.* The Report of the Conference of European Churches' Assembly VIII, 18-25 October 1979. Crete. Geneva: CEC, 1980. 337pp.

The Conference on Security and Cooperation in Europe and the Churches. Study Material for Use in Churches and Congregations. Report of a Consultation at Buckow, GDR, 27-31 October 1975. Conference of European Churches. Geneva: CEC, 1976. 70pp. (CEC, Occasional Paper No. 7).

Europe After Helsinki and the Developing Regions. Spiritual, Moral and Practical Responsibilities of our Churches. Study Material for Use in Churches and Congregations. Report of a Consultation, 7-11 March 1977, Gallneukirchen near Linz. Geneva: CEC, 1977. 100pp. (CEC, Occassional Paper, No. 9).

European Security and the Churches. Report of a Consultation Held at Gwatt (Lake Thun), Switzerland, 25-28 November 1969. Geneva: CEC, 1970. 44pp. (CEC, Occasional Paper, No. 3).

European Theology Challenged by the Worldwide Church. Study Material for Use in Churches and Theological Faculties, Seminaries and Congregations. Report of a Consultation at Geneva, 29 March-2 April 1976. Geneva: Conference of European Churches, 1976. 145pp. (CEC, Occasional Paper, No. 8).

The Groaning of Creation, European Christians in Quest of Their Responsibility Today. Report of the Study Consultation of the CEC, 22-26 March 1982, Bucharest, Romania. Geneva: CEC, 1982. 102pp. (CEC, Occasional Paper, No. 14).

Holmes, Ann. *Church, Property and People.* A Study of the Attitudes of Churches to Their Property in Three Multi-Racial, Multi-Faith Areas, Bradford, Derby and Lambeth. London: British Council of Churches, 1973. 57pp.

Jesus Christ: Contemporary Europe. A Reflection on Some Church Activities. Report of a Consultation at Götzis, Austria, 4-9 March 1973. Geneva: CEC, 1973. 73pp. (CEC, Occasional Paper, No. 5).

Milligan, W.J. *The New Nomads: Challenge Facing Christians in Western Europe.* Geneva: WCC, 1984. 130pp. (The Risk Book Series, No. 21).

Pastoral Care for the Traveller. Report of a Consultation Held at Glion sur Montreux, Switzerland, 19-24 January 1970. Geneva: CEC, 1970. 60pp. (CEC, Occasional Paper, No. 4).

Peace in Europe — the Churches' Role. Report of a Consultation Held at Engelberg, Switzerland, 28 May-1 June 1973. Geneva: CEC, 1973. 109pp. (CEC, Occasional Paper, No. 6).

Relations Between Western Europe Countries and Southern Africa. The Responsibility of Churches in the Struggle for Justice and Liberation. Rotterdam: Ecumenical Research Exchange, 1975. 73pp.

Security, Disarmament and Economics. Socio-Ethical Challenges for European Churches and Christians after Helsinki and Belgrade. Report of the Third Post-Helsinki/Belgrade Consultation of the Conference of European Churches, 26-29 September 1978, Siofok, Hungary. Geneva: CEC, 1979. 126pp. (CEC, Occasional Paper, No. 11).

A Short Bibliography on Muslim-Christian Relations. Consultative Committee on Islam in Europe of the Conference of European Churches. Compiled by Jan Slomp. Leusden: Committee on Islam in Europe of the CEC, 1982. 17pp.

Tschuy, Theo. *An Ecumenical Experiment in Human Rights.* Geneva: The Churches' Human Rights Programme, 1985. 47pp.

Will, James E. *Must Walls Divide?* The Creative Witness of the Churches in Europe. New York: Friendship Press, 1981.

Witness to God in Secular Europe. Report of a Consultation Held in St. Pölten, Austria, 5-10 March 1984. Geneva: CEC, 1985. 75pp.

LATIN AMERICA

¿Cómo enfrentar el racismo en la década del 80? Consulta de Iglesias Latinoamericanas. Lima: Celadec, 1980. 77pp.

La condición social de los jóvenes. Lima: ULAJE, 1979. 52pp. (Documentos ULAJE, No. 2).

Consejo Latinoamericano de Iglesias. *Comprometidos con el Reino.* Recopilación de declaraciones, resoluciones y cartas del CLAI, 1978-1982. Lima: CLAI, 1982. 110pp.

Consejo Latinoamericano de Iglesias. *Jesus Cristo — vocação comprometida com o reino.* São Paulo: CLAI, 1982. 126pp.

Consejo Latinoamericano de Iglesias. En Formación. *Oaxtepec 1978.* Unidad y misión en América Latina. San José: CLAI, 1980. 228pp.

Consejo Latinoamericano de Iglesias. *Semilla de comunión.* Carlos A. Valle editor. Buenos Aires: La Aurora, 1983. 164pp.

Consejo Latinoamericano de Iglesias. *Semente de comunhão, 11-18 de novembro de 1982.* Assembléia Constitutiva do CLAI, Lima. São Paulo: CLAI, 1983. 188pp.

De Panamá a Oaxtepec. El protestantismo latinoamericano en busca de unidad. San José: Centro Evangélico Latinoamericano de Estudios Pastorales, 1978. 172pp.

Declaración de los derechos del niño. Fundamentación bíblica. Buenos Aires: CLAI, 1984. 32pp.

Elementos de pastoral ecuménica. Guía y léxico, sección de ecumenismo. Buenos Aires: CLAI, 1982. 162pp.

En defensa de los pueblos indígenas. Lima: Comisión Evangélica Latinoamericana de Educación Cristiana, 1980. 190pp.

Encuentro Evangélico Latinoamericano de Juventudes. Lima, 21-27 de Febrero de 1982. CLAI, 1982. Pagination varies.

La esperanza en el presente de América Latina. Ponencias presentadas al II Encuentro de Científicos Sociales y Teólogos sobre el tema "El discernimiento de las utopias", Costa Rica, 11-16 de julio de 1983. Raúl Vidales y Luis Rivera Pagán editores. San José: DEI, 1983. 479pp.

Evaluación crítica de la práctica ecuménica latinoamericana. Reflexiones sobre el desarrollo y las perspectivas de las relaciones ecuménicas en el ámbito latinoamericano. Buenos Aires: Tierra Nueva, 1979. 38pp.

Evangelization and Politics. Addresses and Related papers. Matanzas, Cuba, 25 February-2 March 1979. Editors: Sergio Arce Martínez, Oden Marichal Rodríguez. New York: New York Circus, 1982. 224pp.

El futuro del ecumenismo en América Latina. By Julio Barreiro, Oscar Bolioli and Jorge E. Monterroso. Buenos Aires: Tierra Nueva, 1977. 55pp.

International Ecumenical Congress of Theology. *The Challenge of Basic Christian Communities*. Papers from the International Ecumenical Congress of Theology, 20-February-2 March 1980, Sao Paulo. Ed. by Sergio Torres and John Eagleson. Maryknoll: Orbis Books, 1981. 283pp.

Jesus Cristo a vida do mundo. São Paulo: Centro Ecumênico de Documentação e Informação, 1984. 128pp.

Porque de ellos es la tierra. El derecho a la tierra de los pueblos aborígenes. Lima: CLAI, 1983. 144pp.

Míguez Bonino, José. *Integración humana y unidad cristiana*. Publicado por: Seminario Evangélico de Puerto Rico. Puerto Rico: La Reforma, 1969, 102pp. (Conferencias Ecuménicas, No 1).

Premazzi, Javier. *Reflexiones sobre el ecumenismo en América Latina*. Geneva: 1982. 188pp.

El proceso de urbanización en América Latina. Resultados de un encuentro interdisciplinario. Montevideo: ISAL, 1970. 217pp.

Putting Theology to Work. Papers of the Latin America-UK Theological Consultation at Fircroft, May 1980. Ed. by Derek Winter. London: British Council of Churches, 1980. 93pp.

Tamez, Elsa. *La Hora de la Vida*. Lecturas bíblicas. San José: DEI, 1980. 125pp.

Teología desde el Tercer Mundo. Documentos finales de los cinco congresos internacionales de la Asociación Ecuménica de Teólogos del Tercer Mundo. San José: Departamento Ecuménico de Investigaciones, 1982. 99pp.

A Transnacionalização da América Latina e a Missão das Igrejas. Itaici, São Paulo, Outubro de 1980. Rio de Janeiro: Centro Ecumênico de Documentação e Informação, 1983. 52pp.

MIDDLE EAST

Christian Youth in a Troubled Society. Ayia Napa, Cyprus, 13-20 July 1978. Geneva: WCC, Middle East Council of Churches Youth Programme, 1978. 75pp.

The Ecumenical Popular Education Project (EPEP). WSCF Middle East: 1979. 18pp.

Horner, Norman A. *Rediscovering Christianity Where it Began.* A Survey of Contemporary Churches in the Middle East and Ethiopia. Lebanon: Heidelberg Press, 1974. 110pp.

Horner, Norman A. *A Statistical Survey of Christian Communities in Cyprus, Egypt, Ethiopia, Iran, Iraq, Jordan, Lebanon, Sudan, Syria, Turkey, Beirut, 1972.* 37pp.

Middle East Council of Churches. Documentation Office. *Directory on Christian Communication in the Middle East 1985.* Beirut: MECC, 1985. 76pp.

Middle East Council of Churches. *Minutes of the Inaugural Assembly,* Nicosia, Cyprus, 28-30 May 1974. MECC: 1974, 24pp.

Middle East Council of Churches. General Assembly. *Your Kingdom Come.* Third General Assembly of the Middle East Council of Churches, Nicosia, Cyprus, 28 November-4 December 1980. Beirut: MECC, 1980, 283pp.

Middle East Council of Churches. *A Handbook for the MECC Fourth General Assembly,* 13-19 February 1985, Nicosia, Cyprus. Beirut: MECC, 1985. 99pp.

Middle East Council of Churches. Inaugural Assembly. *Our Common Christian Message Today.* Nicosia, Cyprus, 28-30 May 1974. Nicosia, Cyprus: MECC, 1974. 40pp.

Middle East Council of Churches. *Report of the Activities of the Youth Programme 1983.* Beirut: MECC, 1983. 32pp.

Middle East Council of Churches Consultation. *The Community of Women and Men in the Church.* Beirut, Lebanon, 22-26 January 1980. Geneva: WCC, Community of Women and Men in the Church Study, 1981. 87pp.

Our Service for the Life of the World. Kiev, The Soviet Union, 14-27 September 1983. Beirut: Middle East Churches Youth Programme, 1983. 32pp.

Towards Development and Justice with Palestinians. 1982 Larnaca Consultation. MECC, Department on Service to Palestine Refugees, 1982, 136pp.

Unity in Service with the Palestinians. Consultation on Service to Palestine Refugees: Called by the Middle East Council of Churches in Cooperation with the Commission on Inter-Church Aid, Refugee and World Service of the World Council of Churches, Nicosia, Cyprus, 4-8 November 1979. Beirut: MECC, 1980. 116pp.

NORTH AMERICA

Baptism Confirmation. Implications for the Younger Generation. New York: NCCC, Department of Youth Ministry, 1979. 73pp.

Against the World for the World. The Hartford Appeal and the Future of American Religion. Ed. by Peter L. Berger and Richard John Neuhaus. New York: Seabury Press, 1976. 164pp.

U.S. Catholic Ecumenism — Ten Years Later. Ed. by David J. Bowman. Washington: US Catholic Conference, 1975. 90pp.

Cavert, Samuel McCrea. *The American Churches in the Ecumenical Movement, 1900-1968.* New York: Association Press, 1968. 288pp.

Cavert, Samuel McCrea. *Church Cooperation and Unity in America. A Historical Review, 1900-1970.* New York: Association Press, 1970. 400pp.

The Church and Southern Africa. Report on a Consultation Convened by the National Council of Churches of Christ in the USA and the US Catholic Conference, 7-11 March 1977, Marcy, New York. New York: NCC, 1977. 80pp.

Church Investments Corporations and Southern Africa. New York: Friendship Press, 1973. 242pp.

Conciliar Fellowship. A Study of the Commission on Faith and Order of the National Council of Churches of Christ in the USA. Indianapolis: COCU, 1982. 26pp.

Curry Lerond. *Protestant-Catholic Relations in America. World War I Through Vatican II.* Lexington: University Press of Kentucky, 1972. 124pp.

An Ecumenical Encounter. A Discussion Between the National Council of Churches of Christ in the USA and the NCC in India. Ed. by R.L. Turnipseed and Mathai Zachariah. Delhi: ISPCK, 1984. 97pp.

Emerging Models of Christian Mission. A Special Consultation, Ventnor, N.J. 11-14 May. Co-sponsored by the Future of the Missionary Enterprise Project of IDOC, International, Maryknoll Mission Institute and Overseas Ministries Study Centre. Ventnor: OMSC, 1976. 159pp.

Energy Ethics, a Christian Response. Outgrowth of a Seminar of the Energy-Study Panel of the National Council of Churches in the USA Held at Abiquiu, Summer 1978. Ed. by Dieter T. Hessel. New York: Friendship Press, 1979. 170pp.

Holton, Margaret L., ed. *Spirit of Toronto 1834-1984.* Toronto: Image Publishing, 1983. 336pp.

Hoyer, H. Conrad. *Ecumenopolis USA.* The Church in Mission in Community. Minneapolis, Min.: Augsburg Publishing House, 1971. 159pp.

Life Amid Death in Central America. Conversations Between Church Leaders of North and Central America, Summer 1983. New York: NCCC, 1983. 37pp.

Listening to Lay People. Report of the All Lay National Committee of the Listening-to-Lay-People Project of the NCCC in the USA. New York: Council Press, 1971. 73pp.

Modras, Ronald E. *Paths to Unity.* American Religion Today and Tomorrow. New York: Sheed and Ward, 1968. 309pp.

Muelder, Walter G. *A Comparative Study of Twenty-One North American Churches on Church Unity.* A Report of the Work Group on Education for Ecumenism of the US Conference for the WCC. US Conference of the WCC, 1978. 65pp.

National Council of the Churches of Christ in the USA. *A Guide to the NCC Archives 1950-1972.* Ed. by Donald L. Haggerty and Alan Thomson. Philadelphia: Presbyterian Historical Society, 1984. 2 vols.

Report on Possible Roman Catholic Membership in the National Council of Churches by the Study Committee on the Relationship of the NCC and the RCC in the USA. Washington: United States Conference, 1972. 47pp.

Restructure of the National Council of Churches. A Proposal by the General Board to the Ninth General Assembly, 3-7 December 1972. New York: NCCC, 1972. 47pp.

Solomonow, Allan. *Where We Stand.* Official Statements of American Churches on the Middle East Conflict. New York: The Middle East Consultation Group, 1977. 32pp.

Speight, R. Marston. *Christian-Muslim Relations.* An Introduction for Christians in the USA. Hartford: NCCC in the USA, Task Force on Christian-Muslim Relations, 1983. 85pp.

Stowe, David M. *Ecumenicity and Evangelism.* Grand Rapids, Michigan: Eerdmans, 1970. 94pp.

To Love or to Perish. The Technological Crisis and the Churches. A Report of the USA Task Force on the Future of Mankind in a World of Science-Based Technology, Co-sponsored by the NCCC and Union Theological Seminary of New York. Ed. by J. Edward Carothers, Margaret Mead and others. New York: Friendship Press, 1972. 153pp.

Vanderwerf, Nathan H. *The Times Were Very Full*. A Perspective on the First 25 Years of the National Council of the Churches of Christ in the USA, 1950-1975. New York: NCCC, 1975. 128pp.

Whalen, William J. *Separated Brethren*. A survey of Protestant, Anglican, Eastern Orthodox and Other Denominations in the USA. Huntington: Our Sunday Visitor, 1979. 252pp.

PACIFIC

Biddlecomb, Cynthia Z. *Pacific Tourism*. Contrasts in Values and Expectations. Suva: PCC, 1981. 61pp.

Christen, Philippe, comp. *A Bibliography on the Pacific*. A List of Resources Concerning the Pacific Region Available in the WCC Library. Ed. by Pierre Beffa. Geneva: WCC, 1985. 17pp.

Church and Church Membership: Adult Studies. Ed. by Joyce Trudinger, Inoke Nabulivou and P.N. Wellock. Suva: Pacific Islands Christian Education Council, 1969. 41pp.

Garrett, John. *To Live Among the Stars*. Christian Origins in Oceania. Geneva: WCC, Suva: Institute of Pacific Studies, 1982. 412pp.

Garrett, John and Mavor, John. *Worship the Pacific Way*. Suva, Fiji: Lotu Pasifika Productions, 1973. 76pp.

Hezel, Francis X. *Yesterday's Myths, Today's Realities*. A Second Look at Development Strategies in Micronesia. Port Vila, Vanuatu: Pacific Churches Research Centre, 1980. 10pp.

Mission, Churches, and Sects in Oceania. Ed. by James A. Boutilier, Daniel T. Hughes, Sharon W. Tiffany. London: University Press of America, 1978. 500pp.

Pacific Conference of Churches. *Report of the Third Assembly*, Port Moresby. Fiji: PCC; 1976. 110pp.

Pacific Conference of Churches. *The Fourth World Meets*. Suva: PCC, 1972. 110pp.

Pacific Conference of Churches. *Report of the Fourth Assembly*, 3-15 May 1981, Nuku'alofa, Tonga. Suva: PCC, 1981. 298pp.

Pacific Conference of Churches. *The Dancing Convention*. Youths of the 80s. Suva: Lotu Pasifika Productions, 1980. 45pp.

Pacific Regional Consultation on the Christian Understanding of Health, Healing and Wholeness. Papua New Guinea, 23-29 October 1981. Geneva: WCC, Christian Medical Commission, 1982, 80pp.

Richards, Charles G. *Christian Communication in the South-West Pacific*. Report of Consultation Held at Nobonob, Madang, New Guinea, August 1969. Dodoma, Tanzania: Central Tanganika Press, 1970, 173pp.

Siwatibau, Suliana and Williams, David. *A Call to a New Exodus: An Anti-Nuclear Primer for Pacific People*. Suva: Lotu Pasifika Production, 1982., 96pp.

Tides of Change. Pacific Christians Review their Problems and Hopes. Ed. by Vaughan Hinton. Melbourne: The Commission for World Mission of the Uniting Church in Australia, 1981, 127pp.

What Happened at Waitangi in 1983? A Report to the New Zealand Churches Concerning the Treaty of Waitangi, its Observance, and its Ceremonial Commemoration. Auckland: National Council of Churches in New Zealand, 1983, 108pp.

Winkler, James E. *Losing Control*. Towards an Understanding of Transnational Corporations in the Pacific Islands Context. Suva: PCC, 1981, 82pp.

Women Speak Out. A Report of the Pacific Women's Conference Suva, 27 October-2 November 1975. Ed. and Comp. by Vanessa Griffen. Suva: Pacific Women's Conference, 1976, 141pp.

Wright, Cliff. *New Hebridean Culture and Christian Faith*. Report of Education Workshop, Aulua, New Hebrides, 19 April-3 May 1979. Vila, New Hebrides: Pacific Churches Research Centre, 1980, 35pp.

Wright, Cliff. *Seeds of the World*. Tongan Cultures and Christian Faith. Report of Tonga Workshop, 20 June-3 July 1970. Vila, New Hebrides: Pacific Churches Research Centre, 1980. 43pp.

Orthodox Churches in the Ecumenical Movement

Baker, Derek. *The Orthodox Churches and the West*. Papers Read at the Fourteenth Summer Meeting and the Fifteenth Winter Meeting of the Ecclesiastical History Society. Oxford: Blackwell, 1976, 336pp.

Christian Unity and Ecumenism. Encyclical Letter of the Synod of Bishops of the Orthodox Church in America. 1973, 16pp.

Congrès de théologie orthodoxe. Procès-verbaux du deuxième congrès de théologie orthodoxe à Athènes, 19-29 août 1976. Ed. by Savas Chr. Agouridès. Athènes, 1978, 585pp.

Declaration of the Ecumenical Patriarchate on the Occasion of the 25th Anniversary of the World Council of Churches. Déclaration du patriarcat... Erklärung des Patriarchates... Istanbul: Patriarchal Institute for Patristic Studies, 1973, 64pp.

Hebly, J.A. *The Russians and the World Council of Churches*. Documentary Survey of the Accession of the Russian Orthodox Church to the WCC, with Commentary. Belfast: Christian Journals, 1978, 181pp.

Istavridis, Vasil T. *The Ecumenicity of Orthodoxy*. Geneva: WCC, 1977, 13pp. In: Ecumenical Review, vol. 29, 1977. pp.182-195.

Jesus Christ — the Life of the World. An Orthodox Contribution to the Vancouver Theme. Ed. by Ion Bria. Geneva: WCC, 1982, 121pp.

Meyendorff, John. *Catholicity and the Church*. Crestwood, NY: St Vladimir's Seminary Press, 1983, 160pp.

The New Valamo Consultation. *The Ecumenical Nature of the Orthodox Witness*. New Valamo, Finland, 24-30 September 1977. Geneva: WCC, 1978, 86pp.

Nissiotis, Nikos A. *Interpreting Orthodoxy*. Minneapolis: Light and Live Publishing Co., 48pp.

Orthodox Contributions to Nairobi. Papers Compiled and Presented by the Orthodox Task Force of the WCC. Geneva: WCC, 1975, 35pp.

Orthodox Thought. Reports of Orthodox Consultations Organized by the World Council of Churches, 1975-1982. Ed. by Georges Tsetsis. Geneva: WCC, Orthodox Task Force, 1983, 96pp.

Patelos, Constantin G. *The Orthodox Church in the Ecumenical Movement.* Documents and Statements 1902-1975. Geneva: WCC, 1978, 360pp.

Romita, Angelo. *La Tradizione e le tradizioni nella vita della Chiesa.* Storia di un dialogo ecumenico fra teologi orientali e occidentali. Leumann: Elle di Ci, 1983, 240pp.

The Sofia Consultation: Orthodox Involvement in the World Council of Churches. Ed. by Todor Sabev. Geneva: WCC, Orthodox Task Force, 1982, 129pp.

Stephanopoulos, Robert G. *Guidelines of Orthodox Christians in Ecumenical Relations.* Published by the Standing Conference of Canonical Orthodox Bishops in America and Commended to the Clergy for Guidance. New York: Standing Conference of Canonical Orthodox Bishops in America, 1973, 66pp.

The Roman Catholic Church in the Ecumenical Movement

Achutegui, Pedro S. de, ed. *The Dublin Papers on Ecumenism.* Fourth Congress of Jesuit Ecumenists. Manila: Loyola School of Theology, Ateneo Manila University, 1972, 211pp.

Achutegui, Pedro S. de, ed. *Ecumenism and Vatican II; Select Perspectives.* Manila: Loyola House of Studies, 1972, 198pp.

Aspekte der Ökumene. Anregungen für Theorie und Praxis/mit Beiträgen von Ambrosius Backhaus, Johannes Brosseder, Damaskinos Papandreou and others. Hamburg: Katholische Akademie, 1984, 120pp.

Bea, Augustine. *Ecumenism in Focus.* London: G. Chapman, 1969, 311pp.

Bekes, Gerard and Vajta, Vilmos, eds. *Unitatis redintegratio, 1964-1974.* The Impact of the Decree on Ecumenism. With Contributions by Nikos Nissiotis, Yves Congar, Lukas Vischer, and others. Roma, Ed. Anselmiana, 1977, 176pp.

Bowman, David J., ed. *US Catholic Ecumenism — Ten Years Later.* Foreword by Archbishop William W. Baum. Washington: Publications Office United States Catholic Conference, 1975, 90pp.

Boyer, Charles. *Le mouvement œcuménique, les faits — le dialogue.* Rome: Presses de l'Université grégorienne, 1976, 262pp.

Brunello, Aristide. *Vivere l'ecumenismo.* Roma: Edizioni Paoline, 1971, 95pp.

Butler, B.C. *The Church and Unity.* An Essay. London: Chapman 1979, 271pp.

Catholicisme ouvert par un groupe de spécialistes. Yves Congar, Christophe J. Dumont, Jérôme Hamer, Bernard Lambert, Emmanuel Lanne, Pierre Michalon, Charles Moeller, Jean Willebrands and others. Paris: Apostolat des Editions, 1971, 416pp.

Congar, Yves. *Essais œcuméniques. Le mouvement, les hommes, les problèmes.* Paris: Le Centurion, 1984, 316pp.

Congar, Yves. *Une passion: l'unité*. Réflections et souvenirs 1929-1973. Paris, Editions du Cerf, 1974, 117pp.

Desseaux, Jacques Elisée. *Twenty Centuries of Ecumenism*. New York: Paulist Press, 1985, 103pp.

Dulles, Avery. *Church Membership as a Catholic and Ecumenical Problem*. Milwaukee: Marquette University, Theology Department, 1974, 114pp.

Fiolet, Herman A. *Ecumenical Breakthrough*. An Integration of the Catholic and the Reformational Faith. Pittsburgh, Pa.: Duquesne University Press, 1969, 475pp.

Fouilloux, Etienne. *Les catholiques et l'unité chrétienne du XIXe au XXe siècle*. Itinéraires européens d'expression française. Paris: Le Centurion, 1982, 1007pp.

Fox, Helmut. *Ökumene Hoffnung oder Illusion?* Eine katholische Bilanz. Trier: Spee-Verlag, 1974, 168pp.

Fries, Heinrich and Rahner, Karl, eds. *Unity of the Churches: An Actual Possibility*. Philadelphia: Fortress Press, 1985, 146pp.

Girault, René. *L'œcuménisme, où vont les Eglises?* Paris: Le Centurion, 1983, 239pp.

Gleixner, Christine. *Ökumene heute: Eine Orientierungshilfe*. Wien: Verlag Herold, 1980, 232pp.

Hoppenot, Marguerite Ph. *Pleins pouvoirs à l'Esprit Saint*. Paris: Le Centurion, 1975, 181pp.

Horgan, Thaddeus and Gouthro, Arthur. *Parish Ecumenism*. Garrison: Graymoor Ecumenical Institute, 1977, 77pp.

Iung, Nicolas. *Bilan de l'œcuménisme contemporain*. Les Eglises chrétiennes non romaines à la recherche de l'unité, l'action œcuménique de l'Eglise catholique, points de divergence et d'accord. Paris: Mame, 1971, 336pp.

Jaeger, Lorenz. *Einheit und Gemeinschaft*. Stellungnahmen zu Fragen der christlichen Einheit. Hg. vom Johann-Adam-Möhler-Institut. Paderborn: Bonifacius 1972, 427pp.

Joannes Paulus II. *Addresses and Homilies on Ecumenism: 1978-1980*. Ed. by John B. Sheerin and John F. Hotchkin. Washington: US Catholic Conference, 1980, 172pp.

Lescrauwaet, J.F. *Die Einheit der Ökumene*. Perspektiven nach dem Zweiten Vatikanischen Konzil. Stein a.Rhein: Christiania Verlag, 1969, 153pp.

Margerie, Bertrand de, ed. *Vers la plénitude de la communion*. Paris: Tequi, 1980, 184pp.

Neuner, Peter. *Kleines Handbuch der Ökumene*. Düsseldorf: Patmos Verlag, 1984, 184pp.

L'œcuménisme: Unité chrétienne et identité confessionnelle. Paris: Beauchesne, 1985, 123pp.

Rodriguez, Pedro. *Iglesia y ecumenismo*. Madrid: Ediciones Rialp, 1979, 418pp.

Ryan, Thomas. *Tales of Christian Unity: The Adventures of an Ecumenical Pilgrim*. New York: Paulist Press, 1953, 281pp.

Schütte, Heinz. *Ziel — Kirchengemeinschaft: Zur ökumenischen Orientierung*. Paderborn: Verlag Bonifatius-Druckerei, 1985, 207pp.

Secretariat for Promoting Christian Unity. *Ecumenical Collaboration at the Regional National and Local Levels*. London: Catholic Truth Society, 1975, 32pp.

Toinet, Paul. *L'œcuménisme entre vie et mort: l'heure du discernement*. Chambray: C.L.D., 1981, 223pp.

Vaquero, José Sanchez. *Ecumenismo*. Manual de formación ecuménica. Salamanca: Centro Ecuménico Juan XXIII, 1971, 635pp.

Villain, Maurice. *La prière œcuménique*. Paris: Editions Paulines, 1970, 135pp.
Wacker, Paulus Gerhard. *Ökumene provokativ*. Zur Versöhnung der Christenheit. Paderborn: Ferdinand Schöningh, 1973, 199pp.
Willebrands, J. *Œcuménisme et problèmes actuels*. Paris: Les Editions du Cerf, 1969, 212pp.
Yarnold, Edward. *They Are in Earnest*. Christian Unity in the Statements of Paul VI, John Paul I, John Paul II. Middlegreen-Slough: St Paul Publications, 1982, 257pp.

The Joint Working Group between the Roman Catholic Church and the World Council of Churches

First Official Report. In: *Ecumenical Review*, Vol. 18, No. 2, 1966. pp.243-255.
Second Official Report. In: *Ecumenical Review*, Vol. 19, No. 4, 1967. pp.461-467.
Third Official Report. In: *Ecumenical Review*, Vol. 23, No. 1, 1971, pp.44-69.
Fourth Official Report. In: *Ecumenical Review*, Vol. 28, No. 1, 1976. pp.87-96.
Fifth Official Report. In: *Ecumenical Review*, Vol. 35, No. 2, 1983. pp.198-218.
Catholicity and Apostolicity. In: *One in Christ*, Vol. 6, No. 3, 1970. pp.452-483.
Common Witness. A Study Document. Geneva: WCC, 1981, 54pp. (CWME Series, 1).
Patterns of Relationships between the Roman Catholic Church and the World Council of Churches. In: *Ecumenical Review*, Vol. 24, No. 3, 1972. pp.247-288.
Towards a Confession of the Common Faith. Geneva: WCC, 1980, 13pp. (Faith and Order Paper, No. 100).
Vischer, Lukas. *Die Eine ökumenische Bewegung*. Die gemeiname Arbeitsgruppe zurischen der Römisch-katholischen Kirche und dem Ökumenischen Rat der Kirchen. Bericht und Dokumente 1965-1969. Zürich: EVZ Verlag, 1969, 129pp. (Polis, 40).

The Committee on Society, Development and Peace

Asian Ecumenical Conference for Development. Tokyo, July 1970. Geneva: SODEPAX, 1970, 69pp.
Caribbean Ecumenical Consultation for Development, Chaguaramas, Trinidad, November, 1971. Bridgetown: Barbados, 1971, 80pp.
The Challenges of Development. A Sequel to the Beirut Conference of 21-27 April 1968 at Montreal, 9-12 May 1969. Geneva: SODEPAX, 1969, 37pp.
Church Communication Development. Papers from a SODEPAX Consultation. Driebergen, 12-16 March 1970. Geneva: WCC, 1970, 111pp.
Dunne, George H. *The Right to Development*. New York: Paulist Press, 1974, 141pp.
In Search of a Theology of Development. Papers from a Consultation Held in Cartigny, Switzerland, November, 1969. Geneva: SODEPAX, 1970, 221pp.

Millwood, David. *Help or Hindrance?* Aid, Trade and the Rich Nations' Responsibility to the Third World. Geneva: SODEPAX, 1971, 42pp.

Money in a Village World. Papers from a Colloquium on the Interests of the Developing Countries and International Monetary Reform. Geneva: SODEPAX, 1970, 84pp.

Partnership or Privilege? An Ecumenical Reaction to the Second Development Decade. Geneva: WCC, 1970, 118pp.

Peace — the Desperate Imperative. The Consultation on Christian Concern for Peace. Baden, Austria, 3-9 April 1970. Sponsored by SODEPAX. Geneva: WCC, 1970, 83pp.

Picking Up the Pieces. A Report of a SODEPAX Conference on the Churches in Development Planning and Action, Limuru, Kenya, January 1971. Geneva: WCC, 1971, 77pp.

Towards a Theology of Development. An Annotated Bibliography Compiled by Gerhard Bauer for SODEPAX. Geneva: WCC, 1970, 201pp.

World Development: Challenge to the Churches. The Official Report of the Conference on Society, Development and Peace Held, at Beirut, 21-27 April 1968. Washington: Corpus Books, 1969, 208pp.

INDEXES

GENERAL INDEX

The items which are printed in bold italics are fixed topics raised in official discussion.

INDEX OF AUTHORS IN THE
BIBLIOGRAPHY

THE COMMITTEE ON ECUMENICAL HISTORY
RESPONSIBLE FOR THE PUBLICATION OF THIS VOLUME

The Reverend A. J. van der Bent (*Secretary*)

Dr Eugene Carson Blake

Archpriest Vitaly Borovoy

Professor H. D'Espine (*Chairman*)

Curé L. Gauthier

Dr J. Handspicker

The Reverend V. Hayward

The Reverend P. Hoffman

Dr W. Müller-Römheld

The Reverend P. Rodger

Metropolitan Emilianos Timiadis

Dr W. A. Visser 't Hooft

Dr Hans-Ruedi Weber

Professor H. H. Wolf

280.1
R73
1986
V.2

74339

3 4711 00228 5288